POVERTY, INEQUALITY,
AND THE FUTURE
OF SOCIAL POLICY

POVERTY, INEQUALITY, AND THE FUTURE OF SOCIAL POLICY

Western States in the New World Order

Katherine McFate
Roger Lawson
William Julius Wilson

EDITORS

RUSSELL SAGE FOUNDATION / NEW YORK

The Russell Sage Foundation

The Russell Sage Foundation, one of the oldest of America's general purpose foundations, was established in 1907 by Mrs. Margaret Olivia Sage for "the improvement of social and living conditions in the United States." The Foundation seeks to fulfill this mandate by fostering the development and dissemination of knowledge about the country's political, social, and economic problems. While the Foundation endeavors to assure the accuracy and objectivity of each book it publishes, the conclusions and interpretations in Russell Sage Foundation publications are those of the authors and not of the Foundation, its Trustees, or its staff. Publication by Russell Sage, therefore, does not imply Foundation endorsement.

Library of Congress Cataloging-in-Publication Data

Poverty, inequality, and the future of social policy : Western states and the new world order / edited by Katherine McFate, Roger Lawson, William Julius Wilson.
    p. cm.
Includes bibliographical references and index.
ISBN 0-87154-510-1 (hardbound) ISBN 0-87154-593-4 (paperback)
    1. Income distribution—Europe. 2. Income distribution—United States. 3. Poor—Europe.
4. Poor—United States. 5. Europe—social policy. 6. United States—Social policy—1993– .
I. McFate, Katherine. II. Lawson, Roger. III. Wilson, William J., 1935–
    HC240.9.I5P685 1995
    362.5'094—dc20
    94-21887
    CIP

The paper used in this publication meets the minimum requirements of American National Standard for Information Sciences—Permanence of Paper for Printed Library Materials. ANSI Z39.48-1992.

Book design by John Johnston.

RUSSELL SAGE FOUNDATION
112 East 64th Street, New York, New York 10021
10 9 8 7 6 5 4 3 2 1

For M.T.D.

a joyful, gentle spirit
ever in the heart

CONTENTS

ACKNOWLEDGMENTS

THIS PROJECT was born from frustration with the character of the policy debates occurring in the United States in the 1980s. The two main themes of political discussions in this decade were strangely disjointed: On the one hand, there was much handwringing about the way international trade and commerce were affecting the American economy in general and blue-collar workers in particular. On the other hand, when journalists and politicians lamented the development of an urban "underclass" of nonworking poor, they emphasized individual and moral shortcomings, not the economic context which was such an important part of William Julius Wilson's original conceptualization. We hoped that comparative work showing that other Western industrial nations, even those without a significant indigenous minority group population, were experiencing some of the same troubling trends as the United States (increased joblessness, rising inequality, growing concentrations of poor urban ethnic minorities) and would help to refocus attention on the *structural* factors that are affecting the poor. We believe that this volume contributes to that end.

Unfortunately, the research does not provide any clear answers to the question of where social policy is heading or the direction that it *should* take. While Anglo-American models of the minimalist welfare state have clearly proved inadequate to meet the challenges of a more global system of trade and production, contributions from Europe suggest that the traditional social democratic model is proving to be less resilient than advocates might hope. It seems that new kinds of social policies and new forms of social organization and service delivery will be required for the next century. We hope that this book will inform those struggling to construct an inclusive vision of "social citizenship" and the policies to support that vision.

This volume has been a long time in the making, and the list of individuals to whom we owe thanks has accumulated as one year has slipped into another. The first and most obvious debt is to the scholars that contributed to this volume. They revised and reviewed several edits of their work, most with grace and good humor. We have appreciated their collegiality and patience.

Initial funding for the project came from the Rockefeller Foundation. Without its support, we would not have had the luxury of two meetings with contributing authors. James Gibson, then Director of the Equal Opportunity Division, and Erol Ricketts, the Assistant Director, merit special thanks. Without their encouragement and support, the project would have never come to fruition.

In the spring of 1989, an Advisory Committee to the project met to help us tighten up its framework and provided helpful suggestions about potential contributors in Europe and America. We thank Michael O'Higgins, Lee Rainwater, Timothy Smeeding, Françoise Euvrard, Aldi Hagenaars, and Frank Bonilla for taking time from their bustling schedules to help us with this task.

We had a first meeting with the authors in Paris on December 4 and 5, 1989, and must express special thanks to Françoise Euvrard, Centre d'Étude des Revenus et des Coûts, who graciously arranged for us to meet in a breathtakingly beautiful room at the Commissariat du Plan. The level of our discussions must have been improved by the setting and food provided.

In 1991, the authors met a second time in Paris to go over paper drafts. This time we were hosted by the staff at the Maison Suger of the Sciences de'Homme. They, too, took special care of us. We are grateful to the former Director of the Sciences de'Homme, Mr. Clemens Heller, for his kind hospitality.

We would like to thank our program officer at the Charles Stewart Mott Foundation, Jon Blyth, and the Lynde & Harry Bradley Foundation for support for a two-day policy conference in Washington, D.C., in 1991, at which the findings of the papers were presented. The staff at the Joint Center for Political and Economic Studies did a magnificent job hosting a large and diverse set of policymakers and researchers. The comments of the major discussants at the conference—Henry Aaron, Robert Greenstein, Bennett Harrison, Christopher Jencks, and John Myles—enriched the discussions there and no doubt assisted revisions of the papers presented.

A number of other individuals provided helpful advice along the way. They include: Anthony Atkinson, Benoit Bastard, John Benington, Joss Berghman, John Blackwell, Malcolm Cross, Graham Crow, Margrit Eichler, Godfried Engbersen, Jean-Louis Faure, Maria Giannichedda, Colin Gillion, Janet Gournick, Bjorn Gustafsson, Franz Hiss, Jeffrey Lehman, Stephan Leibfried, Sergio Lugaresi, Rund Meffels, Henri Nadel, David Piachaud, Anthony Rees, Graham Room, Abdelmalek Sayad, Gaston Schaber, Kees Schuyt, Adrian Sinfield, Peter Townsend, and Ken Young.

Glynda Featherstone typed numerous edits and revisions over the life of this project. Molly Ruzicka helped with some initial editing before the 1991 conference. Charlotte Shelby at Russell Sage shepherded chapters through copyediting, galleys, and page proofs with a sure hand. Our thanks to each.

Finally, we owe a special debt to Eric Wanner, President of the Russell Sage Foundation, who not only furnished financial support at a critical point but also provided intellectual succor and encouragement through all phases of the project.

INTRODUCTION:
WESTERN STATES IN THE NEW WORLD ORDER

Katherine McFate

W E ARE LIVING through a period of profound social and economic change. Advances in information, communication, and transportation technologies have tied nation states into an increasingly complex web of global trade and production. Japanese, American, and European firms compete for market share, as engineers in New Delhi and Silicon Valley vie for computer software contracts. Today, the emerging industrial "dragons" of South Asia have a larger percentage of their workforce in manufacturing than the oldest industrial countries of the West.[1] New technologies have redistributed employment opportunities worldwide. As a result, Western labor markets have become more fragmented and the demand for low-skilled labor in industrial nations has dropped substantially, leaving a growing number of individuals excluded from the dynamic sectors of the emerging world system of production.

In both Europe and North America, sluggish and uneven growth has left enclaves of unemployed ethnic minorities in declining industrial centers. Many young people entering the labor market for the first time find themselves consigned to jobs that offer few opportunities for economic security or career advancement. Although more women are participating in the paid workforce than ever before, a growing number have been relegated to part-time and contingent employment. In the midst of the affluence and excess of the 1980s, most Western nations experienced an increase in unemployment and poverty that has left traditional safety nets sagging and policymakers scrambling to adjust programs to fit a changing economic environment. Despite differences in the governing structures, institutional arrangements, and generosity of income assistance among the countries studied here (the United States, Canada, the United Kingdom, France, West Germany, Italy, and Sweden), they all faced the same set of constraints—an aging population whose support is a politically "fixed" but increasingly burdensome expense; rising unemployment among a more ethnically and culturally diverse workforce; and a growing number of economically vulnerable households, headed by single individuals with limited earnings potential. Each of these developments challenges the effectiveness of traditional welfare state operations, as discussed below.

THE PROMISE OF THE WESTERN STATE

The contemporary welfare state is a captive of its past success. In every Western state, economic security among the elderly is at an historical high. Over the last 40 years, significant gains in average life expectancies occurred, largely because of subsidized healthcare and public and private pension schemes. By the year 2000, at least one of every seven citizens in the West will be over 65 years of age; about a quarter of the elderly will be over 79 years old. Thus, an increasing percentage of the population in Western industrial countries live long beyond their "earning years," leaving more elderly citizens dependent on government support (both income and medical care) for longer periods. For this support, they are depending on a non-elderly population that has not been increasing as rapidly as they have.

Between 1960 and 1990, the birthrate in most industrial countries fell by between 25 and 40 percent.[2] By the year 2000 there will be only two *potential* workers for each person under 16 and over 64 years of age in most Western countries. This shifting demographic structure stretches the state's ability to keep honoring its commitments to the elderly, since most of the pension schemes that support them are based on revolving payment systems that require new contributions to pay off previous commitments. Recognition of this impending fiscal crisis has led to a general commitment to create a more "active society"; i.e., a society that encourages female labor force participation and rejects mandatory retirement (Organization for Economic Cooperation and Development (OECD) 1988), but global economics have conspired to make such a society difficult to achieve.

SLOWER GROWTH, MORE EMPLOYMENT INSECURITY

The expansion of the welfare state in the postwar period was based on an explicit assumption of steady and robust economic growth. It was assumed that national economies would expand rapidly enough to absorb new labor market entrants, supporting the goal of (relatively) full employment. Increases in productivity would continuously raise wage levels and national prosperity. In the late 1970s and 1980s, these assumptions broke down.

Following two decades of steady improvements in productivity, Western industrialized countries experienced a precipitous decline in the real rates of growth in gross domestic product (GDP) after the first oil crisis of 1973. Between 1968 and 1973, annual real growth rates in Canada, France, West Germany, and

Table I.1 / Growth of Real GDP (annual average growth rates in percentages)

Country	1963–1973	1973–1979	1979–1983
United States	3.0	2.6	2.6
Canada	5.4	4.3	3.0
United Kingdom	3.3	1.5	2.2
Italy	4.6	3.7	2.4
France	5.5	2.8	2.1
Germany	4.7	2.3	2.1
Netherlands	4.7	2.6	1.3
Sweden	3.8	1.8	2.0

SOURCE: OECD. *Employment Outlook, 1991,* Table 2.4.

the Netherlands averaged over 4 percent. By the early 1980s, average real GDP growth in France, West Germany, and the Netherlands had been cut by more than half. In the 1980s, only Canada had an average growth rate of even 3 percent. The average growth rate in the Netherlands fell to 1.3 in the 1980s (Table I.1).

Not surprisingly, as growth slowed, unemployment increased. "Baby boomers" came of age and women began entering the labor market in larger numbers. As a result of both these trends, unemployment rose sharply. Average unemployment rates in the 1980s were typically double those in the 1968 to 1973 period (Table I.2). The most dramatic increase occurred in the Netherlands. In 1968–73, the Dutch unemployment rate averaged less than 2 percent; by the mid-1980s, one of every ten individuals in the labor force was unemployed. Average unemployment rates in the 1980s were almost as high in Great Britain, Canada, Italy, and France. In the United States, unemployment rose to over 9 percent in the recession years of 1982 and 1983, dropped to under 6 percent in the mid-1980s, and then began to climb again at the end of the decade. West Germany was able to keep its unemployment rate relatively low in the 1980s— at around 6 percent—until Unification. Only Sweden managed to keep the goal of full employment in the 1980s within sight of standards set in the 1960s (Table I.2).[3]

Table I.2 / Average Unemployment Rates for Three Periods

Country	1968–1973	1974–1979	1980–1989
United States	4.6	6.7	7.2
Canada	5.4	7.2	9.3
United Kingdom	3.3	5.0	10.0
Italy	5.7	6.6	9.5
France	2.6	4.5	9.0
Germany	1.0	3.2	5.9
Netherlands	1.5	4.9	9.7
Sweden	2.2	1.9	2.5

SOURCES: OECD. *Employment Outlook, 1991,* Table 2.7, and *Historical Statistics, 1960–1987.*

Table I.3 / Changes in Total Unemployment and Youth Unemployment Rates: 1979 and 1989

Country	General Unemployment Rate		Unemployment Rate Among 16–24 Year Olds	
	1979	1989	1979	1989
United States	5.8	5.2	11.3	10.5
Canada	7.4	7.5	12.9	11.3
United Kingdom	5.0	7.1	10.3	8.6
Italy	7.6	10.9	25.6	33.6
France	5.9	9.4	13.3	19.1
Germany	3.2	5.6	3.4	8.1
Netherlands	5.4	8.3	8.1	11.4
Sweden	2.1	1.4	5.0	3.0

SOURCE: OECD. *Employment Outlook, 1990,* Tables 2.7 and 2.8.

Traditional welfare state programs assume that most spells of unemployment will be relatively short-lived, that workers will be shed and taken on again with the short-term ebbs and flows of the business cycle. But unemployment in the 1980s did not prove to be short-lived or randomly distributed. As the incidence of unemployment increased in First World countries, certain groups were particularly hard hit and suffered long spells of joblessness.

The most marked increase in unemployment has been among the least educated and among young workers. A 1989 cross-national study of industrial nations showed that individuals with the lowest levels of educational attainment consistently suffered the highest unemployment rates in the 1980s.[4] Workers who had not completed higher secondary school had unemployment rates 50

Table I.4 / Unemployment Rates, by Educational Attainment, Gender, and Age: 1988

Country	Males		
	Total	Without Secondary School Degree	20–24 Year Olds Without Secondary School Degree
United States	5.6	10.7	19.1
Canada	7.9	11.2	22.1
United Kingdom	10.4	14.8	19.9
Italy	6.7	6.2	21.4
France	6.9	14.4	17.5
West Germany	7.5	10.9	11.8

SOURCE: OECD. *Employment Outlook: July 1989,* Table 2A.1.

NOTE: Figures for Sweden and the Netherlands unavailable.

to 100 percent higher than the national average. The report concluded that individuals with the least education in Western nations are "increasingly and disproportionately" at risk of being unemployed.[5]

Young workers were also more likely to be unemployed than older workers—especially in Europe. Youth unemployment rates were twice the national average in France, Sweden, the United States, and Italy at the end of the 1980s (Table I.3). (However, unemployment rates among 16–24-year-olds declined in several countries in the last years of the decade.)[6] Among young people with few educational qualifications, unemployment rates were often three times the national average (Table I.4).

The average duration of a spell of unemployment also increased in the 1980s. According to the OECD, the proportion of unemployed unable to find work after a year of searching increased from a quarter to a third of all unemployed persons in OECD countries. The report documenting these trends noted that long-term unemployment was a "main feature of the labor market of the 1980s."[7] By the end of the decade, over 40 percent of all unemployed persons in the United Kingdom and France and almost half of the unemployed in West Germany and the Netherlands had been searching for work for a year without success. Over two-thirds of the unemployed in Italy had been unemployed at least a year (Table I.5).[8] The vast majority of the long-term unemployed were "prime-age" workers; i.e., under 45 years old.

Both these developments—the concentration of unemployment among the least skilled and the increase in long-term unemployment—demonstrate the structural character of current unemployment in the West. Technological advances have automated many low-skilled jobs out of existence and/or allowed companies to move labor-intensive production to cheaper labor markets. When Western firms shed workers today, they are less likely to hire back *the same workers with the same skills* if and when operations expand. Laid-off workers are

Table I.4 *(continued)*

Country	Total	Females	
		Without Secondary School Degree	20–24 Year Olds Without Secondary School Degree
United States	4.8	9.6	22.2
Canada	9.0	12.7	25.0
United Kingdom	9.7	11.3	16.8
Italy	16.3	15.3	33.6
France	9.4	12.9	17.6
West Germany	13.2	16.5	16.9

Table I.5 / Changes in Long-Term Unemployment

Country	Persons Unemployed for at Least a Year as a Percentage of All Unemployed			
	1979	1983	1986	1989
United States	4.2	13.3	8.7	5.7
Canada	3.5	9.8	10.9	6.8
United Kingdom	—	36.5	41.1	40.8
Italy	35.8	41.9	N.A.	70.4
France	30.3	42.2	47.8	43.9
Germany	19.9	28.5	32.0	49.0
Netherlands	27.1	43.7	56.3	49.9
Sweden	6.8	10.3	8.0	6.5

SOURCES: OECD. *Measures to Assist the Long-Term Unemployed*, Table II, p. 12; and OECD. *Employment Outlook 1991*.

less likely to find employment in the same industry or occupation from which they were discharged.

This kind of structural unemployment presents difficulties for traditional social protection programs. Eligibility for unemployment insurance is subject to significant restrictions in all industrial countries. The level of support given to an unemployed worker is generally dependent on the contributions the individual made to an unemployment fund, which in turn depends on the individual's work history and wages. When benefits are determined by employment record and work status, the proportion of new labor market entrants who are able to qualify for unemployment insurance programs is limited. Thus, young people and other new labor market entrants (immigrants, mothers returning to the workforce) are often ruled ineligible for unemployment insurance support. But even an individual with a steady work history may eventually "deplete" his or her entitlement if a spell of unemployment lasts a long time. A European Commission Report on New Poverty in 1990 noted that:

> In the U.K., which has created one of the most comprehensive (if not generous) social insurance schemes, the proportion of unemployed men receiving insurance benefits has fallen from 55 percent in 1970 to 25 percent in 1987. . . . In Germany, the proportion of unemployed with a claim to unemployment compensation or unemployment assistance fell from 86 percent in 1975 to 67 percent in 1987. . . . In France, about one third of the unemployed had no entitlement in the mid-1980s, while another quarter had exhausted whatever entitlement they had.[9]

In the United States, only about 40 percent of the unemployed received unemployment benefits in the 1980s despite the fact that long-term unemployment is rare.

Individuals who do not qualify for social insurance programs fall to a second tier of relief or means-tested income assistance programs. These programs typically offer a much less generous level of support, are often highly stigmatizing, and are usually only available to individuals who have substantially depleted whatever assets or savings they may have had at some time.[10]

Traditional unemployment insurance programs were not immediately or automatically linked to employment counselling or training opportunities. If many of the unemployed need new skills to make themselves more attractive to employers, such services will be key to any strategy of reintegrating them more quickly into the changing economy. All industrial countries have been concerned with improving transitions back into the labor force (i.e., shortening the time it takes for unemployed people to find new jobs). Most national governments attempted to reform their unemployment insurance systems in the 1980s to encourage individuals to enter counselling or training,[11] but the motives for and results of such reforms have not always been laudable.[12] Finding an appropriate, affordable structure for providing the high quality training and retraining required of the "active society" is proving difficult.

Even if unemployment in Western nations was reduced, the economy has changed in other ways that undermine basic assumptions of Western welfare states. Recent trends suggest that the standard assertion that "increased industrial productivity will lead to increased national prosperity" may no longer hold. Automation and technological advance may increase the productivity of each industrial worker and through this leave a larger number and proportion of the workforce in lower-paid service and retail jobs.

In all OECD countries, the share of service jobs in the overall economy rose in the 1970s and 1980s. By 1988, Germany was the only industrialized country with less than 60 percent of its jobs in services. Over 70 percent of U.S. jobs were in service industries.[13] If, as some argue, manufacturing jobs are part of a "primary" labor market characterized by high wages, employment stability, job security, and opportunities for advancement; and the majority of service jobs are part of a segmented "secondary" labor market characterized by low wages, poor working conditions, little upward mobility, and weak trade union protections; then the shift of jobs from manufacturing to services may undermine real median earnings.[14]

In fact, wage inequality among full-time workers increased in many countries over the 1980s. In Europe, highly educated workers saw their real wages rise significantly; the wages of those with only a high school education did not increase as rapidly or were stagnant. In the United States, the real wages of all workers declined, but the wages of the least educated declined more sharply than the wages of the most educated.[15] As production technologies become increasingly mobile, industrial employees in First World countries may find that even large increases in productivity and health and pension plan "give-backs" fail to make them competitive with skilled workers in countries with lower living standards. Stagnant or declining wage levels reduce the tax base on which governments depend for the financing of other social welfare spending and may increase the number of citizens eligible for some kind of assistance, thus

Table I.6 / Size and Composition of Part-Time Employment: 1979–1990

Country	Part-Time Employment as a Percentage of Total Employment			Percentage of All Part-Time Employees Who Are Female		
	1979	1983	1990	1979	1983	1990
United States	16.4	18.4	16.9	68.0	66.8	67.6
Canada	12.5	15.4	15.4	72.1	71.3	71.0
United Kingdom	16.4	19.4	21.8	92.8	89.8	87.0
Italy	5.3	4.6	5.7	61.4	64.8	64.7
France	8.2	9.7	12.0	82.2	84.4	83.1
Germany	11.4	12.6	13.2	91.6	91.9	90.5
Netherlands	16.6	21.4	33.2	76.4	77.3	70.4
Sweden	23.6	24.8	23.2	87.5	86.6	83.7

SOURCE: OECD. *Employment Outlook, July 1991*, Table 2.9.

worsening fiscal problems and, ironically, creating new incentives for cutbacks in social spending.

Related to, but not entirely dependent upon, the shift from manufacturing to service jobs is the increase in "non-standard" forms of employment. The number and proportion of workers in part-time jobs, temporary work, or self-employed increased over the 1980s, and in most countries these workers have limited rights to work-based entitlements and protections. The percentage of employed persons who worked only part-time increased in Canada, France, Germany, the Netherlands, and the United Kingdom and the great majority of all part-time employees in Western countries are women (Table I.6).[16] While many mothers may prefer part-time work when their children are young, their part-time status makes it difficult for them to support themselves if there is no other earner in the household, and it may mean that they cannot qualify for unemployment support should they lose their job.

Temporary or contingent work (fixed-term contracts, temporary employment agencies, seasonal or casual employment, certain types of government employment schemes) increased rapidly in Europe and America, and this also contributed to the growing insecurity of the workforce. Temporary work contracts doubled between 1979 and 1987 in France, increasing from 2 to 4 million. In Germany, temporary work contracts rose from the equivalent of 41,000 full-time workers in 1985 to 79,500 in 1987. An estimated 20 million workers in the United States today hold contingent jobs.[17] Individuals in all these "non-standard" work arrangements typically have few labor force protections. They tend to have less social security protection than salaried workers do, and they may not be covered by work-injury insurance and unemployment benefits.[18]

The same is true of the growing number of individuals who reported themselves to be self-employed in the 1980s. Self-employment as a percentage of all employment rose in the United Kingdom, Sweden, and Italy (Table I.7). Al-

Table I.7 / Number of Self-Employed and Their Percentage of Total Civilian Employment

Country	1979	1983	1986	1989
United States	6,751 (7.1)	7,540 (7.7)	7,833 (7.4)	8,561 (7.5)
Canada	659 (6.7)	718 (7.1)	788 (7.2)	856 (7.2)
United Kingdom	1,620 (6.6)	1,949 (6.6)	2,353 (10.0)	2,986 (11.6)
Italy	3,234 (18.9)	3,683 (20.7)	3,976 (21.6)	4,229 (22.4)
France	2,051 (10.6)	2,047 (10.5)	2,047 (10.5)	2,107 (10.5)
Germany	2,024 (8.2)	1,821 (7.4)	1,932 (7.6)	2,031 (7.8)
Netherlands	400 (8.8)	404 (8.6)	402 (8.2)	446 (7.8)
Sweden	177 (4.5)	190 (4.8)	173 (4.2)	304 (7.1)

SOURCE: OECD. *Employment Outlook, July 1992*, Table 2.12.

though most self-employed individuals are men who are, on average, older than salaried employees, there was a significant increase in female self-employment in the 1980s. The self-employed report working longer hours for less compensation than salaried workers, and many spells of self-employment last only a very short period, suggesting that at least a portion of the self-employed would prefer salaried positions.

Traditional welfare state programs were predicated on the assumption that most workers would have a single occupation for most of their adult lives, and perhaps even remain in the same firm or enterprise. Today, continuous, secure employment is a distant dream for a growing portion of the labor force. There has been a new "flexibility" in private sector work arrangements, but it has not been matched by a new flexibility in social protection programs.[19] As a result, there are wide gaps in the coverage of income support programs as well as "poverty traps."

National governments in the West are struggling to find ways to prevent the economic turbulence of today's labor markets from leaving larger segments of their citizenry economically marginalized. Thus far, traditional welfare policies have not adequately met the adjustment challenges created by global markets. Without major reforms, it seems likely that the number of individuals and families who experience long spells of joblessness or become trapped in jobs that offer little hope of economic security will multiply.

RESTRUCTURED FAMILIES

These economic developments alone increased the vulnerability of many citizens; when combined with social and cultural developments in the West over the past two decades, their negative impacts are magnified. Family roles and structures have changed significantly over the past 25 years, the casualties of more liberal sexual mores, the women's movement, and a greater emphasis on individual independence and personal choice.

In the idealized family of traditional welfare state programs, husbands had primary (even sole) responsibility for wage-earning. An industrial worker received a "family wage"—enough income to support a small family comfortably above the poverty level. Full employment allowed workers to marry, begin families, and establish independent households at relatively young ages. A father's earnings rose with his work experience, so the family's income and security grew as the family matured. Comfort in middle age might have been further enhanced through the inheritance of assets of deceased parents or elderly relatives.

Today, marital households are formed later in life, and reproductive families are smaller and less stable. Young adults no longer expect to move directly from their family of origin into marriage; rather, the norm is to establish an independent household for a time before forming a reproductive family.[20]

In part, the later age at first marriage reflects the labor market's demand for higher-skilled workers. Young adults are delaying marriage and childbearing to complete training courses and/or obtain college and university degrees. But the period of independence in young adulthood is also borne of a desire for more personal (and sexual) exploration before marriage, leaving most young people vulnerable to the possibility of unplanned pregnancies.

In any case, the transition period for young adults (when they move from dependence on parental support to reliance on their own earnings) was particularly risky in the 1980s. The least skilled were likely to experience lengthy spells of unemployment and/or low wage work.[21] Even the most skilled often spent some time in the contingent workforce or in part-time work. Households headed by an individual under 30 had high poverty rates at the beginning of the 1980s, but even with these initial high rates, poverty among young adults increased over the decade. If the household contained dependent children, the risk of poverty increased significantly, and if the household head was a young mother, poverty status was practically assured unless extensive governmental and/or family assistance was forthcoming.[22]

Expectations about the permanence of marriage have also changed dramatically. Adults are more willing to leave unhappy marriages, even if children are involved. Between 1960 and 1986, divorce rates more than doubled in the United Kingdom, France, Germany, the Netherlands, and the United States (Table I.8). Marriage in most Western countries seems to be viewed as a conditional commitment, not an immutable life choice. Reforms in divorce and custody laws over the past two decades reinforced these changes in attitude and behavior.

Although child-rearing has not lost its appeal, married couples are having fewer children, and an increasing number of women are bearing children without the legal sanction of marriage.[23] As a result, a rising proportion of children in Western societies are born out of wedlock. Over 40 percent of all births in Sweden and Denmark, and over 20 percent of all births in the United States, the United Kingdom, and France are to unmarried mothers (Table I.9). While many of these children are born to unmarried cohabiting couples, a large proportion will end up spending some part of their childhood in a household

Table I.8 / Divorce Rates per 1,000 Women

Country	1960	1970	1986
United States	9.4	14.9	21.2
Canada	1.7	—	12.9
United Kingdom	2.2	5.5	12.9
Italy	N.A.	N.A.	1.1
France	2.8	3.1	8.5
Germany	3.4	5.0	8.3
Netherlands	2.2	3.3	8.7
Sweden	4.9	6.7	10.7

SOURCE: Kamerman, this volume, Table 6.2.

with only one biological parent, usually the mother. Whether the fruit of divorce or unmarried motherhood, the rapid increase in children living in households headed by lone mothers is of serious concern to policymakers for a number of reasons.

Lone-parent families with children are more likely to be poor than couple-headed families in all countries except Sweden.[24] The reasons are not difficult to discern. Most lone parents are women. Occupational segregation and wage discrimination leave women with incomes significantly lower than men, and family responsibilities keep many mothers in part-time work. But even when a woman works full-time, there is no guarantee that she will earn a family wage. In fact, over 15 percent of full-time working mothers in the United States and almost 12 percent of full-time working mothers in Canada failed to earn enough to keep themselves and their children out of poverty *even with* government assistance.[25] Financial support from absent fathers is essential to the economic well-being of most mother-headed families. But fathers too often behave as if providing financial support to their noncustodial children is an optional choice. As a result of paternal neglect, most Western nations have moved toward more stringently codifying paternal support responsibilities and establishing more effective systems of collecting income support from absent fathers.

Table I.9 / Percentage of All Births That Are Out-of-Wedlock

Country	1960	1970	1986
United States	5.3	10.7	23.4
Canada	4.3	9.6	16.9
United Kingdom	5.4	8.5	21.0
Italy	2.4	2.2	5.6
France	6.1	6.8	24.0
Germany	6.3	5.5	9.6
Netherlands	1.3	2.1	8.8
Sweden	11.3	18.4	48.4

SOURCE: Kamerman, this volume, Table 6.4.

Table I.10 / Female Labor Force Participation Rates: 1979–1990

Country	1979	1986	1990
United States	58.9	64.9	68.2
Canada	55.5	64.0	68.1
United Kingdom	58.0	61.6	67.4
Italy	38.7	42.3	44.5
France	54.2	55.2	56.6
Germany	49.6	51.3	57.0
Netherlands	33.4	41.3	53.0
Sweden	72.8	78.3	81.1

SOURCE: OECD. *Employment Outlook*, 1990 and 1992, Annex Table H.

Nonetheless, lone mothers are left to shoulder primary responsibility for *both* economic support and nurturing activities associated with child-rearing. In the not-too-distant past, grandparents or other relatives might have been expected to help support a lone mother and her children, and temporary cash support and/or residential sharing are not unusual today. However, these interfamilial transfers are increasingly viewed as a matter of *choice*, not a moral obligation. And with a heavier emphasis on personal independence, neither generation is likely to find a "dependent" relationship satisfactory for long.[26]

In most Western countries, lone mothers are expected to enter the paid work-force, at least after their children begin to attend school. This reflects a general change in public attitudes toward working women or, more particularly, work-ing mothers. Between 1970 and 1988, there was a significant increase in the labor force participation of women of childbearing age, including those with children (Table I.10). Whether motivated by a desire for more individual auton-omy or by the need to shore up an inadequate family income, wives and moth-ers have been entering the labor force in increasing numbers over the past two decades.[27] As norms regarding working women have evolved, child support and/or child allowances have come to be viewed as *supplements to*, not *substitutes for*, a mother's earnings (Table I.11). As working mothers become the norm,

Table I.11 / Labor Force Participation Rates of Women and Mothers: 1986

Country	Married Mothers	Lone Mothers
United States	65.0	65.3
Canada*	67.0	63.6
United Kingdom	58.7	51.9
Italy	43.9	67.2
France	65.8	85.2
Germany	48.4	69.7
Sweden	89.4	N.A.

SOURCE: Sorrentino, 1990, p. 53.

*Data for 1988.

Western governments have come under pressure to establish employment protections for women (maternity leave, wage equity, etc.) and to provide childcare (directly or through tax credits).

In the past, familial roles and responsibilities were reinforced by stable work associations and community networks. Today, individuals often leave the communities in which they were raised to pursue employment opportunities elsewhere. Extended family resources are spread more thinly over wider distances, over numerous independent residences, and over several generations. This may lessen the income support available to any particular family member and weaken the ability of family members to effectively monitor problems. The family's capacity to act as the first catchment net against economic hardship is diminished. In short, social developments have conspired with economic conditions to leave more households with children vulnerable to spells of poverty and public dependency.

MORE DIVERSE COMMUNITIES

As changing family roles challenge the operation of welfare state programs, the increasing ethnic and racial diversity of industrial democracies raises basic questions about the concept of community embedded in the theory of the welfare state. Whether derived from the Anglo-Saxon tradition of local government or the Statist traditions of Europe, democratic welfare state institutions use citizenship and community as a way to define the boundaries of social responsibility. If an individual is part of the community and shares a common identity of citizenship, then the state has a social responsibility to ensure some minimum level of well-being. These "rights of social citizenship" had been slowly, if unevenly, expanding through at least the early 1970s.[28] The process stalled as the poor became more racially and ethnically distinct from the middle class.

The immigrant-built countries of the United States and Canada have always been more culturally diverse than European countries. In 1990, the African American population in the United States represented about 13 percent of the population and 29 percent of the poor. Hispanics represented 10 percent of the population and 18 percent of the poor.[29] Although "visible minorities" represent less than 9 percent of the population of Canada and European countries, the number has significantly increased over the past 25 years, as labor shortages experienced in the 1960s and 1970s led to a relaxation of immigrant restrictions.[30] An estimated 4–4.4 million foreign immigrants now live in France; a little over a third are Muslims from North Africa. In Germany there are currently 1.8 million Turkish guestworkers out of a foreign population of 64 million. Great Britain's population of Afro-Caribbean and Asian citizens numbers about 5 percent of the population. Ethnic minorities in the Netherlands represent only 5 percent of the overall population but comprise up to 20 percent of the population of its largest cities.[31]

In fact, multiethnic large cities have become the norm in most Western nations. Today, even blacks in the United States are disproportionately concentrated in large urban centers despite their historical ties to Southern agriculture. Contemporary immigrants almost always settle in urban enclaves. But such residential patterns often reinforce discrimination and separation from majority institutions and culture:

> . . . The location where migrants are living very often increases the scale of discrimination and latent hostility. Concentration enhances visibility, thus reinforcing existing prejudices. Indeed discrimination, be it legal or de facto, is closely related to spatial settlement. Whatever the reasons for preferring to live in a ghetto—such as the availability of a variety of special services, low rents or emotional support—the creation of such "islands of isolation" defers integration. Furthermore, heavy ethnic concentration increases the awareness of the presence of a particular group and becomes the vehicle for social and political movements against further integration.[32]

The issue of residential segregation becomes even more problematic when, as is often the case, ethnic or racial groups are concentrated in occupational niches and/or industrial regions that have suffered heavy job losses. Areas of high unemployment typically demand heavy expenditures on social services as well as income transfers. Residents of these neighborhoods tend to be stigmatized, and observers charge that "cultures of dependency" develop.[33]

When joblessness is geographically and ethnically concentrated, this may create a new barrier to the integration of the young. Free public education has been viewed as an agent of assimilation, an avenue for intergenerational upward mobility. Today, public education credentialling appears to reinforce rather than mitigate ethnic group differences. The educational performance of minority/immigrant children has become a major policy preoccupation in Western countries.[34] Like ethnic minorities in the United States, Canada, and the United Kingdom, the children of immigrants in Europe tend to have low achievement scores, poor basic skills, and are prone to educational failure. With the reduction in the demand for unskilled labor, these young people will face severe disadvantages when competing for work.

When ethnic or racial differences undergird economic inequalities in societies that adhere to democratic ideals and traditions, intergroup tension appears inevitable. If poor market conditions and discrimination force minorities into informal or illegal sectors of the economy, a damaging dynamic may be set in motion. Minority involvement in illegal or unregulated economic activities reinforces the negative racial/ethnic stereotypes of the "majority" population. The minority poor come to be viewed as outside the boundaries of the political/moral community. Support for public assistance erodes, discrimination increases, more minorities are forced into "extralegal" income-generating activities, and social hostilities deepen. As the community fragments into ethnic and class enclaves, the commitment to provide for the "common good" fades. In short, as societies become culturally diverse and less racially homogenous, and as the poor become more culturally and racially distinct from the nonpoor, support for universalism and redistributive welfare state programs seems to waiver.

THIS VOLUME

The contributions to this volume document the developments discussed above in more detail. Part I contains comparative analyses of income, poverty, and workforce trends in a number of Western nations in the 1980s. Parts II to IV focus on policies affecting young adults, lone parents, and ethnic minorities in specific countries. Part V reviews the trends and findings from the earlier chapters and discusses their implications for future policy.

Chapter 1 provides an overview of poverty rates and trends in seven countries. Despite large differences in the distribution of employment and earnings, the incidence of pretax and transfer poverty was relatively high in the 1980s and increased over the decade in five of the seven countries studied. Although government transfer payments provided enough income to lift a significant portion of poor households out of poverty in every country except the United States, posttax and transfer poverty rates increased—at least among some groups —in every country. This suggests that social protection systems are not providing coverage as effectively as in the past.

Duncan et al. (Chapter 2) use longitudinal surveys from six countries to examine transitions into and out of poverty among families with children. In every country, a decline in work hours or loss of a job—i.e., labor market events not marital dissolution or unwed childbearing—were the most common events associated with the beginning of a spell of poverty. A significant number of households also slipped into poverty because social insurance benefits (primarily unemployment insurance) were stopped.

The authors found no trade-off between the incidence of poverty and the length of poverty spells. Rather, the countries with the highest poverty rates also had the highest percentage of long-term poor. Long-term reliance on public assistance was associated with policy factors not with the incidence of poverty. There was apparently little connection between generosity of support and the length of a spell on public assistance.

Susan Mayer examines the relationship between income and measures of well-being in four countries in Chapter 3. She does not find consistent or systematic differences in housing, health visits, and consumer durables between the poor in the United States and the poor in Canada, Sweden, and West Germany. Mayer hypothesizes that the poor in democratic welfare states may have a more similar level of material well-being than income measures suggest because of informal networks of support and non-governmental transfers. Nonetheless, poor people who are poor for long periods seem to experience more material deprivation. If, as this introductory essay suggests, an increasing number of citizens were at risk of experiencing long spells of poverty in the 1980s, then it is likely that material deprivation has been increasing, too.

Standing (Chapter 4) and Gottschalk and Joyce (Chapter 5) examine labor market developments in Western countries in more detail. Standing outlines seven kinds of labor market insecurities that worsened in the 1980s. He attributes these changes to the weakening of labor's political strength and a decline in government support for the objective of ensuring stable, secure employment for all citizens who want work. The growing insecurity of labor has been accompanied by a universal growth in wage inequality among full-time male workers in industrial societies. Gottschalk and Joyce show that both technology and global trade have contributed to this growth in inequality.

In Parts II to IV we move on to examine the way various countries have dealt with the growing vulnerability of our three target groups—lone mothers, young adults, and minorities. The comparative papers in Part I show that cross-national differences in poverty rates among lone-parent families with children were related to the work behavior of lone mothers and to the generosity and organization of social assistance programs for families with children. The chapters in Part II examine the government policies that affect lone mothers in more detail.

Kamerman (Chapter 6) outlines four general approaches to ameliorating the problem of poverty among lone parents: (a) target programs toward poor families; (b) target programs toward lone mothers with modest incomes, based on the assumption that lone mothers have special needs and warrant special assistance; (c) create universal programs for young children, aimed at giving the mothers of young children the choice of remaining at home or working when the child is small; and (d) establish universal labor market programs, designed to provide benefits and services to all working parents so they can remain in the work force during their child-rearing years. She concludes that, with adequate funding, any approach can provide some protection against poverty but argues universal programs are more likely to garner widespread political support and to provide more positive social outcomes in the long-term.

Nadine Lefaucheur (Chapter 7) tracks the development of French social policies from their pronatalist origins to the present. After the Second World War, a network of local maternal and child health and welfare centers was established across the country, and a number of fragmented categorical programs eventually developed into a comprehensive web of social protection. Today, several kinds of income benefits for lone mothers are available and can be combined with more general family benefits. The objective of current French policy is to encourage and enable lone mothers to combine full-time work with parenthood after their youngest child reaches 3 years of age. An extensive system of publicly subsidized childcare makes it possible for mothers to work. However, the economic well-being of lone mothers depends on their earnings capacity and age. Young mothers with little education are still vulnerable to poverty, but the proportion of lone mothers who are under 24 years old is small.

Siv Gustafsson's chapter provides an historical perspective on Sweden's special mix of active labor market programs and redistributive, egalitarian family policies. She cites Sweden's continuing commitment to full employment, progress in gender pay equity (due largely to reductions in occupational wage in-equality), advance child-support collection, and the availability of publicly sup-ported childcare as the most important elements in the nation's ability to provide income security to lone mothers. Despite some recent reforms that allow income inequality to increase somewhat, Gustafsson argues that the Swedish model remains an effective way of ensuring that lone mothers are full and active participants in society, and that all families with children have ade-quate income support.

Ruth Rose (Chapter 9) documents cutbacks in income support for families with children in Canada during the 1980s, and laments that Canada is fast slipping toward a U.S.-style minimalist, decentralized welfare state. She con-demns these developments, arguing that any solution to growing poverty among lone mothers must include a combination of child-support enforcement, better income support for all families, and policies that guarantee women equal access to jobs and earnings.

The lack of subsidized childcare in the United States, the failure to implement policies that "make work pay," and a heavy reliance on means-tested rather than universal benefits are the primary factors that account for the U.S. failure to provide financial security to lone-parent families with children, according to Sara McLanahan and Irwin Garfinkel (Chapter 10). They conclude that policies for lone-parent families in France and Sweden are more effective than American policies in reducing *dependency* as well as poverty because the former countries invest public funds in universal programs that subsidize the costs of child rear-ing *and* they simultaneously invest in programs that promote work among mothers.

These contributions clearly show that some countries are better than others in providing income support that allows lone mothers to achieve income ade-quacy. The trend in most countries has been to reform policies to encourage lone mothers to work, but in an economic climate of rising unemployment and/or falling wages, skeptics might ask if the support costs involved in helping poor mothers work is a wise investment. If jobs are limited, should lone mothers be at the front of the job queue? On the other hand, can lone-parent families expect to achieve economic parity without earnings income? To date, social policies toward lone mothers have been driven by concerns for children and gender equity rather than by broader questions of the allocation of work in society. Of the countries we studied, only the Netherlands and the United Kingdom made little effort to push poor mothers into the labor market in the 1980s. Given their high unemployment rates, this reluctance is hardly surpris-ing. In the decade to come, if joblessness remains high, the commitment to increasing female labor force participation may weaken.

Part III highlights youth employment problems. The degree to which social security systems are able and willing to provide young workers with assistance varies enormously among countries, and the comparative papers show large differences in the effectiveness of tax and transfer systems in reducing poverty among young adults. About half the households headed by young adults in the Netherlands, France, and the United Kingdom were lifted out of poverty as a result of tax and transfer programs in the first half of the 1980s. (Many of these young people were probably receiving unemployment benefits.) But only about a quarter of young West German householders and a little more than a fifth of young Canadian householders were lifted out of poverty by tax and transfer systems. Despite this government assistance, the posttax and posttransfer poverty rate of young adults rose significantly in the 1980s in every country studied.

In European countries, high youth unemployment rates and fears that new labor market entrants were becoming increasingly marginalized led most governments to put more emphasis on training programs for the young in the 1980s. The United Kingdom, Sweden, France, West Germany, and Italy followed this strategy. Unfortunately, the successes of such programs were limited.

Italy established new work and training programs for young people in the mid-1980s, but Pugliese (Chapter 13) argues that the new programs failed to address the basic causes of youth unemployment: regional disparities in investment and growth, and discrimination by age and gender. Moreover, the training programs established in large firms may be marginalizing the youths that they employ by creating a tier of lower-paid laborers.

Even the much-admired German apprenticeship system was forced to reform in the mid-1980s, when it became clear that the "dual system" was not integrating young people into permanent, "core" employment as effectively as it had in past generations. By the latter part of the decade, the situation was improving, partly owing to a decline in the size of the cohort of school-leavers, and partly because the Federal Training Institute (comprised of employers, union representatives, and the government) had revamped the training system and set new goals for employers, according to Bernard Casey (Chapter 12). It is unclear whether these changes will be sufficient to cope with Unification.

The two authors who write about American youth employment problems (Osterman and Duster) are pessimistic about the potential of government programs targeted at young people. Osterman argues that young people are, to some degree, marginalized everywhere because they have fewer skills and less work experience than adults and that this is appropriate. Nonetheless, he finds it troubling that only a third of male high school dropouts and half of male high school graduates in the United States were in stable jobs by the time they reached age 30. The situation among black youths is considerably worse. Osterman believes that the transition into the labor market could be managed better and more fairly and that extending school and apprenticeship programs may be helpful to some youth. However, he believes the underlying problem is the paucity of well-paid jobs available to low-skilled workers in the United States today and employer discrimination in allocating those jobs.

Troy Duster echoes Osterman's concerns about the employment and earnings prospects of black youth. He focuses more attention on the way sectoral changes in the economy affect minority youths. Service work, in contrast to manufacturing jobs, requires a relatively high degree of cultural assimilation, he argues. Among native-born, but culturally distinct minorities, class-race segregation creates behavioral and language differences that may restrict entry into the postindustrial workforce.

Part IV delves into the dynamics of the cross-national and cross-cultural immigration flows that have made the poor in all Western nations more ethnically diverse over the past two decades. In Europe, the recent growth of the minority population was directly related to the demand for low-wage labor according to Ian Gordon (Chapter 16). Gordon contends that keeping this labor "cheap" depends to some extent on ensuring that it remains "distinct" and "alien" from the native population; assimilation of host-country values and standards makes minorities less willing to be satisfied with "dirty jobs" and low wages, and they become less tractable and financially attractive to employers. If this is the case, immigrant minorities face a trade-off. When they remain socially separate in isolated enclaves, they may be able to find work in segregated niches in the labor market, but it will probably be low-wage, marginal employment. When immigrants attempt to enter the mainstream economy and/or industries in a country, they experience higher rates of joblessness, which leads to greater dependence; both circumstances are likely to stigmatize the group and generate mainstream hostility. In all the industrial countries studied, the "minority problem" refers fundamentally to the high rates of joblessness and consequent poverty among minority groups.

Alejandro Portes and Min Zhou argue that immigrant enclaves can also provide minorities with productive roles and a measure of economic independence. They argue that minority communities create their own form of social capital in the "bounded solidarity" and "enforceable trust" found in immigrant communities separated from a host society by ethnicity, culture, and language. This situation provides fertile ground for entrepreneurship. Although the authors acknowledge that this social capital is contingent on situational factors, they contend that developing enterprises within indigenous minority communities could provide a way of bypassing the employment discrimination that economically marginalizes minorities.

Asians appear to be following this path in Britain. According to Colin Brown (Chapter 19), one in four Indian males is self-employed, as are almost one in five Pakistanis and Bangladeshis—proportions that are much higher than the average for white males. However, Brown believes the trend in self-employment represents a withdrawal from the paid labor force as a response to discrimination, and that such behavior may only further marginalize individuals from the economic mainstream. Afro-Caribbeans, in contrast to Asians, have below-average rates of self-employment, high unemployment rates, and are disproportionately found in public sector jobs. Anti-discrimination legislation has not been very effective in improving the employment situation of minorities in the United Kingdom.

Ethnic minorities in Holland also experience disproportionately high rates of joblessness: unemployment rates for the country's minorities are typically twice those of the native population, and long-term unemployment is three times higher among minorities than among native Dutch. Even when controlling for age, education, and other background characteristics, Justus Veenman (Chapter 20) reports large discrepancies in employment rates according to race, providing evidence of labor market discrimination. However, owing to Dutch policies regulating wage inequality and the country's generous system of income and housing support, the living standards of minorities do not appear to be significantly lower than those of many Dutch people. Although minorities are disadvantaged in competing for jobs with the native Dutch, they do not appear to experience the same degree of economic hardship as a result of labor market exclusion as do minorities in other countries. The welfare system provides a level of income support that keeps all people close to the national norm.

In contrast to European countries, urban poor communities in the United States suffer from the effect of living under a system in which the government fails to regulate the impact of the labor market restructuring and fails to provide a minimum standard of living for those who find themselves outside the labor market, according to Loïc Wacquant (Chapter 17). He compares two urban neighborhoods—one in Chicago and one in Paris—that experienced deindustrialization, depopulation, and demographic change in the 1970s and 1980s, and he finds individuals in the Chicago neighborhood much more isolated from mainstream social institutions. He argues that the exclusionary mechanisms that create ghettos in the United States are "organically linked" to state structures and America's history of racial domination.

However, Sophie Body-Gendrot argues that French handling of immigrant and minority groups has not been exemplary. Immigrants are overrepresented among "social housing" tenants, are much more likely to drop out of school than native French children, and suffer disproportionately high unemployment rates. The French government embarked on a major program to revitalize troubled ethnic neighborhoods in the mid-1980s, but tensions remain.

The chapters in Part IV demonstrate the difficulty of advancing the goal of racial or ethnic equality in the context of slow growth and high unemployment. When jobs are scarce employers can be more "selective." Even if there is no conscious decision to discriminate, minorities tend to have educational and/or language deficits that put them at the end of the hiring queue. And, as joblessness and dependency come to be associated with particular groups that are "foreign" or racially distinct from the middle class, sympathy for their plight and public support for universalist programs often deteriorates.

The final section of the volume reviews the evidence presented in previous chapters and speculates about what these developments portend for the future of social policy. Chapter 21 evaluates government efforts to integrate labor market and social policy programs in the 1980s. The most common way of attempting to link the two more closely was to make income support contingent on participation in some kind of job search or training program. The quality of the training and employment services offered varied widely across countries, however, and the countries with the most advanced systems generally worried most about upgrading their training programs. But even in these countries, the institutional networks that deliver training and employment services have proved to be resistant to change. Policymakers largely rejected public job creation schemes in the 1980s because of cost factors and because of an ideological shift away from the language of rights (the right to a job, the right to a minimum income) to a language of contracts and obligations.

Hugh Heclo explores the language underlying policy debates in the 1980s in Chapter 22. He argues that the "rights of social citizenship" have been a defining aspiration of Western societies for over a hundred years, but that in the 1980s, the ideal and possibility of an inclusive society built on a shared vision of social citizenship came under attack from both sides of the ideological spectrum. Recent social policy discussions have been dominated by cost-benefit policy analysis and group interests, and the result has been political paralysis. Citizens no longer see politics/government as the mechanism by which to solve social problems. Heclo asserts that what is required now is moral leadership, that the new policies called for today must come from a shared vision of the kind of society that "we should want to be."

In the final chapter of the volume, Lawson and Wilson review the demographic and political developments associated with "the New Poverty" of the 1980s and conclude that there is a growing convergence of income and racial segregation in Europe and America. Europe's comprehensive programs to promote social rights have so far prevented the emergence of the ghettos and "underclass" areas that characterize American cities, but the authors wonder whether European welfare state programs will be able to continue to provide such protection.

INTO THE NEW CENTURY

Traditional welfare state programs depended on a relatively static vision of social life: occupational training lasted a lifetime; firms and families were firmly attached to stable communities; marriage was a lifetime commitment. However, over the past two decades, change rather than stability has been the dominant feature of modern life. Although policymakers in many industrial countries have struggled to adjust to the new environment, they are working blind. Innovations in social policies in the 1980s were labored and halting because the policy choices made were charting unexplored territory. There are no blueprints for public policies that will ensure growth and generalized prosperity in the competitive global marketplace of the twenty-first century.

Perhaps the most challenging task facing policymakers in Western democracies today is the need to forge a consensus about our vision of the future—the kind of families, workplaces, and communities that will define First World nations in the New World Order. Some fundamental questions remain unanswered. Can we find a common ideal of "the good society" amid societies marked by deepening ethnic and cultural divisions? Is it possible to reform *national* social programs to protect citizens from the negative effects that *global* trade and production systems may have on *local* labor markets? If the traditional institutions on which the welfare state relies—i.e., the family, occupational and workplace associations, residential community ties—are weakening, can new public programs fill the void that their absence creates or do we need to find new forms of social organization?

The grounding assumptions on which traditional welfare programs were built have melted away in the social and economic transformations of the past two decades. But the contours of the new institutions that will emerge to take their place are still hidden in the dawn of a new century. We hope that this volume will encourage readers to peer into the future and talk together about the society they hope to build.

ENDNOTES

1. West Germany is still on par with these "Asian Dragons," but the percentage in manufacturing is declining in Germany and increasing in the Pacific Rim countries.

2. In Canada, the birthrate was halved; the already low Swedish birthrate fell by only 14 percent. (These numbers are calculated from Kamerman, this volume, Table 6.3.)

3. However, unemployment statistics from the last two years (1992 and 1993) give further cause for concern. Unemployment in the United States has remained stubbornly over the 7 percent range. In France, Italy, the United Kingdom, and Canada unemployment has climbed back over the 10 percent market. In Germany, unemployment is now at 8 percent; even Sweden has seen its unemployment rate reach U.S. levels. Only Holland has experienced a significant decline in its unemployment in recent years (it has been halved). (Figures from *The Economist*, July 26, 1993.)

4. *Employment Outlook, 1989*, Chapter Two: "The Educational Attainment of the Laborforce."

5. However, the converse did not necessarily hold true: those with the highest educational attainment levels did not necessarily have the lowest unemployment rates. Whether highly educated workers were fully employed varied according to the structure of national labor markets and, apparently, levels of gender discrimination.

6. Unemployment rates among the young were lower in 1989 than in 1979 in Canada, the United States, and the United Kingdom.

7. *Employment Outlook, 1991*, p. 40.

8. As early as 1986, over three out of ten of the unemployed in the Netherlands, the United Kingdom, Ireland, and Italy were continuously unemployed for *more than two years*. (*Measures to Assist the Long-term Unemployed*, 1988, Table III, pp. 15–17).

9. G. Room et al. 1990, p. 3.

10. Lawson, 1986, for a discussion of the percentage of the unemployed that dropped from unemployment insurance programs to public assistance schemes in West Germany, the United Kingdom, and the Netherlands in the 1980s.

11. *Employment Outlook, 1991*, Chapter 7.

12. Standing, this volume, and Shapiro and Nichols 1991.

13. *Employment Outlook, 1991*, p. 44. See also Chapter 5, *Employment Outlook, 1989*.

14. Bluestone and Harrison 1982; Harrison and Bluestone 1988; Levy 1987; Burtless 1990; Mishel 1991.

15. Levy 1987; Loveman and Tilly 1988; Gottschalk and Joyce, this volume; Danziger and Gottschalk 1992; Freeman and Katz 1993.

16. In the United States, Sweden, and Italy, part-timers represented a relatively unchanging share of the total employed. By the end of the 1980s, fully one-third of all employed persons in the Netherlands worked only part-time.

17. Rodgers and Rodgers 1989; Belous 1989; Callaghan and Hartman 1991.

18. *Employment Outlook, 1992*, Chapter 4. See also Standing, this volume.

19. Economists use the term "flexibility" to refer to a loosening of worker rights and protections, and the use of temporary and part-time workers. See Standing, Chapter 4, for further explication.

20. However, there are important variations in the age at which young adults leave their parents' homes and the incidence of independent living. This can be seen in the various definitions given of what constitutes a child. For example, a child in France is counted as dependent until reaching 24; in the United States, the legal age of adulthood is 18 or 21 years of age. And Pugliese (this volume) tells us that many Italians remain at home until reaching their late twenties.

21. *Employment Outlook, 1989*, Chapter 2.

22. McFate, Smeeding, and Rainwater, this volume.

23. Blundell and Walker 1988; Roll 1989; OECD 1990b.

24. McFate, Smeeding, and Rainwater, this volume; Kamerman, this volume.

25. McFate, Smeeding, and Rainwater, this volume.

26. Moreover, elderly citizens in Western societies today are often asset-rich, rather than income-wealthy. Geography and space may not allow them to share their residence with an adult child and grandchildren.

27. Rising female labor force participation rates are both cause and consequence of rising divorce rates. A women who cannot depend on the permanence of marriage will want to remain linked to the labor market; a women who has an independent source of income may be more likely to leave an unsatisfying marriage than a woman with no independent income source.

   For men, the trade-off is more ambiguous. A man might be more willing to leave a wife who can support herself than one who is dependent on him (and can claim alimony as well as child support). On the other hand, research in the United States has shown that men tend be better off a few years after a divorce than divorced custodial mothers.

28. T. H. Marshall 1950; Titmuss 1974; Epsing-Anderson 1990.

29. During the 1980s, there was a significant increase in immigrants from a number of Asian countries, but few are overrepresented in poverty statistics. Portes, this volume, 1990.

30. Gordon, this volume.

31. Veenman, this volume.

32. OECD 1987a.

33. Wilson 1987, and Dean 1991.

34. OECD 1989c.

REFERENCES

Belous, R. 1989. "How Human Resource Systems Adjust to the Shift Towards Contingent Workers." *Monthly Labor Review* March: 7–12.

Blank, R. 1993. "Working Under Different Rules." Paper prepared for the NBER/Ford Foundation project on Social Protection vs. Economic Flexibility: Is There a Tradeoff?, Washington, D.C., May 7.

Bluestone, B., and B. Harrison. 1982. *The Deindustrialization of America*. New York: Basic Books.

Blundell, R., and I. Walker. 1988. "The Changing Structure of the Labour Force: Married Women and Lone Parents." Symposium of Population Change and European Society. Florence, Italy: European University Institute, Dec. 7–10.

Burtless, G., ed. 1990. *A Future of Lousy Jobs?* Washington, D.C.: Brookings Institution.

Callaghan, P., and H. Hartman. 1991. *Contingent Work: A Chart Book on Part-Time and Temporary Employment*. Washington, D.C.: Economic Policy Institute.

CBO. 1988. *Trends in Family Income: 1970–1986*. Washington, D.C.: Congressional Budget Office.

Center for Budget and Policy Priorities. 1988. *Holes in the Safety Net*. Washington, D.C.: Center for Budget and Policy Priorities.

Danziger, S., and P. Gottschalk, eds. 1993. *Uneven Tides*. New York: Russell Sage Foundation.

Dean, H. 1991. "Dependency Culture: The Image and Reality of the Claiming Experience." Paper presented to the Annual Conference of the Social Policy Association, University of Nottingham, England.

Economic Council of Canada. 1990. *Good Jobs, Bad Jobs: Employment in the Service Economy*. Ontario: The Economic Council of Canada.

Epsing-Anderson, G. 1990. *The Three Worlds of Welfare Capitalism*. Princeton, N.J.: Princeton University Press.

Freeman, R. 1988. *Evaluating the European View that the United States Has No Unemployment Problem*. Reprint No. 1150. Cambridge: NBER Publications.

Freeman, R., and L. Katz, eds. 1993. *Differences and Changes in Wage Structures*. Chicago: University of Chicago Press.

Garfinkel, I., and S. McLanahan. 1986. *Single Mothers and Their Children: A New American Dilemma*. Washington, D.C.: The Urban Institute Press.

George, V., and R. Lawson, eds. 1990. *Poverty and Inequality in Common Market Countries*. London: Routledge Kegan Paul Ltd.

Harrison, B., and B. Bluestone. 1988. *The Great U-Turn: Corporate Restructuring and the Polarizing of America.* New York: Basic Books.

Korpi, W. 1980. "Approaches to the Study of Poverty in the United States: Critical Notes from a European Perspective." Working Paper Series, No. 64. Swedish Institute for Social Research.

———. 1985. "Economic Growth and the Welfare State: A Comparative Study of 18 OECD Countries." Reprint Series No. 145. Swedish Institute for Social Research, August.

Lawson, R. 1986. "Income Support During Unemployment: Comparison in Western Europe, 1945–1985." In *EISS Yearbook of Social Security in Europe.*

———. 1987. "Social Security and the Division of Welfare." In G. Causer, ed. *Inside British Society: Continuity, Challenge and Change.* New York: St. Martin's Press.

Levy, F. 1987. *Dollars and Dreams: The Changing American Income Distribution.* New York: Russell Sage Foundation.

Loveman, G., and C. Tilly. 1988. *Good Jobs or Bad Jobs: What Does the Evidence Say?* World Employment Programme Labour Market Analysis Working Paper No. 22. Geneva: International Labour Organisation, June.

Maier, C., ed. 1987. *Changing Boundaries of the Political: Essays on the Evolving Balance Between the State and Society, Public and Private in Europe.* Cambridge: Cambridge University Press.

Marshall, T. H. 1950. *Citizenship and Social Class.* Cambridge: Cambridge University Press.

Mishel, L., and J. Bernstein. 1992. *The State of Working America, 1992–93.* Washington, D.C.: Economic Policy Institute.

OECD. 1981. *The Welfare State in Crisis.* Paris: OECD.

———. 1987a. *The Future of Migration,* Paris: OECD.

———. 1987b. *The Future of Social Protection: The General Debate.* Paris: OECD.

———. 1988a. *Aging Populations: The Social Policy Implications.* Paris: OECD.

———. 1988b. *Measures to Assist the Long-Term Unemployed: Recent Experience in Some OECD Countries.* Paris: OECD.

———. 1989a. *Employment Outlook: July 1989.* Paris: OECD.

———. 1989b. *Historical Statistics: 1960–1987, OECD Economic Outlook.* Paris: OECD.

———. 1989c. *One School, Many Cultures.* Paris: OECD.

———. 1990a. *Employment Outlook, July 1990.* Paris: OECD.

———. 1990b. *Lone-Parent Families: The Economic Challenge.* Paris: OECD.

———. 1991. *Employment Outlook, July 1991.* Paris: OECD.

———. 1992. *Employment Outlook, 1992.* Paris: OECD.

Palmer, J., T. Smeeding, and B. Torrey, eds. 1988. *The Vulnerable: The Changing Domestic Priorities Series.* Washington, D.C.: The Urban Institute Press.

Piore, Michael, and Charles Sabel. 1984. *The Second Industrial Divide: Possibilities for Prosperity.* New York: Basic Books.

Portes, A. 1990. *Immigrant America: A Portrait*. Berkeley: University of California Press.

Rainwater, L. 1988. "Inequalities in the Economic Well-Being of Children and Adults in Ten Nations." LIS-CEPS Working Paper No. 19, Luxembourg.

Rodgers, G., and J. Rodgers, eds. 1989. *Precarious Jobs in Labour Market Regulation*. Geneva: International and Institute for Labour Studies, International Labour Organisation.

Roll, J. 1989. *Lone Parent Families in the European Community*. Final report. Family Policy Studies Centre. Unpublished, January.

Room, G., et al. 1990. *Final Report of the Programme Evaluation Team for the Commission of the European Communities*. Bath University, April.

Shapiro, I., and M. Nichols. 1991. *Unemployed and Uninsured*. Washington, D.C.: Center on Budget and Policy Priorities.

Smeeding, T., M. O'Higgins, and L. Rainwater. 1990. *Poverty, Inequality and Income Distribution in Comparative Perspective: The Luxembourg Income Study*. London: Harvester Wheafsheft.

Smith, S. 1986. *The Politics of Race and Residence*. London: Polity Press.

Sorrentino, C. 1990. "The Changing Family in International Perspective." *Monthly Labor Review* March: 41–56.

Standing, G. 1986. *Unemployment and Labour Market Flexibility: United Kingdom*. Geneva: International Labour Organisation.

———. 1988. *Unemployment and Labour Market Flexibility: Sweden*. Geneva: International Labour Organisation.

———. 1989. "European Unemployment, Insecurity and Flexibility Planning: A Social Dividend Solution." Working Paper No. 23. Geneva: International Labour Office.

Teekens, R., and M. A. Zaidi. 1989. "Relative and Absolute Poverty in the European Community: Results from Family Budget Survey." Den Haag. Unpublished paper, September.

Titmuss, R. M. 1974. *Social Policy*. London: Allen & Unwin.

Townsend, P., and David Gordon. 1989. "What Is Enough? New Evidence Allowing the Definition of a Minimum Benefit." University of Bristol. Unpublished paper, July.

Wilson, W. J. 1987. *The Truly Disadvantaged*. Chicago: University of Chicago Press.

Part I

POVERTY, INCOME INEQUALITY, AND LABOR MARKET INSECURITY: A COMPARATIVE PERSPECTIVE

Chapter 1

MARKETS AND STATES:
POVERTY TRENDS
AND TRANSFER SYSTEM EFFECTIVENESS
IN THE 1980s

Katherine McFate, Timothy Smeeding,
and Lee Rainwater

C HANGES in the labor markets of advanced industrial societies over the past decade and a half left significant numbers of working age citizens without adequate private support, so that by the end of the 1980s, both "reluctant welfare states" and "redistributive regimes" found their safety nets straining under the burden of expanding numbers of non-elderly poor. This chapter examines changes in the amount of market-generated poverty in the United States, Canada, France, (the former) West Germany, the United Kingdom, Sweden, and the Netherlands in the 1980s and finds that, despite large differences in the distribution of employment and earnings, the incidence of pretax and transfer poverty rates in most countries was high and increasing. Although government transfer programs provided enough income to lift a significant portion of poor households above the poverty line in every country except the United States, these interventions were unable to prevent posttax and transfer poverty among working age citizens from increasing in most countries.

This chapter provides an overview of changes in the incidence of poverty in these seven countries and discusses differences in patterns of work, earnings, and transfer system effectiveness among non-elderly households and among two particularly vulnerable groups—young adults and lone parents with children. Descriptions of the policies responsible for the results described here can be found in later chapters of this volume.

DATA AND DEFINITIONS

The Luxembourg Income Study (LIS), a comparative data set that undergirds this analysis, consists of a set of national household surveys that include similar social and economic indicators from a number of industrial nations. Specifically, the LIS data files contain detailed information on the level and composition of individual household income, the family structure of the household, and the net effects of various taxes and income assistance programs. Although the various national data sets are not strictly and completely comparable, they do allow for general comparisons of the economic status of national populations and subgroups within nations at two points in time in the 1980s.[1] The two North American and five European countries examined here were selected because they share similar social, cultural, and political histories, and because each national data set had the relevant income and trend data for this analysis.[2] More detailed descriptions of the national surveys used can be found in Tables 1A.1–1A.4.

In this analysis, we are concerned with (a) the way the market and private familial networks distribute income, and (b) the way government policies redistribute this income—by collecting taxes and providing income assistance to households with "special needs" (dependent children, an unemployed family head, etc.). We therefore use two income measures. *Pretax and transfer income* consists of market income (wages, salary, income from self-employment or property income), private transfers among family members (alimony, child support), and deferred earnings (occupational pensions). *Posttax and transfer income* includes all forms of regular cash income (and near cash income) net of direct taxes (income and payroll taxes).[3] Hence, the difference between "pretax and transfer" and "posttax and transfer" household income is attributed to government policies.

For the purposes of this analysis, we defined "poor" or "low-income" as *a household in which the total household income was less than 50 percent of the median adjusted household income of non-elderly households in the country of residence.*[4] We believe that poverty is a *relative* concept—individuals perceive themselves and are perceived by others as poor or economically disadvantaged according to the norms of the society in which they live (Rainwater 1992; Hagenaars 1986). This is particularly the case in affluent societies like the ones examined here. We assume that a family with less than half the income of most non-elderly households in their country of residence would have a living standard below acceptable norms and might have difficulty participating in "mainstream" activities and institutions in their country of residence.[5]

The 50 percent-of-median income poverty line used here to delineate low-income households is somewhat arbitrary, but is becoming conventional in European debates where researchers have struggled with cross-national comparisons for decades (Eurostat 1990; Atkinson 1991; Hagenaars 1980). Table 1.1 shows the percentage of non-elderly households with incomes under 40 percent, 50 percent, and 60 percent of the household median in each country at two points in time. Although incidence rates obviously vary with the measures used, the *rankings* remain remarkably similar regardless of the thresholds (with the exception of the United Kingdom—a country that experienced a precipitous increase in unemployment between the two study years). That rankings remain

Table 1.1 / **Posttax and Transfer Poverty Rates for Households with Heads Aged 20–55 Years Old, Using Three Different Median Income Poverty Measures**

Country, Period	40 Percent of Adjusted Median Household Income		50 Percent of Adjusted Median Household Income		60 Percent of Adjusted Median Household Income	
	Period 1	Period 2	Period 1	Period 2	Period 1	Period 2
United States, 1979, 1986	10.8	13.6	15.6	18.1	21.6	23.9
Canada, 1981, 1987	8.6	8.3	13.4	13.9	18.7	19.6
United Kingdom, 1979, 1986	3.6	7.0	8.5	12.5	14.5	20.0
West Germany, 1981, 1984	2.1	3.2	5.5	6.8	11.5	14.1
Netherlands, 1983, 1987	6.0	5.7	7.9	7.6	12.6	12.6
France, 1979, 1984	5.4	6.1	9.9	9.9	16.3	16.9
Sweden, 1981, 1987	4.3	5.9	6.6	8.6	10.7	12.6

SOURCE: Luxembourg Income Study, authors' calculations.

similar, regardless of the poverty measures used, has been confirmed by Rainwater in other work (1990).

The official measures of income adequacy in the countries that have one all fall within 40 to 60 percent of median income household income, adjusted for size (Buhmann et al. 1988; Rainwater 1990; Smeeding 1992). The United States and the United Kingdom represent the low end of government definitions of income adequacy; both have official poverty lines of about 40 percent of median family income (Smeeding 1992). The British were very effective in limiting the number of households that fell below the official measure of income adequacy at the end of 1970s—less than 4 percent fell below the mark. Americans were much less effective. In the United States, almost 11 percent of non-elderly households were poor by the U.S. definition. Sweden represents the high end of official government definitions of poverty. The standard of income adequacy in Sweden (as measured by their minimum income programs) is about 60 percent of median income. Almost as many households fell beneath this line *after* government interventions as fell below the official poverty line in the United States after transfers. Thus, we find that poverty/low income levels are affected by official measures of income adequacy, but are clearly *not* determined by them. There are no official poverty lines in Canada, France, West Germany, and the Netherlands. (See Table 1A.4 for poverty lines in national currency.)

CHANGES IN POVERTY IN THE 1980s

The incidence of posttax and transfer poverty varied significantly across the countries studied, but relative rankings remained fairly constant (Figure 1.1). The United States consistently had the highest poverty rates and Canada followed it closely. At the beginning of the 1980s, about one in seven non-elderly

Figure 1.1 / Changes in Posttax and Transfer Poverty Rates Among Non-Elderly Households

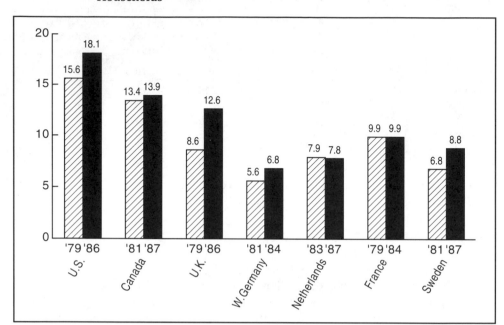

households in the U.S. and Canada were poor—fully twice the proportion as were poor in the Netherlands, Sweden, and West Germany.

Over the period studied, posttax and transfer poverty rates increased significantly in five of the seven countries. The most dramatic increase occurred in the United Kingdom, where poverty increased by 47 percent, but West Germany, Sweden, and the United States also experienced significant increases (33 percent, 30 percent, and 16 percent, respectively). Posttax and transfer poverty rates in France, the Netherlands, and Canada remained stable.

By the second half of the 1980s, an Anglo-American–Continental European divide in the overall incidence of poverty emerges. The average incidence of poverty in the Anglo countries was almost twice the average in the four European countries, 15.2 percent compared to 8.2 percent. These Anglo–European differences are also evident when we examine two subgroups at particular risk of poverty—households headed by young adults and households headed by lone mothers.

Young adults who entered the labor market in the early 1980s faced a very slack labor market with sluggish growth rates. Youth unemployment was particularly high. The work young people found was likely to be of a contingent and/or temporary nature, reducing their ability to qualify for workplace-based insurance schemes when/if they found themselves out of a job. Figure 1.2 shows that posttax and transfer poverty rates among young people rose in every country studied. In most cases, the increase was quite dramatic.

Figure 1.2 / Changes in Posttax and Transfer Poverty Rates Among Households Headed by a 20–29 Year Old

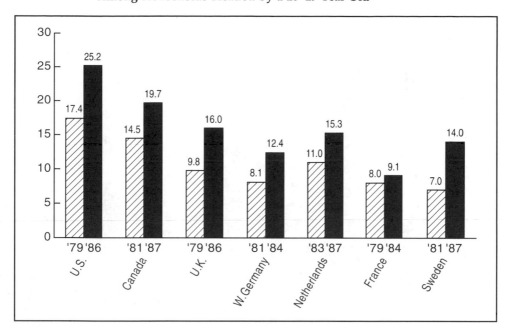

The situation of lone-parent families with children in the United States, Canada, and West Germany was even worse than that of young people. Lone-parent households in these countries had poverty rates two to three times the general rate (Figure 1.3). By the second half of the decade, only Sweden and the Netherlands had lone-parent poverty rates close to the national rate. At the same time, we see that posttax and transfer poverty rates among lone parents declined in France, Britain, and Sweden, even though the overall poverty rate did not. In sum, we find the greatest cross-national variation in posttax and transfer poverty rates among lone-parent families. Not only does the *incidence* of posttax and transfer poverty among lone parents vary widely; change trends are also diverse.

What accounts for the observed differences in overall and subgroup poverty rates in these countries? How much of the variation is due to national economic conditions and how much is due to differences in the effectiveness of income support policies?

Market-Generated Poverty

Beginning in the mid-1970s, low or unsteady growth rates left a legacy of higher overall unemployment, industry-wide depressions, and regional concentrations of long-term joblessness in most industrialized countries. As the share of manufacturing jobs in society fell (Gottschalk and Joyce, Chapter 5 in this

Figure 1.3 / Changes in Posttax and Transfer Poverty Rates Among Lone-Parent Families with Children

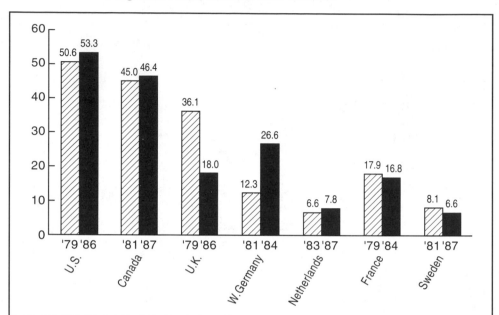

book), and work became more insecure (Standing, Chapter 4 in this book), a growing number and percentage of households found that earnings from work were not providing an adequate, secure income. Since earnings constitute the major source of support for the vast majority of households with heads 20–55 years of age, this resulted in an increase in pretax and transfer or market-generated poverty in every country except the Netherlands and Sweden (Table 1.2).

Market-generated poverty can increase for a variety of reasons. Since high unemployment rates reduce the number of households with earnings and can depress wages (especially among the least skilled), we would expect unemployment rates and pretax and transfer poverty rates to be strongly correlated. But poverty could also increase if a household head and/or secondary worker was working fewer hours (because of part-time or temporary work assignments) or if the real wages of some workers were falling. In fact, the constellation of factors affecting market-generated poverty vary by national economic circumstances and institutions.

The decade of the 1980s was characterized by relatively slow growth rates and high unemployment in all seven nations in this study (Table 1A.5). Most experienced a recession in the early 1980s, and higher, if uneven, growth rates in the latter part of the decade, but higher growth rates resulted in lower unemployment in only two countries—Sweden and the Netherlands.[6] These were the two countries in which pretax and transfer poverty rates declined slightly.

Table 1.2 / The Relationship Between General Unemployment Levels
and Pretax and Transfer Poverty Rates

Country	Unemployment Rate	Poverty Rate Before Taxes and Transfers
United States		
1979	5.8	16.1
1986	6.9	18.0
	+ 1.1	+ 1.9
Canada		
1981	7.5	16.4
1987	8.8	17.4
	+ 1.3	+ 1.0
United Kingdom		
1979	5.6	12.8
1986	11.2	23.2
	+ 5.6	+10.4
West Germany		
1981	4.4	6.9
1984	7.1	10.7
	+ 2.7	+ 3.8
Netherlands		
1983	13.7	20.6
1987	9.6	19.9
	− 4.1	− .7
France		
1979	5.9	18.4
1984	9.7	20.4
	+ 3.8	+ 2.0
Sweden		
1981	2.5	16.0
1987	1.9	15.3
	− .6	− .7

SOURCES: Column 1: OECD: *Main Economic Indicators;* Column 2: Luxembourg Income Study.

Despite the very robust growth rates experienced by the United Kingdom, unemployment doubled over the period examined as did pretax and transfer poverty. France also experienced high unemployment at the end of the decade,
despite its higher growth rates at that time, and its pretax and transfer poverty
rate was quite high. By contrast, growth rates in Sweden were rather anemic
for most of the decade, but unemployment never reached the 4 percent mark
(Table 1.2).

In the second half of the 1980s, Sweden had an unemployment rate one-third
as high as West Germany's but a higher pretax and transfer poverty rate. The
United States had a lower unemployment rate but a higher pretax and transfer

poverty rate than Canada's. In five of the seven countries, the market-generated poverty rate was at least twice as high as the unemployment rate. But in Sweden, the pretax and transfer poverty rate was seven times the unemployment rate, while in West Germany it was only 50 percent higher. In short, although unemployment and market-generated poverty rates moved together in all countries (Table 1.2), the *incidence* of unemployment and market poverty are not strictly correlated.

It is evident that government policies directed at keeping unemployment low have some impact on pretax and transfer poverty rates, but, as the case of Sweden shows, low unemployment does not eliminate market-generated poverty. Nevertheless, it is important to understand that differences in the commitment to full employment and wage-setting institutions have an effect on poverty rates, even before the impact of social protection programs is taken into account.

The data in Table 1.3 show that different patterns of work and earnings lay beneath the varied incidence of pretax and transfer poverty shown in Table 1.2. In the United States and Canada, over two-thirds of all poor households had some earnings. However, the earnings of poor household heads averaged only a fifth of the median household income in each country, and one in every twenty households with a full-time, full-year worker was poor. Despite a declining unemployment rate and a pretax and transfer poverty rate somewhat lower than the American countries, the Swedish pattern of work among the poor was similar to the American pattern. The vast majority of poor Swedish households had some earnings, but full-time, full-year work was not much more of a guarantee against market-based poverty than it was in the United States. In France, too, the great majority of poor households had some earnings. However, the average earnings of the French poor were significantly higher (as a percentage of the median household income) than the other countries.

In the Netherlands, West Germany, and the United Kingdom, poverty and joblessness are more closely tied. In the United Kingdom, it is apparent that joblessness was the major cause of increased poverty. In the Netherlands, even though the unemployment rate dropped by over 20 percent, the percentage of poor households with no earnings increased. Less than 15 percent of poor households in the Netherlands had *any* earnings by the second part of the decade. However, very few households in the Netherlands with full-time, full-year workers were poor. In West Germany, too, there was little poverty among full-time, full-year workers. Unemployment increased in West Germany over the study period as did the pretax and transfer poverty rate, yet the proportion of poor households without earnings did not, suggesting that part-time or temporary work increased with unemployment. The significant increase in pretax and transfer poverty in West Germany may have been fueled by rising unemployment as well as by an increase in part-time workers. Nevertheless, the wage-setting institutions in the Netherlands and West Germany were significantly more effective in ensuring full-time workers an adequate income than the institutions in other countries.

Government policies affect pretax and transfer poverty rates insofar as they

Table 1.3 / Earnings and Market-Generated Poverty (household heads aged 20–55)

Country	Percentage of Pretax and Transfer Poor Households with No Earnings	Average Earnings of the Poor as Percentage of Median Income	Adjusted Median Household Income[a]	Pretax and Transfer Poverty Rate of Households with a Full-Time Worker[b]
United States				
1979	28.5	18.6	$ 23,984	4.8
1986	30.0	17.1	$ 24,540	4.7
Canada				
1981	25.6	19.7	$C 31,666	6.4
1987	34.3	19.3	$C 31,122	5.0
United Kingdom				
1979	34.3	20.9	£ 10,172	N.A.
1986	67.5	8.7	£ 9,298	N.A.
West Germany				
1981	49.3	17.7	Dm 38,774	1.9
1984	49.6	14.7	Dm 37,620	2.2
Netherlands				
1983	84.2	4.7	Dfl. 32,212	4.7
1987	87.8	3.3	Dfl. 34,364	1.2
France				
1979	9.8	28.4	ƒƒ 105,760	N.A.
1984	16.9	25.4	ƒƒ 110,442	N.A.
Sweden				
1981	23.1	20.9	Kr. 145,812	3.5
1987	18.7	20.2	Kr. 151,114	4.8

SOURCE: Luxembourg Income Study, authors' calculations.

NOTES: All figures are for households headed by a person aged 20–55 years old.
　　　 N.A. = Not Available.

[a] Adjusted median income in both periods is shown in the real value of the currency of the country, in the money value of the second year of data.
[b] The U.K. and France data sets do not have a variable that allows identification of full-time, full-year workers.

reduce unemployment and keep the wages of full-time workers high. Anti-inflationary policies may also affect LIS measures of relative poverty, since our poverty rates control for inflation. Consumer price inflation declined across from the first period to the second in every country studied (Table 1A.5). All the countries except West Germany and the Netherlands experienced at least two years of double-digit inflation in the early part of the decade; these high inflation rates could have reduced the real value of wages and non-indexed government benefits in these countries to make their poverty rates look worse than those in the Netherlands and West Germany. But a glance at the pretax and transfer poverty rate of the Netherlands would suggest the low inflation rate did not keep poverty rates low. The low inflation rate in West Germany, however, may have contributed to its low pretax and transfer poverty rate relative to the other countries studied.

To summarize trends in market-generated poverty in the 1980s: overall, pre-tax and transfer poverty in these industrialized nations increased. At the beginning of the decade, the market produced poverty rates of between 6.9 and 20.6 percent; by the second half of the decade, pretax and transfer poverty affected from 10.7 percent to 23.2 percent of non-elderly households. In four out of the seven countries studied (France, Sweden, the United States, and Canada), the great majority of poor households had some earnings—someone was still attached to the labor force. Unfortunately, earnings and private transfers were not enough to provide these families with income adequacy. Even full-time work left one in every twenty households poor in America.

In the United Kingdom, the Netherlands, and West Germany, poverty and joblessness were more strongly associated. Only half the poor households in West Germany had earnings; a third of those in the United Kingdom had earnings (a huge drop from the two-thirds of 7 years earlier), and less than one in nine poor households in the Netherlands had any earnings. However, in West Germany and the Netherlands, full-time work provided good protection against poverty.

The Impact of Tax and Transfer Policies on the Non-Elderly Poor

How effective were income support programs in ameliorating the increase in market-based poverty? After taxes are subtracted and income transfers added, the poverty rate of the Continental European countries fell, so that all of them had poverty rates of less than 10 percent in both periods (Figure 1.1). By contrast, poverty rates in the United States, Canada, and the United Kingdom stood at 18.1, 13.9, and 12.5 percent by the latter period.

The poverty rate among non-elderly household heads in the United States was practically unaffected by tax and transfer policies. It stood alone as the only industrial country whose tax and transfer policies failed to reduce poverty among non-elderly households in the 1980s.[7] The Canadian poverty rate was somewhat reduced by government interventions: about one of every five poor

Figure 1.4 / Percentage of All Poor Households Lifted out of Poverty by Tax and Transfer Programs

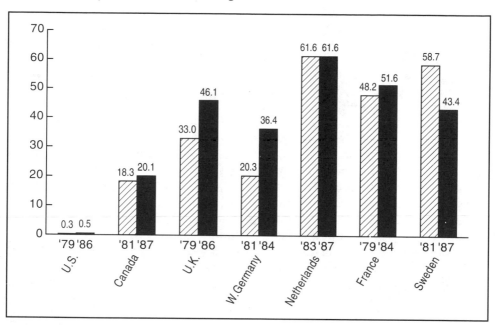

families in Canada were helped out of poverty (Figure 1.4). In the United King-dom, government policies reduced market poverty by half, but the British mar-ket poverty rate rose so steeply over the 7-year period that the posttax and transfer poverty rate in the United Kingdom was close to Canada's by the second half of the 1980s.

Government policies were most effective in reducing poverty in the Nether-lands. Over 60 percent of all non-elderly poor households in the Netherlands were lifted out of poverty by transfer programs, leaving an overall posttax and transfer poverty rate of less than 8 percent despite extremely high rates of market-generated poverty (Figure 1.4). As economic conditions worsened in France and West Germany, public assistance programs actually *improved* in ef-fectiveness—i.e., they helped a greater percentage of the poor move out of poverty. As a result, France was able to prevent an increase in posttax and transfer poverty among the non-elderly. However, despite the fact that West German policies almost doubled in effectiveness during the study period, post-tax and transfer poverty increased from 5.5 to 6.8 percent of non-elderly house-holds. The overall effectiveness of Swedish income support programs declined significantly between 1981 and 1987, in spite of a reduction in unemployment and market-generated poverty rates during this period. Even so, almost 44 percent of poor Swedish households were lifted out of poverty as a result of government interventions, leaving a national poverty rate of less than 9 percent.

VULNERABLE GROUPS: YOUNG ADULTS AND LONE PARENTS

Having examined the effects of tax and transfer policies on aggregate poverty rates in these seven countries, we turn now to look more closely at two groups that seemed at particular risk of poverty in the 1980s: households headed by young adults and households headed by lone parents. To some extent, both these groups are caught between changing cultural norms regarding individual independence and autonomy and a changing economy.

In previous generations, young adults might expect to live with their parents, even in the early years of marriage and childbearing, if they were unable to afford housing or found themselves in unstable employment. Today, young adults who are unable to establish independent households (due to housing costs or poor employment prospects) experience this as a deprivation as do many of their parents. Yet young people who do set up independent households have poverty rates much higher than the national norm. Whether or not these young adults can expect to "age out" of poverty is an open question, addressed by several authors in Parts III and IV of this volume.

Lone parents are similarly squeezed between changing attitudes toward working mothers, marriage, and child-rearing, and the economic reality that it is becoming more difficult for an individual with limited skills and/or education to adequately support even one dependent on his or her earnings alone. Although in most countries mothers are now expected to work, *when* a mother should return to the workforce and *how much* work is expected varies greatly according to national norms. The stigma attached to divorce and single motherhood as well as the legal and social sanctions on fathers who fail to support their children show much cross-national variation. These cultural differences are reflected in maternal work behavior, in the level of paternal transfers to nonresident children, and in the level and kind of government assistance provided to lone-parent households with children. Part II of this volume discusses national policies toward lone parents in more detail.

Young Adults

Young adults entering the workforce for the first time in the 1980s were probably most affected by poor labor market conditions. Pretax and transfer poverty rates among households headed by a young person increased significantly in every country except Sweden over the 1980s, so that at least one out of five households headed by a young person was poor by the second part of the decade (Table 1.4). By contrast, pretax and transfer poverty rates among households headed by older adults (30–55 years old) were stable or declining in every country except the United Kingdom and West Germany, where unemployment increased significantly. This suggests that older workers in the industrial countries studied were generally insulated from the economic effects of labor market restructuring in the 1980s. (However, there are signs that this will not be the case in the 1990s.)

Table 1.4 / Pretax and Transfer Poverty and Joblessness Among Young Adults (household heads aged 20–29)

| Country, Period | Pretax and Transfer Poverty Rate | | | Percentage of Poor Households with No Earnings | | |
	Period 1	Period 2	Percent Change Between Two Periods	Period 1	Period 2	Increase/ Decrease
United States, 1979, 1986						
All households	17.8	24.4	37.0	26.1	27.6	+
All households with children	26.8	39.2	46.0	30.5	30.2	−
Households without children	11.6	14.9	25.8	19.1	23.2	+
Canada, 1981, 1987						
All households	17.7	23.9	35.0	26.8	22.0	−
All households with children	25.8	34.9	35.3	30.1	31.4	+
Households without children	13.3	19.8	48.9	23.5	15.8	−
United Kingdom, 1979, 1986						
All households	14.7	29.8	102.7	47.6	79.9	+
All households with children	20.4	48.6	138.2	34.9	74.9	+
Households without children	8.5	16.0	88.2	80.5	91.2	+
West Germany, 1981, 1984						
All households	12.1	18.5	52.9	68.3	62.8	−
All households with children	5.1	17.6	245.0	45.1	53.0	+
Households without children	15.3	18.7	22.2	71.9	65.4	−
Netherlands, 1983, 1987						
All households	27.6	31.3	13.4	93.3	96.5	+
All households with children	29.0	35.4	22.0	94.7	92.5	−
Households without children	27.2	30.3	11.3	92.8	97.6	+
France, 1979, 1986						
All households	14.1	18.3	29.8	1.3	20.5	+
All households with children	19.3	26.1	35.2	1.4	13.9	+
Households without children	8.8	12.2	38.6	1.3	30.9	+
Sweden, 1981, 1987						
All households	21.3	20.6	−4.6	15.1	10.1	−
All households with children	19.7	27.8	41.1	9.5	6.7	−
Households without children	21.7	19.3	−11.0	16.2	11.0	−

SOURCE: Luxembourg Income Study, authors' calculations.

The increased economic vulnerability of the young adult population in the 1980s was related to the fact that young people tend to have both higher rates of unemployment and lower wages than the general workforce. To some extent, this represents a natural sorting process. However, when large numbers of new labor market entrants are unable to obtain work for long periods of time, they tend to become less attractive to potential employers, and may even be stigma-

Table 1.5 / Unemployment Rates Among Young Adults, by Gender, Age, and Educational Attainment: 1988

Country	All Ages	Male Unemployment Rates, by Age and Education			
		All, Aged 20–24	Least Educated, Aged 20–24	All, Aged 25–34	Least Educated, Aged 25–34
United States	5.6	10.2	19.9	6.4	13.9
Canada	7.9	14.0	22.1	8.6	15.3
United Kingdom	10.4	15.3	19.9	11.5	17.9
West Germany	6.9	10.3	17.5	7.8	19.8
Netherlands	7.5	10.4	11.8	7.3	10.7
Italy	6.7	25.9	21.4	12.0	10.6
Sweden	1.8	4.3	6.6	2.1	3.2

SOURCE: OECD: *Employment Outlook*, July 1989, Table 2A.1.

tized as "unemployable"; and the chances that a segment of the cohort will become permanently marginalized (i.e., resigned to long-term joblessness or relegated to low-skilled, poorly paid employment niches) increase.

Although employment among young adults rose in the latter part of the 1980s, youth unemployment rates were still significantly higher than overall unemployment rates in all countries save the Netherlands by the end of the decade (Table 1.5). In any case, general youth unemployment rates do not convey the limited character of the employment opportunities available to the least skilled. Young people with good educational credentials are eventually able to find employment; it is those without the qualifications who are likely to experience high rates of joblessness. Table 1.5 shows that unemployment among the least educated young people is at least 50 percent higher than the already-high unemployment rate for that age cohort. The only exceptions to this pattern are Italy[8] and the Netherlands.

Moreover, the LIS data suggests that formal unemployment figures underestimate joblessness among the young. According to the LIS data, almost 30 percent of all households headed by a 20–29-year-old in the Netherlands reported no earnings whatsoever in 1987 (Table 1.4), yet official statistics reported unemployment rates of only 10 to 12 percent. In the United Kingdom, about a quarter of 20–29-year-old household heads reported no earnings in 1986, but the official unemployment rate among young people in the United Kingdom was higher than in the Netherlands. The relationship between formal unemployment figures and actual joblessness varies by country. Many unemployed young people probably remain in the homes of parents or relatives, but it appears that a good number of young adult household heads may have withdrawn from the job search process and are not therefore counted as unemployed. Reporting procedures, opportunities for advanced schooling, and the availability (or lack) of income support for new labor market entrants who cannot find work probably all have an effect on official figures.

Table 1.5   (*continued*)

Country	Female Unemployment Rates, by Age and Education				
	All Ages	All, Aged 20–24	Least Educated, Aged 20–24	All, Aged 25–34	Least Educated, Aged 25–34
United States	4.8	8.9	22.2	5.4	13.9
Canada	9.0	11.8	25.0	9.6	16.7
United Kingdom	9.7	13.9	16.8	12.9	15.9
West Germany	9.4	9.6	17.6	11.1	18.0
Netherlands	13.2	12.6	16.9	13.6	19.3
Italy	16.3	38.1	33.6	23.7	23.1
Sweden	1.8	4.3	7.5	2.1	3.4

While joblessness among young adults is clearly a problem, note that in three countries—the United States, Canada, and France—the great majority of poor young household heads worked at least part-time, part-year (Table 1.4). In the United States and Canada, childless young adults were much more likely to have earnings than young people heading households with children. But in France, this situation was reversed: young lone parents were more likely to be working than childless young adults. We presume this difference is related to the availability of high-quality, publicly funded childcare in France (see Lefaucheur, Chapter 7).

The degree to which social security systems are willing to provide young workers with income assistance varies, so it is hardly surprising to see large national differences in the effectiveness of tax and transfer systems in reducing poverty among young adults (Table 1.6). At the beginning of the 1980s, a majority of poor households headed by young adults in Sweden and the Netherlands was lifted out of poverty by government programs. Between 28 and 43 percent of young householders in France, West Germany, and the United Kingdom were also helped out of poverty. Only one in seven young householders were helped in Canada. In the United States, taxes pushed slightly more young adults into poverty than transfers lifted out.

Though transfers lifted a sizable proportion of young people out of poverty in most countries, pretax and transfer poverty rates among adults increased so dramatically in the 1980s that posttax and transfer poverty rates among young adult household heads rose significantly. By the second half of the decade, at least 13 percent of young households were poor *after* taxes and transfers in every country except France. In Canada, about one in five young households was poor by the end of the decade. In the United States, one in four young households was poor. Transfer system effectiveness fell in the Netherlands, Sweden, and West Germany.

One would imagine that schooling systems and school-to-work transition programs would affect unemployment and pretax and transfer poverty rates

Table 1.6 / Effects of Taxes and Transfers on Households with Heads Aged 20–29

Country, Period	Pretax and Transfer Poverty Rate	Posttax and Transfer Poverty Rate	Percentage Lifted out of Poverty by Taxes and Transfers
	Period 1	Period 1	Period 1
United States, 1979, 1986			
All households	17.8	17.4	−2.2
All households with children	26.8	27.2	−1.5
Households without children	11.6	10.7	−7.7
Canada, 1981, 1987			
All households	17.7	14.8	16.4
All households with children	25.8	22.8	11.6
Households without children	13.3	10.5	21.0
United Kingdom, 1979, 1986			
All households	14.7	9.8	33.3
All households with children	20.4	14.2	30.3
Households without children	8.5	5.0	41.2
West Germany, 1981, 1984			
All households	12.1	8.6	28.9
All households with children	5.1	6.8	−33.3
Households without children	15.3	9.4	38.6
Netherlands, 1983, 1987			
All households	27.6	11.4	58.7
All households with children	29.0	4.3	85.2
Households without children	27.2	13.8	49.3
France, 1979, 1986			
All households	14.1	8.0	43.3
All households with children	19.3	8.2	57.5
Households without children	8.8	7.8	11.4
Sweden, 1981, 1987			
All households	21.3	7.0	67.1
All households with children	19.7	6.3	68.0
Households without children	21.7	7.2	66.8

SOURCE: Luxembourg Income Study, authors' calculations.

Table 1.6 (*continued*)

Country, Period	Pretax and Transfer Poverty Rate Period 2	Posttax and Transfer Poverty Rate Period 2	Percentage Lifted out of Poverty by Taxes and Transfers Period 2
United States, 1979, 1986			
All households	24.4	25.2	−.3
All households with children	39.2	39.5	−.1
Households without children	14.9	16.0	−.7
Canada, 1981, 1987			
All households	23.9	19.7	17.5
All households with children	34.9	29.5	15.5
Households without children	19.8	16.0	19.2
United Kingdom, 1979, 1986			
All households	29.8	15.0	33.9
All households with children	48.6	23.2	52.3
Households without children	16.0	8.9	44.4
West Germany, 1981, 1984			
All households	18.5	13.4	27.6
All households with children	17.6	18.8	−6.8
Households without children	18.7	11.8	36.9
Netherlands, 1983, 1987			
All households	31.3	15.3	51.1
All households with children	35.4	13.1	63.0
Households without children	30.3	15.8	47.8
France, 1979, 1986			
All households	18.3	9.1	50.3
All households with children	26.1	9.2	64.7
Households without children	12.2	9.1	25.4
Sweden, 1981, 1987			
All households	20.6	14.0	32.0
All households with children	27.8	5.3	80.9
Households without children	19.3	15.5	19.7

among young people. However, such effects are not evident in Tables 1.5 and 1.6. Certainly Sweden's commitment to full-employment is clear, but this did not keep pretax and transfer poverty rates among young adults low. The much-touted German apprenticeship system did not reduce unemployment rates among the least educated young adults in the 1980s (see Casey, Chapter 12, for an explanation).

The post-government economic circumstances of young adults with children also worsened over the decade: almost 40 percent of households with children headed by a person 20–29 years old were poor in the United States, *after* taxes and income assistance; almost 30 percent in Canada and a quarter in the United Kingdom were poor. Poverty among young families was kept much lower in the Netherlands, France, and Sweden: their figures were 13.1 percent, 9.1 percent, and 5.3 percent, respectively. Swedish transfer policies lifted over 80 percent of young householders with children out of poverty. In France and the Netherlands, almost two-thirds of these households were helped to income adequacy. In the United Kingdom, the poverty rate among young adults with children was cut by more than half. Canadian policies helped almost a third of young householders with children move out of poverty. Government interventions in France, the United Kingdom, and Canada became *more* effective in reducing poverty among young households as need increased over the decade.

In West Germany, taxes pushed more young householders with children into poverty than transfers lifted out. Apparently, a good number of young householders in West Germany were right on the edge of income adequacy before taxes. U.S. policies did little to reduce market-generated poverty among young adults.

Despite the increased effort and effectiveness of income support policies in some nations, no country was able to prevent a significant increase in posttax and transfer poverty rates from occurring among households headed by a young person over the 1980s. Government transfer programs did not counteract the declines in labor market income among young household heads in the 1980s.

A demographic note seems in order here. Poverty did *not* increase because the age of individuals heading households with children declined. In fact, with the exception of the United Kingdom, the proportion of both married-couple households with children and households headed by a parent under 30 *declined* significantly in the countries in the study in the 1980s (Table 1.7). In Britain, the percentage of lone-parent households headed by a young person rose from 25.2 percent to 32.8 percent. The proportion of lone-parent families headed by a young person fell in the United States, Canada, the Netherlands, and France. Young-parent households as a percentage of lone-parent households increased by two percentage points in West Germany and one percentage point in Sweden.

It is difficult to blame the observed increases in poverty on a shift in family structure either—or at least to an increase in female-headed families with children. The percentage of all households headed by a married couple with children declined everywhere, but the primary reason for the decline was a commensurate increase in households headed by *childless* adults. Lone parents with children increased as a percentage of all households with heads 20–55 years old only in the United Kingdom, the Netherlands, and France. However, lone-parent households represented more than 6 percent of prime age households in only the United States, the United Kingdom, and Sweden.

Lone Parents with Children

In most industrial countries, *any* families with children are deemed deserving of some kind of support, the rationale being that society has a special responsibility to ensure the well-being of its children and future citizens. In some countries, family policies are overtly pro-natalist; increasing the national population is viewed as an important social goal that should be encouraged and rewarded with economic support. The United States is the only country examined here that does not give direct child allowances to families with children. However, even the United States gives tax relief to households with children, and the Earned Income Tax Credit provides direct income support to families with children who have working parents. The general commitment to support all families with children clearly affects special policies created for lone parents with children.

Lone-parent families are especially vulnerable to hardship because they contain only one potential earner who must divide his or her time between the paid workforce and child-rearing. If a lone parent, who is almost always a mother, does not work enough hours or earn wages high enough to achieve adequate income support for her household, she must rely on private transfers (principally alimony and child support) or government assistance to make ends meet. Table 1.8 shows the enormous difference in the pretax and transfer poverty rates of lone-parent households relative to couple-headed households in each country examined. The smallest difference was in France, where the pretax and transfer poverty rate among lone parents was not twice the rate of couple-headed families. The largest difference was in the Netherlands, where the pretax and transfer poverty rate among lone-parent households was seven times that of coupled families. In the other countries, lone-parent families were three to five times as likely to be poor as couple-headed families, before taxes and transfers.

These cross-national differences are related to social norms about mothers working in the paid labor force; the degree to which the full-time work (of women) yields "family wages"; and social and legal norms regarding private transfers (alimony and child support). For example, Sweden had the highest labor force participation rate among mothers: almost 90 percent of all mothers were in the labor force. Over 85 percent of lone parents also worked in Sweden, but almost 30 percent of them were still poor before taxes and transfers. Since only 5 percent of lone parents who worked full-time were poor, part-time work among lone-parent households in Sweden must be very prevalent. Nonetheless, it is worth noting that the proportion of poor lone mothers who had some

Table 1.7 / **Demographic Differences in LIS National Surveys**

Country	Percentage of All Married-Couple Households with Children Headed by a 20–29 Year Old		Percentage of All Lone-Parent Households with Children Headed by a 20–29 Year Old	
	Period 1	Period 2	Period 1	Period 2
United States	21.4	17.3	35.6	29.4
Canada	18.8	15.2	31.3	26.4
United Kingdom	19.9	14.8	25.2	32.8
West Germany	12.0	11.0	18.9	20.9
Netherlands	10.3	11.3	23.4	18.6
France	13.5	11.5	22.1	14.4
Sweden	10.3	8.8	18.1	19.4

SOURCE: Calculated from Tables 1A.2 and 1A.3.

earnings was far and away highest in Sweden, and that Swedish lone-parent households with children had the lowest pretax and transfer poverty rates.

In the United States and Canada, about two-thirds of all mothers—whether married or single—participated in the labor force. Since the majority of married-couple households in these two countries (as well as Sweden) have two earners, we would expect most of these families to be protected against poverty, and they are. But a good number of full-time workers in the United States and Canada were poor, and a disproportionate number of the low-earning workers were women and lone mothers. Over 18 percent of full-time working lone mothers in Canada and almost 13 percent of full-time working lone mothers in the United States were poor, before taxes and transfers, by the second part of the decade.

The labor force participation rate of married mothers was much lower than the labor force participation rate of single mothers in France and West Germany in the 1980s. About 85 percent of single mothers in France participated in the paid workforce, but only two-thirds of married mothers did. In West Germany, the difference is even more pronounced: less than half of married German mothers worked, whereas 70 percent of single mothers did. Yet only 15 percent of poor lone mothers worked in Germany, while almost 70 percent of poor lone mothers in France worked by the end of the decade. Despite the enormous difference in the work behavior of poor lone parents in France and West Germany, their pretax and transfer poverty rates were about the same by the second part of the decade. It appears that private transfers (alimony, child support, and help from relatives) provided enough income assistance to give many non-working lone mothers in Germany an adequate income. Relative wage rates in the two countries may also play a role. Couple-headed families with children in West Germany had pretax and transfer poverty rates only a third as high as

Table 1.7 (*continued*)

| Country | Percentage of All Households 20–55 Years Old Comprised of | | | |
| | Married Couples with Children | | Lone Parents with Children | |
	Period 1	Period 2	Period 1	Period 2
United States	45.9	43.3	8.7	8.6
Canada	48.9	44.0	6.4	4.8
United Kingdom	57.8	49.7	5.5	7.3
West Germany	51.3	43.8	3.1	2.0
Netherlands	53.4	43.7	3.8	4.8
France	58.5	53.9	3.1	4.2
Sweden	34.1	28.8	7.6	6.9

couple-headed families in France, despite the fact that more married mothers worked in France than Germany.

In the United Kingdom and the Netherlands, married mothers were somewhat more likely to work than single mothers. In the United Kingdom, only 52 percent of lone mothers worked, compared to 59 percent of married mothers, but only 17 percent of poor lone mothers had any earnings. The Netherlands had the lowest level of maternal labor force involvement: just 30 percent of married Dutch mothers and 24 percent of single lone mothers worked. Only 15 percent of poor Dutch lone mothers had any earnings in the latter part of the 1980s. Consequently, over 70 percent of lone mothers in the United Kingdom and the Netherlands were poor, before taxes and transfers.

If private earnings and private transfers do not provide adequate income support, families with children will be forced to rely on public assistance. Table 1.9 shows the percentage of various kinds of families reliant on government assistance for more than half their total household income. Between two-thirds and 94 percent of poor lone-parent households relied on the government for the majority of their household income in these countries. In the Netherlands and the United Kingdom (both countries with high unemployment rates), at least two-thirds of poor couple-headed families with children also depended heavily on government income support. Sweden and West Germany also provided a large proportion of poor couple-headed families with income support (57.8 percent of poor couples in Sweden and 48.1 percent of poor couples in West Germany relied on government support for more than half their total household income). The three countries that provided the narrowest scope of support to poor lone parents (the United States, Canada, and France) provided support to an even smaller proportion of poor couple-headed families.

While the preceding paragraph provides a sense of the relative scope of support available to *poor* families, it doesn't give us a picture of the incidence

Table 1.8 / Pretax and Transfer Poverty and Joblessness Among the Pretax and Transfer Poor, by Household Type, Head Aged 20–55 Years Old

Country, Period	Pretax and Transfer Poverty Rate, Period 1	Percentage of Poor Households with No Earnings, Period 1	Poverty Rate Among Households with a Full-Time Worker, Period 1	Pretax and Transfer Poverty Rate, Period 2	Percentage of Poor Households with No Earnings, Period 2	Poverty Rate Among Households with a Full-Time Worker, Period 2
United States, 1979, 1986						
All households	16.1	28.5	4.8	18.0	30.0	4.7
All households w/children	19.8	25.0	6.9	23.0	26.3	7.7
Couple-headed w/children	13.7	11.0	6.2	16.4	10.4	6.8
Lone head w/children	52.3	44.6	11.0	55.9	49.7	12.8
Households w/o children	11.6	35.5	2.0	12.5	37.3	1.2
Canada, 1981, 1987						
All households	16.4	25.6	6.4	17.4	27.1	5.0
All households w/children	19.1	20.3	8.7	19.2	25.5	7.0
Couple-headed w/children	14.9	7.4	8.1	14.8	13.7	6.7
Lone head w/children	50.8	49.3	11.6	60.0	52.4	18.1
Households w/o children	13.1	35.0	3.3	15.7	29.0	2.8
United Kingdom, 1979, 1986						
All households	12.8	34.3	N.A.	23.2	67.5	N.A.
All households w/children	15.4	24.9	N.A.	28.9	61.4	N.A.
Couple-headed w/children	11.9	N.A.	N.A.	22.6	51.4	N.A.
Lone head w/children	52.3	N.A.	N.A.	72.0	83.0	N.A.
Households w/o children	8.2	64.8	N.A.	15.7	82.4	N.A.

West Germany, 1981, 1984						
All households	6.9	49.3	1.9	10.7	49.6	2.2
All households w/children	6.0	20.1	3.2	9.5	38.6	2.2
Couple-headed w/children	4.8	6.7	1.9	8.2	28.9	.6
Lone head w/children	26.1	61.1	2.2	38.1	84.2	0.0
Households w/o children	8.0	75.4	.4	11.6	57.2	2.2
Netherlands, 1983, 1987						
All households	20.6	84.2	4.7	19.9	87.8	1.2
All households w/children	17.6	77.9	4.9	15.1	78.3	2.1
Couple-headed w/children	13.0	71.5	.9	9.0	66.2	1.6
Lone head w/children	77.0	93.2	8.3	71.2	92.3	0.0
Households w/o children	24.6	90.2	4.3	24.4	93.3	.3
France, 1979, 1986						
All households	18.4	9.8	N.A.	20.4	16.9	N.A.
All households w/children	23.0	5.0	N.A.	25.2	9.4	N.A.
Couple-headed w/children	22.3	3.8	N.A.	24.2	6.8	N.A.
Lone head w/children	37.8	18.3	N.A.	38.3	31.0	N.A.
Households w/o children	11.1	25.8	N.A.	13.7	35.8	N.A.
Sweden, 1981, 1987						
All households	16.0	23.1	3.5	15.3	18.7	4.8
All households w/children	12.3	12.8	4.9	13.0	8.0	6.7
Couple-headed w/children	7.2	5.1	4.9	9.5	3.9	6.8
Lone head w/children	35.2	20.0	5.6	29.1	14.1	5.1
Households w/o children	18.7	28.0	2.3	16.8	23.7	3.4

SOURCE: Luxembourg Income Study, authors' calculations.

Table 1.9 / Reliance on Government Assistance, by Country and Family Type

| | | Percentage of Households with Children That Rely on Government Assistance for at least 50 Percent of Their Household Income | | | |
| | All Families | All Coupled Families | All Lone Parents | Poor Couple-Headed Families | Poor Lone Parents |
Country, Period					
United States, 1986	10.0	4.4	37.6	26.3	65.1
Canada, 1987	8.2	4.9	38.8	32.9	64.6
United Kingdom, 1986	23.2	15.6	74.9	66.1	90.6
West Germany, 1984	5.6	4.1	39.7	48.1	91.7
Netherlands, 1987	14.4	8.3	70.4	84.5	93.7
France, 1984	7.2	5.8	25.4	23.4	63.7
Sweden, 1987	9.7	6.7	32.6	57.8	92.3

SOURCE: Luxembourg Income Study, authors' calculations.

of income assistance among the general population. The first column of Table 1.9 shows that the United Kingdom had the highest proportion of households with children heavily dependent on public income support. The Netherlands followed and the United States and Sweden were close behind. About one of every seven two-parent families in Britain was heavily reliant on public assistance in the 1980s and three-quarters of all lone-parent households was heavily dependent. In the Netherlands, over 70 percent of all lone-parent households with children relied heavily on government income support, but less than 9 percent of couple-headed families with children did. In most countries, between 4 and 6 percent of all couple-headed families and about a third of all lone-parent families with children depended on income support from the government for over half their household's income.

How successful were various national programs in reducing poverty among families with children? After taxes and transfers, poverty rates among couple-headed households with children were 12 percent or less in every country except the United States and the United Kingdom (Table 1.10). In the Netherlands, West Germany, and Sweden, posttax and transfer poverty rates among couple-headed families were 7.2., 6.0, and 5.0, respectively, in the second part of the decade. French social policies were most effective in reducing poverty among couple-headed families—almost 60 percent were lifted out of poverty by transfers. About half of couple-headed households with children in Sweden and a third in West Germany were so assisted. But less than 27 percent in the United Kingdom, 20 percent in the Netherlands, and 18 percent in Canada were lifted out of poverty by transfers. In the United States, taxes pushed more couple-headed households with children into poverty than transfers lifted out.[9]

In every country except France, income support policies helped a larger percentage of lone-parent than couple-headed families achieve an adequate in-

Table 1.10 / Transfer System Effectiveness, by Country and Household Type

Country, Period	Posttax and Transfer Poverty Rate — Period 1	Percentage of Households Lifted out of Poverty by Tax and Transfer Policies — Period 1	Posttax and Transfer Poverty Rate — Period 2	Percentage of Households Lifted out of Poverty by Tax and Transfer Policies — Period 2
United States, 1979, 1986				
All households	15.6	.03	18.1	−.5
All households w/children	20.2	−2.0	23.8	−3.5
Couples w/children	50.6	−5.8	17.9	−9.1
Lone parent w/children	14.5	3.2	53.3	4.6
Households w/o children	10.0	13.8	11.9	4.8
Canada, 1981, 1987				
All households	13.4	18.3	13.9	20.1
All households w/children	16.2	15.0	15.7	18.2
Couples w/children	45.0	16.8	12.2	14.8
Lone parent w/children	12.4	11.4	48.4	19.3
Households w/o children	9.9	24.4	12.3	21.6
United Kingdom, 1979, 1986				
All households	8.5	33.6	12.5	46.1
All households w/children	10.6	31.2	16.8	41.9
Couples w/children	35.1	N.A.	16.6	26.5
Lone parent w/children	8.2	N.A.	18.0	75.0
Households w/o children	4.9	40.2	6.9	56.0
West Germany, 1981, 1984				
All households	5.5	20.3	6.8	36.4
All households w/children	6.0	0.0	7.9	16.8
Couples w/children	12.3	−16.7	6.0	13.4
Lone parent w/children	5.6	52.8	8.9	33.8
Households w/o children	4.9	38.7	6.6	50.0
Netherlands, 1983, 1987				
All households	7.9	61.6	7.6	61.8
All households w/children	6.3	63.1	7.3	51.7
Couples w/children	5.5	50.3	7.2	20.0
Lone parent w/children	6.6	92.8	7.5	89.5
Households w/o children	9.7	60.6	7.9	67.6
France, 1979, 1984				
All households	9.9	46.2	9.9	51.5
All households w/children	10.7	53.4	10.4	58.7
Couples w/children	17.9	53.8	10.0	58.7
Lone parent w/children	10.3	52.6	15.8	47.0
Households w/o children	8.7	21.6	9.1	33.6
Sweden, 1981, 1987				
All households	6.6	58.7	8.6	43.8
All households w/children	6.5	47.1	5.1	60.8
Couples w/children	8.9	16.6	5.0	47.3
Lone parent w/children	6.0	77.0	5.5	81.1
Households w/o children	6.6	64.7	10.6	36.9

SOURCE: Luxembourg Income Study, authors' calculations.

come. In the Netherlands, almost 90 percent of lone-parent families were lifted out of poverty in the late 1980s (Table 1.10). The Swedish and British systems performed almost as well: at least three-quarters of all lone-parent households were lifted from poverty. (However, since the United Kingdom had a much higher pretax and transfer poverty rate than Sweden, its lone-parent poverty rate remained high.) Almost half of all poor lone-parent households in France were lifted out of poverty by tax and transfer programs, compared to one-third of lone-parent families in West Germany, and one-fifth of lone-parent families in Canada. In the United States, only 5 percent of lone-parent families with children were lifted out of poverty by tax and transfer programs.

Our data suggest that poverty among lone parents is lowest in countries where mothers work and receive income support or in countries where the government is relatively generous in its support of mothers who stay out of the paid workforce. The data provide no definitive answer about whether mixing work with income support is a more effective way of reducing poverty among lone-parent families than simply providing direct income support. Sweden and the Netherlands consistently show the lowest posttax and transfer poverty rates among lone mothers. In Sweden every adult is expected to work. Almost 90 percent of mothers, married or single, are in the labor force. Almost as high a percentage of poor lone parents have some earnings. By contrast, less than a quarter of lone mothers in the Netherlands are in the labor force, and less than 7 percent of poor lone mothers have earnings. Yet the poverty rate among Dutch lone mothers is only 2 percentage points higher than the poverty rate among Swedish lone mothers (7.5 versus 5.5 in 1987). Transfers alone or transfers-with-work can both improve a family's immediate well-being. However, if society expects a lone mother to re-enter the workforce and support herself after her children are grown, then a strategy that encourages a mother to work part-time (to maintain her ties to the paid labor force) might be preferable to an income support program that encourages a woman to completely withdraw from the labor market for long periods of time.

Households Without Children

Poverty rates among childless households were lowest in West Germany, the United Kingdom, and the Netherlands because these countries provided income support to a significant portion of childless households. Between two-thirds and half of childless households in these three countries were lifted out of poverty by transfers, and the effectiveness of income support programs for childless households in these countries increased over the 1980s. In the Netherlands, increased coverage (coupled with reductions in unemployment) resulted in lower posttax and transfer poverty rates among childless households in the second part of the decade than in the first part. In the other two countries, the increased effectiveness of income support programs was not enough to offset increases in market-generated poverty (primarily due to higher unemployment). Since few of the childless households in these three countries had earnings, the lower poverty rates among them were clearly the result of more readily available and/or generous income support in these countries than in the others.

DISCUSSION

Detailed discussions of the policies that underlie the outcomes described above can be found in the next sections of this volume. Our intent here was to identify overall patterns and trends in household poverty among industrial nations and how these patterns affected certain subgroups among the non-elderly population.

When we examined the incidence of market-based poverty, we found that pretax and transfer poverty rates showed less variation than unemployment rates. West Germany consistently had the lowest rates of pretax and transfer poverty, due to high wage levels and a relatively low unemployment rate. Sweden's market poverty rate was a relatively distant second in the latter part of the decade despite its having a lower unemployment rate than West Germany's. The pretax and transfer poverty rates of the other countries clustered fairly closely together: between 17 and 20 percent of non-elderly households were poor. The change in the market poverty rate was dramatic only in the United Kingdom where poverty doubled with the unemployment rate.

There were large differences in the level of joblessness among the poor in these countries. In the United Kingdom, West Germany, and the Netherlands, relatively few poor households had earnings. In fact, in the Netherlands and West Germany, work and poverty were almost mutually exclusive. The poor didn't work; full-time workers weren't poor. Non-work was the norm among poor lone-parent households in these countries. In the United Kingdom and the Netherlands, the majority of lone-parent families relied heavily on the government for income support and were lifted out of poverty as a result of this income assistance. In West Germany, private transfers provided a large proportion of nonworking lone mothers with income support and government assistance helped another third achieve income adequacy.

In the four other countries, poverty was associated with part-time, part-year or low-wage work as well as joblessness. In Sweden and France, the vast majority of all poor households had some earnings and these two countries had the highest proportion of working lone mothers. However, many lone mothers worked only part-time, and when earnings were not enough to provide income adequacy, government transfers often did. Both countries appear to have a child- or family-based system of support: a large proportion of poor couple-headed families, as well as lone-parent families with children were lifted out of poverty by public transfers. In fact, France helped more couple-headed families than lone-parent families out of poverty. Swedish policies helped over 80 percent of lone-parent and almost half of couple-headed families out of poverty.

In the United States and Canada, full-time work did not guard against poverty in couple-headed or lone-parent households. Almost 7 percent of couple-headed families and at least 13 percent of lone-parent families with a full-time worker were poor. At the same time, about half of all poor lone-parent households in the United States and Canada had no earnings. In America, joblessness and low wages contributed to high pretax and transfer poverty rates, especially among lone parents with children. Transfer programs helped only a few lone-parent families with children in the United States escape poverty in the 1980s, and taxes pushed more couple-headed families with children into poverty than transfers lifted out. Canadian tax and transfers did a somewhat better job: about 20 percent of lone-parent households with children and 15 percent of couple-headed households with children received enough income support to escape poverty at the end of the decade.

Posttax and transfer poverty rates among all subgroups of the non-elderly households examined were uniformly higher in America than in the continental European countries, but the most dramatic difference was among lone-parent households. American rates were about four times those in Europe. Posttax and transfer poverty rates among lone-parent households with children were about four times higher in America than in the continental European countries. Posttax and transfer poverty rates among couple-headed households with children in Canada and the United States were twice as high as couple-headed poverty rates in Sweden, West Germany, and the Netherlands.

Although Europeans may celebrate the effectiveness of their social protection policies relative to those in America and the United Kingdom, the trend figures reported here should give pause. Over the course of the 1980s, market-generated poverty increased in five of the seven countries examined. Joblessness among the poor increased in every country except Sweden, and the increase in market-based poverty was most dramatic among 20–29-year-old household heads.

Although income support policies helped a greater proportion of the poor out of poverty in the second half of the decade in every country except the United States, posttax and transfer poverty—at least among some groups—increased in every country. Poverty among households with children increased in the United States, the United Kingdom, West Germany, and the Netherlands. The poverty rate among young household heads increased in every country except France. Whether joblessness, working poverty, and income inadequacy continue to increase in the 1990s or can be halted by government intervention is the question that lies at the heart of the chapters that follow.

ENDNOTES

1. The reader should be aware of four potential shortcomings of the LIS data used in this analysis. First, the data sets were not collected for the same purposes or by the equivalent agencies in each country. Some of the data sets were taken from nationally representative income surveys and others from expenditure surveys that also contain detailed income source questions. The LIS data for West Germany came from two different data sets, making trend analysis somewhat tenuous. The French data are

unique in that the survey is based on a survey of income tax records to which transfer data have been imputed and take-up rates estimated. Some changes in the method used for measuring annual income and coding several key income variables occurred in the United Kingdom data over the 1979–1986 period.

Second, the time periods covered vary somewhat. The periodicity was determined by data availability and the capacity of the LIS staff to produce comparable data sets. Third, the unit of analysis in most countries is "households" (all persons sharing the same living quarters, whether related or not). Unfortunately, in Canada, household data are not available so we must use families (all persons living together *and* related by blood or adoption) as our base unit. However, our estimates suggest that the use of the Canadian unit definition presents few if any problems for working with the non-elderly living units that are the basis for this analysis. The Swedish "household" definition *is* problematic because it corresponds more closely to tax units than to living arrangements. As a result, young single adults (18 or older) living with their parents may be (improperly) classified as single-person households. This would create a bias toward *over*-estimating income inadequacy among young Swedes.

Finally, our definition of a single-parent household (one adult plus children) does not allow us to identify and separate out young single parents who are living with relatives or other individuals for analysis. This may mask some important differences between countries with regard to poverty among young, mother-headed families with children. For example, in the United States, births to unmarried teenage mothers accounted for a large part of the growth in single-parent families in the 1980s. However, many of these mothers live with an older relative (mother, father, aunt, sibling, etc.) and these other relatives would be counted as the household head. By contrast, many of the younger unmarried mothers in the United Kingdom, Sweden, France, and the Netherlands are living with their children's father without being legally married (e.g., Ermisch 1987; O'Higgins 1987; Blundell and Walker 1988). Neither of these groups of young mothers would appear as a single household head in our analysis, yet both are at special risk of experiencing a spell of poverty during early adulthood. Tables 1A.2 and 1A.3 provide more detailed comparisons of differences in the demographic composition of the household samples. Despite the differences among the surveys, the core of the data remains comparable enough to provide us with estimates of significant differences and similarities in income distributions over time and across countries.

2. The data base now contains information for 11 countries for 1979 or 1981 and data for 16 countries for a second period (1984–87 period). Data availability concerns led us to exclude European countries such as Italy, Luxembourg, Switzerland, and Norway, for which only one wave of LIS data is currently available. The uniqueness criterion led us to exclude Australia and Israel. Eastern European countries for which LIS has data from the 1980s (Poland, Hungary, Czechoslovakia) were excluded due to their recent economic upheaval.

3. For example, the cash value of food stamps is included in "posttax and transfer income" in the United States. Housing allowances are included in "posttax and transfer income" in several of the European countries. Medical coverage has not been cashed out and added to income, but this is an issue only in the United States because in other countries, all citizens have access to healthcare. Thus, if one "costed out" and added the value of medical benefits to the income of the poor in the United States, the same procedure would have to be done in every other country. Since

direct cash transfers, not the value of public medical services, are the focus of this study, we did not attempt to add in the value of healthcare benefits.

4. We do want to adjust for family size and have used equivalence scales to do so. The number of equivalent adults per household is determined by a weight of 1.0 for the first adult, .7 for each subsequent adult, and .5 for each child.

5. Table 1A.4 shows what would happen if the poverty measure we use (50 percent of median adjusted household income of households with heads aged 20 to 55 years old) was expanded to include households headed by individuals over 55 years old. In every case, the median would be lowered somewhat. This can only be true if the elderly have incomes somewhat lower than household heads aged 20 to 55; the elderly in the U.K. and Sweden seem to have income significantly lower than younger households. However, the income-poverty of the elderly may not necessarily reflect a lower standard of living of these households, since they often own their own homes and hence have marginal housings costs. Housing is a major expenditure for most non-elderly households, and one that has been growing rapidly in recent years in many countries. Since our study focuses on the economic vulnerability of the non-elderly, we felt that using an income-median that included only non-elderly would provide a more accurate sense of relative economic well-being. Using a median income measure that included the elderly would shift the poverty line down toward the 40 percent mark—particularly in Sweden and the U.K.—and so would reduce poverty rates in those countries somewhat.

6. The LIS data survey years cut at different points in the business cycle in each country. In the United States and the United Kingdom, the LIS sample years fall before and after a deep recession. West Germany and Sweden were in the midst of recession in the first take-up year. The first survey year for the Netherlands comes *after* its recovery had begun. The worst years of unemployment in France occurred *after* the second survey year.

7. Simulations performed by the Congressional Budget Office reprinted in *The Green Book* (1991, Table 8, p. 1166) indicate that on a "percent of persons poor" basis, using official U.S. poverty thresholds and equivalence scales, making some adjustment for underreporting of market income, and including housing benefits, the U.S. tax and transfer system reduced pretax and transfer poverty among families with related children by 6 percentage points in 1979 and by only 3.7 points in 1986. The posttax and transfer poverty rates calculated by CBO and presented in *The Green Book* were 10.5 and 15.8 percent in 1979 and 1986, respectively. Several factors can account for the differences between these and our estimates. In particular, the different level of the poverty line and implicit equivalence scales explain a large part of the story.

At the 40 percent poverty line, the U.S. figures for posttax and transfer poverty rates for households with children are 13.5 and 17.5 percent in 1979 and 1986. Hence, on a persons basis, the CBO-estimated poverty rates increased by 5.3 points (15.8 minus 10.5). Our household-based estimates for 20–55-year-olds with children increased by 4 points (17.5 minus 13.5) over this period.

A recent paper (Smeeding, 1991, Table 3) using the same LIS data set and definitions used here, reported that taxes and transfers affected the poverty rates among children in the United States in a way that coincides reasonably with the CBO results from *The Green Book* and results reported in this paper. Using a 50 percent poverty measure, pretax and transfer poverty rose from 23.0 in 1979 to 26.8 percent in 1986;

posttax and transfer poverty rates rose from 22.5 percent to 27.3 percent. Thus, program effectiveness declined, so that more children lived in households hurt by taxation than helped by transfers. At the 40 percent poverty line, government interventions reduced child poverty from 19.0 to 14.7 percent in 1979, and from 22.3 to 20.4 percent in 1986. Thus, even at the 40 percent line, program effectiveness declined.

8. In Italy, youth unemployment in general is very high, but as Enrico Pugliese explains in Chapter 13, the least educated fare somewhat better in the short run than the most educated because it takes time for the most educated to adjust their expectations downward to the realities of the labor market.

9. However, improvements in the Earned Income Tax Credit for families with children should have improved this situation.

Table 1A.1 / An Overview of LIS Data Sets and Units Definitions

Country	Data Set Name, Income Year (and Size)[a]	Population Coverage[b]	Basis of Household Sampling Frame[c]	Unit of Analysis[d]
Canada	*Survey of Consumer Finances*, 1981 and 1987 (37,900)	97.5[e]	Dicennial Census	Economic Family[f]
U.S.	*Current Population Survey*, 1979 and 1986 (65,000)	97.5[e]	Dicennial Census	Household[g]
Sweden	*Swedish Income Distribution Survey*, 1981 and 1987 (9,600)	98.0[e]	Income Register	Administrative Unit[h]
West Germany	*Transfer Survey,*[i] 1981 (2,800)	93.5[j]	Electoral Register and Census	Household[g]
West Germany	*German Panel Survey*, 1984 (4,900)	96.8[e]	Electoral Register and Census	Household[g]
Netherlands	*Survey of Income and Program Users*, 1983 and 1987 (4,850)	99.2	Address Register of the Postal and Telephone Companies	Household[g]
France	*Survey of Individual Income Tax Returns*, 1979 and 1986 (11,000)	97.0[k]	National Tax Register and Household Survey	Household[g]
U.K.	*Family Expenditure Survey,*[i] 1979 and 1986 (6,800)	96.5[l]	Electoral Register	Household[g]

[a]Data set size is the number of actual household units surveyed.
[b]As a percentage of total national population.
[c]Sampling Frame indicates the overall base from which the relevant household population sample was drawn. Actual sample may be drawn on a stratified probability basis, e.g., by area or age.
[d]Unit definition used in this paper. All unit definitions are the same in both periods.
[e]Excludes institutionalized and homeless populations. Also some far northern rural residents (Inuits, Eskimos, Lapps, etc.) may be undersampled in Sweden.
[f]The economic family in Canada includes all related members which share resources. Unrelated persons living in the same unit are considered as separate units even though they share the same household.
[g]All persons living together and sharing the same living arrangements (housing unit).
[h]Persons age 18 or over plus related children, if there are any, are regarded as one unit. Older children living with their parents are therefore treated as separate units and not as cohabiting members of a single household.
[i]The United Kingdom and Germany surveys collect subannual income data which is normalized to annual income levels.
[j]Excludes foreign-born heads of households, the institutionalized, and the homeless.
[k]Excludes the homeless, institutionalized, and those living in mobile homes.
[l]Excludes those not on the electoral register, the homeless, and the institutionalized.

Table 1A.2 / Demographic Table—Weighted Population Percentages

Household Characteristics	US79	US86	CN81	CN87	GE81	GE84
Total Households	100.0	100.0	100.0	100.0	100.0	100.0
Households with head age 20–55	65.9	66.1	68.3	69.8	58.4	59.2
Other households	34.1	33.9	31.7	30.2	41.6	40.8
Households with Head Age 20–55	100.0	100.0	100.0	100.0	100.0	100.0
With children	54.6	51.9	55.3	48.8	54.4	45.8
Married	45.9	43.3	48.9	44.0	51.3	43.8
Single	8.7	8.6	6.4	4.8	3.1	2.0
Without children	45.4	48.1	44.7	51.2	45.6	54.2
Married	19.8	23.8	21.7	25.1	26.6	31.0
Single	25.6	24.2	23.0	26.1	19.0	23.3
Single Parents as a Percentage of all Households with Children	15.9	16.6	11.6	9.8	5.7	4.4
Persons in Families (20–55)	100.0	100.0	100.0	100.0	100.0	100.0
Head Age (20–29)	31.1	25.4	30.8	26.4	20.3	20.1
With children	12.7	9.9	10.3	7.2	6.5	4.5
Without children	18.4	15.5	19.3	19.2	13.8	15.6
Married	5.7	5.7	7.2	6.6	6.2	5.5
Single	12.7	9.8	12.2	12.6	7.6	10.1
Head Age (30–55)	68.9	74.6	70.4	73.6	79.7	79.9
With children	41.9	42.0	45.0	41.6	47.9	41.3
Married	36.4	36.0	40.3	38.0	45.4	39.7
Single	5.5	6.0	4.7	3.5	2.5	1.6
Without children	27.0	32.6	25.4	32.0	31.8	38.6
Married	14.1	18.1	14.5	18.4	20.4	25.5
Single	12.9	14.5	10.8	13.6	11.4	13.1

SOURCE: Luxembourg Income Study.

Table 1A.2 (*continued*)

Household Characteristics	SW81	SW87	UK79	UK86	NL83	NL87	FR79	FR84
Total Households	100.0	100.0	100.0	100.0	100.0	100.0	100.0	100.0
Households with head age 20–55	57.1	58.1	58.7	59.7	65.5	67.0	61.3	62.3
Other households	42.9	41.9	41.3	40.3	34.5	33.0	38.7	37.7
Households with Head Age 20–55	100.0	100.0	100.0	100.0	100.0	100.0	100.0	100.0
With children	41.6	35.7	63.3	57.0	57.3	48.5	61.5	58.1
Married	34.1	28.8	57.8	49.7	53.4	43.7	58.5	53.9
Single	7.6	6.9	5.5	7.3	3.8	4.8	3.1	4.2
Without children	58.3	64.3	36.7	43.0	42.7	51.5	38.5	41.9
Married	15.0	17.2	24.5	29.9	28.2	24.6	25.4	26.0
Single	43.3	47.1	12.2	13.2	14.5	26.9	13.0	15.9
Single Parents as a Percentage of all								
Households with Children	18.3	19.3	8.7	12.8	6.6	9.9	5.0	7.2
Persons in Families (20–55)	100.0	100.0	100.0	100.0	100.0	100.0	100.0	100.0
Head Age (20–29)	32.3	33.0	24.8	23.1	24.5	27.0	20.2	20.4
With children	5.5	4.2	12.9	9.8	6.2	5.4	10.1	8.9
Without children	26.8	28.8	11.9	13.3	18.3	21.6	10.1	11.5
Married	4.4	4.5	6.9	8.1	10.6	8.3	5.4	5.1
Single	22.4	24.2	5.0	5.2	7.7	13.4	4.7	6.4
Head Age (30–55)	67.7	67.1	75.2	76.9	75.5	73.0	79.8	79.6
With children	36.1	31.5	50.4	47.2	51.0	43.1	51.4	49.2
Married	29.9	26.0	46.3	42.3	48.2	39.5	49.0	45.6
Single	6.2	5.5	4.1	4.9	2.8	3.6	2.4	3.6
Without children	31.6	35.6	24.8	29.7	24.5	29.9	28.4	30.4
Married	10.6	12.7	17.6	21.8	17.6	16.3	20.0	20.9
Single	21.0	22.9	7.2	8.0	6.9	13.6	8.4	9.6

Table 1A.3 / Unweighted Household Count

Household Structure by Age	US79	US86	CN81	CN87	GE81	GE84
	Total Non-Aged Households Head Age 20–55					
All Households	10,045	8,038	10,103	7,822	1,775	3,597
Married w/ Children	4,716	3,563	5,372	3,842	1,050	1,899
Single w/ Children	877	704	594	496	67	105
Married w/o Children	1,993	1,876	2,094	1,802	458	1,005
Single w/o Children	2,459	1,895	2,043	1,682	200	588
	Households Head Age 20–29					
Total Head, 20–29	3,178	2,031	3,038	1,975	307	658
Married w/ Children	1,011	596	1,012	587	127	210
Single w/ Children	312	207	186	131	12	22
Married w/o Children	602	459	684	444	103	200
Single w/o Children	1,253	769	1,156	813	65	226
	Households Head Age 30–55					
Total Head, 30–55	6,867	6,007	7,065	5,847	1,468	2,939
Married w/ Children	3,705	2,967	4,360	3,255	923	1,689
Single w/ Children	565	497	408	365	55	83
Married w/o Children	1,391	1,417	1,410	1,358	355	805
Single w/o Children	1,206	1,126	887	869	135	362

SOURCE: Luxembourg Income Study.

Table 1A.3 (*continued*)

Household Structure by Age	SW81	SW87	UK79	UK86	NL83	NL87	FR79	FR84
	Total Non-Aged Households Head Age 20–55							
All Households	6,698	6,532	4,042	4,285	3,276	2,929	7,113	8,401
Married w/ Children	3,611	2,705	2,336	2,130	1,754	1,450	4,264	4,746
Single w/ Children	706	288	222	311	132	102	181	291
Married w/o Children	1,230	1,542	990	1,280	897	723	1,818	2,145
Single w/o Children	1,151	1,997	494	564	493	654	850	1,219
	Households Head Age 20–29							
Total Head, 20–29	1,019	1,632	1,003	988	811	762	1,192	1,352
Married w/ Children	371	237	464	316	181	164	574	547
Single w/ Children	128	56	56	102	31	19	40	42
Married w/o Children	183	365	280	347	348	259	290	314
Single w/o Children	337	974	203	223	251	320	288	449
	Households Head Age 30–55							
Total Head, 30–55	5,679	4,900	3,039	3,297	2,465	2,167	5,921	7,049
Married w/ Children	3,240	2,468	1,872	1,814	1,573	1,286	3,690	4,199
Single w/ Children	578	232	166	209	101	83	141	249
Married w/o Children	1,047	1,177	710	933	549	464	1,528	1,831
Single w/o Children	814	1,023	291	341	242	334	562	770

Table 1A.4 / Alternative Adjusted[a] Median Income Based Poverty Lines in Own Currency, Excluding and Including Households Headed by a Person Over 55 Years Old

Country	Year	Half Adjusted Median Income, Households with Head 20–55 Years Old	Half Adjusted Median Income, All Households	Comparison of Adjusted Median for Entire Population and for Non-Elderly Households
United States	1986	$US 12,270	11,964	97.5
Canada	1987	$C 15,561	14,899	95.7
Sweden	1987	Kr. 75,557	69,157	91.5
West Germany	1984	Dm. 18,810	18,662	99.2
France	1984	ff 55,221	53,875	97.6
Netherlands	1987	Dfl. 17,182	16,838	98.0
United Kingdom	1986	£ 4,649	4,216	90.7

SOURCE: Luxembourg Income Study.

[a]Median disposable income adjusted using an equivalence scale of 1.0 for first adult, .7 for the second adult, and .5 for children and normalized to a family of three persons.

Table 1A.5 / The Economic Context: 1979–1989[a]

	1979	1980	1981	1982	1983	1984	1985	1986	1987	1988	1989	Average
Economic Growth[b]												
U.S.	**2.5**	(0.2)	1.9	(2.5)	3.6	6.8	3.4	**2.7**	3.4	4.5	2.5	3.1
Canada	3.6	1.1	**3.4**	(3.2)	3.2	6.3	4.7	3.3	**4.0**	4.4	3.0	3.3
U.K.	**2.8**	(1.9)	(1.1)	1.6	3.6	2.1	3.6	**3.9**	4.7	4.6	2.2	2.9
West Germany	4.0	1.5	**0.0**	1.0	1.9	**3.3**	1.9	2.3	1.6	3.7	3.9	2.3
Netherlands	2.1	1.2	(0.7)	(1.4)	**1.3**	2.9	2.4	2.7	**0.4**	2.7	4.1	1.7
France	**3.2**	1.6	1.2	2.5	0.7	**1.3**	1.9	2.5	2.2	3.8	3.6	2.2
Sweden	4.0	1.4	**0.0**	1.1	1.8	4.0	2.2	2.3	**2.9**	2.3	2.1	2.2
Unemployment[c]												
U.S.	**5.8**	7.0	7.5	9.5	9.5	7.4	7.1	**6.9**	6.1	5.4	5.2	7.0
Canada	7.4	7.4	**7.5**	10.9	11.8	11.2	10.4	9.5	**8.8**	7.7	7.5	9.1
U.K.	**5.6**	6.9	10.6	12.3	13.1	11.7	11.2	**11.2**	10.3	8.5	6.9	9.8
West Germany	3.2	3.0	**4.4**	6.1	8.0	**7.1**	7.2	6.4	6.2	6.2	5.6	5.8
Netherlands	5.4	6.0	8.6	11.4	**13.7**	11.8	10.6	9.9	**9.6**	9.2	8.3	10.0
France	**5.9**	6.3	7.4	8.1	8.3	**9.7**	10.2	10.4	10.5	10.0	9.4	8.7
Sweden	2.1	2.0	**2.5**	3.1	3.5	3.1	2.8	2.7	**1.9**	1.6	1.4	2.4
Consumer Price Inflation[d]												
U.S.	**11.3**	13.5	10.4	6.1	3.2	4.3	3.5	**1.9**	3.7	4.1	4.6	6.0
Canada	9.2	10.2	**12.5**	10.8	5.9	4.3	4.0	4.2	**4.4**	4.0	5.2	7.6
U.K.	**13.4**	18.0	11.9	8.6	4.6	5.0	6.1	**3.4**	4.2	4.9	7.7	8.0
West Germany	4.1	5.5	**6.3**	5.3	3.3	**2.4**	2.2	0.1	0.2	1.3	2.9	3.0
Netherlands	4.2	6.5	6.7	6.0	**2.8**	3.3	2.2	0.1	0.7	0.7	1.2	3.1
France	**11.3**	13.6	13.4	11.8	9.6	**7.4**	5.8	2.7	3.1	2.7	3.6	7.7
Sweden	7.2	13.7	**12.1**	8.6	8.9	8.0	7.4	4.3	**4.2**	5.8	6.5	7.9

SOURCES: OECD: *Economic Outlook* 48, December 1990, Tables R.1, R.18; OECD: *Main Economic Indicators*, January 1990, pp. 44–45.

[a]Figures shown in bold indicate the year to which the income survey data refer.
[b]Annual percentage change in real GNP/GDP in the OECD area.
[c]Percentage of total labor force: standardized basis.
[d]Annual percentage change in consumer prices.

REFERENCES

Atkinson, A. 1990. "The Department of Social Security Report on Households Below Average Income 1981–87." Welfare State Programme Research Note No. 22. London School of Economics, December.

———. 1991. "Comparing Poverty Rates Internationally: Lessons from Studies in Developed Countries." *World Bank Economic Review* 5(4): 3–21.

Blundell R., and I. Walker. 1988. "The Changing Structure of the Labor Force: Married Women and Lone Parents." Presented to the Symposium on Population Change and European Society. Florence, Italy, December 8.

Buhmann, B., et al. 1988. "Equivalence Scale, Well-Being, Inequality, and Poverty: Sensitivity Estimates Across Ten Countries Using the Luxembourg Income Study (LIS) Database." *Review of Income and Wealth.*

Burkhauser, R., V. Halberstadt, and R. Haveman. 1984. *Public Policy Toward Disabled Workers: A Cross-National Analysis of Economic Imports.* Ithaca, N.Y.: Cornell University Press.

Dooley, M. 1989. "Demography of Child Poverty in Canada: 1973–1986." Presented to the Population Association of America, Baltimore, MD, March 28.

Duncan, G., et al. 1991. "Poverty and Social Assistance Dynamics in the U.S., Canada, and Europe." University of Michigan mimeo, May 20.

Duskin, B. 1990. *Lone Parents and Their Children.* Paris: OECD.

Ellwood, D. 1988. *Poor Support.* New York: Basic Books.

Ermisch, J. 1987. "Demographic Aspects of the Growing Number of Lone Parent Families." Presented to the OECD Conference on Lone Parents: The Economic Challenge of Changing Family Structures. Paris: OECD, December 8.

Eurostat, 1990. "Poverty in Figures: Europe in the Early 1980s." Theme 3, Series C, Office for Official Publication of the European Community, Luxembourg.

Gottschalk, P., and M. Joyce. 1991. "Changes in Earnings Inequality—An International Perspective." LIS-CEPS Working Paper No. 66, June.

Green, G., J. Coder, and P. Ryscavage. 1990. "International Comparisons of Earnings Inequality for Men in the 1980s." LIS-CEPS Working Paper No. 58, October.

Hagenaars, A. J. 1986. *The Perception of Poverty.* Amsterdam: North Holland Publishers.

Hanratty, M., and R. B. Blank. 1990. "Down and Out in North America: Recent Trends in Parenting Rates in the U.S. and Canada." Mimeo. Evanston: Northwestern University, September.

O'Higgins, M. 1987. "Lone Parent Families in OECD Countries: Numbers and Socio-Economic Characteristics." Presented to the OECD Conference on Lone Parents: The Economic Challenge of Changing Family Structures. Paris: OECD, December 8.

Rainwater, L. 1990. "Changing Inequality Structure in Europe: The Challenge to Social Science." LIS-CEPS Working Paper No. 46, March.

———. 1992. "Poverty in American Eyes." LIS-CEPS, Working Paper No. 80, July.

Smeeding, T. 1990. "Poverty in the United States and Other Nations: Toward a Fund for American Children and Their Families," *FORUM for Applied Research and Public Policy* 5 (2):65–70, Summer.

————. 1991. "Briefing: Cross-National Perspectives on Trends in Child Poverty and the Effectiveness of Government Policies in Preventing Child Poverty in the 1980s: First Evidence from LIS." Presented to the George Washington University Forum, Washington, D.C., February 25.

Smeeding, T., and B. B. Torrey. 1988. "Poor Children in Rich Countries." *Science* 242:873–877, November 11.

Smeeding, T., B. B. Torrey, and M. Rein. 1988. "The Economic Status of the Young and Old in Eight Countries." In Palmer, Smeeding, and Torrey, eds. *The Vulnerable.* Washington, D.C.: Urban Institute Press.

Wolfe, B., et al. 1984. "Income Transfers and Work Effort: The Netherlands and the United States in the 1970s." *Kyklos* 37 (4):609–632.

Chapter 2

POVERTY AND SOCIAL-ASSISTANCE DYNAMICS IN THE UNITED STATES, CANADA, AND EUROPE

Greg J. Duncan, Björn Gustafsson, Richard Hauser,
Günther Schmaus, Stephen Jenkins,
Hans Messinger, Ruud Muffels, Brian Nolan,
Jean-Claude Ray, and Wolfgang Voges

ALL MODERN industrialized countries have developed sophisticated government programs to reduce the adverse financial consequences of labor market and demographic events and establish minimum living standards for poor families. Most combine social insurance against specific labor market events such as unemployment, disability, and retirement; social assistance that distributes benefits to low-income families according to their means; and universal benefits like child allowances or tax credits that have weak or no links to a family's income.

Despite the long history of such programs, we know very little about their collective success in mitigating the risks of economic insecurity and promoting financial independence. Comparative income-distribution data from the Luxembourg Income Study show large differences across countries in the incidence of poverty as well as differences within countries in poverty risks as they affect specific demographic groups (Chapter 1, this volume). But these snapshot pictures tell us nothing about the dynamic nature of family economic mobility. For example, after accounting for government transfers, how often and why do families fall into poverty? Are periods of poverty and social-assistance receipt typically long- or short-term? For those in need, how well do social-assistance programs match the dynamic nature of families' situations?

Our study is the first to use longitudinal household data from a number of Western countries to address these kinds of questions. Our perspective is decidedly comparative, based on the belief that assembling comparable data on poverty transitions and social-assistance receipt across a number of countries provides valuable leverage in drawing conclusions about social policy. A number of interrelated issues motivate our work.

First, at odds with the stereotype of the poor as an unchanging "underclass," longitudinal household data in the United States show frequent, although far from universal, transitions out of poverty, often as the result of economically favorable events such as employment or marriage. For example, the U.S. Census Bureau's Survey of Income and Program Participation found that one-quarter of all individuals living in households with incomes below the U.S. poverty threshold in 1984 were *not* poor in 1985 (U.S. Bureau of the Census 1989). One-quarter of the exits could be linked readily to increased employment and about one-tenth to marriage. Whether upward economic mobility is as extensive in other Western countries is an open question, addressed with panel data for the first time in this chapter.

A dynamic perspective on the distribution of family income raises a set of important but little-discussed issues about social insurance and assistance. We find that while the incidence of poverty is generally lower in Western European countries than in the United States, all countries studied share remarkably similar patterns of economic mobility that produce a mixture of long- and short-term poverty experiences. Poverty for some families is only a temporary condition, beginning with a job loss or divorce and ending with reemployment or remarriage. But poverty for other families is more persistent, the likely result of less tractable deficiencies in health, skills, or structural opportunities. An implication, also borne out by our data, is that the need for social assistance is equally heterogeneous.

How does and should social policy deal with this heterogeneity? Our first task in this area is to describe the dynamics of social-assistance receipt across a number of countries—Canada (Quebec), Germany (Bremen), the United Kingdom, and the United States. Although all of these countries are found to have both short- and long-term recipients, the countries differed greatly in their relative numbers of long-term recipients, with lone-parent recipients in the United Kingdom clearly having the longest spells. In attempting to account for this diversity, we assemble evidence on likely explanations—demographic characteristics of recipients, labor market conditions, the generosity of benefits, employment norms regarding lone parents and the likely stigma attached to social-assistance receipt.

We next turn to a more normative discussion of how social-assistance programs ought to be designed in light of the diverse patterns of need. For example, should the duration of receipt be a key parameter in the design of social-assistance programs? The French Allocation de Parent Isolé (API) supplemental-assistance program limits its benefits to children of lone parents to the period between birth and the third birthday and to divorced or separated women to one year. The German Erziehungsgeld parental allowance program provides benefits to mothers working little or not at all until the child's first birthday. Other countries have no set duration for social assistance. Which approach makes more sense in light of the dynamics of need for such income?

A second issue is targeting: how to channel resources for income-support and skill-augmentation programs most effectively when the duration of need is so much shorter for some low-income families than others. Recent changes in social-assistance policies in the United States have attempted to target training resources on likely long-term recipients.

We address these various issues in three remaining sections. The next section presents our results with regard to poverty transitions and their links with family and labor market events. In the section following, we present data on the duration of social assistance. Finally, we discuss social-policy approaches in the context of the dynamic evidence presented earlier.

POVERTY TRANSITIONS AND EVENTS

Our analysis of poverty transitions is based on longitudinal data gathered from representative samples of the population of eight countries during the 1980s: Canada, (the Lorraine province of) France, the Federal Republic of Germany (before reunification), Ireland, Luxembourg, the Netherlands, Sweden, and the United States. Details on the data sets and procedures are presented in Appendix 2A. Poverty data from three countries—France (Lorraine), Luxembourg, and the Netherlands—should be viewed with caution: sample sizes are small in the French and Luxembourg panels, and with the Dutch data there appears to have been selective attrition among low-income households in several of the early waves.

In brief, and with exceptions noted in Appendix 2A, the heart of our measure of family economic status is total family income, including social assistance and other government and private transfers, but subtracting income and payroll taxes. Samples drawn from all countries consisted of families with minor children. We adjusted for family-size differences using an equivalence scale that gave respective weights of 1.0, 0.7, and 0.5 to the first adult, subsequent adults, and children in the family.

We used size-adjusted family income to examine economic mobility in two ways. First, we defined a family to be in "median-income-based poverty" if its size-adjusted income was below 50 percent of the median in that year.[1] An "escape from median-income-based poverty" is defined as a transition from income below 50 percent of the median in a given year to income 60 percent or more of the median one year later. (We required income to jump at least 20 percent in order to avoid the ambiguity associated with transitions involving very small income changes from just below to just above a poverty line.)[2]

A second—"bottom-decile"—definition of poverty was based on the point of the size-adjusted income distribution that divided the bottom 10 percent of all families from the top 90 percent. By definition, a constant percentage of each country's population of families is "bottom-decile" poor each year. An "escape from bottom-decile poverty" is defined as a transition from the bottom decile to a point at least 20 percent higher than the bottom-decile breakpoint. Given the large variation across countries in the economic position of the worst-off families, the bottom-decile poverty line cuts the income distributions of the various countries at very different points. The bottom-decile threshold is thus not a "poverty line" in any meaningful sense but is used here to standardize on the proportion of the population in relative low-income status.

Poverty Rates and Characteristics of the Poor

We begin by showing the incidence of poverty in the various countries in our study (Table 2.1, Column 1). Rates of median-income-based poverty varied widely across countries, with Canada, foreign residents of Germany, Ireland, and the United States having double-digit rates, and continental countries generally having rates of less than 10 percent.[3] Nearly half of all black families in the United States were poor by this definition, reflecting the much worse economic position of U.S. blacks than whites relative to the median for blacks and whites taken together.

Certain characteristics of poor families themselves—especially lone-parent status, large family size, and the presence of very young children—might be expected to retard transitions out of poverty. A look at these characteristics showed that poor families in Ireland have the most members, while U.S. poor families are most likely to be headed by a lone mother. While the incidence of lone-mother status is also relatively high among poor families in Canada and among native Germans, family sizes are typically small.

Poverty Transitions

Our findings on transitions out of median-income-based poverty are presented in the second column of Table 2.1. Figures there indicate the fraction of poor families in a given year making the transition out of median-income-based poverty by the following year.

Taken as a whole, these figures show a remarkable amount of economic mobility, with all countries but the United States and Canada having at least one-fifth of their poor climbing from below 50 percent of median income to above 60 percent of the median. However, differences in the prevalence of transitions out of median-income-based poverty are nearly as great as the incidence of median-income-based poverty itself. Nearly half of the Dutch poor escape poverty in a typical year, whereas less than one in twelve U.S. black families does so.

Closer examination of the data reveals a marked inverse relationship between the estimated incidence of poverty and escape rates. Countries associated with larger fractions of their populations below the poverty line (e.g., U.S. blacks and whites, German foreigners, Canadians) have lower escape rates, while countries with the smallest proportions poor (e.g., the Netherlands, Sweden) have the highest.

In other words, the median-income-based poverty lines cut the income distributions of the different countries at very different points, but it is uniformly true that the higher in the distribution the poverty line cuts, the smaller the

Table 2.1 / Poverty Rates and Transitions out of Poverty for Families with Children

Country	Using Median Size-Adjusted Income of Population			Using Bottom Decile of Families	
	Poverty Rate: Percentage with Income <50 Percent of Median in t	Transitions: Percentage of Poor Becoming Nonpoor (of those with income <50 percent of median in t, percent with income ≥60 percent of median in t+1)	3-Year Poverty Rate: Percentage of Population with Income <50 Percent of Median in all 3 Years of a 3-Year Period	Transitions: Percentage of Poor Becoming Nonpoor (of those in the bottom decile in t, percent with incomes at least 20 percent above bottom decile in t+1)	Income Changes: Percentage Change in Income for Typical (median) Poor Family
Canada					
All	17.0	12.0	11.9	26.0	20.6
Quebec	20.8	11.1	12.7	23.2	16.7
France-Lorraine	4.0	27.5	1.6	21.0	10.2
Federal Republic of Germany					
All	7.8	25.6	1.5	22.8	17.9
German	6.7	26.9	1.4	24.9	21.0
Foreign	18.0	20.0	4.0	17.1	11.6
Ireland	11.0	25.2	N.A.	26.7	21.5
Luxembourg	4.4	26.0†	0.4	14.5†	10.4†
The Netherlands	2.7	44.4	0.4	21.3	7.5
Sweden	2.7	36.8	N.A.	16.2	8.5
United States					
All	20.3	13.8	14.4	22.6	15.1
White*	15.3	17.0	9.5	29.1 (21.1)	22.2 (13.5)
Black*	49.3	7.7	41.5	13.8 (41.9)	8.2 (39.6)

*Numbers in parentheses for U.S. white and black families show escape rates when "bottom decile" is defined by distribution of income within race subgroup.
†Based on 10–30 cases.

proportion of poor families escaping poverty. This is only logical since, every-thing else the same, the higher up into the income distribution the poverty threshold cuts, the farther away the typical poor family is from that threshold and the higher the income increase required to escape poverty.[4]

The essential similarity of patterns of economic mobility across countries can be seen most clearly by examining escape rates based on the bottom decile. In this case, defining the poor to consist of the bottom 10 percent of families within each country standardizes the relative size of the poor populations across countries, with the result that rates of economic mobility across countries be-come much more uniform (Table 2.1, Column 4). Escape rates for the United States (22.6 percent) are quite high and very similar to those in Canada (26.0 percent), France (21.0 percent), Germany (22.8 percent), Ireland (26.7 percent), and the Netherlands (21.3 percent) and somewhat higher than in Sweden (at 16.2 percent) and Luxembourg (14.5 percent).[5]

As shown in the fifth column of Table 2.1, calculation of the typical percent-age change in size-adjusted income between t and $t+1$ among families defined to be "bottom-decile poor" in year t also produces fairly similar—and quite positive—results across countries, with the typical bottom-decile poor family experiencing income increases ranging from 8 to 22 percent. So while the pov-erty rates displayed in the first column of Table 2.1 show dramatic differences in the relative positions of low-income families across the various countries, the evidence displayed in the right half of Table 2.1 leads us to conclude that the extent of economic *mobility* among low-income families in Canada and Europe is similar to that in the United States, especially for white families in the United States.

Relative Poverty over Three Years

Although low-income families in the countries in our study experienced simi-lar changes in income, their very different starting positions—closer to the me-dian in most European countries, far below the median in Canada and, espe-cially, the United States—lead to dramatic differences in the extent to which families are persistently excluded from living standards that are within the nor-mal range.

The third column of Table 2.1 presents poverty estimates using a 3-year window. Specifically, the estimates are of the fractions of the populations (in the five countries with appropriate data) that failed to enjoy incomes at least 50 percent of the median in at least one of the 3 years.[6] For the continental Euro-pean countries—Germany (native and foreign residents), France, Luxembourg, and the Netherlands—the combination of modest inequality and extensive mo-bility among the poor left very few families with persistently low relative in-comes. However, even with substantial mobility among the poor in Canada and the United States, many were left with incomes less than 50 percent of the median in all 3 years. Specifically, one in eight Canadians as well as one in seven white and two in five black families in the United States were persistently poor over the 3 years by this definition.

Events Associated with Entries

Additional insights into the social and economic processes underlying poverty transitions are provided by linking transitions to demographic and economic events. With varying degrees of comparability (see Table 2A.2), most surveys were able to provide information on whether the following events occurred at approximately the same time as the transition into poverty: a divorce/separation; "job loss," defined as a change from considerable to very little work by family members; "less work," defined as a major decrease in work hours of still-employed family members; and the termination of social insurance benefits.[7] The "job loss" and "less work" events are defined to be mutually exclusive, while neither marital nor social insurance events are exclusive of one another nor of the employment-based events.

An examination of the linkages between poverty entries and unfavorable events (Table 2.2) shows that employment events are clearly the most important correlates of entries into poverty. Loss of work and reduction in work together accounted for more than half of all poverty entries in Canada, the United States, and Luxembourg, and at least one-quarter of entries in all other countries.[8]

Interestingly, divorces and separations figured less prominently in the United States than in most other countries. This may seem surprising given the array of income-support programs available to divorcing women outside the United States. However, the effects of these programs may be overrated. A detailed examination of income changes surrounding divorce in the United States and in the Federal Republic of Germany showed very similar patterns (Burkhauser et al. 1991).

The final event, the termination of social insurance benefits, is tied to between one-tenth and one-fifth of the poverty entries. All in all, the picture that emerges from Table 2.2 is one of similarities in poverty-producing events across countries, with employment clearly the most important factor in all countries.

DYNAMIC ASPECTS OF SOCIAL-ASSISTANCE RECEIPT AMONG SINGLE-PARENT FAMILIES

Since they restrict their benefits to families with low income, social-assistance programs have often been the subject of vivid and memorable case-study accounts of long-term dependence. But such case studies are selected with precisely such dramatic impact in mind. Whether they represent the experiences of *typical* recipients is an important research and policy issue, especially in light of our findings indicating frequent transitions out of poverty. If most people receiving social assistance do so for only a short time, then the social-assistance

Table 2.2 / Marital and Labor Market Events Associated with Transitions _Into_ Poverty for Families with Children, Using Percentage of Median Income

Country	Percentage of Families Falling Into Poverty (size-adjusted family income ≥60 percent of median in t and <50 percent of median in $t+1$) Experiencing Marital and Labor Market Events				Number of Observations
	Divorce/ Separation	Job Loss	Less Work	Social Insurance Terminated	
Canada-Quebec					
All families entering poverty between t and $t+1$	17	29	48	12	9,550
France-Lorraine					
All families entering poverty between t and $t+1$	12	7	19	7	32
Federal Republic of Germany					
All families entering poverty between t and $t+1$	16	17	21	9	152
All German families entering poverty between t and $t+1$	19	17	21	6	85
All foreign families entering poverty between t and $t+1$	0	11	21	19	65
Luxembourg					
All families entering poverty between t and $t+1$	14*	5*	62*	19*	21
The Netherlands					
All families entering poverty between t and $t+1$	6	12	18	5	89
Sweden					
All families entering poverty between t and $t+1$	15	12	41	9	206
United States					
All families entering poverty between t and $t+1$	8	18	48	9	639
All white families entering poverty between t and $t+1$	8	17	46	9	303
All black families entering poverty between t and $t+1$	9	19	53	7	336

*Based on 10–30 cases.

system might better be regarded as providing most recipients with short-term insurance against income losses. But if most social-assistance receipt is indeed long-term, then the issue of dependence arises, and it is important to determine the nature and extent of such dependence and whether the social-assistance system itself causes recipients to become dependent.

We were able to assemble roughly comparable data on the duration of social-assistance experiences of lone-parent families from four countries—Canada (Province of Quebec), with the Social Assistance program; the Federal Republic of Germany (city of Bremen), with the Sozialhilfe program; the United Kingdom, with Supplementary Benefit (changed to Income Support in 1988); and the United States, with the Aid to Families with Dependent Children program. In all but the U.K., comparable information was available for social-assistance receipt among two-parent families. All of the social-assistance programs we chose to analyze shared similar characteristics, in particular allocating benefits according to the income of recipients.

An appendix describes the data sets and procedures. Two sources of noncomparability are worth noting here. First, the U.K. data come from a 1989 survey of lone parents which asked for information about current and previous periods of social-assistance receipt. Since the social-assistance experiences of women who remain lone parents are undoubtedly longer than those of the "average" recipient, this will almost certainly impart an upward bias to the estimated duration of social-assistance spells in the U.K., although we present some evidence below that suggests that the bias may not be very large. Second, the German data are from the city of Bremen and the Canadian data are from the Province of Quebec. The economic conditions in both of these areas were somewhat worse than in most other areas of the two countries; and the political climate in Bremen is less conservative than in most other parts of the country. This, too, ought to impart an upward bias to the estimated duration of the social-assistance experiences relative to what would be observed for all of the Federal Republic of Germany or Canada.[9]

A useful way of describing the nature of social-assistance experiences is with data on the duration of completed spells (i.e., continuous periods of receipt observed from beginning to end). For example, it is important to know about the extent of short-term receipt—how many individuals ever starting to receive social assistance complete their spell of receipt within, say, one or two years. Even more crucial is the extent of long-term receipt—how many are still receiving social assistance 5, 10, or even more years after starting their spell.

Since our survey and administrative-record data contain a great deal of information on the length of spells still in progress at the time of the most recent survey wave or when records were drawn, we use event-history methods to construct estimates of the duration of completed spells. The key piece of information required is the fraction of recipients leaving social assistance after any given number of years of continuous receipt. Information on the exit rates and durations of social assistance is presented in Table 2.3 and summarized in Figure 2.1.

Table 2.3 / **Duration of Social-Assistance Spells for Families with Children, by Family Structure**

Country	Lone-Parent Family at Beginning of Spell		Two-Parent Family at Beginning of Spell	
	Number of Observations at Start of Year	Cumulative Survival Rate: Percentage of Spells still in Progress after t Years	Number of Observations at Start of Year	Cumulative Survival Rate: Percentage of Spells still in Progress after t Years
Canada-Quebec				
$t=1$ year	850	85	2,075	69
2 years	625	62	1,175	40
3 years	600	58	1,075	36
Federal Republic of Germany-Bremen				
$t=1$ year	93	39	138	27
2 years	33	29	35	15
3 years	23	26*	18	10*
4 years	19	20*	12	7*
United Kingdom				
$t=1$ year	701	90	N.A.	N.A.
2 years	517	87		
3 years	388	84		
4 years	312	83		
5 years	234	80		
6 years	170	78		
United States				
All				
$t=1$ year	291	57	197	51
2 years	151	45	83	33
3 years	93	36	50	26
4 years	57	34	29	21*
5 years	32	24	18	19*
White				
$t=1$ year	79	59	N.A.	N.A.
2 years	38	47		
3 years	19	38*		
4 years	13	36*		
Black				
$t=1$ year	212	53	N.A.	N.A.
2 years	113	42		
3 years	74	35		
4 years	44	32		
5 years	23	29*		

*Based on 10–30 cases.

Figure 2.1 / Percentage of Social Assistance Spells Lasting at Least Three Years, by Family Structure

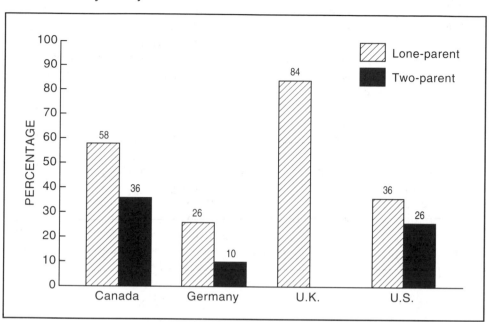

In contrast to the cross-country similarity in poverty dynamics, there appear to be very different patterns of social-assistance receipt across countries. Receipt tends to be relatively short-term in Germany and the United States, somewhat longer-term in Canada, and much longer-term in the United Kingdom. The proportion of lone parents still receiving social assistance after 3 years was 26 percent in Germany, 38 percent and 35 percent for whites and blacks, respectively, in the United States, 58 percent in Canada, and 84 percent in the United Kingdom. After four years these proportions fell to 20 percent and 34 percent in Germany and the United States, respectively, but remained at a very high level—83 percent—in the United Kingdom.[10] Within countries, not surprisingly, social-assistance spells involving lone-parent families were substantially longer than spells involving two-parent families.

Events Associated with Exits and Entries

As with the poverty analysis, one can gain more direct evidence on the similarity across countries of social and economic processes underlying social-assistance transitions of lone parents by linking transitions to demographic and economic events. Again, each of our data sources was able to gauge whether or not the following events occurred at the same time as the transition: a divorce/ separation or marriage/remarriage; substantially more or less employment for household members[11]; and the termination or beginning of social-insurance benefits.

Patterns of events associated with spell *beginnings* are shown in the left half of Table 2.4. Job losses were generally most important and appeared to initiate between one-sixth and one-third of the social-assistance cases. The onset of a marital disruption proved quite important in Germany, although this result may be an artifact of the data.[12] Termination of social insurance was as important as job losses in Germany.

Employment generally figured most prominently in spell *endings* across the four countries as well (right half of Table 2.4). Social-insurance payments brought an end to about one-fifth of social-assistance cases in Canada and Germany, but were less important in the United States. This suggests a role for other components of a country's safety net—labor market programs, other income-tested programs delivered through the tax system or directly. For example, a detailed look at the Bremen transitions involving social insurance revealed a combination of causes—an inefficient social-insurance bureaucracy delaying payments to the point that the recipient had to rely on social assistance, the failure of people to fulfill administrative demands, and perhaps the eagerness of the Bremen social-assistance system in helping potential social-insurance recipients bridge the time until their insurance payments began.

Why Are the Patterns of Social-Assistance Receipt so Different?

What is it about Germany and the United States that produces fairly short social-assistance spells, and why do spells tend to be quite long in the United Kingdom? We see five possible explanations:

Characteristics of recipients. As with poverty transitions, we would expect that certain demographic characteristics of families—in particular, large family sizes, very young children or young mothers—would make exits less likely. Table 2.5 summarizes a number of these demographic characteristics of lone-parent recipient families at the beginning of their spells of receipt.

When compared with other countries, social-assistance recipients in the United Kingdom are disadvantaged in two ways that might well help account for their longer spells. First, although the family sizes of British recipients are among the smallest, the proportion of British recipient families containing very young children is clearly much higher than in the other countries. Some 80 percent of British Income Support recipients had preschool children. A second and related factor is the youth of the British mothers themselves, with nearly half under the age of 25 at the beginning of their spells. Although the stereotypes of recipients in other countries may also be of young mothers, the facts presented in Table 2.5 indicate otherwise.[13]

Employment conditions underlying possible exits from social assistance. These varied widely across the countries (Table 2.6). Among the countries providing social-assistance spell data, the United Kingdom had the highest rates

Table 2.4 / Marital and Labor Market Events Associated with the Beginnings and Endings of the Receipt of Social Assistance for Lone Parents

Country	Percentage of all Spell *Beginnings* Associated with				Percentage of all Spell *Endings* Associated with			
	Number of Spells	Divorce/ Separation	Job Loss	Social Insurance Terminated	Number of Spells	Marriage/ Remarriage	Job Gain	Social Insurance Began
Canada-Quebec	1,275	14%	29%	16%	1,250	14%	13%	20%
Federal Republic of Germany-Bremen	93	53*	16	16	72	8	29	22
United Kingdom	971	8	N.A.	N.A.	159	10	N.A.	N.A.
United States†	291	24	33	18	157	10	20	6

*Divorce/separation in the Bremen data may have preceded the spell beginning by several years.
†For the United States the 157 spell endings were the sample of (un-right-censored) spells already in progress at the beginning of the panel period. As a result, these spells have a longer average duration than those beginning during the panel period.

Table 2.5 / Characteristics of Lone-Parent Social-Assistance Families at Beginning of Spell of Receipt

Country	Average Number of Persons in Household	Percent with Child under 6	Percent Minority	Percent with Age of Lone Parent			Sample Size*
				<25	25–34	>34	
Canada-Quebec	2.7	48%	N.A.%	13%	23%	64%	7,025
Federal Republic of Germany-Bremen							
All	3.0	43	8	13	43	44	93
German	2.8	44	0	14	45	41	86
United Kingdom	2.5	80	N.A.	47	37	16	964
United States†							
All	3.2	61	43	24	43	34	259
White	2.9	57	0	29	47	24	75
Black	3.7	66	100	16	38	46	184

NOTE: These are characteristics of the families as of the first year of the first observed spell.

*The number of observations for lone parent can be lower here than in Table 2.4 because Table 2.4 can include multiple spells.

†In U.S. data, a "lone parent" can be either the mother or grandmother of the children living in the family.

TABLE 2.6 / Economic Conditions in Various Countries in the Mid-1980s

Country	Average Employment Growth: 1984–86[a]	Male Unemployment Rates: 1984–86[a]	Percentage of All Unemployed Males Who Were Without Jobs for 12 Months or More 1984–86[a]
Canada-Quebec	2.7%	10%	12%
France	−0.3	8	41
Federal Republic of Germany	0.6	7	33
Ireland	−2.0	18[b]	46
Luxembourg	1.2	1[b]	N.A.
The Netherlands	1.4	14	57
Sweden	0.3	3	9
United Kingdom	1.3	13	45
United States All	2.8	7	13
White		5[c]	
Black		13[c]	

[a] From OECD: *Employment Outlook*, September 1987.
[b] 1984 and 1985 only.
[c] From *Monthly Labor Review*, September 1986, 1987 and 1988, Table 7, age 20 and older.

of unemployment and extensive long-term unemployment. The United States and Canada had the most favorable growth in employment during this period. Unemployment rates in the United States averaged only about 7 percent in the mid-1980s, as compared with rates twice as high in the United Kingdom and half again as high in Canada.[14] The unemployment data are consistent with the longer spells in the U.K., but do not appear to explain the relatively short-duration spells in Bremen.

Employment norms for working mothers. These differed in ways that are somewhat consistent with the patterns of social-assistance receipt. Table 2.7 assembles evidence from all countries in our study on employment rates among mothers, by family structure and age of the youngest child. While it should be noted that some estimates are based on small case counts, it appears that far fewer British single mothers with young children were employed than their counterparts in Germany and the United States, with single-parent employment

Table 2.7 / Employment Rates of Women with Children and Prevalence of Publicly Funded Childcare Services

Country	Mothers in Lone-Parent Families (percent employed)		Mothers in Two-Parent Families (percent employed)		All Mothers (percent employed)	Publicly Funded Childcare Services for Preschool Children 3 Years and Older as a Percentage of All Preschool Children 3 Years and Older
	Youngest Child Under 6	Youngest Child 6 or Older	Youngest Child Under 6	Youngest Child 6 or Older		
Canada	39%	60%	51%	62%	57%	N.A.%
France	70	85	60	66	66	95+
Federal Republic of Germany						
All	50*	55	30	41	38	65–70
German	60*	54	30	41	39	
Foreign	N.A.	82*	29	44	36	
Ireland	7*	30	23	26	24	35–40
Luxembourg	47*	52*	34	26	30	55–60
The Netherlands	12*	36	24	39	32	50–55
Sweden	83	89	83	92	87	74
United Kingdom	20	55	34	68	54	35–40
United States (1987)						
All	52	72	56	71	64	N.A.
White	57	76	55	71	65	
Black	47	63	59	69	58	

SOURCES: Canadian data are from the Labour Force Survey, French data are from Sorrentino (1990) and are labor force participation rates. United Kingdom data are from "The General Household Survey 1987," Office of Population Censuses and Surveys (Social Survey Division), HMSO, London, 1989. Swedish data are from the Labour Force Survey (AKU, Råtabeller). All other labor force data are from the surveys used to generate the poverty-transition data. Childcare data, for all but Sweden, are from Joshi and Davies (1991). Swedish childcare data are from the 1990 Survey of Childcare Needs and apply to children 4–6.

French figures are labor force participation rates. French data in column "youngest child under 6" are for cases with youngest child under 3. Data in column "youngest child 6 or older" are for all mothers with children under 18 years old. Data in column "mothers in two-parent families" are for all mothers with children.

*Based on fewer than 50 cases.

rates in Canada falling between these two extremes. Although employment rates for British lone mothers with older children are as high as in Germany, the very high incidence of very young children in British social-assistance cases suggests that the low employment rates of single mothers with young children are the more appropriate norm for understanding the length of British social-assistance spells. All in all, the (inverse) rankings by lone-parent employment generally matched rankings by social-assistance spell duration as well.

A related and reinforcing factor is the reduced availability of publicly funded childcare for employed mothers in the United Kingdom as compared with continental European countries (Table 2.7, Column 6).

Higher benefit levels. These might be expected to lead to longer durations for two reasons. First, higher benefit levels generally increase eligibility for benefits. Identical increases in, say, earned income from taking on a part-time job for low-income families in countries with different benefit levels may cause the termination of social-assistance benefits in the less generous country but not in the more generous country. And second, higher benefit levels may induce behavioral changes such as reduced work effort, which would also increase the number of families eligible for social assistance.

Table 2.8 assembles evidence on the generosity of cash and near-cash social-assistance benefits available to single-parent families with two children with: (1) no earned income; (2) income from a half-time job at the minimum wage; and (3) income from a full-time job at the minimum wage.[15] These benefit and earnings levels are then expressed as a fraction of the size-adjusted median family income in the given country. Across-country comparisons of benefit levels are complicated by the fact that some countries target benefits to certain family configurations and that additional noncash benefits vary widely from country to country. Common to all countries is a dilemma involving program generosity, benefit-reduction disincentives, and thresholds for existing programs. A program that is generous to families with no earned income must either "tax" increments to earned income at a high rate by reducing incremental benefits sharply as labor income increases or else continue to pay benefits to families with relatively high levels of earned income. It is obvious from Table 2.8 that the different countries have opted for a variety of strategies to address this dilemma.

These data show that the United States is the only real outlier among countries, with benefit levels that are very low relative to median family income.[16] This may well be a factor producing shorter assistance spells in the United States; however, the other country with typically short spells—the Federal Republic of Germany—has benefit levels that are about as generous as the country with the longest spells—the United Kingdom.[17]

Nor do the benefit-reduction disincentives associated with part- or full-time work appear to correlate with the duration patterns. After adjusting for reductions in benefit levels and possible increases in taxes, the income increment in going from no work to a part-time job is highest in Canada and lowest in the

Table 2.8 / Social Assistance and Earned Income of Lone Parents with Two Children with and without Labor Force Participation in 1986

Country	Size-Adjusted Social Assistance Plus Earned Income (if any) as a Percentage of Size-Adjusted Median Family Income		
	No Earned Income	Half-Time Work at Minimum Wage	Full-Time Work at Minimum Wage
Canada-Quebec	41%	60%	62%
France			
2 children <3	38	66	94
1 child <3, 1 age 3–10	28	56	84
2 children 3–10 and:			
Recent divorce (API)	54	54	74
No recent divorce (no API)	18	46	74
Federal Republic of Germany			
No child under 1	47	42	60
Child under 1 (receives Erziehungs-geld if no or part-time worker)	67	62	60
Ireland	55	62	84
Luxembourg	51	60	57
The Netherlands	61	68	65
Sweden	64	67	85
United Kingdom*	60	69	79
United States	27	39	43

NOTE: All percentages are derived from 2A.1. See Notes to Table 2A.1.

*United Kingdom figures are for 1989.

Federal Republic of Germany, with the United States and the United Kingdom roughly halfway in between.[18] The incongruence between spell length and work disincentives is most striking in the German case, where high benefit levels and a one-to-one reduction in benefits for additional DM of earned income would lead one to expect longer durations and relatively fewer employment-related exits.

Stigma. We would expect shorter spell lengths the more social-assistance benefits stigmatize recipients. Not only does stigma lead recipients to leave the program, it may also translate into administrative practices that restrict eligibility

Table 2.9 / Public Support for Universal Income Support and Education

Country	Percent Either "Strongly Agreeing" or "Agreeing" that the Government Should Provide a Basic Income for All or Help the Poor Attend College		
	(1) Basic Income for All	(2) Help Poor Attend College	(3) Difference (2)–(1)
Federal Republic of Germany	51%	84%	33%
The Netherlands	48	74	26
United Kingdom	59	83	24
United States	20	75	55

SOURCE: Smith (1990), p. 22.

for benefits. Surveys asking comparable questions about public support for government action against poverty and inequality reveal large differences across countries. Table 2.9 summarizes data from Smith (1990) on responses to statements on support for universal income-maintenance programs and for a program targeted at providing educational support for poor people.[19] We take the (complement of the) first to indicate likely stigma attached to social-assistance programs[20] and the second to indicate support for a more targeted (and perhaps cheaper) role for government with regard to income redistribution.

Differences are striking, with nearly three times as many British (59 percent) as Americans (20 percent) supporting universal transfers. Germans and the Dutch are close to the British end of the spectrum. On the other hand, cross-country differences regarding support for targeted education programs are relatively small. If we take the difference between support for these two kinds of programs as an indication of the likely stigma attached to a universal program of social assistance (Table 2.9, Column 3), the much greater likely stigma in the United States is most clear, with little difference among Germany, the Netherlands, and the United Kingdom in their relative lack of likely stigma. Stigma may help account for the shorter spells in the United States, but it cannot help explain the spell-length differences between Germany and the United Kingdom.

Summary

A summary of support found for the various hypotheses regarding cross-country differences in the duration of social assistance is presented in Table 2.10. Patterns of social-assistance receipt differed markedly across countries, with typical recipients in the United Kingdom having the longest spells and recipients in the United States and Germany the shortest. Poor employment

Table 2.10 / Summary Table of Support for Hypotheses about Cross-Country Differences in the Duration of Social Assistance

Hypotheses

Country	Relative Duration of Social Assistance	Relative Proportion of Young Recipients Who Are Young Mothers or Have Young Children	Relative Employment Conditions	Relative Norms About Single-Parent Employment	Relatively Generous Benefits?	Work Disincentives for Part-Time Work?	Relative Stigma
United States	short	medium	good	favorable	no	medium	high
Federal Republic of Germany	short	low	fair	favorable	yes	high	low
Canada	medium	low	fair	favorable	yes	medium	N.A.
United Kingdom	long	high	poor	unfavorable	yes	medium	low

conditions and norms, demographic factors, relatively generous benefits, and substantial public support for income maintenance programs are all consistent with the longer U.K. spells. Why recipients in Germany, with its high benefits levels, work disincentives, and low stigma should have spells as short as recipients in the United States emerges as an interesting issue in need of further research.

POLICY DISCUSSION

Our basic findings about poverty are easily summarized. The relative economic position of families varies widely across countries, with substantial numbers of families in the United States and Canada quite badly off. Although favorable income changes among low-income families with children were widespread and quite similar across the eight countries in our study, the very low starting position of the typical poor family in the United States and Canada made it impossible to elevate the living standards of substantial numbers of families to a level of even half that enjoyed by a typical family. In this section we discuss policy options in light of these similarities and differences.

Economic Mobility

In saying that the structure of economic mobility is similar for black and white families in the United States, as well as for families in Canada and Europe, we do not mean to imply that economic opportunities themselves are similar. Rather, given the static distribution of family incomes in each of the countries, transitions out of poverty appear to be similar. Left unaddressed is the question of why the cross-sectional distribution of family income is so much lower for some groups, most notably blacks in the United States and foreign residents of the Federal Republic of Germany.

Thus, before delving into the policy distinctions associated with short- and long-term poverty, we begin with an obvious but vital point: *the best situation is one in which neither kind of poverty exists.* Some of the countries in our study did much better than others in minimizing both short- and long-term poverty. For example, the Luxembourg panel data were not very useful in our poverty-transition analysis because very few families in Luxembourg met our definition of poverty. Despite a considerable influx of foreign workers from poorer EC countries, Luxembourg has combined extremely favorable employment conditions and a safety net of social insurance and assistance programs to reduce (although not eliminate) poverty among its residents. It should serve to remind us of what might be possible in the rest of the countries.

Persistent versus Transitory Poverty

For countries with substantial poverty, our dynamic perspective on the distribution of family income raises new issues in the debate over social insurance and assistance. Above all, the static dichotomy of "poor" versus "not poor" is misleading and needs to be replaced by at least four dynamic categories of economic position—persistent poverty, transitory poverty, economic vulnerability, and financial security.

The distinction between persistent and transitory poverty is especially important. Low-income families observed at any given time are really a heterogeneous mixture of families who have fallen into relatively brief periods of poverty as well as families unable to meet their basic needs for prolonged periods. In U.S. data (e.g., Duncan et al. 1984) and, we suspect, in other countries as well, the characteristics of the temporarily poor are not very different from the characteristics of the rest of the population. Relatively few families are immune to the possibility and economic consequences of a bout of unemployment or the departure or death of a spouse. For these families, social assistance can be viewed as a kind of insurance program, available if necessary to cushion them against the severity of their temporary misfortunes. With time, their departure from poverty will again place them in the ranks of the taxpayers, supporting the very social-assistance programs that once aided them.

Although surprisingly widespread, movements out of poverty are by no means universal, and long-term poverty probably exists in all of the countries in our study. How should social-assistance programs deal with the distinction between short- and long-run poverty? For some purposes the temporal dimension is unimportant. Social-assistance programs aimed at fulfilling short-term needs—food or heating for example—need not distinguish between the short- and longer-term poor.

However, it is vital that programs aimed at curing long-term poverty make such a distinction, recognizing which poor people are most likely to remain poor as well as which of the long-term poor would profit the most from these programs. It makes little sense to devote scarce resources, say, to provide job training for someone who would have found a job quickly in any case.

But we should also note that not all longer-term recipients would profit from the training. Using U.S. data, Adams and Duncan (1990) found that fewer than half of the long-term poor lived in households where the head was neither elderly nor disabled. And even able-bodied individuals may not be candidates for employment-related programs if they are entrusted with the care of very young children or handicapped persons. The most effective targeting is directed at the employable individuals most likely to have long-term poverty and social-assistance experiences (Ellwood 1986).

Although most of the data sets available to us have not yet accumulated enough information, the longer-running panels have produced helpful information to aid in targeting resources for income-support and skill-augmentation programs. Two examples from the United States: Ellwood (1986) identified younger, never-married mothers as the most likely long-term recipients of social assistance and therefore most in need of skill-augmenting programs. His analysis led in 1988 to changes in social-assistance programs in the United States, giving such women highest priority for training opportunities.

Newman and Struyk (1983) found in an analysis of poverty and housing that several readily available pieces of information about the family situation could be used to predict which families ran the greatest risk of long-run poverty. These examples provide encouraging evidence that the transitory-persistent distinction can be built into the design of intervention programs.[21]

Social Assistance in a World of Transitory and Persistent Poverty

By plugging holes in the safety net not covered by social insurance systems, social-assistance programs play a vital role, particularly in providing support for families that, for various reasons, are unable to support themselves through paid employment. Few would argue against families with able-bodied adults supporting themselves through work and private transfers rather than social assistance. Indeed, social-assistance programs may well stigmatize recipients, rarely provide a standard of living that allows full participation in society and may reduce recipients' desire to support themselves. With these results and our findings on income mobility in mind, how can social-assistance programs provide the most effective help with the least adverse consequences?

First, let us note that the relatively short duration of many experiences with social assistance observed in German and U.S. data is broadly consistent with the idea that social assistance functions as a kind of insurance against temporary misfortune for the majority of recipients in those countries. Nevertheless, the fact that a substantial minority of recipient families in Germany and the United States and larger fractions of recipient families in Canada and, especially, the United Kingdom have longer-term experiences suggests that not all social-assistance recipients are recovering from temporary misfortunes.

One idea is to gear social-assistance benefit levels or eligibility to the duration of receipt, in the case of employable recipients. Although duration-dependent unemployment benefits are common, the French and, to a lesser extent, the Germans are the only ones to have this feature in their social-assistance system.[22] As with all countries in our study other than the United States, France makes means-tested payments available to most of its citizens through the Revenu Minimum d'Insertion (RMI) program. Supplementing this basic support for lone parents is the Allocation de Parent Isolé (API) program. In one portion of the API program, eligibility for means-tested social-assistance benefits for families with children is limited to the period between the child's birth and third birthday, even if low-income status persists beyond this point. In effect, the API program acknowledges a special need for support during this period, especially if a parent wishes to care for very young children and forgo income from work. The elaborate state-funded system in France for providing childcare beginning at age 3 lessens the problems associated with the parent's transition into the labor force. In Germany, a more modest parental allowance (Erziehungsgeld) is available to mothers working less than 20 hours per week until the child is 12 months old (18 months beginning in 1991).

Another part of the Allocation de Parent Isolé program extends means-tested benefits for a period of up to one year to recently divorced or separated women and their children. In this case, the time limit turns the program into a kind of insurance against income losses associated with divorce. Unfortunately, no program-evaluation data are available on how well the API program is meeting its goals.[23]

A number of liberal policy analysts in the United States have called for an explicit limit on the duration of receipt of social assistance to able-bodied recipients. (Conservatives like Charles Murray [1984] conduct "thought experiments" in which all durations are limited to zero!) For example, Ellwood's (1988) recommendations for social-assistance reform include a limit on the duration of assistance to able-bodied recipients to between 1½ and 3 years, depending on the situation. This idea is coupled with a number of other reforms, including assured child-support benefits, a higher minimum wage, and the government as employer of last resort if the recipient is unable to find a job at the end of his or her period of receipt. Kamerman and Kahn (1988) make a similar recommendation about a fixed duration to social assistance.

In European countries, social assistance is viewed as a right, irrespective of the causes of poverty, and is generally available to citizens with low family incomes, regardless of family status, age of children, and so forth. In the United States, only the food stamp program has this element of universality. Proposals to limit the duration of these basic social-assistance programs in Europe would probably be viewed as an unacceptable reversion to unenlightened nineteenth-century social policy.[24]

With social assistance available as an ever-present safety net, the task of reducing the need for it becomes one of minimizing entries into the program and hastening exits. The often sharp distinction between social insurance and social assistance hinders this task. Training and other labor-market programs offered to unemployed workers as part of the social insurance system are not often readily available to current or potential social-assistance recipients whose problems are not linked directly to unemployment. A useful idea here might be to expand the labor-market-based programs such as unemployment insurance by defining, for example, divorced women and young people with difficulties establishing careers as "unemployed" and therefore eligible for training and other labor-market benefits even if they had worked little or not at all. This would reduce the contributory-based and earned-right approach of unemployed insurance, but would deliver needed services to these excluded groups.

The Risk of Marital Disruption

Perhaps surprisingly, marital disruption was even more important in producing poverty spells in Canada and several Western European countries than in the United States. This is consistent with the more detailed examination taken in Burkhauser et al. (1991), which found very similar patterns of adverse economic changes for divorcing women in the United States and the Federal Republic of Germany.

These results point out the unfortunate fact that while social security programs may have succeeded in helping families cope with the economic consequences of work-related events such as unemployment, retirement, and disability, they have yet to come to terms with family-related events such as divorce. In all of the countries in our study, social-insurance programs were developed in a time when the main risks were to the primary wage earner (almost invariably the father), with the presumption that his insurance would cover his family. The rising number of female-headed families presents a risk that is not well covered by social-insurance programs.

What steps could be taken to reduce the economic impact of marital disruption on the women and children involved? As mentioned before, labor market training and employment programs are rarely available to recently divorced women because their work histories do not place them in the "unemployed" category on which these programs are focused. It would appear a relatively straightforward matter to make the necessary changes.

Evidence from both the United States and the Federal Republic of Germany (Burkhauser et al. 1991) suggests that very little of the ex-husband's income is transferred to his former spouse on a voluntary basis. Laudable initiatives, several of which are in place (e.g., in Sweden and Germany) or proposed (e.g., in the U.K.), are aimed at improving the economic status of divorced and separated women, and involve advance maintenance payments, guaranteed support in the absence of payments from the father, and more vigorous enforcement of child-support awards.

APPENDIX 2A

Data used in the paper are drawn from a variety of sources and, despite our persistent efforts, retain a number of inconsistencies. In this appendix, we summarize the data sets, procedures, and remaining inconsistencies.

Data

Canada: the Longitudinal Administrative Database for both poverty and social assistance analyses. **Federal Republic of Germany:** the Socioeconomic Panel (SOEP) for the poverty analyses; the Bremen Longitudinal Social Assistance Sample (LSA) for the social assistance analyses. **Ireland:** a two-wave household panel study conducted by the Economic and Social Research Institute for the poverty analyses; no data available for the social assistance analyses. **Luxembourg:** the Liewen zu Letzebuerg household panel for the poverty analyses; no data available for the social assistance analyses. **France:** the Lorraine Household Panel for the poverty analyses; no data available for the social assistance analyses. **The Netherlands:** the Dutch Socioeconomic Panel Project (SEP) for the poverty analyses; no data available for the social assistance analyses. **Sweden:** the Household Income Survey (HINK) for the poverty analyses; no data available for the social assistance analyses. **United Kingdom:** no data available for the poverty analyses; the 1989 Lone Parents Survey for the social assistance analyses. **United States:** the Panel Study of Income Dynamics for both the poverty and social assistance analyses.

Poverty Analyses

In brief, and with some exceptions noted below, our poverty analyses took all families with children[25] and classified them in year "t" according to whether their posttax, post-transfer income was sufficiently low for us to consider them "in poverty." Repeating this procedure in year "$t+1$" produces a two-way table showing whether or not family income had increased sufficiently for them to be "out of poverty."

All data used in the poverty-transition analyses come from longitudinal household surveys, which provide data on changes in the economic status of the same families between years t and $t+1$. Calendar years corresponding to t and $t+1$ vary from survey to survey. For **Canada,** years t and $t+1$ consist of four pairs of consecutive years from 1982-83 to 1985–86. For **France,** years t and $t+1$ consist of two pairs of consecutive years—1984–85 and 1985–86. For the **Federal Republic of Germany,** years t and $t+1$ consist of three pairs of consecutive years from 1983–84 to 1985–86. For **Ireland,** years t and $t+1$ are not consecutive and correspond only to 1986 and 1988. In addition, the Irish panel reduced the costs of its second wave by following all Wave 1 poor families but only a random subset of Wave 1 nonpoor families. As a consequence, information on transitions into poverty between the two waves is not available. For **Luxembourg,** years t and $t+1$ consist of two pairs of consecutive years—1984–85 and 1985–86. For **The Netherlands,** years t and $t+1$ consist of three pairs of consecutive years from 1984–85 to 1986–87. For **Sweden,** years t and $t+1$ consist of 8 pairs of consecutive years from 1980–81 to 1987–88. For the **United States,** years t and $t+1$ consist of six pairs of consecutive years from 1980–81 to 1985–86.

In all cases the unit of analysis is families with children age 17 or younger at the time of both the year t and year $t+1$ income reports. The family at year $t+1$ must include at least one of the children and one of the adults present in year t to be kept in the sample. Where the family at year t splits into two or more families at year $t+1$, the family unit in which the youngest child (and one of the adults) remain is kept in our analyses and other derivative families are eliminated.

Income in most cases is annual, posttax, post-transfer family cash income. Exceptions are the **French** income data, which are gross of income taxes, and are obtained by multiplying how many of the 12 months prior to the November-December interview a given type of income was received by the amount of such income received in the month prior to the interview; the **Dutch** data, in which the family income total refers to the household's "normal" income at the time of the October interview; and the **United States** data, in which the value of food stamps, a near-cash transfer program, is counted as part of family income.

To form the median-income-based poverty line, we obtained a median size-adjusted income figure in a given year from our survey data as follows. We (1) took all individuals present in that year as the units of observation (including individuals who were not part of families with children); (2) divided the household income by a family-size adjustment factor, which is the sum of: 1 for the first adult, .7 for each additional adult, and .5 for each child (under age 18); and (3) assigned that size-adjusted income to each individual in the household (e.g., each individual in a four-person household containing two adults and two children and a $20,000 household income has a size-adjusted household income of $20,000/(1 + .7 + .5 + .5) = $20,000/2.7 = $7,407). We then (4) found the (weighted) median of size-adjusted household income of all individuals in the sample; and (5) repeated this for each of the years t and $t+1$ used in the poverty analysis. A check to see if the median size-adjusted income changes by a percentage that is comparable to the percentage change in per capita disposable income and inflation rate was generally reassuring.

Once these medians were calculated, it was a simple matter to categorize our samples of households with children according to whether household income was less than 50 percent, 50–60 percent, or 60 percent or more of the median. These four categories, calculated for pairs of t and $t+1$ years, produce the poverty-transition tables that form the heart of our analysis of poverty dynamics.

Social-Assistance Analyses

It proved considerably more difficult to find comparable data bases for the analyses of social assistance. Here we provide country-by-country details on data sets and comparability problems.

Canada: Social-assistance data from the Longitudinal Administrative Database is based only on the Province of Quebec, which represents about one-third of the national caseload. For the analysis we selected a subset of families with dependent children under the age of 18 from a large sample of annualized social-assistance records that were merged with family taxation records. This enabled us to track individuals and families through time, whether or not they were on social assistance, and having information on both spouses allowed us to follow parents with dependent children in cases where families did not remain together.

"Spell beginnings" occurred in a year when a family receiving social-assistance income had not received any benefit in the previous year (i.e., spells could begin in 1983, 1984, 1985, or 1986). Similarly, social-assistance spells would end in a year in which a social-assistance recipient no longer received benefits. A given family could experience multiple spells over the five-year period. Spells in progress are measured from the first year in the sample in which a family received social assistance, regardless of what may have happened prior to 1982.

Federal Republic of Germany: Data are from the Bremen Social Assistance

Sample, a data base of social-assistance (Sozialhilfe) case files in the city of Bremen. Somewhat atypical of the Federal Republic as a whole, Bremen in the 1980s was characterized by relatively high rates of unemployment (up to 15 percent) and social-assistance receipt (around 8 percent). One would expect these conditions to lead to longer durations of social-assistance receipt in Bremen than in the country as a whole.

The sample drawn for the analysis consisted of new social-assistance applications made by families with children in 1983. These families were tracked in the records for a total of 6 years. Cases in which social assistance was still being received at the end of the 6-year observation period were treated as censored.

"Social assistance" consisted of income from the Sozialhilfe program, the primary instrument in Germany for providing a minimum income. Available to all legal residents of the Federal Republic, Sozialhilfe has no limitations on duration. In some areas of Germany other than Bremen benefits are reduced in some circumstances if a recipient refuses to accept work offered to him. Benefit levels vary slightly by region.

United Kingdom: Data are from the 1989 Lone Parents Survey, which was conducted between May and September of 1989 and based on a national sample of lone parents as of April 1989. The necessary spell-based information came from retrospective questions on receipt of income from the Supplementary Benefit Program (converted to the Income Support in April 1988) while a lone parent. (The key question in the survey was "Did you receive Supplementary Benefit/Income Support at all after you [last] became a lone parent?") The analysis in this paper was restricted to spells begun after April 1970 and to the most recent spell in the case of reports of multiple spells; neither of these restrictions is likely to affect the analysis, however, since very few spells began prior to 1970 and very few multiple spells were reported.

It is important to note that the sampling scheme for the survey introduces a peculiar bias in the spell data, since women who received social-assistance income but were not lone parents in April 1989 had no chance of falling into the sample. This will almost certainly impart an upward bias to the estimated duration of the social-assistance spells, since durations for women who remain lone parents are undoubtedly longer than for the "average" woman who receives social assistance.

The Supplementary Benefit/Income Support program is available to individuals age 16 or over who were not engaged in full-time work and had (family) incomes less than the applicable amounts. (Changes instituted as part of the transition to the Income Support Program made it very difficult for 16- and 17-year-olds to receive benefits.)

United States: Data are from the Panel Study of Income Dynamics, an annual household panel survey designed to provide annual information on transfer-income usage for a representative sample of the U.S. population. The fact that the transfer-income data are annual rather than monthly creates some comparability problems with the other data sources. (Monthly dating of transfer income receipt was not introduced into the PSID until 1983.)

The sample drawn for the analysis consisted of families with children from the 1980 interview, plus families reporting a first child born into the family at the time of the 1981–1986 interviews. As with the poverty analysis, in cases where a family split into more than one family, the unit with the youngest child was kept in the sample. We required that the family remain in the panel through the 1987 interview to be included in the sample.

"Social assistance" consisted of income from the Aid to Families with Dependent Children program, along with the PSID's category "other welfare" (often misclassified AFDC), of all family members. Spells of social assistance lasting one, two, three, etc. years correspond to one, two, three, etc. consecutive years in which at least $1 of AFDC or "other welfare" income was reported. The AFDC program is the principal income-tested cash social-assistance program for families in the United States. Benefit levels and other program parameters are set by individual states and vary widely. About half of the states limited benefits to single-parent families during the 1980–87 period.

"Spell beginnings" are spells where we observed a year of no social-assistance income prior to observing the first year of social-assistance income. For the 1980 families, a spell could start with social-assistance receipt in calendar years 1980 (if no such income was reported for 1979) through 1986 (if no such income was reported for 1985). For families with first newborns after 1980, a spell could start with social-assistance income reported for the year after the birth (if zero social-assistance income was reported in the year of the birth) through 1986 (if no such income was reported for 1985). A family could have multiple spells. Any spell with social-assistance income reported in 1986 is censored by the end of the panel period.

"Percentage of year t spells still in progress in year $t+1$" for $t=1$ is the ratio of families observed in both years 1 and 2 who received at least $1 of social assistance in year 1 and year 2 relative to the number of families observed in both years 1 and 2 who received at least $1 of social assistance in year 1. For $t=2$, it is the percentage of families observed in years 1 to 3, receiving $1 of social assistance in years 1 and 2, who continue to receive at least $1 of social assistance in year 3. The "cumulative survival rate" is a standard life-table cumulative survival rate for discrete event-history data such as ours.

Benefit Levels in Tables 2.8 and 2A.1

France: Benefits here include Allocations Familiales (a basic benefit, to which any family with two or more children living in France is entitled), the Allocation d'Orphelin (targeted to both orphans and other children in one-parent families), the Allocation de Rentree Scolaire (intended to cover part of special disbursements linked to school furniture), and the Allocation de Jeune Enfant (available until the child reaches his third birthday). The AF, AO, and AJE (during pregnancy and 3 months after the birth) are not means-tested, the ARS and AJE (from the 4th to the 36th month) are means-tested. The income ceiling is about 90,000 FF per year for the ARS and about 110,000 FF per year for AJE. As a consequence, the marginal benefit-reduction rate may equal or exceed 100 percent at higher earnings levels.

Income taxes are not taken into account in our calculations because, at these income levels, special deductions for children under the "quotient familial" result in no tax liability. Moreover, housing benefits (APL and AL) and special benefits allowed to families with handicapped children (AES) are not included.

Federal Republic of Germany: There is no minimum wage in Germany. In its place, we used the 1986 gross earnings of gainfully employed women of performance group 3 of the Federal Statistical Office (industrial workers of the lowest wage bracket) with a weekly working time of 40 hours (for "full-time" work) and 20 hours (for "half-time" work). To arrive at a net income figure, social security contributions were subtracted from earnings, while housing and child allowances were added to them. A single-parent household containing two children was assumed throughout the calculations. For the housing allowance, it was assumed that the household rented a flat for 3 persons of a size of 646 square feet and an average rent of DM 6.31 per square meter. Income-related expenses of DM 47. were deducted from gross earnings and an additional 30 percent was deducted from the remaining amount for housing costs.

In the table, "typical cash and near-cash benefits" consist of housing plus children's allowances and, in the case of families with children 12 months or younger in which the mother works 19 hours per week or less, Erziehungsgeld. Social-assistance benefit levels vary by only a small amount across areas within Germany. The equivalence scale implicit in German benefit scales attaches higher relative weights to additional children than does the equivalence scale used to adjust the income amounts listed in Table 2.8.

Ireland: The social assistance amounts shown for Ireland are means-tested (long-term) unemployment assistance plus universal Child Benefits at 1986 rates. For half-time work, gross earnings of 3 pounds per hour for a 20-hour work week are assumed, less income tax and National Health Insurance contributions. Such a family would still qualify for some Unemployment Assistance. For full-time work, earnings of 3 pounds per hour are assumed and Family Income Supplement is included in transfer income. Child Benefits are paid in both cases.

Luxembourg: Listed amounts are for one-parent families with two children, one of whom is 6–12 years old and the other older than 12. "Typical cash and near-cash benefits" include child allowances and the Revenue Minimum Garantie (RMG). The minimum wage is set by law. Contributions for health insurance must be paid from the amount of the RMG and have been subtracted from the table's figures. The principal reason that total income associated with half-time work is higher than total income associated with full-time work is that the full-time work situation involves a much higher contribution to the old-age pension system.

The Netherlands: Listed amounts are for the year 1986 for one-parent households with two children ages 5 and 11 years old. Benefits include the basic social-assistance amounts, the holiday allowance, the family allowance for two

Table 2A.1 / Income Packages of Lone-Parent Families with Two Children with and without Labor Market Participation in 1986

Country (unit of exchange)	Social Assistance and No Labor Market Participation			Size-Adjusted Family Median Income[a]
	Typical Cash and Near-Cash Benefits	Medical Insurance Coverage?	Childcare Provided or Subsidized for Preschool Children?	
Canada-Quebec ($)[b]	10,762	Yes	Yes	13,300
France (FF)				
2 children under 3	35,100	Yes	Yes	46,644
1 child under 3, 1 age 3–10	25,860	Yes	Yes	
2 children 3–10 and:				
Recent divorce (API)	50,400	Yes	Yes	
No recent divorce (no API)	16,620	Yes	Yes	
Federal Republic of Germany (DM)				
No child under 1	16,884	Yes	Yes	18,056
Child under 1 (receives Erziehungsgeld)	24,084	Yes	Yes	
Ireland (£)	3,562	Yes	No	3,247
Luxembourg (FLux)	392,832	Yes	Yes	381,660
The Netherlands (Dfl)	20,240	Yes	Yes	16,720
Sweden (SEK)	77,712	Yes	Yes	60,276
United Kingdom (£)[c]	5,323	Yes	No	4,143
United States ($)	6,432	Yes	No	11,730

[a] Size-adjusted family median incomes in 1986, for all countries save the U.K., were calculated using each country's panel data. The social-assistance and labor income figures shown in this table are not adjusted for family size. Table 2.8 figures, showing size-adjusted social assistance and earned income as a percentage of size-adjusted median family income are derived from the numbers in this table, by first scaling the social-assistance and earned income figures by the family-size factor (2, for a lone parent with two children) and then dividing by the size-adjusted median family income of all families shown here in column 4. See note (c) below for details on U.K.

[b] Canada-Quebec social assistance figures reflect 1990 reforms that have improved work incentives. They have been deflated to 1986 price levels. Canadian median income figure is for 1986.

[c] All U.K. figures (social-assistance, earned income, and median family income) are for 1989. The parent, when in the labor force, is assumed to earn a low wage of £3 per hour. (The U.K. has no national minimum wage.) The 1989 U.K. median family income figure, used to calculate the numbers in Table 2.8, is the 1986 size-adjusted family median income inflated to 1989 values, by applying the annual rate of change in per capita Gross Domestic Product, 1986–89.

Table 2A.1 / *(continued)*

Country (unit of exchange)	Half-Time		
	After-Tax Labor Income	Typical Cash and Near-Cash Benefits	Total Income
Canada ($)	5,200	10,758	15,958
France (FF)			
2 children under 3	26,400	35,100	61,500
1 child under 3, 1 age 3–10	26,400	25,860	52,260
2 children 3–10 and:			
Recent divorce (API)	26,400	24,000	50,400
No recent divorce (no API)	26,400	16,620	43,020
Federal Republic of Germany (DM)			
No child under 1	10,638	4,512	15,150
Child under 1 (receives Erziehungsgeld)	10,638[d]	11,712	23,350
Ireland (£)[e]	2,800	1,220	4,020
Luxembourg (FLux)	151,994	303,900	455,844
The Netherlands (Dfl)	10,000	12,777	22,777
Sweden (SEK)[f]	34,812	45,866	80,678
United Kingdom (£)[c]	2,964	3,139	6,103
United States ($)	3,652	5,568	9,220

[d] In Germany, Erziehungsgeld (the supplemental child benefit) stops if the mother works more than 19 hours per week. This half-time work figure then assumes 19 rather than 20 hours of work.
[e] Labor income figures for Ireland assume a low wage of £3 per hour; Ireland has no minimum wage.
[f] Labor income figures for Sweden assume a low wage; Sweden has no minimum wage.

After-Tax Labor Income	Full-Time Typical Cash and Near-Cash Benefits	Total Income	Medical Insurance Coverage?	Childcare Provided or Subsidized for Preschool Children?
10,400	6,195	16,595	yes	yes
52,800	35,100	87,900	yes	yes
52,800	25,860	78,660	yes	yes
52,800	16,620	69,420	yes	yes
52,800	16,620	69,420	yes	yes
19,187	2,652	21,839	yes	yes
19,187	2,652	21,839	yes	yes
4,400	1,089	5,489	yes	no
303,900	135,000	438,900	yes	yes
19,133	2,610	21,743	yes	yes
61,933	40,475	102,408	yes	yes
5,212	1,877	7,089	yes	no
6,894	3,204	10,098	yes	no

Table 2A.2 / Definition of Marital and Labor Market Events in Poverty Analysis

Country	Marriage/Remarriage [divorce/separation]	Job Gain [job loss]	More Work [less work]	Social Insurance Began [social insurance terminated]
Canada-Quebec	Parent without [with] spouse or cohabitant in year t and with [without] spouse or cohabitant in year $t+1$	Earnings of household members were <$2,500 (86 $) in year t [>$3,750 in year t] and >$3,750 in year $t+1$ [<$2,500 in year $t+1$]	Earnings of household members were >$3,750 (86 $) in year $t+1$ [>$3,750 in year $t+1$] and increased by $2,500 or more in year $t+1$ [decreased by $2,500 or more in year $t+1$]	Family income from unemployment insurance and pensions was $0 in year t [>$0 in year t] and >$0 in year $t+1$ [$0 in year $t+1$]
France-Lorraine	Household head without [with] spouse or cohabitant in year t and with [without] spouse or cohabitant in year $t+1$	"Normal" weekly work hours of all household members were <10 in t [>15 in t] and >15 in $t+1$ [<10 in $t+1$]	"Normal" weekly work hours of all household members were ≥10 in t [≥10 in $t+1$] and rose 5 or more from t to $t+1$ [fell 5 or more from t to $t+1$]	Income from social insurance was 0 in year t [>0 in year t] and >0 in year $t+1$ [0 in year $t+1$]
Federal Republic of Germany	Household head without [with] spouse or cohabitant in year t and with [without] spouse or cohabitant in year $t+1$	Work hours of all family members were <500 hours in year t [>750 hours in year t] and >750 hours in year $t+1$ [<500 hours in year $t+1$]	Work hours of family members were ≥500 hours in year t [≥500 hours in year $t+1$] and rose 250 hours or more in year $t+1$ [and fell 250 hours or more in year $t+1$]	Family income from unemployment insurance and pensions was 0 DM in year t [>0 DM in year t] and >0 DM in year $t+1$ [0 in year $t+1$]
Ireland	Household head without [with] spouse living in household in year t and with [without] spouse living in household in year $t+2$	Number of household members at work increased [decreased] between t and $t+2$		Income from social insurance was 0 in year t [>0 in year t] and >0 in year $t+2$ [0 in year $t+2$]

Luxembourg	One household member without [with] spouse or cohabitant in year t and with [without] spouse or cohabitant in year $t+1$	Work hours of all household members were <10 hours per week in t [>15 in t] and >15 in $t+1$ [<10 hours in $t+1$]	Work hours of all household members were ≥10 hours per week in t [≥10 in $t+1$] and rose 5 or more hours per week from t to $t+1$ [fell 5 or more from t to $t+1$]	Family income from old age, accident, and illness pensions was 0 in year t [>0 in year t and >0 in $t+1$ [0 in $t+1$]
The Netherlands	Household head without [with] partner in year t and head with [without] partner in year $t+1$	Work hours of all household members were <10 hours per week in t [>15 in t] and >15 in $t+1$ [<10 in $t+1$]	Work hours of all household members were ≥10 hours per week in t [≥10 in $t+1$] and rose 5 or more hours per week from t to $t+1$ [fell 5 or more from t to $t+1$]	Income of any family member from unemployment benefits, disability benefits, or pensions (old-age, survivors) was 0 in year t [>0 in year t] and >0 in year $t+1$ [0 in year $t+1$]
Sweden	Sampling unit without [with] spouse or cohabitant in year t and with [without] spouse or cohabitant in year $t+1$	Work hours of family were <500 in year t [>750 in year t] and >750 in year $t+1$ [<500 in year $t+1$]	Work hours of family were >500 in year t [>500 in year $t+1$] and rose [fell] by more than 250 from t to $t+1$	Family income from unemployment insurance, labor market assistance, and pensions was 0 in year t [>0 in year t] and >0 in year $t+1$ [0 in year $t+1$]
United States	Family has a female head [male head with wife] at the time of the year t income report and a male head with wife [female head] at the time of the year $t+1$ income report	Work hours of family members were <500 hours in year t [>750 hours in year t] and >750 hours in year $t+1$ [<500 hours in year $t+1$]	Work hours of family members were ≥500 hours in year t [≥500 hours in year $t+1$] and rose 250 hours or more in year $t+1$ [and fell 250 hours or more in year $t+1$]	Family income from unemployment insurance, workers compensation, and social security was $0 in year t [>$0 in year t] and >$0 in year $t+1$ [$0 in year $t+1$]

Table 2A.3 / Definition of Marital and Labor Market Events in Social-Assistance Analysis: Spell Beginnings

Country	Divorce/Separation [marriage/remarriage]	Job Loss [job gain]	Social Insurance Terminated [social insurance began]
Canada-Quebec	Parent was with spouse or cohabitant in year t [without spouse or cohabitant in year $t+1$] and without spouse or cohabitant in year $t+1$ [with spouse or cohabitant in year $t+1$]	Earnings of household members were <\$3,750 (86 \$) in year t [<\$2,500 in year t] and <\$2,500 in year $t+1$ [>\$3,750 in year $t+1$]	Family income from unemployment insurance and pensions was >\$0 in year t [\$0 in year t] and \$0 in year $t+1$ [>\$0 in year $t+1$]
Federal Republic of Germany-Bremen	Case record documents a divorce or separation [marriage or remarriage] occurred up to several years prior to beginning of the case [occurred at end of case]	Case record shows loss of a job by any member of the household, unemployment after vocational training, failure to find an apprenticeship, or too low unemployment benefits	Case record documents a pending application for insurance benefits
United Kingdom	Recipient response to "What is main reason you came onto (social assistance)" was coded "became a lone parent"		
United States	Family has a female head [male head with wife] at the time the spell's first year of welfare is reported and a male head with wife [female head] in the preceding year	Either the family head or head's wife worked <500 hours [≥750 hours] in the first year of the spell and ≥750 hours [<500 hours] in the preceding year	Family income from unemployment insurance, workers compensation, and social security was \$0 [>\$0] in the first year of the spell and >\$0 [\$0] in the preceding year

Table 2A.4 / Definition of Marital and Labor Market Events in Social-Assistance Analysis: Spell Endings

Country	Marriage/Remarriage [divorce/separation]	Job Gain [job loss]	Social Insurance Terminated [social insurance began]
Canada-Quebec	Parent was without spouse or cohabitant in year t [with spouse or cohabitant in year $t+1$] and with spouse or cohabitant in year $t+1$ [without spouse or cohabitant in year $t+1$]	Earnings of household members were <\$2,500 (86\$) in year t [\$3,750 in year t] and >\$3,750 in $t+1$ [<\$2,500 in $t+1$]	Family income from unemployment insurance and pensions was \$0 in year t [>\$0 in year t] and >\$0 in year $t+1$ [\$0 in year $t+1$]
Federal Republic of Germany-Bremen	Case record documents marriage or remarriage [divorce or separation]	Case record shows reason for ending social assistance was a new job by any member of the household or getting a higher income from existing jobs	Case record shows reason for ending social assistance was because nonsocial assistance transfer income (social security or alimony) began or amounts paid had increased
United Kingdom	Recipient response to "What is main reason you were no longer able to receive (social assistance)" was coded "no longer eligible because married, remarried, or living with partner"		
United States	Family has a female head [male head with wife] at the time the spell's last year of welfare is reported and a male head with wife [female head] in the following year	Either the family head or head's wife worked >500 hours [≥750 hours] in the last year of the spell and ≥750 hours [<500 hours] in the following year	Family income from unemployment insurance, workers compensation, and social security was \$0 [>\$0] in the last year of the spell and >\$0 [\$0] in the following year

children of ages 5 and 11 years, and the incidental benefit amount available to households living on one income at or below the social minimum level. The basic amounts, the incidental benefit amount, and the holiday allowance differ according to household composition and age of recipient. The family allowance differs according to number and age of children. Housing allowances and near-cash benefits are excluded from the calculations. The higher total net income for a one-parent family working half-time compared to the same family working full-time may be attributed to a lower tax liability and social-insurance contributions and a lower benefit reduction rate.

Sweden: Listed amounts are for a lone mother with two children in 1986. The "no work" figures assume receipt of social assistance at scales recommended by "Socialstyrelsen," the central authority for the municipalities that are responsible for the provision of social assistance. They include housing costs equal to the average rent for a three-bedroom apartment. For the "half-time work" column, the mother is assumed to earn 44,849 SEK, an amount equal to the average wage of a cleaning woman employed by a municipality. She is assumed to live in a municipality where the local tax rate is equal to the average rate (30.5 percent) and receives housing benefits, child allowances, and advance maintenance payment. Similar assumptions apply to full-time work. Figures on taxes and transfers are obtained from the BEST model (Schwarz and Nyman 1989).

United Kingdom: Listed amounts are for a lone mother with two children (ages 4 and 6) in 1989. The "no work" figures assume receipt of Income Support (IS), the Child Benefit (CB), and One Parent Benefit (OPB). For the half-time work column, the mother is assumed to earn £3 per hour, less £3 pounds per week for National Insurance (NI), with no income from saving, but income from IS, CB, and OPB. Recipients are allowed to keep £15 per week of earned income, but then benefits are withdrawn at a 100 percent rate. Similar assumptions apply for full-time work; in this case, however, NI takes £10.80 and income taxes £8.97 per week and there is a Family Credit of £16.40. As with half-time work, CB and OPB sum to £19.70 per week.

United States: Benefits include AFDC and food stamps paid to one- and two-parent families with no other income in the median state—Colorado. It is assumed that childcare expenses are at least as large as the maximum permitted to be deducted by Federal AFDC regulations at the time—$320 per month. If actual childcare expenses were less than $320 per month, then AFDC income and gross family income would be correspondingly less (but disposable income would be the same). If actual expenses were more than $320, AFDC benefits and gross income would remain the same but disposable income would be correspondingly less. With maximum childcare deductions, full-time, minimum-wage single parents still qualify for AFDC and Medicaid medical insurance. Benefit levels vary widely across states in the United States. The equivalence scale implicit in U.S. benefits attaches lower relative weights to additional children than does the equivalence scale used to adjust the income amounts listed in Table 2.8.

This paper is the result of a collaborative research project sponsored by the Rockefeller Foundation, the Russell Sage Foundation, and the European Science Foundation as part of its Network on Household Panel Studies. CEPS/INSTEAD provided substantial in-kind support. The authors were assisted by Jos Berghman, Petra Buhr, Tim Callan, Bengt-Olof Gert, Pierre Hausman, Bruno Jeandidier, Kjell Jansson, Deborah Laren, Udo Neumann, Willard Rodgers, Daniel Stripinis, Hedwig Vermeulen, and Brendan Whelan. Hauser and Neumann are at Frankfurt University; Ray and Jeandidier are at the University of Nancy; Berghman, Muffels, and Vermeulen are at Tilburg University; Hausman and Schmaus are at the CEPS/INSTEAD in Luxembourg; Messinger and Stripinis are at the Economic Council of Canada; Jenkins is at the University of Bath; Gustafsson is at Gothenburg University; Jansson and Gert are at Statistics Sweden; Callan, Nolan, and Whelan are at the Economic and Social Research Institute in Dublin; and Duncan, Laren, and Rodgers are at the University of Michigan. Voges and Buhr gratefully acknowledge support from the University of Bremen. Tim Smeeding and Katherine McFate provided helpful advice in the early stages of the project, as did Dorothy Duncan, Peter Gottschalk, Heather Joshi, Alfred Kahn, Sheila Kamerman, Anders Klevmarken, Jeffrey Lehman, Gaston Schaber, and participants at a seminar at the Economic Council of Canada at later stages.

ENDNOTES

1. The 50 percent line was defined using the distribution of size-adjusted family income for the entire population of each country each year. Since median-income-based poverty lines are relative to each country's own median, the resulting poverty estimates reflect the degree of inequality of the distribution of size-adjusted family income. Since our medians are based on estimates of the size-adjusted family income of *all* individuals in the population (not just individuals living in families), median-income-based poverty thresholds also reflect the comparative status of family and nonfamily households in the population.

2. The 20 percent figure is admittedly arbitrary. It was chosen because it was larger than the likely extent of most measurement error and because experimentation with alternatives proved it to produce representative results. Note that families starting far below the 50 percent of the median line could have large income increases without crossing the 60 percent of the median threshold. Use of thresholds like 50 percent or 60 percent of median presume such families do not experience "sufficient" mobility.

3. Where possible, data for the Federal Republic of Germany are presented separately for native Germans and for foreign residents (the majority of whom are Turks), while data for the United States are presented separately for blacks and whites. (Both sets of minorities were oversampled in their respective surveys, although weights have been used to calculate unbiased combined national estimates.) We suspect that the nature of poverty experiences of ethnic minorities in most of the other countries of our study deserves separate study, but only in the F.R.G. and the U.S. were there sufficient numbers of observations for separate estimates.

4. Poverty thresholds cutting higher into the income distribution may produce substantial numbers of families crossing the threshold, but the proportion of all poor crossing the threshold will be lower.

5. When the bottom decile is defined on the basis of the incomes of blacks and whites taken together, escape rates for blacks in the United States are relatively low. This is due mainly to the large distance between the typical low-income black family and a poverty line drawn from blacks and whites taken together. When the bottom decile is defined by the black population alone, the escape rate (41.9 percent) is much higher.

6. Note that these three-year estimates are *not* of long-run poverty, since a family poor in, say, the first of the 3 years could have just ended a very long spell of poverty. Rather, the estimates should be taken for what they are—poverty estimates for each country over a 3-year period in the mid-1980s.

7. We were not able to construct comparable measures of another kind of family event—birth to a never-married mother. Duncan and Rodgers (1988) show that 28 percent of all child-years of poverty in the United States could be linked births into an already poor family. They also find that children born to never-married mothers have substantially higher-than-average amounts of poverty during childhood.

8. Data limitations forced us to calculate entry events only for the Quebec province of Canada. Sample sizes for poverty entries are quite small in Luxembourg, owing to the infrequent occurrence of poverty in that country.

9. We considered using the German SOEP for the social-assistance analysis but discovered that very strong assumptions were necessary to be able to link events to the beginnings and endings of spells. Patterns of receipt in the SOEP are quite similar to patterns in the Bremen Social Assistance Sample (Voges and Rohwer 1992).

10. Recall that the U.K. data come from retrospective reports from a survey of lone parents, which will almost certainly impart an upward bias to the estimated duration of social-assistance spells. In an attempt to ascertain how serious this bias might be, we imposed a similar requirement on U.S. data; namely, that lone-parent recipients had to remain lone parents as of the most recent interview date in the PSID. The estimated fraction of recipients still receiving benefits after four years rose modestly, from 35 percent to 42 percent, which suggests that the bias in the U.K. data does not account for the bulk of the cross-country differences.

11. In contrast to the poverty-transition event analysis, we were unable to construct a measure showing instances in which already-employed family members enjoyed a substantial increase in work hours.

12. In contrast to their treatment in data from other countries, divorces/separations in the German data may have preceded the onset of a spell of social assistance by several years.

13. As noted at the bottom of the table, the U.S. data record the age of the household head, who may well be a grandparent of the young child.

14. Unemployment rates in Bremen were nearly twice as high as the national average during the 1980s, in part because of massive layoffs in Bremen's shipbuilding industry in 1983. These layoffs created dismal employment conditions throughout the period during which social-assistance episodes took place.

15. More complete evidence is presented in Table 2A.1; an explanation of assumptions underlying the benefit calculations is given at the end of Appendix 2A.

16. French benefit levels vary enormously by family structure and whether a divorce or separation has occurred recently. The strong pro-natalist position adopted by the national government is reflected in the relatively generous benefits available to women with young children. Benefits available to women with children older than three (and with no recent divorce) are actually lower than available in the median U.S. state.

17. Since its benefit levels vary widely across states, the United States also provides a way of assessing in a crude way whether social assistance spells are longer in states with higher benefits. Dividing the PSID sample into three parts according to the generosity of benefits in the state of residence and calculating the fraction of spells lasting two or more years produces evidence that does not support the hypothesis. Survival rates after two years were 52 percent for families in the lowest benefit states, 46 percent for families in middle-benefit states, and 40 percent for families in high-benefit states.

18. Canada-Quebec social-assistance figures reflect 1990 reforms that have improved work incentives. They have been deflated to 1986 price levels and then compared with 1986 median income figures.

19. The statements were: "The government should provide everyone with a guaranteed basic income" and "The government should provide more chances for children from poor families to go to university," with response categories "strongly agree," "agree," "neither agree nor disagree," "disagree," "strongly disagree," and "can't choose."

20. The imperfect correspondence between the subject of our inquiry—*income-conditioned* social-assistance programs—and the subject of the survey statements—*universal* programs that provide benefits to all individuals, regardless of income—reduces the utility of the results of the survey for our purposes.

21. Apart from possibly stigmatizing recipients, targeting can have other undesirable effects as well. In the United Kingdom, social-assistance recipients who entered through unemployment were paid lower benefits under the Supplementary Benefit program. Under the recent RESTART program, the unemployed (but not other categories of recipients) can lose eligibility if they fail to show satisfactory job-search activity.

22. Until the 1988 social security reforms, the United Kingdom Supplementary Benefit program increased benefits after one year of receipt, provided that the reason for receipt was not unemployment. (Elderly recipients were given the higher rate throughout their spell.)

23. For example, as with the U.S. AFDC social-assistance program, there is a popular perception in France that the API program encourages out-of-wedlock births. Systematic studies using U.S. data generally do not support this hypothesis for the AFDC program. Similar studies in France of the API program would be valuable.

24. Some European countries can and sometimes do reduce social assistance benefits (e.g., by about 25 percent in Germany) in the case of able-bodied recipients who refuse to work. But these reductions are linked to the behavior of the recipient, not the duration of the social-assistance spell.

25. An alternative unit of analysis would have been children themselves rather than families with children. Use of children as analysis units would give increased weight to larger families.

REFERENCES

Adams, Terry K., and Greg J. Duncan. 1992. "Long-term Poverty in Rural Areas." In Cynthia M. Duncan, ed. *Rural Poverty in America.* New York: Auburn House.

Burkhauser, Richard V., Greg J. Duncan, Richard Hauser, and Roland Berntsen. 1991. "Wife or Frau, Women Do Worse: A Comparison of Men and Women in the United States and Germany Following Marital Dissolution." *Demography* 28 (3): 353–361.

Duncan, Greg J., Richard D. Coe, Martha S. Hill, Saul D. Hoffman, and James N. Morgan. 1984. *Years of Poverty, Years of Plenty.* Ann Arbor, MI: Institute for Social Research.

Duncan, Greg J., and Willard Rodgers. 1987. "Longitudinal Aspect of Childhood Poverty." *Journal of Marriage and the Family* 50: 1007–1021.

Ellwood, David T. 1986. *Targeting "Would-be" Long-term Recipients of AFDC.* Washington, D.C.: Mathematica Policy Research.

———. 1988. *Poor Support: Poverty and the American Family.* New York: Basic Books.

Joshi, Heather, and Hugh Davies. 1991. "Childcare Institutions in Europe and Mothers' Foregone Earnings." Paper presented for ESPE91 Conference, Pisa, Italy, June.

Kamerman, Sheila B., and Alfred J. Kahn. 1988. *Mothers Alone: Strategies for a Time of Change.* Dover, MA: Auburn House Publishing Co.

McFate, Katherine, Timothy Smeeding, and Lee Rainwater. Chapter 1, this volume.

Murray, Charles. 1984. *Losing Ground.* New York: Basic Books.

Newman, Sandra, and Raymond Struyk. 1983. "Housing and Poverty." *Review of Economics and Statistics* 65 (2): 243–253.

Schwarz, B., and K. Nyman. 1989. *Skatter och transfereringar till hushallen.* BFR rapport R28.

Smeeding, Timothy, and Lee Rainwater. (forthcoming) "Cross-National Trends in Income Poverty and Dependency: The Evidence for Young Adults in the Eighties." Prepared for the Joint Center for Political and Economic Studies Conference "Poverty and Social Marginality." Washington, D.C., September 1991.

Smith, Tom W. 1990. "Social Inequality in Cross-National Perspective." In Duane Alwin et al. *Attitudes to Inequality and the Role of Government.* Rijswijk, The Netherlands: Sociaal en Cultureel Planbureau.

U.S. Bureau of the Census. 1989. Current Population Reports, Series P-70, No. 15-RD-1. *Transitions in Income and Poverty Status: 1984–85.* Washington, D.C.: U.S. Government Printing Office.

Voges, Wolfgang, and Götz Rohwer. 1992. "Receiving Social Assistance in Germany: Risk and Duration." *Journal of European Social Policy* 2 (3): 175–191.

Chapter 3

A COMPARISON OF POVERTY AND LIVING CONDITIONS IN THE UNITED STATES, CANADA, SWEDEN, AND GERMANY

Susan Mayer

B OTH AMERICANS and Europeans worry about poverty in part because the poor suffer from important material deprivations such as inadequate housing, medical care, and food consumption. Deprivations such as these not only reflect individuals' life chances, they may also affect those life chances. Even those who deny that money can buy happiness usually believe that money can buy homes, cars, food, and medical care, and that those who have these things are more likely to be full participants in society than those who go without them.

Since 1960, American social welfare policy has tried to eliminate absolute material deprivations such as hunger and dilapidated housing by targeting non-cash goods and services to the very poor population. Western European countries have been more likely to emphasize social inequality, placing less emphasis on economic deprivation per se. These different emphases have been reflected in the size and development of the welfare state. In 1980 government expenditures on social welfare programs (excluding education and pensions) were 29.4 percent of Gross Domestic Product (GDP) in West Germany, 29.4 percent of GDP in Canada, 43.6 percent of GDP in Sweden, but only 22.5 percent of GDP in the United States (O'Higgins 1988). Western European countries are also more likely to have universal rather than means-tested programs and to have more redistributive taxes and transfer programs (Aguilar 1987; Hicks and Swank 1984; McFate, Smeeding and Rainwater, this volume).

Comparisons of economic well-being across countries consistently show that poverty rates are higher in the United States than in most Western European countries. This research also shows that poor Americans are poorer than the poor in most Western European countries. For instance, Smeeding et al. (1988) show that poor families with children in the United States need on average 40 percent more income than they currently have to reach the official U.S. poverty threshold. Similar families need 33 percent more income in Canada, 35 percent more in Sweden, and 26 percent more in Western Germany to have the same buying power as the U.S. poverty threshold. The same study shows that poor elderly Americans need on average 30 percent more income to reach the official poverty threshold. But poor, elderly Canadians need only 22.6 percent more income, poor, elderly Germans need 26.7 percent, and poor, elderly Swedes need only 2.3 percent more income to reach the official United States poverty threshold. If families with more money live better than families with less money, the poor in Sweden, Canada, and Germany ought to live better than the poor in the United States.

Because this chapter focuses on the living conditions of the poor, it compares the living conditions of different proportions of the population in each country. For instance, it compares the living conditions of 19 percent of Americans to the living conditions of only 6.8 percent of Swedes. An alternative would be to compare the living conditions of the same proportion of the population, say the poorest 10 percent, in each country. Such a comparison yields the same basic conclusions as those found here (Mayer 1993). This chapter focuses on the poor using a common relative definition of poverty, because most people seem to believe that poverty implies a similar set of deprivations across countries.

However, evidence from previous research suggests that within countries income is not a very good proxy for the conditions in which people live. This means that poverty may not imply the same degree of material deprivation in all countries and, consequently, countries may not rank the same on measures of living conditions as they rank on poverty rates or other income-based measures of economic well-being. These rankings are important because nations assess their successes and failures in social welfare policy in light of such rankings.

In this chapter, I compare the conditions in which the poor live in the United States, Sweden, Western Germany (prior to reunification), and Canada. I consider four different types of living conditions: (1) housing amenities, (2) consumer durables, (3) health status and use of medical service, and (4) expenditures on necessities. I also compare the living conditions of poor American blacks with the living conditions of other poor Americans as well as poor Swedes, Canadians, and Western Germans.

The results strongly suggest that we ought to reconsider many previous conclusions about poverty that are based solely on income comparisons.

POVERTY AND LIVING CONDITIONS

Empirical evidence in the United States shows a weak link between income measures of living conditions such as housing amenities, food consumption, access to medical care, and consumer durables (Mayer and Jencks 1989 and 1993). Social scientists in other countries also find a surprisingly weak relationship between income and a variety of measures of living conditions (Townsend

1978; Ringen 1987; Glatzer 1986; Travers and Richardson 1989). Adjustments for family size only modestly improve the relationship. There are many reasons why we would expect the association between income and living conditions to be weak within countries as well as across countries.

In all social surveys many families seriously underreport their income. This is an especially serious problem at the top and bottom of the income distribution (see, e.g., Coder 1991). The degree of income underreporting is likely to vary across countries, but we do not know by how much.

Income measures usually cover only money income. They do not include noncash income such as housing subsidies, the value of owner-occupied housing, "free" health insurance, or home-grown food. This is an important omission. In the United States, noncash benefits account for about 70 percent of all federal government expenditures for means-tested programs. In the United States, including the value of noncash goods and services (using the recipient value approach) reduced the poverty rate from 13.6 percent to 11.6 percent in 1986 (U.S. Bureau of the Census 1987). Other countries also have extensive noncash transfers. For instance, Canada, Sweden, and Germany all have some form of national health insurance and Sweden subsidizes childcare for all families. All four countries have some form of subsidized housing construction and public housing. But governments are not the only source of noncash transfers. In all of these countries employers provide important noncash transfers, and interfamily transfers of services such as childcare and transportation can significantly reduce families' needs for income. Because it is difficult to determine the value of noncash goods and services, we do not know how their importance varies across countries. Thus, we cannot tell whether including their value in measures of income would increase or decrease the disparity in poverty rates across countries.

Income measures seldom take into account disparities in economic resources that derive from disparities in wealth and credit.[1] The distribution of wealth over income groups varies considerably across countries (Greenwood and Wolff 1988). The availability of credit and its distribution across income groups presumably varies across countries too, but we do not know by how much.

Income measures usually cover an accounting period of a year, which may be too long for assessing some aspects of living conditions and too short for others. Permanent income is probably more closely associated with homeownership and ownership of consumer durables such as cars and refrigerators than current income is. But, at least among the poor, short-term fluctuations in income may be more important than permanent income for recurring expenditures like food consumption.

Measured income is seldom fully adjusted for variation in families' need for income. Poverty measures usually try to adjust current income for family size, but the "correct" adjustment (the adjustment that would equalize the well-being of families of different sizes) is likely to vary across countries (Buhmann et al. 1987). Income-based poverty measures seldom take into account other differences in families' needs such as medical expenses, work-related expenses like transportation and childcare, local variations in the cost of living, or the efficiency with which families spend their money.

The limitations of income measures suggest that if we want to know about the living conditions of poor families, we should try to measure these conditions directly. If we want to understand either the causes or the consequences of differences in living conditions across countries or subgroups within countries, we need to check the validity of conclusions based on income against direct measures of living conditions.

COMPARISON OF LIVING CONDITIONS ACROSS COUNTRIES

The Data

U.S. data on housing amenities and some consumer durables are from the 1980 decennial census, data on health and use of medical and dental care are from the 1980 Health Interview Survey (HIS), and data on other consumer durables and household expenditures are from the 1984–85 Consumer Expenditure Survey (CEX). Swedish data are from the 1981 Level of Living Survey. This is the latest Level of Living Survey (LOL) for which data are available. Canadian data are from the 1982 Survey of Family Expenditures. German data are from the 1984 Socioeconomic Panel Survey. All surveys are weighted to be representative of the civilian noninstitutionalized population of the country in which they were collected. A description of each data set is in Appendix 3A.1.

The samples used in this chapter vary in two important ways from the samples used by Duncan et al. and McFate, Smeeding, and Rainwater in this volume. First, I weight individuals equally in all analyses. In these other chapters households are weighted equally. At least in the United States, poverty rates vary depending on whether we count families or individuals (Mayer and Jencks 1993).

Second, the estimates in this chapter are for individuals in families headed by someone who is between 18 and 76 years old. All of the other chapters in this volume include only the non-elderly population or some subset of the non-elderly population. For instance, McFate, Smeeding, and Rainwater use households with children whose head is aged 22 to 55 years old for their poverty estimates. Duncan et al. include all households with children regardless of the age of the head, but most families with children are headed by someone who is not elderly. Appendix 3B shows that including the elderly does not change the qualitative results discussed in this chapter.

Cross-national comparisons should, in theory, be made at comparable points in each country's business cycle. The poverty rate increases during recessions, but much of this increase is attributable to people who are poor for only a short period of time. People who are poor for only a short time can draw on past accumulations of resources and borrow against future earnings to maintain their living standard. Thus, we expect a higher poverty rate during recessions, but we also expect a higher standard of living among the poor.

Germany, Sweden, Canada, and the United States all experienced the worldwide recession of the early 1980s. In 1980 all four countries were close to a peak in the business cycle. By 1983–1984, Canada, the United States, and West Germany were near a trough. In Canada unemployment increased from 7.4 percent in 1980 to 10.9 percent in 1982. In West Germany unemployment increased from 3.0 percent in 1980 to 7.1 percent in 1984. Unemployment in the United States increased from 7.0 percent in 1980 to 9.5 percent in 1982 and then decreased to 7.4 percent in 1984 (OECD 1990). If the recession increased short-term poverty more than long-term poverty, the living conditions of poor Canadians in 1982 and poor Western Germans in 1984 may have been somewhat better than the living conditions of the poor in these two countries in 1980. Therefore, comparisons between Canada in 1982 and West Germany in 1984 and the United States in 1980 may be somewhat biased, but the difference is not likely to be large.

Measuring Living Conditions

There are several important obstacles to comparing living conditions across countries. Most people agree that families should have adequate food, housing, medical care, and clothing. But there is little agreement on what is adequate, and in wealthy nations such as the United States and the countries of Western Europe these may not be the only items that are considered necessities. For instance, televisions and telephones have become increasingly important means of communication and may be seen as necessities in countries where they are common. Cars may be necessities in places where public transportation is not readily available.

None of the surveys that I use includes all of the living conditions that most people agree are important. For instance, none asks about food consumption. Nor do any of the surveys select randomly among possible living conditions. Each survey collects data on a different subset of living conditions, so that only a few of the measures available in any one country can be compared across all countries.

I compare living conditions from four important domains, namely housing, health status and use of medical services, consumer durables, and expenditures on necessities. Each living condition is defined in Appendix 3A.1. I had to use three different American surveys to cover these domains. This means that I cannot assess the degree to which families that experience one problem also experience another problem in the United States.[2]

Living conditions are likely to vary across countries because of country-to-country differences in wealth, available substitutes, culture, relative prices, and other factors. For instance, cars may be very important to individuals living in areas with no public transportation. Thus, all other things being equal, we expect average levels of car ownership to be higher in countries with large rural populations or weak public transportation systems than in urban countries or those with lots of public transportation. In addition, many people suggest that Americans have a particular culturally based affinity for cars that is not shared by citizens of other countries. If true, we would expect higher rates of car ownership in the United States than in countries less enamoured with the automobile. If the poor in some countries lack cars because they do not want them or do not need them, then comparing the proportion of the poor owning cars across countries could mislead us about the well-being of the poor. In this chapter I compare the proportion of the poor with each living condition across countries, but I also compare how the poor fare relative to the normative standards of their own country. To do this I subtract the proportion of a country's residence with a living condition from the proportion of the poor with that living condition.[3]

Poverty Measures

I use a relative poverty measure to assess differences in living conditions among the poor in these countries. In each data set I adjust household income (before taxes and after cash transfers) for family size by counting the first adult as 1, subsequent adults (anyone over 18 years old) as .8, and children as .5. I call this adjusted income.[4] I then classify individuals by the ratio of their households' adjusted income to the adjusted median income for the sample as a whole. I refer to individuals with less than half of the adjusted median income as poor. Below I discuss the implications of using this particular adjustment for family size.

The income data used in this chapter vary in two important ways from the income data used in the chapters by Duncan et al. and McFate, Smeeding, and Rainwater in this volume. First, since after-tax income data are not available in any of the United States data sets that I use except the CEX, I use before-tax income. Smeeding and Rainwater and Duncan et al. use after-tax income. Since there are few differences in the distribution of goods and services over before-tax and after-tax income groups in Canada, Sweden, or Germany, the conclusions in this chapter would probably be the same if I substituted after-tax for before-tax income.

I use income data from the 1980 decennial census to compute U.S. poverty rates. McFate, Smeeding, and Rainwater's U.S. data are from the Current Population Survey (CPS) and Duncan et al.'s U.S. income data are from the Panel Study of Income Dynamics (PSID). Income is more unequally distributed in the 1980 decennial census than in the 1980 CPS (Mayer and Jencks 1993). The PSID income distribution is more unequal than the census distribution, but more equal than the CPS distribution. Thus, estimates of the size of the poverty population depend on what data set one uses.

Table 3.1 shows that the proportion of Americans with incomes below half the median size-adjusted income is more than 50 percent greater than the proportion of Swedes, Germans, or Canadians with income below half the median size-adjusted income.[5]

Not only are there more poor Americans, but poor Americans are poorer than the poor in these other countries. Table 3.2 shows that the average size-adjusted

Table 3.1 / Distribution of Persons Across Income Groups, by Country

Country	Percentage of Individuals in Households with an Adjusted Income of:					
	Less than 50 Percent of National Median	50 to 75 Percent of National Median	75 to 125 Percent of National Median	125 to 175 Percent of National Median	175 to 225 Percent of National Median	Over 225 Percent of National Median
United States, 1979	19.0	13.9	30.2	19.3	9.0	8.7
Canada, 1982	12.7	16.7	36.5	20.0	8.4	5.6
Germany, 1984	10.6	17.0	38.6	20.1	8.2	5.5
Sweden, 1981	6.8	17.9	47.8	20.3	4.8	2.3

SOURCE: Own calculations from data sets described in Appendix 3A.1.

NOTES: Household income is adjusted for size as described in the text. Rows may not sum to 100 percent due to rounding.

Table 3.2 / Average Household Income as a Proportion of the National Average Household Income

Country	Adjusted Income as a Percentage of Median Adjusted Income					
	Less than 50 Percent of National Median	50 to 75 Percent of National Median	75 to 125 Percent of National Median	125 to 175 Percent of National Median	175 to 225 Percent of National Median	Over 225 Percent of National Median
United States, 1979	.242	.528	.833	1.24	1.66	2.77
Canada, 1982	.314	.558	.867	1.27	1.71	2.57
Germany, 1984	.329	.554	.875	1.29	1.73	2.52
Sweden, 1981	.330	.566	.946	1.52	1.80	2.21

SOURCE: Own calculations from data sets described in Appendix 3A.1.

NOTE: Household income is adjusted for family size.

income of the poor in the U.S. is 24.2 percent of the average U.S. size-adjusted income. The average size-adjusted income of poor Swedes, Germans, and Canadians is at least 30 percent of the average size-adjusted income in their country. The difference between the United States and these other countries is large. The mean size-adjusted income of poor Americans is $3,066. If it were 32.9 percent of the size-adjusted mean it would be $4,167, or 36 percent greater than it is currently. Thus, we would expect the gap in living conditions between the poor and the middle class to be greater in the United States than in these other countries.

Housing Amenities

Housing policies, especially those aimed at the poor, vary greatly across countries. Housing policy can subsidize consumers or producers or both. Both Germany and Sweden have universal housing allowances intended to assure that families do not spend more than some fixed share of income on rent. Consequently, all poor households get a direct subsidy. In the United States, only about 20 percent of poor households get direct housing subsidies (in the form of either public housing or Section 8 subsidies). The United States also provides fewer government subsidies to producers. In the United States nearly all housing units are built by private investors. In 1985 about 90 percent of dwellings completed in Germany and only 42.4 percent of those completed in Sweden were built by such private builders (Heidenheimer et al. 1990). On the other hand, the United States offers greater tax incentives to homeowners than these other countries. Thus, we would expect differences across countries in the quality of housing for the poor.

Nearly everyone in rich industrial democracies believes that adequate housing includes a bathroom and a kitchen. Table 3.3 shows that the poor in the United States are more likely than poor West Germans or poor Swedes to have a complete bathroom, and poor Americans are more likely than poor Swedes to have a complete kitchen. The Canadian survey does not include information on kitchens or bathrooms.[6]

The importance of homeownership depends in part on tax policies covering interest and mortgage payments and on the social meaning of homeownership. Thus, we expect variations across countries in the proportion of people owning their own homes. Table 3.3 shows that West Germans are much more likely than Americans, Swedes, or Canadians to rent their home. Table 3.3 also shows that poor Americans are more likely to rent their homes than poor Swedes, Germans, or Canadians.

Since the normative standards for homeownership and other living conditions vary across countries, Table 3.3 also shows the difference between the proportion of the entire sample who are renters and the proportion of the poor who are renters. This difference is shown in parentheses in Table 3.3. Relative to the average person, poor Americans are more likely to rent their homes than the poor in these other countries.

Table 3.3 / Percentage of Individuals with Housing Conditions in the United States, Sweden, Germany, and Canada, by Income Groups

Housing Conditions	Adjusted Household Income as a Percentage of Median Adjusted Income						
	Less than 50 Percent of National Median	50 to 75 Percent of National Median	75 to 125 Percent of National Median	125 to 175 Percent of National Median	175 to 225 Percent of National Median	Over 225 Percent of National Median	Mean
Rents Home							
United States	55.1 (25.1)	38.8 (8.8)	26.3 (−3.7)	19.0 (−11.0)	14.7 (−15.3)	13.1 (−16.9)	30.0
Sweden	43.6 (7.6)	48.0 (11.8)	35.3 (−0.9)	30.3 (−5.9)	25.2 (−11.0)	16.5 (−19.7)	36.2
Germany	68.7 (15.6)	59.0 (5.9)	53.0 (−0.1)	49.1 (−4.0)	43.3 (−9.8)	35.3 (−17.8)	53.1
Canada	52.8 (23.9)	36.8 (7.9)	26.7 (−2.2)	20.6 (−8.3)	16.3 (−12.6)	14.5 (−14.4)	28.9
Crowded							
United States	20.6 (11.4)	13.3 (4.1)	7.9 (−1.3)	4.1 (−5.1)	2.0 (−7.2)	1.6 (−7.6)	9.2
Sweden	8.8 (6.2)	4.4 (1.8)	2.2 (−0.4)	0.5 (−2.1)	1.0 (−1.6)	0.0 (−2.6)	2.6
Germany	15.0 (−0.8)	20.0 (4.2)	18.9 (3.1)	11.5 (−4.3)	9.6 (−6.2)	6.7 (−9.1)	15.8
Canada	8.5 (4.2)	8.5 (4.2)	3.9 (−0.4)	1.6 (−2.7)	0.1 (−4.2)	0.3 (−4.0)	4.3
No Kitchen							
United States	4.6 (2.1)	2.1 (0.4)	1.1 (−0.6)	0.7 (−1.0)	0.6 (−1.1)	0.6 (−1.1)	1.7
Sweden	7.8 (6.1)	2.6 (0.9)	1.1 (−0.6)	0.5 (−1.2)	0.7 (−1.0)	0.7 (−1.0)	1.7
Germany	2.9 (1.7)	1.0 (−0.2)	0.6 (−0.6)	2.0 (0.8)	0.6 (−0.6)	0.5 (−0.7)	1.2
No Bathroom							
United States	6.9 (4.5)	3.0 (0.6)	1.5 (−0.9)	0.8 (−1.6)	0.6 (−1.8)	0.4 (−2.0)	2.4
Sweden	10.0 (7.7)	3.2 (0.9)	1.9 (−0.4)	0.7 (−1.6)	0.7 (−1.6)	0.0 (−2.3)	2.3
Germany	10.0' (5.4)	5.4 (0.8)	4.8 (0.2)	2.1 (−2.5)	2.1 (−2.5)	0.4 (−4.2)	4.6

SOURCE: Own calculations from data sets described in Appendix 3A.1.

NOTES: The first number in each cell represents the percentage of each income group living with a particular condition. The number in parentheses shows the difference between the mean for the income group and the national mean for the living condition (which appears on the right).

There is no consensus on what constitutes crowded living conditions. I follow the U.S. Census Bureau practice, defining a household as crowded when it has more than one person per room. Using this definition, Americans are more likely than Canadians or Swedes, but less likely than West Germans, to live in crowded housing. Compared to the average person in the United States, the U.S. poor are more likely than the poor in any of the other three countries to live in crowded housing.

Health and Access to Medical Care

Most people believe that good health is related to income. Wealthier countries have healthier citizens and, within countries, high-income individuals are usually healthier than poor citizens. Interpretations of physical conditions are influenced by cultural norms about illness and economic and noneconomic incentives to be sick. This means that comparing absolute levels of health across countries is likely to be misleading and that cross-national comparisons of health must be considered with caution. For instance, Table 3.4 shows that twice as many West Germans as U.S. citizens report a limitation of activity due to a health condition. The difference between U.S. respondents and Swedes reporting a limitation of activity due to a health condition is also large. Differences in the age composition of the population do not account for the differences in reported disability (see Appendix 3A.2). It is unlikely that these differences are due solely to variations across countries in individuals' physical conditions.

Sweden and West Germany have generous government disability transfers and more liberal requirements for demonstrating disability than the United States does. This is likely to contribute to a difference in reported illness and disability across countries. A third of Swedes who report a limitation of activity did not visit a doctor during the previous year. Only 2.4 percent of Americans with such a disability failed to visit a doctor in the same length of time. This suggests that Swedes reporting a limitation of activity may be healthier than Americans reporting such a condition.

Even though there appear to be important differences across countries in interpretation of illness, we can get some idea of how the health of the poor compares to the health of the average person in their country. Table 3.4 shows that, as expected, in all three countries the poor are more likely than the affluent to be sick. However, relative to the average individual in their country, poor Americans are about as likely as poor Swedes or poor West Germans to report a limitation of activity due to a health condition, and they are about as likely as poor West Germans to report a chronic health condition.

Canada, Germany, and Sweden have national health insurance programs, while the United States has a universal health insurance program only for those over 65 years old (Medicare). The only other major government health insurance program, Medicaid, is means-tested and reaches only about 40 percent of the poor. About 15 percent of Americans have no health insurance at all. Thus, we

Table 3.4 / Percentage of Individuals with Health Conditions and Doctor Visits in the United States, Sweden, and Germany, by Income Groups

Health Status and Doctor Visits	Adjusted Household Income as a Percentage of Median Adjusted Income						Mean
	Less than 50 Percent of National Median	50 to 75 Percent of National Median	75 to 125 Percent of National Median	125 to 175 Percent of National Median	175 to 225 Percent of National Median	Over 225 Percent of National Median	
Limitation of Activity Due to Health							
United States	32.7 (14.3)	22.4 (4.0)	15.4 (−3.0)	11.8 (−6.6)	11.5 (−6.9)	12.9 (−5.5)	18.4
Sweden	47.5 (14.1)	50.3 (16.9)	30.0 (−3.4)	23.8 (−9.6)	74.3 (40.9)	7.9 (−25.5)	33.4
Germany	51.4 (15.7)	45.5 (9.8)	33.8 (−1.9)	29.9 (−5.8)	26.3 (−9.4)	27.5 (−8.2)	35.7
Chronic Condition							
United States	34.0 (13.1)	24.2 (3.3)	18.0 (−2.9)	14.9 (−6.0)	14.9 (−6.0)	16.9 (−4.0)	20.9
Germany	46.0 (12.9)	41.9 (8.8)	30.7 (−2.4)	28.2 (−4.9)	26.0 (−7.1)	28.2 (−4.9)	33.1

No Doctor Visit in the Last Year							
United States	25.3 (−0.3)	26.7 (1.1)	26.0 (0.4)	26.9 (1.3)	23.7 (−1.9)	22.0 (−3.6)	25.6
Sweden	39.7 (1.8)	32.0 (−5.9)	37.6 (−0.3)	42.6 (4.7)	38.6 (0.7)	45.7 (7.8)	37.9
No Doctor or Dentist Visit in the Last 3 Months							
United States	51.0 (.5)	52.9 (2.4)	51.7 (1.2)	50.0 (−.5)	48.3 (−2.2)	46.1 (−4.4)	50.5
Germany	27.4 (−2.5)	26.6 (−3.3)	31.6 (1.7)	31.0 (1.1)	31.3 (1.4)	27.4 (−2.5)	29.9
Limitation of Activity and No Doctor Visit in the Last Year							
United States	4.9 (2.5)	3.1 (0.7)	1.7 (−0.7)	1.5 (−0.9)	1.3 (−1.1)	1.4 (1.0)	2.4
Sweden	35.6 (2.1)	28.7 (−4.8)	33.6 (0.1)	36.3 (0.1)	31.9 (−1.6)	40.7 (7.2)	33.5
No Dental Visit in the Last Year							
United States	51.8 (16.7)	46.3 (11.2)	34.9 (−0.2)	25.9 (−9.2)	22.0 (−13.1)	18.5 (−16.6)	35.1
Sweden	51.7 (16.2)	52.9 (17.4)	30.8 (−4.7)	26.1 (−9.4)	17.4 (−18.1)	12.0 (−23.5)	35.5

SOURCE: Own calculations from data sets described in Appendix 3A.1.

NOTE: The first number in each cell represents the percentage of each income group living with a particular condition. The number in parentheses shows the difference between the mean for the income group and the national mean for the living condition (which appears on the right).

would expect large differences between the United States and these other countries in access to medical care.

Table 3.4 shows that in both Sweden and the United States the poor are about as likely as the average individual to visit a doctor in a year. Both poor Americans and poor Swedes who report a limitation of activity are less likely than the average person in their country to visit a doctor in a year. Poor Americans are about as likely as the average American to have visited a doctor or dentist in the last 3 months, but poor Germans are slightly more likely than the average German to have visited a doctor or dentist in the last 3 months.[7] Unfortunately, we cannot tell from these data whether poor Germans visit doctors or dentists or both more often than poor Americans. Compared to the average person, poor Germans are a bit more likely than poor Americans to report a limitation of activity due to illness, so it would not be surprising if they were also more likely to visit the doctor. On the other hand, visiting the doctor increases one's awareness of health problems. So poor Germans may report more disabilities because they visit the doctor more often. Poor Americans are about as likely as poor Swedes to have visited a dentist in the last year whether we consider absolute levels or differences from the mean.

The Canadian Family Expenditure Survey does not include information about either health status or visits to the doctor. However, published data (Statistics Canada 1981) show that in 1979, 7 percent of Canadians in the lowest income quintile had visited the doctor in the previous two weeks. In 1980, 15 percent of Americans in the lowest income quintile had visited the doctor in the previous two weeks. Thus, poor Americans were twice as likely as poor Canadians to have visited the doctor in the past 2 weeks. In neither country was visiting the doctor correlated with income since 7.5 percent of all Canadians and 14.7 percent of all Americans had visited the doctor in the previous 2 weeks.[8]

Consumer Durables

Few believe that the government ought to provide poor citizens with consumer durables such as clothes washers and dryers, dishwashers, or cars. However, consumer durables may be proxies for unmeasured aspects of living conditions such as adequate clothing and structurally sound housing. Indeed, there is some evidence that durables may be at least as good a proxy as income for living conditions. For instance, in the United States owning a clothes washer has a higher correlation than income with owning a home, having a refrigerator, and having a stove. Owning a car has a higher correlation than income with living in crowded conditions, having a complete kitchen, and having a complete bathroom. In Sweden having a washing machine and having a dishwasher both correlate more highly than income with whether a household has central heat. Having a dishwasher is more highly correlated than income with having seen a doctor in the last year, and having a stereo is more highly correlated with income than almost all of the measures of housing amenities and use of physician services. Similarly, in both Canada and West Germany some durables are more correlated than income with housing conditions and visiting the doctor.

In addition, if households purchase goods and services in order of their importance, when the poor are as likely as the rich to have consumer durables, they will also be as likely to meet their basic needs for food and shelter. Thus, while dishwashers, clothes dryers, and other durables may be not socially defined as necessities, their distribution is probably a good indicator of the distribution of unmeasured necessities.

The importance of consumer durables varies depending on their social meaning, available alternatives, and other factors. However, since poor Americans are poorer than the poor in other countries, we expect that, relative to the average person in their country, poor Americans will have fewer consumer durables than the poor in other countries. Table 3.5 shows that relative to the national average, poor Americans are more likely to have a car than poor Swedes or poor Canadians, and they are about as likely as poor Canadians to have a clothes dryer and a clothes washer. But relative to the average person poor Americans are less likely than poor Canadians to have a dishwasher and they are less likely than poor Swedes to have a phone or dishwasher.[9]

No single survey includes measures of all of the housing amenities and durables in Tables 3.3, 3.4, and 3.5, but both the Canadian and United States expenditure surveys include information on five measures, namely, whether the household owns its own home and whether it has a car, a clothes washer, clothes dryer, and a dishwasher. I have no way of weighing these measures in terms of their importance to the well-being of respondents, but if I assign a weight of 1 to all measures and sum them, I find that Canadians average 3.5 of these advantages, while Americans average 3.4. However, poor Canadians average fewer of these advantages than poor Americans (2.32 versus 2.42).

Expenditures

Since wealthy families spend a smaller proportion of their economic resources on necessities and a larger proportion on luxuries than poor families, many economists have suggested that one way to assess economic well-being is to examine the proportion of a household's economic resources that it must spend on necessities such as food (Engel 1885). Furthermore, since families probably try to even out their expenditures when income fluctuates, expenditures may be a better proxy than current income for permanent income.

Neither the German nor Swedish data include information on expenditures. However, Table 3.6 shows the percentage of total household expenditures that Canadians and Americans allocate to food, shelter, and medical care by income groups. The Canadian and U.S. surveys differ in ways that might make comparisons of the levels of expenditures in the two countries unreliable. But survey differences are unlikely to effect the distribution of expenditures within countries.[10]

Table 3.5 / Percentage of Individuals with Consumer Durables in the United States, Sweden, and Canada, by Income Groups

Consumer Durables	Adjusted Household Income as a Percentage of Median Adjusted Income						
	Less than 50 Percent of National Median	50 to 75 Percent of National Median	75 to 125 Percent of National Median	125 to 175 Percent of National Median	175 to 225 Percent of National Median	Over 225 Percent of National Median	Mean
No Motor Vehicle Available							
United States	25.1 (17.0)	8.0 (0.1)	3.5 (−4.4)	1.9 (−6.0)	1.4 (−6.5)	1.7 (−6.2)	7.9
Sweden	47.6 (25.7)	39.9 (18.0)	16.9 (−5.0)	2.6 (−9.3)	10.6 (−11.3)	17.4 (−4.6)	21.9
Canada	42.4 (30.2)	16.3 (4.2)	7.5 (−4.7)	4.2 (−8.1)	3.7 (−8.6)	4.9 (−7.3)	12.2
No Clothes Washer							
United States	40.0 (14.0)	31.0 (5.0)	23.2 (−2.8)	20.0 (−6.0)	16.2 (−9.8)	15.9 (−10.1)	26.0
Canada	27.4 (11.9)	16.9 (1.4)	13.7 (−1.8)	12.7 (−2.8)	12.4 (−3.1)	10.3 (−5.2)	15.5
No Clothes Dryer							
United States	58.5 (21.3)	45.8 (8.6)	34.8 (−2.4)	26.9 (−10.3)	20.1 (−17.1)	20.4 (−16.8)	37.2
Canada	47.5 (20.1)	33.0 (5.6)	25.4 (−2.0)	20.5 (−6.9)	18.3 (−9.1)	16.4 (−11.0)	27.4
No Dishwasher							
United States	76.6 (20.8)	69.8 (14.0)	61.7 (5.9)	45.3 (−10.5)	33.4 (22.4)	21.8 (−34.0)	55.8
Sweden	82.8 (17.6)	80.0 (14.8)	64.7 (−0.5)	55.6 (−9.6)	49.1 (−16.1)	30.2 (−35.0)	65.2
Canada	87.8 (17.1)	80.0 (−9.3)	69.5 (1.2)	62.2 (8.5)	59.9 (10.8)	58.7 (12.0)	70.7
No Phone							
United States	19.6 (12.8)	9.8 (3.0)	4.0 (−2.8)	1.6 (−5.2)	1.4 (−5.4)	.9 (−5.9)	6.8
Sweden	4.9 (3.3)	2.5 (0.9)	2.5 (0.9)	.6 (−1.0)	1.4 (−0.2)	.0 (−1.6)	1.6

SOURCE: Own calculations from data sets described in Appendix 3A.1.

NOTES: The first number in each cell represents the percentage of each income group living in a particular condition. The number in parentheses shows the difference between the mean for the income group and the national mean for the living condition (which appears on the right).

Table 3.6 / Percentage of Total Household Expenditure Allocated to Selected Expenditure Categories, by Income Groups in the United States and Canada

Expenditure Categories	Adjusted Household Income as a Percentage of Median Adjusted Income						
	Less than 50 Percent of National Median	50 to 75 Percent of National Median	75 to 125 Percent of National Median	125 to 175 Percent of National Median	175 to 225 Percent of National Median	Over 225 Percent of National Median	National Average
Food							
United States	25.3	22.3	20.4	18.5	17.2	16.6	20.7
Canada	27.1	21.7	17.3	14.5	12.4	10.6	17.9
Shelter							
United States	18.8	18.0	18.4	18.5	19.2	20.2	18.7
Canada	25.6	20.5	17.8	15.9	14.6	13.4	18.3
Shelter for Renters Only							
United States	23.3	23.9	22.9	23.5	22.9	23.1	23.0
Canada	28.3	21.8	18.0	15.9	14.5	13.6	20.6
Medical Care							
United States	5.3	6.7	5.6	4.8	4.7	4.5	5.3
Canada	2.1	2.5	2.1	1.9	1.7	1.6	2.1

SOURCE: Own calculations from data sets described in Appendix 3A.1.

Since poor Canadians have a greater share of income than poor Americans, we expect them to spend a smaller share of their resources on food, shelter, and medical care. We also expect the share of resources that the poor allocate to food, shelter, and medical care to be more like the national average in Canada than in the United States.

As expected, in both countries the poor allocate a greater than average share of total expenditures to food. But in Canada the share of expenditures that the poor allocate to food is over 9 percentage points greater than average, while in the United States the share of expenditures that the poor allocate to food is only 4.6 percentage points greater than average.

Poor Americans allocate about the same share of their total expenditures to shelter as other Americans. But poor Canadians allocate a greater share of their total expenditures than other Canadians to shelter. Shelter expenditures include the cost of mortgage interest and home maintenance and repair. These are at least in part investments for future consumption. If the poor spend a lot on rent while the rich spend a lot investing in their homes for future consumption, the numbers in Table 3.6 would be misleading—the poor would be spending while the rich were saving. Consequently, I also compare shelter expenditures among renters in the two countries. In both Canada and the United States, renters allocate a greater share of expenditures than owners to shelter expenses. But poor American renters allocate about the same share of expenditures to shelter as other Americans while poor Canadian renters allocate a greater share of their expenditures to shelter than the average Canadian renter.

It is not surprising that the out-of-pocket expenditures allocated to medical care are higher in the United States than in Canada, since Canadian medical expenses are more likely to be financed by taxes. But in both countries the poor allocate about the same share of expenditures as everyone else to medical care. Note that, in the United States, individuals whose household income is between 50 percent and 75 percent of the median income spend a greater proportion of their household expenditures on medical care than any other income group.

In Canada the average person allocates 38.3 percent of total expenditures to food, shelter, and medical care, while the average American allocates 44.7 percent of total expenditures to these things. But poor Americans allocate 49.4 percent of total expenditures to these necessities, while poor Canadians allocate 54.8 percent of their expenditures to the same necessities. Thus, the expenditures of the poor are more like the average in the United States than in Canada.

Since expenditures ought to be a better proxy than current income for permanent income, I compare the distribution of durables and expenditures over adjusted expenditure groups in Canada and the United States. I adjust expenditures using the same household size adjustment that I used for income. Table 3.7 shows that although Americans are much more likely than Canadians to have incomes below half the median (19 percent versus 12.7 percent), they are only slightly more likely than Canadians to have expenditures less than half the median expenditure (13.3 percent versus 10.9 percent).[11] If expenditures do reflect permanent income, this means that many fewer poor Americans than poor Canadians are poor for a long time and that permanent income may be distributed very similarly in Canada and the United States.

Table 3.7 shows that in both the United States and Canada, those with low expenditures (less than half the median expenditure) are less likely than those with low incomes to have dishwashers, clothes washers, and clothes dryers.[12] In both countries those with low expenditures also allocate a greater share of their expenditures to food than those with low income. This is what we would expect if expenditures are a better proxy than current income for permanent income. In both countries those with low incomes allocate about the same proportion of their expenditures as those with low expenditures to shelter and medical care.

Table 3.7 also shows that, relative to the national average, Americans with low expenditures are less likely than Canadians with low expenditures to have clothes washers, clothes dryers, and dishwashers. Although Americans and Canadians average about the same number of five living conditions, Americans with low expenditures average only 1.81 of these living conditions while Canadians with low expenditures average 2.31.

Conclusions about which country's poor allocate the greatest proportion of their expenditures to food depend on whether we look over expenditure or income categories. In both countries the share of expenditures allocated to shelter is about the same regardless of whether we look at those with low expenditures or those with low incomes. Americans with low expenditures allocate a smaller share of total expenditures to medical care than Americans with low incomes, but in either case they allocate more to medical care than poor Canadians.

If low expenditures are a proxy for long-term poverty, these results suggest that the rates of long-term poverty may be similar in the United States and Canada, but that the long-term poor in the United States may experience more material deprivation than the long-term poor in Canada.

Summary of the Comparison of Living Conditions

Poor Swedes are better off than poor Americans on four of ten living conditions measured in both countries. Swedes and Americans are about equal on two living conditions and poor Americans are better off than poor Swedes on the other four.[13] Of the six measures common to the United States and Canada, poor Canadians are better off than poor Americans on three and equal to poor Americans on one living condition. Of the six measures common to Germany and the United States, poor Germans are better off than poor Americans on two and equal to poor Americans on three living conditions. Assuming that these living conditions all have a weight of 1, these results suggest that although poor Americans are poorer than poor Swedes, Germans, or Canadians, they do not suffer from appreciably worse living conditions.

Different weighing schemes could, of course, yield different conclusions. Differences from the mean within countries tend to be smaller for "necessities"

Table 3.7 / **Percentage of Individuals with Various Living Conditions and Percentage of Expenditure Allocated to Food, Shelter, and Medical Care, by Expenditure Groups**

	Adjusted Expenditures as a Percentage of Median Adjusted Expenditures						
	Less than 50 Percent of National Median	50 to 75 Percent of National Median	75 to 125 Percent of National Median	125 to 175 Percent of National Median	175 to 225 Percent of National Median	Over 225 Percent of National Median	Mean
Percent Distribution							
United States	13.3	16.8	33.9	19.4	9.2	7.4	
Canada	10.9	16.9	39.5	21.0	7.4	4.3	
			Consumer Durables				
Dishwasher							
United States	8.5	22.6	43.6	63.1	72.6	76.9	44.3
Canada	8.4	21.1	30.5	38.4	39.1	40.8	29.2
Clothes Washer							
United States	51.2	68.0	76.5	81.4	82.8	83.1	73.7
Canada	73.2	83.1	86.1	87.7	85.8	86.2	84.5

Clothes Dryer							
United States	26.1	52.6	66.9	75.2	76.8	79.8	62.5
Canada	49.0	66.2	75.7	80.5	79.3	82.4	72.6
			Percentage of Total Expenditures				
Food							
United States	30.7	24.1	20.8	17.5	15.1	12.7	20.9
Canada	28.7	22.1	17.2	14.1	12.0	10.0	18.1
Shelter							
United States	18.7	18.5	18.9	19.0	18.5	19.4	18.8
Canada	26.1	20.4	17.8	15.8	14.9	13.7	18.4
Medical Care							
United States	4.9	6.4	5.8	4.6	4.3	4.2	5.3
Canada	2.1	2.6	2.1	1.8	1.7	1.6	2.1

SOURCE: Own calculations from data sets described in Appendix 3A.1.

such as kitchens, bathrooms, and visiting the doctor and larger for "luxuries" such as dishwashers and cars. But this is true in all countries. There appears to be no particular pattern to the living conditions on which poor Americans fare worse than the poor in other countries. This means that weighing schemes that assign a higher weight to one domain rather than another are likely to yield results similar to those obtained from assigning the same weight to all living conditions, namely that the living conditions of poor Americans are similar to the living conditions of the poor in other countries.

These results do, however, suggest that although the proportion of Americans who are "permanently" poor may be similar to the proportion of Canadians who are "permanently poor," permanently poor Americans suffer more material deprivations than permanently poor Canadians.

THE SPECIAL CASE OF AMERICAN BLACKS

American blacks are unique in both their current and historical circumstances. Neither Sweden, West Germany, nor Canada has a racial minority anywhere near as big as the black population in America. With the possible exception of reservation Indians in Canada (who are not included in the Canadian sample), no racial minority in any of these other countries has experienced the degree of residential segregation and labor market discrimination that American blacks have experienced.

Table 3.8 shows the distribution of American blacks and nonblacks by adjusted median income groups. Blacks are more than twice as likely as other Americans to be poor using this relative poverty measure. Although overall the average income of American blacks is only about 72 percent of the average income of other Americans, Table 3.8 shows that the average income of poor blacks is about the same as the average income of other poor Americans. Poor black families are bigger than poor white families. But even the size-adjusted income of poor blacks is only 12 percent less than the size-adjusted income of other poor Americans. Thus, among the poor we do not expect big differences in the living conditions of blacks and other Americans.

Table 3.8 shows the percentage of American blacks and nonblacks with each living condition by income groups. On all measures of housing amenities and durables poor American blacks are much worse off than other poor Americans. Poor American blacks are at least twice as likely as other poor Americans to live in crowded conditions, to lack a complete bathroom, and to lack a complete kitchen. Comparing Table 3.6 with Tables 3.3, 3.4, and 3.5 shows that relative to the average in their country, poor American blacks have worse living conditions than poor Swedes, Western Germans, and Canadians.

Poor American blacks are more likely than other poor Americans to have a chronic condition, even though they are only about as likely as other poor Americans to have a limitation of activity due to a health condition. Since they

Table 3.8 / Percentage of Individuals in United States with Various Living Conditions, by Race and Income Groups

	Adjusted Household Income as a Percentage of Median Adjusted Income					
	Less than 50 Percent of National Median	50 to 75 Percent of National Median	75 to 125 Percent of National Median	125 to 175 Percent of National Median	175 to 225 Percent of National Median	Over 225 Percent of National Median
Percent						
Black	39.6	17.0	25.4	11.5	3.8	2.7
Other	18.4	13.5	29.3	19.5	9.7	9.5
Mean Income ($)						
Black	5,767	13,482	21,156	30,409	37,713	59,557
Other	5,778	12,667	20,041	28,850	37,276	60,754
Adjusted Income ($)						
Black	2,784	6,595	10,409	15,561	20,958	32,226
Other	3,158	6,707	10,566	15,705	20,977	35,249
Housing Amenities						
Rents Home						
Black	65.2	52.4	38.4	30.1	28.7	24.5
Other	51.7	36.5	25.1	18.2	14.0	12.7
Crowded						
Black	31.3	24.9	18.1	13.6	6.3	9.1
Other	17.1	11.3	6.8	3.3	1.8	1.3
No Kitchen						
Black	7.7	4.5	3.1	1.2	0.7	4.4
Other	3.6	1.6	0.9	0.7	0.6	0.6
No Bathroom						
Black	10.4	6.2	3.7	1.9	2.4	2.3
Other	5.7	2.4	1.3	0.7	0.6	0.4

Table 3.8 / *(continued)*

	Adjusted Household Income as a Percentage of Median Adjusted Income					
	Less than 50 Percent of National Median	50 to 75 Percent of National Median	75 to 125 Percent of National Median	125 to 175 Percent of National Median	175 to 225 Percent of National Median	Over 225 Percent of National Median
			Durables			
Access to a Car						
Black	52.8	78.7	88.8	93.3	90.7	95.1
Other	81.1	93.0	97.3	98.5	99.0	98.5
Has Phone						
Black	75.2	83.6	92.4	96.0	96.2	97.8
Other	82.1	91.3	96.4	98.5	98.8	99.2
Has Dishwasher						
Black	5.6	14.3	12.6	38.1	*	—
Other	28.2	33.0	41.0	56.1	68.2	79.0
Has Clothes Washer						
Black	49.1	45.3	56.0	75.0	—	—
Other	63.0	72.2	79.0	80.4	84.1	84.5
Has Clothes Dryer						
Black	21.4	29.8	39.1	66.0	—	—
Other	46.8	58.5	67.9	73.8	80.6	80.0

Health Status and Use of Physician Services

Limitation of Activity Due to Health						
Black	33.3	19.4	11.8	10.4	7.3	4.2
Other	32.5	22.8	15.7	11.9	11.7	13.2
Chronic Condition						
Black	36.0	21.6	15.8	15.1	13.8	8.8
Other	33.5	24.5	18.1	14.8	14.9	17.1
No Doctor Visit in the Last Year						
Black	23.9	25.0	23.1	23.5	17.9	16.5
Other	25.6	26.9	26.3	27.0	24.0	22.2
Limitation of Activity and No Doctor Visit in the Last Year						
Black	4.3	2.4	1.4	1.7	0.6	0.0
Other	5.0	3.2	1.8	1.5	1.4	1.4
No Dental Visit in the Last Year						
Black	53.9	53.2	44.0	33.9	29.3	20.6
Other	51.3	45.4	34.0	25.4	21.5	18.4

SOURCE: Own calculations from data sets described in Appendix 3A.1.

*Fewer than 100 cases.

report more chronic conditions, it is not surprising that poor American blacks visit the doctor a bit more than other poor Americans. But even controlling limitation of activity due to a health condition, poor American blacks visit the doctor more than other poor Americans. Poor American blacks are slightly less likely than other poor Americans to have visited a dentist in the last year.

Relative to the national average, poor American blacks are about as likely as poor Swedes and poor Germans to have a limitation of activity due to health conditions, and they are about as likely as poor Swedes to have visited a doctor in the last year. They are slightly less likely than poor Swedes to have visited a dentist in the last year. Thus, relative to the mean, poor American blacks do not appear to be in greatly worse health or to visit the doctor or dentist much less than poor Swedes or Germans.

Although not shown in Table 3.8, 36.9 percent of blacks live in households with adjusted expenditures that are less than half of the median adjusted expenditure. Thus, while other Americans are much less likely to have low expenditures than to have low incomes, American blacks are nearly as likely to have low expenditures as they are to have low incomes. This is consistent with previous research and research in this volume (Duncan et al.) showing that poverty spells are longer for American blacks than for other Americans. Length of poverty spells presumably accounts for much of the difference in living conditions between poor American blacks and nonblacks and between poor American blacks and poor Swedes, Canadians, and Germans. However, among those with low expenditures, American blacks are much less likely than other Americans or Canadians to have a car, a dishwasher, a clothes washer, and a clothes dryer. Nonetheless, total expenditures and the proportion of expenditures allocated to food, housing, and medical care are very similar for blacks and others with low expenditures.

THE ROLE OF HOUSEHOLD SIZE

To get the poverty rates reported in this chapter, I adjust household income for family size. Most people believe that large families need more money than small families to have the same living conditions, but there is no agreement about the appropriate adjustment for family size. In this section, I test the sensitivity of the results in this chapter to the choice of adjustment for family size. Table 3.9 shows the correlation between various measures of living conditions and three measures of income for each country. The income measures are income unadjusted for household size, income adjusted by household size as described above, and per capital household income.

Table 3.9 shows that in general the greater the adjustment for household size the weaker the relationship between income and a living condition. This means that within countries the distribution of living conditions is more equal over per capita income groups than over unadjusted income groups. For housing conditions and consumer durables, but not health and doctor visits, the difference between the correlation with unadjusted income and the correlation with income per capita is smaller in the United States than in other countries. Thus, had I compared the distribution of living conditions over unadjusted income groups, poor Americans would have appeared to fare even better compared to the poor in other countries. But, had I compared the distribution of living conditions over per capita income groups, poor Americans would not have fared so favorably with the poor in these countries on measures of housing and consumer durables.[14] The household size adjustment that I use in this chapter is between 1 and 0, so it yields an intermediate estimate of how poor Americans fare relative to the poor in Canada, Germany, and Sweden.

The fact that housing conditions and consumer durables have a stronger correlation with per capita income in the United States than in other countries is partly explained by the higher correlation between income and family size in Sweden, Germany, and Canada than in the United States. For instance, the correlation between income and family size is .18 in the United States but .49 in Sweden. The correlation between income and family size is presumably at least partly affected by social welfare policies. Canada, Sweden, and Germany all have universal child (or family) allowances that increase with each additional child. (In Germany the rate of increase of the allowance increases with additional children.) Both Sweden and West Germany also have a cash housing allowance based on family size. Together these increase income as family size increases. Ignoring tax policies, only families receiving Aid to Families with Dependent Children (AFDC) in the United States receive an increase in income when they have an additional child, but the size of the increase decreases with additional children.

Regardless of the income measure, these correlations are consistent with previous research which finds a weak relationship between income and measures of living conditions. For instance, per capita income explains less than 20 percent of the variance in having a car in the United States and Canada and much less in Sweden. The correlation between income and a measure of living conditions is biased downward when the living condition is measured by a dichotomous variable. However, in most cases the correlations in Table 3.9 are so weak that even if they were doubled we would still conclude that the relationship was at best moderate.

Because these living conditions do not accurately distinguish the rich from the poor, one might conclude that they are inappropriate for comparing living conditions across countries. However, these are the living conditions about which most governments as well as most ordinary citizens have worried.

These correlations also show that the relationship between income and "necessities" such as bathrooms, kitchens, and visiting the doctor is much weaker than the relationship between income and things like cars and dishwashers that are more likely to be considered luxuries. This is what we would expect if people purchase goods and services in order of their importance.

Table 3.9 / Correlations Between Living Conditions and Various Income Measures

Living Conditions	Before-Tax Income	Adjusted Income	Before-Tax Income per Capita
Owns Home			
United States	.289	.238	.149
Germany	.229	.156	.033
Sweden	.246	.133	−.031
Canada	.307	.208	.064
Complete Bathroom			
United States	.097	.099	.083
Germany	.116	.121	.068
Sweden	.138	.100	.030
Complete Kitchen			
United States	.074	.074	.061
Germany	.060	.029	.009
Sweden	.103	.081	.034
Car Available			
United States	.229	.206	.150
Sweden	.311	.196	.009
Canada	.290	.240	.136
Telephone			
United States	.188	.183	.152
Sweden	.097	.063	−.002
Clothes Washer			
United States	.219	.150	.051
Sweden	.118	.069	−.007
Canada	.216	.097	−.056
Dishwasher			
United States	.354	.335	.266
Sweden	.379	.215	.008
Canada	.232	.177	.082
5 Living Conditions			
United States	.400	.260	.210
Canada	.390	.210	.074
Limitation of Activity			
United States	−.195	−.153	−.090
Germany	−.179	−.177	−.095
Sweden	−.214	−.144	−.038

Table 3.9 / (*continued*)

Living Conditions	Before-Tax Income	Adjusted Income	Before-Tax Income per Capita
No Doctor Visit in Last Year			
United States	− .043	− .011	− .016
Sweden	.055	.034	− .012
Limitation of Activity and Doctor Visit in Last Year			
United States	− .082	− .068	− .045
Sweden	.044	.004	− .033

SOURCE: Own calculations from data sets described in Appendix 3A.1.

CONCLUSIONS

Everyone agrees that material well-being is only a part of the problem we refer to when we talk about poverty and social inequality. Most people are concerned not only that their material needs are met but that their social and psychological needs are met as well. In fact, our concern with money derives in large part from the notion that it can help us achieve these other goals.

There are more poor people in the United States than in Sweden, Germany, or Canada. The social safety net for the poor is weaker in the United States, and poor Americans are poorer than the poor in these other countries. Consequently, most social scientists have assumed that material living conditions among poor Americans are worse than the living conditions among the poor in these other countries. But the results in this chapter do not suggest that poor Americans are more likely than poor Swedes, Germans, or Canadians to live with material deprivation.[15]

The results in this chapter suggest that living conditions are only weakly related to income in all four countries. If even the consumer durables that most people consider luxuries are not strongly correlated with income, it may be time to turn our attention from how much the poor have to how they get what they have.

Although this paper suggests that the United States does somewhat better by its poorest citizens than one might think based on income data alone, it also reveals two serious problems. First, it confirms and broadens conclusions drawn from income measures about the economic insecurity of American blacks. With the important exception of health status and visiting the doctor, the living conditions of poor American blacks are much worse than the living conditions of other poor Americans. The poorest 40 percent of American blacks live in conditions worse than the poorest 7 percent of Swedes, the poorest 10.6 percent of

Western Germans, the poorest 12.3 percent of Canadians, and the poorest 18 percent of nonblack Americans. This is in part because poor American blacks are poor longer than other poor Americans and perhaps longer than the poor in other countries.

Second, a comparison of expenditure data in Canada and the United States suggests that although Americans are not much more likely than Canadians to be "permanently" poor, Americans who are poor for a long time probably live with more material deprivations than Canadians who are poor for a long time.

The United States spends less on social welfare programs than most other industrial democracies. Social scientists have assumed that this stinginess contributes to social inequality in the United States. However, while state expenditures may be greater in other countries, the state is only one possible agent of redistribution. Friends, families, employers, and philanthropic organizations redistribute goods and services as well as income. These "informal" sources of welfare may be more likely to redistribute goods and services than cash, and the cash that they do redistribute may be more likely to be unreported than cash from government transfers or work. Informal sources of welfare may be more important in countries where the state plays a smaller role in redistribution. For instance, charitable giving appears to be greater in the United States than in most Western European countries, and employer-provided pensions play a greater role in the well-being of the elderly in the United States than in other countries. It is likely that formal and informal redistribution systems complement one another in creating more uniform distributions of living conditions in democratic welfare states than formal systems alone provide.

The way families get income may have as much social importance as the amount they receive. Since American welfare mothers are often too poorly trained to make ends meet by working, and welfare payments even in generous states are too meager to make ends meet, they are forced to get income from irregular, often dangerous sources. Edin and Jencks (1992) found that welfare mothers in Illinois got less than 60 percent of their income from AFDC and food stamps. The remainder (which is mostly unreported to the welfare office and is presumably unreported to census interviewers) came from a variety of sources including boyfriends, absent fathers, parents, and other relatives. Other income came from work, including prostitution and selling drugs. Some mothers held regular jobs under assumed names. Because most of the income from these sources is irregular, these families lived with constant insecurity about their well-being. The dangerousness of some of the income sources surely adds to this insecurity. Furthermore, since welfare mothers who "cheat" (even to feed their children) undermine the political acceptability of AFDC, the political will to improve welfare benefits is diminished.

Some social scientists have suggested using material deprivations to determine poverty status (e.g., Townsend 1979). However, since even wealthy individuals can decide to live in homes which lack bathrooms and kitchens and can choose to forgo material possessions, measures of material deprivations alone may confuse poverty with eccentric tastes. Income measures are intended to overcome the problem of variations in tastes since income supposedly represents command over resources. However, the results of this chapter suggest that measured income may not represent the same command over resources in all countries. Command over resources depends on many factors other than current income, and the apparent differences across countries in command over resources are only partly explained by variations in permanent income and variations in family size. Regardless of the explanation, it is clear that simple comparisons of income-based measures of poverty may tell us little about differences in the way families live across countries or across groups within countries. Simple comparisons of the number of people with material deprivations may also be misleading.

Since income alone and living conditions alone may be misleading, other social scientists have suggested that a combination of both low income and material deprivation would be a better indicator of true poverty status than either measure alone. This strategy avoids none of the problems associated with the measurement of current income discussed at the beginning of this chapter, and it ignores variations across countries in the normative importance of living conditions.

Explanations for the better-than-expected living conditions of the poor in the United States fall into one of two categories. The first emphasizes mismeasurement of economic resources. It suggests that correcting measured income to take into account noncash income, wealth, the availability of credit, and permanent income would strengthen the relationship between income and measured living conditions. The results in this chapter suggest that poor Americans may be less likely than the poor in these other countries to be poor for a long time, and that this may account for the better-than-expected living conditions of poor Americans.

The second type of explanation emphasizes the importance of factors other than income, such as age, family living arrangements, household efficiency, and differences in taste. Appendix 3B suggests that age is unlikely to account for why poor Americans appear to live about as well as the poor in these other countries. But variations across families in both the size of families and the effect of family size on living conditions may partly explain these results.

Living conditions among the poor in the United States may appear to be better than they actually are if there is greater variability in the quality of goods and services in the United States than in West Germany or Sweden. This hypothesis implies that if we compared comparable goods and services, we would find more inequality in the United States relative to these other countries. These data do not allow me to test this hypothesis.

As I noted above, there are serious limitations to the data available for comparing the distribution of living conditions across countries. Although these limitations probably are no greater than the limitations to comparing incomes across countries, the reader should consider the results in this chapter cautiously. Nonetheless, although current income is probably the single most important factor in assessing economic inequality, the cross-national comparisons in this chapter cast doubt on the notion that economic inequality can be measured by income alone. They also suggest that focusing on income alone leads us to exaggerate the difference in economic inequality more broadly conceived between the United States and other countries.

APPENDIX 3A.1

Data Sets Used in the Analysis

All data sets used in this paper are representative of the noninstitutionalized population of the respective countries. In all cases, data have been weighted using sampling weights provided on the data sets adjusted so that the unit of observation is the individual. The sample in all cases is individuals living in a household headed by someone 18–76 years old. Data on health and doctor visits in the United States, Sweden, and Germany are for individuals 17–76 years old regardless of the age of the household head.

United States: The United States data are from several data sets. Data on housing, housing amenities, access to cars, and whether an individual has a phone come from the 1980 decennial Census of Population and Housing 1 in 1,000 sample. These analyses are restricted to individuals living in households, so they exclude members of the armed forces living on bases, college students living in dormitories, individuals living in lodging homes, patients in nursing homes, and inmates of institutions. There are 220,918 cases in the 1980 decennial census.

Data on health status and use of physician services are from the 1980 Health Interview Survey (HIS). There are 57,198 cases in the HIS.

Data on consumer durables and expenditures are from the 1984–85 Consumer Expenditure Survey (CEX). CEX data are for consumer units that are complete income reporters. A consumer unit consists of all members of a household that share certain major household expenses. For convenience in the text I refer to consumer units as households. Complete income reporters are consumer units that report income from at least one major source of income, such as wages, social security, self-employment, or social assistance. Complete income reporters may not have provided a full accounting of all sources of income.

CEX respondents are interviewed five times. Information from the first survey is not available in public use data tapes. The recall period for expenditures is 3 months. Total expenditures are then aggregated over four quarters. Respondents are asked income questions in the second and fifth interview. In each they are asked to recall their income over the previous 12 months. Consequently, neither income nor expenditures correspond to a calendar year, but for most respondents expenditures and income are for the same time period. This sample includes all consumer units that potentially had all four quarters of data between the beginning of calendar years 1984 and the first quarter of 1986. For a more complete description of the CEX data and how it differs from both the Census and the CPS, see Mayer and Jencks (1993). There are 8,760 consumer units in the CEX.

CEX and HIS data are weighted to adjust for probability of being sampled.

Canada: Canadian data are from the 1982 Survey of Family Expenditures (SFE). The survey is conducted in urban and rural areas of the 10 provinces as well as Whitehorse and Yellowknife. People living on Indian reservations were excluded.

The consumer unit concept is the same in the United States and Canada. In the Canadian data set, missing income data are imputed using a hot deck procedure. Note that in the United States CEX missing income values are set to zero which may result in lower income estimates. There are 10,631 cases in the 1982 SFE. The data are collected in one survey during which respondents are asked to recall both income and expenditures for calendar year 1982. Note that the recall period for expenditures in the United States CEX is only 3 months, which may result in differences in both the level and distribution of reported expenditures.

West Germany: German data are from the 1984–85 wave of the German Socioeconomic Panel. It contains 15,013 cases. Guestworkers and other foreigners are included in the sample. A full description of these data is in Universitaten Frankfurt (1988).

Sweden: Swedish data are from the 1981 Level of Living Survey. Income data are from Swedish tax records. People aged 16 and over have their own tax record, so even if they live with their parents they appear as having their own household. To the extent that such people live with and share resources with other family members, this inflates the actual number of low income families. The analyses shown in this paper omit heads of households less than 19 years old which diminishes, but does not eliminate this problem.

I do not use the sample weights provided on the LOL survey. The LOL is a survey of Swedish adults. LOL survey weights adjust for the probability that some adults are more likely to be sampled than others, but it does not adjust for the fact that some households are more likely to be sampled than others because they have more adults. The weights used in this paper make this adjustment.

I omit cases with missing data leaving a sample of 4,742 cases. A description in English of the sampling and data collection procedures is in Erikson and Aberg (1987). A more complete explanation in Swedish is in Institutet for Social Forskning (1984).

Explanation of the Variables and Their Source

Gross Income: Cash income before taxes from all sources for all household members. Income includes all cash government transfers in all countries. In the United States income includes the face value of food stamps.

Household Size: The number of people living in the household at the time of the interview.

Home Ownership: Equal to 1 if the respondent lives in an owner occupied housing unit.

More than 1 Room per Person: Equal to 1 if the number of rooms in the housing unit, not counting bathrooms, divided by the number of household members is greater than 1.

Complete Bathroom: Equal to 1 if the housing unit has a shower or tub, a toilet and piped water, 0 otherwise. In the United States data the housing unit must have both hot and cold piped water to be coded as having a complete bathroom. There is no requirement that the unit have hot water for it to be coded as having a complete bathroom in West Germany or Sweden.

Complete Kitchen: Equal to 1 if the housing unit has a stove, refrigerator, and sink with piped water, 0 otherwise. In the United States data the housing unit must have both hot and cold piped water to be coded as having a complete kitchen. There is no requirement that the unit have hot water for it to be coded as having a complete kitchen in West Germany or Sweden.

Car Available: Equal to 1 if the members of the household have a car or truck available for private use, 0 otherwise.

No Doctor Visit in the Last Year: Equal to 1 if the individual has seen the doctor in the previous 12 months, 0 otherwise. Data are for those over 17 years old in all countries.

No Doctor or Dentist Visit in the Last 3 Months: Equal to 1 if the individual has seen either a doctor or a dentist in the previous 3 months. In Germany respondents were asked whether they had seen a doctor or dentist in the last 3 months. In the United States respondents were asked how long it had been since they had seen a doctor and responses were coded as less than 2 weeks, 2 weeks to 6 months, 6 months to a year, 1 to 2 years, and more than 2 years. Respondents were also asked how long it had been since they had seen a dentist, and their responses were coded in the same way. To estimate the proportion of respondents who had seen a doctor or dentist in the last 3 months, I averaged the proportion who had seen either a doctor or dentist in the last 2 weeks and the proportion who had seen a doctor or dentist in the last 6 months.

Limitation of Activity and No Doctor Visit in the Last Year: In the United States this is equal to 1 if the individual has a limitation of activity due to a chronic condition and has not seen the doctor in the last year. In Sweden this is equal to 1 if an individual has a health condition that limits the type or amount of work that he or she can do and has not visited a doctor in the last year.

Chronic Health Condition: Equal to 1 if the respondent reports having a chronic health condition.

Food Expenditure: Includes both food at home and meals eaten away from home.

Shelter Expenditure: Includes expenditures for owned home including mortgage interest, property taxes, maintenance, repairs and replacement (expenditure which maintains or restores the condition of the property but does not increase its value), condominium charges, homeowners insurance premiums, and utilities. For rented living quarters, it includes rent paid by consumer unit, tenants' maintenance, repairs and alterations, tenants' insurance premium. Shelter also includes the cost of other accommodations including owned or rented vacation homes, traveler accommodations, and other accommodations away from home.

Medical Care Expenditure: Includes all out-of-pocket expenditures for prescription drugs, doctor visits, hospital stays, health insurance premiums, dental visits, medical supplies, eye care goods and services.

APPENDIX 3A.2

The Role of Age

Other chapters in this volume focus on the non-elderly population or various subsets of the non-elderly population in the United States and other countries. I do not currently have data on the living conditions of the non-elderly poor in Sweden. Consequently, in this chapter I compare the living conditions of the poor who live in households headed by someone who is 18–76 years old. In this appendix, I use what data I do have to suggest how these results may have differed had I compared poverty and material well-being among the nonelderly in these countries.

Poor Americans are younger than poor Canadians or Germans. In the United States 87.6 percent of the poor are less than 65 years old. In Canada 81.1 percent and in Germany only 71.3 percent of the poor are under 65 years old. The income of non-elderly poor Americans is 85 percent of the income of elderly poor Americans. In both Canada and Germany the average income of the non-elderly poor is greater than the average income of the elderly poor (33 percent and 22 percent greater, respectively). Thus, while poor Americans in households headed by someone 18–76 years old are poorer than poor Canadians or Germans of the same age, non-elderly poor Americans are even poorer relative to non-elderly Germans or Canadians. This suggests that had I considered only the non-elderly poor, poor Americans would have fared worse than poor Germans or Canadians.

Tables 3A.1, 3A.2, and 3A.3 show the percentage of individuals less than 65 years old with each living condition by poverty status in the United States, Germany, and Canada. These tables show that for these measures the qualitative results (the rankings) are the same whether we consider the entire population or just the non-elderly population in these countries. Poor Germans fare better than poor Americans on 3 of 6 living conditions measured in both countries. Poor Canadians fare better than poor Americans on 4 of 6 living conditions measured in both countries.

Table 3A.1 / Percentage of Non-Elderly Individuals with Housing Conditions in the United States, West Germany, and Canada, by Income Group

	Adjusted Income as a Percentage of Adjusted Median Income						
	Less than 50 Percent of National Median	50 to 75 Percent of National Median	75 to 125 Percent of National Median	125 to 175 Percent of National Median	175 to 225 Percent of National Median	Over 225 Percent of National Median	Mean for Entire Population*
Rents Home							
United States	56.0 (26.0)	40.6 (10.6)	26.9 (3.1)	19.1 (−10.9)	15.7 (−14.3)	13.0 (17.0)	30.0
Germany	73.9 (20.6)	57.1 (3.8)	53.7 (−0.4)	50.1 (−3.2)	44.3 (−9.0)	36.1 (−17.2)	53.3
Canada	52.8 (23.9)	39.1 (10.2)	27.0 (1.9)	20.4 (−8.5)	16.4 (−12.5)	14.4 (−14.5)	28.9
Crowded							
United States	23.2 (7.9)	14.8 (5.6)	8.3 (0.9)	4.2 (−5.0)	2.0 (−7.2)	1.7 (−7.5)	9.2
Germany	20.4 (2.5)	26.0 (8.1)	21.0 (3.1)	12.1 (1.7)	9.8 (−8.1)	7.0 (−10.9)	17.9
Canada	10.5 (6.2)	9.3 (5.0)	4.1 (−0.2)	1.7 (−2.6)	0.1 (−4.2)	0.3 (−4.0)	4.3
No Kitchen							
United States	4.7 (3.0)	2.0 (0.3)	1.0 (−0.3)	0.7 (−1.0)	0.6 (−1.1)	0.6 (−1.1)	1.7
Germany	3.6 (2.4)	0.9 (−0.3)	0.6 (−0.6)	2.1 (0.9)	0.6 (−0.6)	0.5 (−0.7)	1.2
No Bath							
United States	6.9 (4.5)	3.0 (0.6)	1.5 (−0.9)	0.8 (−1.6)	0.6 (−1.8)	0.4 (−2.0)	2.4
Germany	11.4 (6.8)	5.7 (1.1)	4.7 (0.1)	3.3 (−1.3)	2.2 (−2.4)	0.1 (−4.4)	4.6

SOURCE: Own calculations from data sets described in Appendix 3A.1.

NOTES: The percentages in the top row represent the share of each income group with a particular condition. The percentage in the parentheses shows the difference from the national norm in the country of residence. Thus, the first cell of the table shows that 56 percent of all non-elderly, low-income Americans rent their homes. Since 30 percent of all Americans rent their homes, this means a poor household is almost twice as likely to rent as the average American household.

*Includes the elderly.

Table 3A.2 / Percentage of Non-Elderly Individuals with Health Conditions and Doctor Visits in the United States, West Germany, and Canada, by Income Group

Health Status and Doctor Visits	Adjusted Income as a Percentage of Adjusted Median Income						Mean for Entire Population*
	Less than 50 Percent of National Median	50 to 75 Percent of National Median	75 to 125 Percent of National Median	125 to 175 Percent of National Median	175 to 225 Percent of National Median	Over 225 Percent of National Median	
Limitation of Activity Due to Health							
United States	24.2 (10.5)	15.6 (1.9)	12.1 (−1.6)	9.8 (−3.9)	9.9 (−3.8)	10.7 (−3.0)	13.7
Germany	42.5 (17.1)	36.7 (11.1)	30.8 (−3.0)	28.7 (−7.6)	25.5 (−10.7)	26.1 (−10.1)	37.8
Chronic Condition							
United States	34.0 (13.1)	24.2 (3.3)	18.0 (−2.9)	14.9 (−6.0)	14.9 (−6.0)	16.9 (−4.0)	20.9
Germany	39.1 (9.9)	33.8 (4.7)	28.1 (−1.1)	27.1 (−2.1)	25.3 (−3.9)	27.1 (−2.1)	29.2
No Doctor or Dentist Visit in the Last 3 Months							
United States	51.0 (0.5)	52.9 (2.4)	51.7 (1.2)	50.0 (−0.5)	48.3 (−2.2)	46.1 (−4.4)	50.5
Germany	33.0 (1.3)	30.5 (−1.2)	32.9 (1.2)	31.5 (−0.2)	31.1 (−0.6)	27.3 (−4.4)	31.7
Sick and No Doctor Visit							
United States	5.3 (2.1)	4.0 (1.2)	2.8 (−0.4)	2.5 (−0.7)	2.2 (−1.0)	2.4 (−0.8)	3.2
Germany	8.5 (2.8)	5.9 (0.2)	5.2 (−0.5)	6.0 (0.3)	5.4 (−0.3)	4.5 (−1.2)	5.7

SOURCE: Own calculations from data sets described in Appendix 3A.1.

NOTE: See Notes to Table 3A.1.

*Includes the elderly.

Table 3A.3 / Percentage of Non-Elderly Individuals with Consumer Durables in the United States, West Germany, and Canada, by Income Group

Durables	Adjusted Income as a Percentage of Adjusted Median Income						Mean for Entire Population*
	Less than 50 Percent of National Median	50 to 75 Percent of National Median	75 to 125 Percent of National Median	125 to 175 Percent of National Median	175 to 225 Percent of National Median	Over 225 Percent of National Median	
No Car							
United States	24.7 (16.8)	8.0 (0.1)	3.1 (−4.8)	1.6 (−6.3)	1.3 (−6.6)	1.5 (−6.4)	7.9
Germany	40.1 (27.8)	14.5 (2.2)	7.9 (−5.2)	4.1 (−8.2)	3.8 (−8.5)	4.5 (−7.8)	12.3
No Clothes Washer							
United States	41.3 (15.3)	31.9 (5.9)	23.7 (−2.3)	19.9 (−6.1)	16.0 (−10.0)	15.7 (−10.3)	26.0
Germany	27.4 (11.9)	17.4 (1.9)	13.4 (−2.1)	12.6 (−2.9)	12.4 (−3.1)	9.9 (5.6)	15.4
No Clothes Dryer							
United States	58.2 (21.0)	46.2 (9.0)	37.0 (−3.2)	26.8 (−10.4)	19.8 (−17.4)	20.2 (−17.0)	37.2
Germany	46.3 (18.9)	31.6 (4.2)	24.7 (−2.7)	20.0 (−7.4)	18.1 (−9.3)	16.1 (−11.3)	27.4
No Dishwasher							
United States	75.7 (19.9)	69.4 (13.6)	60.5 (4.7)	44.1 (−11.7)	33.3 (−22.5)	21.3 (−34.5)	55.8
Germany	85.9 (15.2)	78.6 (7.9)	68.8 (−1.9)	61.9 (−8.8)	59.6 (−11.1)	58.6 (−12.1)	70.7

SOURCE: Own calculations from data sets described in Appendix 3A.1.

NOTE: See Notes to Table 3A.1.

*Includes the elderly.

146 /

Comparing Tables 3A.1 with Tables 3.1 and 3.2 shows that, relative to the mean, elderly poor Germans are worse off than non-elderly poor Germans. The difference between the within-income group mean and the grand mean is greater for the elderly poor than the non-elderly poor on 5 of 6 living conditions. Comparing these two tables shows that non-elderly poor Canadians are better off than elderly poor Canadians and non-elderly poor Americans fare about as well as elderly poor Americans.

Non-elderly poor Americans allocate a smaller share of their total expenditures to food and shelter than non-elderly poor Canadians, but they allocate a greater share to medical care. This is consistent with the results for the Canadian and American samples that include 65–76 year olds.

ENDNOTES

1. In the United States, a family's chances of experiencing serious material hardship depends to a great extent on their ability to borrow money (Mayer and Jencks 1989).

2. Another obstacle to comparing living conditions across countries is that most European countries do not allow researchers in other countries to use their microdata. For instance, to use the Swedish data a researcher must go to Sweden for as long as it takes to learn to use the data and produce correct results. The German data used in this chapter have only recently become available to researchers outside of Germany (except by special permission for German citizens). Neither the Swedish nor German surveys are documented in English. This makes it very difficult for researchers to use data sets from several countries at once, or to use more than one data set in each country.

3. I could have compared the relative well-being of the poor to the middle class using other methods. One plausible strategy is to divide the within-cell mean by the grand mean. However, because this measure is sensitive to the absolute level of the grand mean, when the outcome is dichotomous the proportional difference between the means for two groups depends on whether we look at the probability of having the living condition or lacking it. Some analysts prefer to analyze differences in dichotomous outcomes by computing differences in the logged odds. Like the arithmetic difference between proportions, logged odds yield the same results regardless of whether you count people with an attribute or without it. But when the base rate is very high or very low, a small absolute gain can translate into a very large change in the odds ratio. Changes in odd ratios are, therefore, unlikely to have a plausible linear relationship to any utility function. This problem is not solved by using arithmetic differences, but it is lessened.

   For most living conditions, these procedures rank countries in the same way, but when the grand mean is much greater in one country than another, comparing proportional differences can yield different conclusions than comparing absolute differences. Regardless of which procedure I use, the qualitative conclusions of the paper remain the same, namely that poor Americans fare better than the poor in other countries on some measures and worse on others.

4. In the United States data food stamps are counted as income.

5. If measures of income inequality vary as much across data sets in other countries as they do in the United States, the choice of a data set could make a difference in conclusions about differences in poverty rates across countries. Duncan et al. (this volume) using the Longitudinal Administrative Database (LAD) find a relative poverty rate of 17 percent in Canada in 1982 among families with children. The Canadian Family Expenditure Survey for the same year shows a poverty rate of only 11.5 percent for such families. Indeed, the CPS and the Canadian LAD might yield very similar poverty rates for 1982, rather than showing that the United States poverty rate is much higher than the Canadian rate, as this chapter shows.

6. The sample sizes for all data sets are relatively large, so comparisons across countries of the difference between the grand mean and the mean for those with less than half the adjusted mean income are usually statistically significant. This can be shown with this equation which tests the null hypothesis that the difference of the proportion is 0:

$$Z = \sqrt{\frac{(p_{d1x} - p_{1x'}) - (p_{d2x} - p_{2x'})}{\dfrac{p_{d1x}q_{d1x}}{N_1} + \dfrac{p_{x'}q_{x'}}{N_2} + \dfrac{p_{d2x}q_{d2x}}{N_3} + \dfrac{p_{2x'}q_{2x'}}{N_4}}}$$

where $d1x$ is the mean for the poor in country 1 on living condition x, x' is the within-country grand mean of x, N_1 and N_3 are the within-cell means, and N_2 and N_4 are the country sample means. Sweden has the smallest sample size and Canada the next smallest. If we use the sample size of these countries and conservatively set p_{d1x} and p_{d2x} to .5, we can estimate that differences of differences greater than 3 percentage points will be statistically significant. Smaller difference of differences will be statistically significant for living conditions, such as bathrooms and kitchens, that have smaller variances and for differences of differences between countries such as Germany and the United States with larger samples.

7. German data on health and access to medical care are for 1984–85, while United States data are for 1980. The Omnibus Budget Reconciliation Act of 1982 reduced the number of people eligible for Medicaid and imposed new costs for Medicare patients. Thus, one might suppose that access to medical care among the poor decreased between 1980 and 1985. Published HIS data show that neither the distribution of limitations of activity due to chronic conditions nor the distribution of doctor visits changed appreciably between 1983 and 1988 and that low-income Americans continued to visit the doctor more often than affluent Americans (Mayer 1991). Data from the Survey of Income and Program Participation confirm that in 1984 income had little effect on individuals' chances of seeing a doctor in the previous year (Mayer 1991).

8. Comparisons of published data from both Canada (Statistics Canada 1987) and the United States (NCHS 1986) suggest that in 1985 low-income Americans were more likely than low-income Canadians to visit a doctor in the last year, and in both countries the chances of visiting a doctor in the last year were only weakly related to income.

9. Unlike the CPS and Census, CEX public use tapes do not include imputed values for missing data. Instead zeros are substituted for values not reported by respondents. The analyses in this chapter use only complete income reporters (see Appendix 3A), but many respondents classified as complete income reporters have failed

to report some income. I also eliminate some cases suffering from serious underreporting. Nonetheless, substituting zeros for missing data probably biases the CEX distribution of consumer durables and expenditures over income groups towards equality. Comparing the distribution of homeownership over income groups shows that homeownership is somewhat more equally distributed in the CEX than in the Census. While census data show that 44.9 percent of poor Americans live in owner occupied housing, CEX data show that 49.4 do. CEX expenditure data are assumed to be quite reliable.

10. U.S. expenditure data are collected during quarterly interviews with a 3-month accounting period. Annual data are the weighted sum of these quarterly reports. Canadian expenditure data are collected annually with a 1-year accounting period. The Bureau of Labor Statistics also conducts a diary survey that collects selected expenditure data covering a single week. Data from the diary survey yield higher estimates of expenditures which, at least for food, more closely correspond to the National Income Accounts. This suggests that the shorter recall period in the CEX may lead to higher estimates of expenditures than the longer recall period in the Canadian survey. It is unlikely, however, that the shorter recall period seriously affects the distribution of expenditures.

11. Total expenditures include income and payroll taxes but not down payments on houses, payments of mortgage principals, and expenditures for home improvements on the grounds that these are savings rather than consumption. Due to data limitations, these estimates include the full purchase price of consumer durables, even when the purchase is partially financed by borrowing. This exaggerates inequality in total expenditure. Current consumption would be preferable to total expenditures as a measure of current economic well-being. However, data limitation prevent me from adequately estimating current consumption.

12. These differences are much greater in the United States than in Canada. Some of this difference may be due to the unreliability of CEX income data as discussed above.

13. I count living conditions as equal if the difference of the difference from the mean (shown in parentheses in Tables 3.3, 3.4, and 3.5) in the two countries is less than 2. If I simply count absolute differences of the differences of the means, poor Swedes are better off than poor Americans on 5 of 10 living conditions, poor Germans are better off than poor Americans on 4 of 6 living conditions. Poor Canadians are also better off than poor Americans on 4 of 6 living conditions.

14. Since the variance of income is greater in the United States than in other countries, when the correlation between income and a living condition is the same or greater in the United States, its distribution over income groups is more unequal.

15. Comparing the poorest 10 percent of Americans with the poorest 10 percent of those in other countries yields results similar to these using median adjusted income categories (Mayer 1993).

REFERENCES

Aguilar, Renato. 1987. "Public Sector Transfers and Income Taxes: An International Comparison with Micro Data." LIS-CEPS Working Paper No. 10.

Buhmann, Brigitte, Lee Rainwater, Guenther Schmaus, and Timothy Smeeding. 1988. "Equivalence Scale, Well-being, Inequality and Poverty: Sensitivity Estimates Across 10 Countries Using the Luxembourg Income Study (LIS) Database." *Review of Income and Wealth* 34 (June): 115–142.

Coder, John. 1991. "Exploring Nonsampling Errors in the Wage and Salary Income Data from the March Current Population Survey." Washington, D.C.: Housing and Household Economic Statistics Division, U.S. Bureau of the Census.

Coleman, Richard P., and Lee Rainwater. 1978. *Social Standing in America.* New York: Basic Books.

Edin, Kathryn, and Christopher Jencks. 1992. "Reforming Welfare." In Jencks, Christopher, ed. *Rethinking Social Policy.* Cambridge, MA.: Harvard University Press.

Engel, E. 1885. "Die Lebenskosten beigischer Abeiterfamillen fruher und jetzt. *International Statistical Institute, Bulletin 9.*

Erikson, Robert, and Rune Aberg. 1987. *Welfare in Transition: A Survey of Living Conditions in Sweden 1968–1981.* Oxford: Clarendon Press.

Glatzer, Wolfgang. 1987. "Living Conditions and Their Assessment." *Social Indicators Research* 19:39–46.

Greenwood, Daphne, and Edward Wolff. 1988. "Relative Wealth Holdings of Children and the Elderly in the United States, 1962–83." In Palmer, John L., Timothy Smeeding, and Barbara Torrey, eds. *The Vulnerable.* Washington, D.C.: Urban Institute Press.

Heidenheimer, Arnold, Hugh Heclo, and Carolyn Adams. 1990. *Comparative Public Policy.* New York: St. Martin's Press.

Hicks, Alexander, and Duane Swank. 1984. "Governmental Redistribution in Rich Capitalist Democracies." *Policy Studies Journal* 13: 265–287.

Institutet for Social Forskning. 1984. *Variabler och kodr for LNU81.* Stockholm.

Mayer, Susan E. 1991. "Are There Economic Barriers to Use of Physician Services?" Unpublished manuscript.

———. 1992. "Living Conditions Among the Poor in Four Rich Countries." *Journal of Population Economics.*

Mayer, Susan E., and Christopher Jencks. 1989. "Poverty and the Distribution of Material Hardship." *Journal of Human Resources* 24 (1): 88–114.

———. 1993. "Recent Trends in Economic Inequality in the United States: Income vs. Expenditure vs. Material Well-Being." In Popadimitriou, Dimitri, and Edward Wolff, eds. *Poverty and Prosperity in the U.S.A. in the Late Twentieth Century.* London: Macmillan.

National Center for Health Statistics. 1986. *Current Estimates from the National Health Interview Survey.* Vital Health Statistics 10 (163).

O'Higgins, Michael. 1988. "The Allocation of Public Resources to Children and the Elderly in OECD Countries." In Palmer, John L., Timothy Smeeding, and Barbara Boyle Torrey, eds. *The Vulnerable.* Washington, D.C.: Urban Institute Press.

OECD. 1990. *Main Economic Indicators.* Paris: OECD.

Palmer, John L., Timothy Smeeding, and Christopher Jencks. 1988. "The Uses and Limits of Income Comparisons." In Palmer, John L., Timothy Smeeding, and Barbara Boyle Torrey, eds. *The Vulnerable*. Washington, D.C.: Urban Institute Press.

Rainwater, Lee. 1974. *What Money Buys: Inequality and the Social Meaning of Money*. New York: Basic Books.

Ringen, Stein. 1987. "Poverty in the Welfare State?" In Erikson, Robert, Erik Jorgen Hansen, Stein Ringen, and Hannu Uusitalo, eds. *The Scandinavian Model*. New York: M.E. Sharpe, Inc.

Smeeding, Timothy, Lee Rainwater, Martin Rein, Richard Hauser, and Gaston Schaber. 1990. "Income Poverty in Seven Countries: Initial Estimates from the LIS Database." In Smeeding, Timothy, Michael O'Higgins, and Lee Rainwater, eds. *Poverty, Inequality and Income Distribution in Comparative Perspective*. New York: Harvester Wheatsheaf.

Smeeding, Timothy, Barbara Torrey, and Martin Rein. 1988. "Patterns of Income and Poverty: The Economic Status of Children and the Elderly in Eight Countries." In Palmer, John L., Timothy Smeeding, and Barbara Boyle Torrey, eds. *The Vulnerable*. Washington, D.C.: Urban Institute Press.

Statistics Canada. 1981. *The Health of Canadians: Report of the Canadian Health Survey*. Ottawa, Canada: Minister of Supply and Services.

————. 1987. *Health and Social Support*. Ottawa, Canada: Minister of Supply and Services.

Townsend, Peter. 1979. *Poverty in the United Kingdom: A Survey of Household Resources and Standard of Living*. Los Angeles: University of California Press.

Travers, Peter, and Sue Richardson. "Averages and Talls: The Tenuous Link between Poverty Status and Standard of Living." Working Paper #89–3, Department of Economics, University of Adelaide, Australia.

Universitaten Frankfurt am Main. 1988. "Das Sozio-okonomische Panel," Sonder-forschungsbereich # (Mikroanalytische Grunlagen ger Gesellschaftspolitik), Frankfurt am Main, West Germany.

Chapter 4

LABOR INSECURITY THROUGH MARKET REGULATION: LEGACY OF THE 1980s, CHALLENGE FOR THE 1990s

Guy Standing

"Insecurity is worse than poverty"—Confucius

W ESTERN EUROPE has experienced more than a decade of chronically high unemployment; the United States has experienced more than a decade in which "poor jobs" have grown while "good jobs" have shrunk.[1] On both sides of the Atlantic, poverty and income inequality have grown steadily. As of summer 1992, the short-term and medium-term prospects for reducing both unemployment and the number in poverty remain bleak.

The nature of labor markets in industrialized economies changed in the 1980s. Compared with the long postwar era of full employment and advancing labor security, the 1980s was an era of labor fragmentation and insecurity. The form and consequences of this new labor insecurity are the principal themes of this chapter. The determinants of international labor market developments will not be considered. The context of these labor market developments is that from the mid-1970s onwards policymakers in most industrialized economies abandoned both the Keynesian commitment to full employment and the "neo-corporatist" regulatory framework that underpinned it. As faith grew in market mechanisms, rather than institutional solutions, protective regulations and progressive distributional policies became perceived as labor "rigidities" impeding competitiveness and employment growth. More intense international competition, stemming from Japan and then from the newly industrializing countries, encouraged policymakers and firms to pursue "flexible" labor practices to reduce fixed and overall labor costs.[2] Those corresponded to and facilitated new forms of technology and management that boosted both "external" and "internal" labor flexibility, which in turn contributed to the labor force fragmentation that is the worst legacy of the 1980s.

THE 1980s: FROM LABOR SECURITY TO SUBORDINATED FLEXIBILITY

In Western Europe, Canada, and to some extent in the United States, between the 1940s and the early 1970s, the dominant way of thinking about social, economic, and labor market policy could be characterized as "social democratic," with the welfare state seen as the means of social protection and redistribution of income, wealth, status, and power. There was a social consensus based on the expectation that all forms of inequality would dwindle, and management would preserve the right to manage while labor security would gradually be strengthened. The underlying regulatory approach was one of managing class conflict rather than removing it by abolishing class distinctions altogether.

One can interpret labor market developments in this era as consisting of "corporatist" bargaining and legislation to promote seven dimensions of labor security:

1. *Labor market security.* This was the commitment by all governments—with the partial exception of the United States—to full employment, a notion that evolved over the years to include employment for groups on the edge of the labor market, notably, married women. Essentially, full employment meant a level of open unemployment that was "frictional," i.e., due to labor turnover and job searching. Governments assumed responsibility for preserving aggregate demand for goods and services at a level that ensured that all those wanting and seeking paid employment could obtain it fairly quickly. In practice, this meant trying to keep the level of unemployment approximately equal to the number of job vacancies in the economy. Keynes, Beveridge, and other architects of the postwar welfare state believed that full employment meant having about 3 percent unemployment. However, in the postwar era, West European governments became threatened if unemployment rose much above 2 percent. In some countries full employment was preserved mainly by boosting economic growth by fiscal and monetary policy; others, notably Sweden, put more emphasis on labor market policy, believing that cutting taxes and increasing the money supply to boost employment would be inflationary.

2. *Employment security.* This meant security against arbitrary dismissal, preserved by protective legislation and the imposition of costs on employers cutting employment without giving due notice. Employment security was extended to include measures to prevent discrimination in recruitment and promote "positive discrimination" to increase the employment chances of socially vulnerable groups, such as the physically handicapped.

3. *Work security.* This was the regulated protection of workers in terms of occupational health and safety, often with the onus of proof of adequate safety placed on employers. "Work security" embraced a range of interventions from "minimalist" to "maximalist." Some countries set minimum standards with an inspectorate to check on their observance. Others adopted a more active approach by combining regulations with

legislative encouragement of enterprise-level and "shop-floor" bodies to promote broader notions of occupational health and safety through collective bargaining.

4. *Job security*. This was, in part, the outgrowth of Taylorist management methods popularized in the prewar era. From being a management tool, the preservation of niches in the production process became a goal of many trade unions and groups of workers, with job security being seen as a defense against the advance of the technical and social divisions of labor.

5. *Labor reproductive security*. This was the government commitment to cover the social costs of education and skill development, as well as promote productivity of the workforce through subsidized schooling, training, health facilities, etc.

6. *Labor representation security*. Governments were committed to promote workers' bargaining strength, or the security of bargaining rights, by means of laws, regulations, and procedures enhancing the politico-economic role of trade unions and other institutions protecting workers' collective interests.

7. *Income security*. All governments were committed in principle to poverty eradication and most to the right to a minimum living standard "from cradle to grave." In Western Europe, programs designed to achieve this included minimum wages, collective bargaining rights, and "progressive" fiscal welfare, coupled with a mixture of universal benefits and insurance-based social security. A common theme underlying these measures was the aim of minimizing resort to means-tested public assistance by strengthening and enhancing "first-line," mainly work-related entitlements.

Looking back on this era of social consensus, sometimes called the golden age of welfare capitalism, one can trace improvements in all seven aspects of labor security in most countries. These achievements were mainly the result of making the labor market *less* like a market and of avoiding outcomes of market relations. However, the consensus depended on a few crucial assumptions, which were to be undermined in the 1970s and 1980s and which will not be recreated. Most fundamentally, it assumed rapid and *stable* economic growth, i.e., based on an industrial distribution of production and employment that changed only very slowly, in which the vast majority of jobs were stable, full-time, and well-paid, filled mostly by men belonging to trade unions powerful and secure enough to bargain for improvements in all seven forms of labor security.

The postwar welfare consensus depended also on annual increments to national income that could be shared between the "social partners" (i.e., capital and labor) and those outside protected full-time employment, who had access to rising living standards via the growth of a vast, complex social security system. This was the motivating principle of the regulated market model—that productivity growth would generate income that would be shared between capital and labor. Once the crises of the 1970s slowed economic growth to a trickle and accelerated inflationary pressures already associated with successively harder attempts to preserve full employment, the social consensus on income distribution crumbled into a period of anguished reappraisal. Fiscal crises of the welfare state mounted, as the costs of income support grew, as work-related entitlements were eroded, and as the complex income transfer system became more inefficient and inequitable.

The following sections consider the main forms of erosion of labor security in the 1980s and their consequences for labor and social policy options in the 1990s.

THE GROWTH AND PERSISTENCE OF LABOR MARKET INSECURITY

The most familiar labor market story in the 1980s was a picturesque contrast between the U.S. "jobs miracle"—with millions of new jobs—and the slithering "Eurosclerosis" of Western Europe, where employment fell or remained stagnant while unemployment rose to levels most economists had presumed were a remembrance of things past. Led by the United Kingdom, but followed by most of the European Community (EC), unemployment rates soared to double-digit levels in the early 1980s, and stayed thereabout. Spain, Ireland, and the United Kingdom were the most affected, but the others (except for the special case of Luxembourg) were not far behind. Only the small European Free Trade Agreement (EFTA) countries managed to maintain single-digit unemployment rates, a point of irony insofar as in the early 1990s EFTA is crumbling as its members rush to join the queue for entry into the high-unemployment club of the EC.

Meanwhile, the U.S. economy was lauded for generating millions of jobs, attributed by many to its flexible labor market and absence of protective regulations, by others to a combination of tight monetary policy coupled with a loose fiscal policy that boosted (lower-paid) service employment and hit (higher-paid) export-oriented production. Certainly, unemployment rose less than in Western Europe. But one could attribute the European unemployment in part to a tendency to push low-productivity workers into social security and social assistance, whereas in the United States many similarly placed workers have had to resort to the informal, mostly service sector economy.

As for European unemployment, the debate was long between the Keynesian interpretation in terms of low aggregate demand—with several research teams proposing a coordinated growth strategy[3]—and the "classical unemployment" interpretation claiming real wages were too high. The latter blended into the "Eurosclerosis" perspective, attributing high unemployment to wages, non-wage labor costs, and labor regulations. Considerable rhetoric has been expended on this debate.

The bare facts about unemployment are too well known to bear much repetition. Because of the way labor markets are evolving, mainly because of the trend away from full-time employment, the "headline" unemployment rates not only understate labor slack but do so to an increasing extent. Generalizations are suspect, but in the interest of brevity and the need to capture the main trends we can paint with a broad brush. Considering the EC countries, in 1983—the first year for which relevant comparative statistics were collected by EURO-STAT—not only was conventional unemployment very high but what can be called "labor slack" was higher. The way we measure it, there is no reason for that to be the case. The labor slack index is essentially a "full-time equivalent unemployment rate," a measure of underutilized labor supply, and thus of labor market insecurity, adjusted to take into account that some of the employed work in part-time jobs, some "voluntarily," some "involuntarily," while some of the unemployed seek full-time jobs, some part-time. In terms of labor slack, conventional data overstate both the unemployed and employed, while no account is taken of "visible underemployment."[4] This is important, since one trend has been that part-time and non-regular jobs are displacing full-time, regular employment, particularly in the EC.

By assuming that an average part-time worker was employed for half the time of an average full-time worker, we can estimate a full-time equivalent *labor slack rate*, by stipulating that whereas a person employed full-time (E_{ft}) was fully in the labor force, a person working part-time voluntarily (PT_v) was half in the labor force and half outside it, and someone who was involuntarily part-time (PT_i) was half employed, half unemployed. Similarly, whereas someone unemployed seeking full-time employment (U_{ft}) was fully in the labor force, someone unemployed seeking part-time work (U_{pt}) was half unemployed, half outside the labor force. Thus, we can convert both the enumerator and denominator of the conventional unemployment rate into the labor slack index:

$$LS = \frac{U_{ft} + 0.5\,U_{pt} + 0.5\,PT_i}{E_{ft} + PT_i + 0.5\,PT_v + U_{ft} + 0.5\,U_{pt}}$$

The European Community pattern is displayed in Figure 4.1, showing labor slack rates for 1989 alongside the corresponding unemployment rates for countries for which data were available. All the labor slack rates were higher, but the relative position of some countries changes with the labor slack measure. And in comparing the ratio of labor slack to unemployment over the 1980s, the difference seems to have grown, implying that the unemployment rate had become a less accurate proxy for labor slack. Several factors contributed to this, notably the shift from full-time to part-time employment, a tendency for more of the unemployed to be men seeking full-time jobs and the relative growth of women's employment. Moreover, a period of slow economic growth had left a huge labor slack, with unemployment alone being three or more times the level recorded in the 1960s and 1970s. Finally, as Figure 4.2 indicates, despite a prolonged economic "recovery" in the mid- and late-1980s, labor slack had scarcely declined, and in some countries, including the major economies of

Figure 4.1 / Labor Slack—Unemployment Rate: 1989

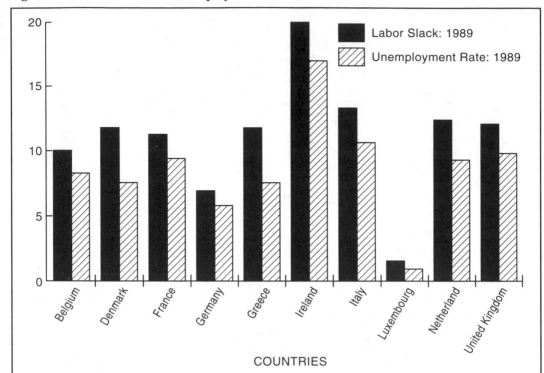

SOURCE: EUROSTAT: Labor Force Survey, 1989 (Luxembourg).

*For Greece, Ireland, and the United Kingdom, the latest available data are for 1988.

France, West Germany, and Italy, it had actually risen, despite falls in official unemployment.

Estimated labor slack rates for the United States in 1989, along with unemployment rates, are given in Figure 4.3, showing that labor slack was higher in all parts of the country, and that the differences were about the same as in the European Community. Figure 4.4 shows that for the United States labor slack was lower in 1989 than in the early 1980s.

In the United States, labor slack rates for women have tended to be higher than for men—this was so in 33 states compared to only 3 in which the male rate was higher (Table 4A.1). In the EC, this was less clear-cut, since in some countries female employment grew relative to men's while their relative unemployment rate fell. In the United States, gender differences narrowed over the 1980s. Though labor slack rates were higher for blacks, the differences were slightly less than for unemployment.

Another index of labor market insecurity in the 1980s was long-term unemployment, which became the main concern of policymakers in Europe by the

Figure 4.2 / Labor Slack: 1983–1989

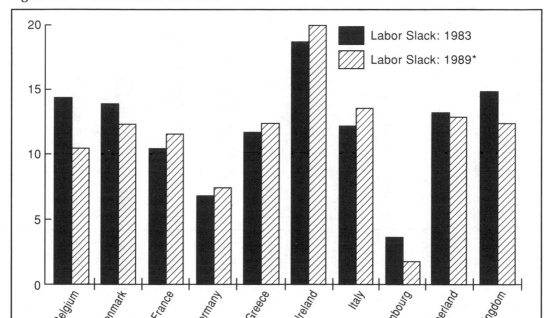

SOURCE: EUROSTAT: Labor Force Surveys, 1983 and 1989 (Luxembourg).

*For Greece, Ireland, and the United Kingdom, the latest available data are for 1988.

mid-1980s. Most commentators have emphasized the divergence between the typical pattern in Western Europe of growing and high levels of unemployment lasting for a year or more, and the United States, where recorded long-term unemployment has been much lower. This may be changing, since the share of the unemployed classified as unemployed for more than six months rose quite sharply in the United States in the 1980s (Table 4A.2). This was so despite lower overall unemployment in the last year covered. The data also indicate the erosion of men's labor market security in the 1980s. In most states men have had a higher long-term unemployment rate than women.[5] And, taking account of the changing overall unemployment rate, men's position worsened. Although more women drop out of the labor force in periods of high unemployment, the deteriorating relative position of men may have as much to do with the changing pattern of labor force participation and with deindustrialization, which led to a sharp decline in male working-class jobs.

One difficulty in international comparisons of long-term unemployment is that it is strongly influenced by the unemployment insurance and social assis-

Figure 4.3 / Labor Slack—Unemployment Rate: 1989

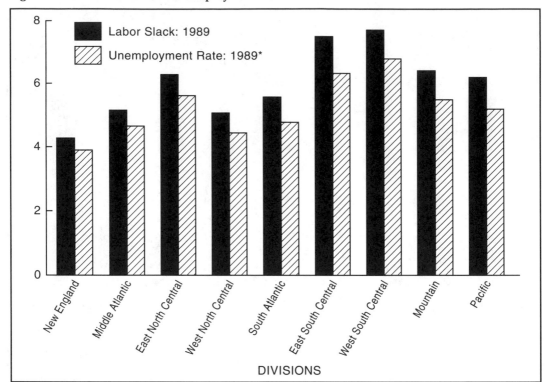

SOURCE: U.S. Department of Labor, Bureau of Labor Statistics. (Washington, D.C.: U.S. Government Printing Office, 1989), Table 1.

tance regime. In the United States, as ordinary unemployment benefits are normally payable for at most 26 weeks (with extended benefits payable in states of high unemployment), long-term unemployment tends to be low, though it is unclear whether this is mainly because the unemployed are forced into job-taking or because they withdraw from the labor force.

In most EC countries, long-term unemployment grew enormously in the 1980s, and remained a high share of total unemployment, although by the end of the decade it had begun to decline in some countries, especially where "special measures" had been directed at those involved.[6] One analysis estimated that by 1985 about half the 15 million unemployed recorded in the EC Labor Force Survey had been searching for work for at least 12 months.[7] In Europe most demographic groups were affected by these trends. One study in the United Kingdom showed that while growth of long-term unemployment had been concentrated in areas of "deindustrialization," all age-sex groups suffered an increase in the 1980s.[8] Many long-term unemployed were in publicly subsidized housing, suggesting not only that such working-class housing had become a residual form, commonly occupied by unemployed manual workers but

Figure 4.4 / Labor Slack: 1980–1989

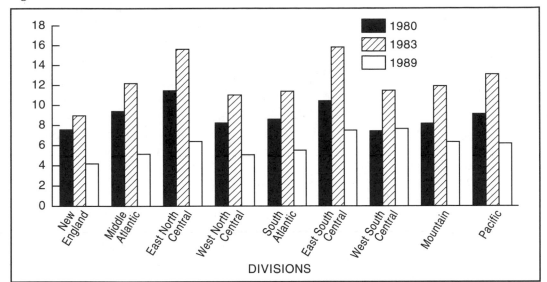

SOURCE: U.S. Department of Labor, Bureau of Labor Statistics. (Washington, D.C.: U.S. Government Printing Office, 1989), Table 1.

that house possession was constraining geographical mobility, making it hard for working-class victims of restructuring to escape from areas of high unemployment.[9]

An issue that has intrigued labor economists has been "insider-outsider" models, particularly as they relate to variants of the hysteresis hypothesis.[10] The basic argument is that the long-term unemployed cease to have the sort of macro-level effect on wages and prices that unemployment is postulated to have in many labor market models.[11] However, one should be skeptical about this. Although, the long-term unemployed search less intensively for jobs,[12] they may still exert downward pressure on wages even if they themselves may be perceived by employers as less employable.

THE CHANGING DEMOGRAPHIC INCIDENCE OF LABOR MARKET INSECURITY

In the early 1980s it seemed as if the unemployment problem of Western Europe was simply one of youth unemployment. Most labor market policies were addressed to this issue.[13] But by the end of the decade, there was talk of a forthcoming shortage of young workers. Although in some countries, notably Italy, unemployment remains primarily a youth labor force entry problem, in most countries the pattern has changed, in part because policies merely shifted the burden of unemployment from teenagers to those in their early twenties.[14] Moreover, *older workers* were among the biggest losers in the 1980s, as governments and the "social partners" responded to unemployment by trying to cut labor supply, with perhaps the most popular policy being early retirement schemes.[15] These cut significantly the labor participation rate of men (in particular) in their late 50s and early 60s. Yet evidence from many countries suggests that they have accentuated poverty among the elderly.

Given widespread resort to early retirement, can one envision older workers reentering the labor market? Is it feasible? And has it occurred very much? Little empirical work seems to have been done, but enabling such reentry seems a prerequisite for reversing the trend to pre-pension age poverty and social marginalization in Europe at least.[16] There are also unresolved questions about substitution effects in employment, particularly between older workers and women, who have become more fully committed labor force participants, and between older workers and immigrants. The latter issue may become controversial in Southern European countries, since demographic pressures in Turkey and the Maghreb countries of Algeria, Morocco, and Tunisia may produce a substantial influx of legal and illegal immigrants.[17] And in the United States it could also become controversial, given that in recent years immigration has been greater than at any time since the 1920s.

In the 1980s, in most of Western Europe, women increased their share of the labor force and employment, as they did in most of the world.[18] Those trends are expected to continue. For instance, women's employment share in the United Kingdom is expected to rise from 40 percent to 44 percent between 1988 and 2000.[19] Some even forecast that they will comprise a majority of the United Kingdom workforce by 2000.[20] Similar forecasts have been made in the United States. Besides changing patterns of labor supply, global "feminization" of labor has been partly due to the changing nature of the labor market—the continuing shift to services, the growth of part-time and other "atypical" forms of employment and changes in tax, benefit, and wage policies. One study of trends in the EC found that (except perhaps in the United Kingdom) the traditional M-shaped age pattern of female labor force participation was fast becoming inverted U-shaped.[21] Male and female workforce behavior will surely become very similar.

Although women in Europe were badly hit by the growth of unemployment in the 1980s, female labor force participation continued to rise, mostly through the spread of low-paid, insecure forms of employment. Despite women's growing share of employment, gender-based job segregation has persisted, and in some countries possibly worsened.[22] The reality seems to be that a growing proportion of women have been in part-time, temporary, or casual jobs, or employed as homeworkers or outworkers, typically without conventional employee rights.[23] There appears also to be a continuing process of stratification within the female labor force, with higher-paid employees having access to career breaks, childcare, etc., while working-class women have not.

As for ethnic minorities, the general growth of labor market insecurity in the 1980s probably weakened the effectiveness of anti-discrimination policies. Yet it is worth making the point here that the erosion of labor market security probably led to a relatively severe deterioration in the position of the white male working class, since it was the shrinking of industrial, unionized, protected jobs that characterized the period. This should not be interpreted as justifying any easing of pressure to combat discrimination, merely that the general erosion meant that those who had made the biggest gains in the previous era drifted backwards. Paradoxically, the stronger the segmentation of jobs the more that would have applied.

So, what can we conclude about labor market insecurity in the 1980s? Although it increased in both Europe and North America, the erosion was greater in Europe, in part because it had been one of the postwar achievements to have created societies in which labor market security had become the overwhelming norm. In the 1980s unemployment and the fear of it affected larger proportions of the population, even though it was concentrated on certain groups who not only have much higher probabilities of unemployment but much lower probabilities of escaping from it. Special measures and what are euphemistically called "active labor market policies" became part of the state response to these manifestations of labor market insecurity, as did workfare tendencies. Such responses partially concealed the erosion of labor market security, as did efforts to reduce labor supply, through early retirement, "training" programs removing youths from the labor force (as in France, for instance), and measures to encourage women to withdraw from or remain outside the labor force.

However, perhaps the most significant long-term development was the spread of labor market disadvantage and insecurity from hitherto "secondary workers," notably women, to prime age and older male workers, who had constituted the norm for social welfare and labor market policy in the postwar era of full employment. This is ironic. The libertarian ideology that dominated public discourse in the 1980s typically supports the notion of the traditional nuclear family, in which the man is in full-time wage or salaried employment while the woman is, first and foremost, a housewife. Yet as that ideology became more strident, the individualistic flexible labor markets were accentuating the erosion of that behavioral norm in practice.

THE SPREAD OF EMPLOYMENT INSECURITY

In the 1980s, there was also an erosion of employment security in most countries. In the welfare state era, it was the objective of policymakers that all those in jobs should be secure from arbitrary dismissal and be enabled to have stable employment. In the 1980s, that ideal faded into the wings, aided by measures derived from the unproven view that employment protection was a rigidity impeding the growth of employment and production. The conventional wisdom became that an erosion of employment security would strengthen labor market security, i.e., cut unemployment. The alleged trade-off has never been demonstrated empirically.

The spread of employment insecurity, rationalized by this new orthodoxy, was probably mainly due to a set of closely linked structural developments. These included the accelerated "deindustrialization" that whittled away industrial jobs, epitomized by the widespread closures and downsizing of manufacturing plants in the United States, which, according to Peter Doeringer's recent book on labor market "turbulence," displaced about two million jobs a year during the 1980s.[24] Other factors that reduced employment security were new managerial strategies of organization, new forms of technology, the pursuit of more flexible production and employment systems, the spread of service jobs, and the desire to avoid non-wage labor costs in the interest of international competitiveness and as a response to increased economic uncertainty.[25] In Europe, it was also associated with widespread privatization of European economies.[26]

The major trends are well known and are mentioned primarily as a means of highlighting labor market disadvantages that they bring in their wake, and which may contribute to their spread.[27] It is worth stressing that although most of the "flexible labor" categories that have been growing involve both employment insecurity and income insecurity as well as a threat of labor market marginalization and a tendency to slip into forms of "social exclusion," one should be cautious about generalizing from conventional work status statistics.[28]

The essence of the dominant trend was a move away from secure, full-time regular wage and salaried employment. Indicative of the growth of "flexiworkers," in the United Kingdom it has been estimated that by the end of 1991 about 40 percent of workers will be in jobs that are not regular, full-time wage employment, a large proportion of whom will legitimately not pay income tax and be excluded from contributory national insurance schemes such as unemployment and sickness benefits.[29] Although the erosion in employment security was most notable in services, similar trends occurred in other sectors, including agriculture, in which in the 1970s and 1980s, there was a shift from regular work to temporary jobs, self-employment, and subcontracting.[30]

The most widely documented trend is the growth of temporary and fixed-term contracts of employment. The growth reflects changes in enterprises' internal employment practices, increasing reliance on employment agencies, and structural changes in production that have propelled the growth of small-scale and other forms of enterprise utilizing large proportions of such forms of labor. We are not discussing a minor phenomenon. In West Germany, for example, by 1986 over a quarter of all workers were on fixed-term, part-time contracts.[31] And in the 1980s, half or more of all new employment created in France, West Germany, the Netherlands, Luxembourg, and Spain consisted of workers on temporary contracts.[32] In Portugal, after a remarkable growth, temporary contracts reached about 14 percent of total employment in 1988 and 40 percent of construction jobs.[33] In Spain, the government tried to reregulate the labor market by legalizing temporary contracts in the early 1980s, and by the late 1980s these accounted for one-third of all new jobs, leading to charges that job creation was largely job rotation.[34] In 1988, 527,000 fixed-term jobs were created, while 149,000 permanent jobs were lost, so that fixed-term contracts rose from 20

Table 4.1 / Change in the Number of Workers
in Full-Time Permanent Employment,
Great Britain: 1981–1988

Year	Male	Female	Both Sexes
1981*	82.2	53.2	70.5
1983	80.3	50.7	68.2
1987	76.1	48.0	64.1
1988	75.4	48.4	63.9

SOURCE: EUROSTAT. Labor Force Surveys, 1981–1988.

*In 1981, the data referred to those in full-time regular employment; from 1983 onwards they referred to those in full-time employment.

percent to 25 percent of total employment, or 29 percent of all private sector jobs.[35] Much the same pattern has been replicated in most of Europe.

The growth of temporary forms of employment has been associated with "deindustrialization." Many workers made redundant in manufacturing have ended up in temporary jobs elsewhere. For instance, in the industrial district of Lorraine, France, hit by the decline in the iron and steel industry, between 1984 and 1988 the number of insecure "interim companies" increased by over 50 percent, and recruitment on fixed term contracts increased from 58 percent of all jobs in 1983 to 65 percent in 1988 and 70 percent in 1989.[36] That was actively encouraged by legislation.

It has been claimed that the "casualization" of labor has grown more in Britain than in Continental Europe because in the former common law allowed a slide into casualization, whereas elsewhere legislative changes were required.[37] It is difficult to say definitively whether casual jobs have grown as a share of total employment, since many temporary jobs are part-time as well, so casualization may have been masked by the unquestioned growth of part-time employment. What is clear is that for both men and women there has been a declining share of full-time, permanent jobs in the United Kingdom (Table 4.1).

In practice, there has been little difference in casualization within Western Europe, since legislative changes in France,[38] Germany, Spain, and elsewhere have encouraged similar trends. Indeed, government's direct role in the growth of temporary employment and labor casualization has been insufficiently emphasized. Yet there is no evidence that the implied erosion of employment security led to more labor market security, via lower unemployment.[39] For example, in Germany, legislative erosion of employment protection and the consequent growth of fixed-term contracts had no effect on total employment.[40]

One way by which casualization has spread has been through the use of private employment agencies—contracting out the employment function—which has been linked to feminization of employment.[41] Although some countries still outlaw temporary work agencies (Greece, Italy, Spain), others (France,

Germany) have eased legislation restricting such employment. In West Germany, temporary work agencies trebled between 1982 and 1987, while labor supplied through agencies rose sharply, as it has in other countries, such as France and the United Kingdom.[42] The number of recognized temporary workers in the United States almost tripled between 1980 and 1988 to 1.1 million.[43] In Canada, employment contracts of under six months rose by nearly 2 percent a year between 1978 and 1988.[44] These short-term contracts have been mainly in traditional services, gone mostly to youths, and most have been part-time in small, nonunion firms where workers have lacked access to fringe benefits or pension plans.

Evidence of this trend can be seen in the growth of temporary help agencies. Already there is an International Confederation of Temporary Work Firms, which reported that temporary contracts grew by between 15 and 20 percent a year in the 1980s, a rate expected to grow after the EC's Single Market in 1992 has been established. Growth has been greatest in the Netherlands, France, Germany, the United Kingdom, and Belgium. The European Commission's concern for "social dumping" has led to consideration of new regulations, but the decision of the European Court of Justice in March 1990 authorizing Spanish and Portuguese firms to transfer their temporaries to work for them in other parts of Europe opened the door to further expansion.

In Canada, the number of people employed by temporary agencies tripled in the 1980s.[45] A 1988 survey found that 41 percent of those doing such work did so because they could not find regular full-time jobs. Mostly it was clerical work, and 70 percent of those involved were women; typically, they earned lower wages than other workers and had minimal fringe benefits.

Besides temporary labor, other means by which employment insecurity has grown have included the shift from large-scale to small-scale firms—as in Spain and the United Kingdom[46]—and the much-discussed growth of subcontracting, outworking, and homeworking, positions overwhelmingly low paid and occupied by women.[47] In the United States, the number employed by subcontractors rose from 3.3 million in 1980 to 5.6 million in 1988.[48]

The growth of subcontracting has reflected the shift to services, and has inflated the statistical growth of service employment insofar as service functions have been shifted from other industrial sectors. This may have given an impression that the new service employment has consisted mainly of "good" jobs, since many jobs contracted out are likely to be production-related services.[49]

The notion of self-employment, like so many labor categories, can be hard to interpret. In the United Kingdom and elsewhere, there has been a growth in those classified as self-employed who in most respects should be called employees but who pay their own national insurance.[50] In the United Kingdom, at least, self-employment has often involved part-time work, with a growing share of both male and female "self-employed" working fewer than 16 hours a week.[51] In Canada, own-account working accounted for 10 percent of job growth between 1978 and 1988. That was mostly in traditional services, involving lower earnings and more variable income. In 1986, just over half of the self-employed workers in Canada earned less than $10,000, compared with 27 percent of paid workers.[52]

The growth of what is covered by self-employment is linked to the so-called informal and "black" economy. Although these notions are conceptual mine-fields, in essence they cover activities beyond the control of government regula-tions.[53] Much informal economy work is illegal, but of immediate relevance is that most activities involve a high degree of employment insecurity, because they are outside the state regulatory framework. While its scale is unknown, the informal economy is widely believed to have grown considerably in the 1980s. In Spain, for instance, the black economy accounted for a quarter of all employment, with about 300,000 out of 800,000 known immigrants in the underground economy.[54] Throughout Europe, incomes in the informal economy are usually low and precarious, and it is likely that such forms of working erode the incomes and benefits of those on lower rungs of the formal labor market.

A third aspect of employment insecurity has been the growth of part-time employment, much of which has been "involuntary."[55] Part-time working has spread more in Europe than in the United States, but has risen in the United States too, albeit slowly as a proportion of total employment.[56] In Europe there have been extreme variations in the rate and level of this growth (Table 4.2). Thus, in Sweden over 20 percent of employment is part-time; in neighboring Finland the official figure has hovered around 8 percent.[57] Yet internationally the dominant trend has been upward. A typical example is Canada, where between 1953 and the 1980s, part-time jobs grew from 4 percent to 15 percent of total employment, and from 1975 to 1988 contributed over 30 percent of employment growth.[58] In other respects too, Canada has been typical. Involun-

Table 4.2 / **Women in Part-Time Employment as Percentage of Total Female Employment, EC Countries: 1979–1985**

Country	1979	1981	1983	1985
Belgium	17	16	20	22
Denmark	46	47	45	44
France	17	17	20	22
FRG	28	29	30	30
Greece	—	7	12	10
Ireland	13	—	16	16
Italy	11	10	9	10
Luxembourg	18	—	18	16
Netherlands	32	49	50	52
U.K.	39	40	42	45

SOURCE: EUROSTAT. *Labor Force Sample Surveys, 1979–1985.*

NOTE: Part-time was based on self-definition, except in the Neth-erlands, the definition of which was changed in 1981 (although in both 1979 and 1981 it was based on under 40 hours) and again in 1983, when the cut-off was lowered to under 35.

tary part-time work grew in the 1980s to 24 percent of all part-time employment, and during the decade nearly half of all new part-time jobs were classified as "involuntary."[59] In the United States, the involuntary share has risen as well.[60]

Part-time jobs tend to be short-term, nonunion, and in small firms, giving the workers fewer benefits and lower wages. This is less true in France than in some other countries, because since legislation in 1981, part-time and full-time workers are supposed to have equal rights. However, even there part-time working has been linked with precariousness.[61] In West Germany, one of the countries where legislation in the 1980s eroded protective regulations, precarious forms of employment multiplied, many on a part-time basis. Wages in so-called marginal part-time jobs there may not be lower, but access to negotiated fringe benefits is much less likely. In the United States as well, part-time workers typically receive much lower hourly wage rates, and make up about two-thirds of those paid at or below the minimum wage.[62]

The growth of part-time employment has been linked to the rise in female employment. In most European countries (except Sweden, where the level of part-time work has long been very high), a growing proportion of women have been working on a part-time temporary or casual basis, or as home- or outworkers, usually without the range of rights of regular employees. A comparative survey of the United Kingdom and the Netherlands showed that those forms of working were associated with lack of access to benefits, employment insecurity, low pay, and exclusion from legal protection available to full-time, regular employees.[63]

The impact of social security and other "non-wage labor costs" on part-time employment is controversial. In the United Kingdom, part-time jobs have been encouraged because employers pay no national insurance contributions on workers earning less than a threshold income. Part-timers are not normally covered by employment protection because they have to be employed continuously for more than two years and/or working for over 16 hours a week, and thus many are not entitled to redundancy pay, maternity pay, unfair dismissal protection, or the right to return to work after maternity leave. In Germany, most part-time jobs are not covered by firm-specific pension plans, negotiated fringe benefits or 13th month pay, bonuses, holiday allowances, etc. Consequently, as much as 30–40 percent of non-wage labor costs, are saved by using casual part-time workers.[64]

In sum, combining part-time, temporary, indirect, and self-employment, there has been a strong international erosion of employment security.[65] To give just one aggregative example, in Canada, "Between 1981 and 1986, these four forms of non-standard employment [part-time, short-term, own-account and temporary agency employment] accounted for about half of all new jobs; they now represent nearly 30 percent of total employment."[66] Some of such growth may have been due to the slack labor market, some to demographic trends. Yet few analysts doubt that it is a long-term trend. It has been growing in manufacturing as well as in services, has been strongly associated with small firms and nonunion enterprises, and has resulted in much more movement between employment, unemployment, and economic inactivity.[67] The overall trend raises questions about access to work-related benefits. But, of course, one's concern over any erosion of employment security would be muted if there were a high degree of labor market security, which as argued is questionable, or if there were a high degree of income and other forms of labor security. Are the trends there any better?

APPREHENSIONS OVER WORK SECURITY

Considering the third form of labor security, the erosion of labor market and employment security has probably resulted in a decline in various aspects of occupational safety and working conditions, partly because the bargaining position of the most insecure in those respects is likely to lead them to have to accept more onerous or risky work. Thus, a recent report by the World Health Organization concluded that as a result of flexibilization of labor contracts there had been a substantial increase in work-related accidents, most notably among the "self-employed" in the construction industry.[68]

So-called shadow work, or undeclared employment, almost definitionally means lack of entitlement to health or disability insurance, and apparently is associated with more exposure to toxic substances and other dangers. Part-time workers are also more unlikely to be covered by health insurance than full-time regular employees in the United States, and in some other countries as well.[69] Moreover, in the United States a growing proportion of involuntary part-time workers have lacked health insurance.[70] Work insecurity is also likely to have been increased by legislation designed to "deregulate" working time.[71] Thus, more workers may be obliged to work "unsocial hours" or long shifts, which are prone to cause physical and medical problems. The example of Japan's workaholism is setting worrying standards that with "deregulation" of working time could be emulated in Europe and North America.[72]

An erosion of work security could also be expected to accompany any erosion of labor representation security, which will be considered in the next section. Thus, in the United States, work-related fatalities have typically been much higher in "right-to-work" states, where unions have been unable to press collective safety demands as effectively as in other states.[73]

In sum, as other forms of labor security facilitate work security, any erosion of those will weaken it and reduce the effectiveness of occupational health and safety regulations.

THE THREAT TO JOB AND OCCUPATIONAL SECURITY

A prominent claim of the 1980s, which will surely continue to be heard in the 1990s, was that workers would have to be more flexible in terms of skills and will be expected to change tasks more often. The old Taylorist "assembly-line" model has supposedly had its day. We now have the prospect of a "post-

Fordist" labor process, based on "flexible specialization." This image may appeal to those who anticipate a working life of variety and autonomy. But for many in the mainstream of society it offers the prospect of job insecurity, necessitating the repeated learning of "new tricks" or the prospect of failing to remain in that mainstream. It is not frequent career changes that beckon but frequent job changes; a career remains the prerogative of an elite.

According to the U.S. Department of Labor, the average worker in the United States will hold about five jobs in two or three different career areas.[74] David Birch estimated, "The career-oriented college graduate today will hold 10 to 12 jobs in more than one industry before retiring. The normal stay of a graduate in one company will average around 3 or 4 years. One in five persons now changes jobs every year; one in ten changes careers."[75] If that process involves a steady expansion of knowledge and valued experience, well and good. But how likely is that?

In that vein, Doeringer's study of industrial turbulence in the United States in the 1980s suggests that career advancement has become less predictable, compensation increases less routine and contingent, and insecure jobs far more common. By the late 1980s, one-third of male workers in manufacturing were ending their career jobs by the age of 55, leaving them to rely on "bridging jobs"—involving substantial cuts in earnings—in the interim before statutory retirement.

One little-discussed aspect of job insecurity is that if there is to be less job and career stability, firms can be expected to seek workers who have different behavioral characteristics than they would seek if long-term job stability was the goal. This may help to alter the labor market patterning of advantage and disadvantage, perhaps contributing to the feminization process and the labor marginalization of older workers.

According to studies in Canada, employers are increasingly seeking workers with the specific qualities of adaptability, communication and interpersonal skills.[76] In Canada, although there was a relative growth of so-called highly skilled jobs, comprising 77 percent of employment growth from 1981 to 1986, compared to a third from 1971 to 1981—the skill distribution has become more polarized, in part it seems because in services there are fewer "intermediate skills" than in manufacturing. The drift away from regular, protected, full-time employment also weakens job security. Part-timers are commonly "dead-ended" in jobs, being given little access to training or promotion. It is unlikely that they will be able to obtain effective skills or training to advance them in any occupation. Job insecurity also implies more labor market risk and uncertainty and more scope for workers to make mistakes and thus fall out of the economic mainstream. A society in which most of its members obtain a niche at an early age, and remain in it until "retirement," requires and tends to generate a very different network of social support and income protection than one in which job changing and shifts between labor market statuses are a recurring, uncertain part of lifetime activity.

LABOR REPRODUCTION INSECURITY: SOURCE OF STRATIFICATION?

Partly because it is covered in other chapters, only a few remarks will be made on what we call labor reproduction security. This should not be taken as suggesting that it is of lower priority than other forms—indeed its significance has surely grown. There are reasons for arguing that a shift to job-oriented schooling and labor market training has been a shift towards market regulation, and that by itself privatization of social policy in this and related areas has meant that labor reproductive security has been strengthened for the more privileged and eroded for lower-income groups.

With the spread of more flexible labor relations and systems of production, broadly based higher-level education or access to craft-based vocational training have become more crucial for gaining socioeconomic mobility and income security than where mass production predominated, based on a hierarchical technical division of labor. As a result, in the 1980s the need for an effective state system for education and skill formation increased. Yet in the United States, United Kingdom, and a number of other countries, it shrunk or stagnated, or at best lagged behind the needs of the time.[77]

One indicator of this failure is that in the United States the expected incomes of secondary school-leavers have fallen sharply relative to those with college education. The stratifying tendency of the schooling system always present has grown, strengthening the economic security of the elite minority, whose academic education enables them to flourish in the international economy, and eroding the labor security of the majority, who cannot obtain entry to meaningful postsecondary education or vocational training. The recent report by the Labor Secretary's Commission on Achieving Necessary Skills (SCANS) concluded that more than half of all young people leave school lacking the skills needed to obtain productive employment.[78] Their disadvantage is then compounded by the fact that few firms provide occupational training, which must be distinguished from job training, based on imparting "minimal modules of employable skill." Most expenditure on training by corporations is actually spent on employees with college education. Formal apprenticeships have practically disappeared, and according to the National Center on Education and the Economy, only a handful of prominent companies (0.5 percent of the total) account for more than 90 percent of all expenditure on training.

With certain exceptions, the situation in Europe (except the United Kingdom) seems to have been much better, with some countries such as Germany, with its "dual system," and Sweden, with its school-based vocational orientation, having provided more effective labor reproduction security than others. However, the stratifying tendencies seem to have grown there as well, in large part because of the growth of flexiworking, which threatens to involve a growing minority in a whirlwind of short-term jobs, short-term "training," and consequent labor insecurity.[79]

This chapter does not go into the links between "skill formation" and job insecurity. Yet the shift from pro-collective regulations to pro-individualistic labor market regulation that has characterized international labor markets in the past decade has surely encouraged an underinvestment in technical skills. If job-changing and career-changing become more common, young people will be less inclined to invest in any one set of skills, because the expected return will be less.[80] Similarly, if the free labor contract is promoted by flexibility legislation, firms will have a lower expected return to investment in training. This means that skills will tend to be underproduced, since they are in essence a "collective good." The problem is that occupational security is reduced by reliance on market regulation, and only if mechanisms for sharing the benefits and costs of skill generation are found will that change.

LABOR REPRESENTATION: THE DIMINISHING VOICE?

When it comes to representative rights, emotion runs high, and with good reason. A basic premise of this chapter is that unless there are effective institutional mechanisms for representing the aspirations, interests, and needs of the vulnerable strata in the labor process, all forms of labor security will be diminished. And, in particular, unless organizations exist to represent the potential losers in more flexible labor markets, the latter will be associated with the growth of all forms of labor insecurity.

Trade unions have been the main vehicle for achieving labor representation security, and though unions have been criticized for having been ineffectual in protecting women and minorities, such claims are controversial and to some extent unfair. Their "sword of justice" effect has been substantial.[81] The problem is that they are ill-equipped to function in flexible labor markets. In many countries, a debate has raged over whether trade unions are fatally in decline, temporarily weakened by the prolonged years of recession, or in fact barely scathed. We cannot dwell at length on this most crucial of issues, since that goes beyond the mandate of this chapter, which is simply to characterize labor market trends. However, one cannot validly analyze the causes and implications of social marginalization and poverty without considering representation rights, mechanisms, and institutions. So, a few points are worth noting.

The 1980s was a period of deunionization, not only in the United States, where the share of the labor force in trades unions shrunk to about 13 percent, but in most industrialized economies. Unionization is probably at the lowest level in France, where it has fallen to 9 percent. In the United Kingdom, membership of the Trades Union Congress declined by a third in the 1980s to a little over eight million. However, there and elsewhere, declining unionization underestimates the real declines, since an increasing proportion of union membership has consisted of retired workers, as in Italy, or nonemployed members. Declines have been concentrated in the private sector, but fairly high and relatively stable unionization in the public sector has been affected by efforts to privatize social services.

The trends in deunionization result from a powerful combination of factors. First, high unemployment and labor market insecurity has eroded membership.[82] The reasons are both direct (fewer workers are employed) and indirect (the unemployed receive fewer benefits from collective bargaining and dues are higher relative to their incomes, so they cease to pay affiliation dues). High unemployment also, of course, makes it easier for employers to resist or derecognize unions and makes it harder for workers to organize or have the confidence to do so.

Second, most of the jobs being generated have been less "unionable." Workers outside regular, full-time employment are much less likely to be in unions.[83] For example, individuals in temporary jobs are rarely unionized, so the growth of such jobs has directly and indirectly weakened representation security. Thus, employment insecurity and job-occupational insecurity have tended to erode industrial and craft unionism. Mostly, this has reflected organizational difficulties, and the difficulty of integrating part-time and intermittent workers into existing union structures. But it is also due to legal factors. As a well-known AFL-CIO report noted, "Working people not classified as 'employees' in the labor laws are subject to open reprisal for seeking to join a union and have no legal right of recourse."[84]

Third, the changing composition of the labor force has been a factor in lower unionization rates; intermittent and marginalized labor force participants being less inclined to join or remain in unions.[85]

Fourth, governments have taken advantage of the changing power base of unions to tighten legislation, making recognition harder and derecognition easier, and limiting the right to strike.

Fifth, employers have been emboldened by the weakness of their institutional adversaries to restrict the capacity of union bargaining or to bypass unions altogether. As the Executive Director of the Confederation of British Industry said in 1990, "Employee relations increasingly feature the culture of the individual."

Sixth, labor decentralization, within existing corporations or through the extension of subcontracting and the spread of small-scale units, makes organization and retention much harder. As one study concluded, "Under a decentralized structure . . . recognition is a vital issue at every plant in an industry. Even allowing for pattern-setting, there will be differences in terms and conditions between plants, and if the non-union sector is or becomes sizeable, it may significantly affect union bargaining power in the organized plants."[86]

Finally, unions themselves have been tempted or forced to concede representation rights, and in so doing have become less able to expand or hold on to members. In the 1960s, unions could often force nonunionized firms to recognize unions; in the 1980s, they were more likely to offer employers job flexibility (occupational insecurity) and no-strike agreements.

The very legitimacy of trades unions has been eroded by the incessant attack on them. One distinguished labor historian has written that "the dissolution of the labor movement [in Britain is] . . . the counter-revolution of our time."[87]

He believes that by the turn of the century private-sector unionized plants will be a rarity, confined to the north of the country. In the United States, it is a remarkable commentary that in early 1990, when unionization was at its lowest and weakest for generations, an opinion poll reported that 40 percent of the public believed that unions had too much power and only 22 percent thought they did not have enough.[88] Somewhat more alarming, to the extent that the poll was fair, was that 50 percent of the public believed that private-sector workers should not have the right to strike without the risk of losing their jobs; only 47 percent stated that they should have that right.

Unions have been shown to help relatively vulnerable groups in the labor market more than others, even though they are frequently castigated for being dominated by white male workers. Often, in the absence of unions the plight of those on the margins of the labor market can be much bleaker, simply because they have such weak bargaining power without a collective voice to give them support. Thus, one study estimated that whereas white men gained a wage premium of about 50 cents an hour from union membership in the United States in the late 1980s, black men gained about $1.61, Hispanic men about $2.18, white women about $0.83, black women $1.23, and Hispanic women $1.53.[89] Another study showed that workers residing in "right-to-work" states in the United States typically have fewer entitlements to fringe benefits, have higher accident rates, and are much less likely to have income security provided by minimum wage laws. In 1989, eight right-to-work states had no minimum wage laws, and only four had minimum wages equal to or above the federal minimum wage.[90]

The weakening of unions is evident in many ways; and the growing inability of workers to have voice in the labor market is one of the most worrying developments of the era. Although distinguished industrial relations talk of an emerging "de facto system of governance for the workforce" and workers as "stakeholders" in modern corporations,[91] this appears to be a minority phenomenon and scarcely meets the requirements of the time.

THE EROSION OF INCOME SECURITY

Corresponding to the regrowth of other forms of labor insecurity, the 1980s witnessed an erosion of income security. In both North America and Western Europe, the number classified as "poor" grew, as did various forms of income inequality, many of which were linked to labor market developments. Many analysts, particularly in the United States, have discussed the trends in terms of the "declining middle"; others, less persuasively, have referred to the growth of a "two-thirds" society, the supposition being that a large minority of marginalized, mostly unemployed or economically inactive people have been unable to share in the income gained by a majority over the past decade. Neither the "declining middle" nor the "two-thirds society" image adequately captures the essence of the changing level and distribution of labor insecurity that has accentuated inequality and poverty. A more useful image is one of labor *fragmentation*, with different groups losing or winning in distinctive ways.[92]

A few stylized facts are worth noting. First, as other chapters have shown, in many countries poverty has increased—larger numbers and larger proportions of national populations are living below national standards of income adequacy—on both sides of the Atlantic. Since 1975, poverty in EC countries has increased quite considerably. According to the European Commission, in 1989 about 44 million people (14 percent of the EC population) were living in poverty, that is, receiving an income less than half their national average.[93]

Second, poverty has been linked to labor market activity much more than it used to be. In the United States, lower government transfers and real wages have been blamed for the increasing incidence of poverty.[94] In Europe, according to a report of the EC's Economic and Social Committee, the resurgence of poverty in the 1980s was due primarily to the growth and persistence of unemployment, underemployment, and precarious low-paid employment, followed by the increase in single-parent families.

The tendency for unemployment to lead to a drift into poverty (defining those in poverty as receiving less than a poverty line of 50 percent of the country's median equivalent expenditure) was demonstrated in a study by Teekens and Zaidi[95] who estimated that households with an unemployed head were usually more likely than most others to be in poverty. In the United States, unemployment due to industrial restructuring has been associated with a lifetime lowering of earnings; between a quarter and a third of workers displaced by plant closures or downsizing suffered permanently lower incomes.[96]

There is also ample evidence that income inequality has worsened in many countries. The United States' story is too well rehearsed to bear much repetition; few question the trend, though some believe it is reversible, others seem to think it is irreversible. In the United Kingdom, inequality has grown sharply since the late 1970s. Using the Family Expenditure Survey and other official data, dividing the population into five strata, Ormerod and Salama calculated annual average growth in real income between 1977 and 1990.[97] The higher the group, the greater the rise in real income. This could not be explained by changes in tax policy alone. At the bottom, it was due in part to the level of benefits being tied to price rises; for the middle groups, a slow rise was apparently due to the impact of technological change being unmatched by any rise in education or training. They concluded, "The increasing premium placed on skill—and the increasing lack of employability of the unskilled—bodes ill for the disappearance of the underclass in Britain" (Table 4.3).

In France, after narrowing for much of the postwar era, income inequality increased in the 1980s, with property owners doing better than wage earners and the old better than the young. This has been attributed to industrial restructuring and financial liberalization; the young paid much of the price for recovery from the crisis of the 1970s. For the first time since 1945, a new generation joined the workforce on less favorable terms than its predecessor, in terms of jobs and incomes. Wage constraint during the 1980s meant that from 1982 to

Table 4.3 / **Changes in Earnings Distribution, Great Britain: 1979–1989**

	Percentage	
	1979	1989
Men		
Top decile male earnings as a percentage of median male earnings	156.9	179.9
Bottom decile male earnings as a percentage of median male earnings	66.0	58.5
Women		
Top decile female earnings as a percentage of median female earnings	158.6	180.5
Bottom decile male earnings as a percentage of median female earnings	69.4	63.1

SOURCE: New Earnings Surveys, 1979 and 1989.

NOTE: Data covered all industries and services, full-time workers on adult rates, with pay not affected by work absences.

1988 real wages fell by 2 percent. But white collar workers were much less affected than blue collar workers, and the higher the management scale the greater the widening of incomes.[98]

In Canada, workers' real compensation peaked in 1977 and had declined slightly a decade later.[99] This has been attributed to slower productivity growth and workers' reduced bargaining power.[100] Whatever the reasons, workers' earnings became more polarized.[101] The Gini coefficient rose to 0.42; the relative size of the middle-income group, defined as having income within 25 percent of the median on either side, shrunk from 27 percent in 1967 to 22 percent in 1986, while there were roughly equal shifts to the upper and lower income groups.

In many countries wage differentials between industries, occupational groups, and the sexes widened or at most stopped narrowing in the 1980s. That was true even where considerable efforts were made to reduce such differentials, such as Sweden and Finland.[102] We need not deal with this in detail, but, as suggested in the chapter by Peter Gottschalk and Mary Joyce, data in many countries suggest that wage differentials have grown, implying increased income insecurity in the lower part of the earnings spectrum.

Conventional data on incomes and wages almost certainly understate the growth of inequality within the labor market, because rather more of the gains at the higher end of the earnings spectrum have been in new forms of payment or in forms not fully captured by more traditional indices, while workers at the lower end of the spectrum have tended to lose such forms of payment, including both enterprise fringe benefits and other forms of non-wage payments, and access to state-guaranteed employment-linked benefits. At best the losers may have only been partially compensated by higher money wages.

Finally, labor casualization and employment insecurity have eroded income security. The growth of part-time and insecure forms of employment worsened inequality by pushing more workers into low-paying jobs; in the United States, over 40 percent of the increase in wage inequality in the early 1980s has been attributed to the growth of part-time employment and the widening gap between the earnings of part-time and full-time workers.[103] This further emphasizes how the various forms of labor insecurity are linked.

Labor casualization has had many indirect effects on income insecurity, such as limiting access to credit or making it more costly for those in irregular forms of employment.[104] In the United Kingdom, one of the paradoxes of so-called "deregulation" in the 1980s was that as a result of more widespread "house ownership" and more flexible forms of employment, numerous working-class households, and many who believed they had middle-class status, sank into a cycle of debt and dispossession.[105] Finally, because the growth of labor insecurity affected mostly those who had gained most from the regulated labor market era, the poverty rates of "demographic" groups (age, gender, ethnic groups) became more alike in the 1980s. In the United States, the rates among blacks and Hispanics actually fell, even though their levels remained nearly three times that of whites.[106] Deindustrialization, erosion of labor representation security, and "market regulation" may all have contributed to the deterioration among the mainstream working class.

CRISIS OF SOCIAL PROTECTION

Developments in European and North American labor markets in recent years have also been associated with an erosion in social protection. In Europe, this has occurred even though all EC countries have ratified 20 ILO conventions guaranteeing protection, and the Council of Europe's Social Charter, introduced in 1965, guarantees the right to social security.[107] Yet disentitlement to state transfers has been widespread, and at the lower end of the labor market those relying on transfers have had lower than average rises in earnings, in some countries because benefits have been linked to prices, which have risen more slowly than earnings.[108] In certain countries, such as Germany, earlier gains in social protection for disadvantaged groups of workers may have been eroded because they were not perceived as the basis for efficient economic policy, as if their social protection has not been seen as consistent with cutting unemployment.[109]

While higher-income groups have improved their access to benefits, the share of workers receiving occupational (enterprise-specific) benefits may have fallen, as the proportion entitled to state benefits has done, along with their income replacement value. All three trends would contribute to a decline in social protection among those at the lower end of the labor market.

A loss has been due in part to sectoral shifts in employment that result in "implicit deregulation." For example, in Italy, the *cassa integrazione guadagni* (payment of subsidies during a firm's restructuring) is in practice only paid to large firms in industry and construction. So, the trend towards small and service-oriented firms implies loss of entitlement. The spread of small firms elsewhere has also been associated with nonentitlement to occupational welfare.

Table 4.4 / **Enrollment in Pension and Health Plans of Firms, by Full-Time and Part-Time Status, by Gender and Occupation; U.S.: 1987**

	Included in Pension		Included in Health Plan	
	Part-Time	Full-Time	Part-Time	Full-Time
Male Family Heads				
All workers	18.3	58.5	37.1	79.0
Professional, managerial, technical	24.5	67.6	43.6	86.1
Sales	18.5	44.2	38.7	75.3
Clerical	17.6	70.0	44.1	84.8
Service	12.9	55.6	27.8	71.8
Craft, operational, labor	17.7	54.5	36.5	75.2
Female Family Heads				
All workers	14.2	50.2	25.6	74.1
Professional, managerial, technical	23.0	62.4	41.3	85.9
Sales	11.8	31.9	20.5	60.3
Clerical	20.6	55.9	36.8	82.1
Service	8.1	28.3	17.2	46.4
Craft, operational, labor	18.8	45.2	22.8	69.1

SOURCE: R.M. Blank, "Are Part-Time Jobs Bad Jobs?" In G. Burtless (ed.). *A Future of Lousy Jobs?* (Washington, D.C.: Brookings Institution, 1990), Table 4, p.30.

The growth of flexible labor relations erodes occupational welfare in various ways. It has particularly affected pension entitlement, and helps explain why women's pensions in European countries are from 20 percent to 60 percent lower than men's. In West Germany, the gender difference was about 60 percent.[110] By being more concentrated in part-time and temporary employment, women are much less likely to receive earnings-related pensions or to belong to occupational pension schemes. In Denmark, women working for fewer than 10 hours a week or fewer than 43.33 hours a month, have no right to the labor market benefit (ATP) entitling them to pension benefits. In the Netherlands, although one can take personal pension insurance with private life insurance companies, about 20 percent of those who change jobs, mostly women, lose supplementary pension (PB1). By such means, employment insecurity, or labor flexibility, is associated with growing income insecurity. In the United States, those in part-time jobs are also far less likely than full-time workers to be enrolled in their enterprise's pension or health schemes (Table 4.4).

Similarly, the emphasis in many countries on earnings-related benefits has penalized those in more flexible or insecure labor statuses. For example, in Germany earnings-related schemes trebly increase women's labor market disadvantage.[111] The effect of wage discrimination that women typically face is transferred fully into the state pension; women in irregular employment lose pension income because of the effect of "missing years," due to child-raising; and under the state pension scheme, workers lose pension income if any months in the working life are missed, a regulation called "Halbbelegung." And in Germany and elsewhere, workers in flexible labor suffer income insecurity through "vesting clauses"; i.e., pension entitlement being a function of time in the company and minimum age when entitlement is gained, which in Germany has been 10 years and age 35. A claim can expire with even a short break in employment, which of course adversely affects women and all those in flexible employment.

Clearly, the income disadvantages of anybody subject to a working life of labor market insecurity will be less where the system relies on tax-financed, flat-rate pension schemes (as operate in Denmark and the Netherlands, for example), than where earnings-related state pensions are the norm (Germany, the United States), or where earnings-related occupational schemes operate (as in the United States, United Kingdom, and Germany).[112] In the 1990s, as part-time, noncontinuous, and nonprotected work gain importance, it will become essential to introduce poverty-preventing minimum standards guaranteed by a basic pension scheme.

EXPLICIT AND IMPLICIT "DISENTITLEMENT"

While growing numbers of labor force participants fail to obtain occupational welfare, the income insecurity of those on the margins of the labor market has increased by what we can call explicit and implicit disentitlement. By the former, we mean that more and tighter conditions have limited entitlement to state (and private) transfers, notably unemployment benefits and "social assistance." By implicit disentitlement is meant the tendency for existing conditions to become more restrictive by virtue of changing labor market statuses, experiences, and behavior. Patchy though the data may be, it seems that the proportion of potential recipients actually receiving state transfers has fallen and that this has had slightly more to do with implicit than explicit disentitlement.

Typically, entitlement to social security has been subject to seven conditions, most of which have led to rising levels of nonentitlement, in part because conditions have been tightened and because of the more flexible, insecure work experience of those in the lower reaches of the labor market. The seven major conditions deserve to be recalled in so far as they relate to unemployment benefits. We have no space to discuss their ramifications in detail, but the hypothesis is that each has become more of a barrier to entitlement.

First, those wishing to receive benefits usually have to register at a local employment exchange. In some countries only those registered and regularly attending an employment office are counted as unemployed, which means that many genuinely unemployed do not qualify for unemployment benefits. The rationale is well known. But employment offices should surely be primarily for the provision of labor market assistance and information. Too often they are regarded by job-seekers with distrust, fear, or skepticism and are ignored by firms that prefer to hire workers by other means. Desired registration will be low unless the exchanges are seen by job-seekers as an efficient avenue to employment and are not seen as primarily administrative offices regulating and monitoring their behavior. Yet often the unemployed register only because it is a condition for benefit receipt, which imparts a stigma from the outset, while many do not register precisely because they believe they will not be entitled to benefits.[113] The difficulty is that in a high-unemployment environment, the regulatory role of employment exchanges will grow, the need for employers to resort to them will fall, and the consequent registration propensity will become weaker.

Second, to be entitled usually a person must have been "actively seeking" employment in a recent period, usually the past 1 or 4 weeks. This too is not without problems. There is not much point searching for work where none is available. But the rule itself invites abuse, notably that of intrusion by employment office officials into the lives of potential recipients. Governments wishing to cut social security expenditure typically tighten the application of such rules, making them more likely to screen out those needing benefits.

Third, a common condition to be counted as unemployed or to be entitled to unemployment benefit is that the person must satisfy some record of past employment. This actually combines two conditions. A typical rule is that an individual must have been in recognized employment for 3 of the previous 12 months. There may be pragmatic fiscal reasons for specifying what is counted as employment and the number of months, but in behavioral terms the rule is bound to be somewhat arbitrary. For example, someone who worked part-time for 4 months might qualify for benefits, while someone who worked full-time for 2 months may not. Given the growing flexibility of labor markets and the tendency for more of the workforce to be in temporary jobs or move in and out of the labor force, this condition may be more responsible than any other for declines in the proportion of the unemployed receiving unemployment benefits in the 1980s. Quite simply, fewer people are likely to have the requisite work record.

A fourth rule is that unemployment should not have started "voluntarily." The rationale is that this discourages workers from being irresponsible in work. Most states in the United States disqualify those reported to have quit their past job "without just cause" and do so for the whole of their unemployment. In other countries the practice is less draconian, disqualifying them from benefits for an initial period. But in some countries the rule has been tightened, discouraging and penalizing labor mobility. Among the many administrative changes introduced in the United Kingdom in the 1980s, the disqualification period was extended from 6 to 13 weeks and then to 26. Such changes can have impressive effects on the official levels of unemployment.

However, the increasingly flexible labor process makes such behavioral rules harder to apply with any consistency or fairness, and more likely to result in the unemployed losing entitlement to benefits. The procedure is subjective, because the distinction between voluntary quitting and being declared redundant or laid off is not always clear. Moreover, workers do not like to admit their enterprise declared them of no use, making the condition a source of embarrassment at the very least.

A fifth condition for entitlement, and sometimes for being counted officially as unemployed, is that the person must not have refused a job deemed "suitable" by an employment office. The rationale is that this demonstrates availability and willingness to work, and that the unemployment is not voluntary. But is the rule needed? There are perfectly good reasons for the unemployed to accept jobs if they believe they suit their skills and aspirations, since remaining unemployed for a long time diminishes the probability of escaping into decent employment. The rule also invites bureaucratic intrusiveness and the presumption that some local official knows better than the job-seeker what is best for him. However, it raises the problem of defining what is "suitable." If the rule is applied tightly, it will often mean that the unemployed is forced to accept a job paying much less than his previous one or lose benefits. This is more likely if employment exchanges are under pressure to demonstrate "success" by increasing their employment placement rate. Such a rush may not be in the best long-term interest of their so-called clients. Several countries, including Australia, have amended their benefit rules to stipulate that the unemployed must accept temporary jobs if offered. Yet this may encourage the trend to labor casualization and undermine the unemployed's subsequent entitlements.

A sixth condition is that the unemployed must have been out of employment for less than a certain number of months, after which benefits expire or are sharply cut. The rationale presumably is that such a prospect concentrates the mind of the unemployed on taking a job. But it is as likely to lead them to make poor long-term decisions, perhaps by taking a temporary job that offers no chance to build up entitlement to benefits before a new spell of unemployment hits them, or taking an unsuitable job from which they subsequently quit "voluntarily," thereby disentitling them to benefits. Above all, where long-term unemployment is high, the condition will encourage many unemployed to withdraw from the legitimate labor force.

The seventh condition for entitlement—applied to unemployment assistance rather than to unemployment insurance schemes—is that the unemployed must have no other source of income. The rationale is that it identifies need for employment. Means tests and income tests may have been reasonable in the early days of the welfare state, when the norm was that the unemployment benefit regime applied in effect mainly to married men, the presumption being that their wives were not working for income. Always dubious, this rule has become increasingly onerous and a source of income insecurity. If an income test is applied on a family-unit basis, an unemployed man with a working wife may be disqualified from all or part of his benefit, making it financially advantageous for the wife to become unemployed as well. So the rule could swell the pool of unemployed, though ironically if a wife quit her job "voluntarily" she herself might not be counted as unemployed or receive benefits. It is for such reasons that, controlling for other influences, in the United Kingdom wives of unemployed men have a lower labor force participation rate than other married women.[114]

The "unemployment traps" and "poverty traps" created by means tests and income tests became more pervasive in the 1980s. They are most likely for those in the lower end of the labor market, if the rule is that they would lose the right to benefits if they obtained any job or other source of income. As the poor can rarely take a long-term attitude to such matters, this is a disincentive to take part-time or low-paying jobs, even though those might offer the prospect of developing into higher-paying jobs. If they took such jobs, they might lose more in benefits than they would gain from working, or the gain would be insufficient to act as an incentive. In the 1980s, such tendencies worsened in various countries, such as the Netherlands.[115] A reason was that many of the new "flexible" jobs are lower-productivity and/or less well-paid than those that have been disappearing. And many are taken by women, who ironically are less likely to be caught in an unemployment trap because they do not qualify for benefits.

Such traps impede labor market efficiency, besides increasing income insecurity in the lower reaches of the labor market. They induce some to remain unemployed "involuntarily," some to work in the informal economy where they can escape being penalized by loss of benefits. Means tests also create a disincentive to personal saving, increasing the unemployed's vulnerability to impoverishment. And it is partly because the eligibility criterion creates unemployment traps that many governments have cut the "income replacement" ratio (the average value of benefit compared to previous income), to increase the work "incentive," even in jobs paying less than previous work.

The irony is that because of the way labor markets have been developing, many benefit regimes have relied increasingly on means-tested and income-tested social assistance. Indeed, in many countries, even though a national unemployment insurance scheme exists, a majority of the unemployed now depend on means-tested or income-tested assistance.

One conclusion is clear. With proportionately fewer in regular, full-time wage employment, and with more labor market and employment insecurity, income security cannot be provided by unemployment benefit systems based on behavioral conditions for entitlement. They become primarily regulatory devices and only partially protect the unemployed, since even if benefits are paid, income protection is far from secure. Thus, in the United States about 20 percent of the long-term unemployed receiving UI (Unemployment Insurance) receive less than the income defined as the poverty threshold. Among UI benefit recipients who were sole earners in their families, the poverty rate was over 40 percent. Similar links between dependence on unemployment benefits and poverty have been found in other countries.

Even worse, mostly as a result of behavioral conditionality, only a minority of the unemployed actually receive unemployment benefits. In the 1980s, in the United States the average figure was about 30 percent.[116] In most "right-to-work" states it was much lower (the lowest being South Dakota with 12 percent, followed by Virginia with 17 percent).[117]

There was also a downward trend in the receipt of unemployment benefits nationally. A 1988 study done for the U.S. Department of Labor estimated that the decline in unemployment compensation coverage reflected:

- A decline in the proportion of the unemployed coming from manufacturing (4–18 percent of the decline).
- Regional shifts in the composition of unemployment (16 percent).
- State program changes (22–39 percent), which involved:
  - an increase in base period earnings requirements (8–15 percent).
  - an increase in income denials for benefit (10 percent).
  - other, nonmonetary eligibility conditions (3–11 percent).
- Changes in federal policy, i.e., partial taxation of UI benefits (11–16 percent).
- Changes in unemployment, as measured by the CPS (1–12 percent).[118]

Obtaining entitlement seems to have grown even harder. In all but 5 of the United States, the person must have been employed in at least two quarters of the base year to qualify for minimum benefits; the other states have a minimum work requirement specified as a wage amount. Between January 1989 and mid-1990, 15 states raised (one lowered) the base year earnings required to qualify for minimum weekly benefit, and 39 states increased the level required for maximum benefit.

Another source of disentitlement has been stricter application of disqualification rules. In the United States, of the 14.2 million "monetarily eligible" initial UI claims in fiscal 1989, 24.3 percent were disqualified—5.9 percent supposedly for not being able to work or for not being available for work, 6.8 percent for leaving a job without good cause, 4.1 percent for being fired for misconduct, 0.3 percent for refusing suitable work, and 7.2 percent for other reasons. Once disqualified, for instance, for "voluntarily" leaving a job or for refusing a job deemed "suitable," the unemployed in a growing number of states cannot receive benefits at any time during the period of unemployment.[119]

In many European countries the situation was not much better. In Spain, less than 30 percent of the jobless receive unemployment benefits, although another 30 percent receive some other income transfers.[120] In France only about 39 percent receive unemployment benefits, in West Germany in the late 1980s about 55 percent, in Sweden (supposedly the model of universalism) it was as high as 68 percent, which is scarcely comprehensive.[121] In the United Kingdom, nearly 20 percent of all those registered as unemployment benefit claimants receive no income whatsoever, not even social assistance, since they do not qualify for one reason or another.

A secular growth in long-term unemployment also contributes to unemployment benefit disentitlement, in the United States and in some other countries. This is primarily due to the exhaustion of claims, and also to the effects of discouragement and anomie. The short duration of entitlement to regular UI benefits in the United States (26 weeks in all but one of the states) surely contributes to its relatively low long-term unemployment rate, by inducing some to take jobs, however menial and low-paying, and some to leave the labor force. Yet a short duration regime combined with a tendency for unemployment duration to grow will mean more people reaching the stage of disentitlement.

In sum, the unemployment benefit system has been found wanting, in that a low and dwindling proportion of the unemployed obtain benefits the system supposedly offers. Yet, with fiscal crises and higher levels of "need" due to labor market insecurity, many governments have shifted to greater reliance on social assistance rather than national insurance social protection.[122] The erosion of the insurance principle, ultimately due to the changing labor market, has meant more resort to means tests, income tests, work tests, and "targeting." That has meant that far more people have come to depend on multiple forms of social assistance. That in turn raises the "take-up" problem.

As more workers have lost entitlement to insurance benefits, reliance on social assistance has multiplied. For instance, in West Germany the number depending on social assistance more than doubled in the 1980s. Yet even access to that has been elusive. For many reasons, the rate of non-take-up (non-use among eligible citizens) of all conditional benefits is extraordinarily high. For instance, in Sweden the non-take-up of *socialbidrag* (a means-tested safety-net benefit) may be about 80 percent.[123] In Germany, non-take-up of *Sozialhilfe* (a similar means-tested benefit) has been estimated as between 36 percent and 79 percent, depending on method of calculation.[124] One could multiply such examples. If the take-up rate has fallen and the number depending on means-tested assistance has risen, then the number entitled to and yet not receiving social assistance must have risen even more alarmingly.

CONCLUDING POINTS

We have dealt only sketchily with some forms of labor security, but in terms of labor market security, employment security, labor representation, and income security one can be reasonably sure that there was a widespread deterioration in the 1980s, in both Europe and North America. One can also be fairly sure that most forms of insecurity have been linked.

Ultimately, a basic question is whether the conventional social security apparatus of either the "institutional redistributive" or "residual" models of the welfare state is appropriate for the more flexible labor markets that are emerging in the 1990s. The problem is that a growing proportion of the working-age population neither contribute to nor gain entitlement to social insurance benefits, and that even among those who are entitled to social assistance a worryingly large number have not been receiving the benefits to which they are entitled. Although that may not represent a crisis, it scarcely amounts to successful social policy. Meanwhile, there is little evidence that labor insecurity in its various forms is going to diminish in the 1990s.

Poverty is about entitlement. In the post-1945 era, European societies in particular developed entitlement through labor security in the multifold sense by which we have defined it. Entitlement depended on a regulated labor market and on the existence of effective institutions to give voice to the disadvantaged. The irony of ironies is that as the most vulnerable groups of all—ethnic minorities, women, and migrants—were gaining some access to mainstream entitlements, the "deregulation" (or market regulation) craze lurched over the horizon. The mainstream went backwards, leaving many more insecure, in numerous ways. Spinoza wrote that our task is not to weep, not to laugh, but to try to understand. Observing the poverty, unemployment, and insecurity of the supply-side experiments of the 1980s and early 1990s, it is hard to be so dispassionate.

For comments, thanks are due to Katherine McFate and Roger Lawson.

Table 4A.1 / Supplementary Tables, Labor Slack Rates, U.S., by State and by Gender: 1980, 1983, and 1988

	Men			Women		
	1980	1983	1988	1980	1983	1988
Alabama	10.3	16.3	8.5	13.9	18.5	11.8
Alaska	12.5	14.1	14.1	12.2	12.2	12.4
Arizona	8.8	12.4	N.A.	8.2	13.1	N.A.
Arkansas	9.3	12.4	8.7	11.3	15.4	13.0
California	8.3	12.6	7.5	9.3	12.6	7.8
Colorado	6.6	9.0	9.3	8.8	10.2	10.0
Connecticut	5.8	8.0	N.A.	8.0	8.4	N.A.
Delaware	8.5	11.1	N.A.	13.0	10.9	N.A.
District of Columbia	9.2	16.2	6.0	8.3	11.7	6.2
Florida	7.1	10.7	6.3	9.5	12.4	7.7
Georgia	6.5	9.6	6.9	11.6	12.3	8.6
Hawaii	6.5	9.5	N.A.	8.2	8.6	N.A.
Idaho	9.3	13.2	8.4	12.3	13.5	10.5
Illinois	9.8	13.9	8.5	10.5	14.6	9.2
Indiana	11.5	14.3	7.4	13.3	15.5	8.1
Iowa	7.5	11.1	5.9	8.4	11.9	5.4
Kansas	5.4	8.3	5.7	6.7	8.2	7.6
Kentucky	10.5	14.9	9.7	11.3	14.9	11.8
Louisiana	8.0	14.4	13.3	10.1	15.3	15.0
Maine	9.1	11.7	N.A.	13.0	13.7	N.A.
Maryland	7.3	8.2	4.9	8.7	9.8	7.0
Massachusetts	6.8	8.3	4.1	7.6	8.8	4.4
Michigan	15.3	17.5	9.4	14.8	18.5	10.7
Minnesota	7.7	11.6	N.A.	7.6	11.2	N.A.
Mississippi	7.7	14.7	9.8	12.9	17.5	13.2
Missouri	8.7	12.5	7.8	10.0	14.0	8.7
Montana	7.1	12.3	10.1	10.6	13.6	11.5
Nebraska	4.9	8.1	N.A.	6.7	10.0	N.A.
Nevada	7.4	12.9	N.A.	8.6	13.1	N.A.
New Hampshire	5.5	5.8	N.A.	7.0	9.3	N.A.
New Jersey	7.5	8.8	4.5	10.1	11.3	5.0
New Mexico	8.4	12.3	10.7	10.0	14.3	11.0
New York	8.8	10.6	5.6	10.4	11.4	5.6
North Carolina	8.0	10.5	4.6	10.4	14.3	6.4
North Dakota	7.1	8.4	N.A.	8.5	8.6	N.A.
Ohio	9.8	15.5	7.7	11.5	15.3	8.8
Oklahoma	6.1	11.8	9.3	7.1	11.6	10.6
Oregon	10.3	14.5	8.1	12.3	15.4	N.A.
Pennsylvania	9.4	16.1	6.8	11.0	14.0	7.5
Rhode Island	7.7	9.2	N.A.	10.1	13.1	N.A.
South Carolina	8.6	11.7	5.5	11.5	16.1	8.1
South Dakota	7.0	6.8	5.6	7.4	10.4	8.0
Tennessee	8.9	14.2	7.5	10.7	16.2	9.0

Table 4A.1 / (*continued*)

	Men			Women		
	1980	1983	1988	1980	1983	1988
Texas	6.1	9.9	9.6	8.2	10.9	10.8
Utah	6.5	12.0	N.A.	9.4	13.9	N.A.
Vermont	7.4	9.0	N.A.	11.0	11.5	N.A.
Virginia	5.8	7.6	4.4	8.6	10.4	7.0
Washington	9.4	14.5	8.3	11.1	15.5	9.1
West Virginia	12.0	24.3	13.1	11.4	17.7	13.6
Wisconsin	8.6	14.6	6.2	9.5	13.4	5.8
Wyoming	4.8	11.9	8.9	7.5	11.7	11.2
U.S.A. Total	8.5	12.2	N.A.	10.1	13.1	N.A.

SOURCE: U.S. Department of Labor, Bureau of Labor Statistics. 1980. *Geographic Profiles of Employment and Unemployment*. Washington, D.C.: U.S. Government Printing Office, Tables 1 and 7; 1983 and 1988, Tables 12, 13, and 22.

Table 4A.2 / **Supplementary Tables, Long-Term Unemployment, U.S., by State and by Gender: 1980, 1983, and 1988 (percentage of unemployed jobless for 27+ weeks)**

	Men			Women		
	1980	1983	1988	1980	1983	1988
Alabama	9.6	31.2	19.1	5.7	22.3	12.4
Alaska	7.9	10.8	16.2	9.4	7.7	14.2
Arizona	5.8	19.6	N.A.	N.A.	10.9	N.A.
Arkansas	6.0	19.0	13.8	4.5	14.1	12.5
California	7.4	24.0	11.1	4.9	16.2	7.9
Colorado	5.3	15.3	21.7	3.2	10.7	10.8
Connecticut	N.A.	10.6	N.A.	N.A.	N.A.	N.A.
Delaware	6.9	24.3	N.A.	N.A.	16.3	N.A.
District of Columbia	7.2	28.6	7.4	6.1	17.7	12.5
Florida	3.2	15.1	8.6	2.8	9.9	5.2
Georgia	1.3	19.1	12.3	2.9	13.7	8.8
Hawaii	17.1	17.1	N.A.	N.A.	N.A.	N.A.
Idaho	2.9	18.6	11.1	7.3	14.6	5.2
Illinois	12.0	35.6	19.3	7.9	22.0	12.0
Indiana	10.0	29.8	7.1	8.7	25.5	3.2
Iowa	9.8	31.5	13.7	N.A.	20.1	9.7
Kansas	N.A.	32.2	11.3	N.A.	N.A.	5.7
Kentucky	7.4	24.7	20.2	6.8	18.0	11.2
Louisiana	4.3	23.4	25.6	N.A.	16.3	14.0
Maine	7.9	19.9	N.A.	5.0	11.7	N.A.
Maryland	7.9	26.8	8.8	4.5	13.0	8.5

Table 4A.2 / (continued)

	Men			Women		
	1980	1983	1988	1980	1983	1988
Massachusetts	6.8	25.5	8.0	4.9	14.2	5.1
Michigan	13.1	37.7	18.7	12.7	24.7	12.7
Minnesota	7.1	23.4	N.A.	N.A.	23.1	N.A.
Mississippi	7.5	30.5	14.1	3.5	21.1	9.3
Missouri	5.9	26.8	22.3	7.4	18.4	8.0
Montana	7.3	16.8	19.2	N.A.	11.0	12.5
Nebraska	N.A.	19.8	N.A.	N.A.	N.A.	N.A.
Nevada	4.3	23.3	N.A.	3.2	15.5	N.A.
New Hampshire	N.A.	N.A.	N.A.	N.A.	N.A.	N.A.
New Jersey	7.5	25.3	11.1	6.7	19.4	7.2
New Mexico	7.0	17.3	13.6	N.A.	13.5	N.A.
New York	11.4	27.0	11.3	6.2	17.7	8.4
North Carolina	7.5	22.6	7.3	5.8	16.8	5.4
North Dakota	N.A.	17.5	N.A.	N.A.	N.A.	N.A.
Ohio	12.0	43.6	21.9	9.9	28.4	12.0
Oklahoma	N.A.	25.2	15.3	N.A.	13.9	11.7
Oregon	9.0	31.0	14.1	6.5	20.1	N.A.
Pennsylvania	10.2	38.7	18.1	6.8	22.1	7.7
Rhode Island	7.7	29.8	N.A.	5.1	17.7	N.A.
South Carolina	4.7	21.6	N.A.	N.A.	15.9	13.4
South Dakota	N.A.	N.A.	21.3	N.A.	N.A.	N.A.
Tennessee	6.8	27.0	17.5	7.5	16.7	4.7
Texas	5.8	17.4	13.3	3.5	9.4	9.1
Utah	5.3	20.2	N.A.	2.3	7.2	N.A.
Vermont	N.A.	22.1	N.A.	N.A.	N.A.	N.A.
Virginia	N.A.	N.A.	N.A.	N.A.	N.A.	N.A.
Washington	7.2	27.8	11.3	9.2	19.4	N.A.
West Virginia	9.8	44.0	32.1	6.1	24.7	18.2
Wisconsin	8.5	37.7	18.3	6.5	17.9	N.A.
Wyoming	N.A.	15.0	13.1	N.A.	6.5	N.A.

SOURCES: U.S. Department of Labor, Bureau of Labor Statistics. *Geographic Profiles of Employment and Unemployment*. (Washington, D.C.: U.S. Government Printing Office, 1980), Tables 1 and 7; 1983 and 1988, Tables 12, 13, and 22.

ENDNOTES

1. Canada has been somewhere in the middle, with high unemployment and a predominance of poor jobs.
2. These developments are elaborated in a set of papers within the International Labour Organisation's research program on labor flexibility.
3. See, for example, O. Blanchard et al. "Employment and Growth in Europe: A

Two-Handed Approach." In O. Blanchard et al. (eds.). *Restoring Europe's Prosperity.* (Cambridge, MA: M.I.T. Press, 1987).

4. The U.S. Bureau of Labor Statistics now publishes a series of unemployment measures broader than the conventional rate. See, e.g., U.S. Department of Labor, Bureau of Labor Statistics. "The Employment Situation: September 1990." (Washington, D.C.: U.S. Government Printing Office, Oct. 1990), Table A.5.

5. The only exception in 1988 was the District of Columbia, where a remarkable reversal occurred between the early and late 1980s.

6. Thus, in Portugal although it remained about 37 percent of total unemployment, it had declined from its peak. Ferreira J. et al. *Caracterizoao de factores e tipos de pobreza em Portugal.* (Lisbon: ISCTE, 1989).

7. J. Sexton. *Long-Term Unemployment: Its Wider Labor Market Effects in the Countries of the EC.* (Luxembourg: EUROSTAT, 1988).

8. A. E. Green and D. W. Owen. *Long-Term Unemployment: JUVOS Analysis.* Final Report of a Project Conducted for the Social Science Branch of the Department of Employment, Department of Employment Research Paper No.72, 1990.

9. M. Munro. "Housing and Labor Market Interactions: A Review." Center for Housing Research, University of Glasgow, Discussion Paper No.12, 1986); A. E. Green, D. W. Owen, A. G. Champion, J. B. Goddard, and M. G. Coombes. "What Contribution Can Labor Migration Make to Reducing Unemployment?" In P. E. Hart (ed.). *Unemployment and Labor Market Policies.* (Aldershot: Gower, 1986).

10. For example, A. Lindbeck and D. J. Snower. *The Insider-Outsider Theory of Employment and Unemployment.* (Cambridge, MA: M.I.T. Press, 1989).

11. For a critique, see O. Blanchard and L. Summers. "Hysteresis in Unemployment." *European Economic Review* 31, 1–2 (1987): 288–295.

12. See, for example, C. de Neubourg. *Unemployment and Labor Market Flexibility: The Netherlands.* (Geneva: ILO, 1990).

13. For one review, see P. N. Junankar. *From School to Unemployment: The Labor Market for Young People.* (Basingstoke: Macmillan, 1987).

14. See the chapters by Pugliese and Casey.

15. G. Esping-Andersen and H. Sonnenberger. *The Demographics of Age in Labor Market Management.* Working Paper No. 89/414 (Florence: European University Institute, 1989); G. Standing. "Labor Flexibility and Older Worker Marginalization: The Need for a New Strategy." *International Labor Review* 125, 3 (1986); de Neubourg (1990), op. cit.

16. B. Casey and S. McRae. "A More Polarized Labor Market?" *Policy Studies* 11, 2, Summer 1990; OECD, 1989a, op. cit.; OECD. "The Economic Dynamics of an Ageing Population: The Case of Four OECD Countries." *OECD Economic Studies* 12 (1989); Standing, 1986, op. cit.

17. See, e.g., W. R. Bohning and J. Werquin. "Some Economic, Social and Human Rights Considerations Concerning the Future Status of Third-Country Nationals in the Single European Market." World Employment Program Working Paper (Geneva: ILO, 1990); J. Widgren, "Europe and International Migration in the Future."

In G. Loescher and L. Monahan (eds.). *Refugees and International Relations.* (Oxford: Oxford University Press, 1989), pp. 49–61.

18. G. Standing. "Global Feminization Through Flexible Labor." *World Development* 17, 7 (1989): 1077–1095.

19. Equal Opportunities Commission. *Women and Men in Britain 1989.* (London, 1989).

20. Henley Center for Forecasting. *Report on Women's Employment.* (Henley, 1989).

21. A. Dale and J. Glover. *An Analysis of Women's Employment Patterns in the UK, France and the USA: The Value of Survey Based Comparisons.* (London: Department of Employment Research Paper 75, 1990).

22. Studies have linked labor market segmentation to employment feminization, in the UK, France, and Italy, for instance. See, e.g., J. Rubery. *Women and Recession.* (London: Routledge & Kegan Paul, 1988); for the UK, see C. Hakim. "Women at Work: Recent Research on Women's Employment." *Work, Employment and Society* 2, 1 (March 1988), pp. 103–113.

23. Low Pay Unit. *What Price Flexibility? The Casualization of Women's Employment.* (London, 1989).

24. P. Doeringer et al. *Turbulence in the American Workplace.* (New York and Oxford: Oxford University Press, 1991).

25. On the managerial strategies, see, for example, P. K. Edwards, *Managing the Factory* (Oxford: Blackwell, 1987).

26. European Trades Union Congress. *Privatization in Western Europe.* (Brussels: ETUC, 1987).

27. Statistics and analyses of these trends have been carried out in such international institutions as the ILO, OECD, and EC, and such institutes as the European Foundation for the Improvement of Living and Working Conditions. See, e.g., Y. Kravaritou-Manitakis. *New Forms of Work and Activity: Their Repercussions for Labor Law and Social Security in the Member States of the European Community.* (Dublin: Report to the European Foundation for the Improvement of Living and Working Conditions, 1988); F. Piotet. *The Changing Face of Work: Researching and Debating the Issues.* (Dublin: European Foundation for the Improvement of Living and Working Conditions, 1988); G. Standing, "European Unemployment, Insecurity and Flexibility: A Social Dividend Solution." Labor Market Research Working Paper (Geneva: ILO, 1989); C. Hakim, "Workforce Restructuring in Europe in the 1980s." *International Journal of Comparative Labor Law and Industrial Relations* 5, 4 (1990): 220–240.

28. Terminological problems have dogged analysis and the development of a valid policy perspective. By lumping too much together, there has been a tendency to take either an excessively positive or an excessively negative view of rather disparate developments. Employers have favored "external flexibility," trade unions have been hostile or suspicious, some groups of workers and professionals welcome the freedom that non-regular, non-full-time working relations offer, others fear not knowing whether a pay check or medical benefit, or whatever, would be coming at the end of the month.

29. Hakim. 1989, op. cit.

30. A. Errington. "The Changing Structure of the Agricultural and Horticultural Work-

force." *Agricultural Manpower* 2, 2 (1985): 21–28; Idem, "Disguised Unemployment in British Agriculture." *Journal of Rural Studies* 4, 1 (1988): 1–7; R. M. Ball, "The Use of Seasonal or Casual Labor in Agriculture and Horticulture: Some Survey Findings." *Agriculture Manpower* 1, 12 (1986): 1–13.

31. "Survey of Fixed-Term Contracts." *European Industrial Relations Review* (Dec. 1988): 20–25.

32. E. Cordova."From Full-Time Wage Employment to Atypical Employment: A Major Shift in the Evolution of Labor Relations." *International Labor Review* 125, 6 (1986): 651; M. Emerson. "Regulation or Deregulation of the Labor Market: Policy Regimes for the Recruitment and Dismissal of Employees in the Industrialized Countries." *European Economic Review* 32 (1988): 797; Y. Kravaritou-Manitakis. 1988 op. cit., pp. 40–44; G. Maurau. "Reglementation, politique des enterprises et dynamique du marche du travail: Le cas de la France." Paper presented to conference on Workers' Protection and Labor Market Dynamics, West Berlin, May 16–18, 1990, organized by ILO and Social Science Center, Berlin; in Buechtemann and Standing forthcoming. Among studies of the growth of atypical forms of precarious employment in France, see Alternative Economiques. "Nouvelles tendances du marche de l'emploi." *Alternative Economiques* (Dijon) 66 (April 1989): 8–9, covering the period 1975–88.

33. Ferreira 1989, op. cit.; Ma Joao. Rodrigues."O mercado de trabalho nos anos 70: Das tensoes aos metabolismos." *Analise Social* 21, 87–89 (1985).

34. L. Toharia. *Unemployment and Labor Market Flexibility: Spain.* (Geneva, ILO, forthcoming).

35. E. Guillen. *La pauvrete en Espagne: Rapport contextual* (Report for the EC's European programme on poverty, 1989, mimeo), p. 21.

36. M.-C. Villeval. "Labor market restructuring and deprivation processes," paper presented at 1990 EALE Conference, University of Lund, Sept. 20–23, 1990, p. 5.

37. Hakim. 1990, op. cit.

38. For instance, the trend in France was aided by government schemes to create "intermediate statuses"—"Travaux d'utilité collective" and "Stages d'initiation a la vie professionelle" for the young, and "Programmes d'insertion locale" and "Stages de reinsertion en alternance" for the long-term unemployed.

39. See, e.g., G. Nerb. "Employment Problems: Views of Businessmen and the Workforce—Results of an Employee and Employer Survey on Labor Market Issues in the Member States." *European Economy* 27 (1986): 5–110; R. Blanpain and E. Kohler (eds.). *Legal and Contractual Limitations to Working Time in the European Community Member States.* (Antwerp and London: Kluwer, 1988).

40. C. F. Buechtemann,"The Socio-economics of Individual Working Time Reduction: Empirical Evidence for the Federal Republic of Germany." In J. B. Agassi and S. Heycock (eds.). *The Redesign of Working Time: Promise or Threat?* (Berlin: Sigma, 1989).

41. Low Pay Unit. 1989, op. cit.

42. "Survey of Temporary Work Contracts." *European Industrial Relations Review* 182 (March 1989): 11–16.

43. R. J. Samuelson. "Temps: The New Workforce." *The Washington Post,* July 12, 1989, p. A23. See, for instance, Bureau of National Affairs. *The Changing Workplace: New Directions in Staffing and Scheduling.* (Washington D.C.: Mimeo., 1986); R. S. Belous. *The Contingent Economy: The Growth of Temporary, Part-Time and Subcontracted Workforce.* (Washington, D.C.: National Planning Association, 1989).

44. Economic Council of Canada. *Good Jobs, Bad Jobs: Employment in the Service Economy.* (Ottawa: Minister of Supply and Services, A Statement by the Economic Council of Canada, 1990), p. 12.

45. Economic Council of Canada. 1990, op. cit., p. 12.

46. L. Fina and L.Toharia. *Las causas del para en Espana: Un punto de vista structural.* (Madrid: Fundación IESA, 1987); for the UK, Fevre. 1987, for steel; Evans. 1990, for construction.

47. ILO, 1990. P. A. Varesi and P. Villa. "Homeworking in Italy, France and the United Kingdom." *Social Europe.* (EC Commission, 1988).

48, Samuelson. 1989, op. cit., p. A23.

49. Some unions have resisted the employers' drive to contract out, including the U.S. Steelworkers' Union. As Lynn Williams, its president, put it in paraphrasing the union's "emotional" position:

    Our people provided you with income and as long as you stay in America there should be an absolute prohibition on contracting out. Our experience is that it is absolutely essential for the industry because American industry needs a quality workforce and this can only come from employment security.

50. C. Hakim. *Employers' Use of Outwork.* (London: Department of Employment Research Paper No. 44, 1984). The trouble is that then the common law distinction between employees and self-employment cannot be sustained. B. A. Hepple. "Restructuring Employment Rights." *Industrial Law Journal* 15, 2 (1986): 69–83.

51. B. Casey and S. Creigh. "Self-Employed in Great Britain: Its Definition in the Labor Force Survey, in Tax and Social Security Law, and in Labor Law." *Work, Employment and Society* 2, 3 (Sept. 1988): 381–391.

52. Economic Council of Canada. 1990, op. cit., p. 12.

53. A major review has been carried out in the EC. R. Pahl. "Conclusion: Whose Problem?" In DGV. *Underground Economy and Economy and Irregular Forms of Employment: Final Synthesis Report.* (Brussels: Commission of the European Communities, 1988, DGV/A/1). For a useful compendium of conceptual and empirical knowledge, see L. Benton, M. Castells, and A. Portes. *The Informal Economy: Studies in Advanced and Less Developed Countries.* (Baltimore: Johns Hopkins University Press, 1989).

54. Guillen. 1989, op. cit.

55. Thus, a survey of the unemployed in the U.K. found that most who took part-time jobs did so only after failing to find full-time jobs. W. Daniel. *The Unemployed Flow.* (London: Policy Studies Institute, 1990), p.129.

56. Some argue that in the USA there has been a part-time "boom"; this seems an exaggeration. C. Tilly. *Short Hours, Short Shrift: Causes and Consequences of Part-Time Work.* (Washington, D.C.: Economic Policy Institute, 1990), p. 4.

57. R. Lilja, T. Santamaki-Vuori, and G.Standing. *Unemployment and Labor Market Flexibility*. (Geneva: ILO, 1990).

58. Economic Council of Canada. 1990, op. cit., p. 12.

59. Ibid. p. 11.

60. Tilly. 1990, op. cit., pp. 4–5.

61. See, e.g., Maurau. 1990, op. cit.

62. E. Mellor and S. Haugen. "Hourly Paid Workers: Who They Are and What They Earn." *Monthly Labor Review* (Feb. 1986): 20–26.

63. Low Pay Unit. 1989, op. cit.

64. Buechtemann. 1989, op. cit., and Idem, *Unemployment and Labour Market Flexibility: Germany*. (Geneva: ILO, forthcoming).

65. As many of these are linked, focusing on one aspect alone may be misleading. For instance, 40 percent of those in the U.S. "temporary help supply" industry work part-time. T. J.Plewes, "Understanding the Data on Part-Time and Temporary Employment." In K. Christensen and M. Murphree (eds.). *Flexible Workstyles: A Look at Contingent Labour* (Conference summary. Washington, D.C.: U.S. Department of Labor's Women's Bureau, 1988). More part-time workers have temporary jobs. Tilly. 1990, op. cit., p. 11.

66. Economic Council of Canada. 1990, op. cit., p.12.

67. A. B. Atkinson and J. Micklewright. *Unemployment Compensation and Labour Market Transitions: A Critical Review.* (Florence: European University Institute, Working Paper No. 90/9, 1990).

68. World Health Organization. *The Submerged Economy and Health.* Summary of Study Group on Unemployment and the Submerged Economy, Barcelona, June 19–21, 1989. (Copenhagen: WHO, 1990).

69. S. A. Levitan and E. Conway. "Part-Timers: Living on Half Rations." *Challenge* (May–June, 1988): 9–16.

70. U.S. General Accounting Office. *Workers at Risk: Increased Numbers in Contingent Employment Lack Insurance, Other Benefits.* Report to the Chairman, Subcommittee on Employment and Housing, Committee on Government Operations, House of Representatives. (Washington D.C.: U.S. Government Printing Office, March 1991), Appendix III, p. 22.

71. Nerb. 1986, op. cit.; Blanpain and Kohler. 1988, op. cit.; Buechtemann and Standing. forthcoming, op. cit.

72. Recent reports have labeled a new industrial disease—karoshi, death from overwork—which may be claiming 10,000 lives a year in Japan, which has not ratified any ILO convention on working time or paid leave. *The Independent*, Aug. 31, 1991.

73. AFL-CIO. 1989, op. cit.

74. C. Kleiman."Changing Jobs at the Drop of a Hat." *The Washington Post*, May 5, 1990.

75. Ibid.

76. Economic Council of Canada. 1990, op. cit., p. 13.

77. The U.K. was particularly bad. In 1989–90, only one-third of Bankok teenagers aged 16–18 were in school; for 19 year-olds, the figure was merely 15 percent. It seems the top strata of students in the U.K. perform as well as in other countries but that the overall average has dropped (S. J. Prain et al.).

78. SCANS. *What Work Requires of Schools.* (Washington, D.C.: U.S. Department of Labor, 1991).

79. For a perspective on this, see Standing, in Scott and Storper. forthcoming, op. cit. In the U.K., firms spent about 1 percent of their payroll on training adults, less than in the United States. Training Agency, Training in Britain (London: HMSO, 1989).

80. W. Streeck. "Skills and the Limits of Neo-Liberalism: The Enterprise of the Future as a Place of Learning." *Work, Employment and Society* 3, 1 (March 1989): 89–104.

81. R. B. Freeman and J. Medoff. *What Do Unions Do?* (New York: Basic Books, 1984).

82. For analyses, see G. S. Bain and R. Price. "The Determinants of Union Growth." In W. E. J. McCarthy (ed.). *Trade Unions: Selected Readings.* (Harmondsworth: Penguin Books, 1985), pp. 245–271; E. Sussex. "Workers and Trade Unions in a Period of Structural Change." *ILO Working Paper* (Geneva: ILO, Oct. 1989).

83. E. Applebaum and J. Gregory. "Union Responses to Contingent Work: Are Win-Win Outcomes Possible?" In Christensen and Murphree. 1988, op. cit., p. 15.

84. AFL-CIO. "The Changing Situation of Workers and Their Unions: A Report by the AFL-CIO Committee on the Evolution of Work." (Washington, D.C., Feb. 1985), p. 4.

85. Thus, although women's unionization rate has not fallen by as much as men's in the USA, it remains much lower. National Displaced Homeworkers' Network. *Unionization: A Way Out of Low-Wage Work.* (Washington, D.C., 1991).

86. Quoted in J. P. Windmuller et al. *Collective Bargaining in Industrialized Market Economies: A Reappraisal.* (Geneva: ILO, 1987), pp. 46–47.

87. H. Phelps-Brown. "The Counter-Revolution of Our Time." *Industrial Relations* 29, 1 (Winter 1990).

88. *Time,* March 26, 1990, p. 56.

89. L. Mishel and D. M. Frankel. *The State of Working America, 1990–91.* (New York: M. E. Sharpe Inc., 1991), pp.114–115.

90. Data compiled by John Zalusky, AFL-CIO, 1989.

91. R. B. McKersie. "Governance: A Framework for our Field." Presidential Address, IRRA Annual Meeting, Washington, D.C., Dec. 30, 1990.

92. For an analysis, see G. Standing,."Labor Fragmentation in an Era of Flexibility." In M. Storper and A. J. Scott (eds.). *Pathways to Industrialization and Regional Development.* London: Routledge, 1992.

93. See, for instance, European Communities, Economic and Social Committee. *Opinion No. SOC/176.* 19 April 1989 (Brussels); *Opinion No. SOC/179.* 12 July 1989 (Brussels).

94. Mishel and Frankel. 1991, op. cit., p.167.

95. R. Teekens and M. A. Zaidi. *Relative and Absolute Poverty in the European Community:*

Results from Family Budget Surveys. (The Hague: Institute of Social Studies Advisory Services, mimeo. Sept. 1989).

96. Doeringer et al. 1991, op. cit.

97. P. Ormerod and E. Salama. "The Rise of the British Underclass." *The Independent,* 19 June, 1990.

98. Maurau. 1990, op. cit.

99. Economic Council of Canada. 1990, op. cit., p. 14.

100. This corresponds to what would be expected by those adhering to a post-Fordist explanation of wage trends. As the official report concluded, "In the decade prior to 1977, real wage increases surpassed productivity growth, but in the decade following that year, wages lagged behind gains in productivity."

101. Ibid. pp. 14–15.

102. See, e.g., G. Standing. *Unemployment and Labour Market Flexibility: Sweden.* (Geneva, ILO, 1988), chap. 3; Lilja, Santamaki-Vuori, and Standing. 1990, op. cit., chap. 3.

103. C. Tilly, B. Bluestone, and B.Harrison. "What Is Making American Wages More Unequal?" *Proceedings of the 39th Annual Meeting of the Industrial Relations Research Association.* Dec. 1986.

104. J. Ford. "Casual Work and Owner Occupation." *Work, Employment and Society* 3, 1 (March 1989): 29–48. Jencks and Mayer show that access to credit is a key difference between blacks' and whites' standard of living. Blacks find it harder to obtain credit even if they have the same income as whites.

105. Repossession of houses reached record levels in 1991.

106. Mishel and Frankel. 1991, op. cit., p. 171.

107. See, e.g., European Commission, Interdepartmental Working Party. "The Social Dimension of the Internal Market." *Social Europe 1988,* Special Edition (Brussels: EC, 1988).

108. Ormerod and Salama. 1990, op. cit. 4. See the article on the FRG in International Labour Organization. "Second Labour Market: Scope and Limits." *Social and Labour Bulletin* 2 (July 1987): 294–296.

109. Ibid.

110. S. Schunter-Kleemann. "Women's Employment in Western European Countries and Deficiencies in Social Security." Paper presented at 1990 EALE Conference, University of Lund, Sept. 20–23, 1990.

111. Schunter-Kleemann. 1990, op. cit., p. 13.

112. Ibid. p. 15.

113. Thus, recent estimates suggest that in the U.K. only 69 percent of the job-seeking unemployed are registered and counted as part of the unemployed. Department of Employment, "Measures of Unemployment and Characteristics of the Unemployed." *Employment Gazette* (Oct. 1988): 534–537.

114. See, e.g., D. Wood. "Men Registering as Unemployed in 1978: A Longitudinal Study." (London: Department of Health and Social Security, The Cohort Study Working Paper 1, 1982).

115. de Neubourg. 1990, op. cit.

116. R. Blank and D. Card. "Recent Trends in Insured and Uninsured Employment: Is There an Explanation?" (Washington, D.C.: NBE Research Working Paper 2871, 1989). Through the 1970s the number of UI recipients was nearly equal to the number of job losers. Congressional Budget Office. *Family Incomes of Unemployment Insurance Recipients and the Implications for Extending Benefits.* (Washington, D.C.: Congress of the United States, Feb. 1990), p. 14.

117. AFL-CIO. *Workers' Compensation and Unemployment Insurance under State Laws, January 1, 1989.* (Washington, D.C.: AFL-CIO, Publication 36, 1989). See also I. Shapiro and M. Nichols. *Unemployed and Uninsured.* (Washington, D.C.: Center on Budget and Policy Priorities, March 1991).

118. Mathematica Policy Research, Inc. *An Examination of Declining UI Claims During the 1980s.* (Princeton, NJ: MPR, Sept. 1988). As all UI benefits are now taxable, the observed tax-induced disincentive to claim will have grown. The time covered by MPR's regressions was 1971–86. None of the decline was due to changes in the demographic composition of the unemployed.

119. W. Corson and W. Nicholson. "Unemployment Insurance Income Maintenance and Reemployment Tradeoffs in a Competitive World Economy" in U.S. Department of Labor, *The Secretary's Seminars on Unemployment Insurance.* (Washington, D.C.: Department of Labor Occasional Paper 89–1, 1989), p. 45. A related factor, identified in the MPR research cited earlier, has been the increase in benefit denials because of other income, most notably following compulsory pension-offset rules, as required under federal law. This has been linked to the rise in income-based denials of unemployment benefit.

120. Guillen. 1989, op. cit.

121. G. Burtless. "Jobless Pay and High European Unemployment" in R. Z. Lawrence and C. L. Schultz (eds.). *Barriers to European Growth.* (Washington, D.C.: Brookings Institution, 1987).

122. In periods of high unemployment, the insurance principle of unemployment insurance is eroded in any case, in that the average spell of unemployment lengthens, so reducing the effective level of insurance protection. *If* the insurance principle is to be maintained, some economists have advocated that the duration of UI benefit should be extended in cyclical downturns. Several U.S. studies have concluded that to maintain the total exhaustion rate for all UI benefits (including extensions) constant over the business cycle, it would be necessary to increase the eligibility duration by 4–5 weeks for every 1 percent rise in the unemployment rate. R. Moffitt, "Unemployment Insurance and the Distribution of Unemployment Spells." *Journal of Econometrics* 28 (1985): 85–101.

123. B. Gustafsson. "Som et isberg? Om underutnyttjande av socialbidrag." *Nordisk Sosialt Arbeid* 3 (1987): 43–51.

124. For a review of the estimates, see W. van Oorschot. "Non Take-up of Social Security Benefits in Europe." *Journal of European Social Policy* 1, 1 (1991).

Chapter 5

THE IMPACT OF TECHNOLOGICAL CHANGE, DEINDUSTRIALIZATION, AND INTERNATIONALIZATION OF TRADE ON EARNINGS INEQUALITY: AN INTERNATIONAL PERSPECTIVE

Peter Gottschalk and Mary Joyce

T HE UNITED STATES has experienced substantial increases in inequality of wage rates and family income during the 1970s and 1980s. Highly educated workers, who were already receiving above-average wages in the 1970s, received substantial raises during the 1980s. At the other end of the spectrum, high school dropouts and high school graduates experienced actual declines in pay.

Inequality increased not only between education groups but also among persons of the same age and with the same education. The increase in dispersion of wages among workers with the same characteristics has further exacerbated the problem for those at the bottom of the distribution—young, low-wage high school dropouts lost ground relative to the average high school dropout as well as to college graduates.

The deterioration in the absolute and relative position of persons with low skills has had a substantial impact on poverty.[1] While the increase in average income during the 1983–1990 recovery should have led to substantial declines in poverty rates, the increase in inequality has kept poverty rates well above the levels achieved during the late 1970s. In fact, changes in the distribution of income have had a larger impact on poverty than changes in economic growth.[2]

While the trends in inequality in the United States are by now well known, their cause is much less well understood.[3] This is largely a result of having many competing explanations—deindustrialization, shifts in technology, demographic shifts, increased international competition, increased generosity of welfare programs—but relatively few observations that can be used to distinguish between explanations. Some progress has been made in eliminating theories. For example, Moffitt (1990) rules out increases in welfare programs as an explanation for the increase in inequality by pointing out that inequality increased among young persons not covered by public assistance programs and that inequality continued to grow during a period when welfare benefits declined. Likewise, Murphy and Welch (1988) conclude that while cohort size explanations were consistent with the data for the 1970s, this supply-side story is not sufficient to explain the continued increase in inequality during the 1980s when cohorts were getting smaller. Although some theories can be eliminated, many of the remaining theories continue to be consistent with the data.

Progress in this field has not been characterized by identifying the "smoking gun" that fully explains the changes but rather by chipping away at existing explanations. Researchers have narrowed the range of possible explanations by identifying theories that are no longer consistent with the data. This chapter continues in that tradition. By using a new source of data that includes information on several developed economies we hope to shed light on the importance of two structural factors—technological change and deindustrialization—that may have influenced the changes in wage inequality.

While related, these two factors are conceptually distinct. One often-heard hypothesis is that technology (or automation) has changed throughout the world in such a way as to devalue the skills of workers with low levels of education and increase the demand for more skilled workers. For example, the computer revolution has led to both an increase in wages and employment for skilled workers.[4] Since such innovations have wide applicability, we would expect to see educational upgrading in a wide variety of countries. Furthermore, if technological change is an important cause of the increase in the demand for skilled workers, we would also expect to see a general upgrading of the skill level used in all industries in the advanced industrialized countries we study— both the skill mix and the skill premium would contribute to an increase in inequality within each industry.[5]

The second structural explanation also focuses on shifts in demand, but these shifts are not technologically driven. Rather, they are driven by shifts in demand for final goods. The increase in openness to foreign competition is said to be largely responsible for the shift in industrialized countries away from production of goods that requires unskilled workers towards service-oriented production that requires skilled workers. The globalization of the Western economies is said to have led to a sharp increase in demand for high-skilled workers. At the same time, competition eroded the position of low-skilled workers, who had to compete with low-skilled workers in the rest of the world. Thus, according to this argument, increased openness led to "deindustrialization," which in turn led to the increase in inequality.[6]

While technological change is likely to be ubiquitous, different countries may have experienced different changes in industrial structure, leaving open the possibility that "deindustrialization" was important for some but not all countries. Thus, if countries differ in the shifts in industrial structure they experienced, then cross-country comparisons may be useful in determining the relative importance of these two structural factors. If, on the other hand, changes in industrial structure were similar across countries, then it is considerably more difficult to access the relative importance of technological change and deindustrialization, since both have similar empirical implications.

The observed decline in the wages of less-educated workers (relative to more-educated workers) could be the result of shifts in industrial structure or broadly applied changes in technology. Both are consistent with the increase in the "skill premium." However, this rise in the "skill premium" was accompanied by an increase in the "skill mix" (ratio of the number of skilled to unskilled workers hired) within each sector. We argue that this increase in demand for skilled workers in the face of rising relative prices cannot be explained solely by changes in industrial structure. Technological change must have increased the relative productivity of skilled workers since more of them were hired in spite of their increased cost to the firm. While the shift in industrial structure cannot be the whole story, it may have reinforced the rise in the demand for skilled workers driven by technological change. If the more skill-intensive sectors were the ones that expanded, then the change in industrial structure would have reinforced the effects of changing technology. We offer a way of decomposing the change in the skill mix into the portion associated with changes in industrial structure and the proportion associated with all other factors. This serves to bound the possible effects of "deindustrialization."

In summary, while we recognize that technological change and deindustrialization are not the only two possible structural factors that can affect inequality, we believe that these two factors have received sufficient attention in both the popular and academic literature to be at the center of this study of international differences. Again we do not pretend to be able to isolate "the smoking gun," rather we hope to be able to use international comparisons to continue to narrow the range of possible explanations.

The chapter is divided into five sections. The next section reviews the literature on inequality in the United States and the emerging literature on international comparisons of inequality. This is followed by a detailed discussion of the links between technological change, industrial restructuring, and inequality. With this as background, we turn to the empirical evidence on these three factors for the industrialized countries we study. The final section draws conclusions from the data presented.

REVIEW OF LITERATURE

Rising earnings and wage inequality among male workers in the United States has led to substantial literature documenting the trends and to a smaller literature attempting to identify the causes of the rising inequality. Changes in the dispersion in the overall wage distribution can be usefully decomposed into changes in between-group inequality and within-group inequality. The former usually focuses on increases in wage differentials between high school and college graduates and between new entrants and older workers. Within-group inequality focuses on increased dispersion in the wage distributions within education and experience groups.

Studies of the United States

Changes in overall distribution. Using the Current Population Survey (CPS), several studies examine the distribution of weekly wages for males.[7] In order to concentrate on changes in wages and not changes in hours worked, the studies select only persons working full-time/full-year. Since the large changes in labor force participation of women confound labor supply and wage effects, most studies focus on the distribution of male earnings. These studies find that wage growth varied dramatically between the upper, middle, and lower ends of the distribution.[8] For example, the median wage of males working full-time/full-year increased by 25 percent between 1963 and 1973 and declined slightly (5 percent) from 1973 to 1987. In contrast, the wages of similar workers at the 10th percentile declined by 21 percent between 1970 and 1987.[9] Thus, the wages of those at the bottom of the distribution fell both absolutely and relatively. In contrast, the real wages of the 90th percentile rose steadily since 1963 and increased considerably (12 percent) from 1970 to 1987 (Juhn, Murphy, and Pierce 1989). Thus, growth in real wages was not shared equally among the labor force. Rather, large wage growth was experienced by those in the upper ends of the distribution and small or no wage growth was experienced by those in the lower tail.

Karoly (1993) finds a similar trend by tracking wages of males in the 90th, 75th, 25th, and 10th percentiles relative to the median. Since 1975, the real wages for the 90th and 75th percentiles increased 10 percent faster than the median while real wages for the 25th and 10th percentiles declined sharply relative to the median. In addition, overall measures of inequality such as the Gini coefficient, the variance of the log of wages, and the coefficient of variation were all relatively stable until 1979 when they increased sharply (Karoly 1993).

Changes in between-group inequality. Part of the observed increase in the overall wage inequality was caused by the large increase in the returns to education. During the 1980s, the returns to education increased dramatically.[10] This is in sharp contrast to the decline in the returns to education during the 1970s (Katz and Revenga 1989; Juhn, Murphy, and Pierce 1989; and Murphy and Welch 1988). The increase in returns to education are largest for the young. Murphy and Welch show that the ratio of college to high school weekly wages for white males with 1 to 5 years' experience increased 50 percent since 1979. A similar but less pronounced increase in the college–high school wage ratio occurred for workers with 26 to 35 years' experience. The returns to experience also increased sharply after 1979 and were especially pronounced for high school educated workers. Thus, young high school workers also lost ground relative to older high school workers.

The result of these trends has been a dramatic decline in the relative position

of young, high school graduates. Juhn, Murphy, and Pierce illustrate this decline by noting that real wages for 10th percentile high school graduates with
1 to 10 years of experience were roughly 18 percent lower in 1987 than wages
for the same group in 1963. The least-skilled workers are rapidly falling away
from the rest of the distribution.

Changes in within-group inequality. In addition to the increased inequality
between education and experience groups, recent studies find a striking increase in wage dispersion within these groups. The increase in within-group
inequality, however, seems to have started earlier, beginning in the early 1970s.
The wage differential between the 90th and 10th percentile has increased within
the distributions of young and old workers and within the wage distributions of
high school and college graduates. In all cases, persons in the upper percentiles
experienced significant growth in real wages while those in the lower percentiles
experienced slight growth or, in most cases, declines in real wages.

Cross-national studies. With the recent availability of cross-country data,
researchers are just beginning to make cross-national comparisons of earnings
and income inequality. Green, Coder, and Ryscavage (1990) examine earnings
inequality in eight industrial countries using data from the Luxembourg Income
Study. Their primary emphasis is on ranking the countries in terms of overall
levels of inequality and seeing how the ranking varies with different inequality
measures. While they take a cursory look at changes in inequality, this is not
their primary focus.[11] Several international studies provide pairwise comparisons with the United States. Freeman and Needles (1991) compare the United
States and Canada; Katz and Loveman (1990) compare the United States with
the United Kingdom and France; while Katz and Revenga (1989) compare the
United States and Japan. Country-specific studies are also available for Australia
(Borland 1992) and Sweden (Hibbs 1990 and Edin and Holmlund 1992).

Freedman and Needles investigate whether the Canadians also experienced
similar changes in the college wage premium and in wage differentials within
education groups over the 1980s. Using data from both the Canadian Survey of
Consumer Finances and the Canadian Census of Population, they calculate
changes in mean log wage differentials between university graduates and high
school graduates and changes in log wage differentials between deciles within
these education groups. They find that Canada also experienced an increase in
the university wage premium during the 1980s. The increase, however, is quite
moderate compared to the United States. In addition, the increase in the university wage premium does not appear to be larger for young workers, as is the
case in the United States. After controlling for changes in weeks worked, Freeman and Needles show the Canadian increase in the university premium among
young workers to be only a sixth of the comparable increase for the United
States. They attribute this smaller rise in the college premium to the much larger
increase in the number of university graduates relative to high school graduates
in Canada. Freeman and Needles also find that Canada experienced increases
in earnings inequality among workers with the same education level. The in-

crease was particularly pronounced for high school educated workers and for young workers.

Katz and Loveman examine trends in weekly and hourly gross wage distributions based on age, gender, occupation, and industry for the United Kingdom. For full-time male workers, they find wage differentials between manual and nonmanual workers were stable over the 1974–1979 period and increased from 1979 to 1989. Wage differentials between experience groups expanded moderately in the later 1970s and substantially in the first part of the 1980s. Wage inequality within distributions based on detailed occupations and detailed occupation-industry breakdowns narrowed in the 1970s and increased greatly in the 1980s. Thus, the United Kingdom's experience is similar to that of the United States.

As for France, Katz and Loveman find the nonmanual/manual differential for full-time male workers narrowed from the mid-1970s through mid-1980s and picked up slightly at the end of the sample period. Thus, unlike the United States and United Kingdom, there is little evidence of a sharp deterioration in the relative wages of young unskilled workers. Data on within-occupation inequality shows relatively little change until 1984 when it begins to increase.

Katz and Revenga examine the changes in between-group wage inequality in the United States and Japan. For the United States, their findings support other studies which show a substantial increase in the returns to education and a large increase in the returns to experience among high school graduates since 1979. The plight of young, low-educated males in Japan contrasts sharply with that of the United States. They find the college wage premium within all experience groups in Japan increased only moderately in the 1980s, whereas much larger increases were found in the United States. During the 1980s, returns to experience did not increase in Japan as they did in the United States. In fact, Japanese new entrants in all education groups gained ground on more experienced workers in the 1980s. Moreover, high school educated new entrants in Japan actually experienced bigger increases in monthly wages in the 1980s than in the 1970s. This contrasts sharply with the decline in real and relative wages for young high school workers in the United States in the 1980s.

Katz and Revenga examine possible supply-side explanations of the observed trends. They show that the growth rate of college graduates from 1979 to 1987 declined in the United States and increased slightly in Japan. This difference partly explains the contrasting changes in the college wage premiums in the two countries. On the other hand, the fraction of new entrants with high school educations declined in the United States in the 1980s. This cohort effect would predict an improvement in high school entrants' wages, yet their wages fell dramatically. In Japan, the fraction of new entrants with high school and college educations declined, which is consistent with the improved position of new entrants in the Japanese labor market.

While Borland (1992), Hibbs (1990), and Edin and Holmlund (1992) do not try to gather comparable data for the United States, they do offer individual country studies on changes in wage inequality. Borland (1992) examines the changes in the distribution of wages for full-time male employees in Australia over the 1982 to 1990 period using individual-level data from the Income Distribution Survey. He finds that average real wages fell and overall wage inequality increased during the period. The rise in inequality is a result of an increase in wage inequality both within and across education-experience groups. Edin and Holmlund (1992) show that the trends in wage inequality in Sweden are similar to those experienced in France. That is, wage inequality has increased in the recent decade, but the increase is moderate and delayed compared to the United States. Overall inequality as measured by the variance in log wages fell from 1960 to 1980 and then began to increase. They also show, using a sample of both men and women, that the returns to education in Sweden declined over the period from 1968 to 1980 and increased thereafter. Hibbs (1990) shows a similar pattern of declining and then the increasing wage inequality among white collar and blue collar workers.

CHANGES IN ECONOMIC STRUCTURE

In this section we start by laying out the analytical links between changes in inequality and several structural changes that may have occurred in the economies of the countries we study. The first set of factors focus on the consequences of increased international competition and the resulting shift away from manufacturing toward services. The second set of factors focus on the implications of technological change on the demand for more skilled workers.[12]

After having established the conceptual links between changes in inequality and these changes in economic structure, we examine three key indicators that may be useful in measuring the relative importance of these factors: (1) changes in the international competition, (2) changes in the industrial structure, and (3) changes in the skill mix within industries. While these three indicators offer only a partial picture of the changes that have occurred in each country, they provide some useful information which can be used to narrow the range of possible causes of the increase in inequality.

Some Analytical Links Between Economic Structure and Inequality

In this section we develop the conceptual links between distributional changes and two commonly cited causes of the trend in inequality: changes in the international competition and changes in technology. Our choice to focus on these factors is motivated largely by the attention that they have received in the popular and academic literature.

The 1980s were marked by substantial shifts in the industrial structure of developed economies. This led to two related hypotheses which suggest that changes in inequality were caused by restructuring. The first hypothesis focuses on "deindustrialization" per se, independent of its cause. The second focuses on changes in industrial structure caused by changes in international competition. Each is considered in turn.

Figure 5.1 / Implications of Alternative Theories

Casual Mechanism	Implication	
	Changes in Skill Premium	Changes in Skill Intensity within an Industry
Changes in Industrial Structure	Increase	Decline
Changes in Technology	Increase	Increase

"Deindustrialization." The hypothesis that changes in industrial structure may have caused distributional changes has been prompted by the observation that manufacturing declined and the service sector expanded in the United States during the same period during which inequality increased. In popular terms, auto workers were being forced to become "hamburger flippers." The resulting shift of workers into industries that had both lower average wages and greater dispersion in wages would increase overall inequality, even if there was no change in the wages paid in each industry.[13]

However, the resulting decline in demand for low-skilled workers in the auto industry and the increased supply of low-skilled workers in the service sector will tend to decrease the wages of low-skilled workers. As a result, the skill premium (i.e., wages of more skilled workers relative to less skilled workers) is bid up. With the resulting increase in the relative cost of hiring more skilled workers, firms would want to substitute less skilled workers for the now more expensive skilled labor.[14] As summarized in the top row of Figure 5.1, the net result of deindustrialization would, therefore, be an increase in the skill premium and a decline in skill intensity within each sector.[15]

Institutions such as unions and governments can partially mediate the effects of these industrial shifts. For example, union-negotiated wages or social contracts can limit the extent to which these market forces alter wages. If all countries lost manufacturing and gained service sector jobs but these same countries experienced different patterns in inequality, then this would call into question the primacy of changes in industrial structure as an explanation for the growth in inequality—deindustrialization either had little impact on inequality or its effects were countered by institutional factors.

International competition.   The change in industrial structure is often attributed to increases in international competition. At the heart of this argument is the hypothesis that foreign competition has its biggest impact on the wages of low-skilled workers—when international trade increases, firms producing tradable goods which require unskilled workers face the largest increase in competition from abroad. This puts downward pressure on the wages of low-skilled workers. At the same time, firms producing skill-intensive tradable goods are able to increase exports. This increases the demand for skilled workers.

The result of the decline in demand for less-skilled workers and the increase in demand for more highly trained workers raises the gap between the wages of low- and high-skilled workers in industrialized countries. Meanwhile, the wage gap is expected to narrow in skill-poor countries. Skilled workers in these countries have to compete with their counterparts in other, more highly educated countries. On the other hand, unskilled workers in less developed countries can effectively compete with unskilled workers in developed countries through exports. These conceptual links between openness and inequality suggest that changes in inequality should be related to changes in openness—if countries that experienced substantial increases in inequality did not experience a concurrent increase in international trade, this is evidence against the international trade interpretation of rising inequality.

Change in Technology

Changes in technology are often cited as an alternative underlying cause of the increase in inequality. According to this argument, the widespread application of computers and automated technologies reduced the demand for less-skilled workers whose jobs were automated out of existence. At the same time there was an increased demand for high-skilled workers to run the automated systems.[16]

This explanation for the increase in inequality has similar empirical implications for the skill premium but different implications for the skill mix within sectors. Both deindustrialization and technological change predict that the wage differential will widen as the demand for less- (more-) skilled workers falls (rises). While the cause of the decline (rise) in demand for less- (more-) skilled workers is different, the prediction for a rising wage differential is identical for the two theories.

Where the theories do differ is in their predictions about changes in the skill mix within each industry. As we argued earlier, the deindustrialization argument implies that each sector will become less skill intensive—the increase in the cost of skilled workers with no offsetting increase in their productivity will induce firms to substitute less-skilled workers for their now more expensive counterparts. If, however, the increase in demand for more-skilled workers came from technological change that made more-educated workers more productive, then one should observe an increase in the skill intensity accompanying the increase in the skill premium. Both reflect the increased productivity of the more highly trained workers. Thus, as Figure 5.1 shows, the two theories have different implications about changes in the skill mix within industries.

EMPIRICAL RESULTS

Data

We use two types of cross-national data in this chapter. The first is the micro survey data from the Luxembourg Income Study (LIS). These data are used to obtain comparable measures of overall inequality, as well as between and within group inequality. The second source of data is published times series on measures of industrial structure and international competition from Organization for Economic Cooperation and Development (OECD). These data are used to try to gain insight into the possible causes of changes in inequality.

LIS data. We use LIS data on Australia, Canada, France, the Netherlands, Sweden, United Kingdom, and the United States.[17] The LIS data are a collection of micro data sets obtained from annual income surveys in various countries.[18] The different surveys are similar in form to the Current Population Survey for the United States and the Survey of Consumer Finances for Canada.[19] The advantage of these data is that extensive effort has been made by country specialists to make information on income and household characteristics as comparable as possible across countries.

Since we are interested in changes in inequality, we are restricted to the countries with two years of data in LIS. Although the years used were dictated by the years covered for each country in LIS, they represent a roughly similar time period—the first wave of data for each country is from the early 1980s and the second wave is from the mid- or late-1980s. For all countries other than Sweden and the Netherlands unemployment rates were higher in the second year than the first year.[20]

Our measure of earnings is real annual gross wages and salaries of male family heads.[21] We use the earning of male heads rather than all males, since data on individuals who are not heads or spouses are not available in LIS for all countries in both years. Studies using the CPS data have found similar patterns of earnings inequality using heads or individuals. We exclude females since we are trying to replicate studies for the United States that have focused almost exclusively on males.[22] In order to focus on people who are not likely to be in school or retired, we limit our sample to males between the ages of 25 and 54. To be consistent with other studies, we attempt to limit the sample to full-time workers.[23] Since no full-time variable is available for France or Canada, we present separate analyses for these countries and contrast their experiences with comparable data from the United States. Finally, in order to focus solely on labor market income we exclude male heads of households that report any self-employment income.

In order to maintain confidentiality, data on income above some upper bound are often reported at the upper bound. For example, in recent years the CPS data is top-coded at $100,000—individual earnings over this amount are recoded to $100,000. This top-coding affects comparisons both across time and across countries.[24] We use two different methods to account for the effects of top-coding. The first is to use summary measures, such as percentile points, which are not affected by top-coding. The second method, which we use when calculating the coefficient of variation, is to measure the dispersion of a truncated distribution by excluding the top 5 percent of the distribution in each year.[25] By providing a consistent cutoff across time and countries we limit the effects of top-coding.[26] Thus, the data we present in this chapter on the coefficient of variation are for the truncated distribution. Medians and percentile points that are not affected by top-coding are for the full distribution.

To explore changes both between and within education groups, we construct three education categories corresponding in the United States to less than 12 years of education, 12 years, and more than 12 years of education. The recoding into the three groups is straightforward for Canada and somewhat more arbitrary for the Netherlands.[27] Since no education information is available for Australia, France, Sweden, or the United Kingdom, we cannot compare changes in inequality between and within education groups for these countries.[28]

Published data. We use published information on the level of trade and the proportion of workers with a university education, by sector in each country over time. The published data on imports and exports (as a share of gross domestic product, GDP) are from the OECD National Accounts 1960–1986. Imports, exports, and GDP in each country are measured in billions of U.S. dollars at current prices and 1980 exchange rates. The employment by sector data are from the OECD Labour Force Statistics 1967–1987. We include females as well as males in these data since structural changes reflect changes in the employment of all persons.

Changes in Economic Structure in OECD Countries

Changes in inequality across countries. In this section we present information on inequality from the seven countries in the LIS data set. We separate our discussion of changes in inequality across countries into three sections: (1) changes in the overall wage distribution, (2) changes in between-group inequality and (3) changes in inequality within groups. Following the tradition of the existing literature we group by age and education.

Changes in the overall distributions. We start by describing changes in the median of the wage distributions in each country. This gives an indication of the underlying rate of growth in each country. Table 5.1 shows the yearly percentage change in median earnings (column 1), in coefficients of variation

Table 5.1 / Yearly Percentage Changes in Median, Coefficient of Variation, and Real Wages and Salaries, by Decile

Country	Yearly Percentage Change Median	Yearly Percentage Change CV*	Yearly Percentage Change 10th Percentile	Yearly Percentage Change 20th Percentile	Yearly Percentage Change 80th Percentile	Yearly Percentage Change 90th Percentile
Full-Time Workers						
Australia						
1981–1985	–.87	1.72	–1.47	–.92	–.41	–.14
Netherlands						
1983–1987	–.11	.90	–.71	–.07	–.27	.67
Sweden						
1981–1987	1.65	1.03	1.41	1.50	2.52	2.14
United Kingdom						
1979–1986	2.06	2.44	.51	.95	3.25	3.31
United States						
1979–1986	–.24	1.79	–.52	–.43	1.44	2.10
All Workers						
Canada						
1981–1987	.73	1.70	–2.08	–.38	1.45	1.31
France						
1979–1984	–.37	1.80	–1.92	–1.38	–.24	.32
United States						
1979–1986	–.48	2.56	–2.35	–1.59	.73	2.10

*The top 5 percent of the sample is truncated in computing the coefficient of variation.

(column 2), and in real earnings by decile (columns 3–6). The top panel is for those countries for which we can limit the samples to full-time workers. The bottom panel shows data for full- and part-time workers in the United States and the two countries for which the full-time variable is not available.

Table 5.1 indicates that median earnings in the United States declined between 1979 and 1986. This is consistent with other studies tracking the growth in real wages over the 1980s (Karoly 1992). The lack of growth was, however, not restricted to the United States—the majority of countries experienced negative growth in median real gross annual wages and salaries. The exceptions are Canada, which experienced a small increase in median wages and salaries, and the United Kingdom and Sweden, which experienced substantial growth.[29]

Our summary measures of inequality replicate the results of others for the United States—a falling median was accompanied by rising inequality during the 1980s. This applies to full-time as well as all workers. Again, this pattern is not isolated to the United States. We find increases in the yearly percentage change in the coefficient of variation for all countries.[30] While the direction of the trend is common across countries, the United States did experience the second to highest increase in inequality, with only the United Kingdom having a higher yearly growth in the coefficient of variation.

Changes in between-group inequality. Previous studies of the United States found large increases in the returns to education and experience since 1979. In Table 5.2, we compute the ratio of median real wage ratios of young (25–30 years old) to older (40–55) workers, low- to high-educated workers, and medium- to high-educated workers in each year. We examine the percentage change in these ratios for each country for which we have data.

In all countries, we find the mean earnings of young workers falling behind the mean earnings of older workers. The ratio of mean wages for workers 25–30 years old relative to 40–55-year-olds declined by 1.97 percent per year for full-time workers in the United States. Thus, the increased returns to experience, which has been an important factor in increasing inequality in the United States, is a widely experienced phenomenon.

Consistent with other studies, we also find that the returns to education increased sharply in the United States, while Canada experienced a much smaller increase in the education premium. The Netherlands, on the other hand, has a different pattern—less-educated workers actually gained on higher-educated workers.[31] Thus, the United States is different from other countries in its exceptionally large increase in returns to education—in the United States, the ratio of mean wages of low- to high-educated workers declined by 2.21 percent per year (for all workers). In contrast, the change in Canada was only 1.07 percent.

Changes in within-group inequality. Previous studies of the United States found that the changes in wage dispersion within the experience and education groups were also large. In Table 5.3, we examine the changes in the coefficient of variation for persons age 25–30 (relatively inexperienced workers) and per-

Table 5.2 / Between-Group Inequality Between Younger and Older Male Workers and Between Those with Low and High Educational Attainment

Country and Year	Ratio of Median Real Earnings of All Male Workers		
	Young/Old	Low/High Educational Attainment	Medium/High Educational Attainment
Australia			
1981	.911	N.A.	N.A.
1985	.862	N.A.	N.A.
Annual Percentage Change	−1.34	N.A.	N.A.
Netherlands			
1983	.820	.520	.666
1987	.741	.650	.819
Annual Percentage Change	−2.41	6.25	5.74
Sweden			
1981	.856	N.A.	N.A.
1987	.833	N.A.	N.A.
Annual Percentage Change	−.45	N.A.	N.A.
United Kingdom			
1979	.956	N.A.	N.A.
1986	.845	N.A.	N.A.
Annual Percentage Change	−1.66	N.A.	N.A.
United States			
1979	.784	.615	.855
1986	.676	.567	.767
Annual Percentage Change	−1.97	−1.11	−1.47
Canada			
1981	.838	.749	.869
1987	.727	.701	.814
Annual Percentage Change	−2.21	−1.07	−1.05
France			
1979	.883	N.A.	N.A.
1984	.763	N.A.	N.A.
Annual Percentage Change	−2.72	N.A.	N.A.
United States			
1979	.753	.615	.872
1986	.679	.520	.733
Annual Percentage Change	−1.40	−2.21	−2.28

*See Table 5A.3 for educational categories used in each country.

Table 5.3 / Yearly Percent Change in the Coefficient of Variation, by Age and Education Group*

| Country | Full Sample | Age | | Education | | |
		25–30	40–55	Low	Medium	High
Full-Time Workers						
Australia	1.72	1.66	1.36	N.A.	N.A.	N.A.
Netherlands	.90	2.09	− .21	5.46	4.38	2.95
Sweden	1.03	− .61	.61	N.A.	N.A.	N.A.
United Kingdom	2.44	1.71	1.72	N.A.	N.A.	N.A.
United States	1.79	2.15	1.24	1.35	1.96	1.35
All Workers						
Canada	1.70	1.77	1.61	1.79	1.04	2.22
France	1.80	1.26	1.40	N.A.	N.A.	N.A.
United States	2.56	2.70	1.95	3.34	2.98	1.69

*The top 5 percent of each sample is truncated in computing the coefficient of variation.

sons 45–55 (relatively experienced workers) to see whether inequality also increased within these groups in other countries. We also look at changes in inequality for persons classified by education for those countries for which education is available.

Inequality among young workers, as measured by the coefficient of variation, increased considerably in all countries except Sweden. While inequality among older workers increased in all countries except the Netherlands, the increase in inequality within this group tended to be smaller. Similarly inequality increased in all education groups in all countries.[32] Thus, the direction of the change in inequality within age and education groups is consistent with the data for the United States.

From the data presented in this section, we conclude that the industrialized countries we have studied have roughly similar patterns of increased wage inequality for every measure other than the rise in returns to education. In the following section we explore whether these countries also experienced similar structural changes in trade and industrial structure.

Changes in Trade and Industrial Structures

Changes in trade. In order to obtain a rough measure of the extent to which these economies were subject to increases in international competition we use OECD data to calculate the proportion of GDP that is directly involved in trade. We use the standard measure of imports plus exports as a proportion of GDP.[33] The time series between 1960 and 1986 for the United States and each country are shown in Figure 5.2.

The United States experienced moderate growth in exports plus imports between 1965 and 1972 and rapid growth between 1973 and 1981. Openness then

Figure 5.2 / Imports plus Exports as Percentage of GDP

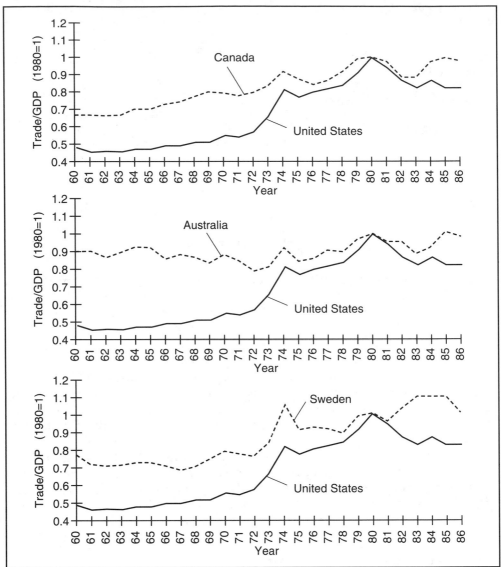

SOURCE: OECD National Product Accounts 1960–1986.

Figure 5.2 / (*continued*)

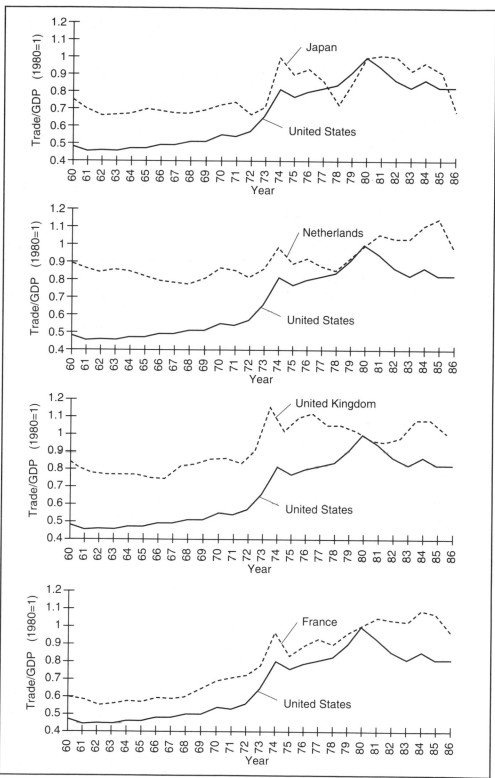

fell in 1982 through 1984, stabilizing at roughly its 1974 level. The trade patterns for France are the most similar to those of the United States. While Canada, the United Kingdom, and Sweden also show increases during the overall period, openness for these countries increased by less than it did for the United States. Only Australia shows much smaller rates of growth in openness. Since it also experienced the smallest increase in inequality, this suggests that inequality and openness may be related.

Given the high degree of industrialization of all the countries we study, it should not be surprising that all the countries that experienced an increase in trade also experienced an increase in inequality. The more-skilled workers in these countries found new markets in the countries with few highly educated workers, while the less-educated workers in these industrialized countries found themselves having to compete with imports made in countries with an abundance of less-skilled workers.

If increased international competition had a large effect, then we would expect inequality to decrease in less-developed countries while it increased in more-developed countries. Highly educated workers in these countries would find themselves competing with their counterparts in industrialized countries. This would decrease the wages of skilled workers in less-developed countries. Meanwhile, the less-skilled workers would experience an increase in their relative wages as the goods they produce compete in new overseas markets. Put another way, jobs lost in the United States as a result of international competition would mean an offsetting increase in demand for low-skilled workers in other countries. Given the high degree of industrialization of all the countries we study, it is not surprising that the increase in trade experienced by these countries was accompanied by an increase in inequality. The more-skilled workers in these countries found new markets in the countries with few highly educated workers while the less-educated workers in these industrialized countries found themselves having to compete with imports made in countries with an abundance of less-skilled workers.

While the evidence on changes in inequality in less-developed countries is very limited, Davis (1992) presents some suggestive evidence on changes in inequality between education groups for South Korea, Brazil, Venezuela, and Columbia. He finds that the skill premium decreased in all four countries. Topel and Kim (1992) who conduct a detailed study of labor market changes in Korea also find that inequality between education groups fell between 1976 and 1989. Unlike the developed countries we study, all these less-developed countries experienced a decline in inequality.

The growth in inequality in developed countries and the decline in less-developed countries is consistent with the view that increases in international competition were partially responsible for changes in inequality. This evidence is, however, at best only suggestive. While the growth in inequality in the developed countries is unusual, the decline in the less-developed countries is consistent with the Kuznets hypothesis that countries in the latter stages of development will experience a decline in inequality. With the data at hand we simply cannot differentiate between a movement along the Kuznets inverted U-shaped inequality profile and a downward shift of the profile that would result from increased openness.

We conclude that the United States was not alone in experiencing an increase in openness during the 1970s, and that trade may be partially responsible for the increase in inequality in industrialized countries. The fact that inequality grew least in Australia, the country with the smallest growth in trade, and the fact that several less-developed countries experienced a decline in inequality suggest that international competition may have been instrumental in raising inequality in the industrialized countries.

Changes in industrial structure. If international competition from less-developed countries is important, then we should expect similar changes in industrial structure among developed countries in LIS. Are there systematic differences between these countries in the degree to which they lost manufacturing and gained service sector jobs?[34] To answer this question, Gottschalk and Joyce (1992) examined the distribution of civilian employment across four sectors: agriculture, services, manufacturing, and a residual sector to see if the other countries studied have experienced changes in industrial structure that are similar to the U.S. experience. They find remarkable similarity across countries in the redirection of employment toward the service sector. Although the relative size of the sectors in each countries varies, the direction of the changes in employment by sector is the same in all countries. Each experienced a decline in employment shares in agriculture and manufacturing and an increase in employment shares in the service sector. We conclude that if inequality is being driven by deindustrialization, which is in turn being driven by increased international competition, then deindustrialization is affecting all these countries in a very similar manner.

Changes in skill mix within sectors. Our initial hope, of distinguishing between the impact of changes in industrial structure and the impact of changes in technology by exploiting cross-national comparisons, has proven to be elusive. The data have shown that the countries we studied experienced similar changes in the inequality and industrial structure. With little variation in either the dependent or the explanatory variable it is difficult to determine the role played by changes in industrial structure.

However, as discussed earlier, deindustrialization and technological change have different implications for changes in the skill mix within sectors. If changing industrial structure is the primary cause of the increased demand for skilled workers, then we would expect to see an increase in the skill differential. This increase in the relative cost of more skilled workers would, however, lead to a decline in the proportion of skilled workers hired as firms had to pay higher prices for workers whose productivity had not increased. In contrast, if technological change was the cause of the increase in the skill premium (documented in Table 5.2) then we would expect to see an increase in skill intensity within all sectors. The rising skill differential would reflect the fact that the productivity

Table 5.4 / Yearly Percent Change in the Relative Proportion of the Labor Force with University Educational Attainment

	Canada 1975–1987	Japan 1974–1987	Sweden 1971–1987	United States 1972–1987	United Kingdom 1981–1987
Agriculture	.58	.31	.42	.50	.40
Mining and Quarrying	.34	.43	N.A.	.28	1.23
Manufacturing	.43	.29	.42	.39	.78
Electricity, Gas, and Water	N.A.	.28	N.A.	N.A.	1.57
Construction	.37	.26	.28	.29	.78
Trade, Restaurants	.43	.25	.39	.29	.45
Transport, Communication	.43	.22	.33	.46	.05
Finance, Insurance, Real Estate Business	.43	.31	.18	.25	.60
Other Services	.23	.26	.18	.16	.33
All Industries	.33	.33	.32	.27	.58

SOURCE: OECD: *Outlook on Employment*, 1987.

of skilled workers had increased enough to induce firms to bid up their relative price.

Table 5.4 presents data on the growth in the proportion of the labor force with a university education by sector and country. The bottom row shows the yearly percentage increase in the proportion of the labor force (in all industries) with a college degree. The growth rates for each country are very similar (ranging from .27 to .58 percent per year).[35] While there is some diversity across sectors, almost all sectors in all countries show an increase in the proportion of university-educated workers. Agriculture, a rapidly declining sector, experienced some of the largest increases in educational upgrading. Likewise, manufacturing and professional services, two sectors with very different employment patterns, had above-average growth in the proportion of their workers with a university degree. This suggests that technological change was increasing the demand for college-educated workers sufficiently fast to offset any effects of the rising skill premium coming from deindustrialization. Without some outside force to drive up demand for skilled workers, we would have observed firms cutting back on their demand for skilled workers whose wages had risen sharply relative to other workers. Thus, changes in technology are a necessary part of the explanation for the rise in inequality.[36]

CONCLUSIONS

There are two types of conclusions that can be reached on the basis of the data in this paper. The first are purely descriptive. Our review of the evidence shows broadly similar patterns in inequality, international competition, and industrial structure in the seven industrialized economies we studied. All countries experienced an increase in inequality both within and between groups, though the United States experienced the second to highest increase in overall inequality and the largest increase in returns to education. Viewed in this light, the U.S. experience may be more acute but qualitatively is not atypical. Furthermore, the deindustrialization and increased openness of the United States are not aberrations. All countries experienced increases in trade, declines in manufacturing, and increases in service sector jobs.

While the widespread increases in inequality suggest that the economic pressures were sufficiently large to partially overcome the institutional barriers to market forces, this is not to say that these countries were not able to redistribute income to offset the effects of market forces. In fact, Blank and Hanratty (1991) show that Canada's social safety net kept poverty from rising in spite of the increase in wage inequality. Likewise, Gottschalk (1992) shows that many of the LIS countries in this study were able to offset the impact of growth in earnings inequality. While earnings inequality increased in all countries, the distribution of family income actually became more equal in some countries.

Some causal conclusions are also offered on the basis of data in this chapter. These are offered much more tentatively since cross-national comparisons do not provide the type of natural experiment which one would need to draw causal inferences. The data we have presented suggest that both internationalization of competition and changes in technology were important. The fact that less-developed countries experienced a decrease in inequality, while all the industrialized countries we studied experienced an increase in inequality suggests that the relative wages of more-skilled workers were being bid down in less-developed countries while they were being bid up in the more-developed countries. This is consistent with the effects of increased international competition. On the other hand, the fact that the proportion of the labor force with a college degree increased in all sectors despite its higher price implies that deindustrialization could not be the whole story—without technological change industries would have become less skill-intensive as a result of the increase in the cost of skilled workers.

In summary, the rise in inequality is not unique to the United States. While there is still no "smoking gun" to explain the rise in inequality in all these industrialized countries, this study shows that both international competition and technological change played a role in rising inequality.

Gottschalk is Professor of Economics at Boston College and Research Affiliate at the Institute for Research on Poverty, Madison, Wisconsin. Joyce is an Economist at the Bureau of Labor Statistics. We would like to thank Tim Smeeding for the years of work it has taken to put the LIS data set together. Participants in the Poverty and Public Policy Project and members of the Industrial Relations workshop at MIT provided useful comments on an earlier draft.

Table 5A.1 / Household Surveys in the LIS Data Base

Country	Survey	Sample Size
United States	*March Current Population Survey*	1979–15,225
		1986–13,707
Australia	*The Income and Housing Survey*	1981–15,985
		1985–7,560
Canada	*Survey of Consumer Finance*	1981–15,136
		1987–10,999
France	*The Survey of Individual Income Tax Returns*	1979–11,044
		1984–12,693
Netherlands	*The Survey of Income and Program Users*	1983–4,833
		1987–4,190
Sweden	*The Swedish Income Distribution Survey*	1981–9,625
		1987–9,421
United Kingdom	*The Family Expenditure Survey*	1979–6,888
		1986–7,178

Table 5A.2 / Unemployment Rates, by Country: 1975–1989*

Country	1975	1976	1977	1978	1979	1980	1981	1982
United States	8.5	7.7	7.1	6.0	5.8	7.1	7.6	9.7
Australia	4.4	4.6	5.6	6.3	6.2	6.1	5.8	7.2
Canada	6.9	7.1	8.1	8.4	7.5	7.5	7.6	11.0
France	4.0	4.4	5.1	5.5	6.3	6.8	7.4	8.2
Netherlands	—	—	—	5.0	5.1	5.9	9.0	12.6
Sweden	1.6	1.6	1.8	2.2	2.1	—	2.5	3.2
U.K.	3.9	5.3	5.8	5.7	5.4	8.8	10.6	9.8

	1983	1984	1985	1986	1987	1988	1989
United States	9.6	7.5	7.2	7.0	6.2	5.5	5.3
Australia	10.0	9.0	8.2	8.1	8.1	7.2	6.4
Canada	11.9	11.3	10.5	9.6	8.9	7.8	7.5
France	8.5	10.0	10.2	10.4	10.5	10.0	9.4
Netherlands	17.1	17.2	15.7	14.7	14.0	6.4	5.7
Sweden	3.5	3.1	2.8	2.7	1.9	1.6	1.4
U.K.	10.7	11.1	11.3	11.4	10.1	8.1	6.3

SOURCE: OECD *Main Economic Indicators.*

*Underlined values are for LIS survey years.

Table 5A.3 / Recoding from LIS Education Categories

Canada 1981 and 1985	
High	University degree
	Postsecondary diploma
	Some postsecondary
Medium	11–13 years
Low	No schooling
	Less than 10 years
Netherlands 1983 and 1987	
High	University
Medium	Secondary
Low	Primary and extended primary
United States 1979 and 1986	
High	13 years or more
Medium	12 years
Low	Less than 12 years

Table 5A.4 / Between-Group Inequality—Real Wages and Salaries, by Age and Education Groups

Country	Sample Size		Median Real Wage		Yearly Percentage Change
United States	1979	1986	1979	1986	
Full	5,419	4,396	26,559	25,561	− .50
Age					
25–30	1,433	1,066	21,668	20,394	− .80
40–55	2,206	1,729	29,144	29,822	.33
Ratio			.743	.684	− 1.14
Education					
Low	1,025	638	18,572	16,615	− 1.50
Medium	1,779	1,622	26,311	23,431	− 1.60
High	2,615	2,136	30,629	31,952	.62
Ratio					
Low/High			.606	.520	− 2.03
Med/High			.859	.733	− 2.10

/ **219**

Country	Sample Size		Median Real Wage		Yearly Percentage Change
Canada	1981	1987	1981	1987	
Full	5,664	4,459	29,701	31,111	.79
Age					
25–30	1,425	1,018	26,426	25,075	−.90
40–55	2,243	1,845	30,959	33,681	1.47
Ratio			.853	.744	−2.12
Education					
Low	2,028	1,319	25,710	25,656	−.04
Medium	1,679	1,388	29,643	29,857	.12
High	1,957	1,752	34,105	36,299	1.07
Ratio					
Low/High			.754	.707	−1.04
Med/High			.869	.822	−.90
Netherlands	1983	1987	1983	1987	
Full	2,444	2,184	44,995	44,743	−.10
Age					
25–30	450	424	38,692	37,774	−.60
40–55	725	756	47,708	50,805	−1.62
Ratio			.811	.743	−2.10
Education					
Low	1,070	1,416	39,899	42,336	1.53
Medium	769	307	51,136	51,062	−.04
High	154	217	73,585	60,776	−4.40
Ratio					
Low/High			.542	.696	7.10
Med/High			.695	.840	5.65
Australia	1981	1985	1981	1985	
Full	5,660	2,928	29,529	28,734	−.67
Age					
25–30	1,234	520	27,260	26,162	−1.00
40–55	2,212	1,157	29,798	29,949	.13
Ratio			.915	.874	1.12

Table 5A.4 / (*continued*)

Country	Sample Size		Median Real Wage		Yearly Percentage Change
Australia (*cont.*)	1981	1985	1981	1985	
Education					
Low	2,207	941	26,145	26,438	.28
Medium	2,831	1,581	30,141	28,956	−.98
High	622	406	40,317	37,538	−1.72
Ratio					
Low/High			.648	.704	2.16
Med/High			.748	.771	.77
Sweden	1981	1987	1981	1987	
Full	3,047	2,749	72,745	72,602	.03
Age					
25–30	530	644	63,845	63,502	−.09
40–55	1,439	1,620	77,708	78,721	.22
Ratio			.822	.807	−.31
France	1979	1984	1979	1984	
Full	4,049	4,843	93,652	91,372	−.50
Age					
25–30	820	847	84,247	75,624	−2.00
40–55	1,933	2,186	95,415	100,308	1.03
Ratio			.833	.754	−2.92
United Kingdom	1979	1986	1979	1986	
Full	2,402	2,694	10,117	11,210	1.54
Age					
25–30	531	449	9,578	9,850	.416
40–55	1,052	996	10,059	11,344	1.82
Ratio			.952	.868	−1.26

Table 5A.5 / Industry Categories, by Country

Sector 1 Agriculture	Sector 2 Manufacturing	Sector 3 Services	Sector 4 Other
United States 1979 and 1986 Agriculture production, Agriculture services, Forestry/fisheries	Ordnance, Lumber, Furniture, Primary metals, Stone/clay/glass, Fab metals, Machinery, Electrical equipment, Autos, Aircraft, Other transport instruments, Other durables, Food, Tobacco, Textiles, Apparel, Paper, Printing, Chemicals, Petroleum, Rubber/plastics, Leather/other	Railroad/railway, Other transportation, Communication, Other public utility, Wholesale trade, Eating/drinking place, Other retail, Banking/other finance, Insurance/real estate, Private HH service, Business service, Repair, Personal services, Entertainment/Recreation, Medical service exc. H, Hospital, Welfare/religious, Educational, Other professional service, Public adm. Postal, Public adm. federal, Public adm. state, Public adm. local	Mining, Construction
Netherlands 1983 and 1987 Agriculture/fish/forestry	Light industry, Heavy industry	Public utilities, Trade, Repair, Communication/transportation, Storage, Banking/insurance/public services	Mining, Construction
Sweden 1981 and 1987 Agriculture/hunting, Forestry/logging, Fishing	Food, Beverage, Textile/apparel/leather, Wood/furniture, Paper/print/publish, Chem./pe-	Electricity/gas/stream water works/supply wholesale trade, Retail trade, Res-	Metal/ore/mining, Other mining construction

Table 5A.5 / (*continued*)

Sector 1 Agriculture	Sector 2 Manufacturing	Sector 3 Services	Sector 4 Other
Sweden (*cont.*)	tro/plastic, Non-metal mineral prod., Basic metal industry, Metal machine/equip., Other manufacturing industry	taurant/hotel, Transport/storage communication, Financial institution, Insurance, Real estate/business services, Public adm./defense, Sanitary service/rel, Social community services, Culture/recreation, Personal/household	
Australia 1981 and 1985 Agriculture, Forestry	Food, Beverage, Textile/clothes, Paper/print, Chemical/petrol. metal product, Transport equip	Elec./gas/water, Special trade, Wholesale trade, Retail trade, Road transport/storage, Other transport/storage, Communication, Finance/business finance/investment/insurance property/business public admin./defense community services, Education/library recreation/personal restaurant/hotel/club, Other service N.E.C.	Mining, General construction
United Kingdom 1979 and 1986 Agriculture/fish/forestry	Food/drink/tobacco coal/petroleum chemical ind./related manufacture metal mechanical/instrument/electri-	Gas/electricity/water, Railroad transportation post/other transport, Wholesale/retail distr., Insur-	Mining, Quarrying construction

Table 5A.5 / (*continued*)

Sector 1 Agriculture	Sector 2 Manufacturing	Sector 3 Services	Sector 4 Other
United Kingdom (*cont.*)	cal engineering/ shipbuilding vehi- cles, Other metal goods, Textiles leather/fur./ clothing/footwear/ brick/pottery glass, Timber, Furniture, Paper, Print, Pub- lish, Other manuf. industry	ance/bank, Bus pro- fessionals/scien- tific, Clean/repair service, Armed forces, Exc. police nation gov. ser- vices, Local police/ fire services, Other local gov. services, Other services	

Table 5A.6 / **LIS Industry Weights in Each Year, by Country**

Country/Year	LIS Industry Weights			
	Sector 1	Sector 2	Sector 3	Sector 4
United States				
1979	1.85	39.21	45.74	13.20
1986	2.49	35.30	50.54	11.67
Australia				
1981	3.18	25.40	65.54	6.87
1985	3.39	22.48	64.73	9.45
Netherlands				
1983	1.85	25.27	61.94	11.89
1987	1.18	20.85	68.04	9.93
Sweden				
1981	4.88	32.37	51.08	11.67
1987	1.97	32.56	53.25	12.22
United Kingdom				
1979	1.60	31.03	47.94	19.43
1986	2.00	26.98	58.89	12.14

ENDNOTES

1. Throughout this chapter we use the term "skilled" to mean persons with more education or experience. Whether these traits lead to higher wages because of screening or higher productivity is not important to the argument.

2. See Gottschalk and Danziger (1985).

3. See Danziger and Gottschalk (1989) for a review of alternative explanations.

4. We use the economist's definition of technological change as a change in methods of production that increase the productivity of a given number of skilled workers. Technological change could arise because of the discovery of new methods of production or managers choosing different methods. The increase in productivity will raise the demand for skilled workers, which will lead to more workers being hired at higher wages.

5. Inequality measures reflect both changes in prices (the wage rates paid to workers of different types) and quantities (the proportion of workers of each type). In the case of the technological change, both prices and quantities contribute to the change in within-industry inequality.

6. We focus on shifts to industries with low mean wages. The term "deindustrialization" can also imply shifts to industries with large variations in wages. Thus, deindustrialization may increase both between-group and within-group inequality. In either case, inequality is affected by changes in the weights put on different industries.

7. For recent studies see Juhn, Murphy, and Pierce (1989) and Karoly (1993).

8. Throughout this chapter all values are in real terms (they are adjusted for inflation).

9. A male at the 10th percentile has a wage that exceeds the wages of 10 percent of male workers.

10. The return to education is the percentage increase in wages that is associated with an extra year of education.

11. Blackburn and Bloom (1990) use the LIS data to compare changes in family income inequality (not wage inequality) between the United States, Canada, and Australia in the 1980s.

12. Bound and Johnson (1992) offer a more formal treatment of these issues.

13. In many European countries the change in demand resulted in lower employment rates as well as some decrease in the wages of less-skilled workers.

14. This is a movement along the demand function.

15. The aggregate skill intensity would still have risen, even though each industry became less skill intensive. The reweighting toward the more skill-intensive sector would more than offset the decline in skill intensity within each sector, since the net change in demand for more-skilled workers must have been positive if their wages rose.

16. The demand for less-skilled workers falls relative to the demand for skilled workers. The absolute change in demand depends on the aggregate demand for the goods produced by the firm.

17. The German data in LIS were not used because the 2 years of data were obtained from two different surveys, the German Transfer Survey and the German Panel Survey. All other countries had data from the same surveys in the two years.

18. The data are stored in Luxembourg under the sponsorship of the Luxembourg government. See Smeeding (1986) for a detailed description of the data source and methods for accessing the data.

19. Table 5A.1 lists the surveys used in each country.

20. Table 5A.2 provides the country specific unemployment rates between 1975 and 1989.

21. Current dollar values have been inflated to 1988 prices (each in their own currency) using the implicit price deflators from the OECD National Product Accounts.

22. Since there were large inflows of women into the labor markets during the 1970s and 1980s, the distribution of the earnings of females was affected by selection (which women entered) as well as by changes in supply and demand for persons of given characteristics. Focusing on males partially avoids these selection issues.

23. The Australian and Netherlands data are for full-time last week rather than for the reference year.

24. Even if the nominal upper bound does not change, inflation will erode its real value.

25. In computing the CV within groups, the top 5 percent of the age or education specific distribution is excluded. For example, when calculating the coefficient of variation for high school graduates we trim the top 5 percent of high school graduates.

26. An alternative would be to impute values to persons who are top-coded. This has the advantage of maintaining information on all persons but the disadvantage of introducing substantial measurement error, which may have a large effect on second moments.

27. See Table 5A.3 for more detail on education categories.

28. An education variable is available for Australia but the coding is not consistent in the 2 years. This makes the changes in inequality between and within education groups less reliable.

29. Katz and Loveman also find high real wage growth rates for the United Kingdom in the 1980s. They attribute the difference in wage growth between the U.K. and the U.S. to the sharp rise in unemployment in Britain relative to the U.S. This suggests that low-skilled workers in the U.K. experienced high rates of unemployment rather than wage reductions, and thus mean wages actually increased in the U.K.

30. Our data match the results of other individual country studies except for France. Katz and Loveman (1990) find little increase in inequality among full-time workers. The data in Table 5.1 suggest that the inclusion of part-time workers leads to a deterioration over time at the bottom of the distribution.

31. While we do not have data on education for the other countries, Borland (1992) finds an increase in the log wage differential between educated and less-educated workers in Australia over the 1982 to 1990 period. The increase is however less dramatic than in the US.

32. Borland (1992) shows that in Australia wage inequality within education groups increased over the 1982–1990 period within all education groups except the least educated group.

33. Very similar patterns emerge when we plot exports as a percentage of GDP.

34. Topel and Kim (1992) find a massive increase in the employment shares in manufacturing for Korea. This is supportive of the hypothesis that world manufacturing production is shifting away from developed countries to middle income economies.

35. This table does not address the cause of the increase in skill intensity. It could have come about because the fast growing sectors were the more skill intensive (i.e., the deindustrialization explanation) or because each sector became more skill intensive (the technological explanation).

36. Bound and Johnson (1992) also stress the importance of technological change in explaining increases in inequality in the United States.

37. The skill intensities for all industries were computed by weighting each sector by its percentage of the civilian employed. The employment percentages were taken from the OECD Labor Force Statistic 1967–1987, while the data on skill intensities by sector were taken from the special 1987 OECD study on education and the labor force.

REFERENCES

Blackburn, McKinley, and David Bloom. 1990. "The Distribution of Family Income: Measuring and Explaining Changes in the 1980s for Canada and the United States." Paper from NBER Conference on U.S. and Canadian Labor Markets. October.

Borland, Jeff. 1992. "Wage Inequality in Australia." Paper from NBER Conference on International Labor Markets. April.

Bound, John, and George Johnson. 1992. "Changes in the Structure of Wages in the 1980s: An Evaluation of Alternative Explanations." *American Economic Review* 82, 3. June.

Danziger, Sheldon, and Peter Gottschalk. 1989. "Increasing Inequality in the United States: What We Know and What We Don't." *Journal of Post Keynesian Economics* XI, 2. Winter.

Davis, Stephen. 1992. "Cross-Country Patterns of Change in Relative Wages." Preliminary draft. February.

Edin, Per-Anders, and Bertil Holmlund. 1992. "The Swedish Wage Structure: The Rise and Fall of Solidaristic Wage Policy." Mimeo.

Freeman, Richard, and Karen Needles. 1991. "Skill Differentials in Canada in an Era of Rising Labor Market Inequality." Preliminary draft.

Gottschalk, Peter. 1992. "Changes in Inequality of Family Income in Seven Industrialized Countries—Responses to Growing Earnings Inequality." December.

Gottschalk, Peter, and Sheldon Danziger. 1985. "A Framework for Evaluating the Effects of Economic Growth and Transfers on Poverty." *American Economic Review.*

Gottschalk, Peter, and Mary Joyce. 1992. "Is Earnings Inequality Also Rising in Other Industrialized Countries?" Unpublished paper.

Green, Gordon, John Coder, and Paul Ryscavage. 1992. "International Comparisons on Earnings Inequality for Men in the 1980s." *Review of Income and Wealth*, Series 38, March.

Hibbs, Douglas A. Jr. 1990. "Wage Dispersion and Trade Union Action in Sweden." In Persson, Inga, ed. *Generating Equality in the Welfare State.*

Juhn, Chinhui, Kevin Murphy, and Brooks Pierce. 1989. "Wage Inequality and the Rise in the Returns to Skill." Preliminary draft, October.

Karoly, Lynn A. 1992. "Changes in the Distribution of Individual Earnings in the United States: 1967–1986." *The Review of Economics and Statistics.* February.

———. 1993. "The Trend in Inequality among Families, Individuals, and Workers in the United States: A Twenty-Five-Year Perspective." In Danziger, Sheldon, and Peter Gottschalk, eds. *Uneven Tides: Rising Inequality in the 1980s.* New York: Russell Sage Foundation.

Katz, Lawrence F., and Gary W. Loveman. 1990. "An International Comparison of Changes in the Structure of Wages: France, The United Kingdom, and The United States." Preliminary draft, December.

Moffitt, Robert. 1990. "The Distribution of Earnings and the Welfare State." In Burtless, Gary, ed. *A Future of Lousy Jobs.* Washington, D.C.: The Brookings Institution.

Murphy, Kevin, and Finis Welch. 1988. "Wage Differentials in the 1980s: The Role of International Trade." Preliminary draft.

Topel, Robert, and Dae-il Kim. 1988. "Labor Markets and Economics Growth: Lessons from Korea's Industrialization, 1970–1990." Paper from NBER Conference on International Labor Markets, April.

Part II

CHANGING FAMILY STRUCTURES: PUBLIC POLICY AND LONE-PARENT FAMILIES

GENDER ROLE
AND FAMILY STRUCTURE CHANGES
IN THE ADVANCED INDUSTRIALIZED WEST:
IMPLICATIONS FOR SOCIAL POLICY

Sheila B. Kamerman

CHANGES in gender roles and in family structure are entwined with changes in marriage, divorce, childbearing, women's employment, and parenting. As Larry Bumpass said in his 1990 address to the Population Association of America, "Changes in one family domain may contribute to further changes in that domain or others."[1] In effect, changes in gender roles and family structures are both cause and effect; together they interact with the family economy and have major consequences for child and family economic well-being.

Although there are differences in degree, the pattern and rate of change in family structure and female work roles in most Western industrialized countries are extraordinarily similar. However, the policy strategies designed to respond to these developments do vary, and these differences have important consequences for children and their families.

This chapter begins by describing the demographic and social changes of particular concern in the United States and compares them with developments in Canada and Western Europe. It then reviews the different policy strategies employed by a range of countries to cope with these developments and assesses the outcomes of these policies, to the extent that they are known, for children and their families. Finally, it highlights the policy option(s) that could lead to improved child and family well-being and discusses which policies may be appropriate for the United States.

THE CHANGING FAMILY

Decline in Marriage Rates

Conventional wisdom to the contrary, the United States remains an anomaly with regard to marriage. Americans continue to marry at significantly higher

Table 6.1 / Marriage Rates per 1,000 Women in Selected Countries

Country	1960	1970	1988*
United States	8.5	10.7	9.7
Canada	7.3	8.8	7.4
Austria	8.3	7.1	6.1
Denmark	7.8	8.0	5.6
Finland	7.4	8.6	5.9
France	7.0	7.7	5.1
Federal Republic of Germany	9.4	7.1	5.9
Italy	7.8	7.4	5.2
Netherlands	7.8	9.5	5.7
Norway	6.6	7.6	5.0
Sweden	6.7	5.4	4.4
United Kingdom	7.5	8.5	7.0
Average	7.6	8.0	6.1

SOURCES: 1960 and 1970 figures from OECD: *Child and Family Developments in the OECD Countries.* Paris: OECD, 1979. Table I–IV, p. 59; for 1988 figures, EEC: *Basic Statistics.*

*Some of these figures are for earlier years, for example, 1984 or 1986.

rates than almost all other people living in the advanced industrialized Western countries (Table 6.1).[2] The average marriage rate (per 1,000 unmarried women) among the 12 countries examined here is 6.0. By contrast, the U.S. rate is 9.7, more than 50 percent higher than the average. The Canadian and British rates, although closest to the U.S. average, are still almost 30 percent below it. France, Norway, and Sweden have the lowest marriage rates (5.1, 5.0, 4.4).

In all the continental European countries studied, the 1987 marriage rate was significantly lower than the 1960 marriage rate, and in all the countries, including the United States and Canada, the 1988 rate was significantly lower than the 1970 rate. Thus, overall, marriage rates are declining throughout the advanced industrialized countries. Remarriage rates are declining even more sharply.

Marriage rates have declined in part because divorce rates have increased and marriage no longer constitutes a form of lifetime security; therefore, it seems a less valuable investment than in previous periods. Marriage has also become less important as more and more women achieve some economic independence by entering the labor market and as more remain in the labor market, even after having children. Moreover, the legal line between marriage and cohabitation is disappearing, further lessening the value of marriage. Whatever the cause, the results are the same—a declining rate of marriage.

Increase in Divorce Rates

Divorce rates rose dramatically over the past 30 years, especially after 1970. Between 1969 and 1985, divorce laws in nearly every Western country underwent major reform, easing the laws governing divorce considerably (Glendon 1987). Civil divorce was introduced in Catholic countries such as Italy, Spain, and Portugal. Other countries moved to accept or expand no-fault grounds for divorce and to accept or simplify divorce by mutual consent. In some countries—the Netherlands, Sweden, and West Germany and in 19 American states—fault grounds for divorce were eliminated entirely. In several other places (like Great Britain and other American states), the grounds for divorce were substantially relaxed. A dramatic rise in divorce in the years immediately after the new legislation ensued was followed by a leveling off of the divorce rate in many countries in the 1980s. Countries where divorce was first permitted only in the 1970s and where the legal grounds for divorce are still restrictive have not yet experienced the dramatic rise, but it seems likely to occur within the next 5 to 10 years.

The U.S. divorce rate (21.2 per 1,000 married women in 1986) is higher than that of any of the other 11 countries (Table 6.2), so it is not surprising that the U.S. divorce rate has increased less since 1960 than in other countries, save Denmark and Sweden. Denmark's divorce rate was also relatively high in 1960, second only to that in the United States. The Swedish divorce rate probably rose so little between 1960 and 1986 because more Swedes were choosing not to get married, and therefore the "divorces" and family breakups that occurred were outside of marriage. By contrast, Canada and Great Britain experienced a startling increase in divorce. Nonetheless, divorce rates in most countries seem to be leveling off, but at a high level. The result has been a striking increase in the number and proportion of families headed by divorced women; this has

Table 6.2 / Divorce Rates per 1,000 Women in Selected Countries

Country	1960	1970	1986	Percentage Increase 1960–1986
United States	9.4	14.9	21.2	+126
Canada	1.7	—	12.9	+659
Austria	5.0	5.9	N.A.	N.A.
Denmark	6.0	7.5	12.8	+113
Finland	4.1	6.0	N.A.	N.A.
France	2.8	3.1	8.5	+204
Germany	3.4	5.0	8.3	+144
Italy	—	—	1.1	—
Netherlands	2.2	3.3	8.7	+295
Norway	2.8	3.7	N.A.	—
Sweden	4.9	6.7	10.7	+118
United Kingdom	2.2	5.5	12.9	+350

SOURCES: 1960 and 1970 figures from OECD: *Child and Family Developments*. 1986 data from EEC. *Basic Statistics*.

N.A. = Not Available.

clearly contributed to the significant increase in lone-parent, female-headed families, which will be discussed later.

The interactive effects of these social processes should be noted. Divorce has increased because of the loosening of restrictive laws; as divorce rates increase, women have less confidence in the security of marriage and therefore are more likely to seek to establish personal economic security through work in the paid labor force. And, as women achieve some degree of economic independence, they are less willing to remain in unsatisfactory marriages. The perceived insecurity of marriage encourages women to become more financially independent; financial independence enables women to leave unhappy marriages.

Lowered Fertility Rates

Fertility rates have declined fairly steadily in all 12 countries since 1960, but the decline was most dramatic in those countries with the highest rates in 1960—United States, Canada, Italy, and the Netherlands (Table 6.3). In Austria, Canada, Denmark, the Netherlands, the United States, and West Germany, the rates declined by between 40 and 55 percent. The Swedish fertility rate declined least of all (by 18 percent), perhaps in part because Sweden's rate was already very low by 1960. France, with average fertility rates in 1960, experienced only a moderate decline over the last 30 years. At the end of the 1980s, the United States, Canada, France, Norway, Sweden, and the United Kingdom had similar fertility rates—just under or at replacement level. Fertility rates in West Germany, Italy, and Denmark were very low—below replacement level.

Table 6.3 / Births per 1,000 Women Aged 15–44, in Selected Countries: 1960, 1970, and 1988

Country	1960	1970/ 1971	1986	Percentage Change 1960–1988
United States	3.6	2.5	2.1	−1.5
Canada	3.8	2.3	1.9	−1.9
Austria	2.7	2.3	1.6	−1.1
Denmark	2.5	2.0	1.6	−0.9
Finland	2.7	1.7	1.7	−1.0
France	2.7	2.5	2.0	−0.7
Federal Republic of Germany	2.4	2.0	1.4	−1.0
Italy	2.4	2.4	1.4	−1.0
Netherlands	3.1	2.4	1.7	−1.4
Norway	2.9	2.5	2.0	−0.9
Sweden	2.2	2.0	1.9	−0.3
United Kingdom	2.7	2.4	2.0	−0.7

SOURCES: *OECD in Figures, 1990* for 1971 and 1988 figures. For 1960 figures, Sheila B. Kamerman and Alfred J. Kahn, eds. *Child Care, Parental Leave, and the Under 3s: Policy Innovation in Europe.* (Westport, CT: Greenwood Press, 1991.)

Analyzing fertility trends in Europe, Chantal Blayo (1987) concluded that fertility rates *within* countries now diverge more than the aggregate rates *between* countries. Moreover, she noted that in many countries, fertility rates are sustained only by the significant increase in out-of-wedlock births; in countries where there has not been an increase in out-of-wedlock births, fertility rates actually declined.

Here, too, the social processes responsible for these trends interact with one another. Low fertility rates permit women to leave home and seek employment; women who work are less likely to have more children than women who don't—the opportunity costs of childbearing are too high. Smaller families with fewer children are better off economically, since family resources do not have to stretch to cover additional members, and higher income levels are associated with lower fertility rates.

Rising Out-of-Wedlock Births

As marriage rates declined, divorce rates plateaued at a high level, and as fertility rates declined, illegitimacy rates soared. Between 1960 and 1986, out-of-wedlock births increased fivefold in the Netherlands, Norway, and Denmark, and more than quadrupled in the United States and Sweden (Tables 6.4 and 6.5). The only countries in which out-of-wedlock births did not at least double during this period were Austria and West Germany. By 1986, only Italy, the Netherlands, and West Germany had illegitimacy rates of under 10 percent. However, there are large cross-national differences in the proportion of children born out-of-wedlock who live with cohabiting couples rather than single mothers living alone.

Table 6.4 / Out-of-Wedlock Births as a Percentage of Total Births

Country	1960	1970	1986	Ratio 1986/1960
United States	5.3	10.7	23.4	4.4
Canada	4.3	9.6	16.9	3.9
Austria	13.0	12.8	21.0	1.6
Denmark	7.8	11.0	43.9	5.6
Finland	4.1	5.5	15.0	3.6
France	6.1	6.8	24.0	3.9
Germany	6.3	5.5	9.6	1.5
Italy	2.4	2.2	5.6	2.3
Netherlands	1.3	2.1	8.8	6.8
Norway	3.7	6.9	24.0	6.5
Sweden	11.3	18.4	48.4	4.3
United Kingdom	5.4	8.5	21.0	3.9

SOURCES: OECD: *Child and Family Developments* for 1960 and 1970 data; 1986, various national and EEC sources.

Table 6.5 / Mother-Only Families, by Marital Status (in percentages)

Country	Year	Widowed	Divorced	Separated	Unwed	Total
Austria	1984	7	43	9	41	100
Finland	1977	29	50	4	17	100
Germany	1985	18	46	16	20	100
France	1982	31	39	15	15	100
Italy	1981	41	7	40	12	100
Sweden	1985	4	31	4	61	100
United Kingdom	1985	8	42	25	25	100
United States	1985	7	42	22	29	100

SOURCE: Sheila B. Kamerman and Alfred J. Kahn. *Mother-Only Families in Western Europe: Social Change, Social Problem and Societal Response.* New York: Columbia University School of Social Work, 1987.

NOTE: We have not attempted to break out cohabitating couples within the mother-only group because there are no consistent definitions and clarifications even within countries, let alone across countries.

Increase in Cohabitation

Cohabitation has emerged in much of Northern Europe as the accepted pattern for premarital relationships. More than 97 percent of all couples who now marry in Sweden have lived together previously. Perhaps more important, cohabitation has become not only a premarital experience but is increasingly viewed as an alternative to marriage. In the United States, cohabitation is still a very small phenomenon, involving less than 3 percent of families with children. By contrast, a growing proportion of young couples in Sweden are living together, having children, breaking up, and merging again with another partner, all without ever having been legally married. In effect, the line between marriage and cohabitation is increasingly disappearing in Scandinavia. In Sweden, this development is occurring with legislative support.

Although cohabitation may be better for children than a single-mother family, research shows that such families are more likely to "divorce" than legally married couples (Kamerman and Kahn 1987). Thus, cohabitation gives a child the advantage of two parents in his or her initial development and perhaps ensures a higher probability of financial support from both parents, but it assures neither the child nor the mother ongoing social or psychological support and security.

Expanded Labor Force Participation by Women

Increased participation in the paid labor force, especially by married women living with their husbands, has been the most dramatic change in gender roles to occur in the advanced industrialized world during the last 30 years. These working mothers contribute to the economic well-being of their children and families in all countries. In some countries, the increase in working wives has

Table 6.6 / Labor Force Participation Rates of Married Women in the United States, by Presence and Age of Own Children: 1960–1990

Year	All Married Women with Children	Children 6 to 17 Years	Children Under 6 Years	Children Under 3 Years	Children 1 and Under
1960	27.6	39.0	18.6	—	—
1970	39.7	49.2	30.3	25.8	24.0
1990	66.3	73.2	59.5	56.7	53.6

SOURCE: Bureau of Labor Statistics. *U.S. Working Women: A Data Book.* 1977. Table 22.

also contributed to the growing trend toward greater income disparity between families headed by a lone woman and families headed by two adults. The trend is easier to document with systematic data in the United States, but illustrative data are available for some of the other countries studied here as well.

The labor force participation rate of married women with children under age 18 in the United States more than doubled between 1960 and 1990. More astonishing, the rates of working wives with children under age 6 more than tripled during these same years, from 18.6 percent in 1960 to 59.5 percent in 1990 (Table 6.6). Although the U.S. Bureau of Labor Statistics (BLS) did not analyze the data for wives with children under age 3 before 1970, since that time the labor force participation rate of married women with small children increased from 25.8 percent in 1970 to 56.7 percent in 1990, and the labor force participation of married women with children aged 1 and younger rose, from 24 percent in 1970 to 53.6 percent in 1990.

Sorrentino (1990) compiled labor force participation data for all women with children under 18, in 10 countries, and presented separate figures for married and single mothers with children (Table 6.7). The data show that the Nordic countries have the highest proportions of both married and solo mothers in the labor force, regardless of the age of the woman's youngest child. The United States, Canada, and France have moderate to high proportions of mothers in the labor force; the United Kingdom has slightly lower rates of working mothers, and West Germany and Italy have the lowest rates. Sorrentino pointed out that the most dramatic rise in labor force participation was for women between the ages of 25 and 34, the prime childbearing and child-rearing ages (Table 6.8). In most of the countries, fewer than half of such women were in the labor force in 1970, whereas by 1988 a substantial majority were.

In 1970, lone mothers in the United States were about 50 percent more likely to be in the labor force than married women, but by 1990 the rates of the two groups had largely converged (Table 6.9). This pattern holds true for most of the other countries, too, except for Canada, the United Kingdom, and Norway where married mothers have *higher* labor force participation rates than single mothers. In general, divorced women are the most likely to be in the labor force in all the countries, and never-married mothers are the least likely to be working, especially in the United States, Canada, and Britain.

Table 6.7 / **Labor Force Participation Rates of Women[a] Under Age 60,
by Presence and Age of Children in Eight Countries: 1986 and 1988[b]**

Country	All Women	All Mothers with Children		Lone Mothers with Children	
		Under 18 Years	Under 3 Years	Under 18 Years	Under 3 Years
United States	68.5	65.0	52.5	65.3	45.1
Canada	66.8	67.0[c]	58.4	63.6[c]	41.3
Denmark	79.2	86.1	83.9	85.9	80.9
Germany	55.8	48.4	39.7	69.7	50.4
France	60.1	65.8	60.1	85.2	69.6
Italy	43.3	43.9	45.0	67.2	68.0
Sweden	80.0	89.4[c]	85.8	N.A.	81.0
United Kingdom	64.3	58.7	36.9	51.9	23.4

SOURCE: Constance Sorrentino. "The Changing Family in International Perspective." *Monthly Labor Review* (March 1990):53.

[a]Women ages 60 to 64 are included in Canada and Sweden. Lower age limits are 16 for the United States and Sweden, 15 for Canada, and 14 for all other countries. For participation rates of women with children, no upper limit is applied for the United States or Canada. These differences do not distort the comparisons because very few women under 16 have children, while few women over 60 live with their minor children. Includes divorced, separated, never-married, and widowed women.
[b]Data for the United States are for March 1988; Canada and Sweden—annual averages for 1988; data for all other countries are for Spring 1986.
[c]Children under 16 years.

N.A. = Not Available.

Table 6.8 / **Labor Force Participation of Women Aged 25–34: 1970 and 1988**

Country	1970	1988
United States	44.7	72.6
Canada	41.2*	74.9
Japan	46.8	54.5
Denmark	N.A.	90.0
France	52.2	74.5
Germany	47.6	61.5
Italy (Ages 25–39)	44.1†	60.8
Netherlands	23.9	55.4
Sweden	60.7	89.4
United Kingdom	43.3	66.0

SOURCE: Constance Sorrentino. "The Changing Family in International Perspective." *Monthly Labor Review* (March 1990):53.

*BLS estimate.
†1977 data.

N.A. = Not Available.

Table 6.9 / Labor Force Participation Rates of Married and Single Mothers
with Children Under Age 18: Late 1980s

Country	Percentage of Mothers in Labor Force	
	Married	Single
Canada, 1988	67	64
Denmark, 1988	87	87
Germany, 1986	48	70
France, 1988	66	85
Italy, 1986	44	45
Sweden, 1988	89	89
United Kingdom, 1988	59	52
U.S., 1990	66	66

SOURCE: Constance Sorrentino. "The Changing Family in International Perspective." *Monthly Labor Review* (March 1990):53.

Increase in Lone-Parent, Mother-Only Families

The growth in lone-parent, female-headed families as a proportion of all families with children constitutes the most dramatic change in family structure experienced throughout the advanced industrialized West over the last 20 to 30 years.[3] In all these countries, mother-only families are viewed as economically "at-risk" and socially vulnerable, and therefore are of growing concern to policy-makers. In earlier years, the concern was with destitute widows and their children, but twentieth century social insurance programs eliminated or lessened the economic problems of these families. Medical progress over the past 3 decades has also dramatically reduced premature death among adult men. Today, the policy concern, for the most part, is with mother-only families that result from divorce, separation, and out-of-wedlock childbirths.[4]

Mother-only families have more than doubled in number and as a proportion of all families with children in the United States since 1970 (Table 6.10). They are the major component in the "feminization of poverty," are the heart of the welfare problem, and constitute a major factor in the pervasive problem of child poverty. However, precise comparisons are not possible across countries because of definitional and measurement problems. For example, the definition of a "child" is not the same in all countries. Cohabiting but not legally married couples sometimes are counted as married couples, sometimes as single parents, and sometimes in a separate category of their own.

Nonetheless, although single-parent families vary in significance as a family type among the countries, the pattern of growth and change is similar across countries. In general, widows have declined as a percentage of family heads in all the countries, constituting a significant group only in Italy and Ireland. The same is true for separated wives. Divorced women constitute the largest group among lone mothers in the United States, Austria, Great Britain, Finland,

Table 6.10 / Distribution of U.S. Families with Children Under Age 18, by Family Type: 1970–1988

Race and Group	1970		1980		1988		Net Change: 1980–1988		Net Change: 1970–1980	
	Number (thousands)	Percent	Number (thousands)	Percent	Number (thousands)	Percent	Number (thousands)	Average per Year	Number (thousands)	Average per Year
Families with Children	29,631	100.0	32,150	100.0	34,345	100.0	2,195	314	2,519	252
Two-parent	25,823	87.1	25,231	78.5	29,977	72.7	−254	−36	−592	−59
One-parent	3,808	12.9	6,920	21.5	9,368	27.3	2,448	350	3,112	311
Mother-only	3,415	11.5	6,230	19.4	8,146	23.7	1,916	274	2,815	282
Father-only	393	1.3	690	2.1	1,222	3.6	532	76	297	30

SOURCE: U.S. Bureau of the Census, *Current Population Reports*, Series P-23, No. 162, *Studies in Marriage and the Family*, Washington, D.C., U.S. Government Printing Office, 1989.

Table 6.11 / Lone-Parent Families with Children Under Age 18,[a]
Various Years (percentages)

Country	Year	Lone-Parent Families as a Percentage of All Families w/Children	Female-Headed	Male-Headed
Austria (children under 15)	1984	13	12	1
Canada	1986	13	—	—
Denmark	1984[d]	26	23	3
Finland	1984	15	13	2
Federal Republic of Germany	1985[d]	13	11	2
France	1981[b]	10	8	2
Italy	1981	6	5	1
Netherlands	1981	12	—	—
Norway (children under 16)	1982	19	18	1
Sweden[c]	1985	32	29	3
United Kingdom (children under 16)[b]	1985	14	12	2
United States	1985	26	23	3

SOURCES: Kamerman and Kahn. *Mother-Only Families in Western Europe.* Table 1, p. 3. Canadian data from Canadian Advisory Council on the Status of Women.

[a] Or other ages as specified.
[b] To age 19, if in school.
[c] To age 19, if in school. The rates include cohabitating (but not legally married) couples. For 1985, 18 percent of families with children were headed by women living alone and 14 percent by cohabitating couples.
[d] These numbers include some percentages of cohabitating couples but the breakdowns are not precise.

France, and West Germany. Unwed mothers are the dominant group in Sweden, Denmark, and Norway, and are a rapidly growing group in all the other countries. However, most of the "unwed mothers" in the Nordic countries, and a significant portion in some other countries, were cohabiting with the child's biological father, at least at the time the child was born. Although increasing, this is true far less often in the United States, Canada, and the United Kingdom.

To offer some comparisons: In Austria, Great Britain, Finland, West Germany, and Norway, between 10 percent and 20 percent of families with children were headed by lone mothers in the mid-1980s (Table 6.11). About 20 percent of these women (40 percent in Austria) had never been married. Denmark and Sweden demonstrate a more dramatic change: between 26 and 32 percent of families with children are not legally married, husband-wife families. In about half of these, two adults are present although not legally married, while the other half are headed by "true" lone mothers living alone. Comparable U.S. rates for approximately the same time period would show that 23 percent of all families with children were headed by women in 1985 (another 3 percent were headed by men alone).

Teenage unwed mothers constitute still another important subgroup among the larger group of single mothers in the United States and are a significant phenomenon only in the United States (Jones et al. 1986). However, they are now becoming more visible in several other countries as well, including Canada and the United Kingdom, and to a lesser extent, France and Germany. Kamerman and Kahn (1987) showed there was a significant increase in unwed adolescent parents in Great Britain during the 1980s, as young girls became more sexually active and perceived that the social benefits available to them as lone mothers (public assistance and priority for publicly subsidized housing) offered greater economic security than the unemployed or low-wage young males with whom they were involved. However, in contrast to the situation in the United States, paternity was acknowledged in most of these cases.

Despite these often-dramatic developments, mother-only families in many of these countries are not viewed as the major policy problem that they are considered to be in the United States. In some countries, the poverty of mother-only families is a potential issue, but social policy often provides them with a protected status and subsidized income. Although in most countries these families are likely to have relatively low income, they are not described as "poor." Earnings and/or transfers protect them from poverty, especially in the Nordic/ Scandinavian countries, to a much larger extent in Europe than in America (see McFate, Smeeding, and Rainwater, this volume). The major concern with mother-only families arises from an interest in assuring that they have a "comfortable" lifestyle and an environment for wholesome child-rearing.

Summary

The demographic picture of gender role and family structure changes in the United States, Canada, and Western Europe is one of delayed marriage and declining marriage and remarriage rates; deferred childbearing, fewer children, and more out-of-wedlock births; increasing or high divorce rates; increasing cohabitation; and increasing rates of lone parenthood. All of these changes raise questions about the future of marriage, the definition of a "family," and the child-rearing roles of the women and men.

The increase in female labor force participation partially accounts (and compensates) for these developments and the rise in solo parenthood. Historically, marriage was equated with economic support for most women. Traditional gender roles assumed that men were in the paid labor force, earning wages that would provide for the family's financial support. Women, in turn, maintained the home and cared for children. Marriage allowed this division of labor to become institutionalized as a life pattern. This is no longer the case. The growth in labor force participation among wives in couple-headed families makes it more viable for women in unhappy marriages to leave their marriage. Given the high risk of divorce, getting or keeping a job means "insurance" against an economic crisis following possible divorce.

Change in the meaning and value of marriage and the consequent greater probability of lone parenthood for women have resulted in increasing economic vulnerability among children and their mothers. The rise in female labor force participation provides new opportunities for some women who head families but has also added significantly to the stress of rearing children alone while coping with paid work. A number of approaches have been developed to address the two most important problems facing families with children: (1) the problem of ensuring lone mothers and their children adequate financial support, and (2) the difficulty of ensuring that working parents have adequate time for child-rearing. These policy approaches are discussed in the following section.

ALTERNATIVE POLICY RESPONSES

Since lone mothers are not a homogeneous group with uniform characteristics, there is no uniform pattern of policy response toward this group across countries or even within countries. Nonetheless, there are some common patterns of policy responses to changing gender roles and family structures.

Until recently, all 12 countries discussed here provided social insurance benefits to the dependents of retired or dead beneficiaries; however, this is now beginning to change. Sweden, for example, recently eliminated widows' benefits. All these countries except the United States provide child benefits (child or family allowances)—universal cash benefits that are based on the presence and number of children in a family and are provided regardless of the family's income. Eight of the 12 nations have established special benefits for children in divorced families, whereby the child is guaranteed a minimum amount of financial support if the noncustodial parent fails to pay support, pays it irregularly, or pays it at an inadequate level (Kahn and Kamerman 1988). All of the countries provide social (public) assistance—a means-tested cash benefit—to poor families; but the significance of this benefit in the lone mother's "income package," the adequacy of the income provided, and the duration of benefit receipt allowed vary significantly across countries. All these countries except the United States provide either national health insurance or a national health service, thereby assuring all children (and their parents) access to health care. Except for the Anglo-American nations, most of these countries provide universal, free or low-cost preschool to all or almost all children beginning at age 2 or 3 (Table 6.12). Thus, except in the United States, an important social infrastructure is in place for single as well as married couples and their children.

Annamette Sorenson (1990) compared the economic situation of solo and married mothers in three countries (West Germany in 1984, Sweden in 1981, and the United States in 1979 and 1986) and concluded that lone mothers are at significant risk of economic hardship for several reasons. Divorced mothers

Table 6.12 / **Labor Force Participation Rates of Women with Children Under Age 18, and Childcare Coverage Rates for Children Aged 0–5: Late 1980s**

Country	Labor Force Participation Rate with Children Under 18 Years Old	Percentage of Children in Childcare Full- and Part-Day	
		0–3 Years Old	3–5 Years Old
Canada, 1988	67	12	31[b]
Denmark, 1988	86	44	85
Germany, 1986	48	2	76
France, 1988	66	24	95
Italy, 1986	44	5	90
Sweden, 1988	89	73[c]	
United Kingdom, 1988	59	2	43[a]
U.S., 1990	65	20	70[d]

SOURCES: Labor force participation rates from Sorrentino, op. cit. Childcare data assembled by author from varied sources. Data for Sweden are for women with children under 16. Childcare data are largely from the mid-1980s.

[a] These data are for children aged 3–4, since compulsory school begins at age 5.
[b] These data are for children whose mothers work or are at school at least 20 hours per week.
[c] These data are for all children aged 1–6, from the time the parent leave ends until compulsory school begins at age 7. The data include part-day programs as well as full-day.
[d] Est., 1984–85; largely part-day.

are at risk because 30 percent more income is required to maintain two households than one household at a pre-divorce standard of living. Thus, if the income available does not increase after a divorce, the living standard of one or both households will fall. Public and private (child support) transfers do not compensate the custodial mother adequately for the loss of the husband's financial contribution in West Germany and the United States.

Never-married mothers are vulnerable in other ways. Child-rearing responsibilities may constrain a lone parent's job opportunities and work schedule. In any case, women's wages remain lower than men's in all these countries today, and one average wage-earner is unlikely to provide sufficient income to support a family in most of these countries. How, then, do different countries mix policy instruments to assist lone mothers, and what is the consequence of various policy packages? A review of the policy packages operating in these countries at the end of the 1980s reveals four alternative strategies.[5] No country constitutes a "pure" model, but all offer a cluster of policies with a particular thrust. In brief, the policies are as follows:

- *A targeted focus on poor families.* This approach provides public assistance to all poor families, on the assumption that assisted mothers, whether in one- or two-parent families, will remain at home with their children.

Meeting the needs of the poor generally helps lone-parent families since they are disproportionately poor.

- *Categorical targeting of lone mothers with modest incomes.* The underlying assumptions of this approach are that most mothers would prefer to remain at home with their children, if it were financially viable; and that lone mothers have special problems that warrant special assistance.

- *Universal support for young children.* This policy aims to provide financial support (and job-protected leaves) to parents with very young children (under age 3), based on the assumptions that most mothers of very young children prefer to remain at home if they can, and that children are better off if parents who want to remain at home can do so. Married and single mothers with very young children are covered by these programs.

- *Combining labor market and family policies.* This policy provides a variety of cash benefits, services, and other policy supports for working families with children. The goal is to enable parents to enter and remain in the labor force without undue burden during the child-rearing years. The premises of this approach: (1) only when earnings constitute a significant component of household income will a family have an adequate standard of living; and (2) women should participate equally with men in generating income as well as in nurturing. Single mothers are covered along with all working mothers.

Descriptions of how these policies operate in specific countries follow.

A Targeted Focus on "Poor Families" Strategy

A lone mother in Great Britain may remain at home and receive a means-tested, indexed cash benefit (called Income Support) until her child or children are 16 years of age.[6] There is no pressure to take on training or a job. Indeed, the tax and welfare system operate to create a disincentive for part-time work. And if mothers of very young children do take a job, childcare is largely unavailable, or unaffordable if available. The single mother who works at least 24 hours per week in spite of the disincentives and is a low-earner is eligible for a special income supplement for working poor families with children (called the Family Credit, originally, the Family Income Supplement). Nonetheless, the at-home role is the norm for single mothers in Britain.

At present, almost half the income of lone-mother families is from public income transfers. Twenty-eight percent of a sample of low-income, lone mothers received child support payments from absent fathers; but 60 percent of the families who received paternal support payments gained no financial advantage, because the payment is deducted from their public income allowance. Family income is further supplemented by a universal child benefit, which equals about 5 percent of average wages and is given for each child, and by a special one-parent benefit for the first child in a mother-only family. Lone-parent families receive priority access to public housing and medical care through the National Health Service.

It appears that the situation of these families in the United Kingdom became worse, not better, in the 1980s (Millar 1989). In 1979, the average gross income of one-parent families equaled about 51 percent of the income of a couple with two children. By 1984, this proportion was down to 39.5 percent. This may be due to two trends. First, the value of the child benefit was not indexed to prices and did not keep up with inflation. Second, the income of two-parent families increased as more married women entered the labor force. Both trends increase the gap between two-parent and single-parent household incomes.

Despite the decline in the value of benefits, the proportion of lone mothers on public assistance in Britain increased substantially in the 1980s, from about 38 percent in 1979 to more than 50 percent in 1985. During this period, the unemployment rate in Britain rose from 5.6 in 1979 to 11.2 in 1985. Lone-parent families are more likely to receive long-term assistance (4-plus years) than are those in the United States, West Germany, Canada, or Sweden (Duncan et al. this volume).

Some view the British targeted policy as a "poverty trap," eliminating part-time work as an economically viable option for single mothers and creating a dichotomy between what is available for at-home mothers and what is available for working, low-income mothers and their children. There is reason to suspect that Britain may change its policy strategy when the employment situation improves.

Both Canada and the United States have followed the same model but with even less "success" than Britain. According to Ruth Rose (this volume) Canadian single mothers are more likely to be in the labor force now than 20 years ago, but in contrast to the earlier times, those with young children (under age 6) are far less likely to be in the labor force than their married sisters. Earnings constitute a larger portion of mother-only family income today than in 1971, but Rose states single mothers "must earn at least 50 percent above the minimum wage to reach a level of income higher than what they receive on social assistance." As a result, single mothers who cannot manage full-time work, in particular those with young children, are unlikely to exit assistance for several years—or to exit poverty.

Using a relative definition of poverty[7] (40 percent of adjusted median disposable family income in each country), 11 percent of the children living in lone-parent families were poor in 1979 in Great Britain compared with 46 percent in the United States (and 40 percent in Canada, which has a policy similar to that in Britain, but for poor, lone mothers only). By 1986, the U.S. poverty rate for children in these families had climbed to 54 percent, whereas the Canadian rate had declined slightly to 37 percent and the British rate was 8.5 percent.

Canadian single mothers on assistance in the mid-1980s may have been better off than their U.S. sisters because they received higher and more consistent benefits; but even these benefits provided incomes of only 50 to 70 percent of poverty (Gundersson and Muszynski 1990). Working single mothers in Canada were better off than their U.S. counterparts as a result of child allowances, refundable child tax credits, and a miscellany of other benefits. British single-mother families were less likely to be poor than American single mothers. However, the British families are better off only in a relative sense, and only in the short term. Moreover, their situation has been deteriorating. The welfare and poverty traps inherent in this approach remain in force.

A Categorical "Lone-Mother" Strategy

Norwegian policy specifies that lone mothers should have the right to choose between staying at home and taking a job. To support this policy of "choice," Norway provides a package of income transfers that includes:

- A universal, tax-free child benefit or child allowance. The youngest children receive the highest benefit, on the assumption that women with very young children need more support so that they can remain at home. Single parents receive a special supplement of one child benefit beyond the number of children they actually have.
- Tax allowances, available to all taxpayers supporting a child under age 20, provide an additional allowance to single parents.
- A childcare tax credit.
- A universal, tax-free, cash childcare benefit for single parents.
- An education benefit covering the costs of an educational or training program for single parents.
- An income-tested "transitional" benefit designed to support lone parents for one year after they become lone parents or until their youngest child is 10 (or even longer under special circumstances). The benefit level is indexed to inflation and is provided to single parents living alone as well as to cohabiting couples, as long as the mother is not living with the child(ren)'s natural father.
- Social assistance, a means-tested cash benefit for the poor. This assistance is relatively unimportant for poor families and largely short-term: families may use assistance more than once in the course of the year (e.g., when school begins, to purchase additional clothing for school-aged children, or around holidays or vacations, when family expenses are unusually high).
- An advanced maintenance or guaranteed minimum child support payment.
- An income-tested housing allowance.

As a result of these policies, a single mother with two children under age 10, with no other income, would be entitled to tax-free cash benefits equaling 70 percent of the average wage of a woman working full-time, or half the median family income of a two-parent family. The lone mother would also be entitled to a housing allowance. Unless well-educated and/or highly skilled, a lone mother is unlikely to earn more by working part-time.

Government income transfers are the major source of income for one-third of all lone-parent families in Norway, but social assistance (the means-tested benefit for the poor) is relatively unimportant for these families. Only 16 percent of lone-parent families used social assistance in the mid-1980s, and lone parents constituted only one of every five social assistance recipients. Clearly, poverty is not an issue for lone-parent families—the child poverty rate in Norway in 1979 was about half the British rate.[8] There are, however, other problems.

In comparing the economic well-being of lone-parent families with husband/wife families, employment status plays a critical role. The well-educated mother, married or single, remains in the workforce after having children; the unskilled mother does not. A well-paying, part-time job and a package of family benefits can add up to a decent income; and, eventually, when the children are older, the mother will probably move into a well-paid, full-time job. Two-parent families who want to sustain a better-than-average standard of living can do so only by having wives that remain attached to the labor force, but adequate support for working families is not yet in place.

There is a shortage of subsidized childcare in Norway, and the school day is short until children are 10 years old. This presents serious problems for lone mothers, regardless of their education. Some Norwegian policymakers contend that women rearing families alone are forced to choose between earning an adequate income and spending adequate time with their children, and that this is not a fair choice. Others are concerned that when the youngest child becomes 10 (or 11, at most), these women must return to the labor force in any case, and would benefit from doing so earlier. Many of the small group of lone mothers who were receiving social assistance for the full 10-year period are having to confront the problem of not being adequately prepared for work.

The Norwegian model, which offers the most generous categorical income support programs for lone mothers, provides at least two lessons. First, the policy offers a good income base to lone-mother families only because there is a generous base of social benefits for *all* families with children. Second, the special transition benefit for lone mothers creates a deliberate work disincentive and can lead to major problems for women who stay out of the paid workforce for long periods when an adequate income ultimately depends on personal earnings.

A Strategy of Universal Support for Young Children

Austrian, Finnish, and French family policies are explicitly designed to benefit all families with children, but each country places special emphasis on families with very young children (under age 3), large families, and low-income families. Each of these countries provides universal child benefits, and France and Finland offer an income-tested supplement. Each provides a guaranteed child support (advance maintenance) benefit to help support children in lone-parent families. France and Finland also offer income-tested housing allowances in addition to subsidized childcare services. In France, preschool programs serve all 3–5 year olds, almost half of all 2 year olds, and about one-quarter of those under 2. In Finland, children under age 3 are guaranteed a place in a subsidized childcare program, and all 3–6 year olds are expected to be guaranteed such a place soon. France targets more generous support for young children in families with three or more children, whereas in Austria and Finland young child benefits are available to all families with at least one child. France also provides a means-tested (income and asset-tested) cash benefit to poor, lone mothers for a maximum of 1 year or until their youngest child is 3.

In addition to the general social or family policy infrastructure just described, the core of this "young child" policy strategy in all three countries is an extended, job-protected, paid parental leave that is available to working parents following childbirth. All the countries provide a basic maternity (or parental) job-protected, paid leave beginning 6 weeks before childbirth in Austria and France (1 month before in Finland) and extending to 10 weeks after birth in France, 8 weeks in Austria, and almost 1 year in Finland. These benefits are wage-related. They replace all or almost all of the mother's (or, as relevant, the father's) wages, and are provided through the social insurance/social security system.

After the basic leave ends, French working mothers are entitled to a job-protected leave until their child is 3, with a cash benefit available to those with a moderate income and at least three children. In Austria, all working mothers can take up to 1 year off after the maternity leave ends, payable at the unemployment insurance rate. Low-income parents can take off another 2 years, at a flat rate, if subsidized childcare is not available. In Finland, parents are entitled to an additional 2-year job-protected leave with a tax-free cash benefit worth almost 40 percent of an average wage in 1991 (allowing them a total leave period of 3 years after their child's birth). They can use this benefit to supplement family income or take a lower benefit (worth 20 percent of an average wage) to purchase private childcare. Or they can obtain a guaranteed place in a publicly subsidized childcare facility.

In these three countries, "choice" is the guiding principle for policymakers. The benefits for families with a child under age 3 have been continually increased to permit parents real choice regarding an at-home or labor force role. But when children reach the age of 3, the expectation is that they will attend the universal preschool provided in France and Finland (but less available in Austria), and that mothers will work if there is an economic need. In France, female labor force participation rates are at about the same level as in the United States, but rates for lone mothers are far higher; in Finland, labor force participation rates for both solo and married mothers are among the highest in the world.

The critical issue for lone mothers in these countries is whether they worked before childbirth. If they did, they will be well protected and their jobs will be

held for them; if they did not, their families may be headed for economic hardship once they no longer qualify for the special benefits, because most of the
other family benefits are important as *supplements* to earnings but cannot provide
an adequate income if used as a *substitute* for earnings. A comparative study of
the economic status of families with children in eight countries in the early
1980s (Kahn and Kamerman 1983) found that "vulnerable" lone-mother families
were better off in France than in Australia, Canada, West Germany, the United
Kingdom, and Israel. Among the three countries discussed here—Austria, Finland, and France—lone-mother families with young children are best off in
Finland. In 1981, Finnish lone-mother families had about 60 percent of the income of husband/wife families, largely as a consequence of government income
transfers. The Finnish family benefit package for lone mothers equals about 25
percent of the average wage; this base benefit package provides an important
supplement to wages and a strong work incentive to young women.

Germany offers a variation on the "young child policy" strategy (Kamerman
and Kahn 1987 and 1991). Germany's modest family benefits include a targeted
child allowance (low and moderate income families receive a higher benefit),
child tax benefits, national health insurance, a modest guaranteed child support
benefit (provided for a maximum of 3 years for a child under age 6), a 14-week
paid and job-protected maternity leave, and a discretionary social-assistance
benefit for the poor. Its newest family policy initiative focuses on very young
children and on providing support for parenting.

Germany's parenting policy provides an extended 2-year job-protected leave
after childbirth and a modest, flat-rate cash benefit to all at-home parents regardless of their prior employment status. The benefit is universal for the first 6
months and income-tested subsequently, but at a sufficiently generous level
that about 80 percent of all new parents qualify for it. The benefit is most helpful
to married couple families with one wage earner, because by itself, the benefit
is not sufficient to support a lone mother with a child. Thus only married
women have the luxury of "choice." However, since the parent benefit is not
counted as income when claiming assistance, it provides a significant supplement to the ordinary social assistance benefit.

German family policy is not particularly supportive of single mothers and
their children, although there is support for solo mothers with children under
age 3 who remain at home. An adequate family income is provided by combining the parenting allowance, the relatively small amount given by the child
support guarantee, and social assistance. When the youngest child is 3, local
social service workers determine the amount of pressure to enter or re-enter
the workforce that will be put onto lone mothers. The usual expectation is that
lone mothers will work at least part-time (if work is available), since part-day
preschools are almost universally available; child allowances, tax credits, and a
housing allowance can all be used as income supplements. This helps explain
the anomaly of Germany as described by Duncan et al. (this volume). Single
mothers in Germany are very likely to work, despite the fact that female labor
force participation rates in general are rather low and that social assistance

benefits are relatively generous. Once German single mothers have an appropriate work history, they have the benefit of generous unemployment benefits (unemployment insurance, and when that ends, unemployment assistance).

Combining Labor Market and Family Policies

In contrast to the countries discussed previously, Swedish social policy has stressed the importance of full employment and the role of labor market policies in achieving social goals (see Gustafsson, this volume). Unlike in the United Kingdom, Canada, or the United States, Sweden's social policies stress reducing marketed-generated income inequality and promoting gender equity (rather than reducing poverty). Like Austria, Finland, and France, the Swedes pay special attention to families with children—particularly those with very young children—but Swedish policies are designed to help all parents balance work and family life. In effect, Sweden created generous family policies and labor-market programs that are mutually supportive.

Earnings from salaried work are viewed as the fundamental source of family income and gender equity in Sweden. Women, like men, are expected to work in Sweden. The Swedes have had an "active" labor market policy: the government invests heavily in job creation, if necessary, and in training, retraining, education, and relocation. Transfer payments—social assistance benefits—are at best either transitional (and very short term) or supplementary when earnings are low. Social policy is designed to facilitate both employment and parenting and this seems unlikely to change even under a conservative government.

Lone-mother families are economically vulnerable in Sweden, as in all countries. It is difficult to earn an adequate family income with only one wage earner, but when wages are low, and/or there is only one earner in the family, Swedish social policy provides a variety of government benefits. None of these is enough to live on if it is the *only* source of income; rather, each serves as a supplement to earned income.

Only a small percentage of Swedish lone mothers—16 percent—used the means-tested social assistance for basic support in the mid-1980s, and lone parents constituted only 25 percent of all social assistance recipients. Among those claiming social assistance, the period of reliance is usually brief—only 3–4 months, largely for emergency and transitional needs.

The major income supplements provided through Swedish social policy are accepted as just and normal and are generous in comparison with the other countries examined here. These supplements include:

- A universal tax-free child or family allowance for each child up to age 18, (and beyond, if the child is in school). Although not indexed, this benefit is usually adjusted each year to equal about 5 percent of average earnings, per child.

- Advanced maintenance allowances are available from the government when noncustodial parents fail to pay, pay irregularly, or pay only a low level of support. Payment is conditional on the custodial parent assisting in efforts to establish paternity. In 1981, these benefits were paid for about half of all children of divorced parents and 14 percent of all children in Sweden, in both single-parent families and "reconstituted" families (which are comprised of cohabiting or married couples in which only one parent is the child's biological parent).

- Income-tested housing allowances that offset some of the costs of housing, whether rental or owner-occupied. In the mid-1980s, the income ceiling allowed about 35 percent of all families and 70 percent of single-mother families to receive a housing allowance.

- A social infrastructure to support working parents that includes benefits and services to ease the tension between work and family life and to reduce the time-crunch working mothers often face. These services are especially important for lone mothers who work (the vast majority of lone mothers in Sweden). In addition to subsidized health care and childcare services, working parents are entitled to a paid and job-protected 15-month parental leave following childbirth, an unpaid but job-protected additional 3-month leave, access to high-quality subsidized childcare at income-related fees, the right to work a 6-hour day until their youngest child is 8, 5 weeks of paid vacation (or more) each year, up to 60 days a year of paid sick leave if needed to care for an ill child, and time off when a child begins a new childcare program, preschool, or school, or to visit a child's school.

- Children from lone-parent families have priority over children from two-parent families for childcare services. Policymakers aim to guarantee childcare coverage for children aged 18 months and older for all parents who want such services for their children when resources permit. Extension of the paid parental leave to 18 months (from the current 15 months) is also planned.

The annual family income, after earnings, taxes, and transfers, of a lone mother with two children working half-time at an average wage was approximately equal to that of the average single male worker, with no children, working full-time in Sweden in 1980 (Kahn and Kamerman 1983). Such a lone-parent family was about twice as well off as a similar family anywhere in the United States. Using the same relative definition of poverty referred to previously (40 percent of adjusted median disposable family income in a country), only 3.7 percent of children in lone-parent families and 1.8 percent of children in two-parent families in Sweden were poor in 1981. By 1986–87, child poverty rates in Sweden had declined still further. The Swedish child poverty rate is lower than the child poverty rate of any of the other countries examined here.

CONCLUSION

I have described various patterns of policy responses to the problems of lone-parent or mother-only families, using the experience of several different countries to illustrate the various approaches and their consequences. Clearly, mother-only families can be supported at home but providing adequate support for this growing number of families is expensive and creates various perverse work disincentives. Moreover, if at-home support is provided for a long period, women who have been out of the workforce for lengthy periods may find themselves at a great disadvantage when they try to reenter it. Providing income support for a transitional period after the dissolution of a marriage seems good in principle, but when the transition period is allowed to extend too long, there are negative consequences. Families are excluded from the mainstream of society, and the sense of relative deprivation they feel in an affluent society may be severe.

As more mothers enter the labor force and as the percentage of children spending some time in lone-parent families increases, the ultimate question for all industrialized countries is: What policy package reduces the risk of poverty for mother-only families and their children and simultaneously provides working mothers with assistance in easing the time pressures and stresses that labor force participation generates? There is great variation in the speed with which national governments have responded to the changing needs of families.

European countries have moved rapidly over the last decade to develop new social policies to alleviate the economic penalties of divorce that fall on children (Garfinkel and Wong 1990; Kahn and Kamerman 1983; Kamerman and Kahn 1987). Some form of "advance maintenance payment" or guaranteed child support is paid by the government in most Western European countries today when noncustodial parents fail to pay or pay too little to provide adequate support. These benefits are available to all custodial parents regardless of income. A government agency assumes responsibility for the collection of support from the noncustodial parent. Creating a system of government-guaranteed (non-means-tested) child support protects lone-parent families from the need to claim a stigmatized social assistance benefit (see the McLanahan and Garfinkel chapter in this volume).[9] In effect, divorce is being redefined in most of Europe as a "social," rather than an individual, risk which can lead to negative economic consequences for women and children; this social risk warrants protection through the social insurance system. The move toward increased protection against divorce and lone parenthood has not yet occurred in the United States, Britain, or Canada.

The United States differs from other countries, especially continental European countries, in its failure to provide direct income transfers (family benefits or child allowances) to all or almost all families with children. But European countries are supportive of parenting in other ways, too. These other countries provide job-protected parental leave to employed women—and often fathers, too—following childbirth. A growing number of countries are providing more extended paid parental leave, lasting from 1–3 years after childbirth. These benefits can often be used flexibly, to make part-time work financially viable for a while by filling all or some of the gap between part-time and full-time earnings. These benefits are designed to give workers time for parenting when children are very young (Kamerman and Kahn 1991).

Family policies in the future should be based on the assumption that women will work (to obtain basic income support and to qualify for benefits contingent on employment) even after they have children. While they may retire from full-time work for a brief interlude (of 1–3 years) after a child is born, they will eventually return to full-time employment. Policy that supports this vision of society will invest in a social infrastructure that supports working parents (single or married), and includes health care, childcare, paid time off to care for an ill child or to visit a child's school, a shorter workday for parents of young children, and parental leave policies like those described above.

The relative economic deprivation experienced by mother-only families will be alleviated, but not eliminated, when women's wages reach closer to parity with men's wages, and/or when low earnings are supplemented with transfer payments. Although the income of one-parent, one-earner families cannot be expected to equal that of two-parent, two-earner families (transfers do not substitute fully for the earnings of the absent spouse), public policies can partially reduce differences, and poverty *can* be eliminated. A reduction in inequality *and* poverty is most likely to be achieved when the policy focus is on supplementing *earned* income with special allowances for children rather than substituting transfer income for earnings. Family policies in most countries are moving away from a focus on income transfers alone toward policies that encourage mothers to mix earnings and income support; and policies that support mothers to stay at home until their children are grown are being replaced by policies that support a parent to stay at home only when a child is very young.

If mothers are expected to work, however, an adequate social infrastructure that supports their work effort must be in place. In this respect, European countries and Canada are far ahead of the United States. Although U.S. policymakers have recognized that motherhood does not preclude paid employment, they have failed to establish public institutions and the social infrastructure that will help American mothers successfully integrate work and parenting roles.

There is a general consensus that society should do as much as possible to provide a healthy environment for children. This means helping parents stay together whenever possible. Toward this end, some countries have established public policies that subsidize parenting, subsidize childcare, increase the supply and subsidize the cost of housing, provide family counseling services, and assure that families with children have adequate incomes. If the couple does separate or a single-parent family is formed in some other way, there is a general consensus that some minimum level of support should be provided to families with children. Although there is some concern that providing lone mothers with special assistance may encourage growth in the number of lone-parent families, the primary issue is that children are assured an adequate standard of living.[10] Ultimately, the choice that every country must make is whether it is more important to protect the economic and social situation of children (even if it means facilitating, or appearing to facilitate, a family lifestyle that is not ideal) or to try to constrain/punish the behavior of adults, regardless of the negative consequences such action may have on children.

ENDNOTES

1. Bumpass (1990), p. 484.

2. The U.S. data in this and the following sections are from *Current Population Reports,* Bureau of the Census, U.S. Department of Commerce; and the Bureau of Labor Statistics, U.S. Department of Labor. International sources are Organization for Economic Cooperation and Development (OECD) and European Economic Community (EEC) statistics, unless otherwise noted.

3. Most of the material in this section is drawn from Kamerman and Kahn (1987). Briefer versions of this monograph are found in Kamerman and Kahn (1988, 1989). For an analysis of the situation of single mothers and their children in the United States, see also Garfinkel and McLanahan (1986). For discussion of developments in specific countries, see Duskin (1990).

4. In light of some of these developments, in summer 1991, the International Social Security Association held a meeting of its members to discuss the changing need for survivor's benefits.

5. These policy options are discussed in greater detail in Kamerman and Kahn (1987, 1989).

6. The United States and Canada also exemplify this model, with some modifications.

7. *Overview of Entitlement Programs,* Committee on Ways and Means, U.S. House of Representatives, 1990.

8. *Overview of Entitlement Programs,* Committee on Ways and Means, U.S. House of Representatives, 1990.

9. These policies also encourage women to work: child support payments do not provide enough income for a family to live on, but do help significantly when added to earnings.

10. Contrary to the fears of American policymakers, the availability of income support for lone mothers does not "cause" women to have babies to qualify for social benefits or couples to break up. However, once an unwed mother has a baby or a couple divorces, social policies can make the lifestyle of lone-parent families more or less comfortable.

REFERENCES

Blayo, Chantal. 1987. "Trends in Fertility in Western Europe After 1980." *Journal of Regional Policy in Europe* 7:493–514; "La Fecondite—en Europe Depuis 1960: Convergence ou Divergence?" Paper presented at European Population Conference, Helsinki, Finland. Central Statistical Office of Finland.

Bumpass, Larry. 1990. "What's Happening to the Family: Interaction Between Demographic and Institutional Change." *Demography* 27, 4 (November):483–498.

Duskin, Elizabeth (ed.). 1990. *Lone-Parent Families: The Economic Challenge.* Paris: OECD.

Garfinkel, Irwin, and Sara McLanahan. 1986. *Single Mothers and Their Children: A New American Dilemma.* Washington, D.C.: Urban Institute.

Garfinkel, Irwin, and Patrick Wong. 1990. "Child Support and Public Policy." In Elizabeth Duskin (ed.). *Lone-Parent Families: The Economic Challenge.* Paris: OECD.

Glendon, Mary Ann. 1987. *Abortion and Divorce in Western Law.* Cambridge, MA: Harvard University Press.

Gunderson, Morley, and Leon Muszynski. 1990. Ottawa, Canada: Canadian Advisory Council on the Status of Women.

Jones, Elsie F., et al. 1986. *Teenage Pregnancy in Industrialized Countries.* New Haven: Yale University Press.

Kahn, Alfred J. and Sheila B. Kamerman. 1983. *Income Transfers for Families with Children: An Eight-Country Study.* Philadelphia: Temple University Press.

——— (eds.). 1988. *Child Support: From Debt Collection to Social Policy.* Newbury Park, CA: Sage Publications.

Kamerman, Sheila B., and Alfred J. Kahn. 1987. *Mother-Only Families in Western Europe: Social Change, Social Problem, and Societal Response.* New York: Columbia University School of Social Work.

———. 1988. *Mothers Alone: Strategies for a Time of Change.* Westport, CT: Auburn House—Greenwood Group.

———. 1989. "Single-Parent, Female-Headed Families in Western Europe: Social Change and Response." *International Social Security Review* 1:3–34.

——— (eds.). 1991. *Child Care, Parental Leave, and the Under 3s: Policy Innovation in Europe.* Westport, CT: Auburn House—Greenwood Group.

Millar, Jane. 1989. *Poverty and the Lone Parent: The Challenge to Social Policy.* Brookfield, VT: Avebury, Gower.

Sorenson, Annamette. 1990. "Single Mothers, Low Income, and Women's Economic Risks. The Cases of Sweden, West Germany, and the United States." Photocopy.

Sorrentino, Constance. 1990. "The Changing Family in International Perspective." *Monthly Labor Review* 113, 3 (March):41–56.

U.S. Congress. House Committee on Ways and Means. 1991. *The 1991 Green Book: Overview of Entitlement Programs.* Washington, D.C.: U.S. Government Printing Office.

Chapter 7

FRENCH POLICIES TOWARDS LONE PARENTS: SOCIAL CATEGORIES AND SOCIAL POLICIES

Nadine Lefaucheur

SOCIAL CATEGORIES mold social policies. It is significant that the term "lone-parent families" (*familles monoparentales*) was not used in France until the 1970s. In the preceding century, families without two married adults were divided into narrower categories like unmarried mothers, widows, and widowers, etc., or were lumped together and mixed with stepfamilies into one large group referred to as "broken families" (*familles dissociées*).

The category of "broken families" appeared at the end of the nineteenth century, when dramatic changes in French economic and social life raised a number of questions regarding the proper socialization of children and the appropriate role of the family and the state in this process. From the early 1880s until World War I, a variety of laws were passed to regulate various aspects of child-rearing (e.g., legislation on compulsory schooling, child welfare protection, limits on parental rights, and juvenile delinquency appeared in this period), as theories about the effects of growing up in an "abnormal" or "broken" family were elaborated by criminologists and child psychologists. Understanding the way contemporary French policies towards lone parents evolved from and built upon earlier social categories and concepts of the family is important to understanding the way current policies operate today.

EARLY SOCIAL POLICY: A PRO-NATALIST EMPHASIS

Throughout the early period of its development, French social policy placed a strong emphasis on increasing the national birthrate. Beginning in the 1870s, and continuing through 1940, defeats suffered by France in wars against Germany made the national birthrate a political issue, and a number of pro-natalist measures were initiated to fight "depopulation." In 1874, a medico-social campaign against maternal and infant mortality won its first battle with the establishment of compulsory medical supervision of young children in childcare (the Roussel Law). In 1893, poor pregnant women were given the right to free medical care and hospitalization. A paid maternity leave of 8 weeks for all working women was mandated in the 1910s.[1] Public maternity hospitals and public or private community clinics for babies (*consultations de nourrissons*) were also established. Maternity homes to shelter pregnant women and new mothers were created and a variety of mother and child welfare associations (*protection maternelle et infantile*) came into operation.

In 1939 and 1943, the *Code de la famille* institutionalized these programs by mandating that each local authority (*département*) establish a maternity home (*maison maternelle*).[2] From 1943 until about 1975, official French maternity homes provided shelter to mothers-to-be during their pregnancy leaves. *Hôtels maternels* were created in the 1950s and 1960s to shelter mothers and babies after the mother's pregnancy leave was exhausted; they provided housing until the babies were 1–3 years old. In 1975, both kinds of shelters were joined and re-named *centres maternels*. Today, there are about 70 *centres maternels* in France, taking in about 2,800 expectant or new mothers, mostly unmarried, each year. Their *crèche* (day nursery) is often open to children in adjacent neighborhoods.[3]

Government income support for poor mothers in France was also established in the nineteenth century. The first income assistance established by the government was a monthly allowance given by *Assistance publique* to poor mothers (who were often unmarried) to discourage them from abandoning their babies.[4] This allowance was designed to give mothers the means to feed their children, and thereby reduce infant mortality, which was especially high among illegitimate children.[5] The current ASE system (*Aide sociale à l'enfance*, formerly *Assistance publique*) is managed by local authorities at the *département* level. Besides monthly allowances, ASE provides educational support to about 105,000 children as well as emergency aid grants. These allowances vary according to the *département* in which the family resides, but are generally about 25 percent of SMIC (minimum salary level–about ff5,300 in 1990), or about 19 percent of the average woman's salary. The level and duration of support is at the discretion of the social workers in charge of ASE. Almost half of the 260,000 grants given each month are to children in lone-parent families. ASE also supports about 150,000 children in the direct care of public authorities; 37,000 of these children are in public institutions and the rest live with families in foster care situations.

In the 1920s, pro-natalist policies led to the repression of abortion and a ban on information on contraception—policies that remained in effect until the 1970s. To aggressively encourage large families, the government also instituted tax cuts for families with children. Some employers also created family allowances (*allocations familiales*) to help offset the costs of large families. By 1932, all workers with at least two children were given a legal right to receive family allowances.

This makeshift system of support for families with young children was reorganized and greatly expanded after World War II. On October 4, 1945, a national law established a social security system to protect the populace against various social "risks." However, access to the social security system depended on an individual being part of a family that had at least one adult worker solidly integrated into the labor force. Not until the unemployment crisis of the 1970s was the requirement of labor force participation as a condition for social security protection relaxed somewhat.

In 1945–46, family allowances were integrated into the social security system. Under the French system, family allowances are paid for by payroll contributions of employers and salaried people. Representatives of both these groups manage the CAF (*Caisses d'allocations familiales,* or family allowances funds). The amount of the allowances, which are tax-free and usually paid monthly, is calculated as a percentage of a monthly base amount indexed to the SMIC.

The 1946 reform provided for four kinds of family benefits. First, family allowances were given to families with at least one working (salaried) parent and at least two children in the household. From 1946 to 1975, disabled or unemployed family heads who could not work were also eligible for family allowances. Since 1975, all families are eligible to receive benefits. The amount of the allowance rises with the third child in the family. Second, single-income allowances were given to families in which only one parent worked. Third, prenatal allowances were paid to all expectant mothers as soon as their pregnancy was medically certified; the amount was based on the amount of the universal family allowance and single-income allowance the family received. Fourth, maternity allowances were owed to families after each birth, regardless of family size.[6] This system was very pro-natalist, giving more to larger families in which only the fathers worked, and rewarding mothers for each birth. Two new benefits were created in 1955: a supplemental benefit (*majoration*) was added to family allowances given for children over age 10, and a housewife allocation (*de la mère au foyer*) for self-employed workers' families.[7]

The tax system was also revised in 1945, so that larger families paid proportionately less in taxes than small families. Today, the first two children of a married couple count as half an individual deduction, and the remaining children and each parent as one deduction. Lone parents benefit from some preferential tax measures too: a widowed lone parent counts as two deductions instead of one, and the first child of a single, separated, or divorced lone parent counts as one deduction instead of half of one. Once their children turn 18 years old, formerly custodial parents have a right to half of one deduction and retain this right until/unless they remarry. Working lone parents can also deduct daycare expenditures from their taxable income (up to 10,000 francs per year for a child under age 7).

Another 1945 law established a network of mother and child welfare centers across France. These centers were charged with the systematic medical supervision of expectant or new mothers and of children under age 6. Today, health insurance is provided to every person who has worked 1,200 hours in the previous year or who has paid social security for at least a year.[8] (The spouse and minor children of insured persons are covered, too.) Lone parents who were previously eligible parties (because they had a working spouse) remain eligible for 1 year after the death of their spouse or a marital separation, or until their last child reaches 3 years of age. A pregnant or recently delivered woman who was eligible for social security because of her late or absent spouse or became eligible because of enrollment in *allocation de parent isolé* (API) is entitled to a "maternal rest allowance" of 16 weeks.[9]

With the reform of the social security system after World War II, the welfare system became more universal and systematic. Although it retained its pronatalist emphasis by establishing a comprehensive support system that included both services and income for families with young children, eligibility was based on the family's direct or indirect links to the workforce. For an overview of the major social programs operating in France today, see Table 7.1.

RECENT TRENDS IN MARRIAGE, FERTILITY, FEMALE LABOR FORCE PARTICIPATION, AND LONE PARENTHOOD

Over the last 25 years, changes in the birthrate and deathrate, in conjugal life, and in female labor force participation have occurred in France. All these changes have had an impact on the circumstances of lone-parent families. Life expectancy has grown in France since World War II. The average life span for women is now 81 (up from 74 in the early 1960s); for men, the average life span is 73 (up from 67). The birthrate dropped after 1950 and has fallen even more since 1963. This declining birthrate has been accompanied by an increase in the average age at first birth (27 years old for women and 28 for men in 1986) and by a drop in the average number of children per marriage. Large families have nearly disappeared. (The number of families with at least four children under age 17 declined from 820,000 in 1962 to 260,000 in 1990.)

The number of divorces in France has doubled since 1975, when divorce by mutual consent was legalized, and the average length of marriages has shortened. Since the mid-1970s, the marriage rate has also declined significantly, and there has been a large rise in cohabitation. In 1990, there were almost two million unmarried, cohabiting couples in France.

It is hardly surprising, then, to find that there has also been a significant increase in illegitimate births in France over the last 25 years. In 1966, only 6 percent of all births were out of wedlock. Today, 32 percent of births are out of wedlock, but most of the parents of illegitimate, newborn children are cohabitating. Although the proportion of children who are not legally recognized by their fathers doubled between 1972 and 1986 (from 5 percent to 9 percent), paternity is still legally established in 90 percent of all births in France.

The labor force participation rates of women, especially of mothers, also rose rapidly over the last two decades. In 1975, 43 percent of mothers living in couples (married or not) worked; in 1982, 59 percent worked; and in 1993, 71 percent worked. Four out of five women in the labor force work full-time. Only mothers who have at least three children, are under age 20, or over age 55 have labor force participation rates lower than 50 percent.

The increased labor force activity of mothers has created the need for daycare for children under age 3. Public *crèches*, created in the middle of the nineteenth century, are the most popular childcare arrangements for children in this age group outside of childcare by the mother. Today, about 1,600 *crèches*, subsidized

Table 7.1A / Income Support in France: 1989

Families with Children	Year of Creation or Reform	Amount (As a Percentage of SMIC)	Number of Beneficiaries		Eligibility		
			All Families	Lone Parents	Family	Parents	Children
Actual Family Benefit (*Allocations Familiales proprement dites*)	(1932) 1946	2 Children: 11% 3 Children: 26% 4 Children: 40% 5 Children: 55% Over 10 Children: +3% Over 15 Children: +6%	3,600,000 families	300,000	—	—	Two or more children under age 17
New School Year (*Allocation de Rentrée Scolaire*)	1974	7% per child	2,000,000 children	—	Eligible for at least one means-tested benefit	—	Schooled
Family Supplement (*Complément Familial*)	1978	15% per child	730,000 families	100,000	Income lower than about twice the SMIC	—	Three or more children under age 3
Total Amount Paid by CAF (Billions)							ff 57.43

Table 7.1B / Income Support in France: 1989 (*continued*)

Lone Parents	Year of Creation or Reform	Amount (As a Percentage of SMIC)	Number of Beneficiaries		Eligibility		
			All Families	Lone Parents	Family	Parents	Children
Family Support Benefit (*Allocation de Soutien Familial*)	(1970) (1973) 1986	10% per child (benefit or advance on unpaid child support)	—	400,000	—	Alone	(Semi-)orphan, or recognized by only one parent—unpaid alimony
Lone-Parent Benefit (*Allocation de Parent Isolé*)	1976	Pregnant: 53% Lone parent: 53% +18% per child	—	130,000	Income lower than guaranteed income	Alone	At least one child expected or living
Total Amount Paid by CAF (Billions)							ff 6.58

Table 7.1C / Income Support in France: 1989 (*continued*)

Young Children	Year of Creation or Reform	Amount (As a Percentage of SMIC)	Number of Beneficiaries		Eligibility		
			All Families	Lone Parents	Family	Parents	Children
Young Child Benefit (*Allocation au Jeune Enfant*)	1985	16%	440,000 families	50,000 families	—	Pregnant mother	Or one child under 3 months of age
			1.2 million families	—	Income lower than twice SMIC		One child over 3 months and under 3 years of age
Parenting Leave (*Allocation Parentale d'Education*)	1985	From 25 to 50%	160,000 children	—	—	One parent having stopped working or reduced his or her working time	Three or more children; last one under age 3
At-Home Childcare Benefit (*Allocation de Garde d'Enfant à Domicile*)	1986	Employer's social security contribution to payroll	—	—	—	Both parents employed	Child cared for at home

Total Amount Paid by CAF (Billions)   ff21.2

Table 7.1D / Income Support in France: 1989 (*continued*)

People with Very Low Incomes	Year of Creation or Reform	Amount (As a Percentage of SMIC)	Number of Beneficiaries		Eligibility		
			All Families	Lone Parents	Family	Parents	Children
Guaranteed Minimum Income for Insertion (*Revenu minimum d'insertion*)	1988	1 person: 40% / 2 persons: 60% / Others: +11% (each one)	325,000 families	About 75,000	Income lower than guaranteed income	—	—

Total Amount Paid by CAF (Billions)   ff 4.91

Table 7.1E / Income Support in France: 1989 (*continued*)

Handicapped People	Year of Creation	Amount (As a Percentage of SMIC)	Number of Beneficiaries		Eligibility		
			All Families	Lone Parents	Family	Parents	Children
Specialized Education Benefit (*Allocation d'Education Spécialisée des Mineurs Infirmes*)	(1963) (1970) 1975	From 11% to 37%	75,000 children	—	Income lower than 55 of SMIC	—	Handicapped
Handicapped Adult Benefit (*Allocation d'Adulte Handicappé*)	(1971) 1975	—	464,000 persons	—	—	Handicapped parents	Or handicapped child over age 20

Total Amount Paid by CAF (Billions)   ff 14.08

Table 7.1F / Income Support in France: 1989 (*continued*)

Housing	Year of Creation or Reform	Amount (As a Percentage of SMIC)	Number of Beneficiaries — All Families	Number of Beneficiaries — Lone Parents	Number of Beneficiaries — Family	Eligibility — Parents	Eligibility — Children
Family Housing Benefit (*Allocation de Logement à Caractère Familial*)	1948	Dependent on income and housing	1,000,000 families	—	—	Conditions of income and size, rent level, and kind of housing	One or more children
Personalized Housing Benefit (*Aide Personalisée au Logement*)	1977	Dependent on income and housing	2,100,000 households	—	—	Conditions of income and size, rent level, and kind of housing	—
Total Amount Paid by CAF (Billions)							ff 38.9

by local authorities, government services, hospitals, or work councils, care for about 90,000 children aged 3 or under. *Crèches* have one qualified employee per five children, and parents pay according to income. Because of the high staff-to-child ratio and the high quality of care, these public *crèches* are costly to run. As a result, local authorities and the CAF have tried to develop other forms of childcare, such as *mini-crèches* (that care for only about 12 children) or parental cooperative *crèches*.[10] *Family crèches* represent another type of young childcare. Under this arrangement, a pediatric nurse, assisted by a secretary, and a part-time pediatrician, supervise about 40 childcare persons, each caring for 1 to 3 children in their own homes. Today, there are about 233 *mini-crèches* caring for 4,400 children, 160 *parental crèches* caring for 2,200 children, and 830 *family crèches* networks with 30,000 childcare workers caring for 52,800 children operating in France.

One out of six children under age 3 (and one out of three children of working mothers), are cared for in nursery schools or in subsidized childcare arrangements. About 40 percent are cared for by their mothers or by other family members. The others are cared for by childcare workers called "mothers' helpers" (*assistantes maternelles*). About 160,000 individuals, including those who work in *family crèches*, are authorized childcare workers. An estimated 140,000 more are working informally in child-minding. France also has about 2,000 "respite care" nurseries (*haltes-garderies*) that take in about 43,000 young children on a part-time basis when their mothers work part-time or need to leave them for a while to shop. Almost all children over age 3 and under age 6 in France attend nursery school (*école maternelle*). This widespread and accessible network of childcare makes it much easier for mothers of young children in France to enter the labor force than is true in many other countries.

Children of lone parents do not have any legal priority on the waiting lists for *crèches* (except for *crèches* run by maternity homes). In any case, the increase in the number of unmarried, cohabiting couples would make it difficult for directors or subsidizers of *crèches* to make "unmarried mother status" a screening criterion for admission. Almost one in five lone mothers in France had children 6 years old or younger in 1982; 7 percent of all children under 3 years old (160,000 children) lived in lone-parent families in France in 1990, but children of lone parents do not have any legal priority on the waiting lists for *crèches* (except for *crèches* run by maternity homes). In any case, the increase in the number of unmarried, cohabiting couples would make it difficult for directors or subsidizers of *crèches* to make "unmarried mothers status" a screening criterion for admission. Nonetheless, some *crèches* do favor the admittance of children of lone parents "in difficulty" who are brought to their attention by social services. As a result of this informal practice, children in lone-parent families are more likely than children in two-parent families to be cared for in *crèches* when their mothers are employed, especially if they are unmarried.

Today, family allowances and a network of childcare providers attempt to simultaneously encourage high birthrates and high female labor force participation. Special income support is provided after the birth of the third child in a family, when children are under 3 years of age, and in order to reduce day-care expenditures for working mothers (*complément familial, allocation au jeune enfant, allocation de garde d'enfant à domicile* and *allocation parentale d'éducation*) (see Table 7.1).

LEGAL REFORMS REGARDING MARRIAGE AND PARENTAL AUTHORITY

From the early sixties, especially between 1965 and 1975, many civil laws concerning family relations were reformed: new laws regarding marriage settlements were passed in 1965 and 1985; adoption procedures were reformed in 1966; contraceptive rights were reformed in 1967; parental authority was redefined in 1970, 1987, and 1993; filiation laws were rewritten in 1972; alimony laws were reformed in 1973 and 1975; and new laws on divorce and abortion passed in 1975. Some of these reforms have significantly affected the formation and living conditions of lone-parent families. Since January 1972, illegitimate children have had the same rights as legitimate children. If not born of incest, these children must be legally recognized by both parents, whatever their marital status. An action to establish paternity can be brought by a mother until the child is 2 years old or by the child himself/herself up until 2 years after he or she comes of age (usually 18 years old).

As of July 1975, three forms of divorce were allowed in France: divorce by mutual consent, divorce for offense, and divorce for the breaking of conjugal life. They constitute, respectively, about 51 percent, 48 percent, and 1 percent of all divorce petitions. The liberalization of divorce laws has been accompanied by an increase in the proportion of divorced mothers in the population. The percentage of lone parents who are divorced almost doubled since 1968 (rising from 35 percent to almost 60 percent).

When divorcing parents have children who are minors, the custody of these children (residence and parental authority) is determined by a judge, who is legally bound to decide "in the interest of the children." In about two out of three such custody cases, judges rule that the noncustodial parent has to pay support to the custodial parent for the care of the children. The amount of support is freely determined by the judge, who takes the needs of the children and the income of the noncustodial parent into account. However, the payments are usually very low. According to a survey conducted in 1985–86, the average amount of child support paid was about 16 percent of the SMIC per child, per month (i.e., 11 percent of the average female's salary), but the median payment was only about 8 percent of the SMIC.[11]

A recent survey of the frequency of contact between fathers and children in lone-parent or reconstituted households (stepfamilies) found that only one out of three children lives with his or her father or sees him at least once a month.[12] However, contact is greater among teenagers and children whose parents are divorced, especially if the parents exercise joint custody.

/ 267

From 1970 to 1993, when parents were not married, the mother was automatically given custody of her children, even if the children had been legally recognized by their father. However, since 1987, judges could order divorced, unmarried, or separated parents to exercise joint custody (parental authority) over their children, and, since January, 1993, that has become the norm for the couples who both recognized their child before he or she was 1 year of age and who cohabitated before this time.

When child support is not paid (as happens in about one-third of cases), the custodial parent can place a claim to garnish the salary or bank account of the debtor or can have the payments collected by a tax collector or bailiff. Since 1986, he/she can request that the CAF (family allowance funds) recover the debt on his/her behalf after 2 months of nonpayment. If a lone parent, he/she can receive an advance on the unpaid child support, called a "family support allowance" (allocation de soutien familial, or ASF), one of the two benefits created for lone parents after 1970. This allowance amounts to about 10 percent of SMIC per child. In 1989, about 400,000 lone-parent families received benefits from this program.

THE PERCEIVED CRISIS OF THE FAMILY

In the mid-1970s, the perception that there was a "crisis of the family" in France became widespread. Fed by declining marriage and fertility rates and the growing propensity for women to work outside the home, the reforms of civil and welfare laws that had occurred over the previous decade both reflected and encouraged these changes.

Lone-Parent Families: A New Statistical Category

The term "lone-parent family" was introduced in France by feminist academics who opposed the traditional view of families headed by unwed and divorced mothers as "psychosocial problems" and "families-at-risk." These researchers argued that the lone-parent family was as noble as, and more "modern" than, the usual type of conjugal family. They favored the new sociological term because they felt it would accord female-headed families the status of "real families." The term was embraced by policymakers and social workers, but rapidly acquired the negative connotations of "abnormality" and "problem families" that had been associated with "split families" and "unmarried mothers."[13]

The proportion of all families with children who are headed by a lone parent has grown gradually since 1975, increasing from 9.4 percent in 1975 to 12.6 percent in 1990.[14] Today, there are about 1.1 million lone-parent families with children under age 25 in France, 87 percent of them female-headed.[15] Lone-parent families today mainly result from divorce or the separation of unmarried couples. In 1968, 56 percent of lone mothers were widows, 9 percent had never been married, and 35 percent had divorced or separated. In 1989, only 21 percent of lone mothers were widows, whereas 21 percent had never been married and 58 percent were separated or divorced (Table 7.2).

Lone mothers are not as young as typically imagined, even if one only considers those with dependent children. Their median age is 37; only 0.2 percent of them are under age 20 and about 62 percent are over age 35 (Table 7.3). Children in lone-parent families are not very young either. In 1990, the median age of a minor child living with a lone mother was 10.[16] In 1982, about 7 percent of all children age 3 and under lived in lone-parent households, but 12 percent of the children 13–17 years old lived in such households. Never-married mothers are, on average, younger than other lone mothers, but only about 13 percent are under age 25 and only about 1 percent are teenagers.

Although sexual relations are occurring earlier and earlier, the pregnancy rate for teenagers is declining, as is the number of teenagers applying for legal abortions. In 1988–1989, only about 20,000 out of almost 3 million teenagers gave birth to a child (and about 5,000 of these were married); and only a little more than 16,000 applied for a legal abortion.

THE UNEMPLOYMENT CRISIS, "NEW POVERTY," AND LONE-PARENT FAMILIES

There was a dramatic rise of unemployment in France after the mid-1970s and a resultant increase in poverty and social segmentation. In response, French policymakers established new programs of basic support as well as programs designed to help the groups most affected by unemployment and poverty become more integrated in the economy and society.

Less than 2 percent of the working population in France was unemployed in the early 1960s, but since then the unemployment rate has grown continually. As of 1991, about 2.2 million (9 percent of the workforce) people were unemployed (Table 7.4). Young people, women, individuals without educational qualifications, and people of foreign origin have experienced especially high unemployment rates. The duration of unemployment has also grown. In 1989, over half of all unemployed persons in France had been unemployed for more than 14 months. The average length of time unemployed increases with the age of the unemployed.

Targeted Benefits for Lone-Parent Families

As unemployment and poverty rose, the benefits created or modified since 1970 have been more targeted to families with special needs (handicapped persons, orphans, and lone parents) and they are often income-tested. Although family allowances in France are available whether the head is employed or not, they are becoming less tied to the principles of universalism and the horizontal redistribution of income (according to family size) than was previously the case. In 1970, less than 14 percent of the total money distributed by the CAF (family

Table 7.2 / Families with Children Under Age 25

	1968 (Census)	1975 (Census)	1982 (Census)	1989 (Employment Survey)
Total Number	7,532,000	8,190,000	8,628,000	8,673,000
Couples	6,874,000	7,464,000	7,781,000	7,576,000
Lone Parents	658,000	726,000	847,000	1,097,000
Lone fathers	132,000	141,000	123,000	147,000
Lone mothers	526,000	585,000	724,000	950,000
Never-married	9.0	13.0	17.0	21.0
Divorced and separated	35.0	44.0	53.0	58.0
Widows	56.0	43.0	30.0	21.0

SOURCES: INSEE. *Census of Population, 1968; Employment and Income Survey, 1989.*

Table 7.3 / Age Distribution and Family Size of Lone-Mother Families, by Marital Status

Lone-Mother Households with Children Under 18 Years Old	All Lone Mothers	Never-Married Mothers
Median Age	37	31
Percentage of Mothers		
Under Age 20	0.2	0.7
Ages 20–24	4.8	14.8
Ages 25–34	32.6	50.0
Over age 35	62.4	34.5
Average Number of Children Under 25 Years Old		
One	56.0	77.0
Two	27.0	15.0
Three or more	17.0	8.0

SOURCES: Data by age groups are from INSEE. *Employment and Income Survey, 1989.* Data by number of children are from INSEE. *Census of Population, 1982.*

Table 7.4 / Unemployment Rates in Working Population in France

	1962	1973	1981	1985	1988	1989
All	1.7	3.0	8.3	10.5	10.2	9.6
Men	1.1	1.7	6.1	8.8	8.1	7.7
Women	3.0	5.1	11.6	13.0	12.8	13.4
Men to Women	2.9	3.4	5.5	4.2	4.7	5.7

SOURCE: INSEE. *Employment Survey* (for years cited).

allowance fund) was income-tested; today, about 50 percent of the total money distributed by CAF is means-tested.[17]

During the 1970s, two income benefits were created especially for lone-parent families. An "orphan allowance" (*allocation d'orphelin*) was created in 1970 for children whose parents were both dead or unknown (full benefit) or who had one parent who was dead or unknown (part benefit). This benefit, which was income-tested until 1973, is now called the "family support allowance" (*allocation de soutien familial* or ASF). Since 1975, the ASF has been available to children with one parent who abandoned them, if the custodial parent lives alone. It is also given to lone custodial parents as an advance on unpaid child support until the CAF has recovered the money due from the noncustodial parent. About 400,000 lone-parent families are entitled to this allowance, but the amount is low—only about 10 percent of SMIC.

Lone-parent families are also eligible for the "lone-parent allowance" (*allocation de parent isolé*, or API), a means-tested and much-criticized benefit created in 1976. The API subsidizes the incomes of about 130,000 lone parents (or pregnant lone women) up to a guaranteed level of about 53 percent of SMIC for a pregnant lone woman and 71 percent of SMIC for a lone parent with one child, plus 18 percent of SMIC for each additional child. A time-limited benefit, the API is available for the first year after the separation of a couple (by death, divorce, or legal separation) or until the youngest child reaches age 3. Almost all beneficiaries of API are women (about 99 percent). The majority (57 percent) have never been married, and about half have only one child. Almost 47 percent of them also receive assistance from the Social Aid to Children's program (ASE); however, since API guarantees support only to a certain level, use of ASE does not result in a higher overall income.

The API has been accused of creating a disincentive for labor force participation and marriage or remarriage among lone parents. The stereotype of allowance recipients is that they try to "cheat" the government by having a "hidden husband" or refusing to marry or live with a man in order to remain entitled to API, and/or that they become pregnant every time the API 3-year entitlement period ends. However, findings from surveys and ethnographic studies of the "coping" strategies of lone parents (conducted by Benoît Bastard and Laura Cardia-Vonèche 1988), as well as results of longitudinal studies conducted by Jean-Claude Ray and colleagues (Ray 1983; Ray and Carvoyeur 1986; Ray, Carvoyeur, and Jeandidier 1986, 1989), indicate that these stereotypes have little basis in reality and that the disincentive effects of the API in work behavior are mild. Those who oppose API because it supposedly creates a "disincentive" to marry forget that API was established as part of a compromise with anti-abortion groups who argued that lone mothers should be supported so that they would not be forced into having an abortion for economic reasons.

It is important to note that, despite the multiplicity of family benefits and the existence of benefits especially intended for lone parents, about 10 percent of lone mothers with at least one dependent child under age 18 do not benefit from any family allowances, because they have only one child, because this child is over age 3, and/or because they have been lone mothers for more than 1 year.

Unemployment, Minimum Incomes, and Insertion Programs

High unemployment rates in the 1970s and 1980s led to a partial reform of the unemployment benefits system and to a conscious "social struggle against unemployment" (as the government dubbed it). The reforms encouraged the early retirement of individuals over age 55 and the creation of new training and "insertion" measures, which focused mainly on young people but also created programs for lone mothers.

In 1983, the Department of Women's Rights in France initiated an experimental program "for the social and occupational insertion of lone mothers," which consisted of individualized training courses (lasting 700 hours, on average) based on the personal career plans or goals of these women. Evaluation studies showed that about 30 percent of the participants attending these programs secured employment, and 28 percent went on to attend specialized occupational training.[18] In 1985, the program was expanded to make all women receiving the API and all other lone mothers eligible to participate. Only about 2,000 (or less than 2 percent of API recipients) women per year attended these paid "insertion"/training courses, but lone mothers who register as job-seekers receive priority for attending paid vocational "insertion" programs.

In 1986, another program, called "local insertion programs for lone women" (*programmes locaux d'insertion en faveur des femmes isolées*, or PLIF) was established for lone women over age 40 with very low incomes (whether or not they were raising children). It combines state and local resources to "insert" about 3,000 lone women per year into public service or general interest activities for at least 760 hours spread over 9 months. Participants are also given special training and an "exceptional aid allowance" of about 40 percent of SMIC. However, both of these programs attempted to "insert" lone mothers in an economy experiencing such high rates of general unemployment that new social insurance measures had to be implemented.

Under the French system of unemployment insurance, all salaried employees who work at least 3 months in the private sector before being dismissed are eligible for unemployment benefits paid by the ASSEDIC (*associations pour l'emploi dans l'industrie et le commerce*). ASSEDIC funds are financed and managed jointly by employers and workers. Unemployed individuals must be registered as job-seekers to receive benefits.[19] The basic benefit of ASSEDIC is normally 40 percent of the previous salary plus about 50 francs (about $9 in 1991) a day or 57 percent of the previous salary of the unemployed worker if that is a higher figure, and it is normally paid for 14 months. However, the amount and duration of unemployment insurance varies according to length of the previous employment, age at the time of dismissal, and length of unemployment. Under age 50, the basic benefit of ASSEDIC cannot be paid for more than 19 months.[20] After exhausting this benefit, individuals can receive "closed-right benefits" (*allocation de fin de droits*) of about 78 francs (about $14 in 1991) a day for 7 to 27 months. After that, they are not entitled to receive benefits under the ASSEDIC. However, if their income is lower than the SMIC, and if they have worked for at least 5 out of the 10 years preceding the "dismissal," they are entitled to a "solidarity benefit" (*allocation de solidarité*) of about 69 francs maximum (about $12 in 1991) per day, paid under the National Employment Fund (*Fonds national de l'emploi*). Homemakers are eligible for solidarity benefits if, during the last 10 years, they worked for at least 2 years and have three children; worked 3 years and have two children; or worked 4 years and have one child.

In spite of the relatively long entitlement benefits for the unemployed described above, the unemployment crisis was so severe by the mid-1980s, that some people were exhausting all available benefits, or were failing to qualify for any benefits because they had been unable to work the minimum amount of time for eligibility requirements. As a result, a means-tested "insertion allowance" (*allocation d'insertion*) was created in 1986. Paid through the National Employment Fund, the allowance provided support for 6 months or at most 1 year to certain categories of people who were registered as unemployed job-seekers but ineligible to receive unemployment benefits. Among those eligible were single people 16–25 years old (who receive about 43 francs per day) and mothers who had been alone for less than 5 years, had an income lower than 170 percent of the SMIC, and had at least one child under age 5 living with them (they receive about 89 francs per day).

In December 1988, a guaranteed minimum "insertion" income (*revenu minimum d'insertion*, or RMI) was established for all individuals over age 24 living legally in France.[21] Individuals rearing at least one child are eligible for RMI regardless of the age of the child. The RMI is granted to people who live alone and have an income lower than about 40 percent of SMIC, or who live with another person and have an income lower than 60 percent of SMIC. Participants receive the difference between their actual income and the guaranteed minimum income (determined by household size, see Table 7.1). They also become eligible for social security and housing support.

To qualify for RMI, individuals must apply to the program every term. They are supposed to sign a "contract of insertion" prepared by a *"commission locale d'insertion."* These contracts commit society to helping "insert" the person and may commit an individual to participate in training programs or in other "prosocial" activities. For example, an individual might agree to enter treatment for alcoholism, to apply for family allowances, to learn to read and write, to take care of his/her children, etc.

In 1991, 400,000 households were supported by RMI in metropolitan France and 90,000 in overseas *départements*. Most of the beneficiaries are individuals, mainly men. One out of four received no benefit from social security, and more than half had no social aid before RMI. However, experts were surprised to find that 20 percent of RMI beneficiaries (or 80,000 individuals) were lone parents. Thus, a much larger number of lone-parent families benefit from the more universal RMI program than was true of the earlier training/insertion programs that targeted lone mothers. The average age of a lone-mother participant in RMI is 36 and most have only one child. Presumably, most of these lone mothers had previously benefited from ASE or API, since RMI benefits are significantly lower than API benefit levels.[22]

A Growing Emphasis on the Labor Market Involvement of Lone Parents

The underlying objective of French family policies is supposed to be choice: public policies should enable mothers to choose freely between being a housewife or a working woman. However, the prevailing pattern in France is for a mother to work, especially if her children are over age 3. Lone mothers are now generally expected to work, especially if they do not have a young child, and there has been an increased emphasis on program activities designed to enable them to enter the labor force as quickly as possible—among lone mothers as well as among other recipients of income support.

It is assumed that mothers will not need more than 1 year (or 3 years, if they have an infant) to cope with the transition from being a "coupled" parent to being a lone mother. French policies assume that lone mothers can raise their children on a combination of their own earnings, child-support payments, and universal family allowances. Therefore, the API and eligibility for social security are given to nonworking lone parents for a limited time—1 year or until their last child is 3 years old—and special programs for lone parents have been mainly concerned with providing training to help integrate them socially and professionally—to help "insert" them in the workforce.

However, since earnings and employment depend not only on the labor force involvement and educational qualifications of the individual but also on the condition of the labor market at the time a worker enters it, lone mothers who entered the workforce after 1975 have had a difficult time. The average earnings of a never-married lone mother under age 30, who entered the workforce after 1975 when unemployment was high, were equal to only 77 percent of the national mean in 1984. By contrast, lone mothers aged 30–39, who entered the workforce before the employment crisis, had average earnings close to the national mean (although significantly lower than those of male workers).[23]

But in the 1980s, the major problem for young mothers has been finding employment. In 1989, over half of the lone mothers under 25 years old who were in the labor force were unemployed and only 31 percent were actually working (Table 7.5). In a time of low unemployment, a specific and short-term aid like API is a necessary and almost sufficient means of helping nonworking lone mothers cope with their situation during a "transitional" period. After a transitional period, it is reasonable to treat poor and/or unemployed lone mothers like all poor and unemployed people unless society makes other choices—like paying lone mothers to stay home and take care of their children, or actively requiring fathers to pay support to their children, or including lone motherhood in the risks covered by the social security system. However, a transitional program like API assumes that a universal and non-time-limited assistance pro-

Table 7.5 / Labor Force Activity of Mothers,
by Family Situation and Age of Mother: 1989

	Coupled Mothers		Lone Mothers	
	Under Age 25	Over Age 25	Under Age 25	Over Age 25
Labor Force Participation Rate	58	64	68	82
Unemployment Rate	34	10	54	15
Working	38	58	31	70
Unemployed	20	6	37	12
Not working	42	36	32	18
All	100	—	100	—
Total Number of Families	255,200	7,583,430	34,550	915,980

SOURCE: INSEE. *Employment Survey* (for year cited).

NOTE: All mothers have at least one child under age 25.

gram like RMI will be available for people who do not fit labor market demand after the transitional period is exhausted, especialy in a time of high unemployment.[24]

LONE PARENTHOOD, POVERTY, DEPENDENCY, AND SOCIAL MARGINALIZATION: A COMPLEX AND INTERACTIVE RELATIONSHIP

Policymakers and social workers often speak of lone-parent families as though they were all poor, unskilled, unemployed, dependent, isolated, and marginalized. But lone parents are a heterogenous group. Does lone parenthood per se create a risk of poverty? How successful are French social policies in providing protection against poverty to lone-mother families? To answer these questions, one must examine the links between lone parenthood, poverty, and social marginalization; the differences between the income and living conditions of one-parent families and two-parent families; and the different subgroups of lone mothers according to their age, marital status, ethnicity, place of origin, and labor force status.

Does Lone Parenthood Result in Poverty?

Does lone parenthood lead to the impoverishment of a household and of its members, as is usually claimed? To determine this, one must compare family disposable income (adjusted for family size), sources of income, property, housing, and consumer durables of one-parent and two-parent households, and, if possible, the condition of the households before and after experiencing lone-parenthood.

Labor Force Participation and Earnings of Lone Mothers

Female workforce participation rates are high in France, but those of lone mothers are higher than the average rate for women (Table 7.6). According to the INSEE Employment Survey of 1993, 70 percent of married mothers, 75 percent of cohabitating women, and 85 percent of lone mothers are working or registered job-seekers. Among lone mothers, divorced women have the highest labor force participation rate (89 percent), followed by never-married mothers (82 percent) and widows (71 percent).[25] Lone mothers are also more likely to work full-time than married mothers. (In 1982, about 90 percent of lone mothers were working full-time, compared to 82 percent of coupled mothers.[26])

A lone mother's experience in the workforce is heavily dependent on her level of education. On average, lone mothers are a little less educated than coupled mothers; they are more likely to have no secondary school diploma and less likely to be university graduates. The oldest lone mothers (usually widows) are the least educated; four out of five widows have no secondary school diploma or have only a primary leaving certificate. The most educated lone mothers are divorced women and/or lone mothers in their 30s.[27] Among never-married mothers, the level of education varies greatly depending on age. Never-married mothers under 30 years of age are the least educated of their age cohort; never-married mothers between 30 and 40 are the most educated.

French lone mothers are a little more likely than coupled women to be professionals or to hold executive positions, but they are about as likely to be office, commercial, or domestic employees as married mothers. Lone mothers usually

Table 7.6 / Labor Force Activity Mothers, by Family Situation and Marital Status: 1989

	Coupled Mothers		Lone Mothers			
	All	Cohabitating	All	Never Married	Divorced or Separated	Widows
Labor Force Participation Rate of Mothers with						
Children under age 18	65	(72)	85	81	83	70
Children under age 25	64	—	81	—	—	—
Activity of Mothers with Children Under Age 25						
Percent employed	57	—	67	—	—	—
Percent unemployed	7	—	14	—	—	—
Percent nonworking	36	—	19	—	—	—
All	100	—	100	—	—	—

SOURCE: INSEE. *Employment Surveys* (for years cited).

do not have the option of staying home, so uneducated lone mothers work and are trapped in low-paying jobs.

The average salary of working lone mothers in France is lower than that of the average male head—whether the male is married or a lone father. However, the average earnings of lone mothers is higher than the average earnings of married women. In 1984, the average salary of a lone mother was 85 percent of the national mean, whereas the salary of a married woman was only 76 percent of the national average. In contrast, the average married man's salary was 139 percent of the mean. Clearly, gender is more important in determining salary levels than marital status. But lone mothers have higher salaries than married women.

Among salaried lone mothers, never-married lone mothers have the highest average earnings (93 percent of the mean salary), followed by divorced mothers (86 percent), widows (77 percent), and married-separated mothers (70 percent). This hierarchy is nearly reversed for lone fathers: widowers and married-separated fathers have the highest average earnings (166 and 140 percent of the mean, respectively), divorced fathers earn 128 percent of the average, but never-married fathers earn only 89 percent. In the labor market, it appears that women who have been strongly involved in a conjugal way of life are penalized, but men who have been strongly involved in conjugal life are rewarded.

The Gross and Disposable Income of Lone-Mother Families

The heterogeneity of the circumstances of lone-mother families is also shown by comparing average gross income (before benefits and taxes) of various family types.[28] The average gross income from work and/or property of a lone-mother family is only 70 percent of the overall gross income of all families.[29] (Among two-parent families, the gross income is about 80 percent when there is one wage earner and 114 percent when there are two wage earners.) However, this average obscures the actual heterogeneity of lone-parent families: if the lone mother is a teacher or a middle executive, her gross income is likely to be twice as high as the income of an unskilled, working lone mother (whose gross income is likely to be barely the SMIC), and three times as high as the gross family income of a nonworking lone mother.

However, gross income levels are less relevant than size-adjusted disposable family incomes when attempting to compare variation in living standards. A survey conducted in 1981 by INED (*Institut national d'études démographiques*) and CERC (*Centre d'étude des revenus et des coûts*) showed that the disposable family income of lone-mother families was about 88 percent of SMIC and that the disposable family income of two-parent families was 116 percent of SMIC. However, there was enormous variation, even within groups, depending on the number of wage earners in the household. The average disposable income of lone mothers was 52 percent of SMIC if the mother was unemployed, but 110 percent of SMIC if the mother worked. The disposable income of two-parent families was 92 percent of SMIC with one wage earner, but grew to 137 percent of SMIC if there were two wage earners. The disposable income of a family headed by an employed lone mother was higher than the disposable income of a two-parent family with only one earner.

Data from the Fiscal Survey of 1984 also show that families headed by an employed lone mother are, on average, better off economically than two-parent families with only one wage earner.[30] In 1984, over half of working lone-parent families had disposable incomes less than 88 percent of SMIC, but more than 63 percent of two-parent families with one wage earner (85 percent of those with three or more children) had low incomes. In sum, although more lone-mother families are poor than are two-parent families, income is very closely related to labor force participation. Lone mothers who work are less likely to be poor than two-parent families with only one wage earner (Table 7.7).

Becoming a lone-parent family does not always result in poverty. The drop in disposable family income that is often associated with becoming a lone-parent family is sometimes temporary; sometimes it does not occur at all. A survey of non-elderly widows conducted by CERC in 1981 showed that, on average, disposable income dropped only 5 percent 7 months after the death of the father.[31] In one-third of the cases, the drop in income was over 20 percent, but in other cases income increased as a result of pensions and other support. In half the cases the average disposable family income was at least equal to former family income 19 months after the death of the father. In a quarter of the cases family income had increased by 30 percent. This stability or increase in income was due mainly to insurance payments and social transfers, which accounted for about half of the income of non-elderly widows. Wages accounted for only one-third of their income.

Table 7.7 / Percentage of Families Who Have Low Income, by Family Type: 1984

Percentage of Families	Whose Disposable Size-Adjusted Income Is Lower Than 50% of the Median	Whose Disposable Size-Adjusted Income Is Lower Than 60% of the Median	Whose Income Is Mainly Composed of Social Transfers
Lone-Parent Families			
Lone fathers	16	21	5
Lone mothers	—	—	—
Non-qualified workers	14	26	22
Unemployed	38	59	69
Nonworking	56	65	59
Two-Parent Families			
Dual earner	4	7	4
One earner	17	31	7

SOURCES: INSEE. *Fiscal Survey, 1984; Family Budgets Survey, 1984.*

Housing and Consumer Durables of Lone Parents

At the time of the 1982 Census, a quarter of two-parent families but only 17 percent of one-parent families in France owned their own homes.[32] Two-parent families were nearly twice as likely as lone mothers to own a car, a dishwasher, or a refrigerator, and a little more likely than lone mothers to have a washing machine or a telephone. It seems that lone parenthood diminishes one's chances of owning housing or major consumer durables.

However, the likelihood of owning a home and major consumer goods varies greatly with gender, age, and the marital status of lone parents. Lone fathers are one-and-one-half times more likely to own housing than are lone mothers; lone parents over age 40 are four times more likely to own housing than those under 40; and widows are five times more likely to own housing than are never-married lone mothers. Widows are also nearly twice as likely as never-married lone mothers to own a dishwasher or a deep-freeze, and one-and-one-half times more likely to have a washing machine or a telephone. Once-married but separated and divorced lone mothers are the group most likely to own the consumer durables most associated with the image of a "modern working woman"—dishwashers and cars.

On average, never-married mothers have the highest earnings but the lowest rate of homeownership. Widows have the lowest earnings but the highest rate of homeownership. These differences are related to the differential commitment to conjugal life of the two groups. The longer and more strongly involved in conjugal life lone mothers were over the course of their lives, the less they usually were involved in the workforce, and their average earnings reflect this. Conversely, their commitment to conjugal life results in a greater likelihood of ownership of housing and durable goods. Because of the relatively higher standard of living of couples compared with lone-parent families, women who had a longer period of conjugal life are more likely to have accumulated goods. Moreover, social mechanisms (like dowries or wedding presents) and financial mechanisms (like compulsory life insurance for houses or flats bought on credit) increase the probability that previously coupled mothers will have more property than never-married and "never-coupled" lone mothers.

Does Lone Parenthood Result in Dependency?

Today, more than four out of five lone mothers in France are in the workforce. However, the unemployment rate of lone mothers is about 12 percent for those over age 25, and 26 percent for those under age 25. According to the survey conducted by INED-CERC in 1981, the income of working lone mothers was mainly composed of their salary (76 percent); the remainder of their income was accounted for by family allowances (15 percent) and child support (9 percent). On average, then, working mothers, who represent 80 percent of all lone mothers, depend on public transfers for only about 15 percent of their income (Table 7.8). By comparison, dual-earner, two-parent families receive 8 percent

Table 7.8 / Sources of Income, by Family Type,
of Families with Children Under Age 25: 1981

	Dual Earner Couples	Single Earner Couples	Working Lone Mothers	Unemployed and Nonworking Lone Mothers
Earnings (direct earnings or social security payments from previous work activity)				
Of the father	57	78	—	—
Of the mother	35	2	76	23
Child Support (by the father or by insurances when the father is dead)	—	—	9	21
Family Allowances	8	19	14	53
Schooling Grants	0	1	1	3
All	100	100	100	100

SOURCE: CERC. "Familles nombreuses, mères isolées: situation économique et vulnérabilité," 1987.

of their income from public transfers on average, and one-earner, two-parent families receive 20 percent of their income from public transfers. Working lone-mother families rely on public transfers less than two-parent families in which the mother is a housewife.

About 20 percent of lone-parent families have no income or receive only a small amount of income from the labor market (direct earnings or social security payments from previous work activity) and, therefore, are heavily dependent on social transfers at any given point in time. Most nonworking lone mothers benefit from API or RMI. But these programs are means-tested, and recipients can combine income from various programs to achieve only a certain (low) level of income support.

Among unemployed or nonworking lone mothers, the primary sources of income are family allowances (56 percent). Entitlements derived from previous salaried activity (unemployment or social security benefits) account for another 23 percent of their income and child support for another 21 percent. Thus, nonworking or unemployed lone mothers on average rely on public support for 79 percent of their income. Dependency rates among lone-parent families are high only when the family head is not working, and over two-thirds of lone mothers with children are employed.

When Benoît Bastard and Cardia-Vonèche (1988) investigated the economic strategies of 50 lone-parent families, they identified four types of coping strategies: *intensification* or *restoration* of their individual occupational and earnings abilities, *claiming* directed towards the former spouse and/or public assistance, and *coordination* of resources and life with the father to take care of the children after separation or divorce. Lower-class mothers mainly engaged in strategies of intensification or of claiming directed at social aid, while middle-class women had enough educational resources to support themselves and their children by participating in the labor force. Upper-class mothers engaged primarily in restoration and coordination strategies.

Among the 15 poor families studied, the identity and the survival of the family itself took priority over economic concerns. The mother's primary objective was to avoid losing custody of her children to child protective workers. Although these mothers saw participation in the labor force as the only way to improve their family situation, they saw little hope of finding employment, given the increase in the number of qualified unemployed job-seekers over the past decade. The mothers were forced to become dependent on social aid. (The researchers noted that obtaining aid required so much time and energy that it could be considered an actual "job.") These families tended to be young, large, and many suffered from domestic violence, alcoholism, illness, homelessness, chronic unemployment, and racial discrimination. Separation from the conjugal partner was often followed by an improvement of their economic situation and the general climate of the family, "because life [with the male partner] had been so difficult."

Does Lone Parenthood Result in Social Marginalization?

Over the past 3 decades, there has been a strong destigmatizing of single motherhood and divorce in France, and this change is reflected in the increasing number of cohabiting, unmarried couples, illegitimate births, and divorces. Criticism of lone-mother families is no longer couched in moral terminology. However, there is still a sense that the absence of the father has a negative psychological effect on the socialization of children, and so there is still some stigma attached to lone-mother families.

One can think about the issues of stigma and marginality among lone mothers by examining changes in the characteristics of residents of maternity homes. Thirty years ago, they were largely French, white, and employed. Because having a child out of wedlock has become nearly "normal" in French society, this kind of lone mother does not need to hide in a maternity home anymore. Today, lone mothers in maternity homes are mainly unemployed, most of them receive API, and they are a racially mixed group. These mothers are stigmatized by the larger society because of their ethnicity and/or because of their poverty and reliance on social transfers, rather than their status as lone mothers.[33]

A number of studies have shown that the more strongly committed a woman has been to a "coupled life-style," the less stigmatized by society she is for becoming a lone mother.[34] However, when the women who have been heavily involved in homemaking find themselves lone parents, they are more likely to *feel* socially isolated and marginalized. And, if their role as wives and mothers took them out of the labor force for a long period, they may find themselves unable to easily reenter working life. In other words, the social marginality that lone mothers feel appears to be related to the degree of commitment the mother felt toward conjugal life and the degree to which marital life excluded work in the paid labor force.

CONCLUDING OBSERVATIONS:
FAMILY POLICY AND LONE PARENTS IN FRANCE

In the past, French family and social policies had two objectives: to encourage French citizens to have large families and to provide parents with the income support and social services (such as childcare) so that mothers could choose to be full-time homemakers or to enter the labor force. Although there is still some tension between various policies and departments regarding the latter objective, the Department of the Family supports the idea that women should freely choose between being homemakers or workers, while the Department of Women's Rights is dedicated to increasing female labor force participation, employment has increasingly come to be viewed as the appropriate goal of all women without very young children—whether they are lone parents or part of a couple.

Today, 81 percent of lone mothers and 65 percent of coupled mothers are in the labor force. The national system of childcare available to all families in France is key to these high labor force participation rates, although French mothers feel the system is not adequate to meet their needs.

Nonetheless, it is important to note once again that lone-parent families are a heterogenous group, and the nature of their ties to the workforce reflects this diversity—some lone parents do better than others on the labor market. Most lone parents (85 percent of male and 81 percent of female lone parents) participate in the paid workforce. Lone-father families are typically better off than lone-mother families, since men still earn higher salaries than women on average. However, because lone parenthood obliges a family head to play both mother and father, it seems to induce men to behave more like women and women to behave more like men with regard to labor force participation. Lone fathers participate less in the workforce than coupled fathers (85 percent versus 93 percent), while lone mothers participate much more than coupled mothers (81 percent versus 65 percent).

Among lone mothers, those who have the highest educational qualifications (typically women in their 30s) are the most economically secure. However, continuity of the participation in the labor force and intensity of work effort can compensate for educational qualifications. Among mothers with the same educational qualifications, there appears to be an inverse relationship between the length and intensity of conjugal involvement and earnings ability: mothers who leave the labor force for extended periods have lower earnings that those who continue to work. Never-married lone mothers who were employed when they gave birth or who entered the labor force shortly after they became lone mothers are unlikely to have left the workforce for any extended period; so unmarried mothers in their 30s or 40s are likely to have been continuously employed full-time for many years and to be among the highest female wage earners. Lone mothers who are continuously employed as full-time workers for most of their adult lives are very rarely poor.

Nearly four out of five lone mothers are able to provide relatively solid support to their families through a combination of their own earnings, child allowances, and child support from the absent father. Lone mothers of children with identifiable fathers receive official help in recovering unpaid child support (about 16 percent of SMIC on average) if such help is needed. Lone mothers with children whose father died or "abandoned" them can receive ASF, a public child support allowance of about 10 percent of SMIC per child. Lone mothers who are in the labor force usually do fairly well economically, and as all workers benefit from generous work-related protections like universal child allowances, health coverage, maternity leave, disability, unemployment and retirement, and access to subsidized childcare. Most working lone mothers do not receive much from the few government programs specifically dedicated to lone-parent families.

About 20 percent of lone mothers in France are not able to support their families with their own earnings and are therefore heavily dependent on social transfers, at least for a period of time (Table 7.8). These mothers tend to fall into two groups: elderly ex-wives who have been out of the workforce for long periods of time or young mothers with little education.

Social insurance programs in France also provide fairly good protection against economic hardship to widows who were tied to the labor market through their own or their husband's employment. If the late husband was self-employed, the widow's social insurance provisions would not be as generous as they would be if he was a salaried worker, but the widow would receive more social insurance today than in the past.

API gives lone mothers with young children a level of support that keeps them out of poverty while they stay home to care for young children or a year of transitional support as they try to reenter the workforce. It is adequate as a transitional allowance if a lone mother previously had an educational or occupational qualification that only needs to be updated. But if a lone mother has many children or physical and mental health disabilities, API is insufficient to provide the kind or level of support required for the mother to be "inserted" in the workforce. Recognizing this, new programs have been established for lone mothers in recent years, focusing on combining training and income support so as to make these mothers more "employable." Several social and occupational "insertion" programs have tried to help poor, unskilled mothers train for employment, but it is too soon to evaluate their effectiveness.

Lone mothers who have exhausted API benefits and who are unable to find work do experience a drop in income, but continue to qualify for child allowances, housing allowance, ASF benefits, and RMI assistance. Since the RMI top-off is adjusted for family size, these benefits leave nonworking lone mothers in an economic situation no better or worse than other long-term unemployed citizens.

Family laws and the social insurance system in France were changed in the 1970s to treat lone parenthood as a social risk rather than as social deviance. ASF and API were created to ensure that a change in family status was not accompanied by serious material hardship. These programs, coupled with a national commitment to quality childcare for young children, have proved successful in providing working lone mothers with enough support to keep themselves and their children fairly well within normal living standards in France.

ENDNOTES

1. Nowadays, maternity leave lasts for 16 weeks, but it may be extended to 28 weeks if the mother already has one child, gives birth to twins or triplets, or has a high-risk pregnancy; maternity allowances are worth 84 percent of the previous salary, but no more than 176 percent of the guaranteed minimum wage. In July 1990, the *salaire minimum interprofessionnel de croissance,* or SMIC, was worth 5,286 francs per month, while the average monthly salary for males was about 9,600 francs and the average monthly female salary about 7,200 francs. In this chapter the amount of the different benefits is given as a rough percentage of SMIC.

2. A *département,* or local authority, is a regional unit of government. There are 100 *départements* in France.

3. Since 1975, a law giving social aid to shelters that were formerly dedicated to homeless individuals has been extended to families *en difficulté,* usually lone-parent families. Some homeless shelters take in lone women, mainly separated or divorced ones, with older children; most of the shelters were created for victims of marital abuse.

4. This allowance was created in Paris in 1837 and was slowly extended to all *départements.*

5. *Assistance publique* does not only or predominantly involve income assistance. *Assistance publique* is still, in the minds of most French, synonymous with public orphanages. However, nowadays, the administrations in charge of the public care of orphans or children taken from their families (*aide sociale à l'enfance*) are D.D.A.S.S. (*Directions Départementales de l'Action Sanitaire et Sociale*) in the Ministry of Health, while assistance publique is in charge of public hospitals.

6. Prenatal and postnatal allowances were suppressed in January 1985; maternity allowances were suppressed in January 1987. They have been replaced by the young child allowance (*allocation au jeune enfant*), paid by *Caisses d'Allocations familiales.*

    Maternal rest allowances (*indemnités journalières de repos*) are paid by *assurance maternité* of *Caisses de Sécurité Sociale* to working women. During the 16 weeks, they receive 84 percent of their salary or no more than *ff*310 per rest day (in 1990). Maternal rest allowance (*allocation de repos maternel* and *indemnités de remplacement*) is an inclusive benefit paid to salaried women and to the wives of non-salaried workers who help their husbands.

7. Two other benefits deserve mention here. A family housing allowance (*allocation de logement à caractère familial*) established in 1948 was the only means-tested benefit created before the 1970s. It was initiated during a housing shortage, at a time when rent legislation was also being reformed. An allowance for the special education of disabled minors (*allocation d'éducation spécialisée des mineurs infirmes*) was also established in 1963 (see Table 7.1).

8. Workers contribute about 14 percent of their gross salary to social security, and employers about 28 percent. A widower or widow who is contributing to or whose late spouse contributed to, social security is entitled to a death capital, equal to three times the monthly salary of the late spouse or no more than about six times the SMIC; a widowhood insurance, if he or she is a lone parent under age 55 with an income lower than about two-thirds of SMIC; a payment of 52 percent of the retirement pension of the social security that his or her late spouse would have received, if a lone parent over age 55 whose income is lower than the SMIC who was married for at least 2 years or had a child with the deceased; 60 percent of the supplementary pensions of her late husband if the widow does not remarry and if she and her husband had two children under age 21 at the time of his death. Children under age 21 are entitled to receive 30 percent to 50 percent of the supplementary pensions of their late father.

9. This allowance is given to mothers who have three prenatal and three postnatal follow-up visits to a doctor (i.e., women who demonstrate good healthcare practices while pregnant). The total amount of the allowance varies from twice the SMIC for a normal pregnancy and delivery, to 3.4 times the SMIC for an abnormal and/or multiple pregnancy and delivery. *Assurance maternité* of *Sécurité Sociale* also provides for the repayment of medical and surgical expenses for pregnancy and delivery.

10. The latter grew out of the unofficial *crèches* created in universities by the May 1968 Movement. They are managed and staffed by parents, who care for the children either one full day or half a day per week. They are now supported by the family allowance funds if they employ one or two qualified pediatric nurses.

11. Léridon and Villeneuve-Gokalp: "Entre père et mère," pp. 1–4. (Table 4, page 3). Results of a survey on *situations familiales* conducted by the *Institut National d'Etudes Démographiques* in 1985–1986, which included about 5,000 households.

12. Ibid.

13. In 1981, lone-parent families became a main category of the nomenclature of households and families used by INSEE (*Institut National de la Statistique et des Études économiques*) to present data from the census and other surveys. As a result, data on the structure and conditions of lone-parent households (defined until 1990 by INSEE as households consisting of a person living without a partner with at least one child under age 25, providing that this child has never been married and does not live with a partner or a child of his or her own) emerged during the 1980s. Since the 1990 Census, all persons who live without a partner with at least one child, regardless of the age of their child, are categorized as lone parents.

14. Lone-parent families had slightly decreased in the mid-1960s, because widowhood was declining as a cause of lone parenthood (as a result of rising life expectancy). Also divorce and separation were not important causes of lone parenthood until the mid-1970s.

15. Of all families with children under age 18, 8.7 percent were lone-parent families in 1982 and 15.4 percent were so categorized in 1993 (when there were 812,000 lone-parent families with children under age 18).

16. Data used for 1990 are those of the last census, while data for 1989 or 1983 are from yearly Employment Surveys.

17. The increase in percentage in CAF payments that are means-tested is mainly due to the increase in the payments of housing benefits and *allocation d'adulte handicapé* (both have more than doubled since 1978) and to the creation in 1986 of the *allocation au jeune enfant*, which is a means-tested allowance for children over 3 months old. In 1990, CAF paid 12 billion francs in housing benefits, 17 billion francs in benefits for handicapped people, and 14 million francs in means-tested AJE payments. API payments were only worth 4 billion francs and RMI payments 10 billion. Other means-tested allowances are the *allocation de rentrée scolaire* (2 billion francs) and the *complément familial* (8 billion francs). Only one benefit which was formerly means-tested is not now—ASF.

18. François Aballéa and Michel Goetz (February 1985) *Programme d'action d'insertion en faveur des mères isolées; rapport d'évaluation.* Culture et Promotion, rapport au Ministère des droits de la femme, au Ministère de la formation professionnelle et à la Caisse nationale d'allocations familiales, mimeo.

19. Almost all employees in the public sector are guaranteed jobs.

20. Some changes have occurred since this chapter was written, when employees and workers renegotiated these rights and the amount of their payroll contributions because ASSEDIC was having difficulty paying claims.

21. The 1988 Law on RMI was a provisional law, passed for 3 years, which was renewed in 1992. Extending its coverage to include young people aged 18–24 has been discussed, but not passed.

22. A lone mother with 3 children over age 3 could receive API (107 percent of SMIC) for no more than 1 year. After that, she would benefit from RMI, which would "fill in" her income up to 82 percent of SMIC (for a family of 4) unless her income was already over 82 percent of SMIC when the following were added: family allowances (26 percent of SMIC) + family supplement (15 percent of SMIC) + ASF (10 percent of SMIC x 3 = 30 percent SMIC if she received no support from the father) + a housing benefit (that could cover almost all her rent).

    On the other hand, if a lone mother had only 1 child and this child was under 3 years old, she would receive API (71 percent of SMIC) and could have her rent almost paid through a personalized housing benefit (if she lived in a building which allows this benefit). When her child turned 3 years old, she would no longer be eligible for API and would receive only 10 percent of SMIC from ASF (if the father paid no support); thus, RMI could lift the family income from 10 percent SMIC to 60 percent SMIC (or even around the SMIC if she gets a personalized housing benefit).

23. Never-married lone mothers over age 40 benefited from entering the labor market when there was a shortage of labor. Even those without high educational qualifications were able to find and retain jobs, and they had the highest average earnings among mothers—108 percent of the mean.

24. When the transition to work is complicated by other factors—for example, the young age of the mother—the appropriate public policy response would seem to be to focus on those other factors (preventing teenage pregnancy by providing access to free contraceptives and abortion).

25. INSEE. Employment Survey 1989, women under age 55.

26. Lone mothers, especially never-married ones, are more likely than married or cohabiting mothers to live in someone else's household or in a collective household—and, in these situations, are less likely to work than other lone mothers. Since both these kinds of households are not taken into account by the INSEE Employment Surveys, it is likely that the actual labor force participation rate of never-married lone mothers is a little lower than that indicated by the Employment Surveys, but nevertheless higher than that of coupled mothers.

27. Regardless of marital status.

28. The reference year here is 1984, and the average initial income (from work and property) of all households equals 100.

29. The disposable family income equals the initial income of the household (from work and/or property), plus benefits, less taxes. In this paragraph, the disposable family incomes are size-adjusted, that is to say, the family incomes are divided between the number of persons in the household, each person being weighed according to his or her age or rank in the household.

30. Geneviève Canceill (1989). *Les revenus fiscaux des ménages en 1984.* Paris: INSEE.

31. This study, entitled, "Le veuvage avant soixante ans: ses conséquences financières," was conducted in 1981 by CERC.

32. See note 15.

33. However, they may face other difficulties from *within* ethnic group stigmatization. Women of Arab origin are likely to be castigated by their families and ethnic group because of their status of never-married mother. Their parents or grandparents belonged to a culture in which illegitimacy was highly condemned and could even be used to justify the murder of the pregnant girl and/or her seducer. Thus, a never-married Arab young mother is likely to shelter in a maternity home during her pregnancy to hide herself and then to abandon her baby. By contrast, among West Indians and metropolitan French women, illegitimacy rates are high for an out-of-wedlock pregnancy, but the group may still stigmatize a member because the group experiences an illegitimate pregnancy as a handicap on the economic and social prospects of the young mother (and other as an added burden upon an already large family). Thus, self-perceptions of social marginality and isolation may not be directly related to the stigma attached to lone motherhood by the larger society, but to the smaller social networks to which the mother belongs and to their personal commitment to a coupled lifestyle.

34. See, for instance, Nadine Lefaucheur (1987) : *Les familles monoparentales: une catégorie "spécifique"?* Rapport de recherche pour le Plan Construction (Ministère de l'Equipement et du Logement), mimeo.

REFERENCES

Bastard, Benoît, and Laura Cardia-Vonèche. 1988. *Les Familles monoparentales face à leur situation économique.* Rapport de recherche pour la Caisse nationale d'allocations familiales. Paris: Centre de sociologie des organisations.

Centre d'étude des revenus et des coûts [CERC]. 1986, 1989. *Le veuvage avant soixante ans: Ses conséquences financières. 1. Les premiers mois du veuvage. 2. La deuxième année du veuvage.* La Documentation française, documents du CERC, nos. 81 and 95, respectively. Paris: CERC.

———. 1987. *Familles nombreuses, mères isolées, situation économique et vulnérabilité.* La Documentation française, documents du CERC, no. 85. Paris: CERC.

Hatzfeld, Henri. [1971] 1989. *Du Paupérisme à la Sécurité sociale, 1850–1940: Essai sur les origines de la Sécurité sociale en France.* Paris: Presses universitaires de Nancy.

Laroque, M. Pierre. 1985. "Ministère des affaires sociales et de la solidarité nationale. Commissariat général du Plan. 1985. *La politique familiale en France depuis 1945: groupe de travail sous la direction de M. Pierre Laroque.* Paris: La Documentation française (documents "affaires sociales").

Lefaucheur, Nadine. 1986. "How the One-Parent Families Appeared in France." In *One-Parent Families in Europe.* Deven, F., and R. L. Cliquet (eds.). Proceedings of the CBGS International Workshop on One-Parent Families, Brussels, October 8–10, 1985. Publications of NIDI and CBGS, vol. 15. The Hague and Brussels: NIDI and CBGS.

———. 1987. *Les Familles monoparentales: Une Catégorie spécifique?* Rapport de recherche pour le Plan construction. Paris: Centre national de la recherche scientifique/Institut de recherche sur les sociétés contemporaines, mimeo.

———. 1988a. *La Situation des familles monoparentales en France.* Rapport à la Communauté économique européenne. Paris: Centre national de la recherche scientifique/Institut de recherche sur les sociétés contemporaines, mimeo.

———. 1988b. "Les Conditions et niveaux de vie des enfants de parents séparés." In Institut de l'enfance et de la famille (ed.). *L'Enfant et ses parents séparés, suites au colloque de Paris, octobre 1985,* 135–68. Paris: Institut de l'enfance et de la famille.

———. 1988c. "Les Familles monoparentales en questions." *Dialogue* 101:28–44.

———. 1991. "Les Familles dites monoparentales." In *La famille: L'état des savoirs.* de Singly, François (ed.). Paris: Editions la Découverte, pp. 67–74.

Lefaucheur, Nadine, and Claude Martin. 1993. "Lone Parent Families in France: Situation and Research." *Single Parent Families: Perspectives on Research and Policy.* Hudson, Joe, and Burt Galaway (eds.). Toronto: Thompson Educational Publishing, pp. 31–50.

Léridon, Henri, and Catherine Villeneuve-Gokalp. 1988. "Entre père et mère." Population et sociétés, n° 220, janvier 1988.

Ray, Jean-Claude. 1983. *Allocation de parent isolé et désincitation au travail.* Rapport de recherche pour le Commissariat général du plan. Nancy: Université de Nancy II, LASARE, mimeo.

Ray, Jean Claude, and Laure Suzanne Carvoyeur. 1986. *API et réinsertion professionnelle,*

2 vols. Rapport de recherche pour la Caisse d'allocations familiales de Meurthe et-Moselle. Nancy: Université de Nancy II, ADEPS.

Ray, Jean-Claude, Laure Suzanne Carvoyeur, and B. Jeandidier. 1986. *Transferts sociaux et modes de cohabitation: Le cas des femmes ayant des enfants à charge.* Rapport de recherche pour le Commissariat général du Plan et la Mission Recherche Expérimentation auprès du Ministère des Affaires sociales. Nancy: Université de Nancy II, ADEPS and LASARE.

———. 1989. *Prestations familiales, activité féminine et isolement: Un parallèle Lorraine/Luxembourg.* Nancy: Université de Nancy II, ADEPS.

Chapter 8

SINGLE MOTHERS IN SWEDEN:
WHY IS POVERTY LESS SEVERE?

Siv Gustafsson

F AMILIES HEADED by single mothers in Sweden are much less likely to be
poor than lone-parent families in the United States, West Germany, the
United Kingdom, or Canada according to research relying on Luxembourg
Income Study data.[1] Less than 6 percent of lone-parent families in Sweden were
poor in 1987 compared to over 25 percent in West Germany (in 1984) and 53
percent in the United States (in 1986). Nonetheless, single-mother families are
still an economically vulnerable group compared to dual-earner families (Gustafsson 1990), even though the evidence shows that the economic hardships
associated with being a single mother are less severe in Sweden than in other
Western industrial nations. This chapter reviews the historical development of
public welfare policies operating in Sweden today and the mechanisms used to
ensure that Swedish lone-parent families with children have an adequate living
standard.

"The Swedish model" describes a welfare state system characterized by full
employment, active labor market policies, a large public sector, and a very
egalitarian income distribution. The model is not without its problems: In the
1980s, Sweden experienced slower economic growth and higher inflation than
other countries in the Organization for Economic Cooperation and Development
(OECD) (Bosworth and Rivlin 1987). However, the strong emphasis in the
Swedish system on work rather than income subsidies has proved to be a resilient method of providing support to the great majority of the nation's citizens,
including single mothers with children.

In Sweden, women as well as men are included in the goal of full employment. Moreover, equality between the sexes in the labor market was listed as
a Labor Market Board goal in 1977. The Swedish policy approach assumes that
every married mother is potentially a divorced single mother; thus, keeping the
labor force participation of married women high is key to assuring that divorced
mothers will be integrated into the labor force.

Although the Swedish model includes strong family policies, since 1937 the
government has provided child-support payments from public funds when fa-

thers fail to provide support. I argue here that the primary reason Swedish single mothers are less likely to experience poverty than single mothers in other countries is because they are more likely to work and to have fairly good jobs with important benefits. This is the result of deliberate government policies designed to include all women in the labor force, whether or not they are mothers, and whether or not they are married. Programs targeted exclusively at single mothers have been of minor importance.

THE PREVALENCE OF SINGLE MOTHERHOOD IN SWEDEN

Recent data pertaining to the situation of single parents in Sweden can be found in two official reports (SOU 1983:51 and SOU 1990:8) compiled as the government attempted to reform its administratively costly "child-support advance" system.[2] The first report was based on a special survey conducted by Holmström et al. (1981) comparing the circumstances of single parents to those of nuclear families and stepfamilies. (For a summary of results, see Gustafsson 1990.) Statistics Sweden Children (Statistics Sweden 1989), another important source of information on lone-parent families, compiles data on families with children from a number of different sources.

Unmarried Cohabitation

The proportion of women giving birth for the first time who were unmarried increased from 12.6 percent in 1963 to 48 percent in 1986, a fact that has amazed foreign observers of Swedish demographic trends (e.g., Popenoe 1988) (Table 8.1).[3] However, this figure reveals almost nothing about the incidence of single parenthood in Sweden, because most of these mothers are living with their child's father. The high rate of out-of-wedlock births simply reflects the fact that young Swedish couples often choose unmarried cohabitation instead of marriage. In 1986, the average age at first marriage was 27.7 years for Swedish women, whereas their average age at the birth of their first child was 26.6 years. Changes in Swedish tax laws over the last two decades made this choice essentially cost-free.

During the 1970s and 1980s, the economic incentives for couples to legally marry were removed. Today, earnings are taxed separately and nonworking spouses do not constitute a deduction from income taxes, so tax codes do not encourage marriage. As of 1990, one of the last remaining benefits that was dependent on legal marriage—the widow's pension—was also abolished. Sweden no longer has a widow's pension for women born in 1944 or after, but older women are still entitled to the pension if they were legally married in 1989 or earlier. Over twice as many marriages (108,765) were recorded in 1989 as the annual average recorded between 1970 and 1989 (40,000). Presumably, a large number of cohabiting women married in 1989 to become eligible for the widow's pension (Hoem 1990).

Table 8.1 / Demographic Change in Sweden: 1963–1989

Year	Births per Females of Childbearing Age	Percentage of Mothers Not Married	Divorces per 1,000 of Population	Marriages per 1,000 of Population
1963	2.33	12.6		
1964	2.47	13.1		
1965	2.47	13.8		
1966	2.37	14.6		
1967	2.28	15.1		
1968	2.09	15.8	5.9	6.6
1969	1.94	16.3	6.3	6.1
1970	1.94	18.4	6.7	5.4
1971	1.98	21.6	7.1	4.9
1972	1.93	25.0	8.0	4.8
1973	1.88	28.4	8.5	4.7
1974	1.89	31.4	14.5	5.5
1975	1.78	32.4	14.3	5.4
1976	1.69	33.2	11.7	5.5
1977	1.65	34.7	11.2	4.9
1978	1.59	35.9	11.2	4.6
1979	1.66	37.5	11.3	4.5
1980	1.68	39.7	11.3	4.5
1981	1.63	41.2	11.5	4.5
1982	1.62	42.0	12.0	4.5
1983	1.65	43.6	12.0	4.4
1984	1.65	44.6	11.9	4.4
1985	1.73	46.4	11.7	4.6
1986	1.79	48.4	11.4	4.6
1987	1.84			4.9
1988	1.96			5.2
1989	2.00			

SOURCES: SOS Befolkningsförändringar del 3. Hela riket länen mm (Population changes). Statistics Sweden, individual years.

The concept of illegitimacy has also been removed from Swedish legislation. Children inherit from their parents equally, whether born within marriage or not, and parents as a general rule establish joint custody of their children in the case of separation because the default case in Swedish law is joint custody.

These legal changes reflect the fact that Swedish society accepted the legitimacy of unmarried cohabitation much earlier than most other countries. Demographic research (based on a retrospective survey) shows that 34 percent of women born between 1936 and 1940 lived with a partner before marriage, and that 83 percent of the cohort of women born between 1951 and 1955 lived with a partner before marriage (Hoem and Rennermalm 1985).

A number of historical factors may account for Swedes' more liberal attitudes toward unmarried cohabitation. Among working-class people in Stockholm, unmarried cohabitation was common by the end of the nineteenth century, a fact related to the failure of the law to protect the legal rights of married women to their own earnings. Until 1920, a husband had ownership rights over his wife's earnings. The possibility that a husband might take her earnings and spend them on alcohol, for example, made working women prefer unmarried cohabitation to marriage. These living arrangements were referred to as "Stockholm marriages" (Matović 1984). Married women were not granted the legal right to enter into work contracts and to control their own earnings until the marriage act of 1920.[4]

Premarital sex was also common in rural communities in nineteenth century Sweden. Carlsson (1977) estimates that a third of farmers' daughters who married in the eighteenth and nineteenth centuries were pregnant at the time of the marriage. Agricultural production was very sex-segregated, and farm operations required the work of women, so very few farmers' daughters remained unmarried throughout adulthood.

Thus, the risk of pregnancy was acceptable to Swedish women and unmarried parenthood was not as socially stigmatizing as in many other countries. Of course, an out-of-wedlock pregnancy could still produce a personal catastrophe—when the man refused to acknowledge paternity, when there was no marriage promise, and/or when the woman was dismissed from her job because of pregnancy. However, Sweden has a rather long history of experience with and acceptance of unmarried cohabitation.

Children in Single-Mother Households

In 1985, about 12 percent of Swedish children under 18 years old lived with a single mother. Table 8.2 shows the extent to which Swedish children live with both parents, from 3 months old until their 18th birthday, the day of achieving legal adulthood. Almost 90 percent of preschoolers live with both parents, but a quarter of these couples are not legally married. However, the proportion of couples who remain unmarried declines as their children mature. At the same time, the percentage of all children who live with a single parent increases with a child's age. It seems, then, that unmarried couples with small children make the decision to separate or marry as their children grow older. If a couple stays together, the chances that they will eventually marry are high.

The total number of Swedish children who live with a lone mother increased from 10.1 to 12.2 percent between 1975 and 1985—not a very dramatic increase. In fact, the Swedish figures are similar to those in France, where the percentage of children in lone-mother households increased from 9.3 percent in 1975 to 12.4 percent in 1988 (Lefaucheur 1989). By contrast, 11 percent of children in the United States lived with a lone mother in 1970; by 1988, the figure had increased to 21 percent.

Regional and class differences in the proportion of children living with a single mother are also evident in Sweden. Census data show that the rate of lone parenthood is highest in Stockholm, followed by Göteborg and Malmö.

Table 8.2 / Changes in the Living Arrangements of Children: 1975 and 1985

Living Arrangements	Age of the Child			Total for Children 0–17 Years	Total Number of Children 3 Months–17 Years
	3 Months–6 Years	7–12 Years	13–17 Years		
Children with Parents Living Together					
1975	90.8	88.2	86.1	88.6	1,771,733
1985	89.0	85.3	82.8	85.9	1,545,313
Of Which the Following Were Not Married					
1975	13.4	4.8	3.0	7.6	151,672
1985	23.2	15.5	7.2	14.4	259,323
Children with Parents Not Living Together Single Father					
1975	0.7	1.4	2.2	1.3	26,632
1985	0.8	2.1	3.1	1.9	34,984
Single Mother					
1975	8.5	10.4	11.7	10.1	200,956
1985	10.2	12.6	14.1	12.2	218,910
Number of Children					
1975	751,168	716,932	531,221	—	1,999,321
1985	645,190	609,121	544,898	—	1,799,209
Children Who Have Set Up Their Own Households					
1975	—	—	6,082	—	6,082
1985	—	—	2,907	—	2,907

SOURCES: Statistics Sweden (1989). Primary source: Censuses 1975 and 1985.

When these three largest cities are excluded from national totals, the proportion of single parents in the general population is much lower. Lower-class children are more likely to be found in lone-parent households than are middle-class children. In 1984/85, about 83 percent of the children of white-collar workers lived with both biological parents, whereas only 75 percent of the children of blue-collar workers did (Statistics Sweden 1989).

A new living arrangement for children of separated parents has also emerged. Since 1982, the legal "default option" for divorcing or separating parents is to share joint legal responsibility for their children. Under this arrangement, a child may spend every second week with the alternate parent. However, only about 5 percent of children with separated parents divide their residence equally between the two. Most spend almost all their time with one parent, and a third of the children living in stepfamilies have no contact whatsoever with the absent parent (Statistics Sweden 1989, Table 2.11).

SWEDISH WOMEN IN THE LABOR MARKET

Swedish mothers, single and married, typically have a paid job. During working hours, their children are cared for in government-subsidized childcare. They also enjoy a 15-month paid parental leave following the birth of a child, which can be shared by the child's father. Although women's wages are still lower than those of men (see Table 8.4; also Löfström and Gustafsson 1991), the discrepancy is not large by international standards. Modern Swedish equal opportunity policies are described in detail in other work (Gustafsson 1984; Gustafsson and Jacobsson 1985; Petterson 1990; Sundström 1991).

The History of Legal Protection for Female Workers

The legal protections afforded to women in Sweden have a lengthy history. In 1939, Sweden passed a law that made it unlawful to lay off a female employee because of pregnancy, birth, or marriage (Hatje 1974, p. 43). This was the most progressive national legislation of its time, protecting a woman's right to work. By contrast, the Dutch government introduced an act in 1934 mandating that a female civil servant lose her job on the day of her marriage (Pott-Buter, Van Kessel, and Kuperus 1986, p. 30). In the United States, a federal law prohibited two people from the same household from being employed by the civil service during the Depression (Hobson 1990, p. 5). Repressive attitudes toward married women working also appeared in France during the 1930s (McIntosh 1983).

In fact, there was hostility toward married women working in Sweden during this period, too. As in other European countries, objections to the employment of married women were tied to arguments about the priority rights of "breadwinners" to employment, coupled with strong pro-natalist sentiments. Legislation demanding restrictions on a married woman's right to work was proposed to the Swedish Riksdag in 1935 (e.g., SOU 1935:6), but Alva Myrdal and other feminists in Sweden were able to turn the political debate about a married woman's right to work into a debate about a working woman's right to marry and have a family.

In a 1934 book entitled *Crisis in the Population Question*, Alva and Gunnar Myrdal contended that Sweden could stop its worrisome population decline by giving financial support to families with children. The Swedish working class had been very influenced by neo-Malthusian theories arguing that they could improve their standard of living only by limiting the size of their families (Hatje 1974), so they were very suspicious of pro-natalist arguments like those in the Myrdal book.

Nevertheless, Social Democrats and intellectuals saw the Myrdals' work as a breakthrough in arguments for social policy. At the 1936 Social Democrat Party Congress, the Minister of Social Affairs, Gustav Möller, stated:

> I will not hesitate to frighten... Conservatives, Farmer's Unionists and members of the Liberal Party with the threat that our people will otherwise die out, if with this threat I can get them to vote for social proposals I put forward. This is my simple view of the population issue and it is good enough for me. [quoted in Hatje 1974, p. 31 and Popenoe 1988, p. 112].

Pro-natalist policies were framed as social welfare policies, and the latter were made acceptable to conservative politicians because of their intended pro-natalist effects.

A special government committee on women's right to work was formed with Alva Myrdal as secretary. Its members argued that if working women were dismissed as a result of their marriage, they could not afford to marry and have children. The illegitimacy rate would therefore increase, as would illegal abortions, and those couples who depend on two incomes to maintain a household (the norm among working-class families) would refrain from having children. Hobson (1990) has suggested that Swedish feminists were successful in winning a consensus on social policy issues supportive of women's work roles because: (a) they linked married women's right to work with the national concern with low birthrates; (b) they formed alliances with unions and conservative women's groups; and (c) they were able to use the centralized policymaking system in Sweden to achieve systemwide reform.[5]

The 1930s political debate in Sweden demonstrates that demographic arguments can be powerful tools for winning female workforce rights.[6] However, they can also be used against women, as McIntosh (1983) has argued was the case in France.[7]

Family Benefits

In the 1930s and 1940s, a fierce debate raged in Sweden over whether families with children should be assisted by tax deductions or by child allowances. The debate was waged between conservatives (*högern*) and agrarians (today the center party), who favored tax deductions, and Social Democrats, supported by the liberals (*folkpartiet*), who favored benefits.[8] The main proponent of tax deductions was Professor Sten Wahlund, who wanted to spread the cost of children evenly between childless persons and families with children within each income group. He pleaded for "horizontal equity" (Hatje 1974:95). However, working-class families often had incomes so low that they did not pay any taxes. Tax deductions would therefore not provide additional support for children in these families (Hatje 1974:91). Social Democrats wanted to reduce income inequality *between* social classes as well as provide support for children and argued for vertical income redistribution.

With the Social Democrats the victors in these debates, "the enthusiastic welfare state" began to be built (Rainwater et al. 1986). General child benefits, mailed directly to all mothers, were introduced in 1948. Sending child benefits to mothers, rather than to fathers, was totally new, as all money matters had previously been considered to be in the male domain. The decision was motivated by a desire to indicate that the child benefit was a kind of "wage" for the work of mothering. This type of support for children is still in effect in Sweden.[9]

The income tax system, on the other hand, has been reformed into a completely separate tax system. The current income tax scheme, first introduced in 1971, takes no account of the number of dependents in determining tax liability. The child benefit is a lump-sum benefit of 750 crowns per month per child (as of July 1992) until the child is 16 years old. It is mailed to every mother irrespective of family income. There is no child deduction in the tax system.

Taxation of Wives' Earnings

Joint taxation for married wage earners was introduced in 1902, but a parliamentary action against it was issued by the Swedish Riksdag in 1904, when it was argued that joint taxation was disruptive to marriage and encouraged "sinful liaisons." When, in the fall of 1947, a new "tax-at-the-source-of-earnings" was introduced, there was a strong public outcry against the high marginal taxes this placed on married women's earnings. Taxes at source were deducted as if each wage earner was single. Then, after filing tax returns, the authorities recalculated the tax on the income of married women based on the earnings of their husbands. New taxes were then collected on the family's combined income, making the marginal tax on married women's earnings very visible. (See Elvander 1974 for a history of the shift from joint to separate taxation.)

In response to the outcry, a committee was formed to consider the introduction of separate taxation. It decided to keep joint taxation, but introduced a deduction for working married women (called *förvärvsavdraget*) to acknowledge that working women could do less work around the house than housewives.

By the mid-1960s, an increasing number of female university graduates in Sweden complained about the prospect of "lifetime imprisonment within the four walls of a home" because women could not "afford a career" owing to a tax system that took most of the income they added to the family. However, the governing Social Democrat party showed little interest in separate taxation, arguing that it was a "luxury" problem for the upper classes that had no impact on the majority of women.

Feminist writers like Eva Moberg responded by charging that women were only conditionally liberated—they were allowed to work, but raising children and care of the home were supposed to be their first duty. "The Conditional Release of the Woman," an extremely influential article in feminist circles, argued that men's roles as well as women's had to change. In contrast to Myrdal and Klein's (1956) argument that women had to have two roles, as mothers and wage earners, Moberg charged that both men and women should have one role—as human beings. Moberg's philosophical position was bolstered by the work of Sonja Lyttkens, who showed that when a husband is allowed to deduct two basic allowances from his income (because of a non-wage-earning wife), he receives a tax rebate, which is taken away from him if his wife starts to earn and uses her basic allowance. This creates a large disincentive for married women to work—even among low-income couples (Gustafsson and Bruyn-Hundt 1991).

Ultimately, the feminists convinced the reigning political parties and the powerful labor organizations of the justness of separate taxation. The campaign was aided by a 1965 economic survey that warned of a growing labor shortage and argued that married women, particularly mothers of young children, were the only remaining reserve of labor to tap. This argument finally convinced Gunnar Sträng, then Swedish minister of finance, to support separate taxation.

Today, Sweden taxes the earnings of wives and husbands separately. Moreover, the progressivity in the tax system until 1991 created a strong incentive for married women to work, because more family income is left after taxes if a secondary earner works part-time than if the main earner works overtime.[10] A fundamental tax reform, taking effect in January 1991, has turned the Swedish tax system into a practically proportional one.

A recent OECD study (1990b) examined the after-tax income of a family in which a wife starts from zero and increases her earnings from 0 to 33 percent of an average industrial worker's income versus the after-tax income of the same family if the husband increases his income an equal amount. Sweden's tax system gives the first family (husband full-time/wife part-time) the greatest income advantage over the second family (husband only earner) among all the 18 OECD countries in the study. In the Netherlands, France, Germany, and Ireland, after-tax family income increases *more* if the main earner works overtime than if the secondary earner works part-time. In the United States, tax policy is close to neutral in this respect.

Recent Macroeconomic Developments in Sweden

In the mid-1980s, foreign observers expressed alarm about rising unemployment especially among young people in Sweden (Bosworth and Rivlin 1987; Standing 1988). These concerns were shared by Swedish economists (see, for example, the Swedish government report on the *Medium Term Economic Survey* of 1987). Although, as Figure 8.1 shows, unemployment rates dropped dramatically in the latter half of the 1980s, over the decade of the 1980s, the average number of hours in the work week increased, reversing three decades of declining work hours (due to shortened work hours and increased vacation and parental leave, etc.). The total number of hours worked by Swedes between 1980 and 1989 increased by an average of over 11 percent, according to the 1990 government report on the *Medium Term Economic Survey* (SOU 1990:14) (Table 8.3).

In 1990, after several years of low GDP and high inflation, Sweden experi-

Figure 8.1 / Unemployment for Men and Women (from Björklundm, Anders 1992)

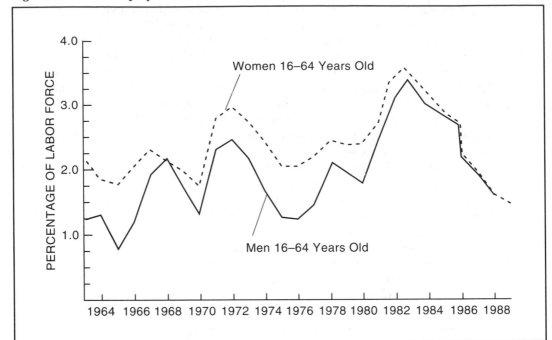

SOURCE: Labor Force Surveys, Statistics Sweden.

enced a bank strike and a government crisis.[11] As a result, political debate and commentary concerning Sweden's economy have been awash in images of catastrophe.

Although Sweden has historically dealt with unemployment by emphasizing active labor market policies, according to a recent paper by Calmfors and Forslund (1990), the emphasis will now shift from job creation to job training. Indeed, the traditional Swedish consensus on active labor market policies may be undergoing a profound transformation. The private sector employer organization (known by its Swedish acronym SAF) has withdrawn from the three-partner corporate structure (of government, labor unions, and employers) that

Table 8.3 / Changes in Employment in Sweden (per decade)

	1950s Decade	1960s Decade	1970s Decade	1980s Decade
Percent Increase in the Number of Employed Persons	5.7	8.2	8.2	7.1
Percent Increase in the Number of Hours Worked Each Week	−1.3	−2.6	−5.1	11.1

SOURCES: SOU 1990:14; Primary sources: Statistics Sweden and the Ministry of Finance.

has been the mainstay of the Swedish model. As of March 1991, SAF no longer participates on the national Labor Market Board or on the 24 regional labor market boards, the institutions that have handled active labor market policies. SAF employers have announced that they no longer support "corporatism" and want to act as an independent pressure group. However, wage negotiations between employers and unions, which have never included the central government, will still be a two party arrangement and include SAF.

The tax structure is also being reformed. A 1991 change in the tax laws lowers marginal taxes on earned income to 30 percent for about 90 percent of Swedish wage earners; the top marginal tax rate will now be 55 percent. This is in marked contrast to recent years when full-time, blue-collar workers often faced tax brackets of 70 percent, and the top marginal tax rate was 84 percent. At the same time, sales taxes have been extended to previously exempt sectors of the economy (like restaurants and hotels), to "totally finance" the tax reform.[12]

Nevertheless, despite what one observer called "the new paradigm [in which] everything changes," Swedish politicians and social scientists continue to proclaim the achievements of Swedish social policies. The Swedish model will continue to exist, but in a revised form. The following subsection reviews the way these recent macroeconomic developments can be expected to affect the labor market position of Swedish women.

Current Problems and Prospects for Women's Work

The condition of Swedish working women today can be characterized as follows: (a) they are clustered into a small number of occupations; (b) they are highly concentrated in public-sector employment; (c) a large proportion are in part-time work (i.e., they work between 20 and 34 hours a week); (d) they receive lower wages than men; and (e) they have a high rate of absenteeism. In comparison to other countries, the male to female wage differential in Sweden is small, but has been fairly constant (although it has tended to increase since 1982).

Figure 8.2 illustrates recent changes in the wage distribution of gender-segregated jobs in Sweden.[13] The horizontal axis of the figure ranks existing occupations according to their perceived status. The vertical axis represents wages. One would expect higher status jobs to generally be accompanied by higher wages. Thus, there should be a positive association between high status and high wages. The *slope* of the line will depend on how much wage inequality exists between occupations. The greater the wage inequality between occupations, the steeper the slope. So, line A in Figure 8.2 represents an occupational-wage distribution with a higher degree of inequality than line B.

Women in Sweden are concentrated in relatively few occupations which tend to be low wage, low status. The point in the occupational-wage distribution where the average woman falls is marked toward the left-hand corner of each line on Figure 8.2. Men, on average, are in higher-wage, higher-status jobs (the average is marked at the top right of the figure). The female–male wage ratio

Figure 8.2 / Wage Distribution, Occupational Segregation, and the Female–Male Wage Differential

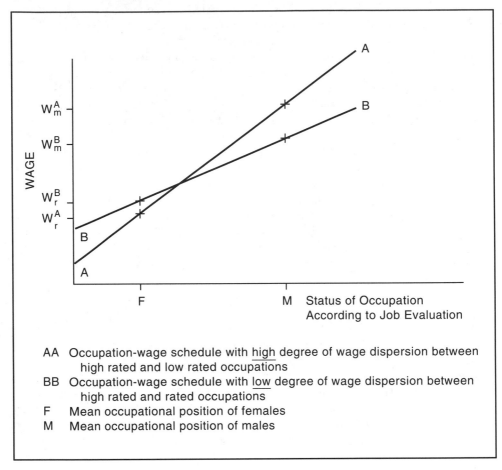

AA Occupation-wage schedule with <u>high</u> degree of wage dispersion between high rated and low rated occupations
BB Occupation-wage schedule with <u>low</u> degree of wage dispersion between high rated and rated occupations
F   Mean occupational position of females
M   Mean occupational position of males

under Regime A is W_{af}/W_{am}. With equal levels of occupational gender segregation in each regime, there will be a substantially larger wage differential between men and women under Regime A than under Regime B. A more equal wage distribution in general helps to reduce male–female wage differences when occupational segregation is high.

The wage differential between men and women in Sweden decreased continuously from 1963 to 1982, but since then has tended to grow. The decrease in wage differentials during the 1960s and 1970s resulted primarily from a more equal distribution of wages across occupations, not from an improvement in the position of women on the occupational status continuum.[14] A job segregation index computed on the basis of the 320 different occupations in the Swedish censuses of 1960, 1970, and 1980 showed that occupational segregation decreased relatively little—from 74.5 to 70.6 to 67.9 respectively, over this 20-year

Table 8.4 / Female Labor Force Participation Rates
and Female—Male Wage Ratios: 1963–1988

Year	Labor Force Participation of Women 16–64 (a)	Female—Male Wage Ratio Blue Collar (b)	Female—Male Wage Ratio White Collar (b)
1963	54.5	72.2	51.7
1964	54.0	73.6	52.4
1965	53.8	74.9	53.2
1966	55.1	76.5	53.9
1967	54.9	77.6	54.3
1968	56.4	78.2	55.8
1969	57.6	79.1	57.1
1970	59.3	80.0	58.6
1971	60.9	82.0	60.7
1972	62.0	83.5	61.5
1973	62.7	83.9	63.2
1974	65.2	83.8	64.5
1975	67.9	84.8	67.2
1976	69.1	86.6	69.1
1977	70.6	87.1	70.0
1978	72.1	88.4	70.8
1979	73.8	89.1	71.1
1980	75.1	89.8	71.4
1981	76.3	89.9	72.1
1982	76.9	90.2	72.7
1983	77.6	90.0	73.5
1984	78.2	89.8	72.2
1985	79.2	89.7	72.4
1986	80.0	90.2	73.6
1987	81.1	89.9	74.0
1988	81.8	89.8	74.1

SOURCES: (a) AKU Årsmedeltal (Labor Force Surveys), yearly, Statistics Sweden.
(b) SOS löner del 1, del 2, Statistics Sweden.

period (Jonung and Persson 1990).[15] However, the female–male wage ratio improved substantially, increasing from 72.2 to 90.2 for blue-collar workers and from 51.7 to 72.7 for white-collar workers between 1963 and 1982 (Table 8.4). Moreover, the public sector in Sweden—where the majority of women are employed—is characterized by more occupational-wage equality than the private sector (Gustafsson 1976).

Swedish women are highly concentrated in public-sector employment. Close to 60 percent of all female workers are employed by the government. Health care, education, and childcare are the occupational fields in which women are most concentrated, and in Sweden these services are administered almost completely through the public sector. However, as part of the political reorganization that is occurring, the public sector is likely to decrease its share of total employment. This may depress the demand for women's labor and increase female unemployment.

The decrease in male–female wage differences in Sweden from the early 1960s to the early 1980s was largely the result of solidaristic wage policies that supported the use of tax and transfer policies to create a relatively narrow distribution of income, the effect of which was to raise all low wages. Now, however, these wage policies have lost popularity, and international factors are affecting occupational wage structures. Thus, the market has become more influential in determining the wage structure, and the occupational-wage distribution is becoming more unequal; one would thus expect male–female wage differences to increase again.

Other factors may partially counterbalance these trends. For example, occupational segregation by gender may decrease as women improve their educational levels. Analyses of Swedish data show that as the education, work experience, and labor force attachment of Swedish women approach levels similar to men, wage differentials decrease, but a smaller part of the remaining wage differences are accounted for by differences in human capital accumulation (Löfström and Gustafsson 1990).

Swedish women today earn less than men because they are more likely to work part-time. In 1986, almost 43 percent of Swedish women worked less than 35 hours per week. Most of these women worked what the Swedish call "long part-time"—that is, from 20 to 34 hours per week. In fact, the average work week for female workers is 30 hours per week. Moreover, mothers working full-time can use parental leave to decrease their hours to 30 paid hours a week until their youngest child is 8 years old; they then have the right to return to full-time hours in the same job. A high proportion of Swedish women use this option. Nonetheless, the number of women working full-time has grown since 1982 (when the number of women working part-time peaked at 46.2 percent of all employed women). More women working part-time switch to full-time work today than the reverse (Sundström 1987). Single mothers are still more likely to work long hours than are married mothers. Only 1.9 percent worked less than 20 hours per week, and 47.9 percent worked full-time (Table 8.5).

Nonetheless, absenteeism remains an issue in debates about the "Swedish model." When workers make use of paid parental leave, they are counted as employed but absent from work. The labor force participation rate for women with children under 6 years of age was 85.8 percent in 1988, but only 55.2 percent were actually "at work" on an average day; the rest were making use of the parental leave program.[16] This program (along with a liberal sick leave policy) contributes to a high absenteeism rate in Sweden. In March 1991, the government lowered the compensation received during sick leave from 90 percent of pay to 70 percent for the first 3 days of absenteeism, and the absenteeism rate immediately declined.[17]

Table 8.5 / **Employment Status of Single Parents in Sweden, by Child's Age: 1986–1987**

Employment	0–6	7–12	13–15	16–17	All	Number of Children 0–17 Years of Age — One Child	Number of Children 0–17 Years of Age — Two Children
Employed, Number of Hours Worked Each Week							
35 or more	28.4	44.5	67.7	63.7	47.9	56.1	44.7
20–34	42.8	36.1	18.4	22.6	32.2	25.1	33.5
1–19	0.7	2.2	—	4.7	1.9	2.0	2.6
Farmer or Other Self-Employed	1.0	1.1	—	—	2.6	4.7	0.9
Not in Labor Force	27.1	16.2	6.8	4.5	15.4	12.2	18.3
TOTAL	100.0	100.0	100.0	100.0	100.0	100.0	100.0
Number of Children (in thousands)	71	78	42	49	240	117	123

SOURCES: Statistics Sweden 1989; Primary source: *Survey of Living Conditions* 1986–1987.

THE ECONOMIC SITUATION OF LONE MOTHERS IN SWEDEN

This section examines the economic situation of single mothers in Sweden more closely—their earnings, sources of income, and the child-support advance system (the one program in Sweden specifically targeted at lone mothers).

Employment, Earnings, and Income Packaging of Lone Mothers in Sweden

The term "income packaging" was introduced by Rainwater et al. (1986) to describe the mix of sources from which families derive their disposable income. Practically all Swedish lone mothers have earnings. In 1986–87, over 84 percent of all lone mothers were in the labor force. About 27.1 percent of those who had children under school age were not in the labor force, but a large share of the mothers who were not in the labor force were students. Close to half of all single mothers (47.9 percent) were full-time workers, and another third (32.2) worked between 20 and 34 hours per week. Less than 2 percent of solo mothers worked less than 20 hours per week. Only 2 percent of lone mothers consider themselves full-time homemakers, compared to 18 percent of women in nuclear families and 11 percent of women in stepfamilies, according to a survey by Holmström et al. (1981) (Table 8.6).

Table 8.6 / Labor Force Status of Mother, by Family Type in Sweden: 1980 (in percentages)

	Lone Parent	Nuclear Family	Step-family	All Mothers
Labor Force Participant	87	76	79	78
Unemployed	2	1	1	1
Full-time homemaker	2	18	11	16
Student	7	3	6	4
Other	3	2	4	2
TOTAL	100	100	100	100
Hours of Work per Week	34.6	26.9	33.2	29.1
Commuting Time (hours per week)	5.0	3.6	4.3	3.7

SOURCE: Holmström et al. 1981.

Over 98 percent of solo mothers received some government support in Sweden in 1970, compared to 89.3 percent of solo mothers in the United Kingdom and 56.8 percent in the United States. Government assistance in Sweden and the U.K. included child allowances, which are not means-tested in Sweden; they are sent to all mothers with children aged 16 and under. Over half (50.7 percent) of Swedish lone mothers also received means-tested subsidies in 1970, compared to 46.7 percent of British lone mothers and just 37.7 percent of U.S. lone mothers (Rainwater et al. 1986:109). But a much larger proportion of Swedish single mothers (44.5 percent) combine work and welfare than is the case in the United Kingdom (22.5 percent) or the United States (20.7 percent). Only a tiny percentage of lone mothers in Sweden (6.2 percent) rely entirely on public assistance for support, while 2.4 percent of single mothers in the United Kingdom and 17 percent of those in the United States depend entirely on public support. Recently published labor force participation rates of single mothers suggest these percentages have probably not changed much since the 1970s.

The major means-tested subsidy in Sweden is the housing subsidy. In 1979, 80 percent of lone parents in Sweden received housing subsidies, compared to only 26 percent of nuclear-parent households and 31 percent of stepparent families. The housing subsidy is an important contribution to the income package of lone parents. It covers 40 percent of their rent costs, compared to only 11 percent of the rent of nuclear families and 17 percent of the rent of stepfamilies' (Table 8.7). Rainwater et al. (1986) noted that:

> needs-tested transfers are more often received in Sweden than in the two other countries [United States and United Kingdom], but when received they represent a very small amount of money. Thus in Sweden recipients

have a median dependency on welfare of only 4 percent and fewer than 10 percent of them receive as much as a fifth of their income from this source. In contrast, the recipients in the two other countries derive on average more than half of their income from means-tested sources.

Earnings are thus the major component of a lone-mother income package in Sweden; lone mothers receive 60 percent of their aggregate income from earnings, compared to only about 40 percent among American and British lone mothers (Rainwater et al. 1986, p. 108).

Nevertheless, a lone mother runs a higher risk of experiencing economic hardship than a coupled mother in Sweden. Table 8.8 compares three degrees of economic vulnerability according to family structure and size. Over 25 percent of lone parents with one child were reported to be at economic risk, compared to only 6.3 percent of couple-headed, one-child families. The risk of hardship increases somewhat with the number of children, regardless of family type. In the late 1980s, the economic situation of solo parents is still somewhat worse compared to that of two-parent families.[18]

Table 8.7 / Housing Subsidies in Sweden, by Family Type: 1979

	Lone Parent	Nuclear	Step
Proportion Receiving Housing Subsidy	80	26	31
Percentage of Rent Covered by Subsidy	40	11	17

SOURCE: SOU 1983:51.

Table 8.8 / Households Distributed by Disposable Income and Number of Children in Sweden: 1979

	Below Subsistence	At Risk	Hard Pressed	Not at Economic Risk	Number of Households (in thousands)
Number of Children					
One child					
Lone-parent	3.8	3.0	14.6	78.6	106
Two-parent	2.0	1.5	2.9	93.7	357
Two children					
Lone-parent	8.4	2.9	13.2	75.5	38
Two-parent	2.6	7.0	6.2	84.2	394
Three children					
Lone-parent	—	—	—	—	—
Two-parent	11.5	12.6	12.4	63.5	100

SOURCE: SOU 1983:51.

The Child-Support Advance System

Child-support advance legislation was introduced in Sweden in 1937. According to this law, if a father fails to pay the court-ordered or agreed-upon amount of child support, the mother will receive the amount as an advance from the state. Passage of this law was linked to the debates about abortion during the 1930s. The committee studying abortion legislation in 1935 recommended that women be granted legal abortions for medical, eugenic, and social reasons. Eugenic reasons included rape and genetic causes—for example, if the mother was mentally retarded. Two "social" reasons for abortion were put forward: first, if the woman already had many children, abortion would be allowed as birth control. Second, women who became pregnant as a result of infidelity in marriage or sex outside of marriage, would be allowed to obtain an abortion so as not to suffer "disgrace."

At this time, between 10,000 to 20,000 illegal abortions were carried out every year. The Myrdals, taking a pro-natalist stand, argued that society had to change its view of single mothers. "Grace" rather than disgrace, they said, should be given to those women who took on the hardships of raising a child alone. Furthermore, motherhood should always be seen as a social good, and the state should support single mothers in the absence of fathers. The Myrdal view dominated and resulted in the child-support advance law. It also led to 1938 abortion legislation, which did *not* allow abortions for "social reasons" except for women with many children.[19]

The first child-support advance law was means-tested but was changed in 1947 so that all single mothers received child-support advances irrespective of their financial situation. At this time, children whose fathers were unknown were also allowed to receive the state child-support advance—after they were 3 years old.[20] The child-support advance became gender-neutral in 1956, so that when a father is the custodial parent and the mother pays support, the same rules apply. An additional act in 1957 stipulated that when a child's "support payer" (in most cases a father) could pay only an unacceptably low level of support, the government would provide income up to a certain minimum level of support.

In 1964, an act was passed (and is still in effect) that dramatically changed the child-support advance program. Instead of individual awards being agreed upon or decided in court, a certain amount of support per child was set—initially 25 percent of the "base individual amount" of support on which most of the Swedish Social Security system is based. This was seen as a way to give all children a basic means of subsistence. The amount of child-support advance has been increased over time and is now about 40 percent of the "base amount." The state takes responsibility for getting the money from the father. To reclaim the money, the state can have the child support deducted from the support payer's paycheck.

Since 1979, custody laws have changed so that divorced parents have joint custody of their children as the default option. As a consequence, "support payers" can make deductions against support awards according to the time children spend with them, and can claim part of state subsidies given through the child-support advance system (administered by the National Health Security System). This has made the task of deciding the amount the "support payer" must pay much more complicated. Child support is to be determined according to the needs of the child and the joint economic capacity of the parents. The needs of the child are computed from a schedule; other support the child receives is subtracted from this "need" amount. Determining the economic capacity of each parent is very complicated (Socialstyrelsen 1982). For example, is the "support payer" (e.g., father) entitled to lower his support to his first child because of his second marriage and/or responsibilities for new children? Can he be allowed to support his new wife if she is a housewife before paying for his child in his previous relation? Does the father have a right to lower his payments if he changes careers and lowers his income?

As Table 8.9 shows, over half of all lone parents in 1980 made use of the child-support advance program. However, the Swedish state has been able to recover a diminishing percentage of child-support over time, as shown by Table 8.10. Part of the explanation for the decrease is structural: the amount that fathers have to pay back has been lowered.

Because the child advance system is very complicated and costly, two different governmental committees have been appointed to study the system and recommend reforms. In 1983, the first of these committees suggested that each parent should pay exactly half of the needs of each child. This suggestion was criticized as unfair to women, since they earn much less than men; and the recommendation of the committee did not become law. In 1990, a new government report (SOU 1990:8) proposed three alternative "models" for simplifying child support. A new report from the Ministry of Social Affairs (Socialdepartementet 1992) proposes that government support to single mothers be altered in a way that will contain elements of means-testing.

In the present system, all single mothers are assured a certain benefit amount each month for their child irrespective of whether the father pays any support or not—the government "fills in," after the father pays, up to 1,123 Swedish crowns. Under the new system proposed, the maximum government support

Table 8.9 / Families Receiving Child Support Advance Payment in Sweden, by Number of Children and Family Type: 1980

Number of Children	Lone-Parent		Stepfamilies		Total
	Number	Percent	Number	Percent	
1	62,339	(53)	16,333	(43)	78,672
2	33,707	(58)	31,725	(67)	65,432
3	8,013	(68)	12,550	(46)	20,563

SOURCE: SOU 1988:51. Primary source: HINK, Statistics Sweden 1980.

Table 8.10 / Child Support Paid by Noncustodial
Parent as a Percentage of Child Support
Advance Paid by Government

Year	Ratio
1974	100
1975	98
1976	95
1977	87
1978	70
1979	53
1980	46
1981	46

SOURCES: SOU 1983:51. Primary source: Derived from data from the National Board of Statistics, Series 5, 1975–1982, Statistics Sweden.

will be raised to 1,300 Swedish crowns, but the benefit will be means-tested. If the mother earns more than 9,000 Swedish crown per month, the government will fill only a proportion of the maximum amount, which will decrease and reach zero when the mother's gross monthly earnings equals 15,000 crowns for one child; 22,000 crowns for two children; and 25,400 crowns for three children. Also, the income of a new partner will be considered in determining the need for government support. Mothers who earn less than 9,000 will gain from the reform, but all mothers earning more than 13,000 crowns a month (the average earnings of a full-time female industrial worker) will lose.

It will be more important to secure support from the father when the government does not fill in. Under the new plan, the state will still forward money to the mother and collect money from the father, but only the amount that has been agreed upon in court. The reform has been effective from July 1993; its financial impact on the government budget is projected to be the same as the present system.

COMBINING WORK AND MOTHERHOOD

The ability of Swedish women to combine work and parenthood rests on two important programs: a nationwide system of public childcare and *paid* parental leave. Sweden's system of publicly subsidized childcare is run by the country's 285 units of local government. Single mothers receive preferential treatment in the allocation of limited childcare, and their children are also charged a lower fee than children of nuclear families in most communities. Arguments for the extension of the childcare system were largely based on the premise that a woman should combine work and family; it is sometimes also argued that it is good for children to be in daycare, especially if the child lives in a family with social problems ("children with special needs").

Under Sweden's parental leave program, one parent can stay home to care for a new baby for 12 months with full pay and with per diem pay for an additional 3 months. As mentioned earlier, the parental leave program increases the share of women who are employed but "absent from work" at any given time.

From Maternity Protection to Parental Leave

Beginning in 1900, maternity protection in Sweden prohibited employers from employing a woman earlier than 4 weeks after childbirth, but it did not guarantee women the right to return to their jobs. New legislation in 1939 prohibited women from being dismissed because of childbirth, and mandated that a woman be allowed a 12 weeks' leave of absence due to childbirth; thus, women in Sweden received 12 weeks of job security. Of course, the right to a period of leave is useful only if a parent can afford to take time off from work. The population committee of 1935 suggested a general subsidy to all new mothers and a means-tested supplemental subsidy for poor mothers (Hatje 1974:33), but there was strong political opposition to programs that broke with the "insurance concept" of social benefits; i.e., the idea that support should compensate for a loss of income in certain situations like retirement, sickness, unemployment, or maternity leave. The resulting compromise simply gave all mothers below a certain income level an additional cash benefit. Over time, the maternity period was gradually extended, and in 1974, fathers were given the right to share parental leave in Sweden. (See also Sundström 1991 for a description of parenting policies.)

Swedish parents today (1992) have the right to 15 months of paid parental leave: 12 months are paid at the same compensation rate as for sickness—in most cases 90 percent of current earnings; the last 3 months are compensated according to a per diem grant. Job security is guaranteed for 18 months. The parent can use child/parental leave until the child is 8 years old. This allows parents to "bank" parental leave in case the parents need time off when the child starts a new childcare group or begins primary school later on (see Sundström 1992.

Because women are compensated on the basis of their lost earnings during the 12 months leave period, maternity leave policies create an incentive for women to establish themselves as workers before having children. If they do not have any earnings previous to giving birth, they receive only a low guaranteed amount during their 12 months leave period. Paid parental leave policies also influence the timing of births. Since 1986, if a second child is born within 2½ years of the first, the mother is compensated on the basis of her earnings before the birth of her first child. This encourages mothers to space children by no more than 2½ years. Previously, a mother would have to return to work before the birth of her second child in order to get parental leave based on her earnings rather than the low guaranteed amount. In 1979, full-time employed parents in all sectors of the economy received the right to reduce their work hours to about 30 hours per week until their child is 8 years old; they then have the right to return to full-time work after giving 3 months' notice. Furthermore, working parents have the right to paid leave for occasional care of sick children or when their normal caregiver is sick.

Much of the political debate in the 1988 election centered on family policy. The Social Democrats proposed extending the paid parental leave period to 18 months. (An extension would also have made it easier to fulfill a pre-election promise of childcare for all who wanted it.) The opposition proposed introducing a *benefit* for the first 3 years, which the parents could use to buy childcare instead of receiving subsidized childcare if they work. The Social Democrats won the election, but they were unable to finance an extension of the paid parental leave to 18 months and settled for 15 months instead.

The 1991 election was won by a coalition opposing the Social Democrats. Family policies were not in the foreground of the political election campaigns: the economic situation and European integration were more prominent issues. However, the idea of taking resources from the daycare system to give as a child benefit to families with children under 3 is being put forward by the new government and is a threat to the system.

In 1988, about 48.2 percent of all Swedish children under 6 years old were cared for under the publicly subsidized daycare system (Table 8.11). Daycare in Sweden is available in two forms: a daycare center and a host mother or daycare mother. The latter are women who take children into their own homes and are paid by the local government, which then collects fees from parents. Fees from parents cover, on average, only 10 percent of total daycare costs (Gustafsson and Stafford 1992). The majority of working parents in Sweden have a child in the public childcare system: 64.6 percent of preschoolers who live with two parents who are both working or studying and 84.2 percent of children of single parents who work or study are in public childcare (Table 8.12). Privately paid-for childcare is used by only 4.5 percent of children with single mothers. Private childcare is not an attractive option for Swedish parents because it is very expensive and must be paid out of posttax income, because no tax deduction for childcare costs is allowed.

Ergas (1990) has classified childcare provision on a continuum of private and public responsibility. Great Britain and the United States come closest to "maximum private responsibility for children," and Sweden comes closest to maximum public responsibility. The expansion of the public daycare system in Sweden did not come until relatively late in the development of the welfare state—the 1970s and 1980s, when working mothers began to demand greater availability of childcare (Gustafsson and Stafford 1992). Before this, maternal leave and public subsidies allowed working women to take time off from work to care for small children themselves, but for a shorter interval than currently is the case.

Table 8.11 / Daycare of Preschoolers: Third Week of January 1988

	4–11 Months	One Year	Two Years	Three Years	Four Years	Five Years	Six Years	All
One Parent at Home on Childcare Leave Plus Only								
Part-Day Kindergarten	90.5	43.3	36.2	36.2	31.2	29.7	32.3	41.8
Of these, mother is a daycare mother	1.6	3.2	3.6	5.0	4.0	3.8	4.0	3.7
Public Childcare								
Daycare center	1.7	22.9	33.2	35.5	39.0	41.8	36.7	30.6
Daycare mother	2.2	18.1	20.2	19.6	20.3	19.2	21.3	17.6
TOTAL	3.9	41.0	53.4	55.1	59.3	61.0	58.0	48.2
Private Daycare								
Paid for	3.6	10.6	7.0	6.1	6.1	5.6	5.8	6.5
Not paid for* plus only part-day kindergarten	1.9	4.9	3.3	2.5	3.2	3.5	3.8	3.4
TOTAL	5.5	15.5	10.3	8.6	9.3	9.1	9.6	9.9
Of these only part-day kindergarten	—	—	—	—	1.7	8.3	30.2	—

SOURCES: Statistics Sweden 1989. Primary source: A special analysis of the 1988 Child Care Survey.

*Free of cost—relatives or friends provide care without asking for money.

Table 8.12 / Activity of Parents and Childcare Arrangements for Preschoolers: January 1988

Living Arrangements and Activities of Child's Parents	Parent Provides Childcare in Home	Parent Is a Childcare Provider	Public Childcare	Private Paid Care	Private Not-Paid Care	Not Reported Care*	Sum	Number of Children (in thousands)
Parents Living Together, Both Work or Study at least 20 Hours per Week with Children Aged:								
0	52.7	6.7	18.5	19.2	9.5	0	100	11
1	23.6	4.9	54.4	15.6	6.3	0.1	100	62
2–3	18.8	5.8	68.3	9.0	3.8	0	100	119
4–5	18.3	5.2	69.8	7.6	4.3	0.1	100	122
6	22.6	5.5	65.4	7.4	4.6	0	100	63
TOTAL	20.0	5.4	64.6	9.7	4.7	0	100	377
Parents Living Together, One Parent Is on Childcare Leave While the Other Works or Studies, with Children Aged:								
0	97.9	—	1.0	0.7	0.4	0.1	100	56
1	89.2	—	8.6	1.5	0.6	0.1	100	14
2–3	78.5	—	18.1	2.8	0.6	0	100	28
4–5	73.2	—	23.8	2.2	0.8	0	100	16
6	77.9	—	18.6	1.9	1.4	0.3	100	6
TOTAL	87.9	—	9.9	1.6	0.6	0	100	121

Parents Living Together, One Parent Is Unemployed and the Other Works or Studies	59.8	3.1	33.0	5.3	1.9	0	100	18
One or Both Parents Living Together at Home Full-Time or Single Mother Is Home Full-Time	93.8	—	4.3	0.8	0.6	0	100	68
Other or No Information	52.6	—	36.9	3.4	4.2	2.1	100	7
Children of Single Parents Who Work with Children Aged:								
1	5.1	1.8	74.4	7.4	13.0	0.1	100	16
2–3	8.6	5.7	83.0	4.6	3.8	0	100	21
4–5	3.1	1.4	89.3	4.4	3.2	0	100	11
6	5.3	1.8	86.2	4.6	3.9	0	100	8
TOTAL	5.8	2.8	84.2	5.2	4.9	0	100	56
On Parental Leave	77.7	—	18.9	2.3	1.1	0	100	6
Unemployed	36.0	—	60.6	1.5	1.8	0.1	100	6
Other	—	—	—	—	—	—	—	2
All Children of Single Parents	16.1	2.3	75.5	4.5	4.3	0	100	69

SOURCES: Statistics Sweden 1989. Primary source: A special analysis of the 1988 Child Care Survey.

*Free of cost—relatives or friends provide care without asking for money.

Childcare and School Hours

Nonetheless, the ideological justification for public daycare in Sweden can be traced to early discussions of family policy in the 1930s. The Myrdals (1934) believed that childcare specialists hired by childcare centers would do a better job of raising children than would ordinary mothers without any education in child development. This aspect of the Swedish solution—"the social engineering"—has been recently criticized by feminists (Hirdman 1990) and conservative males (Popenoe 1988) alike. As a direct result of the Myrdals' 1934 book, the government created a population committee, which recommended public childcare institutions. Such institutions were viewed as a "last resort" form of childcare and partly as poverty relief. However, the committee tried to remove the connotation of poverty by urging that part-day childcare be made available to all children. Although state subsidies for childcare were discussed during the 1940s, no government action was taken because the Social Democrats believed that the problem for working-class mothers was not that there was no place to leave their children, but that they could not afford to spend time with them.[21]

Working mothers do not stop worrying about childcare when their children reach school age. As a recent OECD study (1990a) notes, primary school is a very imperfect child minder. The kind of childcare that is needed to supplement school time varies widely among countries according to school hours, whether or not a hot lunch is served at school, and school vacation time (which in all countries exceeds the maximum paid vacation days of adult workers).

Comparison of female labor force participation rates and the childcare/school relationship in Sweden and Germany is instructive. In Sweden, the labor force participation rate of mothers of school-age children is not lower than the rate of women without children. But being a mother of a school-aged child is still a major obstacle to working in Germany (Gustafsson 1992). Part of the explanation is the difference in the organization of school hours in the two countries. German schools leave a large share of the education of young children to the parents. Parents are expected to actively help their children with extensive homework. School hours end at one o'clock in the afternoon, and mothers are expected to fix lunch for their children, who come home at this time. The afternoon must be spent helping children with homework. If a teacher is ill, her class is simply sent home. School hours can begin and end at different hours every day.

By contrast, in Sweden school always begins at eight o'clock in the morning and includes a hot lunch at noon. All schoolwork is done at school, at least among younger children. School hours end relatively late in the afternoon, and children have little homework. On the other hand, Swedish children start school at the age of 7—later than in most other countries. This is an important factor in the need for universal public childcare. Within the public childcare system, young children are prepared for school and taught materials similar to what children who start school at 4 or 5 years old are taught in other countries.

The increasing strain on public budgets in Sweden in the 1980s, and the growing demand for more childcare as work hours increased, caused a national change in attitude toward childcare. Today, more flexibility and parental initiative in the provision of childcare services are allowed. Many Social Democrats fear that if parents are allowed to create their own institutions with public subsidies, community centers will suffer and a greater percentage of spaces will have to be given to "children with special needs." In that case, single mothers might find themselves in a more vulnerable position than they are today. However, public daycare is still the preferred form of childcare among both single mothers and couples in Sweden today.

CONCLUSIONS

The relatively good economic situation of single mothers in Sweden is the result of universal policies that promote women's involvement in the paid workforce and encourage combining work and family, rather than special policies targeted at single mothers. Virtually all mothers in Sweden—single and married—have jobs. This policy reflects the traditional Swedish emphasis on full employment.

The "Swedish model" has been based on the assumption that women—whether single or married—can and should contribute paid wages to the support of their families. Public policies to support this goal were created early in the development of the Swedish welfare state. Three main programs to help integrate mothers in the workforce are universally available throughout Sweden. First, the parental leave program is crucial to helping women cope with the double demands of work and family and allows women to enter and leave the workforce to bear (and raise) children without losing wages or status accrued from previous work experience. Second, a national system of public daycare also supports the labor force participation of mothers. Solo mothers receive preferential treatment in the allocation of scarce spaces in the public daycare system and pay a lower parental fee than do two-parent families. In 1988, 84 percent of children of solo mothers were in public childcare, but because daycare is so universally used, the program does not stigmatize those children who attend. Third, all lone mothers, regardless of income, benefit from the child-support advance system.[22]

In sum, lone mothers in Sweden are less poor than in other countries because the state has actively encouraged them to enter the labor market through parental leave and tax policies, the provision of public daycare, and a solidaristic wage policy that resulted in greater pay equity between men and women. Moreover, from a very early period, the government established the principle that absent parents must support their children, and that if they are unable to do so adequately, the government will assume this responsibility. The universal programs that have formed the basis of Sweden's "enthusiastic welfare state" since the 1930s have been most effective in protecting lone-mother families in Sweden from poverty and material hardship. By promoting the use of contraceptives, teenage pregnancy in Sweden is very low. Single mothers in Sweden are therefore very likely to be previously married women and older than in a country like the United States, where teenage pregnancy is much higher. (See also Kamerman in this volume.)[23]

Sweden has distinguished itself from other West European countries by its ability to keep its open unemployment rate below 3 percent for the entire period between 1963 and 1990 (with the exception of a short period between 1982 to 1984 when it rose to 3.5 percent). However, the commitment to full employment in the 1980s was maintained at the cost of rising inflation, decreasing productivity, and the decreasing competitiveness of Swedish industry internationally. The current 1992 recession has led to rising unemployment rates in Sweden, and the economic forecasts project that unemployment will increase to levels comparable to those in Denmark. According to prominent economists, the fact that Sweden escaped high unemployment in the 1980s (unlike other Western European countries) was due to devaluations of the Swedish crown and a boom that resulted from deregulation of the credit system, which made people borrow for consumption and housing. Now that these sources of increased demand for labor are gone, the prospects that Sweden will be able to keep its unemployment rate lower than neighboring countries seem poor. There is a growing feeling among employers and higher paid professionals that macroeconomic conditions are undermining the "Swedish model," and this concern has resulted in a decline in political support for the Social Democrat party and a weakening of the commitment to solidaristic wage policies.

Wage inequality increased in Sweden in the 1980s (see also Gottschalk in this volume), resulting in an increase in the wage differential between men and women. This growing wage differential occurred as women entered full-time work in increasing numbers in the 1980s. The recent tax reform (cutting marginal tax rates to 30 percent for most workers and to 55 percent for the top bracket) is also expected to encourage more women to enter full-time work.[24] Thus, women are likely to contribute even more to family incomes in the future, but may have less time for family and parenting. This increasing male–female wage differential may hurt lone-mother families disproportionately.

Nonetheless, Swedish lone mothers are old enough so that most have finished their schooling and are employed, and the Swedish system encourages women to combine work roles and family life. Although Sweden has had a non-Socialist coalition in control of the state since 1991, this government supports the major aspects of the Swedish system—the general child benefit, the active labor market policies, and the paid parental leave. The childcare system is getting decreased subsidies, but dramatic changes are not expected—at least not dramatic enough to undermine the Swedish lone-mothers' high labor force participation rates, and hence, the widespread economic security they experience relative to lone mothers in other Western democracies.

ENDNOTES

1. These studies define a poor household as one with 50 percent of median family income, adjusted for size.

2. The child-support advance system was introduced in 1937, owing largely to the efforts of Alva Myrdal and Gunnar Myrdal. As a result of very low fertility rates in Sweden in the 1930s, government public support for single mothers was introduced. Under this system, still in effect, the state steps in and pays child support to a mother-headed family; the government then tries to locate the father and retrieve the child support advanced from him (Socialstyrelsen 1982, p. 1 and Riksförsakings-verket 1982, p. 1).

3. SOS Befolkningförändringar del 3 (Population Changes), Statistics Sweden, Stockholm. From 1987 onward this statistic has not been reported in Sweden.

4. By contrast, married women in the Netherlands had to wait until 1957 to obtain similar rights (Pott-Buter, Van kessel, and Kuperus 1986).

5. By contrast, American feminists had to fight in each state legislature. They used the argument of economic need to argue for the right to work, which made them vulnerable since it was the same argument used against married women's right to work (namely, that if married women worked, they took the jobs away from the breadwinners, the men, who had to support a family). However, toward the end of the 1930s, U.S. feminists linked their arguments to the fight for democracy in a free world and were more successful.

6. At least one observer (Popenoe 1988), has charged that these policy developments in the 1930s are the source of the current "devastating" decline of the traditional nuclear family in Sweden, the low marriage rate, the high rate of nonmarital cohabitation, the high percentage of lone-parent households, and the extensive involvement of mothers in the labor force. He laments that no one in Sweden defends the family, that there is no political spokesperson for what he calls "familism," which he believes is in conflict with feminism. However, Popenoe himself admits there is no evidence that Swedish children spend more time in one-parent families than American children.

7. Qvist (1978) argued in fact that demographic arguments were powerful in granting unmarried, single women in Sweden the right to work in the decades after 1850. At that time, males were more likely to emigrate from the country than females, but females moved from rural to urban areas. This left an unusually large number of unmarried women in the cities. The economic burden on fathers and brothers to provide for these adult women, who were not allowed to educate themselves or to take jobs, was a strong factor pressing for the granting of women's rights.

8. A recent study (Wennemo 1990) has indicated that this type of division is international, with Christian Democrats generally favoring child deductions and Social Democrats generally favoring child benefits. The results are received from an analysis of 18 Organization for Economic Cooperation and Development (OECD) countries over the period 1930–85.

9. West Germany's system, on the other hand, put a higher stress on child deductions, although there also was a child benefit. In the tax reform of 1986, the Federal Repub-

lic of Germany considerably increased the amount of the tax deduction for children. At the same time, single mothers were granted a double basic deduction like married couples have. The German system aspires to tax families according to the number of people who must live off the income.

10. The German tax system has the opposite effect. Part-time earnings are taxed at the marginal tax rate of the higher full-time earning, so part-time work among married women is not very profitable. Gustafsson (1992) compares the tax effects on married women's labor supply in Sweden and Germany.

11. One example was that bank employees went on strike for 3 weeks during which period no cash could be handled. Shops had to allow customer credits and see turnover decrease substantially.

12. The Swedish sales tax on value added tax is now 25 percent, which makes it one of the highest in the world.

13. The following analysis of the male–female wage gap was previously presented in Gustafsson (1988). See also Löfström and Gustafsson (1990) for an explanation of the female-to-male wage ratio and its development over time in Sweden.

14. The United States and many Western European countries have a steeper occupational-wage slope than Sweden's. The wage ratio of an accountant V (highest level) and a typist I in 1980 was 457/100 in the United States; the corresponding figure for Sweden was 199/100 (Klevmarken 1982, pp. 56–67). According to Jonung (1984), however, sex segregation in Sweden is as prevalent as in the United States.

15. Jonung (1984) reported segregation index numbers of 74.5, 70.6, and 69.5 for the years 1960, 1970, and 1975, respectively, whereas Leinio reported 69.0 for 1980. Jonung and Persson (1990) computed the number 65.0 for 1985, but warn against comparing this figure to earlier years because of the reclassification of the occupational structure between 1980 and 1985.

16. Statistics Sweden, AKU Årsmedeltal 1988 (Labor Force Survey) (see Jonung and Persson 1990).

17. The sick leave reform dramatically changed hospital care. To account for the high rates of absenteeism, employers of hospital workers kept large numbers of employees on the employment rolls. When workers suddenly began to show up, hospital budgets ran into serious difficulties because they had to pay wages which had been previously taken care of by the national health insurance.

18. A Swedish teenage mother, who got pregnant before ever having a job who lives with her parent(s) would get the following support: paid parental leave (guarantee amount 60 crowns/day equals 1,800 crowns per month, child support advance 1,123 crowns per month, child benefit 750 crowns per month, housing subsidy 1,000 crowns per month, which adds to 4,623 crowns per month. That is 4,623/13,924 equals 33 percent of average earnings of a female industrial worker in 1992. This support is meant to be a complement to earnings and she keeps all of it if she starts earning. If she is a normal girl with normal parents, she will have the initiative to get an education or a job. If she has special problems, poverty social assistance officers will take care of her.

19. Both pro-natal interest and the social reform lobbies fought against more liberal abortion laws. The latter argued that allowing abortion would remove the impetus

for social reforms to improve the situation of single mothers. If a mother applied to get an abortion and was refused by the doctor, she would be prosecuted if she then got an illegal abortion. The 1938 abortion legislation was in effect until 1975, demonstrating the patriarchic reasoning of policymakers.

20. Swedish social authorities are very efficient at finding the fathers. Fathers are even searched for abroad and made to pay child support. This fact supposedly made Swedish female tourists on the Riviera less attractive to Italian gigolos because they had to worry about the risk of having to pay for child support if the woman was Swedish (NRC, the Netherlands 1991).

21. Although it was not possible to form a coalition in favor of state-subsidized childcare in the 1940s, support was garnered for free school lunches. Conservatives supported the provision of free school lunches to poor children in the belief that they would improve the health of the children. But an important minority of Social Democrats arranged that school lunches should be free and compulsory to *all* children, so that poor children would not be labeled and stigmatized because of their poverty. This argument has always been an important argument against means-tested programs among Social Democrats. The Social Democrat Prime Minister Tage Erlander realized it would be financially impossible to make free school lunches available to all children immediately, so the principle of supplying free lunches to all children who wanted to participate was established. In 1943, 15 percent of all school children in compulsory school education participated. Today (1991) a hot school lunch is a universally available option and is taken by practically all students.

22. If the parents can agree among them on the child support, the state does not participate. As shown above (Table 8.9) about one-half of all single mothers make use of the child support advance system, and it is probable that those who do not use it are to be found among the better paid.

23. In 1981, the pregnancy rate for U.S. women aged 15–19 years old was 83.4 pregnancies per 1,000 teens, compared to a Swedish rate of only 34.6 pregnancies per 1,000 teens (Jones et al. 1986).

24. The Social Democrat government has increased sales taxes to fully compensate for the decrease in income taxes, by extending the basis for sales taxes to include previously exempt areas like restaurants and hotels. This is however one of the political targets of the "moderates" who rightly claim that there is no tax decrease, only a reorganization of the sources of tax receipts.

REFERENCES

Björklund, Anders. 1992. "Why is the Swedish Unemployment Rate Low?" *Issues in Industrial Economics-Celebrating 50 Years of Research*. IUI: Stockholm.

Bosworth, Barry P., and Alice M. Rivlin, eds. 1987. *The Swedish Economy*. Washington, D.C.: Brookings Institution.

Burtless, Gary. 1987. "Taxes, Transfers, and Swedish Labor Supply." In *The Swedish Economy*. Barry P. Bosworth and Alice M. Rivlin, eds. Washington, D.C.: Brookings Institution.

Calmfors, Lars, and Anders Forslund. 1990. "Wage Formation in Sweden." In *Wage Formation and Macroeconomic Policy in the Nordic Countries*. Lars Calmfors, ed. Stockholm: SNS Förlag; Oxford: Oxford University Press.

Carlsson, Sten. 1977. *Fröknar, mamseller, jungfrur och pigor. Ogifta kvinnor i det svenska ståndssamhället* (Unmarried Women in the Swedish Class Society). Stockholm: Almqvist & Wiksell International.

Edin, Per-Anders, Bertil Holmlund, and Johnny Zetterberg. 1990. "Lönestruktur och rörlighet på den svenska arbetsmarknaden" (Wage Structure and Mobility in the Swedish Labor Market). In *Tid och råd. Om hushållens ekonomi* (Time and Money. The Financial Situation of Families). Stockholm: Industrial Institute for Economic and Social Research—Klevmarken (ed.).

Ergas, Yasmine. 1990. "Child-Care Policies in Comparative Perspective. An Introductory Discussion." In *Lone-Parent Families: The Economic Challenge*. Paris: OECD.

Flanagan, Robert J. 1987. "Efficiency and Equality in Swedish Labor Markets." In *The Swedish Economy*. Barry P. Bosworth and Alice M. Rivlin, eds. Washington, D.C.: Brookings Institution.

Gustafsson, Siv. 1976. Lönebildning och lönestruktur inom den statliga sektorn (Determination and Structure of Salaries in the Government Sector of Sweden). With a 25 page summary in English. Stockholm: The Industrial Institute for Economic and Social Research. Ph.D. Diss.

————. 1984. "Equal Opportunity Policies in Sweden." In *Sex Discrimination and Equal Opportunity. The Labor Market and Employment Policy*. Günther Schmid and Renate Weitzel, eds. West Berlin: Wissenschaftzentrum; London: Gower Publishing Co.

————. 1988. Löneskillnader mellan kvinnor och män—gapet ökar igen (Wage Differences between Women and Men—The Gap Increases Again). *Ekonomisk Debatt* 3.

————. 1990. "The Labor Force Participation and Earnings of Lone-parents. A Swedish Case Study with Comparisons to Germany." In *Lone-Parent Families: The Economic Challenge*. Paris: OECD.

————. 1992. "Separate Taxation and Married Women's Labor Supply, A Comparison of West Germany and Sweden." *Journal of Population Economics* 5:61–85.

Gustafsson, Siv, and Marga Bruyn-Hundt. 1991. "A Comparison between the Netherlands, Sweden, and West Germany." *Journal of Economic Studies* 18(5/6):30–65.

Gustafsson, Siv, and Roger Jacobsson. 1985. "Trends in Female Labor Force Participation in Sweden." *Journal of Labor Economics* January (pt. 2).

Gustafsson, Siv, and Frank Stafford. 1992. "Day-care Subsidies and Labor Supply in Sweden." *Journal of Human Resources* 27:204–230.

Hatje, Ann-Katrin. 1974. "Befolkningsfrågan och välfärden. Debatten om familjepolitik och nativitetsökning under 1930-och 1940-talen" (The Population Issue and Welfare. The Debate on Family Policies and Increase in Fertility during the 1930s and 1940s.) Stockholm: Allmänna Förlaget.

Hirdman, Yvonne. 1989. "Att lägga livet till rätta–studier i Svensk folkhemspolitik" (To Guide and Organize People's Life–Studies in Swedish People's Home Policies). Stockholm: Carlssons.

Hobson, Barbara. 1990. "The Debate about Married Women's Right to Work in Sweden and the U.S. During the 1930s: A Comparative Perspective on Gendered Discourses and Strategies in Welfare States."

Hoem, Jan M. 1990. *"Att Gifta sig om utifalatt...Änkepensionen och giftermålen i december 1989"* (To Get Married if . . . The Widow's Pension and Marriages in December 1989). *Stockholm Research Report in Demography* 60. Stockholm: University of Stockholm, Section of Demography.

Hoem, Jan, and Bo Rennermalm. 1985. "Cohabitation and Social Background. Trends Observed for Swedish Women Born Between 1936 and 1960." *European Journal of Population* 1.

Holmström, Leif, et al. 1981. "Ensamförälder 1980" (The Single Parent in 1980). *Ds S, 1981* 18. Stockholm: Allmänna Förlaget.

Jones, Elise F. 1986. "Teenage Pregnancy in Industrialized Countries." Study sponsored by the Alan Guttmacher Institute. New Haven and London: Yale University Press.

Jonung, Christina. 1984. "Patterns of Occupational Segregation by Sex in the Labor Market." In *Sex Discrimination and Equal Opportunity. The Labour Market and Employment Policy.* Gunther Schmid and Renate Weitzel, eds. West Berlin: Wissenschaftzentrum; and London: Gower Publishing Co.

Jonung, Christina, and Inga Persson. 1990. *Hushållproduktion, marknadsproduktion och jämställlhnet, part I* (Household Production, Market Production and Gender Equality, Part I). In *Kvinnors roll i ekonomin* (Women's Role in the Economy). Supplement no. 23 to LU 90, The Medium-Term Economic Survey, 1990. Stockholm: Ministry of Finance.

Klevmarken, N. Anders. 1983. "Löbebildning och lönestrukur. En jämförelse mellan Sverige och USA" (Wage Discrimination and Wage Structure. A Comparison Between Sweden and the USA). Stockholm: The Industrial Institute for Economic and Social Research.

Lefaucheur, Nadine. 1989. Outline presented to authors conference on poverty. Paris, December 4–6. Photocopy.

Leiniö, Tarja-Liisa. 1988. "Sex and Ethnic Segregation in the 1980 Swedish Labor Market." *Economic and Industrial Democracy. An International Journal* 4(7).

Löfström, Åsa, and Siv Gustafsson. 1991. "Policy Changes and Women's Wages in Sweden." In Steven Willborn, ed. "Stability and Change in Six Industrialized Countries." *International Review of Comparative Public Policy* 3:313–330.

Matović, Margareta R. 1984. *Stockholmsäktenskap. Familjebildning och partnerval i Stockholm 1850–1890* (Stockholm Marriages. Family Formation and Choice of Partner in Stockholm, 1850–1890). Stockholm:Liber.

McIntosh, Alison C. 1983. *Population Policy in Western Europe. Responses to Low Fertility in France, Sweden, and West Germany.* New York/London: M.E. Sharpe, Inc.

Moberg, Eva (ed.). "Kvinnans villkorliga frigiving" ("The Conditional Release of the Woman"). Stockholm: Hederberg.

Myrdal, Alva, and Viola Klein. 1956. *Women's Two Roles: Home and Work.* London: Routledge & Kegan Paul.

Myrdal, Alva, and Gunnar Myrdal. 1934. *Kris i befolkningsfrågan* (Crisis in the Population Question). Stockholm: Bonniers Förlag.

Organization for Economic Cooperation and Development. 1990a. "Child Care in OECD Countries." In *OECD Employment Outlook 1990*. Chap. 5. Paris: OECD.

———. 1990b. "Child Care in OECD Countries." In *OECD Employment Outlook 1990*. Chap. 10. Paris: OECD.

Petterson, Gisela, ed. 1990. *Zeit-Puzzle Modell Schweden: Arbeitszeit und Familienpolitik* (Jigsaw Time Puzzle. The Swedish Model. Work Hours and Family Policies). Hamburg: VSA-Verlag.

Popenoe, David. 1988. *Disturbing the Nest, Family Change and Decline in Modern Societies*. New York: Aldine de Ruyter.

Pott-Buter, Hettie, Ellen Van Kessel, and Marga Kuperus. 1986. *Hoezo, gelijk belast? Invloed van arbeid, belasting- en premieheffing op het leven van vrouwen* (Indeed the Same Burden? The Impact of Taxes and Social Security Payments on the Lives of Women). Amsterdam: De Populier, Amazone.

Qvist, Gunnar. 1978. *Konsten att blifva en god flicka. Kvinnohistoriska uppsatser* (The Art of Being a Good Girl. Essays in Women's History Studies). Stockholm: LiberFörlag.

Rainwater, Lee, Martin Rein, and Joseph E. Schwartz. 1986. *Income Packaging in the Welfare State. A Comparative Study of Family Income*. Oxford: Clarendon Press.

Socialdepartementet 1992. (Ministry of Social Affairs) Ensamförälderstöd (Support for Single Parents). *DS 1992* 53. Stockholm: Allmänna Förlaget.

Socialstyrelsen and Riksförsäkringsverket. 1982. *Underhållsbidrag och bidragsförskott*. Child-Support and Child-Support Advance.

Sørensen, Annemette. 1990. "Single Mothers, Low Income, and Women's Economic Risks. The Cases of Sweden, West Germany, and the United States." Photocopy.

SOU. 1935:6. *Arbetslöshetsutredningens betänkande* (The Government's Study on Unemployment). Stockholm: Allmänna Förlaget.

———. 1983: 51. *Ensamföräldarna och deras barn* (Single Parents and their Children) Betänkande från Ensamförälderkommittén (Government Report from the Committee on Single Parents). Stockholm: Allmänna Förlaget.

———. 1990: 8. *Samhällsstöd till underhållsbidragsberättigade barn. Betänkande av underhållsbidragskommitten, Idéskisser och bakgrundsmaterial* (Government Support to Children Entitled to Child-Support. Report from the Child-Support Committee. Ideas and Background Material). Stockholm: Allmänna Förlaget.

———. 1990: 14. *Långtidsutredningen 1990* (The Medium-Term Economic Survey of Sweden, 1990). Government Report. Stockholm: Allmänna Förlaget.

Standing, Guy. 1988. *Unemployment and Labour Market Flexibility: Sweden*. Geneva: International Labour Office.

Statistics Sweden. 1989. *Barns levnadsvikor* (Children's Living Conditions). Living Conditions Report 62. Stockholm: Statistics Sweden.

Sundström, Marianne. 1987. "Deltidsarbetets utveckling." ("The Development of Part-time Work.") *Ekonomisk Debatt* 8.

————. 1991. "Sweden: Supporting Work, Family and Gender Equality" in Kamerman S. B., and R. Fred Kahn (eds.). *"Child-Care, Parental Leave and the Under 3s."* Westport, Conn.: Auburn House.

————. 1992. "Women's Return to Work from Parental Leave of the Swedish Telephone Company." Paper presented at the Sixth Annual Meeting of ESPE in Gmunden, June 1992.

Wennemo, Irene. 1990. "Familjepolitikens framväxt- en jämförande studie av barnbidrag och Skatteavdrag for barnfamiljer i 18 OECD-länder" ("The Development of Family Policy—A Comparative Study of Child Benefits and Child Tax Deductions for 18 OECD Countries"). Stockholm: SOFI, University of Stockholm. Photocopy.

$$\mathscr{Chapter}\ 9$$

LONE PARENTS:
THE CANADIAN EXPERIENCE

Ruth Rose

"THE FEMINIZATION of poverty" was an expression heard with increasing frequency in Canada during the 1980s. However, the proportion of the Canadian adult poor who are women has not been rising. In 1975, women represented 59 percent of all poor adults in Canada. By 1981 the figure rose to 61 percent but by 1987 returned to 59 percent. It is the increase in poor families headed by women in Canada over the past three decades that is striking. Since 1961, the percentage of poor families headed by a lone mother has grown from 13.2 percent to 16.6 percent in 1969, 35.4 percent in 1980, and 36.8 percent in 1988 (National Council on Social Welfare 1990b: 2).

This chapter examines the reasons why lone-mother families comprise an increasing share of all poor families in Canada and the ways that Canadian policymakers have responded to this growing problem. I argue that the economic condition of lone mothers is tied integrally to their position in the labor market. Deteriorating economic conditions in Canada in the late 1970s and 1980s have had a severe impact on lone mothers—especially the young and the least educated. While Canadian social policies provide some protection against severe economic hardship for lone-parent families with children, significant changes in the tax and transfer system in recent years have created special difficulties for single mothers.

Before we move to an analysis of Canadian social policies, a word about federal–provincial relationships is in order. In most policy areas (labor market regulation, welfare, health, and education), direct authority for the design and implementation of programs is left to the 10 provincial and 2 territorial governments, so it is difficult to generalize about "Canadian" policy. In employment policy, the federal government has direct jurisdiction over its own employees and those of federal Crown corporations, banking, and interprovincial or international transportation and communication.

In social policy, the federal government exerts leadership by offering to finance a part (usually 50 percent) of program costs incurred by the provinces in exchange for their agreeing to abide by certain national standards or requirements. (Much of Canada's constitutional discussions are related to national standards and to requirements the federal government may impose without violating the constitutional guarantee of provincial jurisdiction.) But because Canada has great regional disparities in wealth, the effect of most cost-sharing programs is to provide federal money to the richest provinces—Ontario, Alberta, and British Columbia—which already have the most money for programs and the lowest poverty rates. These provinces spend more per capita on social policy than the four provinces with the highest poverty rates—New Brunswick, Nova Scotia, Newfoundland, and Prince Edward Island.

Quebec, Manitoba, and Saskatchewan, all of which have had social democratic governments at some time, have often been leaders in the development of innovative social policy, although their spending levels are typically lower than those of the richest three provinces.[1] For a variety of reasons, Quebec has experimented most in social policy. It is the only province that collects its own income tax, and its exemptions and tax credits for children differ from those of the other provinces. It also has its own public pension plan and has taken the lead in providing pension credits for nonworking mothers with young children.

CANADIAN LONE PARENTS: A STATISTICAL PROFILE

As in most countries, the number of lone-parent families in Canada has grown since 1951. By 1986, nearly 16 percent of all families with children under the age of 18 were headed by a lone parent, up from 13.5 percent in 1981. About 84 percent of these 541,000 lone-parent families were headed by a woman (Table 9.1). It is important to bear in mind, however, that the percentage of lone-parent families in 1986 was *lower* than the percentage in 1931. The First World War produced many widows, and the Great Depression resulted in many abandoned

Table 9.1 / The Number and Distribution of Family Types in Canada: 1986

	All Families	Husband– Wife Families	All Lone-Parent Families	Lone-Parent Families as a Percentage of All Families	Percentage of All Lone-Parent Families Headed by a Female
All Families	6,734,980	5,881,335	853,645	12.7	82.2
Families with Children	4,533,430	3,679,785	853,645	18.8	82.2
Families with Children <18	3,475,280	2,934,050	541,230	15.6	84.0

SOURCES: Statistics Canada, Canada 1986 Census, *Families, Part 1*, cat. no. 93-106, compiled from Tables 3 and 4.

Table 9.2 / Marital Status of Canadian Lone Parents: 1951, 1981, and 1986

	1951	1981	1986
Single, Never Married	1.5	9.8	13.4
Separated	28.9	31.3	24.4
Married—Spouse Absent	N.A.	N.A.	5.2
Divorced	3.1	26.3	29.9
Widowed	66.5	32.7	27.0
TOTAL	100.0%	100.0%	100.0%

SOURCES: 1951 and 1981: Statistics Canada, 1981 Census, *Canada's Lone Parent Families*, cat. no. 99-933; 1986: Statistics Canada (1990: 16).

NOTE: Columns may not add up to 100 percent because of rounding errors.

N.A. = Not Available.

wives and children. Proportionally, there were as many lone-parent families at the beginning of World War II as in the 1980s.

However, as might be expected, the marital status of lone parents changed during this period. In 1951, there were few never-married lone parents; by 1986, 13.4 percent of lone parents had never married (Table 9.2). According to Margrit Eichler, 4.3 percent of all live births in 1960 were "illegitimate." According to a somewhat broader definition (births to single, widowed, or divorced mothers), about 6 percent of births in 1974 and 16.7 percent of births in 1984 were to lone mothers; there is no sign that this trend is slowing (Eichler 1988: 232).

The age at which unmarried mothers give birth shows a definite upward trend. In 1974, 55.7 percent of single mothers giving birth were under the age of 20, and 30.3 percent were between the ages of 20 and 24. Less than 15 percent of births to single women were to mothers over 24 years old. By 1984, only 26.6 percent of single mothers giving birth were under 20 years old, 38.5 percent were between 20 and 24, and a third were over 24 years old. Presumably, those in the oldest group are having babies by choice and not by accident.

Before the 1960s there were also few divorced lone parents. Canada did not have a uniform federal divorce law until 1968. When this law was passed, divorce rates jumped from 54.8 per 100,000 population in 1968 to 124.2 per 100,000 in 1969 to 285.9 per 100,000 in 1982 (Eichler 1988: 58). Divorces declined between 1982 and 1985 and then surged again in 1986 and 1987, undoubtedly due to another revision of the divorce law (Statistics Canada 1990: 19).[2] The percentage of lone parents who are separated has remained fairly steady in spite of all the other changes, while the percentage of widows and widowers has declined dramatically.

The proportion of divorces that involved children remained fairly steady between 1970 and 1985, at between 52 percent and 59 percent, then declined sharply in 1986 and 1987.The percentage of divorces in which the custody of children is awarded to the father remained fairly constant between 1970 and

1987: about 15 percent. However, joint custody awards (or custody awarded to someone other than the parents) expanded from 3.5 percent in 1970 to 12.7 percent of all child custody arrangements in 1986.

On average female lone parents are older than married women with children, but the age of lone mothers varies with their marital status. Over three-quarters of never-married lone parents are under the age of 35. About two-thirds of separated and divorced women are between the ages of 25 and 44. Widowed lone parents are heavily concentrated in the older age bracket–two-thirds are at least 55 years old. The youthfulness of never-married lone parents has important implications for their average years of schooling and their ability to support themselves economically. Because divorced lone mothers are older and are less likely to have preschoolers, they are probably better able to support themselves and their children than younger mothers.

Table 9.3 shows that families headed by lone mothers are much more likely to be poor than other family types. In 1989, after 7 years of economic recovery, over half of all lone-mother families were poor. The poverty rate of lone mothers jumped from 53.0 percent in 1981 to 59.3 percent in 1983 and did not fall below 1981 levels until 1989.

The 1982–1986 recession increased poverty rates for all types of families, but the rate of poverty among young, lone mothers today is shocking. In 1987, four-fifths of lone mothers aged 16 to 24 were poor; among those aged 25 to 34, about two-thirds were poor.[3] In 1990, with a new economic recession, poverty rates shot up again by nearly 8 percentage points. Single women between the ages of 15 and 24 also had an extremely high poverty rate of 53 percent in 1987 suggesting that the 1982–1986 recession hit all marginal groups particularly hard (National Council on Social Welfare 1990b: 105).[4]

THE LABOR MARKET AND LONE MOTHERS

Labor Force Participation

Marital status, age, and the presence of children are all related to the labor force participation and, hence, the poverty status of lone-mother families. Within age groups, separated and divorced mothers had higher rates of labor force participation in 1981 and 1986 than never-married or married mothers (Table 9.4). Never-married women tend to have the lowest labor force participation rates, especially among the youngest age groups. As discussed later, this is linked to their lower levels of schooling.

Over the 12-year period between 1976 and 1988, labor force participation rates increased for all women but especially among married women with children under age 6. In 1976, among mothers with young children, a higher proportion of lone mothers than married mothers worked (43.9 percent vs. 34.9 percent, respectively). By 1984, the inverse was true: 54.2 percent of married women compared with only 51.3 percent of lone parents with young children were in the labor force. Labor force participation rates among both married

Table 9.3 / Poverty Rates in Canada, by Family Type: 1980 to 1989

Family Type	Poverty Rates									
	1980	1981	1982	1983	1984	1985	1986	1987	1988	1989
Husband-Wife with Children	9.0	9.3	11.1	12.0	12.4	11.0	10.2	9.7	8.3	8.0
Female Lone-Parent Families	54.5	53.0	57.1	59.3	59.5	59.6	55.5	56.6	53.4	50.9
Male Lone-Parent Families	24.9	15.6	22.8	28.5	26.0	27.0	22.7	17.0	N.A.	N.A.
Unattached Women	36.6	34.6	31.9	38.1	36.9	36.8	34.0	33.3	35.3	31.7
Unattached Men	24.4	24.6	28.7	33.1	30.2	29.9	29.2	29.5	27.2	24.1

SOURCES: For 1980 to 1987: Statistics Canada (1990: 25, 113); for 1988 and 1989: Statistics Canada, *Income Distribution by Size in Canada, 1988* (or 1989), cat. no. 13-207 (table is also based on "economic families"—see Appendix A for definition). Married couples with children and lone parents are those with at least one child under age 18. Table is based on 1978 low-income cutoffs, indexed for inflation. In 1989, the figure was $16,027 for a family of two living in a city with a population of 500,000 or more.

N.A. = Not Available.

Table 9.4 / Labor Force Participation Rates of Canadian Women, by Age, Marital Status, and Presence of Children: 1981 and 1986 (in percentages)

Marital Status and Presence of Children	Labor Force Participation Rate	
	1981	1986
Women Aged 15–24		
Without children	63.7	66.4
With children	44.2	52.1
Never married	39.1	44.6
Separated	51.0	53.6
Divorced	53.1	54.5
Widowed	49.6	36.3
Married	44.1	53.3
Women Aged 25–34		
Without children	88.5	90.2
With children	54.2	63.5
Never married	54.3	55.8
Separated	64.7	67.2
Divorced	66.6	68.9
Widowed	56.1	62.0
Married	53.3	63.4
Women Aged 35–44		
Without children	79.1	82.7
With children	61.3	69.6
Never married	63.6	67.1
Separated	70.8	77.0
Divorced	73.0	77.0
Widowed	63.5	68.2
Married	60.1	68.8
Women Over Age 45		
Without children	25.6	24.9
With children	43.8	49.0
Never married	54.6	57.2
Separated	55.7	59.6
Divorced	66.7	68.0
Widowed	31.1	29.0
Married	44.4	50.6

SOURCES: Statistics Canada, 1986 Census, *Labor Force Participation*, cat. no. 93-111, Table 2.

Table 9.5 / **Labor Force Participation Rates of Canadian Women,
by Marital Status and by Presence and Age of Children (in percentages)**

	Labor Force Participation Rates			
Marital Status and Presence of Children	1976	1980	1984	1988
Women with a Spouse and Children Under 6	34.9	44.3	54.2	62.2
Women with a Spouse and Children 6 to 15	49.0	57.1	63.9	73.0
Women with a Spouse and no Children Under 16	43.5	47.2	49.7	52.8
Women with no Spouse and Children Under 6	43.9	53.3	51.3	51.0
Women with no Spouse and Children 6 to 15	58.7	66.4	68.3	72.3
Women with no Spouse and no Children Under 16	40.7	42.7	48.4	48.6

SOURCE: Statistics Canada (1990: 80).

women and lone mothers with children aged 6 to 15 rose significantly during this period. In 1988, both groups had labor force participation rates of over 70 percent (Table 9.5).

Unemployment Rates and Unemployment Insurance

Unfortunately, increased labor force participation rates do not always translate into increased employment and earnings. Lone mothers with young children have astronomically high unemployment rates. Since 1979, their unemployment rates have been almost twice as high as those of married mothers (Table 9.6). Among mothers with children aged 6 to 15, the unemployment gap is smaller, but it widened substantially between 1981 and 1982 and has hardly narrowed since. The 1982 recession hit lone mothers hard. Between 1983 and 1986 one out of four lone mothers with children under age 6 was unemployed. Lone mothers with children aged 6 to 15 also saw their unemployment rate rise by more than 50 percent. By 1988, the figure had not yet fallen back to its 1981 level.

Table 9.6 / **Unemployment Rates of Canadian Women,
by Presence or Absence of Spouse and Age of Youngest Child: 1976–1988**

	Unemployment Rates			
Marital Status and Presence of Children	1976	1980	1984	1988
Women with a Spouse and Children Under 6	11.9	9.9	13.5	10.2
Women with a Spouse and Children 6 to 15	7.3	7.0	10.2	7.7
Women with a Spouse and no Children Under 16	6.4	6.4	9.0	6.9
Women with no Spouse and Children Under 6	15.7	18.3	26.0	18.6
Women with no Spouse and Children 6 to 15	8.0	9.9	14.6	12.8
Women with no Spouse and no Children Under 16	5.6	7.5	9.1	7.3

SOURCE: Statistics Canada (1990: 95).

Unfortunately, the rules surrounding the receipt of unemployment insurance benefits often operate to exclude women. The first Unemployment Insurance Act was not adopted in Canada until 1940[5] and was fairly conservative, covering only 42 percent of the labor force. Until 1957, married women were excluded from receiving benefits unless they could prove they had a permanent attachment to the labor force. After 1971, major revisions in the program enlarged eligibility to all those who had worked for 8 weeks during the previous year and extended coverage to some 96 percent of the labor force. However, until 1975 women usually received lower benefits than men because it was assumed that they did not have dependents.

Throughout the 1970s and 1980s, unemployment and the number of unemployment insurance (UI) beneficiaries rose steadily. Instead of attacking the causes of unemployment, the government responded by attacking the unemployment insurance program. Women and young people, in particular, were accused of entering the labor force only to qualify for benefits. Since 1975, there has been a progressive tightening of rules governing the program, so that fewer unemployed persons are now eligible for benefits. In 1991, benefits replaced only 60 percent of previous earnings, compared to the 66 percent to 75 percent rate of replacement of the early 1970s. The duration of benefit receipt is also much shorter.[6] Because women are frequently confined to unstable employment in the service sector or seasonal employment, it is increasingly difficult for them to qualify for unemployment benefits if they find themselves jobless. Moreover, family responsibilities are likely to handicap a female's competitiveness in the labor market and her eligibility for unemployment insurance. If a woman has to quit a job because her childcare arrangement has fallen through, or she is fired for absenteeism because her child is sick, she may be subject to penalties of 7 to 12 weeks without benefits.

Lone Mothers Have Low Earnings and Low Incomes

One might assume that lone mothers are more likely to work part-time than full-time and that this helps account for the high poverty rate among these families. However, Table 9.7 shows that married women with children are much more likely to work part-time than lone mothers, regardless of the age of the child. Except for a nominal amount, earnings are deducted dollar for dollar from welfare payments, so part-time work does nothing to increase income levels for single mothers who receive these benefits.

Even if lone mothers are employed and work full-time, they do not earn as much as men. Although details on the earnings of lone parents per se are not available, a comparison of the earnings of full-time, full-year working women and men show large differences (Table 9.8). Even single women, the group least likely to have had a career interruption, earn less than their male counterparts (except for single men aged 45 to 54, the number of which is so small as to make the group statistically insignificant).

Married women also earn considerably less than married men of the same

Table 9.7 / **Percentage of Employed Women Working Part-Time in Canada, by Family Status and Age of Youngest Child, Selected Years: 1976–1988**

	Percent Working Part-Time			
Marital Status and Presence of Children	1976	1981	1986	1988
Women with a Spouse and Children Under 6	31.4	34.1	33.1	32.6
Women with a Spouse and Children 6 to 15	26.1	29.6	28.7	27.5
Women with a Spouse and no Children Under 16	15.1	19.0	20.4	20.6
Women with no Spouse and Children Under 6	17.1	16.8	19.4	19.7
Women with no Spouse and Children 6 to 15	14.0	13.1	15.9	12.8
Women with no Spouse and no Children Under 16	11.1	12.9	13.2	15.1

SOURCE: Statistics Canada (1990: 88).

age group. Marriage appears to enhance the earnings capacity of men while reducing the earnings capacity of married women—even those currently employed full-time. This may be the result of interruptions in work careers that result from the demands of family life.[7]

As a result of these wage differences, the average income of families headed by women is significantly lower than the average of families headed by men.[8] Lone-mother families have incomes only about half as high as those of lone fathers and only 40 percent as high as those of husband–wife families. This changed very little between 1971 and 1987.

During the 1982 recession, the real value of all family incomes declined. The income of husband–wife families climbed back to their real 1981 income level by 1986, and the income of male lone-parent families returned to 1981 levels by 1987. However, not until 1989 did the real income levels of female lone parents return to 1981 levels. In 1990, their real income declined 7.3 percent on average, while that of other groups remained stable or declined only slightly.

Female lone-parent families and unattached women not only have much lower incomes than male-headed households, but the relative importance of various kinds of income sources in lone-mother families differs from that of other households (Table 9.9). In 1971, only 54.8 percent of female lone-parent families' income came from earnings; 32.4 percent came from government transfers—mainly social assistance and family allowances—and 9 percent from pensions and other kinds of income (including alimony and child-support payments as well as benefits for surviving spouses and orphans from public and private sources).

Between 1971 and 1981, lone mothers reduced their dependence on transfer payments and pensions and other sources, due to their increased labor force participation. By 1981, 64.7 percent of their income came from earnings and only 23 percent and 7.3 percent, respectively, from transfers and "other" income. But the 1982 recession reversed the trend toward greater reliance on labor market earnings. By 1987, earnings as a share of income for lone mothers had declined to 62.3 percent, and their dependence on transfer payments and "other income

/ **335**

Table 9.8 / Average Earnings, by Marital Status, Age, and Sex of Persons Working Full-Time, Full-Year in Canada: 1987 (in Canadian dollars)

Age and Marital Status	Average Female Earnings	Average Male Earnings	Ratio of Female–Male Earnings
15 to 24 Years Old			
Single	15,235	17,542	86.8
Married	15,680	21,674	72.3
Other	N.A.	N.A.	N.A.
TOTAL	15,423	18,558	83.1
25 to 34 Years Old			
Single	22,116	23,846	92.7
Married	20,392	30,778	66.3
Other	21,381	28,701	74.5
TOTAL	20,982	28,715	73.1
35 to 44 Years Old			
Single	26,446	29,187	90.6
Married	22,504	36,291	62.0
Other	23,309	36,541	63.8
TOTAL	23,092	35,728	64.6
45 to 54 Years Old			
Single	31,331	26,627	117.7
Married	21,358	37,605	56.8
Other	23,738	35,783	66.3
TOTAL	22,595	36,972	61.1
55 and Over			
Single	N.A.	23,623	N.A.
Married	18,383	32,616	56.4
Other	21,242	27,887	76.2
TOTAL	19,814	31,846	62.2
All Ages			
Single	21,007	22,472	93.5
Married	20,742	34,140	60.8
Other	22,488	33,019	68.1
TOTAL	21,012	31,865	65.9

SOURCE: Statistics Canada (1990: 99).

N.A. = Not Available.

Table 9.9 / Sources of Income of Non-elderly Households in Canada, by Family Type: 1971, 1981, and 1987 (constant 1987$)

Family Type and Income Source	1971	1981	1987
Husband–Wife Family	$36,924	$47,150	$48,708
Earnings	92.6	88.8	88.3
Investment	3.1	5.3	3.7
Government transfers	3.1	4.6	5.7
Other[a]	1.0	1.3	2.4
Female Lone-Parent Family	$14,681	$19,590	$18,946
Earnings	54.8	64.7	62.1
Investment	3.8	5.0	2.1
Government transfers	32.4	23.0	26.5
Other[a]	9.0	7.3	9.0
Male Lone-Parent Family	$30,905	$35,499	$38,892
Earnings	95.5	88.7	86.2
Investment	−1.3	2.8	5.6
Government transfers	4.2	7.1	7.7
Other[a]	1.6	1.4	0.6

SOURCES: Statistics Canada (1990: 113–14). Table is also based on "economic families" (see Appendix A for definition).

NOTE: Columns may not add up to 100 percent because of rounding errors.

[a] Includes alimony and child-support payments as well as benefits for surviving spouses and orphans from public and private sources.

sources" rose to 26.5 percent and 9 percent, respectively. Greater reliance on transfer payments occurred among all other groups, too, probably as a result of greater use of unemployment insurance, but by 1987 the real income of these other groups had returned to 1981 levels.

Almost a quarter of all lone-mother families in Canada had no wage earner in 1987 compared to only 7.3 percent of lone-father families. Only 1.4 percent of husband–wife families with children had no earner. In both male and female lone-parent families, the parent is the only earner 45 percent of the time, but the earnings of lone fathers are on average *40 percent higher* than the earnings of lone mothers ($35,605 compared with $20,947[9] in 1987). The difference in earnings is explained by several factors: (a) women are more likely to work part-time than men, (b) lone mothers are younger on average than lone fathers, and (c) continuing wage and labor market discrimination against women keeps their wages low.

Support from Father's Earnings

To what extent can Canadian lone mothers count on support from absent fathers? In principle, absent fathers (and noncustodial mothers) have an obligation to contribute to the support of their children. The practice, however, is very different. A study of all couples divorcing or legally separating between 1981 and 1983 in Quebec found that of the 80 percent of mothers who took custody of children, only 58 percent received a court order for child support. Average payments were about $4,400 a year, and half were under $3,100. Of those who had court orders, only 63 percent were paid regularly; 14 percent were partially paid; 23 percent received no payments, even though 83 percent of the defaulting spouses were employed. Moreover, the rate of payment tends to decline over time (Odile Tremblay 1987, cited in National Council on Social Welfare 1990b: 85–86).

A 1985 study (Steel 1985: 204–205) showed that only 68 percent of divorced mothers with dependent children in Alberta had a legal child-support order and that some 75 percent of the fathers were in default. A 1983 study in Ontario showed that the mean amount awarded for support payments was only 17 percent of the husband's income.

Most provinces now have a public enforcement mechanism for child support. However, the main purpose of such mechanisms is to ensure payment for women who are on social assistance and, therefore, to save money for the province. Because welfare payments are reduced by the entire amount collected, the living standards of the poor women and children are not improved by paternal support payments. Women who are not welfare beneficiaries must initiate court proceedings themselves to obtain child support. Delays are long, and the resulting legal hassle usually increases tension between the ex-spouses as well as between them and their children. Despite evidence that women who receive child support or alimony payments are less likely to be poor than those who do not, the government does little to help nonwelfare recipients collect child support.

In short, much of the poverty of children living with their mother alone is attributable to the fact that fathers do not contribute sufficiently to their mainte-nance. The legal mechanisms for stipulating that child support be paid and for enforcing court orders are far too weak to ensure adequate paternal support to lone-mother families with children.

POLICIES TO IMPROVE THE LABOR MARKET POSITION OF WOMEN

Even if fathers contributed fairly to the support of their children, the lower earnings of women would leave lone mothers at a disadvantage relative to male-headed families. Thus, programs to promote pay equity and employment equity are crucial to improving the economic position of lone-mother families.

Education and Training

The lack of educational qualifications is a major disadvantage for lone moth-ers who attempt to enter and compete in the labor market. Whatever their

Table 9.10 / Highest Educational Level Attained, by Age, Gender, and Family Status in Canada: 1986 (percent distribution)

	Women			Men		
Age and Educational Level	Wives	Lone Mothers	No Family	Husbands	Lone Fathers	No Family
Under Age 35						
Less than 9 years	4.4	8.4	3.3	6.1	9.0	4.8
9–13 years	45.4	51.9	33.4	36.5	46.1	39.5
Other nonuniversity	30.7	28.6	30.9	33.8	29.8	28.0
Some university	19.4	11.1	32.3	23.7	15.2	27.6
Aged 35–44						
Less than 9 years	11.7	13.1	9.6	13.6	13.7	11.6
9–13 years	39.5	36.2	28.2	28.7	33.3	29.8
Other nonuniversity	27.3	30.0	26.0	29.9	28.6	25.4
Some university	21.6	20.8	36.1	27.8	24.5	33.2
Aged 45–54						
Less than 9 years	24.3	25.7	22.5	26.7	25.0	28.4
9–13 years	41.0	35.0	33.2	29.8	30.2	30.4
Other nonuniversity	22.6	23.9	23.8	25.7	24.9	21.5
Some university	12.2	15.4	20.5	17.8	19.8	19.7
Over Age 55						
Less than 9 years	37.0	48.8	43.8	38.7	46.3	48.7
9–13 years	38.8	31.1	33.2	29.5	25.1	27.0
Other nonuniversity	16.4	13.7	14.9	19.1	16.2	13.6
Some university	7.7	6.5	8.0	12.7	12.3	10.8

SOURCES: Statistics Canada, 1986 Census, *Families, Part 2*, cat. no. 93-107, Tables 4, 11, and 17.

NOTE: Columns may not add up to 100 percent because of rounding errors.

age or family status, fewer women have a postsecondary degree (university or nonuniversity) than men. Overall, lone mothers have less education than either married women or nonfamily (single) women.

Age is also an important determinant of educational credentials. Table 9.10 shows that men and women aged 35 to 44 are more likely to have a university degree or certificate than those under age 35. The difference in education according to age is particularly marked for lone parents but is also apparent among individuals without families. Lower educational levels among lone parents may reflect interruptions in schooling that occur when an unplanned child arrives.

In Canada, the federal government is responsible for adult training programs that are associated with the Unemployment Insurance Act and administered by the Canadian Employment and Immigration Commission as part of the "Canadian Jobs Strategy." Although one of the explicit objectives of the Canadian Jobs Strategy is to give women training in nontraditional occupations and correct some of the disadvantages they experience in the labor market, access to training programs is conditional on being eligible for UI benefits. Individuals unable to *enter* the labor force because they lack educational qualification or individuals in unstable or temporary jobs are not eligible to participate in these programs. Thus, many lone mothers cannot participate in the more effective federal training programs and are confined to those offered to provincial welfare recipients.

Over the past 25 years, Canada has had a very low level of expenditure on adult retraining and specialized professional training, by private firms and by the government. In 1987, Canadian firms spent only $100 per worker on training, compared with $500 spent per worker in the United States.[10] Until recently, the training that did take place was financed by general government revenues as part of the federal government's contribution to the UI fund, but as of January 1990, the government withdrew all contributions to unemployment insurance, and training programs are now financed by employer–employee contributions only. This withdrawal of federal funding greatly reduces the countercyclical stabilizing role of unemployment-related training and means that fewer funds will be available during recessionary periods; in other words, less training will be available when the labor force needs it most. Enrollment in government-sponsored institutional training courses declined by almost half between fiscal year (FY)1983–1984 and FY1988–1989, falling from 235,000 to 126,600 (Canada, Office of the Auditor General 1986, cited in Ontario Ministry of Community and Social Services 1988: 95), and funding for the Canadian Jobs Strategy for FY1991–1992 was cut by $100 million (Wilson 1991).

Another strategy for improving skill levels would be to increase general educational achievement levels by investing in postsecondary educational grants and loans. But the federal government has been reducing funding to higher education over the last decade or so, and provinces have also reduced grants and loans available to students. Lone mothers receive priority in certain grant/loan programs for students, but the programs are available only to those who are able to study full-time.

Employment Equity

The 1960 Canadian Bill of Rights guarantees "equality before the law and protection of the law without discrimination because of . . . sex," but the 1970 *Report of the Royal Commission on the Status of Women in Canada* found that federal law did little to protect women from even blatant discrimination in the labor market. Provincial and territorial antidiscrimination legislation was just as inadequate. The commission recommended that the Fair Employment Practices Act and its accompanying regulations "be amended to include 'sex' and 'marital status' as prohibited grounds for discrimination" and that the provisions apply to all employees of the government of Canada.

In 1977, the Canadian Human Rights Act was adopted and the Canadian Human Rights Commission established. Discrimination in hiring was expressly prohibited for the 750,000 workers covered by federal labor laws. Most provincial legislatures adopted similar laws at this time, offering some protection against hiring discrimination for the vast majority of Canadian women. However, the legislation was complaint-based, which meant that individuals who felt they had been the victim of discrimination had to initiate proceedings. The burden of proof was essentially on the plaintiff, and the scope of remedies was limited.

Affirmative action in hiring, even on a voluntary basis, was considered discriminatory and essentially illegal in Canada until 1982, when the Canadian Charter of Rights and Freedoms was adopted. Article 15, particularly subsection (2), now states that:

1. Every individual is equal before and under the law and has the right to the equal protection and equal benefit of the law without discrimination and, in particular, without discrimination based on race, national or ethnic origin, colour, religion, sex, age or mental or physical disability.
2. Subsection (1) does not preclude any law, program or activity that has as its object the amelioration of conditions of disadvantaged individuals or groups including those that are disadvantaged because of race, national or ethnic origin, colour, religion, sex, age or mental or physical ability.

The 1986 Employment Equity Act requires employers with 100 or more employees under federal jurisdiction to implement an affirmative action hiring program aimed at four target groups: women, aboriginal peoples, persons with disabilities, and members of visible minority groups. In the words of the act, employers must "identify and eliminate employment barriers, implement employment equity plans and programs, achieve a representative work force and report annually on their results" (Employment and Immigration Canada 1989a: 1). The term *representative work force* means that the target groups should be present in numbers proportionate to "their representation (i) in the work force, or (ii) in those segments of the work force that are identifiable by qualification, eligibility or geography. . . ." (Employment Equity Act 1986: Section 4). Employment equity programs are also mandatory for companies receiving federal contracts worth more than $200,000. Many provinces have similar programs in various stages of implementation, but affirmative action programs are, by and large, voluntary in the private sector except for firms bidding on large government contracts.

It is still too early to judge the effectiveness of these laws in improving the employment and occupational position of women. As of 1988, 2 years after implementation of the Employment Equity Act, compliance was high (companies covered by the law are adopting plans and filing required reports), and the proportion of women in companies covered by the act had increased from 40.9 percent to 42.1 percent. (Overall, 44 percent of the Canadian labor force is female.) However, a 1989 report on the act noted that "the bulk of women's net employment growth from hirings and terminations was in Clerical, Sales and Service occupations. There were more terminations than hirings for women in Middle and Other Managers, Supervisors, Forewomen and Professional occupations." It also reported that the "full-time wage gap (now 28.74 percent) has not narrowed significantly since the first reporting year. . . . Women were also more likely to be paid less than men in almost all occupational groups in all sectors" (Employment and Immigration Canada 1989a: 29).

Wage Equity

Legislation mandating pay equity between men and women has also been passed in Canada. This legislation parallels the history of affirmative action laws. The 1977 Human Rights Act requires "equal pay for work of equal value in the same establishment." Between 1978 and 1985, some 4,000 federal public servants, mainly women, were awarded $39.1 million in retroactive or permanent awards. Permanent increases awarded as a result of suits were worth about $3 million annually (Ouimet 1989: 36–43).

It was not until 1986, however, that systematic, large-scale evaluation programs began to compare jobs within firms, across firms in a particular industry, and within the public sector. The Canada Labor Code now gives inspectors the right to inspect records of federally regulated employers and to take the initiative in filing a complaint before the Human Rights Commission when there are reasons to believe that an employer has been discriminating on the basis of sex. Unions have been taking a much more aggressive stance as well, and recent settlements at both the provincial and federal levels have included substantial corrections in pay scales for groups in which women predominate. However, preliminary evaluations suggest that these settlements are often based on bargaining power rather than on a systematic job evaluation scheme, and that they only partly correct inequities with the concomitant danger that the remaining discrepancies will never be corrected.

Occupational segregation remains a major problem in improving female wages relative to male wages. Large numbers of women work either in firms or in occupations where there is no comparable male group. Job evaluation plans can help establish reference points in large firms where there are male groups working in different job categories, but in small firms, where no male comparison groups exist, the problem of low wages will not be solved until female labor becomes scarce enough to allow women to demand higher wages.[11]

To sum up, Canada is beginning to make some progress in establishing pay equity and rectifying some of the gross discrepancies in salaries between occupations dominated by men and those in which women are heavily represented. However, it is still too early to evaluate the full impact of the laws and collective bargaining efforts.

Childcare Policies

Two serious problems for mothers in the labor force or in training programs in Canada are the inadequate supply of licensed childcare places and the high cost of childcare. Table 9.11 compares the number of childcare spaces with the number of children whose mothers are in the labor force, a maximum estimate of need. Although nearly a quarter of children aged 3 to 5 whose mothers are employed can be accommodated in licensed daycare centers or licensed family homes, only a small fraction of infants and toddlers find spaces.[12] Until recently, virtually no daycare was available for school-aged children.

Each province has its own childcare policies. Some provide operating subsidies to daycare centers and to agencies that supervise licensed family-home care. All provide financial aid to low-income parents, although the amounts and income levels at which aid is available vary widely from province to province.[13] The federal government also provides financial support for childcare services with income-tested tax credit, tax deductions, and by paying 50 percent of the cost of provincial aid to low-income parents through the Canada Assistance Plan.[14]

Parental Leave

Maternity benefits were introduced in Canada in 1971 as part of unemployment insurance. The right to take leave upon the birth or adoption of a child is generally covered by provincial labor legislation and is dependent upon conditions set down in each province.[15] In 1988, all provincial labor standard acts granted 17 or 18 weeks' leave at the time of the birth of a child, but the conditions for eligibility varied widely—from no conditions in New Brunswick and British Columbia to 63 weeks with the same employer in Ontario.[16] Before November 1990, the mother of a newborn could receive 15 weeks of paid maternity leave at 60 percent of her salary after a 2-week waiting period. In November 1990, the Unemployment Insurance Act was amended so that either the father or the mother could receive an additional 10 weeks of parental benefits at 60 percent of salary.[17] To be eligible for either maternity or parental benefits, the beneficiary must have worked in insured employment for at least 20 weeks of the previous 52 weeks.[18] Most civil servants and employees of para-public institutions such as hospitals, colleges, and universities have considerably better maternity and parental leave clauses—sometimes with full pay—than employees in the private sector.

In some provinces the right to maternity leave means the right to return to the same job with accumulated seniority and continuity in all insurance plans and other benefits. In others it means returning to a comparable post with at least the same salary and benefits. Although these laws guarantee the right to return to a job, they do not specify how long the employer must retain the returned mother, and in most cases they provide no protection against arbitrary firing. Thus, a mother who is frequently absent because of a sick child, unreliable childcare, or her own illness may lose her job. Leave for family responsibilities for parents with older children is just beginning to be recognized in some provincial labor standards acts and some union contracts. For lone mothers, such leave is essential.

Table 9.11 / **Number of Canadian Children Whose Mothers Work and Ratio of Licensed Daycare Spaces to This Measure of Need[a]: 1978 to 1990**

Year	Children Aged 0-2 with Working Mothers	Ratio of Daycare Spaces	Children Aged 2-5 with Working Mothers	Ratio of Daycare Spaces	Children Aged 6-16 with Working Mothers	Ratio of Daycare Spaces
1978	209,000	5.7	486,000	12.7	2,236,000	0.4
1979	217,000	4.1	504,000	15.5	2,318,000	0.3
1980	229,000	3.8	531,000	15.8	2,443,000	0.7
1983	305,172	5.4	650,581	16.1	1,319,822[b]	1.3

Year	Children Aged 0-17 Months with Working Mothers	Ratio of Daycare Spaces	Children Aged 18 Months-3 Years with Working Mothers	Ratio of Daycare Spaces	Children Aged 3-5 Years with Working Mothers	Ratio of Daycare Spaces	Children Aged 6-13 Years with Working Mothers	Ratio of Daycare Spaces
1984	204,869	5.7	215,557	10.7	419,727	24.9	1,612,567	2.0
1987	303,018	4.6	319,357	8.6	633,937	24.3	1,777,250	2.7
1988	303,954	5.2	320,761	11.6	652,922	23.4	1,634,010	3.6
1989	317,374	5.0	319,024	10.7	639,358	27.0	1,682,475	4.5
1990	307,063	5.4	316,277	9.7	641,893	27.7	1,720,310	5.6

SOURCE: Health and Welfare Canada, *Status of Day Care in Canada*, various years. Numbers of children needing daycare are estimated by Health and Welfare Canada based on census data and on information from the Women's Bureau of Labour Canada.

[a] This ratio of the number of licensed daycare spaces to the number of children whose mothers work is only an approximate measure of the percentage of needs being met, because many families where the mother does not work may want or need daycare. On the other hand, some of the families measured here may be able to arrange parental care for the children and may not want or need daycare.
[b] Children aged 6–13.

BENEFITS TO FAMILIES WITH CHILDREN:
ALLOWANCES, CREDITS, AND EXEMPTIONS

Public support to Canadian families with children is comprised of a complicated set of programs that, like archaeological strata, have been built up by successive governments as a result of election promises and changing policy objectives. None of these programs provides much income, and the whole system is in need of simplification. However, it is difficult for the government to eliminate programs that are perceived by the public as an acquired right, even if the programs are to be replaced with a more coherent system of benefits.

The first child benefit tax exemption for children under the age of 16 was granted in 1918, and tax exemptions for children have existed in one form or another ever since.[19] In general, tax exemptions benefit upper-income families most and, therefore, are not a very equitable way to distribute public funds. Recently, as part of a rationalization of the family benefit system, tax exemptions for children (including the larger tax exemption for lone parents) were converted to nonrefundable tax credits so that all families (except the poorest who pay no taxes) receive the same benefit. At the same time, the *value* of these child tax exemptions has been greatly reduced.

In 1945 the Canadian government established a universal family allowance with benefits of $60 to $96 per year per child under age 16, payable to the mother. This program was supposed to encourage women, who had been recruited on a massive scale to work in war industries, to return home. Family allowances were supposed to take the place of a second income for the family, to put money directly into the hands of the mothers, and to encourage families to have more children.

A major revision of the family support program for children occurred in 1974. Family allowances were increased to $240 per year per child under age 18 and were indexed to the consumer price index (CPI) at a time when inflation was high and accelerating. At the same time, allowances were made taxable in the hands of the parent who claimed the child tax exemption (which was also indexed). This is an example of the incoherence of the system, because the tax exemption had the effect of annulling the tax on family allowances while still giving greater benefits to higher-income families.

The period from 1978 to the present marks a move away from universality and toward income-tested programs. Family allowances were cut significantly in 1979, and a refundable child tax credit of $218 per year was introduced for families with net incomes below what was then the median family income. The credit was reduced at a rate of $5 per $100 of income above this threshold level.[20] By 1990 the child tax credit had been increased to $565 per child, while the real value of family allowances (at $399 per year) had fallen, and the tax exemption, with a value of only $68 per child, was virtually nonexistent. On the one hand, as Figure 9.1 shows, the system is fairer, and some low-income families have benefited. On the other hand, there has been a significant cutback in overall support to families with children and, in particular, to middle-class families, a move that may jeopardize political support for this kind of program. Even more alarming, the threshold above which families receive only a partial child tax credit or none at all has lost nearly half its value since 1979 and now stands at only a little above 50 percent of median family income. It continues to be de-indexed at a rate of 3 percent per year. As shown in Figure 9.1, only those lone parents with incomes below the low-income cut-off level (about $22,500 in 1990 for a family of three) made any gain from 1984 to 1990, and those with incomes above $30,000 received considerably less in real terms in 1990 than they did in 1978.

Figures 9.2–9.4 show that a very large part of the benefits for lone parents now comes from the "equivalent to married persons exemption." This exemption is granted to heads of lone-parent families and other unmarried persons with certain dependents and has the same value as the exemption granted a married person for a dependent spouse, $874 in 1990. If this analysis had been done for a two-parent family, it would show that benefits for families with incomes above $50,000 are almost nil and that families at all income levels have lost in real terms. In practice, even many of the poorest families were hurt by the reforms because most of the provinces reduced their welfare benefit level by the amount by which the child tax credit (a federal benefit) was increased. (Quebec is unusual because it has introduced a pro-natalist policy targeted to two-parent families with three or more children. However, support for poor lone mothers in the province has been curtailed. See Appendix B for a description of these programs.)

INCOME SUPPORT OF LAST RESORT

Until 1966, Canadian social assistance for the needy took the form of a compli-cated set of programs targeted to specific groups (blind persons, the elderly, needy mothers, widows, veterans, handicapped persons), each with its own eligibility criteria and scale of support and financed either in part or entirely by the federal government or by various provincial governments.[21]

In 1966, the federal government adopted the Canada Assistance Plan, which provided funds for a single social assistance plan "of last resort" in each prov-ince. The only criterion for eligibility under this plan is a gap between needs and resources, resources being defined in terms of current income and assets. Needs are generally defined according to a fixed scale based on family composi-tion, with provisions for special needs (rents above a certain threshold, disabili-ties, prescription drugs, moving costs, and so forth). The federal government sets maximum scales that it will finance, but each province establishes its own level of support, and, in some provinces, each municipality has its own scale.

Until 1990 the federal government financed 50 percent of all provincial expen-ditures that met federal guidelines. However, since 1990 the government has limited increases in payments to the three provinces with above-average per capita income (Ontario, Alberta, and British Columbia) to 5 percent annually.

Figure 9.1 / Value of Family Benefits, Lone Parent with 2 Children under 12 (1990$)

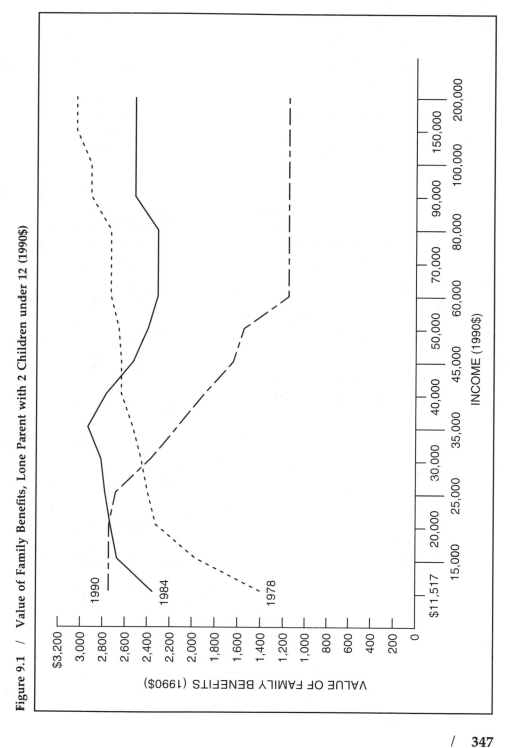

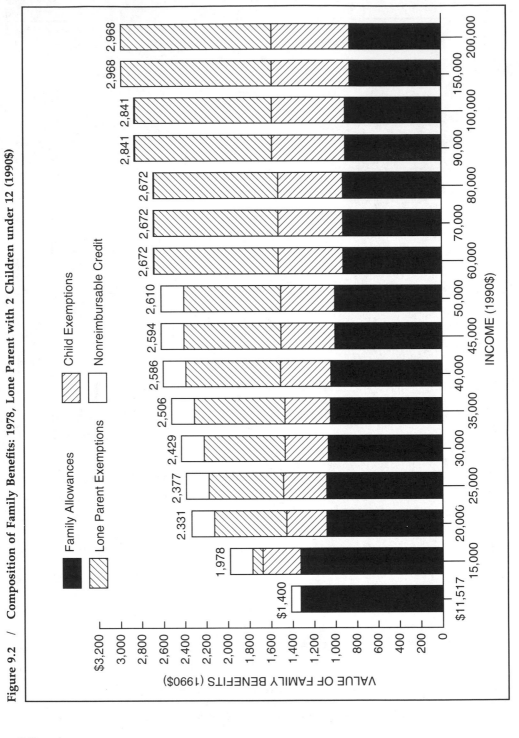

Figure 9.2 / Composition of Family Benefits: 1978, Lone Parent with 2 Children under 12 (1990$)

Figure 9.3 / Composition of Family Benefits: 1984, Lone Parent with 2 Children under 12 (1990$)

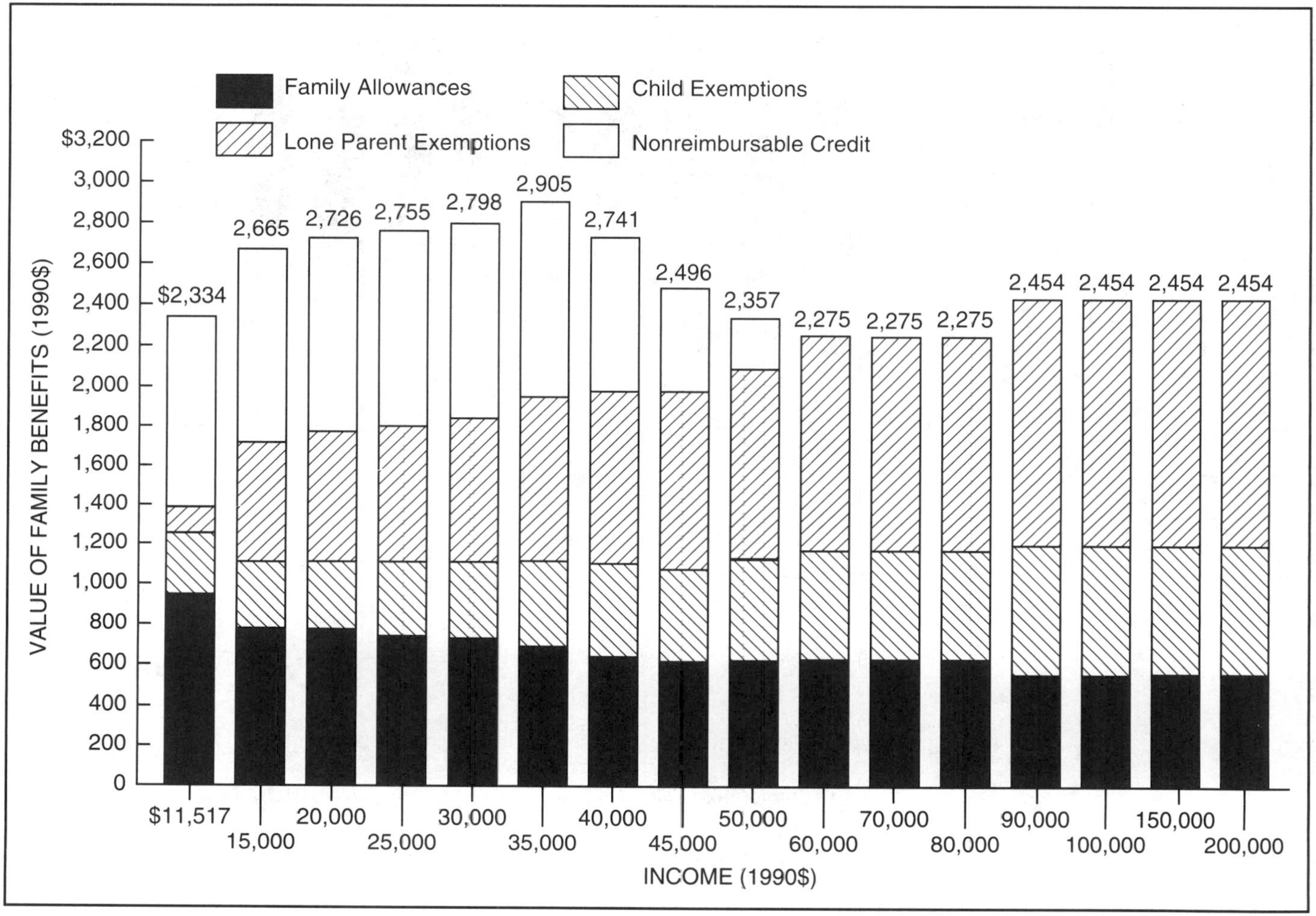

Figure 9.4 / Composition of Family Benefits: 1990, Lone Parent with 2 Children under 12 (1990$)

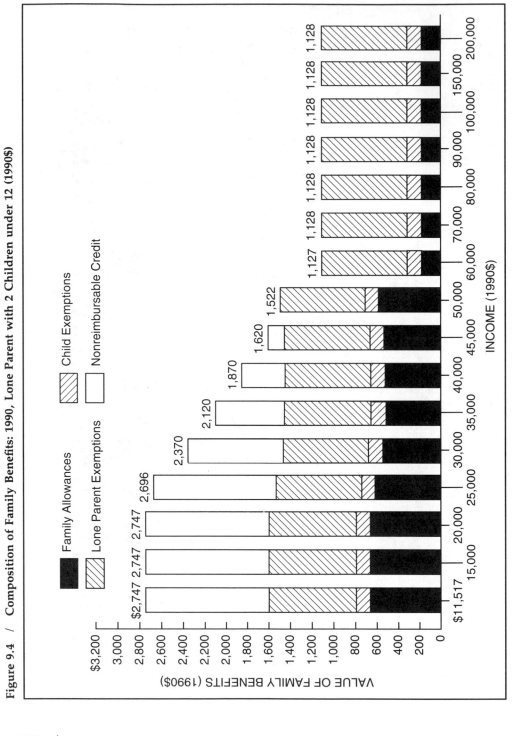

Table 9.12 / Welfare Benefits for Lone-Parent Families in Canada with one 2-Year-Old Child, by Province: 1989

Province	Welfare Payments ($)	Total Income[a] ($)	Government Assistance as a Percentage of the Low-Income Cutoff Line[b]
Newfoundland	9,486	10,678	66.6
Prince Edward Island	9,570	10,762	66.6
Nova Scotia	9,408	10,600	66.1
New Brunswick	7,624	8,816	55.0
Quebec	8,583	9,845	61.4
Ontario	10,806	12,539	78.2
Manitoba	7,887	9,079	56.6
Saskatchewan	9,927	11,119	69.4
Alberta	9,006	10,115	63.1
British Columbia	9,714	10,976	68.5
Yukon	11,132	12,872	80.3

SOURCE: National Council on Social Welfare (1990a: 23–30).

[a]This total includes federal and provincial family allowances, the federal reimbursable child tax credit, and the federal sales tax credit, as well as special provincial tax credits or allowances.
[b]Statistics Canada low-income cutoffs distinguish as to the size of the municipality in which households live. However, this distinction has been widely criticized because costs of living are not necessarily related to this criteria. The figure used here is $16,027, or the low-income cutoff (1978 base indexed for inflation) for a family of two living in a city of 500,000 people or more. Median family income in Canada in 1989 was $44,460 (all families) and $35,251 (a family of two).

The government has argued that these provinces can afford to finance any extension of social welfare programs they wish to implement (Wilson 1990: 76–77). However, over half of the Canadian poor live in these three provinces, and the limitation was put in place just at the beginning of a major recession.[22]

Table 9.12 shows the amounts provided by various provinces in 1989 to a lone mother with a 2-year-old child. "Total Income" includes the value of all family support programs and is expressed as a percentage of Canadian low-income cutoffs. As can be seen, the highest level of benefits represents less than four-fifths of the most widely used measure of poverty in Canada. Most provinces offer about two-thirds of this level.

The percentage of lone mothers who receive social assistance in any area is dependent on such factors as the state of the labor market, eligibility rules, the level of support given, and the zeal with which provincial authorities enforce the "spouse-in-the-house rule." In Quebec, lone mothers comprised only 21 percent of social assistance beneficiaries in 1987. The province has had a punitive attitude toward lone mothers, carrying out an aggressive campaign of home visits in search of single mothers who were living with a man. Both single persons and lone parents who share housing with another adult have had their benefits reduced by more than $90 a month since 1989.

Ontario represents the other extreme. In Ontario, lone mothers make up more than a third of social assistance beneficiaries. The "spouse-in-the-house" rule was relaxed in 1987, and the penalty for shared housing was recently abolished. A lone mother is considered to have a spouse only if the man has a legal obligation to support her or her children—specifically, if the couple is legally married, has lived together for at least 3 years, or has lived together and are the biological or adoptive parents of the child(ren) (Health and Welfare Canada 1989).

Federal guidelines specify the maximum amount of earned income that a social assistance beneficiary can keep without a reduction in his or her welfare check. All other income, including alimony or child support, is deducted at a rate of 100 percent. Thus, strict means testing is one of the main obstacles to leaving welfare, particularly for lone-mother heads of families.

Social assistance benefits are so low that it is generally advantageous for a single person to take a job even at the minimum wage. In the case of two-parent families or couples without children, it is possible for the family to improve their income with paid work if both parents are working.

However, single parents must earn at least 50 percent above the minimum wage to be better off than they are on social assistance, given the additional costs of working and the fact that welfare beneficiaries are eligible for special benefits such as glasses, dental care, and prescription medicines. Although all provinces provide for a full or partial subsidy of childcare costs for low-income, lone-parent families, it may be difficult for parents to find a subsidized childcare center, and most provinces do not cover informal, nonlicensed care. Moreover, in many provinces, the maximum childcare subsidy is so low that a lone mother will still have to pay as much as $1,500 a year in childcare costs.

"Employable" Welfare Beneficiaries

In the last decade, all the provinces have changed their welfare programs to distinguish beneficiaries who are "employable" from those who are not. Those who are permanently disabled receive somewhat higher benefits, although they are still far below the poverty line. Most lone parents, however, are classified as employable. In some provinces, lone mothers are considered temporarily unavailable for work (and receive a slightly higher benefit) if they have a young child.[23]

A beneficiary who is considered employable and available for work must actively look for work and/or enroll in a training program. (However, this varies by province.) Enrollees in one of these training programs typically receive a bonus to cover some of the costs of working or studying outside the home, including childcare (in addition to the regular program for low-income parents). Refusal to participate in a program, refusing a job, or insufficient zeal in looking for a job can lead to a serious reduction in benefits. In the case of a lone-parent family, this could result in losing one's apartment and having to place one's children in a foster home.

Programs to encourage welfare beneficiaries, and particularly lone mothers, to enter the paid labor force are not new. Unfortunately, most of these programs have never been systematically evaluated. According to one recent study of training programs for social assistance beneficiaries in Ontario:

> Recent reports suggest that current training programs do not always succeed or accomplish what we expect. The most recent report of the federal Auditor General underscores some of the failures of Canada's institutional training programs, for example. It discovered that 44 percent of trainees were not working 90 days after completion of their course, and of those employed, only half were working in areas directly related to their training. A previous evaluation had shown no significant increase in earnings for trainees, as compared with a control group of non-trainees. (Canada, Office of the Auditor General 1986, cited in Ontario Ministry of Community and Social Services 1988–1995)

Several provinces are also experimenting with earned-income supplement programs, the purpose of which is to alleviate the disincentive effect of dollar-for-dollar deductions of earned income from welfare benefits, especially for families with children. For example, the Manitoba Child Related Income Support Program (CRISP) provides a maximum nontaxable benefit of $30 per month per child ($360 per year) to families with a net annual income of less than $10,894 (in July 1987). Above this threshold, benefits are reduced by .25 for each additional $1.00 in earnings. In March 1987, some 9,083 families, about half of whom were lone parents, received benefits (Health and Welfare Canada 1989).

In Saskatchewan, the Family Income Plan (FIP) provides a nontaxable benefit of $1,200 per year for the first, second, and third children and $1,080 for any other children to families with annual earnings below $8,700 (excluding federal family allowances and child tax credits). In March 1987, nearly 50 percent of the 7,678 beneficiaries were lone parents.

In Quebec, families with at least one dependent child (including full-time students over 18) are eligible for the APPORT program (*Aide aux parents pour leurs revenus du travail*—aid to parents with earned income).[24] The amount awarded is calculated according to a complicated formula based on the number of children and adults in the family, the amount of earned income, and the cost of child care. Eligibility is based on income earned each month, and 75 percent of the estimated benefits are paid immediately to ensure that families receive the money when they need it and to reinforce the perceived link between work effort and benefits. This program, along with a special reduction of provincial taxes given to low- and middle-income families with dependent children, has the effect of lowering the real marginal tax rate from 75 percent to about 50 percent on earnings between $4,000 and the social assistance level (about $10,000 for a family of three). The marginal tax rates on earnings between the social assistance cutoff and the poverty line fell from about 65 percent to about 58 percent (Ruth Rose, with François Aubry 1988).[25] However, by December 1990 (nearly 3 years after APPORT was established), the program was used by less than half of the 44,000 families thought to be eligible for participation. About half of the current beneficiaries are lone parents.

The Ontario WIN (Work Incentives) Program has been in operation since 1981, serving single heads of families with children and handicapped or disabled persons. Benefits range from $150 to $240 a month (1987) for a sole-support parent. This amount is reduced by 50 percent of the income earned above $675 per month. A lone parent is also allowed to keep $100 of earnings plus $40 (less than the cost of a monthly transit pass in Toronto) for work-related expenses with no reduction in welfare or WIN benefits. Participants are also allowed to keep health benefits such as Ontario Health Insurance Premiums, prescription drugs, dental care, eyeglasses, and hearing aids. However, by 1987, only about 2 percent of the nearly 100,000 lone parents receiving general assistance were participating in the program (Ontario Ministry of Community and Social Services 1988: 272–275).

While earned-income supplements look good on paper and help alleviate some of the worst effects of dollar-for-dollar reductions in welfare benefits, they are not very generous, and the complexity of administering them results in their being used by only a fraction of their intended clientele.

DISCUSSION

Although tax and transfer policies helped reduce the incidence of poverty among lone-parent families in Canada during the 1980s, almost half of all lone mothers are still poor today (McFate, Smeeding, and Rainwater, this volume). Furthermore, high and rising levels of unemployment and recent cutbacks in social programs suggest that the situation of lone-mother families in Canada may worsen.

Until recently, there was an assumption that a woman's first duty was to her children. As a result, lone mothers were not expected to work. Rather, a combination of insurance-based widows' and orphans' benefits and income-tested social assistance benefits (which were often subject to "moral conduct" tests) provided support to poor families. None of these programs were ever very generous, and lone-mother families (and elderly widows) have always been at the bottom of the Canadian income distribution.

Today, lone mothers are no longer given the choice of making do with inadequate welfare benefits or working. During the last 10 to 15 years, social expectations have changed, and it is now widely held that women should earn their own living. This has led to attempts to convert welfare programs into "work-fare" programs. Unfortunately, the conversion is being attempted during a period of growing unemployment and stagnating wages, particularly for those at the bottom of the occupational structure.

If we are serious about reducing poverty among lone-mother families, then we must design policies to address three different problems. First, we must increase the capacity of lone mothers to support their families through paid work. Second, we must increase the contributions by noncustodial parents to the support of their children. Third, we must reform social policies that provide help to families with children; these include basic health and education programs, direct money transfers to families with children, and social-assistance and other income-tested programs.

Labor Market Policies

Helping lone mothers attain economic independence will require macroeconomic policies to promote full employment at decent wages and attack labor market discrimination against women. The reinforcement of employment and pay equity programs will be a necessary part of improving the labor market position of female workers. But lone mothers face specific handicaps on the labor market, too—in particular, they suffer because family responsibilities may interrupt their educational pursuits and work history. Improving access to higher educational opportunities and high-quality occupational training programs for lone mothers could help them overcome early educational deficits.

Paid parental leave is also crucial to helping lone parents mix work and family responsibilities. Paid leave is needed not only at the time of birth or adoption of a child; a certain number of days per year should be given throughout the time when children are young. Although budget constraints may prevent Canada from providing completely free childcare programs at this point, high-quality childcare for preschool and primary-school-aged children should be available without charge to families with incomes below the poverty line and with a partial subsidy to those with incomes just above this level. In Canada, this would require a rapid expansion of the number of licensed childcare spaces.

The Obligation of Both Parents to Help Support Their Children

Lone mothers typically get very little economic support from the absent father. Social policy should guarantee supplementary income to lone mothers to compensate for the fact that there is only one actual or potential wage earner in the family to support several people. It is scandalous that fathers take so little responsibility for supporting their children. The governments should enforce the regular payment of child support—without the custodial parent having to initiate court action.

If the noncustodial parent is unable to provide at least a minimal level of support or if the state cannot ensure payment, then government should guarantee the payment so that the children are not penalized. Such a system is preferable to welfare programs, which disrupt family life, and has already been extensively used in some Scandinavian countries.

General Social Policies

Although Canadian social policies provide much more protection from hardship than those operating in the United States—especially in the areas of healthcare and income support to families with children, Canada tends to rank fairly low in international comparisons that include European countries. Nonetheless, Canada's universal health and hospitalization insurance programs provide a basic measure of justice and prevent sickness from impoverishing groups who are otherwise self-sufficient. Universal, free primary and secondary education is also a great economic leveler, although it is much taken for granted.

Canada has experimented with a wide variety of tax and transfer programs for families with children, although the amount per child devoted to these programs is not overly generous. Recent federal reforms have targeted more benefits to low-income families and reduced benefits to middle- and upper-income families to achieve this end. Unfortunately, many provincial governments have reappropriated whatever federal increases/refunds were granted to welfare families by lowering their own support to poor families.

If the concern is to not only alleviate poverty but to prevent it as well, then universal family allowances and income-tested child tax credits that operate to benefit a fairly broad span of families are preferable both to tax exemptions that disproportionately benefit higher income families and to narrowly targeted, means-tested programs that contribute to "poverty traps" at the low end of the income ladder.

But even if all of the programs described previously were in place and working, a significant number of lone-parent families would probably need at least temporary income assistance. A number of guaranteed minimum income experiments and earned-income tax credits or allowances have been attempted in both Canada and the United States. Most economists are skeptical of the possibility of designing welfare programs that provide a decent standard of living without creating a disincentive to work (Burtless 1990). In general, policymakers want to maintain a substantial gap between welfare benefits and the minimum wage. Tax-back rates below 100 percent significantly increase the cost of income assistance and raise the number of potential beneficiaries whose income and marital status must be monitored on a monthly basis. In practice, earned income supplements have not been very generous, they tend to reach only a fraction of their targeted clientele, and they reduce only marginally the problems of high tax-back rates.

By ensuring lone mothers a minimum income through guaranteed child support and general family allowances, it would be possible to reduce the amount of income-tested benefits and thereby narrow the range of the "poverty trap." With a certain part of their income guaranteed, lone mothers with labor market earnings even as low $10,000 would be better off than on welfare. Two other policies should be made more accessible to low-income working families: special benefits (such as subsidized prescription drugs, glasses, and dental care) and targeted housing subsidies. This too would help eliminate the disincentives to work.

The Prognosis for Canadian Lone Mothers

Certain trends in the labor market lead us to fear that the circumstances of lone mothers in Canada will get worse before they get better. Job cutbacks in both public- and private-sector firms are occurring. Large firms are contracting out business to small firms that offer low wages and little job security. Increased international competition is likely to result in no growth or even job losses in the industries that employ large numbers of women—the garment industry, textiles, and footwear. As the computer revolution matures, other "female occupations" like data processing, office work, and bank telling are also declining. These changes will not help lone mothers already struggling in the labor market.

Unfortunately, over the last 10 to 15 years, federal and provincial governments have been cutting back on income transfer programs and public services. Income taxes have become much less progressive, and corporate taxes have declined. Regressive sales taxes at the federal and provincial levels have increased, and responsibility for funding services has been shifted down to municipalities, which must also rely on regressive property taxes for revenue. The result is greater social polarization and a shrinking middle class. The combined effect of rising taxation and cutbacks in programs for middle-income families is likely to jeopardize public support for social programs.

Rather than backing away from the "welfare state" as policymakers have been doing over the last 10 or 15 years, Canada needs to find new ways to invigorate it. Universal programs like health care and public insurance against unemployment, work-related accidents, illness, and disability were designed to maintain standards of living during a crisis and, therefore, to *prevent impoverishment*, not just palliate the effects of poverty. Similarly, paid parental leave, affordable quality childcare, and monetary support for families with children (with low or zero tax-back rates) are intended to provide these families with an adequate income while allowing parents, particularly lone mothers, to take good care of their children.

Rich countries like Canada and the United States can afford these programs if they fully use their resources. The key is a full-employment policy (with decent wages) that would not only provide jobs but also reinforce the tax base needed to finance social programs and mobilize the human resources required to provide social services.

APPENDIX A: DISCUSSION OF TERMS

Some Definitions

The definitions of a number of terms in the text are drawn from the 1986 Canadian census. According to the census, *"Lone parent* refers to a mother or a father, with no spouse present, living in a dwelling with one or more never-married children." Furthermore, "persons living common-law are considered, for census purposes, as now married, regardless of their legal marital status, and accordingly appear as a husband–wife family in most of the published tables."

Unless otherwise specified, data in this chapter refer to the *census family*, that is, "a husband and a wife (with or without children who have never married, regardless of age), or a lone parent of any marital status, with one or more children who have never married, regardless of age, living in the same dwelling."

The other definition used in Statistics Canada publications, notably for data on income, is that of an *economic family*, that is, a "group of individuals sharing a common dwelling unit and related by blood, marriage or adoption."

The term *children* here refers to "sons and daughters (including adopted children and stepchildren) who have never married, regardless of age, and are living in the same dwelling as their parent(s). Sons and daughters who have ever been married, regardless of their marital status at enumeration, are not considered as members of their parents' family, even though they are living in the same dwelling."

Non-family persons or men and women with "no family" are defined relative to a census family: "household members who do not belong to a census family. They may be *related* to the household reference person—Person 1 (e.g., brother-in-law, cousin, grandparent) or *unrelated* (e.g., lodger, roommate, employee). A person living alone is always a non-family person."

APPENDIX B: QUEBEC: A PRO-NATALIST POLICY

A French enclave of some 6 million people in a North American sea of close to 300 million, Quebec is particularly concerned by its exceedingly low birthrate, which fell from one of the highest in the Western world (four children per woman throughout the 1950s) to one of the lowest (1.4 children per woman in the mid-1980s) (Dionne 1989: 10). Accordingly, Quebec has introduced a series of pro-natalist policies that have been particularly favorable to two-parent families with at least three children and a wife at home. Lone-parent families, on the other hand, have lost ground.

In 1986, Quebec introduced an exemption of $1,870 for the first child under age 18 and $1,370 for additional children. Dependent children over age 18 who were full-time students were also eligible, and an additional exemption of $2,690 was granted for any child enrolled full-time in a postsecondary institution. (Previously, there had been only an $810 exemption for children 16 and 17 years of age and an exemption of $1,320 for full-time students.) All exemptions are indexed at the full rate of inflation, although the exemption for the second and succeeding children has been increased at a slightly higher rate in recent years.

At the same time, a married person's exemption was increased from $3,960 to $5,280 (the same level as the basic personal exemption), but the exemption for the first child in a lone-parent family was frozen at the $3,960 level until 1989, and part of this amount became conditional on the family not sharing lodging with any other adult.[26]

Quebec has had its own modest provincial family allowances since the mid-1970s, and, like the federal allowances paid in Quebec, they are weighted toward the third and subsequent children. In 1990, combined federal and provincial allowances amounted to $373 for the first child, $910 for the second child, $2,066 for the third child, and $3,260 for the fourth and subsequent children. Children between the ages of 12 and 17 get an additional $98 per year from the federal government, and those under age 7 get a special "allowance for young children."

The most spectacular measure introduced by the provincial government in 1989, however, was the "allocations de naissance," or birth allowances. By 1991, these allowances had risen to $500 for the first child born, $1,000 for the second child, and $7,500 (spread out over 5 years) for the third and subsequent children. Many municipalities and local credit unions have followed suit and offered their own baby bonuses to new parents. The province also provides a partial interest subsidy to young couples with children who are buying their first home.

Finally, in 1988 Quebec introduced a special tax reduction for families with children. In 1990, the maximum reduction was $1,180 for a two-parent family, $925 for a lone-parent family maintaining a separate lodging, and $710 for a lone-parent family living with another adult. A lone parent with two children who was not sharing lodging with any other adult and had an income below $18,600 in 1990 paid no provincial income tax.

ENDNOTES

1. The two territories, the Yukon and Northwest Territories, are a separate case. With huge geographical areas and very small populations, mostly Inuit and Amerindian, they have a special constitutional status. The cost of living is very high in the territories, their tax base is very low, and they receive special financial assistance from the federal government. Because of their unique situation, they are largely excluded from this discussion.

2. Under Canada's 1968 Divorce Act, and until 1986, two kinds of grounds for divorce were recognized: (1) matrimonial offense including "adultery, sodomy, bestiality, rape, homosexual acts, a form of marriage with another person, and mental or physical cruelty which renders continued cohabitation impossible"; and (2) marriage breakdown, including "prolonged imprisonment, gross drug addiction with no ex-

pectation of rehabilitation, lack of knowledge of the petitioner of the whereabouts of the respondent for at least three years . . . , having lived separate and apart for at least three years (five years if the deserting party petitions for divorce)" (Eichler 1988: 359–360).

In 1986, a new Divorce Act specified only one kind of grounds for divorce: marriage breakdown:

> [I]f: (a) the spouses have lived separate and apart for at least one year immediately preceding the determination of the divorce proceeding and were living separate and apart at the commencement of the proceeding; or (b) the spouse against whom the divorce proceeding is brought has, since celebration of the marriage, (i) committed adultery, or (ii) treated the other spouse with physical or mental cruelty of such a kind as to render intolerable the continued cohabitation of the spouses (Eichler 1988: 359–360).

Because divorce became easier, the numbers of divorces, particularly among younger or older couples without children, increased dramatically.

3. National Council on Social Welfare (1990b: 69).

4. Young males under age 25 also have relatively high poverty rates. In fact, any declines in poverty have occurred almost exclusively among older men and women (those aged 55 and over) as a result of improvements in income-tested transfer programs for this group.

5. This history is taken mainly from Dingledine (1981). The description of developments since 1980 is based on legislation adopted—in particular, Bill C-21, An Act to Amend the Unemployment Insurance Act and the Employment and Immigration Department and Commission Act, which took effect in November 1990.

6. The duration of benefits is a function of the number of weeks of insured employment during the previous years as well as the regional unemployment rate. For example, under the old law, in a region with an unemployment rate of 6 percent, a person needed 14 weeks of insured employment to qualify for 22 weeks of benefits. In 1991 that person would require 20 weeks to qualify for 17 weeks of benefits.

7. A 1984 study asked women whether they had interrupted their work activity for a year or more in order to meet family responsibilities. Over 60 percent of those aged 30 and over said they had done so once, and close to 20 percent said they had done so more than once (National Council on Social Welfare 1990b: 55).

8. Although lone-parent families with a male head earn a lower average income than do husband–wife families, it should be remembered that lone-parent families are also smaller on average. Other figures show that, in fact, male lone parents have as high an income, and in some years a higher income, than the male spouse in a husband–wife family.

9. Unless otherwise specified, all money amounts are given in Canadian dollars.

10. Canada spent only 0.57 percent of its gross national product (GNP) on employment promotion measures, compared with 1.86 percent of GNP in Sweden and 0.74 percent to 0.99 percent in France, Finland, West Germany, and the United Kingdom. In this respect, however, Canada did better than Australia, the United States, or Japan (Industry, Science and Technology Canada 1989: 32–43).

11. The most advanced pay equity law is found in Ontario. All public- and private-sector employers with more than 500 employees were required to develop and post a pay equity plan as of January 1, 1990, and to start paying adjusted salaries as of January 1, 1991, with adjustments occurring at a minimum rate of 1 percent per year. Private-sector employers with between 100 and 499 employees were to follow 1 year later and employers with between 10 and 99 employees in the following 2 years.

12. For infants and toddlers in particular, most provinces have emphasized family home care, which allows women to take children into their own homes under the supervision of a provincial agency or a private agency licensed by the provincial government. The agencies are supposed to ensure minimum safety standards as well as some training in child development for the childcare workers. They also provide backup caregivers in case of illness and handle the administrative work. Unfortunately, fewer and fewer women are willing to do this kind of work, which generally pays less than the minimum wage for a 10-hour day, without social insurance benefits or paid holidays or vacations.

13. For example, in 1984 New Brunswick provided a maximum subsidy of $11 per day for children aged 2 to 13 years old and $13 per day for those under age 2 to families with annual net incomes below $10,000–$11,500 (depending on the number of adults and children in the family). Above this threshold, the subsidy was reduced at a rate of 50¢ per $1 of additional income. At the other extreme, in some municipalities in Ontario, in 1984 a lone parent with one child and an income below $17,000 would have been eligible for a subsidy that covered the entire fee. For a two-parent family with two children, the comparable threshold was $23,000. On the other hand, the use of a needs test (as opposed to an income test) meant that the tax-back rate was 100 percent (Blain 1985: 166–231).

14. In principle, the federal government will subsidize only those parents who use nonprofit, childcare services that are licensed and supervised by the provincial government. However, some provinces have circumvented this limitation by administering their childcare services through the municipalities. The municipalities contract for childcare with commercial (for-profit) centers but claim the subsidy directly. Because the municipalities are a nonprofit, public agency, they are eligible. Other provinces have skirted this clause by using a needs rather than an income test. The net effect is that in some provinces, the federal government pays half of the cost of provincial expenditure on aid to low-income parents, while in others it pays considerably less (see Townson 1985: 1–37).

15. The Canada Labor Code governs employees of banks, interprovincial transportation and communication, and federal Crown corporations such as the post office. Civil servants and armed services personnel are covered under separate legislation.

16. Information on provincial and federal laws is taken from the Canadian Advisory Council on the Status of Women (1988). The information was compiled in April 1988 but may be out of date, because provincial governments are in the process of revising their labor standards acts, and unions are renegotiating their collective bargaining contracts to harmonize them with the new unemployment insurance benefits.

17. If the father takes the benefits, an additional 2-week waiting period without salary is imposed. In the case of adoption, either parent is eligible for 10 weeks of "childcare" benefits.

18. Almost all salaried employment in Canada is covered by unemployment insurance. A person must have worked at least 15 hours per week or earned at least 20 percent of the maximum insurable earnings to be covered.

19. Unless otherwise noted, the chronology is taken from Health and Welfare Canada (1985: 17–19).

20. According to the Health and Welfare Canada chronology (1985), this child tax credit was introduced in 1978 at a rate of $200 per child for families with net incomes below $18,000. However, it was not actually applied until the 1979 taxation year, at which time it had been indexed by 9 percent for an increase in the cost of living.

21. For a description of the creation and evolution of some of these programs, see Vaillancourt (1988). For a description of their current form, see Health and Welfare Canada, *Inventory of Income Security Programs in Canada, January 1988* (or subsequent years). See also National Council on Social Welfare (1987).

22. The initial "cap" was for 2 years, but in 1991 the government announced that it would be extended for an additional 2 years. The unilateral revision of a federal-provincial cost-sharing agreement with no forewarning was challenged in the courts by British Columbia. However, the Canadian Supreme Court has ruled in favor of the federal government.

23. In Saskatchewan the child must be under 1 year old; in Alberta, under 4 months old; in British Columbia, under 6 months old if there is only one child; and in Quebec, under 6 years of age (National Council on Social Welfare 1990a: 16).

24. From 1978 to 1988, the Quebec plan, called SUPRET (*Supplement to earned income*), also gave benefits to single persons and couples without children over age 30. Early evaluations of the program suggested that it did not reach large numbers of the targeted poor, because those persons with an annual income sufficiently low to qualify almost always received some other form of government transfers, which in effect canceled their potential SUPRET benefit. In addition, payments were made the year following that in which eligibility was established, which meant that people did not receive the money when they needed it and there was little perceived linkage between the level of benefits and work effort. The new program, APPORT, attempted to correct some of these problems, but only families with children are eligible.

25. The tax-back rates calculated before APPORT came into effect take into account the previously existing SUPRET program. Without either program, tax-back rates below the social assistance level are 100 percent for all practical purposes and between 35 percent and 40 percent for incomes between the social assistance and poverty levels. Tax-backs on childcare subsidies above the social assistance level would increase this rate an additional 25 percent.

26. In 1988, following the lead of the federal government, all exemptions were converted to nonrefundable tax credits at a rate of 20 percent, thus making them more equitable.

REFERENCES

Burtless, Gary. 1990. "The Economist's Lament: Public Assistance in America." *Journal of Economic Perspective* 4(1): 57–78.

Brouillette, Liliane, et al. 1990. *L'évolution de la situation économique des familles avec enfants au Canada et au Québec depuis 15 ans (The evolution of the economic situation of families with children in Canada and Quebec over the last 15 years).* Research Report 55. Montreal: University of Quebec at Montreal, Center for Research in Economic Policies.

Dandurand, Renée. 1987. "La monoparentalité au Québec: Aspects socio-historiques" ("Lone-Parent Families in Quebec: Some Socio-historical Aspects"). *International Review of Community Development* 18(58): 79–85.

Dionne, Claude. 1989. "L'évolution récente de la fécondité en Québec" ("The Recent Evolution of Fecundity in Quebec"). In *Dénatalité: des solutions (Falling Birth Rates: Some Solutions).* Quebec: Publications du Québec: 5–17.

Eichler, Margrit. 1988. *Families in Canada Today, Recent Changes and Their Policy Consequences,* 2nd ed. Toronto: Gage Educational Publishing.

Krashinsky, Michael. 1987. "The Cooke Report on Child Care: A Critique." *Canadian Public Policy* 13: 294–303.

Ouimet, Lise. 1989. "Les expériences fédérales en matiére de parité salariale: 1980–1988" ("Federal Experiences with Wage Parity: 1980–1988"). In *Équité en matiére de salaire et d'emploi, Dix-neuviéme colloque relations industrielles, 1988 (Wage and Employment Equity, Nineteenth Industrial Relations Colloquium, 1988).* Michel Brossard (ed.). Montreal: University of Montreal Press, 36–43.

Raymond, Myriam. 1988. *La vie maritale sous la Loi d'aide sociale (Marital Status Under the Act for Social Assistance).* Montréal: La Ligue des Droits et Libertés.

Rose, Ruth. 1987. "La nouvelle politique fiscale québécoise: Retour à la famille nucléaire?" ("The New Quebec Tax Policy: A Return to the Nuclear Family?"). *International Review of Community Development* 18/(58): 35–43.

———, with François Aubry. 1988. *Fiscalité et aide sociale: Pour une réforme juste et équitable (Taxation and Social Assistance: For a Fair and Equitable Reform).* Montreal: University of Quebec at Montreal, Services aux collectivités.

Schlesinger, Benjamin, ed. 1979. *One in Ten—The Single Parent in Canada.* Toronto: University of Toronto, Faculty of Education.

Sirard, Guylaine, et al. 1986. *Des méres seules, une étude sur la situation des femmes cheffes de famille monoparentale du Centre-Sud de Montréal (Mothers Alone—A Study of Lone Mothers in South Central Montreal).* Montreal: Le journal LA CRIEE.

Steel, Freda M. 1985. "The Role of the State in the Enforcement of Maintenance." In *Women, the Law and the Economy.* E. Diane Pask, Kathleen E. Mahoney, and Catherine A. Brown (eds.). Toronto: Butterworths.

Vaillancourt, Yves. 1988. *L'évolution des politiques sociales au Québec, 1940–1960 (The Evolution of Social Policies in Quebec, 1940–1960).* Montreal: University of Montreal Press.

Government of Canada Documents

An Act Respecting Employment Equity (Royal Assent, June 27, 1986).

Bill C-21, An Act to Amend the Unemployment Insurance Act and the Employment and Immigration Department and Commission Act, effective November 1990.

Blain, Christine. 1985. "Government Spending on Child Care in Canada." Background paper for *Report of the Task Force on Child Care*. Series 1: 166–231. Ottawa: Status of Women Canada.

Brown, Mona G., and Delia J. Power. 1985. "Child Care and Taxation in Canada: Who Pays?" Background paper for *Report of the Task Force on Child Care*. Series 1: 38–84. Ottawa: Status of Women Canada.

Canadian Advisory Council on the Status of Women. 1988. *Becoming a Parent*, Ottawa.

Canadian Charter of Rights and Freedom. 1982. *Status of Women*.

Canadian Labor Market and Productivity Centre. 1990. "Labor Market Trends." *Quarterly Labor Market Productivity Review* Fall: 12–17.

Dingledine, Gary. 1981. *A Chronology of Response: The Evolution of Unemployment Insurance from 1940 to 1980*. Ottawa: Supply and Services Canada.

Employment and Immigration Canada. 1989a. *Employment Equity Act, Annual Report*. Ottawa: Supply and Services Canada.

———. 1989b. *Success in the Works, A Policy Paper*. Ottawa.

Health and Welfare Canada. 1985. *Child and Elderly Benefits*, Consultation Paper by Jake Epp, Minister, Ottawa.

———. 1987. *Survivor Benefits Under the Canada Pension Plan*. Consultation Paper.

———. 1989. *Inventory of Income Security Programs in Canada, January 1988*. Ottawa.

Industry, Science and Technology Canada. 1989. *Adjusting to Win, Report of the Advisory Council on Adjustment* [also known as the *De Grandpré Report*]. Ottawa.

National Council on Social Welfare. 1987. *Welfare in Canada—The Tangled Safety Net*. Ottawa.

———. 1988. *Poverty Profile*. Ottawa.

———. 1990a. *Welfare Incomes, 1989*. Ottawa.

———. 1990b. *Women and Poverty Revisited*. Ottawa.

Report of the Royal Commission on the Status of Women in Canada. 1970. Ottawa: Information Canada [also known as the Bird Commission].

Report of the Task Force on Child Care. Status of Women Canada 1986. Ottawa: Supply and Services Canada.

Revenue Canada Taxation. 1989. *Taxation Statistics, 1989 Edition, Taxation Year 1987*. Ottawa.

Statistics Canada. 1990. *Women in Canada*, 2nd ed. Cat. no. 89–503, Ottawa.

Townson, Monica. 1985. "Financing Child Care Through the Canada Assistance Plan." In *Financing Child Care: Current Arrangements*. Background paper for Report of the Task Force on Child Care. Series 1: 1–37. Ottawa: Status of Women Canada.

Wilson, Michael H. 1989. *Budget '89, Budget Papers*. Ottawa: Minister of Finance 1989.

———. 1990. *The Budget February 20, 1990*. Ottawa: Minister of Finance.

———. 1991. *The Budget February 26, 1991*. Ottawa: Minister of Finance.

Government of Ontario Documents

Doherty, G. 1990. *Highlights Paper. Factors Related to Quality in Child Care: A Review of the Literature.* Toronto: Ontario Ministry of Community and Social Services, Child Care Branch.

Ontario Ministry of Community and Social Services. 1988. *Transitions, Report of the Social Assistance Review Committee.* Toronto: Queen's Printer for Ontario.

Pay Equity Commission, The. 1990. *Newsletter* 2 (22, February/March).

Government of Quebec Documents

Bellware, Jo-Ann, and Diane Charest. 1986. *Monoparentalité féminine et aide sociale* (Female lone parents and social assistance). Service des politiques et de la recherche en sécurité du revenu. Quebec: Les Publications du Québec.

De Gagné, C., and M. Gagné. 1988. *Garderies à but lucratif et garderies sans but lucratif subventionnés . . . vers une évaluation de la qualité (For-Profit and Nonprofit Subsidized Day Care Centres . . . Toward an Evaluation of Quality).* Working paper. Montreal: Office des services de garde à l'enfance.

Guide descriptive des programmes de sécurité du revenu, édition 1990 (Guide to Income Security Programs, 1990 Edition) 1990. Quebec: Les Publications du Quebec.

Lévesque, Gérard D. 1991. *Budget 1991.* Quebec: Minister of Finance.

Chapter 10

SINGLE-MOTHER FAMILIES
AND SOCIAL POLICY:
LESSONS FOR THE UNITED STATES
FROM CANADA, FRANCE, AND SWEDEN

Sara McLanahan and Irwin Garfinkel

THE DEBATE over policy toward single mothers takes place in the context of a more general debate over who shall pay the social and economic costs of raising children. This debate is taking place on both a private and public front. On the private front, the controversy is between mothers and fathers; the issue is how to distribute child-rearing obligations in a way that is equitable to both sexes. On the public front, the controversy is between society and parents; the issue is how much of the costs of raising a child should be borne by the government and how much should be borne by parents.

The emergence of this debate during the past two decades is due in large part to changes in women's roles and marital stability. As Sheila Kamerman points out in Chapter 6 in this volume, the labor force participation rate of mothers has increased dramatically since 1960, which, in turn, has reduced the amount of time mothers have available for taking care of children. In 1950 less than 30 percent of married women with school age children in the United States were working outside the home. By 1990, the percentage was 73, about two and a half times as great (U.S. Department of Labor 1985).

At the same time, increases in marital instability and single parenthood have reduced the amount of time children spend with their fathers and the amount of money fathers contribute to their children's support. With regard to time, less than a third of the children who live in single-mother families see their fathers on a weekly basis, whereas children who live with both parents see their fathers on a daily basis. With regard to money, married fathers contribute between 20 and 25 percent of their income to support their children, whereas nonresident fathers contribute less than 10 percent.[1] Overall, these changes tend to decrease the resources available to children as a whole and increase the responsibilities of mothers vis-à-vis fathers. In response, child welfare advocates, policy analysts, and feminists have become increasingly critical of the

/   367

existing system insofar as it simultaneously discriminates against women and impoverishes children.

The decline in children's access to parental resources and the disparity between mothers' and fathers' contribution to children are highlighted in the mother-only family. Whereas in two-parent families the loss of the mother's time is more or less offset by the gain in economic resources, in single-mother families there is an absolute loss of both parents' time as well as a loss of fathers' economic support. Not surprisingly, the children who grow up in single-mother families are disproportionately poor, and many suffer long-term disadvantages. Their educational attainment is lower; their earnings are lower; they are more likely to become single parents themselves, either through out-of-wedlock births or divorce; and they are more likely to be dependent on the government for income support (McLanahan and Booth 1989).

Many of the disadvantages associated with growing up in a mother-only family can be traced to the economic insecurity and poverty of these families. As much as 50 percent of the difference in children's educational attainment is due to differences in family income (McLanahan 1985). Government can reduce these problems by strengthening the labor market opportunities and earnings of single mothers, by forcing nonresident fathers to provide more economic support to their families, and by supplementing the incomes of single mothers via government transfers.

Reducing poverty and economic insecurity in single-mother families will clearly make children better off. But making single parenthood more attractive may also increase the prevalence of such families. The first policy dilemma faced by U.S. policymakers is whether to minimize prevalence or economic insecurity of mother-only families.

Increasing the public's share of the costs of child rearing may also increase dependence on government. Many people believe this is undesirable—for taxpayers and perhaps for mothers and their children. Because all people depend on government for some things (e.g., education, social security, defense, etc.), the concern over dependency is obviously limited to certain types of dependency. In particular, most Americans are concerned about dependency if it is too high, if it lasts too long, and if it occurs among individuals who are expected to be self-sufficient. Here we define a single mother as dependent if she receives over 50 percent of her income from government transfers. Given the high value placed on self-reliance and independence in our society, heavy, long-term dependence on public assistance isolates and stigmatizes recipients. The trade-off between providing public support for single mothers and reducing dependence on government support is the second dilemma facing U.S. policymakers.[2]

In the United States, the dilemma over whether to minimize the poverty and insecurity of lone-mother families or to minimize their prevalence and dependency has generally been resolved in favor of reducing the latter. To minimize costs and discourage both the formation of mother-only families and dependence on government, we restrict eligibility for the bulk of benefits to mothers who are poor, and we provide very low levels of assistance. As a result, about half of all single mothers derive very little help from government. Among the less fortunate half of single mothers who rely heavily on public assistance, nearly all remain below the poverty line.

A key question facing U.S. policymakers in the 1990s is whether we can devise a better system for aiding single mothers than the one we now have, a system that does a better job of reducing poverty and economic insecurity in mother-only families without increasing their prevalence and dependence. Cross-national comparisons are an excellent means of gaining insight into this question, because all industrialized countries have been experiencing a growth in mother-only families, and all have had to deal with the issues of "Who shall pay?" and whether to minimize economic insecurity or prevalence and dependence. The chapters presented in this volume allow us to examine the Swedish, Canadian, and French systems in considerable detail with an eye for identifying particular lessons for U.S. policymakers.

The remainder of the chapter is divided into three sections. The first section presents quantitative estimates of how well single-mother families are doing in Canada, France, Sweden, and the United States. We look not only at the relative poverty and inequality of single mothers in different countries but also at the role of government in reducing poverty. We also present data on the relative prevalence of single parenthood and dependence on government. The analysis allows us to address the question of whether government transfers inevitably increase prevalence and dependence or whether some countries do a better job than others at minimizing both poverty and prevalence/dependence.

The second section of the chapter discusses key policy lessons—both positive and negative—that can be drawn from the comparisons among U.S., Canadian, French, and Swedish policy toward single mothers. The discussion is designed to identify those areas in which the countries differ and those areas in which their differences might be related to differences in poverty, prevalence, and dependence. We conclude that the major differences between the U.S. system and that of more successful countries, that is, Sweden and France, are (1) the U.S. system's lack of subsidized childcare, (2) its heavy reliance on means-tested as opposed to universal benefits, and (3) its lack of employment policies that "make work pay" for mothers. We conclude that the U.S. system forces single mothers to choose between two alternatives, neither of which is particularly attractive: total dependence on government, poverty level incomes, and time for children *or* little to no support from government, slightly higher than poverty level incomes, and very little time for children. The final section of the chapter discusses the need for additional information.

SOCIAL POLICY AND WELL-BEING

How well are single mothers doing in different countries, and what is their relative status vis-à-vis two-parent families? Table 10.1 presents two measures of single mother's well-being: single-mother's family income as a percentage of

Table 10.1 / Relative Economic Well-Being of Single-Mother Families in Four Countries

Country	Income as a Percentage of Two-Parent Family Income	Percent Living Above One-Half the Median Income
Canada	.52	.55
France	.74	.84
Sweden	.87	.94
United States	.47	.47

SOURCES: The first indicator is taken from Yin-Ling Irene Wong, Irwin Garfinkel, and Sara McLanahan, "Single Mother Families in Eight Countries: Economic Status and Social Policy," Institute for Research on Poverty, October 1991. The second indicator is taken from McFate, Smeeding, and Rainwater, Chapter 1 in this volume.

two-parent family income (column 1), and the percent of single-mother families living above the poverty line (column 2). The latter is the inverse of the poverty rate. Poverty is defined as having an income less than one-half of the median family income. Both measures compare the incomes of single-mother families to a measure of average family income in the country. The first encompasses the entire income distribution of single mothers, whereas the second focuses on the bottom of the distribution.

Neither of the measures is a perfect indicator of well-being. There is much in life besides income that contributes to well-being. Health is a good example.[3] Income is not even a perfect measure of economic well-being. Property in general, and home ownership in particular, may play a significant role.[4] Nonetheless, income is a very important component of well-being. Therefore, while not perfect, these are good indicators.

The story that emerges from the well-being measures is clear and simple. Single mothers in the United States are the worst off, single mothers in Canada fare a bit better, and single mothers in France and Sweden are the best off. The magnitudes of the differences between the United States and France and Sweden are startling. Whereas the average income of single mothers in the United States is less than half the average two-parent family income, in France their average income is nearly three-fourths that of couples, and in Sweden it is close to nine-tenths. Similarly, whereas only 47 percent of single mothers in the United States live above poverty, in France and Sweden the numbers are 84 percent and 94 percent, respectively.

Of course, part of the difference in the relative position of single mothers across countries may be attributable to differences in demographic characteristics. Very young single mothers have less earnings capacity. Large numbers of children both inhibit the utilization of earnings capacity and increase the family's need. Indeed, differences in the age of the mother and the number of children account for 19 percent of the difference between France and the United

States and 28 percent of the difference between Sweden and the United States in the relative incomes of single mothers as compared with two-parent families (Wong, Garfinkel, and McLanahan 1991). These are hardly negligible figures. But they still leave the bulk of the differences unaccounted for.

What is the role of government in accounting for the relative well-being of single mothers in France and Sweden? To what extent is government responsible for reducing economic insecurity and does this come at a cost of prevalence and dependence? Table 10.2 provides some preliminary answers to these questions.

Columns 1 and 2 report pretransfer poverty rates and the percentage reduction in pretransfer poverty due to government transfers in each of the four countries. Column 3 reports the prevalence of single-mother families in each country, and column 4 reports dependence on government. We should point out that in-kind transfers such as childcare and health care are not counted in either the poverty reduction measure or the dependence measure. This omission clearly understates transfers and degree of dependence of single mothers in Sweden and in France. Column 5 of Table 10.2 reports labor force participation rates for single mothers in each of the countries. These figures provide us with another estimate of the extent to which single mothers are "independent," that is, the extent to which they rely on market income.

The most important story conveyed by these data is also relatively simple and clear. The biggest differences across countries are in the effectiveness of government transfers in reducing poverty (column 2). The U.S. income transfer system reduces pretransfer poverty by only 5 percent, Canada reduces pretransfer poverty by 19 percent, France by 59 percent, and Sweden by 81 percent.

Table 10.2 / The Effects of Welfare State Transfers on Poverty, Prevalence, and Dependence

	Percent				
Country	Pretransfer Poverty	Reduction in Poverty	Prevalence[a]	Dependence	Labor Force Participation
Canada	60	19	13	39	65
France	38	59	12	25	70
Sweden	29	81	12	33	83
United States	56	5	22	38	71

SOURCES: Pretransfer poverty rates and reduction in poverty are taken from Table 7 and dependency ratios are taken from Table 10 of Timothy M. Smeeding and Lee Rainwater, "Cross-National Trends in Income Poverty and Dependency: The Evidence for Young Adults in the Eighties," Aug. 7, 1991 draft; the prevalence figures are taken from the country chapters; and the labor force participation rates are taken from Yin-Ling Irene Wong, Irwin Garfinkel, and Sara McLanahan, "Single Mother Families in Eight Countries: Economic Status and Social Policy," Institute for Research on Poverty, October 1991.

[a]The prevalence figures in Canada and the United States refer to the percentage of families with children that are headed by single mothers, while the figures for France and Sweden refer to the percentages of all children who live in families headed by single mothers.

Thus, there is no mystery as to why single-mother families do so much better in Sweden and France. Clearly, government plays a major role in their relative success.

It is important to keep in mind that *pretransfer* poverty rates are also effected by social policy. For example, column 1 indicates that single mothers in France and Sweden are much better off than their counterparts in the United States and Canada even before government transfers are counted. This is due in part to very generous childcare policies in France and Sweden, which are not counted in the data on government transfers, but which encourage work, and also to labor market policies such as full employment and minimum wages. Each of these policies will be discussed in more detail below. Note also that pretransfer poverty rates in Canada are higher than in the United States. This explains why even though government transfers are more generous in Canada as compared with the United States, the well-being of single mothers in the two countries is very similar. The higher levels of pretransfer poverty in Canada could be due either to lower earnings of single mothers or less adequate private child support.

Columns 3–5 in Table 10.2 present data on the prevalence of single mothers and their dependence on government. The first point to mention is that the proportions of single-mother families in Canada, France, and Sweden are all lower than in the United States—13 percent, 12 percent, and 12 percent vis-à-vis 22 percent. That Sweden has a lower proportion of single-parent families than the United States may come as a surprise to many. As Siv Gustafsson points out (Chapter 8, this volume), however, this is because of the confusion between marital status and residence patterns. Children who live with unmarried mothers are sometimes included in the Swedish count of single-mother families. About half of these children, however, are living with their natural fathers and, therefore, should be counted as two-parent families. The figures in column 3 clearly belie the argument that the high prevalence of single parenthood in the United States is attributable to overly generous aid. Rather, the international comparison suggests that even large increases in the generosity of provision will have only small effects on the prevalence of single parenthood.

This inference from the cross-national data is consistent with the empirical research that has been carried out during the past two decades on the effect of income transfers on the growth of mother-only families in the United States. Compared with other factors such as women's greater economic independence, the decline in earnings of low-skilled men, and shifts in social norms for divorce and out-of-wedlock birth, government benefits account for a very small portion of the growth of mother-only families since 1940 (Garfinkel and McLanahan 1986).

Similarly, there is not a close correspondence between generosity and dependence. Note that the dependency ratios in Sweden and France are actually lower than the dependency ratios in the United States and Canada. As noted above, these ratios probably understate the degree of dependence on government in France and Sweden, because they do not include childcare transfers. Yet, labor force participation rates for single mothers (column 5) are consistent with the dependency ratios, suggesting that single mothers in France and Sweden contribute a substantial amount to the support of their children and are just as work-oriented as single mothers in the United States despite the greater generosity of their governments. That the French and Swedish income transfer systems do much more than the United States to reduce pretransfer poverty (column 2), and yet have substantially lower prevalence and somewhat lower dependence, suggests that the United States could be doing more to simultaneously reduce poverty, prevalence, and dependence.

LESSONS FROM EUROPE AND CANADA

Single mothers in the United States have substantially higher poverty rates than single mothers in Sweden, France, and, to a lesser extent, Canada. In previous work we have argued that the higher poverty rate of single mothers vis à vis other groups in the United States is due to three factors: meager government support, low earnings of mothers, and lack of child support from nonresident fathers. If income in any or all of these domains were increased, poverty rates of single mothers in the United States would be substantially lower. We believe that the chapters on Sweden, France, and Canada contain a number of important lessons for U.S. policymakers in each of these three areas: public support, mothers' earnings, and private child support. While these lessons cannot tell U.S. policymakers exactly what to do—policy decisions must ultimately reflect choices among values, and U.S. values will always be somewhat unique—they can teach us something about the consequences of alternative choices.

The most important *general lesson* that comes out of the readings is that France and Sweden do a much better job than the United States not only in reducing poverty but also in minimizing dependence and prevalence. Canada does a little better than the United States but not nearly as well as the European countries. We believe the secret to success in the two European countries lies in an interaction between two sets of policies: a heavy investment in universal benefits accompanied by a heavy investment in policies that promote work. Whereas in Sweden and France the general strategy is for single mothers to work *and* receive public transfers, in the United States it is *either* to work *or* to receive benefits. This combining of work and public support is not a matter of making income-tested benefits more generous but rather of restructuring public benefits so that "work pays" and "work and family go together." The following lessons elaborate briefly.

LESSON 1

The three other countries examined here go well beyond the United States in terms of socializing the cost of raising children. France, Sweden, and Canada all provide free medical care for all children and child allowances. France and Sweden also provide respectively modest and quite generous parental leaves and advanced child support maintenance. And, most important, we suspect, both Sweden and France provide very generous publicly financed and provided childcare.

Unfortunately, comparable data on each country's expenditures on children, let alone on the degree to which each country has socialized the costs of child rearing, is not currently available. Thus, for the moment, we are unable to measure exactly the degree to which the countries differ in total, public, and private expenditures on children. Ironically, given how important we hypothesize it to be, the biggest omission is comparative data on national public and private expenditures on childcare. Neither the OECD data nor the comparative expenditure studies by O'Higgins (1988) and Kamerman and Kahn (1991) provide such data.[5]

Despite the inadequacy of existing data, the O'Higgins and Kamerman-Kahn studies reinforce our reading of the four country studies: Canada spends marginally more on children than the United States, while France and Sweden spend much more than the United States on children. According to Kamerman and Kahn, for example, family transfers per child up to age 15 equaled $244 in the United States, $318 in Canada, $808 in Sweden, and $1,305 in France. Government social expenditures as a percentage of gross domestic product in the four countries were equal to 18, 23, 32, and 34, respectively.

Thus, based on the papers and other evidence, we conclude that compared with U.S. social policy, Canadian social policy assigns somewhat greater responsibility to the government vis-à-vis either parent in providing for the economic costs of rearing children, whereas Swedish and French policy assign quite a bit more responsibility to government. Recall from the previous section that compared with single mothers in the United States, Canadian single mothers fare somewhat better, French single mothers fare much better, and Swedish single mothers fare even somewhat better than the French.

The first lesson seems pretty obvious. Single mothers and their children do well to the extent that the public bears an appreciable share of the costs of child rearing. This lesson not only conforms to the economist's maxim of "There is no such thing as a free lunch" but suggests as well that social policy works.

LESSON 2

Compared with the United States, the European countries and Canada spend a greater proportion of their child welfare budget on universal as opposed to income-tested programs. Universal programs make all single mothers a little dependent on government, whereas income-tested programs make a large minority of single mothers nearly 100 percent dependent.

For example, whereas the other countries provide health insurance to all children, the United States has Medicaid, an income-tested program that covers only poor children. Similarly, whereas other countries have a child allowance that is available to all children, the United States has food stamps available only to poor children. Using the LIS data, we find that income-tested benefits account for about 90 percent of U.S. transfers, and for about 60, 55, and 45 percent in Canada, France, and Sweden, respectively (Wong, Garfinkel, and McLanahan 1991). These data omit health insurance and childcare benefits and thereby understate the real differences between the United States and the other countries with respect to reliance upon income-tested benefits. On the other hand, they also omit some tax relief benefits, such as the childcare tax credit and the child deduction in the United States, which overstate the real differences. On balance, we feel pretty confident that more comprehensive measures would not change the qualitative picture conveyed by the LIS data: The United States relies much more heavily upon income-tested benefits than Canada, France, and Sweden.

Heavy reliance on welfare programs both increases dependence among single mothers and fails to reduce poverty. Dependence is increased because single mothers must forego income from other sources in order to receive public assistance. In effect, high levels of dependence are a condition for receipt of government support. Moreover, because other benefits such as health insurance are linked to welfare receipt, many single mothers are forced to stay on welfare in order to ensure that their children have access to healthcare.

Not only does U.S. welfare policy encourage dependency, it does a poor job of reducing poverty, as noted in Table 10.2 earlier. This is no accident. Because income-tested programs encourage dependence, and because too much dependence is a bad thing for everyone, policymakers must worry about negative incentives. Therefore, they keep benefits low in order to make dependence less attractive. Conservatives support income testing because they want families to be entirely independent of government. Many liberals support income testing because they want to target benefits on the most needy. The European countries provide a very different example. In the context of making a much greater commitment to children, they maintain a set of income-tested programs but add on top of that a set of generous universal programs.

LESSON 3

French and Swedish policies promote work among all single mothers, whereas U.S. and Canadian policies are ambivalent about whether mothers should work. This point is critical insofar as we believe that differences in labor supply and the returns to work explain a great deal of the difference in single mothers' well-being across these four countries. We also believe that work policy is the key to transcending the dilemma between economic well-being and dependence. Mothers who work are, almost by definition, not dependent on government for more than half of their income. Thus, money spent to promote work is money spent toward reducing dependence. This is quite different from the usual way of framing the problem: to spend money and create dependence or to not spend money and reduce dependence. France and Sweden both spend more, but their investments promote independence as well as reducing poverty.

Childcare Policy

Of all the work-related policies, childcare is probably the most important. Under childcare we would include both parental leave policy, which allows mothers (or parents) to care for infant children in the home, and childcare provided outside the home. In France and Sweden excellent institutional childcare is available to parents from all income classes, and the bulk of the cost is paid for via taxes. The Swedish childcare subsidy for each child is twice as large as the combined value of the Swedish child allowance, housing allowance, and advanced maintenance payment (Garfinkel and Sorenson 1982). Based on the Lefaucheur chapter, we would guess that the French childcare system is of equally high quality. Free childcare increases the net, after expenses, wage rate of mothers both by eliminating a major employment expense and by increasing the demand for female labor.

Childcare policy in Sweden and France contains a number of lessons that are important to U.S. policymakers. First, by increasing work and wages, generous provision of childcare transcends the dilemma between reducing poverty and reducing dependence. Because childcare subsidies complement rather than substitute for earnings, generous government support in Sweden and France does not lead to high levels of dependence on government. Mothers who make the greatest use of the subsidy will always have an independent source of income. Childcare policy also reduces long-term dependence insofar as single mothers who work while raising their children are in a position to support themselves after their children have grown.

Second, paid maternity or parental leave reinforces work in the long run—by making previous labor force attachment a condition for eligibility and by limiting eligibility for the benefit to a short period of time—even as it encourages mothers to remain at home to provide personal care during infancy. Current U.S. policy results in a bimodal distribution of work experience in which some mothers work continuously and others work very little. The French and Swedish cases illustrate a third alternative—combining work and care for children. The notion that promoting work *and* family is superior to promoting work alone may not sit well with some feminists in the United States who have been reluctant to acknowledge that family-based care for infants is superior to outside care. Their position reflects the fact that in the United States, there is still considerable debate over whether or not mothers should work outside the home, with many conservatives arguing that mothers' employment is harmful to children. In defending women's right to work, many feminists have taken the position that mothers' employment has *no* negative consequences for children, even during infancy. Unfortunately, this position undermines the argument for parental leave, because it undermines advocates ability to argue that parental leave is in children's interest. As noted above, the French and Swedish examples suggest that rather than promoting domesticity, allowing women to combine family and work promotes women's employment over the long run. On this point, it is worthwhile noting that while Swedish mothers are more likely than U.S. mothers to stay at home during the first year after the birth of a child, they are more likely to work outside the home once that child reaches age 2.

Fourth, the French and Swedish childcare policy teaches us that childcare is in part an extension downward in age-of-education policy. By providing high-quality care to all their children and by using childcare centers to screen and identify early childhood problems, France and Sweden go a long way toward reducing inequality and increasing social and economic mobility among their children. The United States was once the leader in free education, and there is considerable evidence that programs such as Head Start have positive cost/benefit ratios. Yet we remain reluctant to make a major public commitment to provide good childcare for all of our nation's children.

Finally, the French and Swedish experiences suggest that expanding child-care services not only reduces the costs of working for single mothers but may also increase the demand for women workers. Since women are the primary childcare workers, socializing childcare provides jobs for women, including single mothers. While the conference papers do not provide direct evidence of this potential benefit, the fact that Sweden has a large public sector and the fact that Swedish women are disproportionately employed in public sector jobs suggests that the "jobs creation" benefit of publicly provided childcare may be substantial. The job creation benefits that may accrue from socialized childcare should be pursued in future research.

Making Work Pay

In addition to active childcare policies, the two European countries do a lot to enhance the earnings of mothers who work outside the home. In France, the minimum wage is equal to 55 percent of average male earnings. The comparable figure for the United States is under 40 percent.[6] The ratio of female to male wage rates in Sweden is the highest in the Western world—78 percent (McLanahan, Casper, and Sorenson). This is achieved in part through a general wage solidarity policy that results in one of the most egalitarian wage distributions in Western Europe. As was the case with childcare policy, wage enhancement policy encourages work and discourages dependence. Nonincome-tested benefits also supplement rather than replace earnings. For example, among working single mothers, family allowances in France raise income by 18 percent.[7]

The Earned Income Tax Credit is the major earnings subsidy available to working single mothers in the United States. The credit has recently been expanded, and by 1996 it will add as much as $3200 to the earnings of poor or near poor single mothers. While the benefit is income-tested, the break-even point is nearly twice as high as the U.S. poverty line for a single mother with two children. Consequently, the tax credit represents a substantial earnings supplement and work incentive for poor single mothers.

Sweden also promotes work by directly employing a large proportion of single mothers in public sector jobs. As noted earlier, childcare is an example of how socializing domestic production increases women's earnings not only by reducing the costs of working but also by increasing the demand for women workers. Here we would offer one note of caution. While the expansion of public-sector jobs makes it easier for government to keep women's wages high and allow for flexible work schedules, it also encourages occupational segregation. As Gustafsson notes in Chapter 8 of this volume, Sweden has the highest rates of occupational segregation of all countries. Due to recent declines in productivity and increases in unemployment, Swedish employment policy has now come under attack. Whether or not a government-based strategy of wage enhancement can be sustained during hard times is another issue that deserves monitoring.

Apart from political opposition to employment policy, it is not clear whether encouraging high levels of occupational segregation can lead to gender equality in the long run. While differences in economic well-being can clearly be reduced, the Swedish system appears to have institutionalized a gender-based division of labor that encourages women to work part-time and be responsible for children while men pursue high-status jobs in the private sector. In contrast, U.S. women have made some progress during the past decade in closing the wage gap with men and in breaking down occupational segregation. They have done this by entering the private market as well as the public sector, which in the long run may lead to great equality between the sexes. Of course, their advance has been achieved under a system that forces women to choose between family and work. What we don't know is whether a market-based strategy of achieving gender equity is consistent with a strategy that allows mothers to combine work and family. This is a key question for the 1990s.

With respect to other approaches to wage enhancement for single mothers, policies such as pay equity, affirmative action to attack occupational segregation, equal pay for equal work, and comparable worth as pursued in Canada and the United States seem to have had less effect on the economic status of single mothers (and we would guess, women in general) than the other policies we have identified here.

Finally, in addition to childcare policy and wage enhancement policies, France's *time-limited* welfare benefits for single mothers are another way of sending a clear message about work expectations. Time-limiting benefits, along with other changes in the welfare system, have been proposed by the Clinton Administration as a way of transcending the poverty dependence dilemma in the United States (see Garfinkel and McLanahan 1986; Ellwood 1989). Again, it is worth emphasizing that time limits alone will not reduce poverty among single mothers because many mothers have very low earnings capacity and would be poor even if they worked full-time. As the Swedish and French examples show, societies that want and expect single mothers to work outside the home must ensure that "work pays" and that children are cared for while mothers are out of the home.

The lesson about the importance of clear expectations for and concomitant support of work among single mothers must be qualified by an alternative example that is not represented in the four country chapters. Our own research indicates that single-mother families in Great Britain fare about as well as those in France. Yet, unlike France and Sweden, Great Britain does not encourage single mothers to work, and, not surprisingly, most single mothers do not work in the United Kingdom. Instead, Great Britain increases the incomes of single-mother families by providing much higher public transfers and by enforcing private child support. Thus, it is clear that work is not the only solution to reducing poverty among single mothers. If a society is willing to support single mothers to stay at home and care for their children, it can do so simply by making up the difference between private child support and the poverty line. Of course, this greatly increases single mothers' dependence on government.

We doubt that the British model is applicable to the United States for several reasons. First, most taxpayers in the United States do not like our current system of public assistance, and most believe that families receiving welfare are not doing enough to contribute to their own support. This applies to the contribution of single mothers on welfare as well as to the commitment of nonresident fathers. In short, most Americans believe that the present distribution of the costs of children among low-income families puts too much of the burden on the public and too little on the parents. While the American dislike of welfare is often attributed to racism and lack of compassion, there is a simpler and more compelling explanation. Americans place a very high value on independence and self-sufficiency, which means that they place a high value on work. Recent trends in women's labor force participation and the fact that a majority of mothers work outside the home have only increased the emphasis on women's independence and the expectation that women will help support their families. It is hard to envision garnering political support for a social policy that encourages single mothers to remain outside the labor force when married mothers are entering the labor force in increasing numbers every year. Such a policy would be viewed as *not* in children's best interest or in mothers' interest by most policymakers.

LESSON 4

The first three lessons described earlier point to the fact that France and Sweden have socialized more of the cost of raising children than either the United States or Canada. While the lessons suggest that single mothers in the United States could be doing more to help support their families, they also indicate that the U.S. government could be doing much more to help them become independent and at the same time promote economic security. The final lesson has to do with private child support and the distribution of child-raising costs between mothers and fathers.

Although the data in the foreign papers are fragmentary, in conjunction with other data, they suggest pretty clearly that the higher economic status of single mothers in Canada, France, and Sweden is *not* attributable to superior enforcement of private child support. In Canada, for example, only 58 percent and 68 percent of divorced mothers in Quebec and Alberta had child support awards; in France, the proportion is 66 percent. In the United States, the proportion is over 80 percent. Furthermore, the LIS data indicate that child support received by single mothers in both France and the United States is about 9 percent of the mean income of two-parent families (Wong, Garfinkel, and McLanahan 1991). Although Sweden clearly does a superior job in establishing paternity— over 90 percent of out-of-wedlock births compared with less than 40 percent in the United States—it is not clear how much support the Swedes actually collect (Nichols-Casebolt and Garfinkel 1991; Garfinkel and Sorenson 1982).[8] Gustafsson notes that the proportion of the advanced maintenance payments that are recovered via private support payments declined from 100 percent in 1974 to only 46 percent in 1981 and that in part this was due to a decline in private payments (Gustafsson, this volume). Quite clearly, the greatest advantage single mothers in Sweden derive from child support comes from their advanced maintenance system. Similarly, estimates for the United States suggest that a publicly assured child support benefit—the U.S. term for advanced maintenance—could substantially reduce poverty (Meyer, Garfinkel, Oellerich, and Robins 1992).

On the other hand, two elements of our research indicate that private support can make an important difference. First, as noted earlier, cross-national comparisons that include Great Britain suggest that single mothers there fare better than their counterparts in the United States at least in part because of much higher private transfers—alimony and child support. Similarly, microsimulations suggest that the economic status of single mothers in the United States could be raised appreciably through improved enforcement of private child support. For example, the poverty gap in the United States would be reduced by 25 percent if nonresident fathers paid as much child support as they should according to child-support guidelines (Oellerich, Garfinkel, and Robins 1991).

FINAL QUESTIONS

The chapters on the two European countries and Canada contain many useful insights for U.S. policymakers concerned with improving the economic security of single mothers and their children. They also leave some questions unanswered, questions that we would like to see pursued in the future.

First, we should begin by noting that a comparison of four selected countries is always somewhat precarious. Here, for example, we find a strong correspondence among countries that promote work among single mothers and countries with low relative poverty rates for single mothers. And yet we know from other sources that single mothers in the United Kingdom do as well as mothers in France, even though Great Britain does not promote work, and even though most single mothers in the United Kingdom do not work outside the home. While we do not believe that the U.K. example nullifies the importance of the Swedish and French examples for U.S. policymakers, it does suggest that the relationship between adequate income support and promoting work among lone mothers may not be as simple as we imply. At a minimum, we need information on other countries that promote work if only to help identify the conditions under which work reduces economic insecurity.

Second, with regard to the three countries examined here, we would like more information on overall levels of public spending on children, including cash transfers as well as in-kind transfers such as childcare, health/medical care, and education/training, including elementary and secondary education. Such information would be very useful in helping to determine absolute levels of public spending as well as the distribution of costs between parents and society. To complete this picture, we also need information on the prevalence and amount of private child support payments in each country, including support for children born out-of-marriage as well as for children born in-marriage. What percent of nonresident fathers pay support to their children? What is the average value of child support awards?

Finally, we would like to know what happens when a single mothers lacks education or motivation to work and yet is physically capable of working. What types and level of public assistance are available to such mothers in each of the countries? The chapters on French and Swedish policy present a vivid picture of the benefit of work for single mothers in these countries, but they do not tell us very much about the "costs" of not working. As the United States intensifies its efforts to move welfare mothers into work and training programs, it would be very helpful to know more about the relative efficacy of using the "stick versus the carrot" to promote work and independence.

Finally, reducing economic insecurity *without* increasing dependence on government means placing a greater burden on parents. It means requiring nonresident fathers to pay more child support and requiring single mothers to work more hours outside the home. And this, in turn, gives rise to a new question: Will placing a greater burden on parents increase or reduce child well-being in the long run? Here there are two concerns. The first has to do with the consequences associated with increasing fathers' economic responsibility. Some analysts fear that forcing fathers to pay more support may increase parental conflict and thereby reduce child well-being. The key issue is whether the gains associated with greater economic security will outweigh the psychological costs associated with greater potential parental conflict. The second concern has to do with the consequences associated with mothers' employment. Some analysts fear that encouraging (or forcing) mothers to work outside the home will increase family stress and undermine parental supervision. Again, the issue is whether the gains associated with mothers' higher earnings will outweigh the potential costs associated with more demands on mothers' time.

More research on the magnitude of these effects on child well-being is warranted.

ENDNOTES

1. The estimate for married fathers' contribution is based on consumption survey data. The estimate for nonresident fathers' contribution is based on Oellerich, Garfinkel, and Robins (1991).

2. Whether to give priority to reducing insecurity or to reducing prevalence and dependence applies not only to single mothers and their children but more generally to all those with low incomes.

3. The effect of excluding health is ambiguous. Although the availability of national health insurance in each of the other countries presumably means that an absolute measure of the well-being of single mothers overstates the U.S. position compared with those of other countries, our measures are relative. Universal health insurance covers two- as well as one-parent families in these countries. Furthermore, poor single mothers in the United States have Medicaid coverage. So they do better than poor two-parent families.

4. We would guess that including homeownership would make the United States look somewhat better because we have such high homeownership rates. But to our knowledge the analysis has not been done.

5. Perhaps the second most important omission is the lack of comparable data between France and Sweden on private expenditures on child support and public expenditures on advanced maintenance. This clouds our ability to understand why Sweden does a bit better than France.

6. The less than 40% figure comes from the following: Mean annual earnings in the U.S. for prime age males in 1983 was $19,000 and the minimum wage was less than $4.00 per hour. Multiplying $4.00 per hour times 2,000 hours yields $8000 which is 42 percent of $19,000. Clearly this figure is too high.

7. Lefaucheur (p. 24) notes that family allowances comprise 15 percent of income, which implies that they raise income by 15/85 or 18 percent.

8. For data on U.S. paternity establishment rates, see Ann Nichols-Casebolt and Irwin Garfinkel (1991). For the Swedish record, see Garfinkel and Sorenson (1982).

REFERENCES

Ellwood, David. 1989. *Poor Support.* New York: Basic Books.

Garfinkel, Irwin, and Sara McLanahan. 1986. *Single Mothers and Their Children: A New American Dilemma.* Washington, D.C.: Urban Institute Press.

Garfinkel, Irwin, and Annamette Sorenson. 1982. "Sweden's Child Support System: Lessons for the United States." *Social Work* 27:509–515.

Gustafsson, Siv. "Single Mothers in Sweden: Why Is Poverty Less Severe?" Chapter 8 of this volume.

Higgins, Michael. 1988. "The Allocation of Public Resources to Children and the Elderly in OECD Countries." In *The Vulnerable*. Edited by John Palmer, Timothy Smeeding, and Barbara Torrey. Washington, D.C.: The Urban Institute Press.

Kamerman, Sheila B., and Alfred J. Kahn. "Government Expenditures for Children and their Families in Advanced Industrialized Countries, 1960–85." Innocenti Occasional Papers, Economic Policy Series, Number 20, September 1991, forthcoming in *Child Poverty in Industrial Countries: Trends and Policy Options*. Edited by Giovannia Andrea Cornia.

McFate, Smeeding, Rainwater. Chapter 1 of this volume.

McLanahan, Sara. 1985. "Family Structure and the Reproduction of Poverty." *American Journal of Sociology* 90:873–901.

McLanahan, Sara, and Karen Booth. 1989. "Single Parenthood: Problems, Prospects, and Policies." *Journal of Marriage and the Family* 51:557–580.

McLanahan, Sara, Lynne Casper, and Annamette Sorenson. "Women's Roles and Women's Status in Eight Industrialized Countries." *Gender and Family Change in Industrialized Countries*. Edited by K. O. Mason and A. M. Jensen. Oxford: IUSST/Oxford Univ. Press: forthcoming.

Meyer, Daniel R., Irwin Garfinkel, Donald Oellerich, and Philip K. Robins. 1992. "Who Should Be Eligible for An Assured Child Support Benefit?" In *Child Support Assurance: Lessons from Wisconsin*. Edited by Irwin Garfinkel, Sara S. McLanahan, and Philip K. Robins. Washington, D.C.: The Urban Institute Press.

Nichols-Casebolt, Ann, and Irwin Garfinkel. 1991. "Trends in Paternity and Adjudications and Child Support Awards." *Social Science Quarterly* 27:89.

Oellerich, Donald T., Irwin Garfinkel, and Philip K. Robins. 1991. "Private Child Support; Current and Potential Impacts." *Journal of Sociology and Social Welfare* 18:3–23.

U.S. Department of labor. June 1985. *Handbook of Labor Statistics*, bulletin 2217. Washington, D.C.: Government Printing Office.

Wong, Yin-Ling Irene, Irwin Garfinkel, and Sara McLanahan. 1991. "Single Mother Families in Eight Countries: Economic Status and Social Policy." *Social Services Review* 67:177–197.

Part III

YOUTH LABOR MARKET POLICIES

Chapter 11

IS THERE A PROBLEM
WITH THE YOUTH LABOR MARKET,
AND IF SO, HOW SHOULD WE FIX IT?

Lessons for the United States
from U.S. and European Experience

Paul Osterman

THE EMPLOYMENT difficulties facing American youth have long been at the center of labor market policy. In the early 1960s the initial emphasis of the Manpower Development and Training Act (MDTA) on "mainstream" adults quickly shifted to focus on inner-city youths. Much, if not most, of the job training associated with the War on Poverty (the Neighborhood Youth Corps, the Job Corps, and the summer jobs program) was targeted toward young people. The expansion of the Comprehensive Employment and Training Act (CETA) in the 1970s consisted of Public Service Employment and Youth Demonstration Projects. Young people still receive a disproportionate fraction of training funding today despite recent competition from welfare recipients. Even though these programs are characterized as "youth programs," in fact, they have been more specialized and have typically targeted poor, minority youths.

Yet over the past decade or so, there has been a subtle shift in emphasis. Although no one would profess disinterest in the problems of inner-city youths—and a vigorous discussion of their difficulties has been incorporated in the debate around the underclass issue—more attention is being paid to the larger group of noncollege young people.[1] This new emphasis is driven less by a concern with high unemployment or racial/urban problems than by a broader interest in competitiveness and skill development. The consensus diagnosis that there has been a decline in American competitiveness assigns important emphasis to the inadequate human resource practices of American firms and the weak training of the U.S. labor force. (See Kochan and Osterman 1991 for an analysis along these lines.) The typical comparison is between the United States, Germany, and Japan, with the first one coming off third best with respect to workforce preparation. This view has led to an explosion of national commissions and proposed reforms centering on providing better vocational training to young people.

An additional element in this new view is the argument that shifting product demand and technology has undercut opportunities for noncollege youth. This is seemingly reflected in wage data that show a decline in the relative wages of high-school versus college-educated young people (Blackburn, Bloom, and Freeman 1990).

The foregoing represents what is perhaps the current mainstream view toward youth employment problems. There is, however, an alternative perspective. This holds that youth employment problems have always received much more attention than they deserve. The transition from school and living with parents to self-sufficiency and an adult job is bound to be full of stops and starts. This is particularly true in the United States, a country with a much less structured labor market entry process than Germany or Japan. This lack of structure might seem to cause problems if viewed at a single slice in time, but one could argue that over the longer term, the vast majority of American youth successfully settle into jobs with no discernable adverse effects. Although particular groups, like inner-city minorities, may have problems, there is little about which to be concerned overall. Which view is correct? Before examining possible policies to "fix" the youth employment problem, we need to understand better what the youth employment "problem" is.

YOUTH EMPLOYMENT PATTERNS

The School-to-Work Transition Process

How well does a given youth cohort manage the transition into adult status? The standard story for noncollege youth is that, regardless of the quality of general education, high school does not do much in the way of vocational training and preparation. The average American high school student takes 4.5 vocational education courses (National Assessment of Vocational Education: p. 1–6). However, enrollment figures have been falling, and evaluations of the quality of vocational education efforts are almost uniformly pessimistic. Instead of learning job skills in school, youths go through an extended period of labor market adjustment after they leave. During this period, they experience spells of casual work and nonwork while searching for an adult job (Osterman 1980). Eventually, most young people settle down into an adult job, but the paths to this end are many and varied.[2]

If one compares this process cross-nationally, the conventional wisdom is to emphasize the contrast between American training and labor market entry patterns and those of other countries. Germany sweeps the overwhelming majority of every cohort along a well-marked route of part-time schooling and apprenticeships, which culminates in examinations and placement into a first adult job. In Japan, non-college-bound high school students are placed in their first job by their teachers and are expected to remain there (Rosenbaum and Kariya 1989). The U.S. process appears chaotic compared with these models. Moreover, there are important questions about the quality of the skills American youths learn along the way. On the other hand, there is much greater scope for individual choice and for experimentation and mind changing. These very important benefits are often overlooked. The question is, What price do U.S. citizens pay for these virtues?

There is another way to view the school-to-work transition in other countries, a view that is perhaps less romanticized and more realistic than the dominant vision described previously. In some European nations the process appears to be virtually identical to that in the United States. In France, much like in the United States, young people first work in a secondary sector, gain work experience in high turnover jobs, and eventually land more stable employment in the adult sector of the workforce (Germe 1986). This pattern of youths working more intensively in some sectors than others characterizes most European nations (Marsden and Ryan 1986). The employment situation of youths in some countries, such as Italy, has been catastrophic (Garonna 1986, Pugliese, this volume). Even in Germany, youths were overly represented in small firms during their apprenticeship period in the 1980s and had to move when their training ended (Casey 1986, and this volume). This movement between apprenticeships and stable work often entailed a period of unemployment. Thus, while teenage unemployment in Germany is low, some youth unemployment is simply deferred to older age groups. In short, one could argue that American youth is not significantly more isolated from adult jobs than its counterparts overseas. Nonetheless, legitimate questions remain about whether youths in other nations reap some benefits from the way labor market entry is structured in their countries. Moreover, the costs of the U.S. process may be too high to justify the benefits.

To assess the validity of these competing views, we need to track the progress of a cohort of young Americans making the school-to-work transition. The National Longitudinal Survey of Youth (NLSY) follows the labor market experiences of 11,406 young people who were between the ages of 14 and 22 in 1979 through the 1980s. Table 11.1 follows a national sample of individuals who were 16 to 19 years old in 1979.[3] The activity status categories are mutually exclusive; all individuals who are in school are so classified even if they worked while enrolled. The data show work commitment growing steadily with age. Only 3.5 percent of the oldest cohort of men and 4 percent of the oldest cohort of women were unemployed at the time of the last interview.[4] The most striking difference between men and women is the higher fraction of women in the "other" category, a reflection of commitment to family. There is little in these data to indicate a crisis in the school-to-work transition.[5]

These patterns vary with educational attainment but perhaps not as much as one might expect. Both male and female high school dropouts work less than their cohort as a whole and have higher unemployment rates. However, even this most vulnerable group is overwhelmingly employed, and this pattern holds

Table 11.1 / Activity Patterns, by Gender, Educational Attainment, and Age Group

	Age Group			
	16–19	20–23	25–28	29–31
Men: All				
Working	21.9	53.9	81.2	85.7
Unemployed	4.7	11.1	4.4	3.5
In school	68.5	23.4	5.4	5.0
Armed forces	0.4	6.5	4.0	2.2
Other	4.5	5.2	5.0	3.6
Women: All				
Working	18.9	49.3	67.9	66.1
Unemployed	5.8	8.6	4.6	4.0
In school	65.6	21.4	4.9	4.8
Armed forces	0.1	0.7	0.6	0.1
Other	9.6	20.0	22.0	25.0
Men: High School Dropouts				
Working				85.4
Unemployed				6.8
In school				0.5
Armed forces				0.0
Other				7.2
Women: High School Dropouts				
Working				63.4
Unemployed				6.8
In school				0.2
Armed forces				0.0
Other				29.6
Men: High School Graduates (no college)				
Working				92.1
Unemployed				3.4
In school				1.3
Armed forces				0.6
Other				2.6
Women: High School Graduates (no college)				
Working				66.0
Unemployed				4.0
In school				1.1
Armed forces				0.0
Other				28.9

SOURCE: National Longitudinal Survey, Youth.

NOTES: The first three columns follow those aged 16–19 in 1979 until they were 25–28 in 1988. The final column is for a separate cohort, those aged 29–31 in 1988. The activity categories are mutually exclusive and individuals in schools are recorded as in that status regardless of whether they also worked.

for both sexes. On examining these data, one does not come away with the sense that there is a major dysfunction in the school-to-work transition process. It would be desirable to reduce high school dropout rates, but we already knew that. If there is a problem with the process, we have to search further.

The most cogent criticism of the foregoing is that is does not provide any sense of the *quality* of the outcome. While virtually everyone progressively moves into work or family responsibilities, does this necessarily represent a successful transition? In previous work (Osterman 1980), I argue that the desirable outcome is for a youth to settle into a "career job." Is there evidence that employed young people in their late 20s have found such a niche? Two reasonable measures are whether the employment is long-lasting and whether the young people enjoy long stretches without unemployment. The findings, shown in Table 11.2, are not comforting.

Table 11.2 presents data on three groups: all youth, high school dropouts, and high school graduates. In all three panels the sample is limited to those who had not been in school or in the armed forces since 1985.[6] As an additional control, the third panel of Table 11.2 is limited to those women who were in the labor force continuously since 1985, to account for the fact that many women drop out of the labor force for limited periods.[7]

At the beginning of their 30s, a bit over a third of all men had failed to find a job that had lasted for at least a year, and another 16 percent were in their current job for only a year. Among high school graduates, the picture is slightly better but still troubling: Over 30 percent had not held a job for a year, and another 12 percent had only 1 year of tenure at their current job. Among *all* women the picture is somewhat worse, but among women who were in the labor force for the 4 years prior to the survey, the female pattern was very similar to the pattern among males.

It is important to note that these patterns cannot be explained away by occupational differences. A high job-changing rate among upwardly mobile professionals would not explain these results for high school graduates and dropouts. When individuals employed in construction were excluded,[8] the patterns were the same.[9] However, there is no evidence that the pattern has *worsened* in the 1980s.[10]

If one turns to unemployment, the picture is complicated. Very few respondents are what might be termed chronically unemployed, but a substantial fraction experience some long-term unemployment. A third of men and 30 percent of the women had at least one spell of unemployment that lasted 4 weeks or more within the past 3 years. These rates seem to me to be sources of concern.[11]

The conclusion I would draw is that whether there is a general school-to-work transition problem depends upon the standard one uses. Most young people enter the labor market and become increasingly attached to the workforce. However, probing more deeply into the *quality* of the process raises difficult questions. Roughly a third of all high school graduates, and a higher proportion of high school dropouts, fail to find stable employment by the time they are 30. Even if some of this group improves its employment situation in the next few

Table 11.2 / Job Tenure and Unemployment Spells, for Individuals Aged 29–31 Years Old in 1988, by Gender and Educational Attainment

	Men			Women			Women Continuously in the Labor Force Between 1985 and 1988		
	Total	High School Dropouts	High School Graduates (no college)	Total	High School Dropouts	High School Graduates (no college)	Total	High School Dropouts	High School Graduates (no college)
Job Tenure									
In current job 2+ years	42.8	27.7	54.8	31.7	19.4	30.7	52.3	41.7	52.4
In current job 1–2 years	15.8	23.0	12.8	16.6	20.6	14.4	15.8	18.0	14.1
In current job less than 1 year	37.0	49.3	32.4	51.7	60.0	54.9	31.9	40.3	33.5
Unemployment									
Unemployed 4 or more weeks in none or 1 of past 3 years	87.8	78.2	85.4	92.6	87.3	92.4	91.9	80.5	91.9
Unemployed 4 or more weeks in 2 of past 3 years	9.4	16.2	11.5	6.0	9.9	6.4	6.2	15.1	5.7
Unemployed 4 or more weeks in 3 of past 3 years	2.8	5.6	3.1	1.4	2.8	1.2	1.9	4.4	1.4

SOURCE: National Longitudinal Survey, Youth.

NOTES: Individuals were excluded if they had been in the armed forces or school in any year between 1985 and 1988. The final 3 columns also exclude women who had been in the "other" activity category sometime between 1985 and 1988.

years, this leaves a substantial fraction of the cohort in trouble. For this group, the loosely structured American system does not work well.

By way of comparison, a 1985 survey in West Germany showed that only 9.5 percent of 29–31-year-old men and 8.2 percent of 29–31-year-old women had held their job for less than a year, and another 8.7 percent of men and 9 percent of women report between 1 and 2 years of tenure.[12] These figures are much lower than those found in the United States.

Should we be concerned that high job turnover persists into the early 30s in the United States? After all, as already noted, a virtue of the U.S. labor market is the opportunity it offers youth to experiment with moving in and out of work and education[13] and trying different employment options. Such experimentation necessarily entails reduced job tenure. How much turnover is too much? And when should the period of experimentation stop?

One reason to be concerned with high turnover rates has to do with training. The probability that an individual will receive high-quality, firm-based training increases with job stability. Firms are reluctant to train employees who may leave.[14] Moreover, in my judgment (and this is only a judgment), most young people with 10 years or more of work experience should be in a stable job by the age of 30. The fact that substantial numbers are not is troubling.

The Transition Process for Minority Students

The gap between minority and white employment rates has long been at the center of youth policy concerns. In the late 1970s, when black youth unemployment reached into the 40-percent range, a widespread sense of crisis resulted in the Carter Administration's Youth Employment Demonstration Projects Act. How has the employment situation of minority youths changed with the overall employment growth of the 1980s?

Table 11.3 presents October 1992 employment rates for 16–24-year-old youths who were not enrolled in school and shows that unemployment rates of high school dropouts, both black and white, are terrible; the jobless rate of black dropouts is nothing short of catastrophic.[15] Less than 30 percent of black youths in this age group are employed. As education levels improve, so do employment outcomes, and the employment differences among black and white college-educated young people are within the range of reason. However, there is a very substantial racial gap among high school graduates; only slightly over half of the black high school graduates are employed.

Table 11.4 presents measures of labor market activity and "job settling" derived from the National Longitudinal Survey, broken out by race and education. Among men, the racial gaps in employment stability are quite substantial for both high school dropouts and graduates but narrow considerably for those with some college. Women show a similar racial gap for high school dropouts, but the racial differences are not striking among females with a high school diploma or some college. All of this is consistent with the pattern we will observe in the unemployment data: Blacks who attend at least some college

Table 11.3 / **Employment Indicators for 16–24-Year-Olds Not Enrolled in School in October 1992, by Educational Attainment and Race**

	Whites	Blacks
Less Than High School		
Labor force participation rate	66.1	50.2
Unemployment rate	21.0	48.1
Employment/population ratio	52.2	26.0
High School		
Labor force participation rate	84.0	73.4
Unemployment rate	10.0	26.7
Employment/population ratio	75.6	53.8
Some College		
Labor force participation rate	91.6	81.4
Unemployment rate	05.8	18.8
Employment/population ratio	86.2	66.0

SOURCE: Calculated from Employment and Earnings, November, 1992.

do reasonably well relative to whites, but very substantial differences remain among those with less than a college education.

The foregoing should not be interpreted to mean that white high school dropouts are in good shape. They are not. High school dropouts of all races are in difficulty. But the employment situation of black dropouts is truly terrible, and the employment situation of black high school graduates, while better, is still quite grim. When combined with other information, such as indicators of involvement with the criminal justice system, it is clear that minority youths without some college are in crisis.

The Competitiveness of American Youth: The Skills Issue

The foregoing assessment of the American school-to-work transition process examined the experience of individuals. One might also ask if American youth as a group is receiving adequate skills to enable it, and the nation, to compete in the international economy.

There has been considerable discussion about whether new technologies and new production systems require greater skills and, if so, whether Americans are as likely to receive these skills as overseas youth (for a review, see Kochan and Osterman 1991). Contrary to the spirit of the older Braverman-inspired "de-skilling" debate, the evidence suggests that when new technologies are combined with new forms of work organization (which emphasize team production, statistical process control, and total quality management), the skill demands on the labor force do indeed increase. This conclusion is based partly on enterprise surveys of skill requirements; these surveys provide mild support

Table 11.4 / Activity Patterns and Job Tenure of Individuals Aged 29–31 Years in 1988, by Educational Attainment, Gender, and Race

	Men		Women	
	White	Black	White	Black
High School Dropouts				
Activity				
Working	91.8	69.1	71.4	50.0
Unemployed	5.8	9.7	2.8	15.9
In school	0.2	1.8	0.0	1.0
Armed forces	0.0	0.0	0.0	0.0
Other	2.2	19.3	25.7	33.1
Job tenure				
2+ years	28.5	21.4	21.6	17.5
1–2 years	25.4	21.3	21.4	20.5
<1 year	46.1	57.3	57.0	62.0
High School Graduates (no college)				
Activity				
Working	94.3	79.7	66.2	67.8
Unemployed	2.7	8.3	2.5	13.0
In school	1.6	8.7	1.1	0.9
Armed forces	0.1	0.0	0.0	0.0
Other	1.3	3.3	30.2	18.3
Job tenure				
2+ years	58.3	33.9	30.9	34.4
1–2 years	12.0	16.3	14.2	18.6
<1 year	29.7	49.8	55.7	47.0
Some College				
Activity				
Working	79.8	74.3	65.6	65.4
Unemployed	3.1	7.3	1.5	7.9
In school	9.3	9.2	12.5	8.0
Armed forces	3.3	4.8	0.1	0.0
Other	4.5	4.5	20.4	18.7
Job tenure				
2+ years	41.4	43.3	44.4	35.9
1–2 years	13.7	16.6	14.3	10.6
<1 year	44.9	40.1	41.3	53.5
College				
Activity				
Working	82.0	78.5	68.7	75.0
Unemployed	1.4	2.6	2.8	3.7
In school	8.9	14.8	5.5	13.6
Armed forces	5.4	4.0	0.2	2.3
Other	2.3	0.0	22.8	5.3
Job tenure				
2+ years	54.6	50.1	32.4	59.5
1–2 years	17.4	27.2	23.0	12.4
<1 year	28.0	22.7	44.6	28.1

SOURCE: National Longitudinal Survey.

for the upskilling conclusion but are likely to understate skill *shifts*.[16] More striking evidence of the need for higher skills comes from case studies of firms that have undertaken innovations in workplace organization. Moreover, when researchers have created matched comparisons of American and foreign firms in various industries, and compared work organization and skill requirements, American firms have not fared well in comparison with Japanese and European firms.[17]

Concerns about a skills gap are heightened by recent wage developments in the United States. The wage rates of both high school graduates and high school dropouts have fallen sharply relative to college graduates, with the fall being the sharpest for dropouts. Numerous authors have documented this trend. For example, a representative paper by Blackburn, Bloom, and Freeman (1990) shows that the hourly wage differential (in log points) of white male high school and college graduates aged 25 to 34 increased from .19 in 1973 to .35 in 1987; the comparable figures for high school dropouts relative to college graduates showed an increase of .34 to .60 during the same period.

Nonetheless, there is little evidence of a direct link between increasing wage differentials and growing skill deficits among American youth. It is hard to argue that the current trends reflect a declining quality of schools or the skill of youths, because older workers (who attended school many years earlier) show a comparable, although less dramatic, pattern[18] of growing wage inequality. Moreover, relative wages can decline for a number of reasons that are unrelated to the skills of the labor force—for example, shifts in product demand, a decline in union power, etc. In fact, recent research has shown that skills and wages moved in *opposite* directions in many occupations over the past two decades.

More importantly, my field work shows that firms with more highly skilled workers are most likely to shift to new forms of workplace organization that attempt to utilize those skills, but that American firms vary widely in their willingness to adopt such changes. The reasons for this reluctance are complicated and include considerations such as managerial ideology, lack of strong employee voice, and the unwillingness of American firms to stabilize employment. Given this uneven adoption of new production systems, the size and scope of the "skill deficit" in the United States is unclear.

This raises the most difficult question regarding the existence of a possible skills problem. Would an improvement in the skills of youth entering the work force *lead to* the widespread adoption of production systems that utilized higher skills? Would supply create its own demand? I will discuss this question at greater length later, but it is important to understand that any policy focused on reducing the "skills gap" rests on an implicit assumption that increasing the supply of skilled workers will result in an increase in the demand for them. If this is true, then it is plausible to believe that we are in a low-level equilibrium trap that we can escape via training. If this assumption is false, then we need to focus on policies directly related to the creation of high-quality jobs instead of focusing on training.

YOUTH LABOR MARKET POLICY

There are two ways to think about reforming youth labor market policy in the United States. One could take the position that the overall structure of the entry process is adequate but does not serve a relatively small group very well; thus, specific policies should be designed for this group. Alternatively, one could take the view that something deep and fundamental is wrong with the entry process and that we need to consider more structural remedies to "fix" the school-to-work transition process. Which view more accurately reflects the situation in the United States?

It is obvious that there is an identifiable group—minority youths—whose problems run deeper than others. Whether there is a more general youth labor market problem is in the eye of the beholder. However, the fact that over 30 percent of 30-year-old men, and a much larger fraction of 30-year-old women, are in jobs that they have held for less than a year suggests that the "settling in" process is not working well.

The evidence on wages and skills is ambiguous. The fact that the wages of young people with a high school degree or less are declining is clearly a problem, but it is not clear if this should be seen as a problem that can be addressed by improving the skills of young workers and the school-to-work transition or if falling wage levels reflect broader shifts in the national economy that require other strategies. Nonetheless, even if the problem is more general, as is suggested by the decline in the earnings of adult workers with high school educations, we should still focus supply-side solutions on the youth labor market, because it is more feasible to alter the characteristics of younger workers than older workers. However, if the more fundamental need is for a demand side response—reinvigorating unions or establishing a national industrial policy, for example—then a focus on the youth labor market is misleading.

These qualifications aside, I will move on to discuss youth policy options, beginning with targeted programs aimed at disadvantaged youths and then turning to more general efforts to restructure the youth labor market.

Targeted Policies

As noted at the beginning of the chapter, the main focus of U.S. youth labor market policies has been on non-college-bound minority youths, although even the targeted programs have served only between 5 and 10 percent of the American youth eligible for participation (Smith and Gambone 1991: 7).[19] Other aspects of the youth labor market have been left alone.

A rough but useful way to classify youth programming is to divide federal policy into three periods. The first period began with the Manpower Demonstration Projects Act and ran through the War on Poverty to the beginning of the Youth Employment Demonstration Projects Act (YEDPA) in 1977. This period saw substantial experimentation, but few if any evaluations were adequate enough to allow us to reach conclusions about what works and what does not.[20] In the YEDPA period (1977 and 1981), there were a number of careful evaluations of demonstration programs, and in the post-YEDPA years (1981 to the present), several demonstration projects were launched with the benefit of the YEDPA experience. Taken together, these studies allow us to draw reasonable conclusions about employment interventions for disadvantaged youth.

The only youth employment program of the YEDPA era in which participants experienced long-term employment and earnings gains was the Job Corps (which was designed prior to YEDPA).[21] This expensive residential program appears to "pay off" in that it improves employment and earnings and results in declines in criminal activity and welfare receipt among participants. (However, even with this program, there is more uncertainty about its positive outcomes than popular discussions suggest).[22] Other programs either failed to achieve their objectives (e.g., the Youth Entitlement program did not reduce dropout rates) or had effects that decayed rapidly over time. (Various job search assistance programs fall into this category.) An additional important (although negative) finding was that work experience—simply the experience of holding a job—had no long-term effect on employment and earnings. This is important in that many youth programs are designed to provide work experience and offer little additional training.

The YEDPA experience left one major question unanswered: if a Job Corps-like program were run on a larger scale for out-of-school youths, would it yield positive results? To answer this question, the Manpower Demonstration Research Corporation launched the JobStart program. JobStart provides intensive services—both educational and skills training—to high school dropouts in 13 sites around the nation. The average enrollee was in the program nearly twice as long (6.6 months vs. 3.4 months) as the average high school dropout who participated in a regular Job Training Partnership Act (JTPA) training program. Because the program was a demonstration, it is reasonable to conclude that it was executed better than the typical youth program.

The JobStart program used a random assignment design. The program paid off in terms of improving educational attainment. At the end of a year, 27 percent of the participants had obtained a General Educational Degree (GED)[23] compared with 9 percent of the controls; 94 percent of the participants had received some kind of education and/or training compared with 29 percent of the controls. The very bad news is that these achievements did not translate into earnings gains. After 24 months, the male participants' annual earnings were a little *below* those of the control group, and the female participants were essentially even with the controls. Remedial education degrees and occupational training did not result in increased earnings.[24] JobStart was exactly the right experiment to run, and, unless the 48-month evaluation shows a complete turn-around, it is hard to be optimistic about the program. Other youth demonstration programs have had similarly discouraging outcomes.[25] And analyses based upon a very different methodology (creating a comparison group via Census data) also reach generally negative conclusions (Bassi et al. 1984).

However, certain demonstrations have had more encouraging results. A number of programs aimed at young welfare mothers seem to be able to modestly increase their participation in the labor force and, hence, decrease the reliance on income support programs. However, these welfare mothers start from such a low base that even significant gains in work hours by participants still leave the participants with very low employment rates.

Jobs for America's Graduates, which provides counseling and mentoring activities for high school seniors, appears to increase postschool employment rates among disadvantaged youth but has little impact on their wages or upon job quality. Finally, Career Beginnings was able to increase college attendance rates of high school students by 5 percentage points relative to controls (Cave and Quint 1990).[26]

If our remedial efforts to improve the employment outcomes of disadvantaged American youths have not worked very well, do European countries offer better models? At one level the answer is no: Experimentation with and the evaluation of targeted remedial training programs is better in the United States than in Europe. For example, the two leading French programs—TUC and SIVP—that Faure (1991) describes appear to be little more than subsidized work experience of the sort that our evaluations have shown to have little payoff in employment or earnings gains. He refers, in language very reminiscent of the U.S. discussion, to the "chronic lack of stability" and "multiplicity and transitory" nature of remedial programs.

Although this review of targeted efforts that focus upon disadvantaged youths is not encouraging, it does not mean that we should just give up our efforts to help such individuals; that would be morally unacceptable if nothing else. In small ways (and surely for some individuals in big ways) the programs help. But in the end we are driven to consider the need for more structural changes in the youth labor market. Structural changes, by their character, will affect not only the disadvantaged, but the general youth population and the broader functioning of the youth labor market.

Three major strategies for structural change are currently being discussed. They include (1) increasing time spent in school, (2) introducing new school-to-work transition systems, and (3) attempting to alter the broader allocation/stratification system that maps individuals into jobs of a given quality.

Extending School

Throughout the difficult economic decade of the 1970s and into the 1980s, young people in most nations stayed in school longer. Faure reports that in France the school attendance rates of 18- and 19-year-olds increased by over 20 percentage points. This is remarkable and must reflect a cyclical as well as secular component; nonetheless, it indicates that a broad shift in school and work patterns occurred. Even in Germany, the fraction of 18- and 19-year-olds in school or formal vocational training increased from 23 percent in 1960 to 81 percent in 1986 (Casey 1994).

The American story is similar but contains a twist. Between 1970 and 1990, the percentage of white 16–24-year-olds not enrolled in school and not high school graduates remained constant (between 12 and 13 percent). However, there was a sharp *increase* in black school attendance: the percentage of black 16–24-year-olds out of school and without a high school degree fell from 26.5 percent in 1970 to 13.5 percent in 1990.[27] School enrollment rates among whites have remained essentially constant, while black high school attendance rates have gone up considerably, and black college rates have increased mildly. In this sense, the youth group most vulnerable to unemployment—blacks— has responded in ways similar to its European counterparts. The question is whether this strategy improves matters or simply delays reckoning.

Given the clear relationship between labor market outcomes and education, and given the earlier discussion of the skills gap among American youth, one must be pleased with the increased schooling of minority youths. Individuals clearly improve their employment prospects by graduating from high school instead of dropping out, and they do even better by attending college. Although simple tables and means are confounded by selectivity issues (the more able and/or motivated remain in school, and the better employment outcomes they experience may partly reflect this self-selection rather than the direct effect of extra schooling), we must believe that improvements in school retention are in the individual's and society's interest.[28]

Having said this, we also recognize that simply extending school is not enough. To a certain extent, all that is bought is delay: In Germany the unemployment of youths in their mid-20s is high, not the unemployment rate of teenagers. The structure of the entry process delays—but does not entirely eliminate—transition difficulties.

Even so, the entry process works reasonably well in Germany, and the same cannot be said for the United States. As we saw, black high school *graduates* are very disadvantaged in the labor market. Hence, even if dropping out could be magically eliminated, serious difficulties would remain for the "new" minority high school graduates and the 50 percent of white youth who do not currently go to college.

Linking School and Work

This then brings us to the second major strategy for structural change: altering the relationship between schools and the workplace. There has been an explosion of interest in this recently, inspired in part by growing awareness of the German system, and we should note that European nations have trod this path. In France, there has been a growing enrollment in the vocationally oriented intermediate level CAP and BEP school degrees and a shift toward "alternance" training, in which work is mixed with schooling (Marsden and Ryan 1990). In Britain, the Youth Training Scheme was at least partly motivated by an effort to redesign the school-to-work transition to be more like the German system. Even in Sweden, a country with a very well developed high school vocational track, recent educational reform efforts have taken the tack of adding an additional year of rotation between schools and the workplace to the basic education program.

To date, the American experience along these lines largely involves only traditional vocational education programs. In spite of indications that the quality of vocational education has improved somewhat recently, it is difficult to be very enthusiastic about the impact of vocational training in the United States— either in terms of wage gains or occupational placement subsequent to training.[29] One would expect school-based vocational education programs to perform poorly for a number of reasons. Schools make considerable investment in both capital equipment and staff with job-specific skills, yet both the physical and human capital can quickly become obsolete. However, because of the investment they have made, the schools maintain enrollment in out-of-date training programs, and, in effect, the system becomes supply driven rather than demand driven. Because it is so difficult for schools to maintain up-to-date knowledge of actual production technologies, it stands to reason that on-the-job training is simply more effective than classroom work in most occupational areas. Moreover, because many youths spend several years after high school drifting through the labor market, the effectiveness of school-based training will be further reduced.

On the other hand, school-based training is likely to be more general than training offered by firms and, hence, may be more useful to workers over the course of their careers. As I will discuss later, community colleges seem to provide useful and relatively effective vocational training.

The German model is attractive because it appears to represent a balance between firm- and school-based training, and all observers agree that the quality of training participants receive is high. For this reason, recent American discussions of reforming the school-to-work transition have centered on efforts to transplant the German model here.

There is considerable irony in the current American fascination with the German model. In the first two decades of the twentieth century, a heated debate raged in the United States over the desirability of including vocational training in general high schools versus setting up separate vocational schools. The rationale for a dual system was that technologies were changing, and the U.S. labor force lacked adequate skills; thus, efficiency and equality of opportunity required separate tracks for the "vocationally inclined." Then, as now, Germany was the model.

The Chicago superintendent of schools at that time became the major advocate of establishing a dual system in the United States after making a trip to Germany, and business support for the effort was strong. Consider the following comments by a Chicago businessman, which could easily be mistaken as excerpts from the current debate:

> There is perhaps no greater object lesson of the possibilities of vocational training than the phenomenal industrial advance of Germany during the

last generation. . . . This has been accomplished primarily because forty years ago German statesmen were sufficiently farsighted and progressive to inaugurate the comprehensive system of vocational education by which German youth acquire a better training for their life's work than youth of any other nation.[30]

Unions and progressive reformers bitterly fought the plan on the grounds that it would enshrine class distinctions and remove education from democratic control to place it in the hands of business. The apprenticeship plan was defeated, but this struggle over the proposal to create a dual system was one of the key events in the formation of the current structure of American education.[31] In the end, unions did support the establishment of vocational tracks within comprehensive high schools, and these vocational tracks became both ineffective and stigmatizing.

Despite this history, there has been a flurry of activity in the United States designed to set the stage for establishing new forms of apprenticeships here. Numerous national conferences have been held, and the U.S. Department of Labor's Office of Work Based Education and several national foundations have underwritten a number of demonstration programs. The Clinton Administration has introduced new school-to-work legislation inspired by this discussion. The ideas put forward range from fairly modest work-study efforts to an almost verbatim adoption of the German system.[32]

How should we evaluate these various efforts? At the broadest level, these proposals are attractive because they directly address the inadequate skills that American youths bring to the workplace in a way that somewhat promises a structural reform of the school-to-work transition process. The initiatives seem to offer a way to escape from the trap of remedial programs and old employment patterns, and so are very compelling. Nonetheless, it is important to probe a little deeper to examine the principles and the practicality of establishing a dual system in the United States. In thinking about these proposals, we need to consider the issues raised if they were to be introduced "at scale," that is, for a substantial fraction of the youth cohort. This is a more difficult problem than simply implementing small demonstration programs.

One of the strengths of the American system is the opportunity it gives young people to experiment and to change their minds. A second strength is its relative lack of tracking compared with European systems. Both of these advantages are at risk in a German model. It is very hard to imagine Americans willing to accept a system that requires most youth to select career paths in the 10th or 11th grade.[33] If such a system were established, it would have to be designed to accommodate the enormous amount of mind changing that would inevitably ensue. (Second thoughts are not a central part of the German system.) As a result, it would be impossible to specialize classroom or occupational training very much because the skills taught would have to be transferable to other training programs. However, when specialization is downplayed, the program begins to look more like work experience and less like a serious apprenticeship.

The United States is a long way from the uniformity of 400 recognized occupations with standard national examinations for each that exists in Germany.

A related problem concerns portability. Americans are very mobile. Any apprenticeship program must result in credentials recognized throughout the country. However, the highly decentralized structure of American education means that the new apprenticeships would have to be organized on a district-by-district basis.

An additional concern is whether firms can be induced to cooperate in offering apprenticeship openings. In Germany, smaller firms have geared their production system around these slots. Large firms have training staffs for their trainees, and the staff in these firms (and many employers) have gone through the dual system themselves and, hence, are committed to the program and to quality training.

Employers in the United States would presumably be motivated to participate in an apprenticeship program through public service appeals or because apprentices were viewed as a way to guard against labor shortages. Both motives are weak foundations upon which to build fundamental change. Imagine what the current status of an apprenticeship program in New England would be today if it had been set up 8 years ago to take care of expected labor shortages in real estate and financial services.[34]

Even if an executive or owner of a company committed him- or herself to a given number of slots, the quality of the training given might be problematic. Most observers agree that American firms do a poor job of training their *incumbent* workforce. Given this fact, why should we expect these firms to provide high-quality training to individuals in apprenticeship programs? Moreover, because the quality of any training provided depends on the behavior of supervisors, it is difficult to imagine how quality training within firms could be mass-produced.[35]

A related concern is how firms would be compensated for the cost of training. In Germany, apprentices are paid at rates far below those of regular workers. Indeed, according to Casey (1986), 16-year-old German apprentices are compensated at about 20 percent of the adult rate and 18-year-olds at 33 percent. Particularly in small firms, employers find the system worthwhile because the youths are actually part of the production system. American proposals tend to be silent on the issue of pay and the related issue of how to compensate firms for the cost of the training they provide. The cost issue exacerbates concerns about quality.

Some advocates of an American apprenticeship system might argue their case from an equity perspective. They might argue that apprenticeships can provide a formal path into the labor market for minorities who lack the informal contact networks enjoyed by whites. Yet why would apprenticeships meet this objective when vocational education programs have failed to do so? Only a comprehensive apprenticeship system that encompassed a large share of the non-college-bound youth and, hence, avoided stigmatizing its clients, could achieve this end. An additional concern is that the need to provide productive youth to employers (in order to "sell" an apprenticeship) precludes targeting the most disadvantaged youngsters for apprenticeships. School-to-work transition programs cannot be aimed at those least competitive in the labor market—at individuals with very low academic skills who have dropped out or are close to doing so.[36] So this returns us to the earlier discussion about whether it is realistic to think that a broadbased, comprehensive system could be built in the United States.

The foregoing discussion focused on the difficulties of implementing school-to-work transition programs on a large scale in America. Although these difficulties are serious, I nonetheless believe that it is worthwhile proceeding with efforts to implement programs along these lines. We are unlikely to succeed in re-creating the German model on our shores, but we do have the possibility of succeeding along three dimensions. For some youths who leave high school and go directly into the labor market, well-run programs can connect them to employers. For these youths, the program acts as a more effective guidance or career counselor. Other youths may be encouraged by their exposure to the labor market to further their education. This is the objective of a health careers program in Boston that provides after-school and summer jobs in the health sector and that encourages youths to take courses at local community colleges. Finally, situating academic learning in the context of the labor market may make the high school experience more rewarding and may enhance the learning environment for many youths. In this sense the apprenticeship models become a tactic of school reform as much as a labor market program.

The Broader Distribution of Jobs

The third broad policy option for improving school-to-work transition outcomes is to try to alter the overall distribution of occupational opportunities that new labor market entrants face. Let us assume that a certain fixed distribution of jobs exists in the economy and that these jobs are characterized by wage and skill differences. A "good" youth labor system moves young people into this distribution without pain and without discrimination (e.g., young people do not experience extended spells of unemployment, and minority youths do not land a larger share of the bad jobs than white youths), but in the end, the distribution is what it is, and people find a place in it.[37] To alter this situation, we would need to design policies that could transform the underlying distribution of opportunities.

Such a goal raises many other deep issues, ranging from the question of whether social policy can influence social mobility[38] to what determines the pattern of a firm's demand for labor. I obviously cannot do justice to these issues here. A more narrow formulation directly related to youth labor market policy and the school-to-work transition process might be, Will an increase in the skills of American youth induce employers to alter the content of their jobs so as to upgrade the quality of employment?

Advocates of increased training frequently argue that employers will respond to an increased supply of skilled workers by restructuring work; however, hard evidence on this is scarce. It is obviously difficult to prove the point using American evidence because there are few, if any, identifiable local labor markets in which the experiment has been executed (i.e., where training has been sharply improved and then firm behavior observed). In the absence of such natural experiments, advocates typically cite research comparing matched samples of firms in similar industries producing similar products (e.g., Maurice, Sorge, and Warner 1980; Steedman and Wagner 1989; Daly, Hitchens, and Wagner 1985; MacDuffie and Krafcik forthcoming). Most of these studies find that firms with a more skilled labor force also have broader jobs, are more likely to devolve authority to employees, to use teams, etc. The problem, of course, is that it is very hard to know whether increased training *induced* firms to adopt these systems or whether firms chose "transformed" production systems for other reasons and then developed the skilled workforce that such systems require.

It seems to me that the best way to think about this issue is to conceptualize increases in the skill levels of potential new hires as a reduction in the costs firms face should they choose to adopt new production systems. In this view, improving skills would *increase the chances* that a transformation occurs but would in no way guarantee the change.

Any theory explaining why firms adopt production systems must identify a number of important factors in this decision—such as worker voice, management values, and product market strategy. Those nations that have highly skilled workforces and production systems with more broadly skilled jobs significantly differ from the United States on these dimensions. There is no reason to give "labor force skills" any particular causal primacy. Indeed, there are reasons to think that it may be secondary. Case studies of American firms that have chosen to move in new directions—firms such as Corning and Motorola—show that the decision to change came first, and *then* the firm moved to train its workforce. Some international evidence also supports this view: Japanese young people do not leave school with high levels of vocational skills[39]; Japanese schools are known to be weak in vocational training. Rather, Japanese graduates have a strong academic background, and firms provide the vocational training to their new employees. Vocational training follows, rather than leads, production system innovations.

This does not imply that training does not help to improve job quality. As already noted, training reduces the cost of production innovations and, hence, will improve the chances that change will occur. Moreover, training provides a useful platform from which policymakers can work with firms on a variety of issues. Training can provide entry into the private sector, and through this access, other kinds of actions can be encouraged. Nonetheless, our expectations about the direct impact that skill enhancement will have upon the quality of jobs generated by the private economy should be modest. Simply upskilling new entrants will not improve the distribution of job quality very much.

However, Europeans can teach a lesson about the broader distribution of jobs. Until very recently, Europeans used a combination of laws, union power, and custom to raise the bottom of the labor market. As a consequence, the earning distribution in Europe is narrower than in the United States, layoffs are typically more difficult, and temporary or short contract work (and part-time work) is scarcer. It would seem reasonable to conclude that young people in Europe who do find permanent work are better off relative to the average adult than are young people in the United States. This suggests that it is possible to use political power to alter the distribution of labor market outcomes.

There are, however, several reasons to qualify this conclusion. Until the mid-1970s, Europe enjoyed lower unemployment than the United States and, therefore, had it both ways: high-quality jobs and plenty of them. This has changed, and European unemployment has risen above American levels, especially among the young. By way of example, Katz and Loveman (1990) show that France faced the same increase in demand for more skilled labor as the United States, but the wages of employed unskilled young French workers did not deteriorate in the 1980s. They attribute this to the French industrial relations system, which extends collectively bargained wage scales to all employees, and to high and binding minimum wages in France. However, while young *employed* French workers were relatively better off than their counterparts in the United States, young people in France had a very hard time *finding* employment. Unemployment, especially long-term unemployment among young people in France is very high.

As a result, Europeans have had to reconsider the optimum amount of labor market regulation desired, and in recent years most governments loosened a number of labor restrictions. While European labor markets remain more regulated than those in the United States and arguably still produce better jobs as a consequence, the case for emulating Europe is now shakier than in the past.

CONCLUSION

Does the United States have a youth labor market problem? If so, how do we deal with it? The answers are less clear than we might like. In all countries, young people are marginalized in the labor market. Young people in France appear to have experiences like young workers in the United States—they enter marginal sectors of the economy and suffer high unemployment rates as they try to move into the adult economy. Even Germany marginalizes young workers, although in a more subtle way. Young people are "confined" to a youth sector: They disproportionately take their apprenticeships in small firms, but do not remain there as they age. In small firms, young people are viewed as low-wage labor as much as trainees enrolled in an educational program. Furthermore, while teen unemployment in Germany is low, the unemployment of young adults rises more sharply in Germany than it does in other nations, because the effect of the dual system is to delay the entry process. Youth are marginalized everywhere because they have fewer skills and less work experience than adults and because it is a reasonable distributional rule to parcel out good jobs to adults rather than young people.

Given these facts of life, the process of entry into the adult world can be managed well or badly. A well-managed process would include a period in which genuine skills appropriate to future economic demands were gained. It would ensure that the process was fair—that no subgroup suffered disproportionately from unemployment or low wages. By these standards, the United States leaves much to be desired. However, difficulties arise when one attempts to prescribe solutions for the problem. The following seems to me to be a fair summary of long-term policies that could ease the entry process:

1. The most obvious solution, and one that many nations have followed, is to *extend the time spent in school*. For most youth, this may only delay the entry process, but for minority youths, it seems crucial. Blacks who have had some college do much better relative to whites with regard to both employment and earnings than those with high school or less. Selectivity can account for some but not all of these differences.

The extended-schooling strategy should focus on the "real thing," that is, real degrees from high schools, community colleges, and 4-year colleges. The evidence we have on the returns from GEDs and various certificate programs suggests that these do not pay off. This finding throws into question various proposals for community-based "second-chance" programs. The evidence on targeted training programs reinforces this conclusion.

2. The United States has experimented with a wide range of targeted training programs aimed at disadvantaged youths. In this regard we are far ahead of European nations. But the results have been discouraging. Even well-designed and carefully thought-out programs do not seem to pay off in a substantial way. To the extent that there are any benefits, they are modest and accrue largely to young women.

A reasonable response to the failure of targeted programs is to *emphasize broader reforms of the school-to-work transition process*. Disadvantaged youths could benefit from such reforms along with others. Although an adaption of the German dual system is under widespread discussion, it is difficult to imagine an American version having a great deal of fidelity to the German model. Nonetheless, even modest reforms in this direction are worth pursuing. But it is unlikely that these programs will be of much benefit to the young people in the greatest difficulty.

3. It would also be desirable to *change the demand side of the market by altering both the allocation rules employers use and the distribution of high-quality, high-skilled jobs* available in the economy. The former would involve increasing equal employment opportunity recruitment efforts. But it is difficult to determine how to accomplish the latter. Despite considerable discussion of training-oriented policies based on the assumption that better educated and trained youth would in themselves constitute an incentive for employers to adopt more skill intensive production systems (with better-quality jobs), the evidence supporting this view of firm behavior is very weak.

To summarize, my policy recommendations would be: keep youth in school longer, connect them to the labor market earlier, and induce them to enroll in some form of higher education—if only community colleges. These are the best lessons that can be drawn from my review of the literature. Unfortunately, these policies are clearly not enough to help substantial numbers of inner-city minority youth in the United States find decent jobs. What we have learned, from here and abroad, suggests that interventions in the youth labor market are too narrow a way to understand this issue. A more expansive macroeconomic policy and broader and deeper interventions in communities, families, and schools will be required if we are to improve the employment and earnings capacity of non-college-bound youths entering the labor market today.

The author is grateful to Frank Levy, Katherine McFate, Richard Murnane, and Paul Ryan for comments.

ENDNOTES

1. This is explicit in the title of the influential Grant Foundation report, *The Forgotten Half: Pathways to Success for America's Youth and Young Families.*

2. Just how diverse these routes are is demonstrated by the results of a national survey that asked technicians how they learned their skill. Five percent cited high school vocational education, 21 percent post–high school vocational education, 20 percent community colleges, 24 percent colleges, 14 percent formal firm-based training, and 32 percent informal firm-based training (U.S. Department of Labor 1985: 36).

3. The same people are followed from ages 16–19 in 1979 to ages 25–28 in 1988. The data for those ages 29–31 are taken from a different group (i.e., those ages 20–22 in 1979) and are included to show the impact of a few additional years of age. If one assumes there are no vintage effects, these data should be representative of the experience of the 16–19 cohort.

4. The unemployment rates are conventionally calculated higher because the denominator includes only those who are in the labor force. Another difference with conventional statistics is that I count those in school as out of the labor force, whereas normally individuals may be classified as both in school and working.

5. It is interesting to note the importance of the armed forces for men. The coming reduction in the size of the military establishment will have an adverse, albeit not overwhelmingly large, effect particularly on young blacks. The group denied access will come from the bottom of the qualifications range of those (almost all high school graduates or better) who in the past would have gotten in.

6. This eliminates the effect of entry/exit from the labor force. High school graduates and dropouts had basically been out of school for 10 years by 1988.

7. This group represents 51.6 percent of all women who were not in school or in the armed forces anytime between 1985 and 1988.

8. I excluded anyone who worked in construction in any year between 1985 and 1988.

9. Of the men, 42.5 percent had been in a job for a year or less.

10. The May 1979 and May 1988 Current Population Surveys collected information on job tenure of employed persons. Among people aged 29–31 in 1979, 53.6 percent of the women and 44.1 percent of the men had 2 years or less of tenure with their employer. In 1988 the comparable figures were 43.7 percent of women and 37.2 percent of men. This improvement no doubt reflects the stronger economy in the late 1980s compared with the late 1970s. Given that the late 1980s were a cyclical peak, these figures are probably as "good" as they can get; even so, a very substantial fraction of young adults were evidently not settled down.

11. These worries are reinforced by data on wages. Among 29–31-year-old-male high school graduates who held the same job for 3 years or more, the average hourly wage was $11.15 compared with $8.67 for those who had not held a job for a year. Among women the average hourly wage of the high tenure group is $8.45 compared with $6.68 for those with low tenure.

12. These data are my calculations from the Qualification and Berufsverlauf survey, which was made available by the Central Archives for Empirical Social Research at the University of Koln.

13. In the NLSY among persons aged 16 to 19 in 1979 who were out of school at the time of their interviews in both 1979 and in 1980, 15.6 percent reported being in school at the time of their interviews in at least 1 year between 1981 and 1988.

14. High turnover reduces the payoff to the firm's investment in training. Indeed, one of the virtues of European and Japanese commitments to employment continuity is that it creates an environment that encourages employers to invest more in their workers.

15. According to the NLSY, among 29–31-year-old whites, 13.9 percent were high school dropouts, 38.5 percent were high school graduates, 23.8 percent had some college, and 23.8 percent were college graduates. The comparable figures for blacks were 28.4 percent, 31.4 percent, 24.1 percent, and 13.2 percent. In effect, then, blacks were twice as likely to be high school dropouts and just under half as likely to be college graduates.

16. Studies of skill trends that typically rely on the Dictionary of Occupational Titles assume that the content of each title—that is, what workers with a given occupation do—remains constant. These studies focus on changes in the relative numbers of the titles. As a result of this procedure, these studies miss out on changes in skill content that occur within a given title. For example, a machine operator using FMS systems needs more skill than in a more traditional assembly line. Even more common, assemblers working in teams require a range of interpersonal skills and cross training that assemblers working alone do not require.

17. This literature is cited later.

18. I am grateful to Richard Murnane for pointing this out to me.

19. Aspirations remain modest: The recently released report of the National Commission on Children called for a gradual increase of Job Corps enrollments from 62,000 to 93,000.

20. There is both controversy and hard feelings in the community of youth program designers, consultants, operators, and researchers about appropriate standards of

evaluation. At one extreme are those who argue that only true random assignment experimental designs allow one to draw conclusions. At the other extreme are those who argue that we can draw useful "lessons from experience" without "scientifically rigorous" research and that to ignore what we can learn from the myriad of programs that have been implemented is wasting information in the name of an abstract standard. My own view falls in between, albeit somewhat shaded toward the former position. Without random assignment (and sometimes even with it), it is very difficult to have any confidence in the statement that this program "works" in the sense of achieving objectives such as increased wages or more work hours. It is simply very hard for even the most knowledgeable observer to have an accurate view of a program's effects, and this is compounded by the fact that in most programs there are enough success stories to make an advocate believe that the program has accomplished something.

At the same time, in the past two decades we have built up a great deal of experience in knowing how to mount and manage programs. This expertise, some of which is in the "field" and some of which is housed in particular consulting firms and universities, is very valuable and is too often ignored in the rush to examine the regression results from econometric evaluations. For a statement of the view skeptical of an exclusive emphasis on random assignment evaluations, see Hahn (1991).

21. This summary of YEDPA evaluations is based on Betsey et al. (1985).

22. First, the evaluations of Job Corps were based on comparison groups, not random assignment. Second, the program does not pay off in a cost/benefit sense if employment effects alone are considered. Reductions in criminal activity have to be added to the benefits side of the calculations of the program to be cost-effective.

23. The academic equivalent of a high school diploma.

24. The data presented in the previous paragraphs were taken from Auspos, Cave, Doolittle, and Hoerz (1989). The reports of the results from the most recent 24-month evaluation were provided to me orally and will shortly appear in an MDRC report. Similar findings regarding the GED, using a different methodology, are reported by Cameron and Heckman 1993.

25. Public/Private Ventures undertook the STEP program that aimed at providing educational remediation during the summer to counteract the finding that many youths lost educational gains during those months. The objectives of the program, which also included some school year services as well as a specifically designed life skills curriculum, was to reduce school dropping out and to reduce teenage pregnancy. The program was evaluated by random assignment, and, although a final report has yet to appear, all indicators are that the program did not achieve a gain for participants relative to controls.

26. Given the importance of college attendance, as demonstrated in the data presented earlier, this is an important effort, and the achievement is worthwhile. However, Career Beginnings provided intensive services (tutoring, mentoring, help in preparing forms, etc.) to middle-range high school students (i.e., not potential dropouts but not obviously headed to college), and the gains were seen as modest relative to the effort. This is explained by the surprisingly high level of similar services received by the controls.

27. These data are from *Employment and Earnings*, various years. The tables are entitled "Employment Status of 16–24 year-olds by Type of School and Enrollment Status, October. . . ." and are calculated from Current Population Survey data.

    On the other hand, high school *graduation* rates are not quite as good as these figures imply: The NLSY data cited earlier showed that among 29–31-year-old blacks, 28.4 percent were high school dropouts in 1988 compared with 13.9 percent of whites.

28. Later I discuss an evaluation of rates of return of community colleges by Norton Grubb. He includes efforts to control for selection bias and finds that the returns are not substantially reduced by such controls.

29. A recent summary of this literature is provided by the National Research Council, *High Schools and the Changing Workplace* (Washington, D.C.: National Research Council), 1984. See also John Grasso and John Shea, *Vocational Education and Training: Impact of Youth* (New York: Carnegie Foundation for the Advancement of Teaching), 1979.

30. The quote is from Theodore Robinson, first vice-president of the Illinois Steel Company, and was delivered in 1913 to the American Steel Institute. It is taken from Julia Wrigley, *Class Politics and Public Schools* (New Brunswick: Rutgers University Press), 1982, p. 69.

31. For additional material see Marvin Lazerson and W. Norton Grubb, *American Education and Vocationalism* (New York: Teachers College Press), 1974.

32. Perhaps the most extensive proposal is that of Robert I. Lerman and Hillard Pouncy. They call for a program in which 7th and 8th grade students learn about occupations through various activities such as site visits and job sampling, and in the 10th grade students decide upon an apprenticeship field (or upon the college track) and sign a contract. During the 11th and 12th grades, they combine school and work with time on the work site increasing to 70 percent, take an interim exam at the end of 12th grade, and for some undetermined time continue at the work site while spending 15 percent of their time in community colleges (Lerman and Pouncy 1990: 10).

33. Of course, some youths may have strong interests or aptitudes that this is appropriate but recall that all of these proposals are aimed at the 50 percent who do not go to college.

34. In England a number of companies have recently stopped participating in the Youth Training Scheme because of the recession.

35. An example of how quality problems can arise when the German system is transplanted is Britain's Youth Training Scheme. The YTS—inspired in part by the German approach—established a 2-year training/school period after the age of school leaving was implemented on a large scale. However, many observers are very critical of the quality of training (Dore and Sako 1986; Marsden and Ryan 1990) and tend to see it largely as an effort to sop up youth employment and provide low-wage workers to employers. On a somewhat more positive note, Main and Shelly (1990) find that participation in the original 1-year version of YTS increased a youth's subsequent probability of employment. However, whether any skills were taught is thrown into some doubt by their other finding that participation in YTS had no effect upon wages. Taken together, these findings suggest that in the long run, the impact of YTS is likely to decay just as was true in many U.S. job finding programs.

36. Furthermore, despite much effort, no youth employment program has had much effect on dropout rates. The greatest failure was the Entitlement Program implemented under YEDPA, but other efforts have had similarly poor results. Nonetheless, there is some evidence that curricular reform, combined with a vocational curriculum, can help reduce the rate of dropping out. For an analysis of the success of the California Peninsula Academies, see Stern, Dayton, Paik, and Weisberg (1989).

37. Such a view seems implicit in Leibfried's contrast of the point at which stratification mechanisms bite in Germany and America. He argues that schools perform the stratification function in Germany and the labor market in the United States; he implies but does not say that the outcomes may be very similar. The only issue is which approach works most smoothly and fairly (Liebfried 1991).

38. For a recent contribution that concludes it is possible to use social policy in this way (written by an author who in the past argued for invariant mobility patterns across societies), see Erikson (1990).

39. However, the academic skills of Japanese secondary school graduates appear to exceed those of Americans. See Bishop (1990) for a convenient summary of the data.

REFERENCES

Auspos, Patricia, George Cave, Fred Doolittle, and Gregory Hoerz. 1989. *Implementing Jobstart: A Demonstration for School Dropouts in the JTPA System.* New York: MDRC.

Barth, Roland. 1991. "Young Workers in Germany." Presented at the Conference on Poverty and Social Marginality, Joint Center for Political and Economic Studies, Paris.

Bassi, Laurie, Margaret Simms, Lynn Burbridge, and Charles Betsey. 1984. *Measuring the Effect of CETA on Youth and the Economically Disadvantaged.* Washington, D.C.: The Urban Institute.

Betsey, Charles, et al. 1985. *Youth Employment and Training Programs: The YEDPA Years.* Washington, D.C.: National Research Council.

Bishop, John. 1990. "Incentives for Learning: Why American High School Students Compare So Poorly to their Counterparts Overseas." In *Research in Labor Economics.* Greenwich, Conn.: JAI Press.

Blackburn, McKinley, David Bloom, and Richard Freeman. 1990. "The Declining Position of Less-Skilled American Males." In Gary Burtless, ed., *A Future of Lousy Jobs.* Washington, D.C.: The Brookings Institution.

Cameron, S., and J. Heckman. 1993. "The Nonequivalence of High School Equivalents." *The Journal of Labor Economics* II(1)(January):1–47.

Casey, Bernard. 1986. "The Dual Apprenticeship System and the Recruitment and Retention of Young Persons in West Germany." *British Journal of Industrial Relations* 24:63–81.

Cave, George, and Janet Quint. 1990. *Career Beginnings Impact Evaluation.* New York: MDRC. 1990.

Daly, A., D. M. Hitchens, and K. Wagner. 1985. "Productivity, Machinery and Skills in a Sample of British and German Manufacturing Plants." *National Institute of Economic Review* February.

Dore, Ronald, and M. Sako. 1986. "The Wider Labor Market Effects of the Youth Training Scheme and The Young Workers Scheme," mimeo.

Erikson, Robert. 1990. "Politics and Class Mobility: Does Politics Influence Rates of Social Mobility?" In *Generating Equality in the Welfare State*. Edited by Inga Persson, 247–265. Oslo: Norwegian University Press.

Faure, Jean-Louis. 1991."Young Adults in France Since the Mid-1970s: Problems Associated with Entry into the Workforce and Public Policies." Presented at the Conference on Poverty and Social Marginality, Joint Center for Political and Economic Studies, Paris.

Germe, J. F. 1986."Employment Policies and the Entry of Young People into the Labor Market in France." *British Journal of Industrial Relations* 24:29–42.

W. T. Grant Foundation. 1988. *The Forgotten Half: Pathways to Success for America's Youth and Young Families*. Washington, D.C.: W. T. Grant Foundation.

Grubb, Norton. 1990. "The Economic Returns to Post-Secondary Education: New Evidence from the National Longitudinal Survey of the Class of 1972," mimeo, University of California, Berkeley: School of Education.

Hahn, Andrew. 1991. "Inside Youth Programs: A Paper on the Limitations of Research," mimeo, Brandeis University.

Hartmann, G., I. Nicholas, A. Sorge, and Malcolm Warner. 1983. "Computerized Machine-tools, Manpower Consequences and Skill Utilization: A Study of British and West German Manufacturing Firms." *British Journal of Industrial Relations* 23(2).

Howell, David, and Edward Wolff. 1991. "Trends in the Growth and Distribution of Skills in the U.S. Workplace, 1960–85." *Industrial and Labor Relations Review* 44:486–502.

Katz, Lawrence, and Gary Loveman. 1990. "An International Comparison of Changes in the Structure of Wages: France, the United Kingdom, and the United States," mimeo, Harvard University.

Kochan, Thomas, and Paul Osterman. "Human Resources Development and Training: Is There Too Little in the U.S.?" prepared for the American Council on Competitiveness. Harvard Business School Press, forthcoming.

Lerman, Robert, and Hillard Pouncy. 1990. "The Compelling Case for Youth Apprenticeship." *The Public Interest* 62–77.

Liebfried, Stephan. 1991."Comments on Young Workers in Germany." Presented at the Conference on Poverty and Social Marginality, Joint Center for Political and Economic Studies, Paris.

MacDuffie, John Paul, and John Krafcik. "Integrating Technology and Human Resources for High Performance Manufacturing: Evidence from the International Auto Industry." In *Transforming Organizations*. Edited by Thomas A. Kochran and Michael Unseem. New York: Oxford University Press, forthcoming.

Main, Brian, and Michael Shelly. 1990. "The Effectiveness of the Youth Training Schemes as a Manpower Policy." *Economica* 57:495–514.

Marsden, David, and Paul Ryan. 1986. "Where Do Youth Work?" *British Journal of Industrial Relations* 83:102.

/ **413**

———. 1990. "Institutional Aspects of Youth Employment of Training Policy in Britain." *British Journal of Industrial Relations* 28:351–370.

———. 1990. "Intermediate Level Vocational Training and the Structure of Labor Markets in Western Europe in the 1980's." In *New Developments in Worker Training: A Legacy for the 1990s.* Edited by Louis Ferman, Michele Hoyman, Joel Cutcher-Gershenfeld, and Ernest Savoie, 309–338. Madison: Industrial Relations Research Association.

Maurice, M., A. Sorge, and M. Warner. 1980. "Societal Differences in Organizing Manufacturing Units: A Comparison of France, West Germany, and Great Britain." *Organization Studies* 1:59–86.

Osterman, Paul. 1980. *Getting Started: The Youth Labor Market.* Cambridge, Mass.: MIT Press.

Packer, Arnold, and John Wirt. 1991. "Restructuring Work and Learning" prepared for Urban Institute Conference on Urban Poverty. Washington, D.C.: Secretary's Commission on Achieving Necessary Skills.

Polit, Denise, Janet Quint, and James Riccio. 1988. *The Challenge of Serving Teenage Mothers: Lessons from Project Redirection.* New York: MDRC.

Rosenbaum, James, and Takehiko Kariya. 1989. "From High School to Work: Market and Institutional Mechanisms in Japan." *American Journal of Sociology* May.

Smith, Thomas, and Michelle Alberti Gambone. 1991. "The Effectiveness of Federally Funded Training Strategies for Youth," mimeo, Public/Private Ventures.

Steedman, H., and K. Wagner. 1987. "A Second Look at Productivity, Machinery and Skills in Britain and Germany." *National Institute Economic Review* November.

Stern, David, Charles Dayton, Il-Woo Paik, and Alan Weisberg. 1989. "Benefits and Costs of Dropout Prevention in a High School Program Combining Academic and Vocational Education: Third Year Results for Replications of the California Peninsula Academies." *Educational Evaluation and Policy Analysis* 11:405–416.

Sum, Andrew, Joseph Franz, Chuang Shi-Feng, and Neeta Fogg. "The Labor Force, Employment, and Earnings Experiences of JAG Program Participants and Comparison Group Members During the First Two Years Following Graduation: Findings of the 1986 Wave II Follow-up Survey of the Class of 1984." Northeastern University, Center for Labor Market Studies.

U.S. Department of Labor. 1985. *How Workers Get Their Training,* Washington, D.C.: U.S. Government Printing Office.

Chapter 12

APPRENTICE TRAINING IN GERMANY: THE EXPERIENCES OF THE 1980s

Bernard Casey

IN THE MID-1980s the German apprenticeship scheme faced what was possibly its most severe challenge. While favorably regarded, and even held up as a model for emulation by outsiders, the dual system's ability to deliver quality training to the large mass of school-leavers was in question. By the end of the 1980s, however, the symptoms of crisis had largely disappeared. A consensus had developed that the "dual system" had passed the test and that it had the potential to provide Germany with the highly skilled workforce it needed to meet the challenges of the twenty-first century. This chapter reviews the developments of the 1980s and particularly those of the last 5 years, drawing upon the publications of the Federal Training Institute (especially BMBW, various years), the federal Institute for Labour Market Research, and a series of "expert interviews," and assesses the extent to which these optimistic conclusions about capabilities of Germany's dual system are justified.

The remainder of this chapter consists of seven sections. A brief introduction to the nature of the "dual system" is given in Section 2. Section 3 summarizes the nature of the crisis that the system underwent in the first half of the 1980s, and Section 4 describes the recovery of the late 1980s. In Section 5 the changes in the nature of apprenticeships and apprentices that have taken place over the last decade are reviewed. Sections 6, 7, and 8 are concerned with the three challenges currently confronting policymakers in the Federal Republic: the challenge induced by the steep fall in the number of young people (6), the challenge induced by the demands of new technologies and new ways of working (7), and the challenge posed by the "disadvantaged" groups who fail to enter or to complete a course of vocational training (8). A final section draws some conclusions and suggests that recent developments in the German Democratic Republic mean the future for the youth labor market and the labor market for skilled workers is very unclear.

CHARACTERISTICS OF THE GERMAN APPRENTICESHIP SYSTEM

The German apprenticeship system is distinguished by two characteristics—first, its broad coverage; and second, its combination of school-based and work-place-based training (hence, its designation as "the dual system"). Apprenticeships provide the pathway into employment for some 70 percent of school leavers (Figure 12.1). Training places are provided for occupations in all sectors of the economy, in services as well as manufacturing, in large firms as well as small, in white-collar as well as blue-collar occupations. The period of training lasts typically between 2 and 3½ years. Rather than a wage, the trainee receives an allowance that, even in the final year, is still only a fraction of the wage of a comparable skilled worker.[1] Practical training is carried out in the place of employment, either on the job or (in larger organizations) in special training centers. More theoretical training is provided by special technical schools that apprentices attend for 1 or 2 days per week.[2]

Since 1969, the in-firm element of apprentice training has been governed by the Vocational Training Act. This act specifies that the regulations determining the content of training are to be determined jointly at the national level by employers' organizations and trade unions.[3] The technical schools that provide the off-the-job element of training are under the jurisdiction of the individual states (*Länder*), although nowadays training regulations will normally also contain the joint recommendations of the state education ministers concerning the content of the college-based training to be given. Responsibility for monitoring the performance of firms lies with the local chambers of industry and commerce or of artisan business, to which all employers are obliged to belong. The chambers set and conduct the final examinations and award certificates of skill competence.

**Figure 12.1 / Activities of a 1-Year Age Cohort
6 Months After Completing Full-Time Schooling***

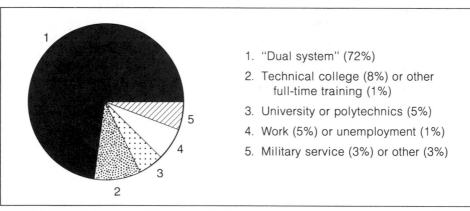

1. "Dual system" (72%)
2. Technical college (8%) or other full-time training (1%)
3. University or polytechnics (5%)
4. Work (5%) or unemployment (1%)
5. Military service (3%) or other (3%)

SOURCE: BMBW, 1989 Kap. 3.2; own calculations.

*Schooling includes full-time vocational preparation courses.

In most of the years of the 1960s and 1970s, the overwhelming majority of young people seeking training places were able to find them. Not all received a place in the firm of their first choice or even in the occupation of their first choice,[4] and there were some regional mismatches in supply and demand for apprenticeships, so that the positive net balances (surplus of places offered over applicants) recorded at a national level in most years did disguise some cases of negative net balances at the occupational or regional level. However, these were generally, if not universally, regarded as of minor significance.

Youth unemployment was considered to be a problem but was viewed as a problem specific to certain "disadvantaged groups" who failed to gain or had difficulty gaining entry into the apprenticeship system, or who subsequently dropped out of their apprenticeships after gaining entry. The magnitude of the problem of youth unemployment in the 1980s and policy responses to it are discussed at more length later in this chapter.

THE CRISIS OF THE EARLY 1980s[5]

At the start of the 1980s, the youth labor market was struck two blows simultaneously. The second oil price rise and the subsequent recession led to a sharp increase in unemployment as firms rationalized and reduced their workforces. In the large-firm sector, training activity—which had tended to follow a procyclical path—was also cut back. At the same time, postwar "baby boomers" were coming onto the labor market in their greatest numbers. Between 1970 and the peak year of 1981, the number of 16–19-year-olds in the population rose by a third, putting maximum demands upon the employment and training system at a time when it seemed least able to meet them. Appeals by the federal chancellor, other national and state politicians, and representatives of industry resulted in more training places being offered in 1984 than ever before, but the shortfall that year was still greater than at any time in the past. Based upon a conventional interpretation of supply and demand statistics (which were criticized for habitually disguising the true extent of the problem), a 5 percent net deficit in training places was recorded for 1984 (Table 12.1). Nearly 60,000 young people were still looking for an apprenticeship slot at the start of the training year in September, while an unknown number had at least temporarily abandoned their plans and either returned to school or technical college or had gone out onto the market to search for unskilled jobs.[6]

At the same time that many German youngsters were experiencing special difficulties in surmounting the "first threshold" in the system (the transition from the school system to the training system), others were experiencing special difficulties in surmounting the "second threshold" (the transition from training to adult employment). This, too, was an almost entirely new phenomenon in Germany. It was generally believed that the large majority of apprentices, and practically all of those who wished to stay, remained with the company that trained them after they had successfully completed their apprenticeships. The

Table 12.1 / Demand for and Supply of Apprenticeship Places: 1974–1989

Year	New Apprenticeship Contracts	Unfilled Apprenticeship Places	Unplaced Applicants	Excess or Shortfalls in Apprenticeships Offered (col. 2 − col. 3)	Excess or Shortfalls/ Applicants (col. 4/col. 1 + col. 3)
1974	450,000	29,000	21,000	+8,000	1.8
1975	462,000	18,000	24,000	−5,000	−1.0
1976	496,000	18,000	28,000	−10,000	−1.8
1977	558,000	26,000	27,000	−2,000	−0.3
1978	602,000	22,000	24,000	−2,000	−0.2
1979	640,000	37,000	20,000	+17,000	+2.6
1980	650,000	45,000	17,000	+27,000	+4.1
1981	606,000	37,000	22,000	+15,000	+2.4
1982	631,000	20,000	34,000	−14,000	−2.1
1983	677,000	20,000	47,000	−28,000	−3.8
1984	706,000	21,000	58,000	−37,000	−4.9
1985	697,000	22,000	59,000	−37,000	−4.9
1986	685,000	31,000	46,000	−15,000	−2.1
1987	646,000	45,000	34,000	+11,000	+1.6
1988	604,000	62,000	25,000	+37,000	+5.9
1989	584,000	85,000	18,000	+67,000	+11.1

SOURCES: BMBW, various years.

NOTE: Due to rounding, totals do not always add.

assumed high costs of providing training suggested that retention of trainees would be in a firm's interests. It was only in the early 1980s, on the basis of large-scale surveys conducted by the federal authorities, that policymakers began to recognize that the picture was rather more complex. Large firms had a much higher retention rate than small firms, and certain occupations had higher retention rates compared with others.

These findings were consistent with propositions advanced elsewhere that the industrial and commercial (or large-firm) sector and the artisan (or small-firm) sector have fundamentally different approaches to the provision of apprenticeship training.[7] Large, industrial firms adjust their training levels in accordance with their short- to medium-term business prospects but do invest substantially in the training they give. Small firms in the artisan sector appear to train anti-cyclically and are much less likely to regard training as an investment.[8] Instead, they appear to give much more weight to apprentices' contribution to production, viewing them as a source of cheap labor. As a consequence, small firms have an almost unlimited demand for trainees.[9] When the number of training places offered by the large-firm sector shrinks (as a result of economic developments) or the number of youngsters seeking apprenticeships rises (as a result of demographic developments), the small-firm sector is better able to satisfy its demand for trainees.[10] Once these apprentices have completed their training, they are no longer so attractive to the small firms, and a substantial proportion are discharged or, seeing few prospects, leave. Many seek jobs in the large-firm sector, often at a semiskilled level (hence the quip about Opel—the motor vehicle manufacturer—being the largest employer of bakers in the country).[11]

In the mid-1980s, as record numbers of young Germans were completing their training, as many as 20 percent of newly graduating apprentices who wanted to stay were reportedly not receiving takeover offers (Herget, Schöngen, and Westhoff 1987)—a figure four times as great as that which prevailed at the start of the decade. Larger firms were not offering the same semiskilled job opportunities as they had previously, and, thus, they were less able to absorb the excess trainees of the small-firm sector. In fact, the large firms found themselves unable to employ all those they had trained themselves, particularly those who, in response to political pressures, they had trained for "social" rather than "economic" reasons.[12] As a consequence, the equivalent of over one in eight of all those completing their apprenticeships in 1983 spent at least some time subsequently unemployed, and in September of that year the stock of unemployed newly graduating apprentices stood at over 50,000 (Table 12.2).

THE RECOVERY OF RECENT YEARS

Within 5 years, the situation had changed substantially. This was only in part the consequence of an about-turn in the German economy. Table 12.3 shows that in the second half of the 1980s, employment grew and unemployment fell at about the same rates as in other major OECD countries, while output growth was comparatively sluggish. Rather, the "recovery" of the dual system was the consequence of the declining of the size of the youth cohort, which fell at a rate even faster than that at which it had previously expanded. Between 1981 and 1989 the number of 16–19-year-olds fell by 35 percent. While this did not translate immediately into an equivalent reduction in the number of young people seeking a training place, the demand for apprenticeships certainly diminished. By 1989, the national balance of apprenticeship places had changed from the 5 percent deficit of training places recorded in 1984 to an 11 percent surplus. The number of young people officially categorized as failing to find an apprenticeship fell at the start of the 1989–1990 training year to only 18,000—only 30 percent of its 1984 level (Table 12.1).

Consistent with the previously discussed proposition of intersectoral differences in training behavior, there was a relative fall in the number of new training places accounted for by the small-firm (artisan) sector and a relative increase in the number accounted for by the large-firm (industrial and commercial) sector.[13] In the same way, there was a decline in the number of youths starting training in those occupations (mainly artisan) for which the number of new apprenticeship contracts had increased rapidly over the previous decade and were out of line

Table 12.2 / Unemployment After an Apprenticeship

	1979	1980	1981	1982	1983	1984	1985	1986	1987	1988
Number Successfully Completing an Apprenticeship (000s)	503.7	567.3	603.4	620.4	616.4	604.8	632.5	675.0	680.1	643.1
Number Registered as Unemployed after an Apprenticeship (000s end September)	7.7[a]	8.7[a]	19.0	40.7	54.4	46.4	37.2	33.1	29.5	21.0
Rate of Unemployment after an Apprenticeship (%)	1.5	1.6	3.1	6.6	8.8	7.7	5.9	4.9	4.3	3.3
Flow into Unemployment after an Apprenticeship (000s Jan.–Dec.)	N.A.	N.A.	N.A.	53.8	77.2	81.1	87.0	87.9	90.6	81.5
Flow as Percentage of Number Successfully Completing an Apprenticeship	N.A.	N.A.	N.A.	8.7	12.5	13.4	13.8	13.0	13.3	12.7

SOURCES: Federal Ministry for Education and Science; Federal Labour Office; own calculations.

[a]Extrapolated.

N.A. = Not Available.

Table 12.3 / Output, Employment, and Unemployment

	1984	1985	1986	1987	1988	1989
GDP (1985 = 100)						
Germany	98.0	100.0	102.3	104.0	107.8	112.1
Major OECD countries[a]	96.8	100.0	102.7	106.4	111.2	114.9
Employment (1985 = 100)						
Germany	99.0	100.0	101.0	106.0	107.0	108.0
Major OECD countries[a]	99.0	100.0	101.0	103.0	105.0	107.0
Unemployment (%)[b]						
Germany	7.1	7.2	6.4	6.2	6.1	5.5
Major OECD countries[a]	7.3	7.2	7.1	6.7	6.1	5.6

SOURCE: OECD Principal Economic Indicators; OECD Quarterly Labour Force Statistics; own calculations.
[a] USA, Canada, Japan, Germany, France, Italy, U.K.
[b] Standardized.

with future employment prospects for workers with the skill concerned (see Casey 1986). There were also indications that the transition from apprenticeship to employment was preceding more smoothly. The relative number of newly graduating apprentices experiencing some unemployment on graduation remained much the same as 4 years previously (13 percent), but the number registered as unemployed in September 1989 was much lower, standing at only 21,000 (Table 12.2). This suggests that the average duration of "unemployment after an apprenticeship" was considerably shorter in the later period.

If, at the end of the day, the most apparent threat to the legitimacy of the "dual system" had been overcome, the employment and training market for young people was not entirely unproblematic. A closer examination of the net demand and supply ratio for apprenticeship places by state reveals mismatches (Table 12.4). The overall positive balance of 11 percent nationally hid a range of variation at the state level that included, among others, a deficit of 2 percent in the city state of Bremen and a surplus of 28 percent in Bavaria. The mismatch phenomenon to which these figures bear testament is a problem of growing importance; interregional disparities have been worsening throughout the 1980s, almost regardless of developments on the national youth labor market. In 1982, Bavaria (still the "best performer") recorded a net surplus of training slots about 4 percentage points better than the national average; by 1989, its surplus was almost 17 percentage points better than the national average. Bremen (still the "worst" performer) recorded a net deficit only 4 percentage points worse than the national average in 1982; by 1989, its deficit was over 12 percentage points below the national average. The dispersion of state mismatch measures was four times as great in 1989 as in 1982.

The performance of the "dual system" throughout the 1980s reflects the widely commented-on growing north-south divide in Germany. The industries

Table 12.4 / Ratio of Supply to Demand of Apprenticeship Places, by State

	1982	1989
Schleswig Holstein	95.9	104.1
Hamburg	95.3	98.1
Lower Saxony	95.3	104.0
Bremen	93.7	98.2
North Rhine-Westphalia	96.8	102.6
Hessen	95.1	110.3
Rheinland-Pfalz	95.6	112.6
Baden-Würtenburg	100.9	119.7
Bavaria	101.2	128.0
Saarland	95.4	108.4
Berlin (W)	95.6	107.3
Federal Republic	97.6	111.1
Coefficient of Variation	0.0248	0.0980

SOURCES: BMBW, 1983 and 1990; own calculations.

NOTE: The table reads as follows: In Hamburg in 1982 there were 95 apprenticeship places offered for every 100 young people seeking one. The coefficient of variation is a standardized measure of dispersion. A value of 0 would indicate that every state had the same balance between demand and supply. The extent of dispersion in 1989 was four times as great as in 1982.

of the south are often more modern than those of the north, and they have more often been growing than contracting. However, the dominance of small firms in the south has also played a part for, as has been pointed out, such firms employ relatively more apprentices (for reasons discussed earlier). So far the federal authorities have proposed no specific measures to counter the problem of the regional imbalances in the market for training places, although young people who leave home to take up an apprenticeship in another part of the country are eligible for special benefits to help meet the costs of accommodation and travel. In addition, it is now generally agreed that regional policy should accord a greater priority to apprentice training provision.[14]

THE CHANGING CHARACTER OF THE SYSTEM

The character of the apprenticeship system has changed in other ways in the course of the last decade. As was hinted at earlier, the age profile of young trainees has changed considerably. The typical new apprentice is not a 16-year-old school leaver and has not been for some time. The average age of an apprentice in 1987 was some 18.5 years, 1 year higher than at the end of the 1970s and 2 years higher than at the start of that decade (Table 12.5).

There are a number of explanations for this. First, in the 1970s, as a growing proportion of young people stayed on at school to complete their matriculation certificate, the effective school-leaving age was rising. More important, however, a growing proportion of those who passed their matriculation examination chose not to go on to university (or at least not immediately) but instead to take up an apprenticeship.[15] In 1988 as many as 16 percent of all apprentices possessed their matriculation certificate, compared to 6.5 percent 10 years previously (Table 12.5). While it cannot yet be said that any training occupations have become the exclusive preserve of those with such a qualification, or that the possession of such a qualification is a necessary requirement for taking up training in a particular occupation, highly qualified school-leavers are to be found concentrated in a very few occupations, mainly in commerce, insurance, and banking.

A second explanation is that a growing proportion of young people are not entering apprenticeships directly from school. Research carried out in the first half of the 1980s drew attention not only to the variety of routes coupling school to the training system but also made an attempt to quantify their relative importance (Brandes, Brosi, and Menk 1986). It was estimated that some 70 percent of those leaving the general school system do eventually take up an apprenticeship, but half of them do not do so immediately. Some 23 percent spend a year or more as a full-time student at a vocational school or on a special preparatory course, and 11 percent spend time working, being unemployed or inactive, or

Table 12.5 / Characteristics of Apprentices

	1970	1979	1988
Average Age	16.6	17.6[a]	18.5[c]
Sex			
Male	64.7	62.2	56.9
Female	35.3	37.8	43.1
Educational Qualification			
Basic high school certificate	N.A.	N.A.	24.3
Matriculation	N.A.	6.5[b]	16.1
Occupation			
Production	46.7	50.7	46.8
Service	46.5	43.3	47.3
Sector			
Artisan	33.0	41.1	34.8
Industry/commerce	57.1	45.4	49.9

SOURCES: BMBW, various years; own calculations.

[a] 1978.
[b] 1980.
[c] 1987.

N.A. = Not Available.

doing their military service. On the basis of this information, it can be estimated that only one-half of new entrants into the "dual system" in the early to mid-1980s came directly from school, a third came from vocational schools and preparatory courses, and the remainder had been away from the general school system. Because not only minimum age school-leavers but older teenagers as well now determine the demand for training places, it is not surprising that the numbers seeking apprenticeships failed to immediately decline with the size of the 16-year-old cohort; there was a lag in the decline in demand for apprenticeships.

There were other ways in which the character of the "dual system" was changing over the course of the 1980s. Some of these changes were of a long-term nature—like the gradual increase in the age of apprentices; others were short-term developments, sometimes reversing trends of a previous period. The most important of the first kind of change was the increase in the proportion of apprentices who are female. At the start of the 1970s, women constituted scarcely a third of the total; by 1988, they comprised 43 percent of all apprentices, and it is generally assumed that the upward trend will continue (Table 12.5). By comparison, the relative shares of apprenticeships in the service and production occupations have been more volatile, as have been the related shares of apprenticeships provided by the large-firm (industry and commerce) sector and the small-firm (artisan) sector. There was a marked increase in the proportion of apprenticeships being undertaken in the small-firm sectors in the 1970s, but this movement was to some extent undone in the latter part of the 1980s. As the share accounted for by the small-firm sectors rose, the share accounted for by service occupations fell but less than proportionately. As the share accounted for by the large-firm sectors grew again in the 1980s, the share accounted for by service occupations grew (Table 12.5). Forecasts of the future structure of the labor force suggest that this trend, too, is likely to continue into the coming decade (Hofer, Weidig, and Wolff 1989).

THE NEW DEMOGRAPHIC CHALLENGE

The aging, higher level of qualification of the apprentice population, and its gradual feminization, are developments relevant to the principal concerns of employers and politicians engaged in thinking about training requirements and training policy for the 1990s and beyond. Once again, the major problem of the German youth labor market is the result of demographic change, but the problem is the opposite of what it was in the early 1980s. Instead of a "surplus" of young people seeking apprenticeships, there is likely to be a shortage of apprentices. The fall in the size of the 16–19-year-old cohort that began in 1981 will continue to the mid-1990s, and in 1995 the number of young people in this age group will represent only 55 percent of the size of the 1981 cohort. A small upswing followed by stabilization is expected thereafter (Figure 12.2).

Aggravating this demographically induced problem is a change in the behav-

Figure 12.2 / Number of 16–19 Year Olds in Population in Britain and Germany: 1970–2000.

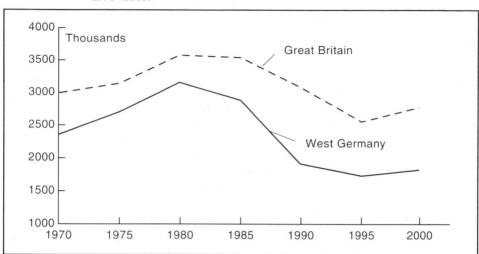

SOURCE: Federal Ministry for Education and Science; Department of Employment.

NOTE: 1990 onward are projections.

ior of young people and their attitude toward training. By the end of the 1980s, the proportion of young Germans in possession of a matriculation certificate who were opting to follow an apprenticeship rather than higher studies leveled off and started to fall, and this fall is expected to continue into the 1990s. Compared with a high of over 700,000 new apprenticeships concluded in 1984, it is estimated that there will be only 500,000 completed apprenticeships in 1995. A commonly expressed fear is there will be a resultant shortfall in the number of skilled workers in Germany and that the economy will be unable to train a sufficient quantity of skilled manpower to assure the preeminence of the country as a supplier of quality goods and services.[16]

Various schemes have been suggested to remedy this potential problem. One solution would be to encourage a more efficient use of the most highly qualified training applicants. While the training regulations for each occupation specify the normal duration of an apprenticeship, they do permit a reduced duration under certain circumstances. Such reductions are made in practice, but there is no systematic knowledge of when and why. Over the last few years, the government and the Federal Training Institute have been exhorting employers to make greater use of the option of accelerated training for those applicants possessing a matriculation certificate. This could make any given intake of apprentices more quickly serviceable in the adult economy and might increase the attractiveness of apprenticeships to more highly qualified young people. This might help overcome the stagnation or decline in the proportion of individuals with a matriculation certificate who are choosing the apprenticeship route. Moreover, if the more highly qualified young people are to be better used, they will have to be pulled into more occupations than the narrow range in which they are currently concentrated. Whether it will indeed be possible to induce them to enter traditional production occupations remains to be seen, but it is possible that the transformation of jobs as a result of new technologies will have a positive impact.

Young women are also seen as an underutilized resource. They have traditionally trained in a very limited number of occupations, mainly in the commercial or personal services sector. In the course of the 1980s the government, through the Federal Training Institute, has promoted a series of demonstration projects under the title "girls in men's occupations" in an attempt to encourage a breakdown of existing patterns of gender segregation. Measures of gender segregation in apprenticeship training that can be extracted from official statistics have shown some movement over the last decade. In particular this has taken place at the extremes, so that the proportion of young women training in heavily male-dominated occupations has increased and the proportion training in heavily female-dominated occupations has decreased (Table 12.6).

Finally, both the government and the Federal Training Institute have been urging employers to reconsider their attitudes to members of the more "disadvantaged" groups on the youth labor market, such as the handicapped, those with no qualifications, and first-generation immigrants. Increased apprenticeship recruitment of members of these groups, it is argued, might help overcome the forecast shortages of skilled labor.

Along with these strategic responses to the potential shortage of skilled labor, employers are also responding more tactically. Principally, this means trying to improve their individual competitive position in the market for trainees. However, in contrast to Britain, this has not resulted in a bidding up of youth wages (or as is more appropriate with respect to Germany, of the "training

Table 12.6 / Female Apprentices in Selected Occupations: 1977 and 1987

	1977	1987
In Male Dominated Occupations (0–20% of apprentices female)	2.5	8.4
In Mainly Male Occupations (20–40% of apprentices female)	6.3	6.9
In Mixed Occupations (40–60% of apprentices female)	19.4	20.0
In Mainly Female Occupations (60–80% of apprentices female)	24.7	24.6
In Female Dominated Occupations (80–100% of apprentices female)	47.1	40.0

SOURCE: BMBW (1989).

NOTE: The table reads as follows: In 1987 8.4 percent of female apprentices were in male-dominated occupations compared to 2.5 percent a decade previously. Occupations are grouped according to the proportion of females training in them in 1977.

allowance"). Instead, a number of larger firms have increased the value of the fringe benefits they offer or have introduced new benefits (such as transportation costs or the costs of a midday meal).[17] Some companies have been more imaginative in combining a strategic with a tactical response. One major motor vehicle manufacturer—Audi—has sought to increase the number of trainees it attracts by offering young women who train and stay with the company guarantees of reemployment valid for up to 7 years if they leave work to bear and raise children.

Given the higher quality of the training, the greater security of future employment offered, and the better remuneration attached to that employment, the large-firm sector as a whole has been relatively successful so far in recruiting the desired number of apprentices. The small-firm sector has performed less well, and it is here that the major shortfalls are experienced.[18]

THE CHALLENGE OF MODERN WORKING SKILLS

The second concern is not with the quantity of skilled labor in the medium term but with its quality. While the thoroughness of the training prescribed in the regulations for each occupation was not questioned, as early as the 1960s there was concern that apprenticeships were not always relevant to the demands imposed by the most modern products and services and the most up-to-date methods of working. In some cases, the outdated nature of apprenticeship training might even have discouraged young people from following training in a particular occupation. For some occupations, training regulations had been laid down before World War II or even earlier, and for many others no revisions had been undertaken since the 1950s or 1960s. Larger and more advanced firms supplement the minimum requirements of the training regulations with their own additional training to take account of changing materials and technology; smaller, less advanced firms are much less likely to do so. Formally, apprentices have to be tested in their final examinations to see if they can meet the requirements laid down in the regulations, but informally a multiplicity of standards prevail. Thus, on the basis of their knowledge of the employing organization, examiners are likely to adjust the rigor with which they test individual candidates and the extent to which the questions they ask make reference to extracurricular skills.

In order to bring young people's skills up-to-date and to increase the transferability of these skills, the Vocational Training Act was passed, and steps have been taken to revise the training regulations falling under its jurisdiction. Each year since 1969, progress has been made in reviewing the training for a number of occupations, and by the end of 1989, 96 percent of all training places covered by the act had been subjected to revised regulations. This review also involved a process of rationalization. The objective was not only to bring minimum requirements into line with present-day skill demands and work conditions but also to eliminate unnecessary duplication by combining closely related courses and abolishing occupations that had become irrelevant to the needs of an advanced industrial society. Consequently, there has been a fall in the number of recognized apprenticeships from 465 in 1980 to 382 in 1988. Some of the most important revisions occurred in recent years. For example, in 1986 new regulations were introduced for occupations in industrial engineering and in 1988 for the engineering occupations in the artisan sector. Some 160,000 young people are training for the first group of occupations, and nearly 200,000 are training for the second. Other major groups for which training regulations have been reformed in recent years include the electrical occupations (for both the industrial and artisan sectors), the commercial and clerical occupations, and the retailing occupations. It is hoped that by the early 1990s, the first round of reforms will be completed and that work can commence on a second round.

The reform process, which involves joint negotiations and consultations between trade union and employer representatives, supported by the resources of the Federal Training Institute, is not a particularly fast one. For example, the initial proposition to reform the regulations for engineering occupations in the artisan sector was made in May 1983, but the new regulations, which were not finally agreed upon until 1988, did not come into operation until August 1989. In the case of the regulations for engineering occupations in the industrial sector, reform procedures were initiated in 1979, but the new regulations were not effective until August 1987. For other occupational groups, the process was shorter (between 3 and 4 years), but the long average time it takes to reform regulations combined with the infrequency with which reforms do take place suggests an inflexibility in the German apprenticeship system that is an inevitable consequence of the high degree of regulation to which it is subject.[19] Therefore, it seems likely that the more progressive training firms will continue to treat the regulations as minimum requirements and to supplement their requirements with their own training in the use of the newest technologies. On the basis of case studies, it has been suggested that the training given in such circumstances is more "specific," than "general," and this has led some commentators to express doubts about its full transferability (e.g., Beuschel, Gensior, and Sorge 1988).

This could be interpreted as a failure to meet the objectives that the reform process professed to have. Yet steps were made in the desired direction. The wider skill bands that were created did expand the range of tasks that a skilled worker was considered capable of performing. Although it represents an extreme example, a good illustration of this is provided by the apprenticeship system for occupations in the industrial engineering sector. Previously, there were 37 separate occupations for which a young person could qualify: after the reform there were only seven. The recommended curriculum for the school-based part of training, which was published simultaneously with nearly all of the new training regulations, has ensured that nationwide standards now apply here too, so that an apprenticeship acquired in one state will be recognized more readily elsewhere. Finally, although not so directly a consequence of the reforms themselves, there has been a growing standardization of examinations, at least in the industrial and commercial sector. Local chambers of industry and commerce have remained the examiners, but over the last decade an increasing number of them have been availing themselves of the services of the Institute for Vocational Examinations and Teaching Material, purchasing centrally produced examination questions rather than constructing their own. The use of common examinations is seen to promote common standards of marking, and this too should lead to a more universal acceptance of qualifications acquired.

The attempt to improve the quality of training has sometimes involved an extension of the duration of apprenticeships. The reformed engineering and electrical apprenticeships last for 3½ years; their predecessors lasted only 3. In retailing, the 2-year apprenticeship (for sales assistant) has been increasingly displaced by the 3-year apprenticeship, and, while the reform did not abolish the former, it seems to have accelerated this process (see Schenkel 1989).[20] Similarly, the reform of the clerical occupations is likely to see the phasing out of the 2-year office assistant apprenticeship.

It is more difficult to determine whether progress has been made in encouraging the acquisition of what can best be termed "general competencies." The new regulations for the engineering and electrical occupations require that apprentices be able "on their own to plan, carry out, and control" their work, and that the final examination should test them in this as well as their ability to perform fragmented, occupationally specific tasks. What is unstated is how these general competencies should be taught and how they should be examined.

THE CHALLENGE OF THE "DISADVANTAGED"

Although the "dual system" is, in comparison with the vocational training systems of many countries, an extremely encompassing one, there remains a not inconsiderable minority of young people who fail or threaten to fail to acquire any vocational qualifications at all. Indeed, over the last decade, an average of nearly 10 percent of each age cohort has passed into adulthood without obtaining a vocational qualification or a university or college degree. If the unqualified are considered in relation to those who undertake an apprenticeship or its equivalent (a more appropriate comparison), then more than one in eight of those who should enter training leave school without going on to further study and fail to secure a vocational qualification.

It is this group that is seen as being among the most "disadvantaged" on the German youth labor market. According to a recent survey (Kloas and Sacks 1991), about half of the young people who fail to obtain a vocational qualification never seek a training place. Among young men this is mainly because they are more interested in trying to earn money immediately; among young women this is because their family requires their help in the house or because of pregnancy. Among those who seek a training place, half do so in vain; the remainder are successful but drop out, because they feel unable to cope, because of difficulties with their employer, or because such personal reasons as pregnancy intervene.

Over and above the group of young people who lack the qualifications or the motivation to apply for or stay in an apprenticeship (a group called the "psychologically disadvantaged") is a second group—the "economically disadvantaged." The latter group is made up of young people who, under normal circumstances, could be expected to find a training place but who, as a result of a particularly unfavorable situation on the national or local youth labor market, fail to do so. Thus, while the size of the first group is largely determined by demographic factors, the size of the second is also related to the economic factors. In the early 1980s, concern for this group became dominant, and at the end of the 1980s it came to the fore again, but only in certain, geographically limited areas of the country where pockets of "economic disadvantage" were still recognizable.

Young "foreigners," particularly those of Turkish or Yugoslavian parentage, are overrepresented in both of the last two groups. Overall, their achievement at school is inferior to that of young Germans (Table 12.7), so that they are four times as likely as German youths to leave school without even a basic high school certificate—20 percent of them leave without a basic certificate. Of those who register to seek an apprenticeship place, twice as many fail to find a place by the start of the training year. (In 1988, the failure rate was nearly 8 percent for foreigners compared to 4 percent for Germans.) This reflects, in part, their lower level of educational qualifications but also a degree of selection discrimination on the part of providers of apprenticeship places—a discrimination that is easier to exercise when there is a surplus supply of youth labor. Those young "foreigners" who start vocational training are more than twice as likely to break it off before completion than are young Germans. In short, young "foreigners" benefit considerably less from the "dual system" than do young Germans. Less than 30 percent of them pass through an apprenticeship, compared to over 70 percent of young Germans.

The policy response to the problem of these three groups who have difficulty in the "dual system" has not been to create an alternative system of vocational training but rather to establish a network of aids that will bring these individuals

Table 12.7 / School Leavers, by Nationality and Qualification Obtained: 1988

	Germans	Foreigners
No Qualifications	4.8	20.2
Basic Qualification[a]	25.0	46.3
Middle Qualification[b]	37.3	24.8
Matriculation[c]	32.9	8.7

SOURCE: Federal Ministry for Education and Science.

[a] *Hauptschulabschluß*—normally at 16.
[b] *Realschulabschluß*—normally at 16.
[c] *Abitur*—normally at 18–19.

up to a standard that will enable them to apply successfully for an apprentice-ship place, or to provide special assistance, to them or to their employers while they are in a training course, or to provide a workplace in which they can pursue a training course for which they are suited. Such a workplace is in an "external" (*überbetrieblichen*) training center,[21] and initially the individual is assigned to it for 1 year only. If, however, the young person fails to find a place in a company for the remainder of his or her apprenticeship, the full period of training can be completed there. The "external" training center-based program benefits "economically disadvantaged" as well as "psychologically disadvan-taged" young people.

The program concentrating on preparing young people for an apprenticeship involves courses of up to 1 year, and the numbers of youth participating in this program have fluctuated considerably over the 1980s, from over 80,000 in the middle of the decade to a little more than 50,000 at the end. The program giving special assistance to "disadvantaged" apprentices has grown rapidly, from little more than 2,000 young people in 1983 to over 37,000 by 1989. The program providing training places in "external" training centers has also grown in terms of the numbers served, although in the last 4 years it has stabilized at about 21,000 participants, of which about 3,500 are classified as "economically disad-vantaged" young people. The total of 40,000 "disadvantaged" apprentices sup-ported under the last two programs represents only 2.5 percent of the total of 1.6 million young people currently in apprenticeships. Four times that many young people—another 160,000 individuals under age 25—are not participating in and have not graduated from a vocational training course.

As was suggested earlier, attempting to make the "dual system" even more encompassing than it presently is might help relieve possible future shortages of skilled labor. However, the price of integration is high. The individual mea-sures and courses mounted under the various programs described earlier are necessarily very labor-intensive, and some require the provision of special ac-commodations and the services of social workers as well as trainers. Federal government expenditure supporting "disadvantaged" young people in appren-ticeships (not including expenditures on pre-apprenticeship, preparatory courses) tripled between 1984 and 1990. Nor is admittance to one of these schemes a guarantee of success: the dropout rate among supported apprentices is well over one-third. Despite the "dual system's" favorable record in helping the majority of young people make the transition from school to work compared with the procedures and institutions of other countries, German politicians and labor market administrators remain as concerned about the problem of youth unemployment as their counterparts abroad.

CONCLUSION: UNIFICATION, THE NEW CHALLENGE

In reviewing recent developments in the German apprenticeship system, it is important to stress that the changes made have been marginal and incremental. There has been no major structural overhaul, because there has been no perceived need for it. In the opinion of most interested parties, the "dual system" overcame the challenge of the early 1980s with its legitimacy intact. Most observers believe the deficiencies identified were not fundamental, although there are a few academics and politicians who point to continuing imbalances in the system, including its tendency to undertrain and overtrain, and the mismatch between the skills needed by the economy and the skills produced by the training system (problems that could only be rectified by greater government intervention). Nevertheless, the calls for a statutory obligation to provide apprenticeship places and for a "levy-grant" scheme to finance training activity[22] that reverberated through the debates of the mid-1970s to mid-1980s have almost completely died away.

Had the crisis experienced been of longer duration, and had the political situation been different, it is possible that reforms along these lines would have been considered. (History also shows they would have been fiercely contested.) As it was, the same factors that contributed to the crisis' onset also contributed to its demise. Thus, although it passed a critical test, thanks to an element of fortuity, supporters of existing arrangements looked forward with some confidence to the challenges of the 1990s. The tone of statements by the federal government and the Federal Training Institute implies that, while the scope of these challenges is considerable, they can be solved within the framework of existing arrangements and institutions.

Moreover, as the shortage of skilled workers was perceived to be one of the most pressing problems of the foreseeable future, events in Germany since the late summer of 1989 appear to have considerably alleviated these concerns. The massive influx of citizens from the German Democratic Republic (GDR) brought more than 500,000 people to West Germany by the spring of 1990, and a further 150,000 arrived by the end of the year. The majority of these "settlers" (*Übersiedler*) were believed to be young and qualified. With monetary and social unification in summer 1990, the former West Germany acquired an almost boundless reserve of labor in the east, which grew as the collapse of the eastern economy threw hundreds of thousands out of work.[23]

Yet if unification was a source of considerable advantage to West German employers, it created new and substantial problems for the training authorities in the united Germany, who were faced with potentially massive youth unemployment in the new *Länder*. The apprentice system in the east, which shares common roots with that in the west, is heavily dependent upon the employer provision of training places. While not all firms have been shedding labor on a massive scale, very few have been recruiting, and school-leavers have been the first to suffer as a result. In the very short run, the youth labor market has been relieved by a more than doubling of the proportion of young people staying on at school beyond the age of 16. (The percentage rose from about 15 to over 30 percent.) In the short to medium term, the establishment of publicly sponsored "external" training centers may provide the training opportunities that cannot be offered by companies themselves. The "unification treaty" (*Einigungsvertrag*) provided for the establishment of a program of aid for "economically disadvantaged" young people to be established in the eastern states. (It will be open to those who lost their jobs while still in training as well as to school-leavers.) It is estimated that up to one in three apprentices in the former GDR will be trained in such centers over the next few years (BMBW 1991).

However, guaranteeing the quality of training is as important as guaranteeing that apprentice training places are available (see Rudolph 1990). Most apprenticeships in the GDR had been of 2 years' duration and had a much more "artisan-like" quality than the apprenticeships in the west. As discussed earlier, during the 1980s much of the effort of those responsible for training in the west was directed at upgrading the quality of training and bringing it closer into line with modern materials, technologies, and methods of working. Materials, technologies, and methods in the east are dramatically underdeveloped in comparison with the west, and the ability of most eastern firms to comply with western standards is limited. Failure to comply, however, will frustrate the ability of eastern firms to attract school-leavers of quality and condemn the east to long-term backwardness.

The challenge that those responsible for apprentice training policy face at the beginning of the 1990s is many times greater than the challenge they faced at the beginning of the 1980s. In their search for solutions for the 1990s, they may take succor in the experiences and (relative) successes of the 1980s. Whether economic "takeoff" (*Aufschwung*) will come to the rescue in the east in the same way that demographic change did in the west in the mid-1980s is uncertain. It certainly cannot be predicted with the same degree of accuracy as changes in age cohort size. Nor, if it were to come, would it be an unmixed blessing, for it would ultimately bring back the problems of skill shortages and shortages in the supply of young workers that dominated the discussions at the end of the 1980s, problems for which no lasting solutions were found.

The research upon which this chapter is based was financed by the Skills Unit of the Training Agency. The author would like to acknowledge this support, together with the assistance of members of the staff of the Bundesinstitut für Berufsbildung (Federal Training Institute), Berlin, and the Institut für Arbeitsmarkt- und Beschäftigungsforschung (Institute for Labour Market Research), Nürnberg. The opinions expressed here are, however, the author's own.

ENDNOTES

1. Estimates put the training allowance at between 20 percent and 27 percent of a skilled worker's wage in the first year and between 27 percent and 53 percent in the final year, with levels toward the lower end being more usual.

2. The law requires that all young people under the age of 18 attend school on a part-time basis for a minimum of 1 day per week.

3. Training regulations (*Verordnungen*) lay down the minimum level of skill and knowledge expected of an apprentice. They are often quite bulky documents, and they are couched in very specific terms, covering what is to be taught, at what stage and for how long, and specifying the periodicity, content, and duration of examinations.

4. In 1987–1988, 53 percent of those who registered with the youth employment service seeking an apprenticeship obtained a training place in the occupation of their first choice. Not all young people were the ones registered, and it is possible that it was those who were least successful in their search who did register.

5. This section draws extensively from an earlier study of the German apprenticeship system (Casey 1986).

6. Contemporary estimates suggest that some 30,000–35,000 took up pre-apprenticeship courses, and some 40,000–50,000 returned to school, either to continue in general education or to start some form of vocational education.

7. The equation of artisan (*Handwerk*) and industrial and commercial (*Industrie und Handel*) with small and large is an approximate one. The distinction is based upon the firm's legal and organizational status, and, hence, the chamber with which it is registered. However, nearly 90 percent of artisan firms have less than 20 employees.

8. In the early 1970s a government commission (the Edding Commission) made a detailed ongoing study of the costs and financing of apprenticeship training. As well as investigating the net costs of training for different types of firm, the commission made an extensive appraisal of the quality of the training in terms of both inputs and outputs. The commission's report made clear the difference in net costs between small and large firms and also illustrated the much higher quality of the training provided by large firms. An in-depth evaluation undertaken in 1980 broadly confirmed the commission's picture of the difference in net costs of training between the two types of firms. More recently (see Damm-Rüger, Dengen, and Grünewald 1988) a fresh attempt has been made to measure the quality of training, although the methodology of the study was considerably less rigorous than that applied by the commission. One of the main findings was that, in relative terms, the quality of training provided by small firms had improved, although it still fell considerably below that of larger firms.

9. It is notable that in firms with less than 10 employees, apprentices make up, on average, 15 percent of the workforce, while in firms with more than 500 employees they make up less than 6 percent.

10. This is referred to as the "sponge function" of the small-firm sector and was first illustrated systematically by Steinbach (1974) in a background study for the Edding Commission.

11. A "pull" as well as a "push" effect has to be recognized here. The earnings of a semiskilled worker in a large firm are usually considerably higher than those of a skilled worker in a small firm.

12. It is uncertain how much of such "training beyond own needs" took place. However, it should be remembered that the marginal costs of offering an additional apprenticeship place could sometimes be very low (see Casey 1986).

13. In 1984, industry and commerce accounted for 48.6 percent of new training places

and the artisan sector for 35.4 percent. In 1988 these proportions had become 51.7 percent and 33.1 percent, respectively.

14. At the Ruhr Conference in spring 1989, called to discuss the structural difficulties of the eponymous region, the federal government's pledge of financial support included the allocation of DM 91 million to support apprentice training in areas affected by firm closures.

15. This reflected in part their assessment of poor prospects on the graduate labor market, in part the fact that a growing proportion of them were from families where university students were not the norm, and in part the perception that a double qualification (apprenticeship followed by a degree) could enhance future employment chances.

16. Some commentators are much more skeptical about the extent and seriousness of current and predicted skilled worker shortages. There are some who argue that the claims of employers' inability to find sufficient skilled workers are made to play down the significance of current high employment levels or to serve as ammunition in the fight against union claims for shorter working hours. At a less emotive level, it has been pointed out that a substantial proportion of skilled (manual) workers—perhaps between a quarter and a third—are currently employed in semi- or unskilled positions, and that they constitute a reserve upon which employers could draw (IAB 1989).

17. This is not to say that the level of the training allowance is insensitive to the state of the youth labor market, rather that the response is a lagged one. Thus, after increasing at between 5 and 7 percent over the years 1976–1982, training allowances grew at only 2 to 3 percent in the years thereafter. While overall wage growth also slowed in these years, at least some of the lower rate of increase in the level of training allowances has also been attributed to the relative oversupply of young people on the labor market. Accordingly, it is expected that in the coming years the rate of increase in the level of training allowances will pick up. In the first part of the 1980s, there were cases of collective agreements, notably that of the chemical industry, freezing the training allowance for a year as a contribution toward improving the position of young people on the labor market. Equally, in the late 1980s, the construction industry, which had suffered a severe shortage of skilled labor and of young recruits, increased the level of the training allowance it paid and now tops the tables as the highest paying sector of all.

18. Of the 85,000 unfilled training places registered with the federal employment service in September 1989, 51,000 (60 percent) were with artisan (small) firms and 26,000 (30 percent) with industrial and commercial (large) firms.

19. Defenders of the reform process argue that there is a difference between an initial revision, such as the large majority of occupations were subject to, and an updating, such as should occur in the future. They would argue that the process now has a momentum, which will make reforms much easier and quicker.

20. The "inferior" 2-year qualification has been kept in existence on a provisional basis, subject to review by the employers' associations and trade unions of the retail sector.

21. These "external" training centers were established by chambers of industry and commerce, industry associations, etc. initially to provide training places for the teach-

ing of skills that some firms could not provide alone. The federal government can contribute toward their capital costs and also meets their running costs where they are serving participants in special programs for the "disadvantaged."

22. On the history of this demand, see Casey (1986). "Pooling systems," governed by collective agreements, do exist in four industries: construction, garden maintenance, (artisan) masonry, and (artisan) roofing. The first of these is by far the most important, covering in excess of 50,000 apprentices.

23. Estimates for the number of unemployed in the former GDR in mid-1991 are some 1.7 million. A further 700,000 will be taken out of the statistics by special employment measures and by early retirement, and a further 500,000 members of the labor force will be working or living in the west. In 1989, the GDR labor force numbered just over 10 million (Autorengemeinschaft 1990).

REFERENCES

Autorengemeinschaft, Zur Arbeitsmarktentwicklung 1990/1991 im vereinigten Deutschland ("The Development of the Labour Market in 1990/1991 in a United Germany"). *Mitteilungen aus der Arbeitsmarkt- und Berufsforschung* 4/90: 474–503.

Beuschel, W., S. Gensior, and A. Sorge. 1988. *Mikroelektronik, Qualifikation und Produktinnovation (Microelectronics, Skills and Product Innovation)*. Berlin: VDI/VDE Technologiezentrum Informationstechnik Gmbh.

BIBB. 1989. *Neue Berufe—Neue Qualifikationen* ("New Occupations—New Qualifications"). (Report of a special conference in 5 volumes). Nürnburg: Wissen Verlag.

BMBW. *Berufsbildungsbericht* (Vocational Training Report). Various years 1986 onward. Bonn: Bundesministerium für Bildung und Wissenschaft.

Brandes, H., W. Brosi, and A. Menk. 1986. "Wege in die berufliche Bildung" ("Pathways into Apprenticeships"). *Mitteilungen aus der Arbeitsmarkt–und Berufsforschung* 2/86: 287–297.

Casey, B. 1986. "The Dual Apprenticeship System and the Recruitment and Retention of Young Persons in West Germany." *British Journal of Industrial Relations* XXIV: 63–81.

Damm-Rüger, S., U. Dengen, and U. Grünewald. 1988. *Zur Struktur der betrieblichen Ausbildungsgestaltung (On the Structure and Character of Enterprise-Based Apprentice Training)*. Bonn und Berlin: Bundesinstitut für Berufsbildung (Berichte zur beruflichen Bildung, Heft 101).

Herget, H., K. Schöngen, and G. Westhoff. 1987. *Berufsbildung abgeschlossen—was dann? (Apprenticeship Completed—What Next?)*. Bonn und Berlin: Bundesinstitut für Berufsbildung (Berichte zur beruflichen Bildung, Heft 85).

Hofer, P., I. Weidig, and H. Wolff. 1989. *Arbeitslandschaft bis 2010 nach Umfang und Tätigkeitsprofilen (The Structure of Employment up to 2010)*. Nürnberg: Institut für Arbeitsmarkt und Berufsforschung der Bundesanstalt für Arbeit (BeitrAB 131.1).

Institüt für Arbeitsmarkt und Berufsforschung. 1989. *Fachkräfteangebot und Fachkräfteeinsatz im Arbeiterbereich in den 80er Jahren (Skilled Worker Supply and Skilled Worker Utilisation in the 1980s)*. (Kurzbericht VII/3) Nürnberg.

Kloas, P.-W., and P. Sacks, 1991. "Junge Erwachsene ohne Berufsausbildung -Ergebnisse einer Repräsentativbefragung des Jahres 1990 in den alten Bundesländern" ("Young People Without Vocational Qualifications—Results of a Survey in the Former West Germany"). *Berufsbildung in der Wissenschaft und Praxis.*

Rudolph, W. 1990. *Die Berufsbildung in der Deutschen Demokratischen Republik (Vocational Training in the GDR).* Berlin: European Centre for the Development of Vocational Education and Training (CEDEFOP).

Schenkel, P. 1989. "Einführung in die Ausbildungsordnung" ("Introduction to the Training Regulations"). In BIBB, Vol. K, *Neue Entwicklungen in den kaufmännischen Berufen,* pp. 49–62.

Steinbach, S. 1974. *Analyse der Konjunkturabhängigkeit der betrieblichen Berufsbildung in der Bundesrepublik Deutschland (An Analysis of the Conjunctural Dependence of Vocational Training in West Germany).* Studien und Materialien der Sachverständigenkommission "Kosten und Finanzierung der beruflichen Bildung," Band 2. Bielefeld: Bertelsman Verlag.

Streeck, W., J. Hilbert, K.-H. Kevelaer, F. Maer, and F. Maier. 1987. *The Role of the Social Partners in Vocational Training and Further Training in the Federal Republic of Germany.* Berlin: European Centre for the Development of Vocational Education and Training (CEDEFOP).

Chapter 13

SPECIAL MEASURES TO IMPROVE YOUTH UNEMPLOYMENT IN ITALY

Enrico Pugliese

U NEMPLOYMENT IN ITALY is found mainly among the young. Unemployment touches young people in all regions of Italy and from every social class. Although young people represent less than a third of the Italian workforce, three-quarters of all unemployed persons in Italy in 1988 were under 30 years old. However, educational credentials, gender, and residence mitigate the severity and length of youthful unemployment.

Young people from middle-class backgrounds with good educational qualifications tend to experience a period of unemployment when leaving school but eventually settle into permanent jobs; those with less education have greater difficulty finding permanent employment. Because the Italian labor market is characterized by severe gender discrimination, young women have the highest unemployment rates in Italy. Unemployment among young males declines with age (as they eventually find work), while young women often end a long spell of unemployment by withdrawing from the labor market. The dualistic nature of the Italian labor market also affects unemployment: The overall unemployment rate is less than 6 percent in the north but more than 20 percent in the south. For young adults aged 25–29 years old, the unemployment rate in 1988 was 10.1 percent in the north but 31.2 percent in the south.

Although youth unemployment has been the object of extensive social legislation in Italy in recent years, the unemployment situation in the south has markedly worsened. I argue that the youth employment policies implemented to date have been ineffective because the causes of youth unemployment in the south have not been adequately understood, and the policies prescribed have therefore been inappropriate to the problem.

UNEMPLOYMENT AMONG YOUNG ITALIANS

In aggregate, quantitative terms, Italian unemployment does not appear to be more severe than in other European countries. According to the results of the 1988 European Community Labor Force Survey, there are about 2.6 million unemployed persons in Italy. This represents about 18 percent of the 14.3 million unemployed individuals in the European Community (EC),[1] which means Italy's share of European unemployment is proportional to its share of the overall working-age population in the EC (Table 13.1). The unemployment rate in Italy is 11 percent, and the unemployment rate in the EC is 10 percent (Table 13.2). At the aggregate national level, therefore, there is no great divergence between the situation in Italy and in most of Western Europe. When one examines unemployment among particular age cohorts, however, the picture changes.

Italians comprise about one-fifth of the total European population under 25 years of age, but they represent more than a quarter of the unemployed who are under 25 years old. The unemployment rate among young Italians is about 33 percent, compared with an average European unemployment rate among young people (including Italy) of 20 percent. When Italy is excluded, the average European unemployment rate among young people falls to about 17 percent. The unemployment rate of young Italians 25–29 years old is also higher than the European average for that age group—16 percent compared with 12 percent for all the EC (Table 13.2).

The situation reverses when we examine those aged 30 and over. The unemployment rate dramatically drops among older age groups in Italy. Unemployment is generally *lower* than in other European countries—2.3 points *less* than the European average among people in the 35–39-year-old age cohort and 2.6 points *less* than the average among 40–45-year-olds (Table 13.2). Thus, Italian youths are much more likely to be unemployed than Italian adults (especially adult males), and the contrast between the young and old in Italy is much greater than anywhere else in Europe—so much so that the Statistical Office of the EC found it necessary to explain the striking results of the 1988 labor force survey: "The relative high number of first-job seekers in Italy reflects the convention and practice of job stability in the Italian labor market. The counterpart of this high number is the relatively low number of unemployed seeking work following the loss of their job" (EUROSTAT 1990: 41).

This "convention and practice of job stability" is directly related to labor relations and to the high degree of protection enjoyed by Italian workers employed in industries of the core sector. In these industries the degree of union protection is higher, and job stability is guaranteed by collective contracts. Moreover, the *Cassa integrazione* system works most effectively in large-scale, major industrial firms.

Cassa integrazione guadagni is a device that allows firms to place workers in "temporary layoff" status when the need for labor falls. Workers get 80 percent of their previous wages paid by the state as a kind of unemployment benefit. This "temporary" layoff may last a year or longer. But laid-off workers are still officially employees of the factory. Therefore, they are counted as employed in the labor statistics. While the statistical bias caused by *cassa integrazione* is not large (only a few hundred thousand workers, mostly male, are involved), the

Table 13.1 / Size of Total Population, Labor Force, Employed, and Unemployed Population in Europe and Italy, by Age: 1988 (in thousands)

Age	Total Population		Size of Labor Force		Number Employed		Number Unemployed	
	Europe 12	Italy	Europe 12	Italy	Europe 12	Italy	Europe 12	Italy
14–19	24,048	5,053	8,649	1,265	6,743	767	1,906	498
20–24	24,940	4,401	18,368	2,980	14,846	2,068	3,522	912
25–29	24,201	4,436	19,351	3,063	16,949	2,579	2,401	484
[25–49]	[109,236]	[19,484]	[86,289]	[14,550]	[79,187]	[13,474]	[7,102]	[1,076]
[50–64]	[55,781]	[10,714]	[27,566]	[4,545]	[25,817]	[4,439]	[1,749]	[106]
>65	46,012	8,382	1,845	358	1,808	354	37	4
TOTAL	318,391	56,496	142,718	23,698	128,403	21,101	14,315	2,596

SOURCES: Labor Force Survey: Results 1988. Bruxelles, Luxembourg: EUROSTAT 1990.

Table 13.2 / Unemployment Rates in Europe and Italy, by Gender and Age: 1988

Age	Males		Females		Total	
	Europe 12	Italy	Europe 12	Italy	Europe 12	Italy
14–19	19.6	32.7	24.9	47.4	22.0	39.4
20–24	17.2	25.8	21.4	36.1	19.2	30.6
[14–24]	18.0	[27.9]	22.5	39.4	[20.1]	33.2
25–29	9.9	11.1	15.9	22.4	12.4	15.8
30–34	6.5	4.8	12.3	13.7	8.8	8.2
35–39	5.6	2.9	10.0	8.8	7.3	5.0
40–44	4.9	1.9	8.0	6.8	6.1	3.5
45–49	4.9	2.1	6.7	6.3	5.5	3.5
50–64	[6.1]	[1.9]	[6.8]	[3.7]	[6.3]	[2.3]
>65	2.1	N.A.	1.9	N.A.	2.0	0.9
TOTAL	8.2	7.4	12.8	17.3	10.0	11.0

SOURCES: Labor Force Survey: Results 1988. Bruxelles, Luxembourg: EUROSTAT 1990.

N.A. = Not Available.

system demonstrates the degree of job protection enjoyed by industrial workers in the core sector. Both union strategies and state legislation in Italy tend to protect workers from firings and layoffs. This approach affects the structure of Italian unemployment. In Italy, fewer of the unemployed are former industrial workers than is the case in other countries like the United Kingdom. This system also affects the gender composition of the unemployed, because workers in the core industries are predominantly male.

The position of women in the Italian labor market does not compare well with those in other European countries. The overall rate of unemployment among Italian women of all ages is much higher than in Europe as a whole (12.8 percent in Europe compared to 17.3 percent in Italy). This difference is due to extremely high unemployment rates among younger groups of women. Among young women 14–24 years old, the unemployment rate in Italy is almost twice as high as in Europe generally (40 percent in Italy compared to 22.5 percent in Europe) (Table 13.2).

Among women over 35, the unemployment rate in Italy is much lower than among younger cohorts of women and lower than in the rest of Europe (Table 13.2). However, these lower unemployment rates do not necessarily mean that the older women have found jobs; rather, the unemployment rate of older women falls because they withdraw from the labor force.

Low labor force participation and high unemployment combine to leave Italian women with very low employment rates (Tables 13.2 and 13.3). In the past, labor force participation among Italian women was very low because the role of housewife was accepted (more or less forcibly) by the majority of women of working age. However, this acceptance has waned—especially among younger

Table 13.3 / Labor Force Participation Rates in Europe and Italy, by Gender and Age: 1988

Age	Males		Females		Total	
	Europe 12	Italy	Europe 12	Italy	Europe 12	Italy
14–19	32.9	27.3	28.7	22.8	30.8	25.0
19–24	79.5	74.5	68.0	61.4	73.7	67.7
14–24	54.6	48.8	47.4	41.1	51.0	N.A.
25–29	92.4	90.8	67.5	61.8	80.0	75.9
[25–49]	[95.4]	[95.4]	[62.6]	[54.2]	[79.0]	[74.7]
[50–64]	[67.9]	[64.9]	[32.1]	[21.2]	[49.0]	[42.3]
>64	6.7	7.7	2.2	1.8	4.0	4.3
TOTAL	68.1	65.7	41.1	34.2	54.1	49.3

SOURCES: Labor Force Survey: Results 1988. Bruxelles, Luxembourg: EUROSTAT 1990.
N.A. = Not Available.

women. An increasing number of young women enter the labor market today, but gender discrimination and the patriarchal character of Italian society, particularly in the south, block their ability to find and keep jobs.

It should be noted that high rates of unemployment among young people in Europe are not unusual. In most European countries, young people experience a period of unemployment after they leave school to enter the labor market. When growth in the national economy is slow, the period of unemployment lengthens. Half of all Europeans 14–25 years of age have been searching for work over a year (Table 13.4). However, over 70 percent of unemployed Italian youngsters are "long-term" unemployed. Thus, current unemployment rates in Italy are much higher than one would expect from the typical short-term, school-to-work transition "churning."

Table 13.4 / Long-Term Unemployment in Europe and Italy: Job-Seekers, by Number of Months They Have Been Seeking Work, by Age: 1989 (in percentages)

Age	Less Than 3 Months	3–5 Months	6–11 Months	12 Months	Total
Europe 12					
14–24	17.1	13.2	19.7	50.0	100
25–49	14.9	12.7	15.7	56.8	100
>50	11.6	11.2	13.3	64.0	100
Italy					
14–24	4.6	7.4	17.6	70.4	100
25–49	6.1	10.2	15.5	68.2	100
>50	11.5	15.3	18.6	54.6	100

SOURCES: Labor Force Survey: Results 1988. Bruxelles, Luxembourg: EUROSTAT 1990.

EXPLANATIONS OF YOUTH UNEMPLOYMENT

Different interpretations of the causes of youth unemployment in Italy place varying emphasis on the importance of demographic, social, and economic variables. Youth unemployment began to be a central issue in the 1970s when the baby boom generation entered the labor market and early explanations of the phenomenon focused on Italy's changing demographic structure. Unemployment is particularly high in the south, it was argued, because the birthrate and natural population increase was much higher there than in the rest of the country; the market simply couldn't absorb the rapid population growth. However, youth unemployment continued to rise, even as the number of baby boom labor market entrants slowed.

More recent interpretations have emphasized the importance of social variables. Young people (most in search of a first job) and women (primarily young women) constitute the great majority of the Italian unemployed. Contrasted with the women of the previous generation, young women—in particular those with high and medium levels of education—want to be part of the labor force. They reject the career of housewife. As a result of these social changes, female participation in the labor market is increasing both in the north and in the south, and neither the high risk of unemployment nor the extremely marginal position of women in the labor force has discouraged these trends (Altieri 1986, 1990; Cavalli 1990; IRES-CGIL 1988; Pugliese 1989). So, although still below the European level, the labor force participation rate of Italian women continues to increase. Their entry into the labor market simultaneously increases female unemployment and general unemployment rates.

One must look at the structure of a society's economic and social policies to understand why unemployment hits particular groups harder than others. In *Why Some People Are More Unemployed than Others—The Strange Paradox of Growth and Unemployment* (1986), Goran Therborn argues that a society's unemployment can be characterized according to the interaction of three factors: the groups most likely to be unemployed, the duration of unemployment, and the type of public support provided to the unemployed. According to Therborn, Italian unemployment is *exclusivist* because unemployment is allowed to fall almost entirely on women and youths and *punitive* because income support for the unemployed is limited and meager. This is the result of the historical development of Italian social protection policies. The Italian labor movement was preventionist rather than interventionist, with regard to unemployment. This meant that the unions preferred to fight against unemployment and for more jobs instead of for a larger and more universal system of unemployment benefits. This approach spawned the *cassa integrazione* system, which has left women very "unprotected" and which provides little to young people who are unable to find a place in the industrial core.

While Therborn's work helps to explain the variation in unemployment across social groups, it provides little insight into the regional differences in unemployment that exist in Italy. Italian economists have filled in this gap.

They point out that the Italian labor market has an extremely dualistic north/south structure (Ciravenga 1990; Frey 1989; Giannola 1990; Vinci 1989). The overall unemployment rate in the north is only a third of the south's: 7.7 percent versus 20.6 percent, respectively. The unemployment rate almost doubled in the south during the 1980s, rising from 11.5 percent to 20.6 percent (Table 13.5). Many young people in the south are moving through their 20s without experiencing employment.

The demand for labor is weak in the south due to a lack of private investment in the region (e.g., SVIMEZ 1989; Vinci 1989). The south is part of the industrial "periphery" of Italy. Until this basic structural problem is addressed, the government is unlikely to have much success in improving employment rates among young adults in that region of the country, despite its declared intention to intervene to do so.

Among young labor market entrants in Italy, there appears to be a hierarchy of access to the labor market. At the top are adult males in the northern regions, who enjoy virtual full employment, and in the bottom position are young women in the south, who experience almost "full unemployment."[2] In between are young women in the north and, below them, young men in the south (Table 13.6).

THE PATH FROM SCHOOL TO WORK: SKILLS, CREDENTIALS, AND REGIONAL DIFFERENCES IN LABOR DEMAND

Economic factors and social policy explain the high levels of unemployment in Italy and its concentration in the south. However, an additional aspect of youth unemployment must be taken into account: the growing difficulty that those with low levels of education have finding work. A brief review of the "school-to-work" transition in Italy may be useful in understanding the impact of educational credentialling on youth unemployment.

As Liebfried and Allmendinger (1991) point out, the timing and risks of dropping out of school and/or of switching to a lower educational track vary according to national school systems. In Italy, the main high-risk points of transition occur when a student moves (a) from one school level to another, (b) from formal schooling into vocational training, and (c) from vocational training (or formal education) to the workforce. At each point along this path, an individual can shift down in the system or out of it, and each downward movement increases the risk of economic marginalization, through either chronic unemployment or employment in a low-wage, occupationally segmented work situation.

Compared with other formal educational systems, the Italian school system can be characterized as semi-stratified. It is less *rigidly tracked*, for instance, than the German system, but less *universal* than the American system. Italian education is universal for the first 8 years: All children go to the same type of elementary school followed by junior high school. Almost all children attend

Table 13.5 / Unemployment Rates in Italy, by Region, Age, and Gender: 1980 and 1988

	Female				Male				Total			
	1980		1988		1980		1988		1980		1988	
Age	North Central	South	North Central	South	North Central	South	North Central	South	North Central	South	North Central	South
14–19	33.0	54.3	39.7	69.0	19.9	33.6	24.3	52.1	26.3	42.0	31.6	59.2
20–24	17.3	43.0	24.9	64.3	12.9	27.6	15.1	44.6	14.9	33.9	19.8	53.2
25–29	9.1	23.0	14.5	45.7	4.1	9.9	6.6	22.3	6.1	14.2	10.1	31.2
30–39	4.5	7.7	6.6	16.0	0.8	1.7	1.8	5.9	1.9	3.4	3.5	9.0
>39	10.4	16.3	1.0	3.3	2.4	4.8	0.9	2.3	4.4	7.6	0.9	2.5
TOTAL	10.2	20.1	12.7	32.0	3.5	7.5	4.7	14.5	5.8	11.5	7.7	20.6

SOURCE: Istituto Centrale di Statistica (ISTAT), Rilevazione delle forze di lavoro, 1988.

Table 13.6 / Labor Force Participation and Unemployment Among Young Italians, by Region, Gender, and Age: 1988

Gender/Age	Labor Force Participation Rate		Unemployment Rate	
	North Central	South	North Central	South
Female				
14–19	47.3	34.6	39.3	65.3
25–29	73.3	49.1	14.5	45.7
Male				
14–19	58.7	47.2	17.8	47.1
25–29	91.7	89.6	6.5	22.3
Total				
14–19	48.2	40.3	23.3	55.2
25–29	82.2	68.2	10.1	31.2

SOURCE: Istituto Centrale di Statistica (ISTAT), Rilevazione delle forze di lavoro, 1988.

public (state run) schools, regardless of region and social class. Education is free and compulsory until the eighth grade (or 14 years of age). There are no alternative tracks in the first 8 years (Moscati 1989). The so-called *class differenziali* schools, where disadvantaged children used to be concentrated, were abolished 20 years ago. Therefore, the degree of formal stratification for the first 8 years is minimal. There is some variation in quality according to differing characteristics of cities and neighborhoods, but the curricula and the funding are essentially the same in schools throughout the country.

Many children in Italy drop out of school before the end of compulsory education. Available estimates, based on data from the Ministry of Education and of the Istituto Nazionale di Statistica, show that about 8 percent of Italian children leave school during the years of Scuola Media del'Obbligo ("middle school" or sixth to eighth grade). About 6 percent of children in the north leave during this time compared to 10 percent in the south. However, cities such as Palermo and Napoli have rates as high as 16 percent. These young people face a bleak economic future. They are likely to become involved in petty criminal activity, and some are recruited into the lowest echelons of criminal organizations like the Camorra and the Mafia.

After the eighth grade, Italian students may select alternative school tracks. They are not formally assigned to a specific track and are free to choose from various alternatives, at least theoretically (Moscati 1989). These alternatives range from the elitist *liceo classico* (classic high school) to an endless variety of technical and vocational (*professionali*) senior high schools. But even with the multitude of diverse career tracks represented by this variety of secondary schools, the formal inclusiveness of the system reasserts itself at the end of senior high school. All graduates from all types of high schools may enter a university, according to their chosen course of study and preferred location. There are no admission tests for Italian universities (except for some medical schools). Tuition is very low, as the state subsidizes all higher education. Therefore, the Italian school system can be considered to be relatively universal and formally democratic; it does not exclude certain students from the best careers as the German system does. All types of schools are formally accessible to all young people. Nevertheless, subtle forms of stratification and discrimination are embedded in the system.

The chances of dropping out of school early are strongly correlated with social class. Moreover, certain kinds of study courses and schools are correlated with dead-end careers—especially those often chosen by girls (Capecchi 1983). For example, graduates of the school for kindergarten teachers and of "commercial" high schools generally end up unemployed in the south. These schools are generally chosen by middle- and lower-class girls because they represent the opportunity to enter "pink-collar" careers (secretarial and teaching occupations). In general, these schools give rather poor training. And in the south they are preparing girls for secretarial jobs that don't exist.

Males also have a choice about what kind of school to enroll in, but they tend to choose schools that provide better opportunities—most enter the male technical high schools. However, a large number are not able to complete the course of study. Most dropouts leave school (or perhaps more accurately, are left by the schools) in the first 2 years after entering high school—at age 15 or 16. Consequently, the *Istituti Tecnici e Professionali* (like the "commercial" high schools) have the highest dropout rates. Although the rates have declined, they are still high. In Italy as a whole, there are more than 200,000 unemployed young people who have not completed the first 8 years of compulsory education and another 700,000 with only a junior high school (eighth-grade) degree. More than two-thirds of these youngsters reside in the south. They do not necessarily have a rural background; many of them are located in metropolitan areas such as Palermo. Dropping out of school early is the most serious mistake an Italian youth can make, because older adult dropouts have the highest rates of unemployment and the worst work careers. But at every educational level, males have much lower unemployment rates than females (Table 13.7).

Besides the formal school system, Italy has a network of vocational training schools that are not part of the regular national school system. These schools (*istituti di formazione professionale* or *centri di formazione professionale*) do not offer a standard national curriculum. They are under the supervision of the local (regional) authorities, provide varying levels of technical skills, and require trainees to have different levels of education to enter (Meghnagi 1989). Local vocational training programs exist in the north as well as in the south and are supposed to provide remediation to those who drop out of the regular educational system. However, despite heavy government investment in the vocational training system, results have been poor. The system of vocational training in Italy cannot effectively rehabilitate the large numbers of young people who have dropped out of regular school (e.g., Moscati 1987). Moreover, the voca-

Table 13.7 / Unemployment Rates, by Gender, Age,
and Educational Attainment: 1988

	14–19 Years Old	20–24 Years Old	25–29 Years Old	30–59 Years Old	Over 59 Years Old
Males					
No education	43.2	29.3	17.2	4.5	1.4
Junior high school[a]	31.4	19.6	9.9	2.9	1.5
High school	58.6	36.2	13.7	2.0	1.0
College degree	—	40.0	20.5	1.3	0.0
Total Unemployment	35.2	25.7	12.5	3.2	1.4
Females					
No education	56.1	45.9	35.0	10.7	1.6
Junior high school[a]	44.5	31.5	21.9	10.5	5.7
High school	70.4	42.8	24.3	8.1	2.5
College degree	—	45.4	28.4	3.9	0.0
Total Unemployment	49.7	37.5	24.4	9.4	1.8
Total					
No education	47.1	34.8	23.0	6.5	1.5
Junior high school[a]	37.2	24.5	14.4	5.2	2.4
High school	66.3	40.0	18.9	4.3	1.4
College degree	0.0	43.7	24.7	2.3	0.0
Total Unemployment	41.5	31.2	17.5	5.3	1.5

SOURCE: Istituto Centrale di Statistica (ISTAT), Rilevazione delle forze di lavoro, 1988.

[a] Eight years.

tional training system is widely believed to be most inefficient and ineffective in the south—where the need for a "second chance" or remedial vocational training is greatest.

The main reason for the difference in the performance of the training system in the north compared with that in the south is due to the relationship between training and labor demand in the two regions. In the North, particularly in regions such as Emilia Romagna (Capecchi 1983), the training centers respond to local firms' demands for better trained manpower. Training programs are developed in response to pressure from the industrial system for workers with particular skills. Vocational training in the north modifies and improves the characteristics of potential workers in a way that makes them better fit existing labor market demand.

The situation in the southern regions is quite different. In the south, labor demand (both actual and potential) is very weak. Even when vocational schools give training that improves the skills of the young unemployed, this skill development is not geared to any local demand for labor. Although sizeable investments of public funds have been channeled into training and vocational institutions, resulting in the development of clientelistic networks of training providers, the positive role of vocational training has been overestimated. Very ambitious programs requiring huge investments have been launched, but they end up being ineffective because the young people who participate in them are then thrown into slack local labor markets. The basic error in the approach is thinking that vocational institutions that focus on supply problems can be effective without parallel programs to increase labor demand. (A paradoxical effect of the vocational training system is that it does create job opportunities for trainers and local politicians [Caroleo and Veneziano 1988].)

The problems created by focusing on training alone are also evident by examining the employment figures of educated young people. Unemployment rates are very high among young people with the lowest and highest educational attainment levels. In fact, young people under 25 years of age *with* college or high school qualifications show the highest unemployment rates. This has led some observers to suggest that there is a great deal of "intellectual" unemployment (i.e., that educated young people have unrealistic expectations about the kind of employment they can and should expect) or that there is an "oversupply" of training and education in Italy. It is true that young people with good educational credentials often have difficulty finding jobs appropriate to their skill levels. In the period immediately after leaving school, they only look for jobs that reflect their qualifications. This "selectiveness" results in high rates of unemployment among high school and college-educated 20–29-year-olds. Eventually, a "cooling down" of expectations occurs, and these young people accept whatever positions are available. Many graduates end up taking jobs requiring a lower level of education/training than they actually possess, so that in the long run people with more education find a place in the workforce. There is a radical improvement in the employment levels of high school or college graduates, especially males, after they reach 25 or 30 years of age (Table 13.7).

Although unemployment rates are higher for females than males of all age groups and educational levels, gender differences are *least* evident among those with some college and among younger age groups (Table 13.7). Higher education lessens the effects of gender discrimination, and a university education reduces the risk of adult unemployment for both men and women.

However, labor demand is clearly as important a factor as schooling levels. Unemployment levels in the south are two to three times as high as those of young people in the north with the same educational qualifications (Table 13.8).

LITTLE GOVERNMENT SUPPORT FOR UNEMPLOYED YOUTHS

Most unemployed people are located in the south, where poverty rates are highest. However, because Italian poverty rates are based on *family*, not individual, income, it is not necessarily true that the poorest families are those with the largest number of unemployed family members. In fact, many families with incomes below the poverty line have family members that are not in the labor

Table 13.8 / Unemployment Rates, by Region, Age, and Educational Attainment: 1988

	14–19 Years Old	20–24 Years Old	25–29 Years Old	30–59 Years Old	Over 59 Years Old
North Central					
Less than 8 years	35.6	20.0	13.6	7.3	3.1
Junior high school[a]	28.0	16.0	8.9	5.1	2.3
High school	53.8	25.6	9.9	3.9	1.3
College degree	—	30.0	18.1	2.7	0.2
Total Unemployment	31.6	19.8	10.1	4.9	2.4
South					
Less than 8 years	53.8	43.9	29.4	16.9	8.1
Junior high school[a]	55.7	44.0	26.2	12.2	4.7
High school	87.1	68.8	37.6	11.4	1.2
College degree	—	67.7	37.7	6.8	0.4
Total Unemployment	59.2	53.2	31.2	12.5	5.9

SOURCE: Istituto Centrale di Statistica (ISTAT), Rilevazione delle forze di lavoro, 1988.

[a]Eight years.

force (i.e., children, the elderly, and retired), and many of the young unemployed are children of families with incomes above the poverty level (Garonna 1984; Morlicchio 1987).

A unique character of Italian unemployment is that few unemployed people are family heads. Even in the south, very few families are poor as a result of the "breadwinner" being unemployed. Nonetheless, both unemployment and poverty are concentrated in the south, and both are a function of slack labor demand and low wages. The south has only 36 percent of the total national population but contains more than 55 percent of the unemployed in Italy and 55 percent of families in poverty (Morlicchio 1987). Job opportunities in manufacturing, agriculture, and the service sector are characterized by low pay and few union and legislative protections. Jobs in the official labor market are scarce; work can only be found in the so-called submerged (informal) sector of the economy. Although the living standards in the south are higher today than in previous generations, they are still much lower than in the north and not high enough to encourage young people to withdraw voluntarily from work.

Jobless young people have no choice except to remain in their parents' households if they are unable to find a job and a source of personal income because income support during periods of unemployment is contingent on having a previous work history.[3] Individuals who have never been employed do not qualify for any kind of benefits. As a result, family support is becoming more and more important in Italy (Saraceno 1988).

In any case, the family is the only source of support for unemployed young people, because unemployment protection in Italy is not provided to all catego-ries of the unemployed according to some universal principle. Instead, unem-ployment insurance has traditionally been linked to industry and occupational distinctions. Although a new scheme linking unemployment benefit levels to the wage level of an employee's most recent job was devised recently, this reform, like previous measures, would apply only to people with previous work experience. Because the great majority of young unemployed are first-time job-seekers, they cannot qualify for unemployment benefits. The exclu-sion of young people from unemployment benefits is, to some extent, an out-growth of the tradition of Italian labor relations and social welfare policies built on particularistic-meritocratic principles, which hold that benefits should only be granted to those who have contributed to the system.

POLICIES OF INTERVENTION

To review the structure of Italian unemployment discussed earlier, over 60 percent of the unemployed are under 30 years old, two-thirds of these have been looking for work for at least a year, more than half are women, and the majority are located in the south. The youthful unemployed belong to all educational levels, but young people with better educational credentials eventu-ally find jobs. Although the overall rate of unemployment was much lower in the 1970s than in the 1980s, most of these characteristics could be observed by the mid-1970s. It was around this time that the government was compelled to pass its first youth employment legislation.

The following part of this chapter analyzes various employment policies targeted toward young people that were implemented from the late 1970s through the 1980s, starting with *"Legge 285"* (*Legge n. 285 del 1 giugno 1977 recante provedimenti volti a incrementare l'occupazione giovanile*), a law that was an object of extensive debate in the late 1970s and early 1980s.

The First Act: *Legge n. 285 per l'occupazione giovanile*

"Legge 285," passed in 1977, provided employment to several hundred thou-sand young men and women throughout Italy in the late 1970s. It was meant to increase private-sector employment through self-employment or the creation of cooperative firms. Unfortunately, it failed to generate employment in the private sector; instead, it provided young people—particularly those born be-tween the late 1940s and late 1950s—with public-sector employment. *Legge 285* deserves some detailed attention because it provided employment for youth on a massive scale and because it was judged to be such a failure that subsequent interventions used it as a negative model. Indeed, the reluctance to enact youth employment legislation in the late 1970s and early 1980s can perhaps best be understood as the result of legislators' preoccupation with avoiding a repetition of the "mistake" of *Legge 285*.

The legislation was enacted in response to a number of economic and political pressures. Youth unemployment had reached unprecedented levels in the early 1970s, and Italy's young people vociferously demanded action by the government to improve their situation. Student unrest in the country climaxed in the mid-1970s, and youth unemployment was a key issue of antigovernment protests. Moreover, the student and youth movements were concerned not just with the *level* of employment; they also criticized the *quality* of existing job opportunities and the overall organization of work. Young people argued that the work available to them was insecure, boring, and noncreative. The search for never-well-defined "alternative forms of work" formed the agenda of the youth movement and of political debates that involved politicians as well as social scientists (Moscati and Pugliese 1978).

The *Legge 285* that grew out of these debates was ostensibly more than a simple active labor policy intervention (Bruno 1978). Its first goal was to correct the mismatch between labor demand and supply by establishing professional training courses for young people. But it also attempted to encourage the creation of new firms able to absorb the surplus labor supply by tapping the innovation and entrepreneurial abilities of young people (Bruno 1978). Thus, the act was concerned with *structural* reform, too.

Legge 285 implicitly accepted one of the dominating myths of the time—that cooperatives were a new and superior way to organize work and production—and encouraged the creation of cooperative enterprises in agriculture, craftsmanship, and the service sector. However, financial support (capital investments or credit at low interest rates) was not provided to the young people accepted as would-be entrepreneurs. The act only provided subsidies for the firms' operation and professional training for the young people involved in the new enterprises.

Legge 285 was intended to be an experiment. It operated primarily as an emergency program and was financed for only 2 years. Many cooperative enterprises were started between 1977 and 1978, but within 2 years all had failed—the casualties of inadequate external support, monitoring, and financing. When the cooperatives closed, the young people who had been employed in them were simply hired by the public sector in activities related to their work in the cooperatives. Almost 700,000 young people, mainly in the southern regions, found steady employment as a result of this act. The fact that they were hired on the basis of universal principles rather than clientelism (the typical mechanism for recruitment to state jobs in southern Italy) was a significant reform. However, government fears of a further expansion of state employment through public-sector job creation halted future programs of this kind.

THE *CONTRATTI DI FORMAZIONE LAVORO* (TRAINEE CONTRACT)

In the wake of *Legge 285*, policymakers demonstrated little interest in the problem of youth unemployment in the late 1970s and early 1980s. However, after 1982, an innovation in hiring procedures and work relations (the *Contratto di formazione lavoro,* or trainee contract) encouraged massive employment of young people and lessened the problem of youth unemployment. These trainee contracts were introduced experimentally for 1 year (by *Legge 79* of 1983), but a more permanent program (*Legge 863*) with comprehensive regulations became law in 1984.

Under *Legge 863* of 1984, young people hired under a trainee contract were to receive on-the-job training in the workplace. Simultaneously, with the establishment of these training contracts, general hiring procedures were deregulated to make it easier for industrial and commercial firms to hire young people under the training contracts. Firms may now directly choose the young people they are going to hire, regardless of their position in the seniority list at the labor exchange. Because the young people on training contracts are paid much less than adults, the new program became a way for employers to reduce their labor costs. According to Frey (1988: 221), this act "greatly enhanced flexibility by allowing for discretionary, individual hiring by employers through the government employment service . . . the labor costs to employers of persons employed under law 863 was reduced to below the ordinary cost of similar labor performed without the benefit of the law's provisions."

Although many young people were hired as a result of *Legge 863,* the training contract places a young person in a rather weak position within the firm. Not only are the training contracts short-term, but often they do not contain all the guarantees of a regular contract in the same industry or even in the same workplace. Moreover, according to most investigations of the subject, little training actually occurs under the contracts. As Guarna (1988: 233) has written, "What is evident . . . is the programs' unquestionable inadequacy in terms of training objectives, not only . . . because very few young people find in the trainee experience a true alternative to the school system as a means of vocational training, but chiefly because of the very low skill level of most of the jobs for which trainee contracts are offered." In other words, the *quality* of the jobs given to "trainees" is very poor, so there are few real skills to learn.

The overall effect of the act on youth unemployment is not clear. A large majority of young people who are employed in the industrial sector today (as well as in service and commerce) were hired under such contracts. But it is difficult to say if the law has *caused* additional employment or if the young people involved would have been hired anyway. The act has been used most extensively in the northern regions where labor demand is dynamic. But the southern regions, which house more than 55 percent of the unemployed, operate only a fraction of all training contracts. In 1989, there were only 55,000 trainee contracts in all regions of the south (10 percent of the national total). This has led critics to observe that because the trainee contracts are most often used in regions with a growing demand for labor, the government is merely allowing employers to hire young workers that they would have hired anyway at lower wages than normal. In 1986, *Legge 863* was reformed by *Legge 113* to provide additional economic incentives to firms in the South to hire young people under trainee contracts. Although it is too soon to assess completely the effects of this reform, early indicators suggest that it has not had much effect on youth unemployment.

Nonetheless, the possibility of hiring young people through the trainee contracts has lessened the age discrimination in hiring policies that seems to characterize Italian employers. Many firms now prefer to hire young people because this lowers their labor costs and increases their flexibility. On the other hand, one could argue that age discrimination has not diminished but has only changed form—young people are discriminated against in terms of wage levels and job security rather than *access* to employment.

The "De Vito Act"

Whereas the trainee contracts were intended to increase employment by making young people more attractive to existing employers, another piece of legislation, *the Legge n. 44 per l'imprenditorialita' giovanile* of 1986 (called the "De Vito Act"), was intended to increase employment through the creation of new enterprises by young people in the south. This act should be viewed as an intervention aimed at enlarging the productive structure in the south.

Under the provisions of the DeVito Act, new enterprises created by 18–29-year-old residents of southern Italy can receive financial and technical assistance if their business projects are approved by a special governmental commission. Technical assistance includes help in planning the enterprises and monitoring the development of projects, and the professional training of staff is provided. The financial incentives (direct financial contributions and low-interest loans) are very generous and may provide up to 75 percent of the initial capital investment required for an enterprise.

There is a striking difference between this program and the *Legge 285* of 1977, which provided little or no support for new enterprises. Whereas the old act targeted the general population of young unemployed persons, the new one targets a special group of people—those with capital resources and/or entrepreneurial abilities. Unfortunately, the overwhelming majority of unemployed young people in the south lack both.

As of 1989, fewer than 3,000 projects had been submitted to the *Commissione per l'imprenditorialita' giovanile* (Committee for Youth Entrepreneurship), and more than two-thirds of these were rejected. A good number of those young people who have benefited from the DeVito Act have families that are already engaged in a business activity. The approved projects could employ *at most* 16,000 individuals; yet there are 1.1 million unemployed people under 30 in southern Italy, so it is clear that this costly intervention will not improve the condition of most young people or significantly reduce youth unemployment.

The "Socially Useful Projects"

The trainee contracts (*Legge 863*) and the "DeVito Act" are the two measures that have attracted the most public attention and the most public money, but another policy (*Legge* 67) was established in 1988, designed to employ young people in the south in "socially useful projects." Under the provisions of *Legge* 67, the state will finance very labor-intensive, short-term activities aimed at improving the quality of life in the southern regions. Firms and cooperatives who offer to carry out these projects are expected to hire unemployed young people who are registered at the local labor exchange. The 18–29-year-olds so hired receive a small salary for 18 hours of work per week—a kind of unemployment allowance conditional on their work contribution. (Their official registration as unemployed at the labor exchange is not canceled while they work in these projects.)

Proposed projects are submitted to a special committee of the *Agenzia regionale per l'impiego* (Regional Employment Agency). Upon approval, the projects are financed for 1 year. At least 80 percent of the total amount received by the project managers must be spent on the wages of the young unemployed, and the remaining 20 percent can be used as expenses for the firm's operations. The range of activities covered by these projects is very wide—from environmental protection to the analysis of health conditions at the local level to surveys of artistic values.

Legge 67 raised the expectations of many young people in the south, because it was the first significant policy measure in 10 years aimed at helping large numbers of unemployed youth. The total number of youngsters involved in each of the 3 years has been roughly 75,000. Only the *Legge 285* in the late 1970s involved such a large number of youngsters in the south. However, despite high hopes for the act, it has proved itself to be at least a partial failure for reasons embedded in the nature and structure of the program.

First, the so-called socially useful projects are not carried out directly by a state agency but by private firms. This makes supervision complicated. Some projects appear to have the sole function of "parking" unemployed youth for some hours a day. There is an excess of underutilized personnel. Second, the demand that activities be labor intensive has proved to be a kind of boomerang. In many projects, the work to be performed is very low-skilled, so the jobs cannot be considered a career "boost" in any way. Third, many projects are not selected strictly on a merit basis; rather, clientelism has reemerged to corrupt the selection process. Finally, because there is no coordinating body to oversee the entire range of activities, the program has created a series of unrelated projects rather than a comprehensive system of new services. All of these criticisms are not made to suggest that the program be canceled; however, to be effective, it must be dramatically reformed. The young people enrolled have not had any chance to use their skills and education.

DISCUSSION

In the 1980s, scholars of several disciplines ranging from economics to regional planning, sociology, and political science called attention to the Italian industrial experience. The international literature frequently presented the Italian case as a successful system of flexible production (Sabel and Piore 1986). Some regions—especially the "NEC" (north-east-central) area—experienced an intensive rhythm of development based on small industrial firms and flexible specialization. But special historic and social conditions were key to the success of this strategy. The literature has not given sufficient attention to the difficulties involved in replicating the model. Were it easy to reproduce the flexible specialization model, one would think the southern region of Italy would be the first to benefit from this production innovation.

In fact, expectations for the spontaneous diffusion of the "flexible production" model to the southern regions actually reduced the commitment of the state to encourage public or private investment in the south of Italy in the 1980s. The result has been a stagnation of productive investments in these regions and growing economic differences between the north and the south over the past decade. The steady high level of unemployment in the south is a primary indication of this "dualism."

Policy measures to reduce youthful unemployment since the 1970s have attempted to create training and employment opportunities with various mechanisms, but with limited results. The most recent training contracts created an incentive for employers to hire young people who were excluded from the labor market, but the contracts then marginalize youths within the firm. Moreover, they have been least effective with those youth most likely to experience long-term unemployment—young people in the south with little education.

The emergency projects have not offered the young much in terms of income, training, or future prospects. They did not operate on a scale large enough to provide activities for the massive number of unemployed young people in the south nor did they offer much in the way of training, future employment, or income. The "socially useful work" programs were an exception to this rule, because they did provide an allowance to participants, but young people were only allowed to participate for 1 year. Moreover, the program is to be closed shortly, without any alternative program to replace it.

Because unemployed youths in Italy are not entitled to any form of unemployment benefits, they are forced to be dependent on their families for support. Discrimination against young people in the labor market, the lack of any form of unemployment benefit for them, and the inefficacy of targeted employment measures have had the cumulative effect of leaving unemployed young people in Italy economically and socially marginalized.

Although the majority of young people in Italy are able to find stable employment by the time they reach adulthood (30 years of age), the proportion of unemployed of all age categories grew over the last decade, and unemployment rates among 20–29-year-olds in the south are particularly severe today. Policy measures aimed at reducing unemployment among the young must be evaluated with regard to their effectiveness in reducing unemployment in the south, where the problem is concentrated. Policies to date have not been successful in this regard.

No active labor policies can compensate for the lack of economic policies aimed at activating labor demand in the south. Most public policy analysts are now convinced that youth employment in the southern regions can only be reduced if training and income maintenance are accompanied by structural interventions like industrial investment, public works, and construction projects (Giannola 1990; Mingione 1990). Labor market demand can be activated through investments in the public sector and by stimulating private investments. For example, if the DeVito Act were expanded and made less selective so that financial support was given to a larger array of firms created by young people, a more effective policy of job creation favoring the development of small firms might be established.

The "socially useful" projects could also be reorganized to be truly useful. The quality of life in the south is worse than in the north not only because of lower private consumption standards, but also because of the quality of the public services. The original concept of the socially useful projects was to simultaneously occupy young people, give them some training, and *create social services*. The objectives are still valid. It is the organization and management of the projects that has been flawed. The programs were not seriously monitored or evaluated, but the general objectives were correct. With over half of 20–25-year-olds and a third of 25–29-year-olds in the south unemployed, an emergency program is urgently required to occupy these young people, if possible in a productive way. The foreclosure of the projects has added to the frustration felt by these young people.

In the short run, a plan for the immediate employment of young people on a large scale in regions of the south is needed. Even if the work performed by the young people is low-skilled, the program would at least guarantee a basic income and counteract the negative effect of long-term unemployment. This idea is now being debated in political circles and the parliament. In the long run, however, the government will only be able to reduce unemployment with a strong economic policy of targeted regional economic development. Only this will alleviate the structural conditions that cause the massive unemployment the South is currently experiencing.

ENDNOTES

1. To allow comparison with other European countries, the analysis of unemployment in this chapter is based on EUROSTAT data (1990). However, international statistical sources on labor markets do not provide data at the subnational and regional levels. Therefore, to give a more understandable and correct picture of the Italian situation, national data provided by INSTAT (Istituto Centrale di Statistica) are not used here for international comparison.

2. The labor force participation rates of young women are much lower in the south than in the north. Only one in three 14–24-year-old women and one in two 25–29-year-old women are in the labor force in the south, compared with almost one in two 20–24-year-old women and three out of four 25–29-year-old women in the north (Table

13.6). However, despite the fact that fewer southern women enter the labor market, female unemployment rates in the south are much higher than in the north. Among 14–24-year-old women, 65.3 percent in the south are unemployed compared with 29.2 percent in the north; almost 46 percent of 25–29-year-old women in the south are unemployed compared with only 14.5 percent in the north. Very low labor force participation rates and massive unemployment among young women in the south combine to leave only about 15 percent of 14–24-year-old young women and a quarter of 25–29-year-old women in the south employed.

3. Unemployment compensation is occupationally determined in Italy. Agricultural and construction workers, who suffer from seasonal unemployment, receive unemployment benefits according to a complex set of rules. Industrial workers receive a rather generous system of unemployment benefits under the *cassa integrazione* system discussed earlier. This type of unemployment benefit is granted to workers in specific plants, under specific circumstances, but it is the typical form of unemployment benefit for workers in the core manufacturing industries.

REFERENCES

Abbate, C. 1989. "Relazione tra tasso di disoccupazione e variabili sociali, demografiche, ed economiche." *Economia e lavoro*, no. 3.

Altieri, G. 1986. "Disoccupazione e occupazione femminile: Una contraddizione apparente." *Politiche del lavoro*, no. 1.

―――. 1990. "Identita' femminile e mercato del lavoro." *Politica ed economia*, no. 3.

Agenzia per l'impiego della Campania. 1989. *I lavori di utilita' collettiva in Campania: Analisi di un'esperienza*. Napoli: Agenzia per l'impiego della Campania.

Bruno, S. 1978. *Disoccupazione giovanile e azione pubblica*. Bologna: Il Mulino.

Capecchi, V. 1983. *Prima e dopa il diploma: Percorsi maschili e femminili*. Bologna: Il Mulino.

Caroleo, E. F., and S. Veneziano. 1988. Mercato del lavoro e politiche dell occupazione nel Mezzogiorno. Napoli: Liguori.

Cavalli, A. 1990. *I giovani del Sud*. Bologna: Il Mulino.

Ciravegna, D. 1990. *I caratteri della inoccupazione*. Milano: Angeli.

EUROSTAT. 1990. Labor Force Survey: Results, 1988. Bruxelles-Luxembourg: EUROSTAT.

Frey, L. 1988. "The Impact of Labor Policy in Italy, 1984–1988." In *Labor and Employment Policies in Italy*. Roma: Ministero del lavoro e della previdenza sociale.

―――. 1989. *La disoccupazione in Italia: Il punto di vista degli economisti*. Milano: Angeli.

Garonna, P. 1984. *Nuove poverta' e sviluppo economico*. Padova: Cleup.

Giannola, A. 1990. "Problemi di sviluppo e problemi di occupazione." In *Quaderni IRES*. Forthcoming.

Guarna, C. 1988. "The Extent and the Nature of Labor Policy in Italy, 1984–1988." In *Report 1988: Labor and Employment Policies in Italy*. Roma: Ministero del lavoro e della previdenza sociale.

IRES-CGIL. 1988. Rapporto sulla disoccupazaione in Italia. Roma: IRES.

Leibfried, S., and J. Allmendinger. 1991. Comments on 7.HISS, "Young Workers in Germany." Presented at the Conference on Poverty and Social Marginality. Maison Suger. January 16–18.

Mingione, E. 1990. "Il sistema italiano delle divisioni regionali e i processi di informazione." *Inchiesta*, no. 88–89: 3–25.

Morlicchio, E. 1987. "Povero? No, Disoccupto." *Politica ed economica*, no. 12: 71–75.

Moscati, R. 1987. "La condizione giovanile nel Messogiorno. *Inchiesta*, no. 75: 71–92.

———. 1989. *La sociologia dell'educazione in Italia*. Bologna: Zanichelli.

Moscati, R., and E. Pugliese. 1978. *Obiettivo giovani*. Roma: Alfani.

Pugliese, E. 1989. "Struttura e comportamenti dell'offerta di lavoro nel Mezzogiorno." *Nord e Sud*, no. 4 (new series): 22–50.

Sabel, C., and M. Piore. 1986. *The Second Industrial Divide.* New York: Basic Books.

Salvati, M. 1989. "Offerta e domanda di lavoro; offerta e domanda di prodotti." *Politica ed economica*, no. 3.

Saraceno, C. 1988. *Sociologia della famiglia.* Bologna: Il Mulino.

SVIMEZ (1990). *Rapporto sul Mezzogiorno*. Bologna: Il Mulino.

Therborn, G. 1986. *Why Some People Are More Unemployed than Others—The Strange Paradox of Growth and Unemployment*. London: Verso.

Veneziano S. 1990. "Interventi locali di utilita' collettiva." *Quaderni IRES*. Forthcoming.

Vinci, S. 1989. "Disoccupazione e domanda di lavoro nel Mezzogiorno." *Nord e Sud*, no. 4 (new series).

Chapter 14

POSTINDUSTRIALISM
AND YOUTH UNEMPLOYMENT:
AFRICAN AMERICANS AS HARBINGERS

Troy Duster

I N BOTH ACADEMIC and policy circles, there is a remarkable consensus about the nature of the great economic and social transformation of Western industrialized societies over the last quarter century. In particular, there is general agreement that the important and decisive shift from predominantly industrial to mainly service economies has been accompanied by select and patterned "dislocations" that are true for all nations that have a declining manufacturing sector. Perhaps most significantly, what is common to declining secondary-sector economies is the attendant sharp increase in youth unemployment without regard to ethnic or cultural variation.[1]

While economists, sociologists, public policy analysts, and social demographers are in bland agreement on these basic facts, there are fierce disagreements on the implications of these developments for policy and the lessons that rising youth unemployment provides about the changes in national economies. All postindustrial societies share this relatively new development, but as Tolstoy told us, "each family (substitute 'nation') is unhappy in its own way."

Those analysts who are inclined to see cycles express a strong faith that "the crisis" of youth unemployment will work itself out. They advise that economies should continue along the same general path as had been their course in the heyday of industrial sector domination. Others see more structural change and thus advise strong readjustments in state policy to limit the hemorrhaging of capital and/or the underwriting of new methods to generate employment. Still others have suggested explicit planning to better articulate schooling with work. In any event, comparative studies across nations and regions hold out the promise of increasing our insights about the larger picture that youth face in the new service economies.

There are two quite distinct approaches to this matter of comparative youth unemployment. First, there is the strategy of comparing whole societies, for example, France with Germany, the United States with Japan, or Australia with England regarding the fate of youth. These comparisons are made with regard to rates of youth unemployment, or with regard to public policy on employment and employment training. As Osterman (this volume) points out, this allows us to see how youth in general are doing in different settings, and how large societal issues and policies (or a lack thereof) relate to the transition from school to work. The other strategy involves comparing the fate of particular segments of the youth population within the same society, for example, comparing youth from the dominant group in a society with youth from immigrant groups or from ethnic, racial, and cultural minorities.

But there is a major methodological problem with the second approach. The Nuremburg injunction against identifying citizens by race means that many nations just do not keep statistics by race and ethnicity, or they have rejected the basis on which such data are collected. Gordon (this volume) mentions this is true regarding Italy, but it certainly applies to several other European nations as well. Moreover, there is no agreed upon poverty line in most countries; even where there is, the differences between rural and urban poverty are considerable. It is difficult to address the issue of the comparative centrality of race or ethnicity in different countries without some minimal agreement on a baseline and an empirical data base for making measurable comparisons. We can nevertheless salvage some important insights from specific kinds of comparative data. For example, most immigrant laborers have "fallen" into secondary labor market employment in the last decade. *There is a general tendency for the largest migrant or ethnic groups in each country to experience the highest rates of unemployment.*

On the surface, immigrant minorities and indigenous minorities would seem to experience much the same fate, that is, the greatest vulnerability to high rates of youth unemployment. But it is a mistake to lump together immigrant youths with indigenous minorities in cross-national comparisons. In the United States, it is the indigenous minorities that have the highest rates of unemployment; immigrant Asian minorities on the two coasts and immigrant Cubans in Florida fare much better (Portes and Rumbaut 1990; Portes and Zhou 1992).

By examining ethnic differences within a single country, we can compare youth unemployment between immigrant minorities recently arrived and long-term indigenous minorities (insofar as such records are kept). The United States has a history of record keeping regarding ethnic differences, at least for the last decade, and there has been some important empirical and theoretical work in this arena. Ogbu (1978, 1983, 1990), Portes and Rumbaut (1990), Light and Bonacich (1988), Bourgois (1991), Bailey and Waldinger (1991), Waldinger (1986) and Wilson and Martin (1982) have each made a contribution to our increased understanding of the relationship between ethnicity and economic destiny in postindustrial nations. Portes shows how immigrant solidarity in ethnic enclaves can be a buttress, even sometimes an economic advantage (trust, working with kin, extended and fictive, etc). But this must be contrasted with Ogbu's work on indigenous cultural minorities where enclaves do not serve this advantage. Theoretically, comparison strategies can be related—that is, one could conduct an examination of internal differentiation in a country and then do cross-national global comparisons. However, as a matter of either practical empirical investigation or social theorizing, analysts tend to make a choice and favor one over the other.

Because of the putative link between socialization, credentialing, and the workplace, comparative research on educational achievement of cultural minorities has been especially instructive. Gordon shows that West Indians fare relatively poorly in the United Kingdom's school system. John Ogbu (1990) points out that West Indians, however, do relatively well in the educational system of the United States. Because American-born blacks do relatively poorly in the United States, Ogbu has theorized that the often dramatically different educational achievement successes of immigrant minorities versus indigenous minorities can be explained by the "active resistance" of the latter and is in sharp contrast to the "active assimilation" strategy of the former. Today's immigrants soon become tomorrow's second and third generation, who either assimilate into occupational structures or act (and/or are treated) increasingly like indigenous minorities, who are visibly isolated in low-wage marginalized employment.

THE TRANSITION TO WORK

With respect to national policy planning regarding the transition from school to work, the German model is at one end of the continuum and the United States at the other. Germany integrates schooling with apprenticeships and has the best integration with industry and posttraining placement into first adult jobs. The United States has one of the looser connections between schooling and employment, with a period of flux, adjustment, and uncertainty. Current critiques argue that U.S. education does not integrate its graduates into either the changing white collar technical segment or the changing vocational economic organization of the service sector well. In the United States, about one-third of those who complete only high school fail to find stable employment by the time they are 30 (see Osterman, this volume). By contrast, only about 10 percent of the German population fails to find stable employment by age 30.

When youth populations are disaggregated by immigrant, native-born, and ethnic or racial minority status, both internal and cross-national comparisons are dramatic and illuminating. At the beginning of the 1990s, unemployment among all American high school dropouts aged 16 to 24 was very high. But among African American dropouts, the unemployment rate is over 70 percent. Germany, Luxembourg, and the Netherlands have virtually no families in persistent poverty, but a substantial portion of the poor in Canada and the United States were persistently poor. While one in seven American whites was persistently poor, 40 percent of African Americans were persistently poor (see Duncan et al., this volume). But policy disagreements surface immediately as various analysts offer explanations for labor market differences in the position of black Americans, especially black male youths, and others.

Let us go on to examine some general trends in income distribution. There is

Figure 14.1 / Income Distributions

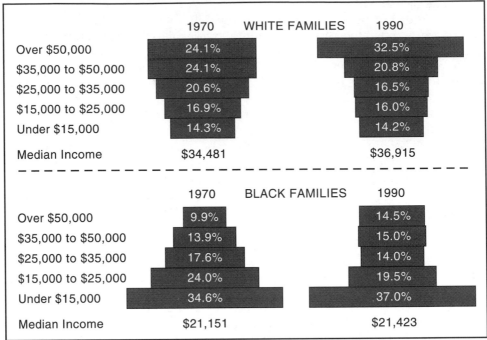

SOURCE: Andrew Hacker, *Two Nations, Black and White, Separate, Hostile, and Unequal.* New York: Scribners, 1992, p. 98.

a pyramidal shape to the income distributions of both agricultural and industrial economies, but income distributions take on an hourglass shape (perhaps a "coke bottle") as the economy shifts from secondary to service sector domination (Plunkert 1990; Tienda et al. 1987). However, notice that when we pull apart the income distribution graph and separate black and white Americans (Figure 14.1), what looked like an hourglass when the national income distribution figures were aggregated became a regular pyramid for blacks but an inverted pyramid for whites. However, as noted previously, the position that one takes as to why blacks are in this particular position is at the core of policy prescriptions about how to attend to the problem.

Sassen's (1988) work on the New York City economy shows that the immigrant population is engaged in the "informalization" of the city's economy. Expanding high-income populations demand customized service, and this can produce a bulge above the middle of the hourglass. Meanwhile, expanding low-income populations increase the demand for low-cost goods and services, thereby producing a bulge below the middle squeeze of the hourglass. It is this lower bulge that is served by the proliferation of new small vendors or services and goods among the immigrant populations. Burgeoning private services can sometimes be handled by highly competitive small entrepreneurs developing out of the secondary labor market, and this is a direct link with what Sassen-Koob (1984) described in New York. In a related way, the work of Light and Bonacich (1988) on Koreans in Los Angeles and Portes and Rumbaut (1992) and Bailey and Waldinger (1991) on ethnic enclaves in Miami (Cubans) and New York (Dominicans and Chinese) make similar points about vertical integration and entrepreneurial success.

If we think that these trends mean that the economy is generally healthy, then we need only tinker with the parts, or direct policies at specific target groups and develop fine-tuned remedial strategies for those groups. If, on the other hand, we believe that economic conditions for young people are generally worsening (opportunities are declining), then more universal policy initiatives need to be considered.

THE CANARIES IN THE COAL MINE

Working in a coal mine can be very dangerous. Not only are there cave-ins and explosions, but there are noxious fumes. However, the levels of toxicity in these fumes are not noticeable to humans until it is too late. The canary is a delicate bird with a small lung capacity. Someone conjured the bright idea to take a canary down into the coal mine so that, at levels of toxicity far lower than those that would be fatal to humans, the canary would succumb—a warning signal to the coal miners.

It may well be that African American urban youths in the United States are socially analogous—they are the most visibly vulnerable "canary" of the international service sector coal mine—and others are well advised to take heed. To put it more directly, black Americans may simply be *the first to have experienced massive structural youth unemployment in the service sector.* They are soon to be followed by parallel developments in a number of other nations experiencing a sharp increase in the service sector of their respective economies. We should not be surprised when skyrocketing rates of youth unemployment occur among the most vulnerable youth populations in industrial countries—for example, the Turks in Germany, North African and Caribbean immigrants in France; Pakistanis and Jamaicans in the United Kingdom; Vietnamese, Greeks, and Italians in Australia; and African immigrants (North and sub-Saharan) in Italy.

Australian youth unemployment has run at about 15 to 20 percent for the last decade (Polk and Tait 1990). Australia obviously has no black youth unemployment problem per se, because the Aborigines are mainly in rural areas. But the fact that Australia has what seems to be an intractable youth unemployment problem forces us to reflect on whether this problem is either a consequence of "neutral systemic forces" or policies and practices that impact one part of the population more than others. Phrasing the issue this way, it is clear that it is a serious analytic error to think of spiraling youth unemployment in tertiary economies as *either* systematic *or* the result of the characteristics of vulnerable populations. Both are true. My basic argument is that by reconceptualizing the systemic character of youth unemployment in tertiary economies, we can see that the first signs of a *systemic* problem show up among the most vulnerable youth populations.

The recent history of Detroit auto production is instructive for understanding how trends in workforce composition affect different parts of the labor market. In the 1940s, there were eight production workers to every skilled worker at General Motors. By the middle of the 1980s, that figure had been halved to four production workers to one skilled worker (Jacobs 1987). This looks like a bland statistic that is hardly race-specific, but African Americans historically were most heavily represented in production jobs (Jacobs 1987: 6). Machine shops that supply screws to the auto manufacturers are a vital ancillary part of that industry. One of the largest concentration of screw machine shops has developed in Jackson, Michigan, a city with a population less than 20 percent black. Moreover, because of the U.S.-Canadian Auto Pact, American auto magnates from Detroit have placed major production facilities in neighboring Ontario province, in the city of Windsor. Indeed, Windsor has become something of an industrial suburb of Detroit, and in recent years, Canadian auto workers have grown to an all-time high number of 120,000. This tells only a part of the story, because new jobs are developing in the area of "high technology." But it is this area in which minorities are doing poorly (Markusen et al. 1986: 177–178). A survey of the 50 largest "high-tech" companies in the state of Michigan revealed that *not a single firm had manufacturing operations within the city limits of Detroit.*

These facts and related evidence presented here are used to show that regional and technological change is connected to the increasing rates of black youth unemployment. As the force of tertiary sector domination penetrates and begins to affect the general youth population, African Americans may well be viewed as a harbinger of things to come for the general population rather than a special case of disadvantage.

Over the last three decades, the United States has witnessed the development of a relatively new phenomenon: An aggregation of people, mainly African American but increasingly Latino, who live in the central cities, participate at unparalleled levels in both alternative and underground economies, and have extraordinarily high rates of youth unemployment and contacts with the criminal justice system. Our cultural memory is so short that there is a tendency to regard this very recent development as endemic and a long-standing feature of American society. In the next section, we examine some of the important social and economic forces that help explain how this happened.

SOCIALIZATION AND ARTICULATION WITH THE ECONOMY

It has long been noted that the movement from an agricultural to a manufacturing society required far less from the schools than does the move from manufacturing to service. People who could and did move from the farms to the cities needed little in the way of formal education to obtain employment. Drop-outs could still find jobs. But if we take a closer look at the issue of school dropouts as an historical phenomenon, we will see that it is not dropping out but the larger economic context in which students drop out that makes dropping out a problem.

In 1910, the rate for white dropouts was higher than it currently is for blacks. But in 1910, teenagers were dropping out of school and dropping into factory jobs in a booming and expanding secondary sector of the economy. Back in the 1940s, blacks could move from rural areas to Gary, Pittsburgh, and Chicago to take factory jobs.

Both conventional wisdom and scholarly analysis have emphasized the importance of schooling as it relates to new service sector jobs (Wilson 1987; Moss and Tilly 1991). In order to sharpen the argument about the differing fates of African American and white youth in the America of the last few decades, we need to review a bit of social history concerning their recent comparative schooling experiences. In 1940, only 70 percent of white youth in America aged 16 to 17 were attending secondary schools, and only 55 percent of black youths were attending secondary schools (Farley 1984: 18). By the early 1970s, that gap was nearly closed, with whites attending at about 90 percent and blacks at 87 percent. Today, there is virtually no difference, with both groups enrolled in excess of 90 percent.[2]

This increase in high school enrollment for both blacks and whites is a major change from 1960, when secondary school enrollment was 70 percent for whites and only 40 percent for blacks. African Americans are experiencing more schooling but also more unemployment than in the 1950s (Table 14.1). If schooling is supposed to connect with jobs and preparation for careers, why this peculiar development?

As we move to the actual employment situation, a two-pronged explanation begins to emerge. In a fascinating study, a group of researchers sent *matched pairs* of white and black high school graduates from the class of 1983 in Newark, New Jersey, out in the world to seek employment (Culp and Dunson 1986). These job applicants were not "faking" an interest in employment. They had been screened as actually seeking work and were "matched" for academic achievement. In the manufacturing sector, blacks and whites had about equal success in obtaining employment. However, in the service sector, the differences in the experiences of these matched pairs were dramatic. The whites were four times more likely than blacks to be fully employed in this sector (Culp and Dunson 1986: 241). For the purposes of the argument that will be developed in this chapter, the most important finding is that *retail establishments were far more likely to discriminate against black youths than were manufacturing establishments.* Yet this is precisely where the economy has grown and will grow (Tables 14.2–14.5).

In a recent update, elaboration, and adjustment of the methodology used by Culp and Dunson in the 1983 study, Turner et al. (1991) conducted a total of 576 hiring audits in the two metropolitan areas of Chicago and Washington, D.C., during the summer of 1990. In this study, two young men, one black,

Table 14.1 / Employment and Unemployment Rates Among Males, by Race and Age: 1954–1981

	1954	1964	1969	1977	1981
Blacks and Other Nonwhites					
Percentage of the population employed					
16–17 years old	40.4	27.6	28.4	18.9	17.9
18–19 years old	66.5	51.8	51.1	36.9	34.5
20–24 years old	75.9	78.1	77.3	61.2	58.0
25–54 years old	86.4	87.8	89.7	81.7	78.6
Percentage of the labor force unemployed					
16–17 years old	13.4	25.9	24.7	38.4	40.1
18–19 years old	14.7	23.1	19.0	35.4	36.0
20–24 years old	16.9	12.6	8.4	21.4	24.4
25–54 years old	9.5	6.6	2.8	7.8	10.1
Whites					
Percentage of the population employed					
16–17 years old	40.6	36.5	42.7	44.3	41.2
18–19 years old	61.3	57.7	61.8	65.2	61.4
20–24 years old	77.9	79.3	78.8	80.5	76.9
25–54 years old	93.8	94.4	95.1	91.3	90.5
Percentage of the labor force unemployed					
16–17 years old	14.0	16.1	12.5	17.6	19.9
18–19 years old	13.0	13.4	7.9	13.0	16.4
20–24 years old	9.8	7.4	4.6	9.3	11.6
25–54 years old	3.9	2.8	1.5	3.9	4.8

the other white, were carefully matched on all characteristics, including education, job qualifications, and experience. Jobs were from classified ads in major metropolitan newspapers. Discrimination is presumably lower for advertised jobs than for those passed by word of mouth. All auditors participating in the study were actually college students described as "articulate and poised" and dressed conventionally. These were all entry-level jobs. The applicants were also coached to be as similar as possible regarding demeanor. The researchers found that when differential treatment occurs, it is three times more likely to favor the white applicant. "Reverse discrimination," where a black is favored, is far less common than the other form of white preference. What might be happening here? Why should whites and blacks have such similar fates in the manufacturing sector of the economy, while there are such dramatically different success and failure stories in the service sector? Education is supposed to be the key to success in the new service sector of the economy, with skin color and race receding in importance over time. Why this apparently anomalous finding that runs so far counter to the conventional wisdom?

There are two reasons, one the flip side of the other. The first relates to active racial discrimination on the part of the employer, something that we have just

Table 14.2 / Employment Change from 1979 to 1989, Various Industry Groups

Industry	1979	1989	Change Number	Change Percent
Total Nonagricultural	89,823.0	108,581.0	18,758.0	20.9
Total Private	73,876.0	90,854.0	16,978.0	23.0
Goods Producing	26,461.0	25,634.0	−827.0	−3.1
Mining	958.0	722.0	−236.0	−24.6
Construction	4,463.0	5,300.0	837.0	18.8
Manufacturing	21,040.0	19,612.0	−1,428.0	−6.8
Durable goods	12,760.0	11,536.0	−1,224.0	−9.6
Nondurable goods	8,280.0	8,076.0	−204.0	−2.5
Service Producing	63,363.0	82,947.0	19,584.0	30.9
Transportation and public utilities	5,136.0	5,705.0	569.0	11.1
Wholesale trade	5,204.0	6,234.0	1,030.0	19.8
Retail trade	14,989.0	19,575.0	4,586.0	30.6
Building materials	629.2	769.8	140.6	22.3
General merchandise stores	2,287.4	2,483.4	196.0	8.6
Food stores	2,296.8	3,269.0	972.7	42.4
Automotive dealers and service stations	1,812.3	2,157.0	344.8	19.0
Apparel and accessory stores	949.4	1,191.9	242.5	25.5
Furniture and home furnishings stores	614.9	811.2	196.3	31.9
Eating and drinking places	4,513.1	6,369.9	1,856.8	41.1
Miscellaneous retail	1,885.7	2,521.7	636.0	33.7
Finance, insurance, and real estate	4,975.0	6,814.0	1,839.0	37.0
Services	17,112.0	26,892.0	9,780.0	57.2
Hotels and other lodging places	1,059.8	1,603.4	543.6	51.3
Personal services	904.0	1,196.1	292.1	32.3
Business services	2,905.9	5,788.7	2,882.8	99.2
Auto repair, services, and garages	575.1	898.7	323.6	56.3
Miscellaneous repair services	281.8	359.9	78.1	27.7
Motion pictures	227.6	265.2	37.6	16.5
Amusement and recreation services	712.0	975.6	263.6	37.0
Health services	4,992.8	7,635.3	2,642.5	52.9
Legal services	459.9	896.3	436.4	94.9
Educational services	1,089.7	1,628.8	539.1	49.5
Social services	1,081.3	1,736.9	655.6	60.6
Museums, botanical and zoological gardens[a]	32.2	52.5	20.3	63.0
Membership organizations	1,516.2	1,761.6	245.4	16.2
Miscellaneous services	940.7	1,459.3	518.6	55.1
Government	15,947.0	17,727.0	1,780.0	11.2
Federal government	2,773.0	2,998.0	215.0	7.8
State government	3,541.0	4,134.0	593.0	16.7
Local government	9,633.0	10,606.0	973.0	10.1

NOTE: Figures shown for 1979 and 1989 are annual average from the CES program.

[a] Although published monthly estimates begin in 1982, the previously unpublished annual average for 1979 was computed and used for these comparisons.

Table 14.3 / The 20 Fastest-Growing Industries from 1979 to 1989 (in thousands)

		Employees		Change	
Rank	Industry	1979	1989	Number	Percent
1	Computer and Data-Processing Services	270.8	763.4	492.6	181.9
2	Outpatient Care Facilities[a]	113.0	317.3	204.3	180.8
3	Personnel Supply Services	526.5	1,315.2	824.7	156.6
4	Mortgage Bankers and Brokers[a]	62.3	148.8	86.5	138.8
5	Correspondence and Vocational School[a]	44.9	105.1	60.2	134.1
6	Business Credit Institutions[a]	30.2	67.1	36.9	122.2
7	Individual and Family Services[a]	161.0	353.1	192.1	119.3
8	Mailing, Reproduction, Stenographic	113.3	245.1	131.8	116.3
9	Residential Care[a]	201.1	426.4	225.3	112.0
10	Sanitary Services	47.0	96.8	49.8	106.0
11	Guided Missiles, Space Vehicles, Parts	101.5	207.8	106.3	104.7
12	Air Transportation Services[a]	47.3	96.8	49.5	104.7
13	Security Brokers and Dealers	164.7	336.5	171.8	104.3
14	Legal Services	459.9	896.3	436.4	94.9
15	Holding and other Investment Offices	111.2	212.0	100.8	90.6
16	Miscellaneous Publishing	46.1	82.8	36.7	79.6
17	Miscellaneous Business Services[a]	1,277.5	2,256.5	979.0	76.6
18	Advertising	145.9	256.4	110.5	75.7
19	Accounting, Auditing, and Bookkeeping	299.0	520.4	221.4	74.0
20	Local and Suburban Transportation	75.8	130.3	54.5	71.9

NOTE: Figures shown for 1979 and 1989 are annual averages from the CES program. Industries are compared at the three-digit Standard Industrial Classification (SIC) level, unless the CES program only publishes monthly estimates at the two-digit level.

[a] Although published monthly estimates begin in 1982, the previously unpublished annual average for 1979 was computed and used for these comparisons.

glimpsed in the previous studies of matched pairs seeking employment. The second is more subtle and relates to the "lack of fit" between the clashing cultures and expectations of employers in the service sector of the economy. However, before moving to this discussion, we will address yet another structural feature—schooling and its problematic relationship with the market economy.

AMERICAN EDUCATION, SEGREGATION, AND COMPETITION IN THE SERVICE ECONOMY

As firms leave American central cities, the revenue base of these cities has deteriorated severely,[3] leaving public education in a shambles, and whites began to abandon the public schools of the central cities. As early as 1980, one white child in five aged 4 to 15 was attending a private school in the United

Table 14.4 / The 20 Most Rapidly Declining Industries from 1979 to 1989 (in thousands)

Rank	Industry	Employees		Change	
		1979	1989	Number	Percent
1	Iron Ores	24.8	9.3	−15.5	−62.5
2	Combined Real Estate, Insurance, etc.	22.8	9.0	−13.8	−60.5
3	Watches, Clocks, and Watchcases	27.7	11.3	−16.4	−59.2
4	Copper Ores	33.3	14.1	−19.2	−57.7
5	Blast Furnaces and Basic Steel Products	570.5	274.3	−296.2	−51.9
6	Rubber and Plastic Footwear	22.7	11.0	−11.7	−51.5
7	Handbags and Personal Leather Goods	32.8	16.1	−16.7	−50.9
8	Railroad Equipment	74.3	39.0	−35.3	−47.5
9	Railroad Transportation	556.3	294.8	−261.5	−47.0
10	Footwear, except Rubber	148.9	79.6	−69.3	−46.5
11	Bituminous Coal and Ignite Mining	255.6	139.3	−116.3	−45.5
12	Musical Instruments	24.0	13.1	−10.9	−45.4
13	Operative Builders	83.3	45.7	−37.6	−45.1
14	Taxicabs	59.6	35.1	−24.5	−41.1
15	Cement, Hydraulic	32.7	19.4	−13.3	−40.7
16	Iron and Steel Foundries	240.7	143.6	−97.1	−40.3
17	Farm and Garden Machinery	182.3	109.8	−72.5	−39.8
18	Construction and Related Machinery	382.8	237.0	−145.8	−38.1
19	Primary Nonferrous Metals	72.5	45.4	−27.1	−37.4
20	Weaving Mills, Cotton	150.9	95.9	−55.0	−36.4

NOTE: Figures shown for 1979 and 1989 are annual averages from the CES program. Industries are compared at the three-digit Standard Industrial Classification (SIC) level, unless the CES program only publishes monthly estimates at the two-digit level.

States (Farley and Allen 1987: 203). That figure has increased in the last decade and is now approaching one in four. In major urban centers, a better estimate would be one in three. Meanwhile, nearly 90 percent of black Americans attend public schools. As the tax base has declined, blacks have become increasingly concentrated in the inner cities. This segregation of our urban life has some obvious consequences and some that are less obvious.

In America, the segregation of blacks has had a distinct outcome in a surprising area—language. William Labov, a linguist at the University of Pennsylvania, has been studying speech patterns of racial and ethnic groups for decades. Labov taped the ordinary speech patterns of British white and black children at play in Battersea Park, London. When he replayed the tapes, neither he nor his English colleagues could tell whether the voices belonged to black or white children.

In sharp contrast, Labov claims that he can detect from his tape recordings of children from Philadelphia whether a child is white or black approximately four times in five. This linguistic segregation is becoming more and more pronounced. Some two decades ago, Labov (1972) published a major empirical study establishing the formalistic underpinnings for the technical argument that

Table 14.5 / The 30 Industries Adding the Most Jobs from 1979 to 1989 (in thousands)

Rank	Industry	SIC	Employees 1979	Employees 1989	Change Number	Change Percent
1	Eating and Drinking Places	58	4,513.1	6,369.9	1,856.8	41.1
2	Miscellaneous Business Services[a]	739	1,277.5	2,256.5	979.0	76.6
3	Grocery Stores	541	2,001.9	2,889.1	887.2	44.3
4	Hospitals	806	2,608.4	3,490.7	882.3	33.8
5	Personnel Supply Services	736	526.5	1,351.2	824.7	156.6
6	Hotels, Motels, and Tourist Courts	701	1,019.9	1,548.9	529.0	51.9
7	Computer and Data-Processing Services	737	270.8	763.4	492.6	181.9
8	Offices of Physicians	801	716.8	1,206.8	490.0	68.4
9	Legal Services	81	459.9	896.3	436.4	94.9
10	Nursing and Personal Care Facilities	805	950.8	1,384.2	433.4	45.6
11	Miscellaneous Shopping Goods Stores	594	568.5	905.4	336.9	59.3
12	Services to Building	734	487.0	807.6	320.6	65.8
13	Machinery, Equipment, and Supplies	508	1,260.8	1,574.0	313.2	24.8
14	Trucking and Trucking Terminals	421.3	1,248.8	1,537.7	288.9	23.1
15	Colleges and Universities	822	716.9	990.9	274.0	38.2
16	Amusement and Recreation Services	79	712.0	975.6	263.6	37.0
17	Engineering and Architectural Services	891	515.0	756.1	241.1	46.8
18	Insurance Agents, Brokers, and Service	64	430.1	659.8	229.7	53.4
19	Residential Care[a]	836	201.1	426.4	225.3	112.0
20	Accounting, Auditing, and Bookkeeping	893	299.0	520.4	221.4	74.0
21	Outpatient Care Facilities[a]	808	113.0	317.3	204.3	180.8
22	Air Transportation	451.2	390.9	595.0	204.1	52.2
23	Commercial and Stock Savings Banks	602	1,369.3	1,572.8	203.5	14.9
24	Individual and Family Services[a]	832	161.0	353.1	192.1	119.3
25	Real Estate Agents and Managers	653	360.2	550.6	190.4	52.9
26	Groceries and Related Products	514	648.1	837.9	189.8	29.3
27	Offices of Dentists	802	322.0	511.6	189.6	58.9
28	Department Stores	531	1,878.1	2,056.2	178.1	9.5
29	Security Brokers and Dealers	621	164.7	336.5	171.8	104.3
30	Savings and Loan Associations	612	236.0	402.8	166.8	70.7

NOTE: Figures shown for 1979 and 1989 are annual averages from the CES program. Industries are compared at the three-digit Standard Industrial Classification (SIC) level, unless the CES program only publishes monthly estimates at the two-digit level.

[a] Although published monthly estimates begin in 1982, the previously unpublished annual average for 1979 was computed and used for these comparisons.

black English was a coherently different linguistic system from standard English. Until Labov, the notion that black English was indeed "a second language" that could be treated as such for the purposes of education and learning was hotly contested.[4] While Labov's research on language use and social segregation is fascinating in and of itself, a particular aspect of this work may bear upon the differential success rates of matched pairs of white and black youth in the secondary and service sectors discussed in the previous section.

Employers in the industrial sector are more likely to be concerned with a worker's productivity than with how that worker relates to the outside world. That is the nature of employment in the manufacturing sector. Conversely, employers in the service sector are more likely to be concerned with a worker's way of relating to the customers, clients, and the general public. This helps explain the different fates of matched pairs of white and black youths seeking employment in manufacturing and service industries cited earlier.

For analytic parsimony, economic and social analysts of employment patterns usually emphasize one or the other side of the *relationship* between employer/employee and the job market. However, in an increasingly competitive economy with a low rate of growth, employment in the service sector involves a complex set of conditions that notably constrain economic opportunities, entry-level employment, and career trajectories for all workers. These problems are exacerbated for young workers and even more particularly for young workers with styles of presentation and demeanor that employers may see as threatening or less attractive. Employers in the service sector are particularly sensitive to behaviors, attitudes, and social and physical attributes that make up a certain "presentation of self," because they assume that prospective customers will find these behaviors and attributes undesirable and take their business elsewhere.

In such a setting, mature female workers replace younger male workers, immigrant workers replace native-born racial and ethnic minorities (Segura 1984, 1989), and suburban workers replace workers from the more ethnic urban cores. The new demographic reality of two-worker households has meant that more women are engaged in the part-time or full-time workforce (Tienda et al. 1987; Bianchi and Spain, 1986). This combines with the flight of retail trade, supermarket grocery, and discount stores to the suburban periphery. It is now taken for granted that jobs migrate away from "certain parts of town."

> For example, nearly all new export and regional-serving jobs moved north of Atlanta during the 1980s; the vast majority of low-income, black neighborhoods are on the south side of town. In Dallas, nearly all new jobs have been created in the north and northwest quadrants of the metropolitan area; the black and Hispanic populations are concentrated to the east and south. In the Philadelphia metropolitan area, from 1970 to 1990 the number of export and regional-serving jobs that located in the high-income Main Line to the north-west of the city, as well as in the white middle-income areas of lower Bucks County to the northeast and New Jersey to the east, increased by more than 50 percent. The number of these types of jobs in the increasingly black and Hispanic city dropped by 15 percent over the same time period. (Leinberger 1992)

A good summary of the empirical literature on this topic appears in Moss and Tilly (1991). There is also recent comparative work on geographical location and employment opportunities for young black males in New York and Los Angeles (Jargowsky and Bane 1990). The misfit between the location of urban young minority workers and suburban service jobs complements the employer preference for female and white workers to serve the predominantly white and female suburban retail trade and services clientele.

UNEMPLOYMENT, UNDERGROUND ECONOMIES, AND THE DARKENING OF U.S. PRISONS

In 1954, unemployment rates among black and white youth in America were equal, with blacks actually having a slightly lower rate of unemployment in the 16 to 19 age group. By 1984, the black unemployment rate had nearly quadrupled, while the white rate had increased only marginally (Table 14.1). As unemployment rates among African American youths were skyrocketing over these three decades, so were incarceration rates for this group. If we turn the clock back just about 50 years, whites constituted approximately 77 percent of all prisoners in America and blacks about 22 percent (Hacker 1992: 197). This provides a context for Table 14.6, which shows an astonishing pattern of recent increases in incarceration rates by race. In 1933, blacks were incarcerated at a rate approximately three times that of whites. In 1950, the ratio had increased to approximately four times; in 1960, it was five times; in 1970, it was six times; and in 1989, the black incarceration rate was seven times that of whites.

During the last two decades, we have seen the greatest shift in the racial composition of prison inmates in U.S. history. According to the most recent figures (Hacker 1992: 197), 45 percent of those in our state and federal prisons are African American. Of the more than 275,000 awaiting trial, more than 40 percent are black. And if those figures are not sufficient to alert us to the special importance of the relationship between race, the economy, and criminal justice, African Americans account for 61 percent of all robbery suspects.[5]

The data in Table 14.7 demonstrate that while *there are more than 10 times as many white males in higher education than incarcerated (4,485,000 vs. 330,258), there are more black males in prison or jail than attending colleges and universities on a full-time basis (341,662 vs. 270,301).*

It is difficult to exaggerate the extent to which the net of the criminal justice system envelops the lives of young African American males. During 1989, 35 percent of all black males between the ages of 16 and 35 were arrested (Freeman 1991). Tillman's (1986) arrest data for the state of California reveal that among white youth aged 18 to 28, the chances of an arrest are 3 in 10; for black youth aged 18 to 28, chances of an arrest are 7 in 10. These data are the result of the increased participation of black males in street sales in the new underground drug economy, the selective enforcement of drug laws for street dealers, and harsher mandatory sentencing guidelines aimed at crack-cocaine versus powder cocaine (Meierhoefer 1992).

In the last decade, America has been building more prisons and incarcerating more people than at any other time in history. Indeed, in the brief period from 1981 to 1991, the state and federal prison population rose from 330,000 to 804,000—more than a doubling in a single decade. (This does not include jail

Table 14.6 / Incarceration Rates, by Race: 1933–1989

Year	Total Population			Number Incarcerated			Rate (%)		
	Total	White	Black	Total	White	Black	Total	White	Black
1933	125,579,000	112,815,000	12,764,000	137,997	102,118	31,739	0.11	0.09	0.25
1950	151,684,000	135,814,000	15,870,000	178,065	115,742	60,542	0.12	0.09	0.38
1960	180,671,000	160,023,000	19,006,000	226,065	138,070	83,747	0.13	0.09	0.44
1970	204,879,000	179,491,000	22,787,000	198,831	115,322	81,520	0.10	0.06	0.36
1989	248,240,000	208,961,000	30,660,000	712,563	343,550	334,952	0.29	0.16	1.09

SOURCES: Series A 23-28: Annual Estimates of the Population, by Sex and Race: 1900 to 1970. *Historical Statistics of the United States, 1976*, Department of Commerce, Bureau of the Census (1976), pp. 9–28; No. 19: Resident Population—Selected Characteristics: 1790–1989; *Statistical Abstract of the United States 1991*, 111th edition, Bureau of the Census, 1991, p. 17; Table 3-31: Characteristics of Persons in State and Federal Prisons, *Historical Corrections Statistics in the United States, Bureau of Prison Statistics*, 1986, p. 65.

NOTES: Data for incarceration reflect the estimated number of prisoners surveyed on a particular date.
　　Population: Total population of the United States by ethnicity (in thousands).
　　Incarceration: Total number of prison population by ethnicity.
　　Rate: incarceration/population.

Table 14.7 / Incarceration Versus Matriculation in the United States: 1986–1988

	Black Males	White Males
Incarceration		
In prisons	240,117[a]	186,879
In jails	101,545[b]	143,379
TOTAL in Prisons and Jails	341,662	330,258
College and University Enrollment[c]		
Four-year	185,407	
Two-year	84,894	
Part-time/4-year	66,272	
Part-time/2-year	99,255	
TOTAL in College or University (full- and part-time)	435,828[c]	4,485,000[d]

SOURCES: "Profile of State Prison Inmates for 1986," U.S. Department of Justice Statistics, January 1988; and "Prisoners in 1987," U.S. Department of Justice, Bureau of Justice Statistics, April 1988; and "Jail Inmates in 1986," U.S. Department of Justice, Bureau of Justice Statistics, October, 1987.

[a] In 1987 figures.
[b] In 1986 figures.
[c] (Full-time total: 270,301, Part-time total: 165,527). SOURCE: "Survey Report," Center for Education Statistics, April, 1988, U.S. Department of Education.
[d] No breakdown available here on full or part-time enrollment in higher education.

populations, persons in drug-related facilities, or juveniles.) Federal drug offense convictions increased 213 percent during this same period, signaling the importance of the "drug war" in this expansion. This represents *the greatest rise in a prison population in modern history.*[6]

There is now a near complete consensus among criminologists that drug control strategies account for most of the increase of the U.S. prison population of the last decade. As late as 1980, only 25 percent of those in federal prisons were incarcerated on drug charges. By January 1992, this figure had risen to 58 percent of the federal prison population (Clark Foundation 1992).

According to the government's own best statistics, blacks constitute only 15 to 20 percent of the nation's drug users (Flanagan and Jamieson 1990; NIDA 1990), but in most urban areas they constitute approximately half to two-thirds of those arrested for drug offenses. Indeed, a recent study in New York City concluded that in 1989 African Americans and Latinos constituted 92 percent of all those arrested for drug offenses (Clark Foundation 1992). We have reviewed the evidence that documents how African American youth are at a disadvantage as job-seekers in the postindustrial service economy. But they are recruited into the underground economy of street drug sellers at such a level as to have a near monopoly on the street portion of the trade. In contrast, drug sales in the fraternity houses or "in the suites" routinely escape the net of the criminal justice system.[7] It is the street sales that are most vulnerable to the criminal justice apparatus, at least as currently constituted and employed.

Moreover, federal law is not race-neutral on these two very much related chemical substances: Possession with intent to distribute 5 grams of powder cocaine brings a variable sentence of 10 to 37 months, but possession with intent to distribute 5 grams of crack brings a mandatory minimum 5-year sentence.[8] Blacks are more likely to sell and consume crack, while whites are more likely to use and sell powder cocaine (Flanagan and Jamieson 1990; NIDA 1990). A study by the Federal Judicial Center has revealed that mandatory minimum sentencing in drug cases has had the effect of dramatically increasing the length of time blacks serve in prison (Meierhoefer 1992).[9]

The drug war has affected black and white incarceration rates quite differently. For example, in Virginia, 63 percent of the new prison commitments on drug offenses were white people in 1983. Just 6 years later, in 1989, the situation was reversed: Only 34 percent of the new drug commitments were whites; 65 percent were minority. The racial differences in incarceration are the result of the cumulative effects of the full net of the criminal justice system, which consistently falls more heavily and selectively on blacks. Table 14.8 shows the steady increase in the proportion of incarcerated black offenders.

There is a direct relationship between the new statistics of race, crime, and incarceration and an emerging group of youths who have been involved with entry-level service sector employment. The National Bureau of Economic Research found that men jailed before 1981 worked 25 to 30 percent less than those who were never locked up. Fifty percent held a job before incarceration but only 19 percent afterward. The researchers, Bound and Freeman (1992), calculated that this soaring rate of imprisonment accounted for nearly three-quarters of the sharp drop in the employment of young black dropouts in the decade of the 1980s.

Recent research by Bourgois (1991) provides us with a good part of the texture of the relationship that is otherwise mired and lost in statistical analyses and marginal totals. Bourgois, an anthropologist and ethnographer, spent 5 years in Spanish Harlem, living in an irregularly heated, rat-filled tenement opposite one of the largest conglomerations of segregated and impoverished public housing projects in the world. He found that many of the crack dealers that he

Table 14.8 / Number of Drug Offenders, by Race

	1984	1986	1988	1990
White	1,394	2,075	2,269	1,431
Black	185	386	861	943
Hispanic	741	1,094	1,673	1,029
Percentage Black	8%	11%	18%	28%

SOURCE: Meierhoefer, Barbara S., "The General Effect of Mandatory Minimum Prison Terms: A Longitudinal Study of Federal Sentences Imposed," *Federal Judicial Center*, Washington, D.C. 1992.

befriended had been employed in marginal factory work. The factory jobs had generated an "oppositional culture" of defiance and resistance; even the most rudimentary factory work produced some measure of collective opposition/defiance.

When the factories closed down or left Spanish Harlem, these individuals were left looking for other kinds of employment. Several found low-paying, entry-level jobs in the service sector. However, jobs in the service sector require more direct contact with the culture of supervisors and a subordination of behavioral and linguistic styles. The youths voice a combination of class and race anger at the subordination of their values, in part because they are unmediated through a union or any other form of collective resistance. The workers in these service jobs routinely complained of being *disrespected*. The nature and quality of the disrespect was different in kind and poignantly experienced. It penetrated their armor and pierced through to their self-worth and self-conception. Too often, it left them with a strong emotional antagonism toward "straight society" quite different from the feelings others report after being "laid off" or experiencing unemployment in the industrial sector:

> The fundamental issue is the qualitative change in the nature of social interaction in service sector employment. When you are sweating in the mail room or behind the xerox machine, you cannot maintain your cultural autonomy. There's no union and there are very few fellow workers protecting you. In fact, you're surrounded by supervisors and bosses from an alien and a dominant culture. If they are not scared of street culture, they ridicule it. You look like a bumbling fool to them, incapable of enunciating all the syllables in the complicated words they mouth at you. You have a hard time deciphering the sloppy abbreviations on the notes they jot out for you each morning. Besides, none of the logic behind the filing of triplicate copies or post-dated invoices makes any sense to you. And worse, you don't even know how to look them in the eye without making them nervous or even how to walk down the hallway without bopping your shoulders. They want you to smile their tight-lipped way every time they tell you what to do. From the prospective crack dealer's perspective, it appears that the supervisors want you to imitate them, hook, line, and sinker. (Bourgois 1991: 10)

In the service sector, the cultural clash between white yuppie power and inner-city "scrambling jive" is much more than style. It is experienced as terror to the dropouts who suddenly realize that they are buffoons in the eyes of the folks with all the power over them. As Julio explained, the humiliation only gets worse when you stick it out and "when they get to know you." Here is a direct quotation from one of Bourgois' informant street dealers who was once among the gainfully employed in the straight economy: "So you, you know, you try to do good, but then people treat you like shit. Man, you be cool at first and then all of sudden when they get to know you they try to 'diss' you. When I first got to my jobs, I was busting my ass and everything but after awhile, it's like, you get to hate your supervisor" (Bourgois 1991: 10). This points to a peculiar conjunction of class-and-race alienation from employment opportunities in entry-level jobs in the service sector.

Wilson (1987) has argued that the exodus of the black middle class from the inner city to housing in more affluent neighborhoods has effectively destabilized the situation for the poor blacks in the urban core. Wilson posits that the absence of role models and the lack of networks (connections or links by way of job referrals) are at the core of the problem. Yet there is a sharp contradiction here that needs to be addressed both theoretically and empirically.

In the early part of the century, it was common for immigrant minorities to settle in working-class and very poor areas of our cities. In succeeding generations, some sizeable proportion of this early group would accumulate enough wealth to move up and out of the area. This is the well-documented social history of the Lower East Side of Manhattan, where working-class Jews and Italians lived for a time, then the more economically successful moved up and out to Scarsdale and New Rochelle and Long Island. The Bowery served in a similar manner as the first home to the Irish. As some of these Irish became more affluent, they moved out. These three groups did not leave behind them an underclass of Jews, Italians, and Irish, trapped in persistent unemployment, persistent and seemingly intractable poverty, and saddled with high rates of teenage pregnancies and high rates of incarceration. Rather, they left behind working-class Jews, Italians, and Irish.

These groups left behind a working class for the elegantly elementary and simple reason that there was still a strong industrial sector at that period in American history. It had little to do with the absence of role models or the "connection to jobs" that is provided by ethnic linkages and kin ties. Indeed, ethnic networks were and are important, and referrals to jobs in the police departments, the garment industry, and the restaurant business were very much intact and in operation *irrespective of the proximity or physical or geographical location* or the making of the net*work* (Glazer and Moynihan 1970). It is important to emphasize that job referrals were done by kin, fictive kin, and ethnic associates and connections, *even from the distance of Scarsdale and New Rochelle.* No underclass developed for the Jews, Irish, and Italians, not because the middle class stuck around to provide role models (they didn't), not because the middle class stuck around to provide referrals (they did, but not from contiguous geographical locations), but because there was a strong manufacturing sector, a vital factory system that sustained a working class. The working class never needed the middle class to provide it with role models in order to work. In fact, where this topic has been the subject of empirical investigation, the working class often rejects the middle class as model and instead configures and creates its own image of appropriate class-related behavior (Bourdieu 1984; Willis 1981; Bernstein 1975; Miller 1958; Cohen 1955).

If we reexamine the question of why the "underclass" (or persistent poor) phenomenon has peculiarly visited itself upon African Americans (Jencks 1992), and if we reexamine why we did not have a Jewish "underclass," despite the exodus of Jews to Scarsdale (Glazer and Moynihan 1970), we can stumble upon the answer because we can't get very far without tripping over it. Why? The data Wilson (1987) presented in the first chapters of *The Truly Disadvantaged* tell an important story about the economic transformation of this society. Wilson's argument about black middle-class exodus is special and interestingly idiosyncratic when we place it up against his earlier formulation about the decreasing significance of race in explaining persistent poverty. If this situation (of leaving behind an "underclass") was experienced only or mainly by blacks, then are we not left with the glaring probability that there is something peculiar and unique about the circumstance of blacks in America? Race, perhaps?

Yet if we leave it only at that, we have only part of the answer. Wilson was actually onto something important in the first part of his analysis of structural change and the effects of a new kind of economic development on African Americans. However, rather than shifting the level of analysis to a general jobs policy and submerging the saliency of race, it makes more sense to acknowledge the saliency of greatest vulnerability. Social policy needs to take into account the specific and particular needs of the most vulnerable youth populations, and to fine-tune those policies in ways that address those particular vulnerabilities. But this is not a zero-sum problem; to accept and promote a fine-tuning strategy does not require that one then abandon a quest for general strategies that will improve the conditions of labor market access for youth in general. It is important to pursue both strategies simultaneously.

CONCLUSION

The United States, like almost every other nation that was an industrial power in the first half of the twentieth century, has experienced a fundamental change in its social and economic organization. The shift to service sector domination has brought along with it substantial and sometimes massive youth unemployment. In the United States, youth unemployment has disproportionately fallen on African Americans.

In an earlier time, there was a need for unskilled and semiskilled labor. Today, we have an economy that has few avenues of access for the young, inexperienced, and unskilled. In the factory system and the ancillary employment connected to factories, there was employment for young males. However, in the service economy, new competition entering the labor force from women to immigrant minorities produces a considerable "displacement" of these youth.

In other countries, a parallel development is occurring and will affect the most vulnerable youth populations. We are bound to see alternative and underground economies springing up with greater frequency and with deeper penetration throughout postindustrial societies across the globe. In these societies, youth from the most vulnerable immigrant, ethnic, and indigenous minority populations will be most recruited to these alternative economies. Africans in Rome and Turks in Berlin will both experience these developments before Italian youths or German youths. Thus, rather than seeing African American youths as possessing particular attributes that make them unique, we may find some useful insights into the future if we see the situation of high black youth unemployment as systemically derived and, thus, a harbinger of things to come for other vulnerable youth populations.

What social policies are available to help us deal with these problems? One approach would be a *control strategy*, to limit the response to policies that attempt to contain and/or control the specific problems of crime that come hand-in-glove with alternative and underground economies. Another I will call a *developmental strategy*, designed to provide positive alternatives to the basic economic problems. Within this approach, urban education will have to play a central role. While control strategies might be appealing in some quarters, they leave the underlying problems intact.

We can expect too much from the schools. The basic source of the contemporary crisis among young blacks resides in the shifting structure of the economy and the nature of work. Any attempt to work with schools must be accompanied by policies designed to address labor market conditions as well. *Put another way, while there may be too many inadequate schools in the United States, the current crisis is not the result of bad schooling.*

If we wish to seriously address the question of how to organize new opportunities for large numbers of young people currently trapped in a cruel structural reality and dominated by despair, we must be willing to consider a broad and wide range of new economic and educational policies. If we are to hold out to young people new hope, then whole new job structures will need to be created. The term job structures is used deliberately here, because more is at issue than simply creating jobs.

Two essential ingredients are required if we are to move in this direction. First, new jobs that make it possible for a person to move upward (in ways not currently possible) in a step-by-step fashion in a career structure need to be created. For an example, at the present time, one becomes a teacher by finishing a university level degree and obtaining a teaching certificate. However, it should be possible to have an additional path to teaching—in which one works first as a tutor, then as a teacher's assistant, then as a teacher's aide, then perhaps as a teaching intern. Such routes would provide an alternative port of entry into the role of teacher. The "career ladder" assumes the creation of a linked set of new jobs and is, therefore, above all else, a job creation strategy.

The second ingredient is some continuous combination of education and training. It is essential to ensure that as individuals move up the career ladder, there is the progressive learning of professional skills and experience, combined with credentialling. Such new forms of schooling would provide settings for the teaching and learning of specific skills, as well as the framework for assuring that such learning is officially recognized through progressively developed qualifications. If explicitly organized to assure movement upward in work careers, these qualifications would have a clear articulation with existing labor markets. The very notion of career ladders would then hold the promise of long-term employment with potential career mobility for young people, a welcome change from the current dominant scene in postindustrial societies.

ENDNOTES

1. To a greater degree than any other nation, Germany, especially the former West Germany, has been able to buck the trend, with a relatively higher employment rate in the industrial sector, by remaining competitive in the manufacture of automobiles, chemicals, and machine tools. In Australia, on the other hand, while there has been a growth in employment overall and for adults in the last two decades, but among youths (aged 19–24), there has actually been a substantial loss of jobs. Indeed, over one-third of the jobs available to teenagers in the 1960s in Australia have now disappeared (Polk and Tait 1990).

2. However, there is still a gap between the races with respect to who is completing high school. In 1980, about 85 percent of whites but only 70 percent of blacks finished high school.

3. For example, between 1960 and 1980, the tax base of the city of Detroit declined by $650 million (Jacobs 1987: 12).

4. After that publication settled the linguistic debate, the matter was no longer contested. It was mainly ignored.

5. Blacks constitute 61 percent of all robbery arrests (Hacker 1992: 181). Data from The Sentencing Project, based upon Justice Department statistics, reported a finding that has been widely cited, but not fully analyzed for its impact on youth unemployment: In mid-1989, 23 percent of the 20–29-year-old age group of black men were either in prison, in jail, on probation, or parole (*New York Times*, Feb. 27, 1990).

6. Bureau of Justice Statistics, U.S. Department of Justice, Office of Justice Programs, January 1992, Vol 1., No. 3, NCJ-133097, Washington, D.C.

7. When the police conducted a raid on a fraternity house in Virginia in 1989, it was national news . . . almost a "man bites dog" story.

8. Section 21 U.S.C.-841(a).

9. In 1986, before the mandatory minimum sentences became effective, the average sentence for crack offenses was 6 percent higher for blacks than for whites. Four years later, the average sentence was 93 percent higher for blacks. While these figures are most shocking for crack, the shift toward longer sentences for blacks also includes other drugs. In the same time period, from 1986 to 1990, the average sentence for blacks vis-à-vis whites (for offenses related to powder cocaine, marijuana, and the opiates) went up from 11 percent to 49 percent greater (Meierhoefer 1992: 20).

    In an interview with a member of the federal judiciary in District 9 of San Francisco, in which drug arrests and sentencing are particularly high, I was given this account as to why this might be the case. The Sentencing Guidelines are actually a misnomer, in that they have statutory status, and judges are generally restricted to remain within these guidelines. These "Guidelines" give very little discretion, except under a formula. One part of the formula is "cooperation with the prosecution."

    Here is an actual empirical case before the judge in question:

The accused, a low-level "runner" for a drug operation, knew only a very few people in the operation. Therefore, he had nothing to "bargain" in terms of giving information to prosecutors. He was sentenced to a minimum of 20 years in prison. In the same courtroom, a drug dealer high up in the organizational structure could and did name over a dozen people around and below him. For his "cooperation with the prosecution," he received a reduced sentence of only 2 years in prison.

REFERENCES

Austin, James S., and Aaron David McVey. 1989. "The Impact of the War on Drugs." *Focus*, San Francisco: The 1989 National Council of Crime and Delinquency Prison Population Forecast, 39:1–7.

Bailey, Thomas, and Roger Waldinger. 1991. "Primary, Secondary, and Enclave Labor Markets: A Training Systems Approach." *American Sociological Review* 56:432–445.

Bernstein, Basil. 1975. *Class, Codes and Control, Volume 3, Towards a Theory of Educational Transmissions.* London: Routledge & Kegan Paul.

Bianchi, Suzanne M., and Daphne Spain. 1986. *American Women in Transition.* New York: Russell Sage Foundation.

Bluestone, Barry, and Bennett Harrison. 1982. *The Deindustrialization of America.* New York: Basic Books.

Bound, John, and Richard B. Freeman. 1992. "What Went Wrong? The Erosion of Relative Earnings and Employment Among Young Black Men in the 1990s." *Quarterly Journal of Economics* February:201–232.

Bourdieu, Pierre. 1984. *Distinctions: A Social Critique of the Judgement of Taste.* Cambridge, Mass.: Harvard University Press.

Bourgois, Philippe. 1991. "In Search of Respect: The New Service Economy and the Crack Alternative in Spanish Harlem." *Working Paper No. 21.* New York: Russell Sage Foundation.

Clark, Edna McConnell Foundation. 1992. *Americans Behind Bars.* New York.

Cohen, Albert K. 1955. *Delinquent Boys: The Subculture of the Gang.* Glencoe, Ill.: The Free Press.

Cole, Robert E., and Donald R. Deskins, Jr. 1988. "Racial Factors in Site Location and Employment Patterns of Japanese Auto Firms in America." *California Management Review* 31:9–22.

Cross, H., with G. Kenney, J. Mell, and W. Zimmerman. 1992. *Employer Hiring Practices: Differential Treatment of Hispanic and Anglo Job Seekers.* Washington, D.C.: The Urban Institute.

Culp, Jerome, and Bruce H. Dunson. 1986. "Brothers of a Different Color: A Preliminary Look at Employer Treatment of White and Black Youth." In *The Black Youth Unemployment Crisis*, edited by R. B. Freeman and Harry J. Holzer, 233–260. Chicago: University of Chicago Press.

Duncan, Gregory J., Björn Gustaffson, Richard Hauser, Günther Shmaus, Stephen Jenkins, Hans Messinger, Ruud Muffels, Brian Nolan, Jean-Claude Ray, and Wolfgang Voges. 1994. Chapter 2 in this volume.

Farley, Reynolds. 1984. *Blacks and Whites: Narrowing the Gap.* Cambridge, Mass.: Harvard University Press.

Farley, Reynolds, and Walter R. Allen. 1987. *The Color Line and the Quality of Life in America.* New York: Russell Sage Foundation.

Flanagan, Timothy J., and Kathleen Maguire, eds. 1990. *Sourcebook of Criminal Justice Statistics 1989.* U.S. Department of Justice Statistics, Washington, D.C.: U.S. Government Printing Office.

Freeman, Richard B. 1991. "Crime and the Employment of Disadvantaged Youth." National Bureau of Economic Research, NEBR Working Paper No. 3875.

Gibbs, Jewelle Taylor. 1984. "Black Adolescents and Youth." *The American Journal of Orthopsychiatry* 54:6–19.

Glazer, Nathan, and Daniel Patrick Moynihan. 1970. *Beyond the Melting Pot: The Negroes, Puerto Ricans, Jews, Italians, and Irish of New York City.* Cambridge, Mass.: MIT Press.

Gordon, Ian. 1992. *The Impact of Economic Change on Minorities and Migrants in Western Europe.* Washington, D.C.: Joint Center for Political and Economic Studies.

Hacker, Andrew. 1992. *Two Nations: Black and White, Separate, Hostile, Unequal.* New York: Scribner's.

Jacobs, James. 1987. "Black Workers and the New Technology: The Need for a New Urban Training Policy." *Industrial Technology Institute,* Ann Arbor, Michigan.

Jargowsky, Paul A., and Mary Jo Bane. "Neighborhood Poverty: Basic Questions." In *Concentrated Urban Poverty in America,* edited by Michael T. McGeary and Lawrence E. Lynn. Washington, D.C.: National Academy of Sciences Press, forthcoming.

Jencks, Christopher. 1992. *Rethinking Social Policy: Race, Poverty and the Underclass.* Cambridge, Mass.: Harvard University Press.

Labov, William. 1972. *Language in the Inner City: Studies in the Black English Vernacular.* Philadelphia: University of Pennsylvania Press.

Leinberger, Christopher B. 1992. "Business Flees to the Urban Fringe." *The Nation* 255: 10–14.

Light, Ivan, and Edna Bonacich. 1988. *Immigrant Entrepreneurs: Koreans in Los Angeles, 1965–1982.* Berkeley: University of California Press.

Lorence, Jon. 1991. "Growth in Service Sector Employment and the MSA Gender Earnings Inequality: 1970–1980." *Social Forces* 69:763–783.

Markusen, Ann, Peter Hall, and Amy K. Glasmeier. 1986. *High Tech America.* Boston: Allen & Unwin.

Meierhoefer, Barbara S. 1992. *The General Effect of Mandatory Minimum Prison Terms: A Longitudinal Study of Federal Sentences Imposed.* Washington, D.C.: Federal Judicial Center.

Miller, Walter. 1958. "Lower-Class Culture as a Generating Milieu of Gang Delinquency." *Journal of Social Issues* 14:5–19.

Moss, Philip, and Chris Tilly. 1991. "Why Black Men Are Doing Worse in the Labor Market: A Review of Supply-Side and Demand-Side Explanations." New York: Social Science Research Council.

NIDA (National Institute on Drug Abuse). 1990. National Household Survey on Drug Abuse, DHHS Publication No. (ADM) 91-1789.

Ogbu, John U. 1978. *Minority Education and Caste: The American System in Cross-Cultural Perspective.* New York: Academic Press.

———. 1983. "Minority Status and Schooling in Plural Societies." *Comparative Education Review* 27:168–190.

———. 1990. "Minority Status and Literacy in Comparative Perspective." *Daedulus* Spring:141–168.

Osterman, Paul. 1994. Chapter 11 in this volume.

Plunkert, Lois M. 1990. "The 1980's: A Decade of Job Growth and Industry Shifts." *Monthly Labor Review* September:3–16.

Polk, Kenneth, and David Tait. 1990. "Changing Youth Labour Markets and Lifestyles." *Youth Studies* February.

Portes, Alejandro, and Reuben Rumbaut. 1990. *Immigrant America, A Portrait.* Berkeley: University of California Press.

Portes, Alejandro, and Min Zhou. 1992. "Gaining the Upper Hand: Old and New Perspectives in the Study of Foreign-Born Minorities," for the Conference, *Poverty, Inequality and the Crisis of Public Policy,* Joint Center for Political and Economic Studies.

Quinn, Jim. 1985. "Linguistic Segregation." *The Nation* Nov. 9:479–482.

Sassen, Saskia. 1988. *The Mobility of Labor and Capital.* New York: Cambridge University Press.

Sassen-Koob, Saskia. 1984. "The New Labor Demand in Global Cities." In *Cities in Transition,* edited by Michael P. Smith, 139–171. Beverly Hills, Calif.: Sage.

Segura, Denise. 1989. "Chicana and Mexican Immigrant Women at Work: The Impact of Class, Race and Gender on Occupational Mobility." *Gender and Society* March:37–52.

———. 1984. "Labor Market Stratification: The Chicana Experience." *Berkeley Journal of Sociology* 57–91.

Tienda, Marta, Shelley A. Smith, and Vilma Ortiz. 1987. "Industrial Restructuring, Gender Segregation, and Sex Differences in Earnings." *American Sociological Review* 52: 195–210.

Tillman, Robert. 1986. "The Prevalence and Incidence of Arrest Among Adult Males in California." Bureau of Criminal Statistics Special Report Series, State of California, Department of Justice, December.

Turner, M. A., M. Fix, and R. J. Struyk. 1992. *Opportunities Denied, Opportunities Diminished: Discrimination in Hiring.* Washington, D.C.: The Urban Institute Press.

Waldinger, Roger. 1986. *Through the Eye of the Needle: Immigrants and Enterprise in New York's Garment Trades.* New York: New York University Press.

Willis, Paul. 1981. *Learning to Labour: How Working-Class Kids Get Working Class Jobs.* New York: Columbia University Press.

Wilson, Kenneth, and Allen Martin. 1982. "Ethnic Enclaves: A Comparison of the Cuban and Black Economies in Miami." *American Journal of Sociology* 78:135–160.

Wilson, William J. 1987. *The Truly Disadvantaged: The Inner City, the Underclass, and Public Policy.* Chicago: University of Chicago Press.

Part IV

MINORITIES IN ADVANCED INDUSTRIAL COUNTRIES

Chapter 15

DIVERGENT DESTINIES:
IMMIGRATION, POVERTY,
AND ENTREPRENEURSHIP
IN THE UNITED STATES

Alejandro Portes and Min Zhou

C ONTEMPORARY IMMIGRATION to the United States is seldom associated
with the traumas of poverty in the specialized literature. This is not due
to the absence of objective indicators of poverty, such as low incomes,
among recent immigrants, but to the low incidence of those social pathologies
commonly associated with the domestic "underclass" (Marks 1991). Instead,
the areas where the foreign born concentrate are characterized by a different
set of social traits including the widespread use of languages other than English,
great diversity in terms of both national origins and socioeconomic backgrounds, the large and semi-open presence of unauthorized aliens, and the rise
of ethnic business enclaves. The research literature on immigration has focused
on these and related topics in contrast to those that most concern students of
domestic poverty.

Indeed, when the two literatures come together, it is in the form of comparisons that point to the relative progress of immigrants relative to native-born
minorities despite initial disadvantages, such as lack of English knowledge and
unfamiliarity with the host culture. These comparisons are notable because immigrants must often endure conditions every bit as harsh, if not worse, than
the domestic poor. The difference is that immigrants' poverty is embedded in
a social context that makes it appear less hopeless and more transitory than the
kind afflicting the native born. We review some of the reasons for this contrast
later following an overview of the magnitude and characteristics of contemporary immigration.

IMMIGRATION TODAY

In 1990, the United Stated admitted 1,536,483 foreigners for legal permanent
residence. This is the single largest annual total in the twentieth century, ex-

ceeding by 240,000 the preceding record year of 1907 (INS 1991b). The 1990 figure is an inflated indicator of new arrivals, however, because it is dominated by legalizations of formerly unauthorized aliens, as mandated by the 1986 Immigration Reform and Control Act (IRCA). A total of 880,372 foreigners already residing in the country legalized their residence in 1990. Added to those who did the same in 1989, the total number of admissions of former illegals under the IRCA regular legalization program reached 1.35 million, of which over 70 percent came from Mexico and another 10 percent from Central America.

Even after discounting the new legalizations, immigration has continued to climb steadily, reaching 656,111 in 1990 or a 15 percent increase over the figure 5 years earlier. For the decade, and discounting legalizations, legal immigration added almost 6 million newcomers to the U.S. population, a total second only to the 1901–1910 decade (INS 1991). To this figure must be added the unauthorized immigrant population. Although the legalization program of IRCA reduced its numbers, the deterrents built into this law for preventing new illegal entries have proven ineffective, leading to a rebound in the unauthorized inflow.

Apprehension of illegal aliens did decline sharply following passage of IRCA in 1986, but then turned upward again, reaching 1.2 million in 1990. Although apprehensions are only an imperfect proxy for new entries, they serve as a rough indicator that the unauthorized movement continues. Adding to the newly legalized, a conservative estimate of the remaining unauthorized population in the United States furnished by Census Bureau demographers (Woodrow et al. 1987), we would have a total of 3–5 million additional immigrants that arrived and settled clandestinely in the country.

The immigration literature has repeatedly noted the geographic concentration of the present U.S.-bound inflow, both in terms of countries of origin and areas of destination. As seen in Table 15.1, only a handful of countries accounted for the bulk of legal, unauthorized, and refugee migrations during the last decade. Only 12 nations out of the more than 100 sending immigrants to the United States accounted for 62 percent of regular admissions for permanent residence, only 10 countries for 90 percent of applications for legalization under IRCA, only 5 countries for 96 percent of new apprehensions of unauthorized arrivals in 1990, and only 6 nations for 80 percent of all refugees during the decade.

A more careful perusal of the figures in Table 15.1 brings to light two additional findings. First, immigration and, in particular, unauthorized immigration to the United States is, to a large extent, a Mexican phenomenon. That country alone accounted for over one-fifth of legal immigrants, three-fourths of legalization applicants, and over 90 percent of apprehended aliens during the last decade.[1] Second, every country sending large numbers of immigrants or refugees has been closely entangled with the United States at some point during its recent history, each having been subject to extensive North American political and economic influence during that period. Although this is not the place to develop this argument in detail, a brief review of the history of the top five countries sending legal immigrants (Mexico, the Philippines, China/Taiwan, South Korea, and Vietnam), the top two sending unauthorized immigrants

Table 15.1 / Sources of Immigration to the United States: 1981–1990

Country	Legal Permanent Residents: 1981–1990[a] N (000s)	%	Legalization Applicants: 1988–1990[b] N (000s)	%	Deportable Aliens: 1990[c] N (000s)	%	Refugees: 1981–1990[d] N (000s)	%
Mexico	1,656	22.6	2,268	74.7	1,092	93.3		
Philippines	549	7.5	29	1.0				
China/Taiwan	347	4.7						
South Korea	334	4.6						
Vietnam	281	3.8					324	32.0
Dominican Republic	252	3.4	28	1.0	6	0.5		
India	251	3.4	22	0.7				
El Salvador	214	2.9	168	5.5	17	1.4		
Jamaica	208	2.8						
United Kingdom	159	2.2						
Canada	156	2.1			6	0.5		
Cuba	145	2.0					113	11.1
	(62.0)[e]							
Guatemala			71	2.3	10	0.8		
						(96.5)		
Haiti			59	1.9				
Colombia			35	1.2				
Pakistan			22	0.7				
Peru			20	0.7				
			(89.7)					
Laos							143	14.1
Cambodia							114	11.2
Soviet Union							72	7.1
Iran							47	4.6
							(80.1)	
TOTAL	7,338	100.0	3,035	100.0	1,170	100.0	1,013	100.0

SOURCE: INS (1991).

[a] Includes legalized aliens under IRCA.
[b] Includes applicants under both the regular legalization program and the Special Agricultural Workers (SAW) program. As of May 12, 1991, 94.4 percent of regular applicants and 93.1 percent of SAW applicants who had received a final decision had been approved for legal residence.
[c] These are workload figures and not persons, since the same individual can be apprehended more than once.
[d] Refugees and asylees granted lawful permanent resident status.
[e] Figures in parentheses are percentage totals for countries listed in the respective columns.

(Mexico and El Salvador), and the four main sources of refugees (Vietnam, Laos, Cambodia, and Cuba) will support this conclusion.[2]

Just as the geographical origins of contemporary immigration are highly concentrated, so are its areas of destination. As during the turn of the century, immigrants today are overwhelmingly urban-bound, going to key metropolitan areas in a few states. As shown in Table 15.2, the states and cities of destination of present-day immigrants differ, however, from the predominantly northeastern destinations of turn of the century arrivals. California is by far the preferred state and, within it, Los Angeles-Long Beach is overwhelmingly the most favored metropolis. In 1990, the 24 percent of legal immigrants intending to reside in Los Angeles exceeded the number going to any *state*, except California itself.

Los Angeles also received more immigrants during that year than the next four most popular metropolitan destinations combined. Although the predominance of Los Angeles is somewhat exaggerated in 1990 because of the residential preferences of the newly legalized, figures for this year are representative of a trend observed during the entire decade. What IRCA legalization did was to bring into the open the absolute dominance of southern California and its displacement of New York as the prime site of destination of contemporary immigration, both legal and unauthorized.

As seen in Table 15.2, just six states, including California, accounted for three-fourths of immigrant destinations during the 1980s; just 12 cities, including Los Angeles, represented 60 percent. Past studies also show that individual immigrant nationalities tend to select different places of destination, giving to each receiving city a different ethnic mix. This is illustrated in Figure 15.1,

Table 15.2 / **States and Cities of Preferred Destination of Legal Immigrants**

States of Destination: 1980–90	N	%	Metropolitan Areas of Destination: 1990	N	%
California	2,331,000	35	Los Angeles-Long Beach	375,000	24
New York	959,000	14	New York	164,000	11
Texas	595,000	9	Chicago	73,000	5
Florida	440,000	7	Anaheim-Santa Ana	65,000	4
Illinois	401,000	6	Houston	58,000	4
New Jersey	266,000	4	Miami-Hialeah	38,000	3
Others	1,759,000	26	San Diego	37,000	2
			Riverside-San Bernardino	36,000	2
			Washington, DC	33,000	2
			San Francisco	29,000	2
			Dallas	29,000	2
			San Jose	26,000	2
			Others	491,000	32
			Nonmetropolitan Areas	82,000	5

SOURCES: Fix and Passel (1991: 6–7); Immigration and Naturalization Service (1991: 82).

Figure 15.1 / Composition of Immigrant Flows to Six Major Metropolitan Destinations, 1987

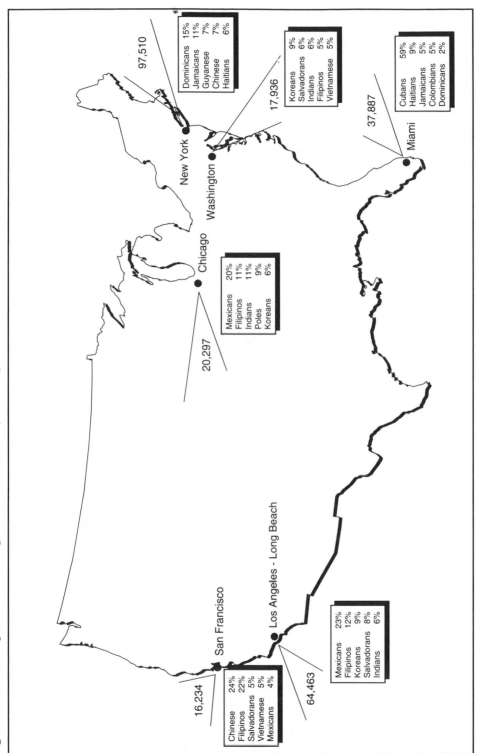

SOURCE: INS (1987: table 18).

NOTE: Chinese include immigrants from mainland China only.

which presents the composition of inflows going to the six major metropolitan destinations in 1987, the year before the IRCA legalization program started. Los Angeles-bound immigration is dominated by Mexicans, Filipinos, and Koreans; New York receives primarily flows from the Caribbean and so does Miami, where Cubans are dominant. Appropriately, given its midcountry location, Chicago is the most diverse of major destinations, receiving large inflows from three continents.

By 1990, the foreign-born population of the United States stood at approximately 19.8 million or 8 percent of the total. This is the largest absolute number of immigrants living in the United States ever. The previous peak of 14 million was recorded in the 1930 census and was surpassed sometime in the 1980s. As a percentage of the total population, however, contemporary immigration does not even come close to the peak years of the 1890s, when 15 percent or one in every seven persons living in the country was foreign-born (Fix and Passel 1991).

The surge of immigration during the last decade has produced two consequences of note. First, it has led to a doubling of the Asian population to more than 7 million in 1990 and to a 53 percent increase in the number of Hispanics to 22.4 million (Rumbaut 1992). Neither group even existed as a statistical category before 1965. Second, immigration prevented serious declines in the population of some of the states where it has concentrated, while contributing to the extraordinary growth of others. An estimated 1 million immigrants to New York State helped compensate for its 1.7 percent loss of people during the decade. Similarly, Illinois' 1 million population loss was partially compensated for by a net immigration of 400,000. At the other end, rapid growth in Florida and California was fueled, in part, by the 439,000 immigrants going to the first state and 2.33 million to the second (Fix and Passel 1991).

Hence, while leaving most American states and cities largely untouched, immigration has had a major impact on those areas where it concentrates. This effect is not only demographic but economic and political as well. In combination with the 1990 Voting Rights Act that mandated better representation of minorities in the electorate, the recent inflow will have, for example, a significant effect in the reapportionment of electoral districts. Already in Miami, where Cubans have been joined by significant Nicaraguan and South American inflows, Cuban-American state representatives are expected to increase to 11 from the present 7, or more than half of Dade County's delegation; Cuban-American state senators are likely to double to four and congressional representatives to two (Fiedler 1991). The economic impact will be as significant although its character will vary with the diverse origin and incorporation of immigrants, as explained later.

MODES OF INCORPORATION

Table 15.3 presents a typology of the patterns of entry used by contemporary immigrants to come to the United States and seek legal permanent residence.

Table 15.3 / Paths of Entry into the United States

Type	Mode of Entry	Residence Status	Next Legal Step	Federal/State Policy	Representative Nationalities
Regular Immigrants	Visa for permanent residence from U.S. consulate abroad	Legal, permanent	Citizenship acquisition in 3–5 years	Eligible for most official aid programs available to citizens	Filipinos, Koreans, Canadians
Refugees	Refugee status granted by INS official abroad	Legal, temporary	Adjustable to legal permanent residence after 1 year	Eligible for special resettlement assistance under 1980 Refugee Act	Russians, Vietnamese, Cambodians
Asylees	Surreptitious (entry without inspection)	Illegal. Temporarily legal if granted asylum	Deportable if asylum petition denied. Adjustable to legal permanent residence in 1 year if granted.	Ineligible for most programs while in illegal status. Eligible for state programs while awaiting adjudication.	Salvadorans, Nicaraguans, Haitians
Unauthorized Immigrants—I	Surreptitious	Illegal	Seek legalization to permanent residence under IRCA or by marrying U.S. citizen. Deportable if unsuccessful.	Eligible for state administered health and education programs. Ineligible for most federal programs while in illegal status.	Mexicans, Guatemalans, Hondurans
Unauthorized Immigrants—II	Temporary visa	Illegal after visa expiration	Same as above.	Same as above.	Irish, Dominicans, Colombians

The diversity of these channels is correlated with the future economic performance of each national inflow and its insertion into American society. In general, regular immigrants tend to come from higher socioeconomic backgrounds. This is especially true of those nationalities that make heavy use of the occupational preferences of the 1965 Immigration Act. These groups come mostly from Asia, Africa, and South America. Refugees are also screened abroad prior to entry, although their socioeconomic backgrounds vary greatly. The initial refugee waves from such countries as Cuba and Vietnam contained high proportions of well-educated, formerly well-off individuals from the elite and middle class of their respective countries. Subsequent waves came from increasingly more modest backgrounds (Portes and Bach 1985: chap. 3; Gold 1992).

Surreptitious entrants are predominantly former urban laborers and rural workers and, hence, tend to have lower educational levels. Those coming from Central America and Haiti are often escapees from political turmoil at home, although their requests for political asylum have seldom met with a sympathetic ear by U.S. immigration authorities. Mexicans represent the overwhelming majority of surreptitious entrants. They seldom claim political asylum but, as seen earlier, have been the prime beneficiaries of the IRCA legalization program. Finally, visa overstayers is a socioeconomically diverse category that includes many immigrants from modest backgrounds, but also skilled workers, artisans, and even university-trained professionals.

This diversity of origins underlies the wide range of educational credentials among contemporary immigrants. Education is commonly used as an indicator of the "human capital" brought by the foreign born to their new country. Table 15.4 compares the educational composition of the immigrant population of the United States and selected nationalities with the U.S. averages on two dimensions: percent completing high school and percent completing 4 years or more of college. The foreign-born population as a whole has 13 percent less high school graduates than the U.S. total population, but the number of college graduates is about the same. As shown in Table 15.4, a number of nationalities exceed the U.S. averages, often by a considerable margin. Notable in this regard are the educational profiles of Iranians, Egyptians, Taiwanese, and Nigerians.

Most highly educated nationalities come from Asia and Africa and, with the exception of Iranians, who often arrive as political refugees, they are regular immigrants. The same is true for all other groups above the U.S. educational averages. Noteworthy as well is the fact that some of the most highly educated immigrants are recent arrivals. This is the case of Iranians, 72 percent of whom arrived during the 5 years preceding the 1980 census and of Taiwanese and Nigerians, over half of whom came during the same period.

At the other extreme are groups formed by refugees and former refugees, such as Laotians. Low average education is also associated with groups whose mode of entry is often surreptitious such as Mexicans, Guatemalans, and Salvadorans. As seen earlier, some immigrants from these countries manage to regularize their status as asylees or permanent residents and, during the 1980s, were the primary beneficiaries of the IRCA legalization program. Given their modest

Table 15.4 / Educational Attainment of Selected Immigrant Groups: 1980

Country of Birth	Persons	Percent High School Graduates[a]	Percent Completed 4 Years of College or More[a]	Percent Immigrated Between 1975 and 1980
U.S. Total	226,545,805	66.5	16.2	—
Foreign-born	14,079,906	53.1	15.8	23.7
I. Above U.S. Average				
Nigeria	25,528	96.7	48.7	68.6
Taiwan	75,353	89.1	59.8	54.6
India	206,087	88.9	66.2	43.7
Egypt	43,424	87.3	50.2	32.4
Iran	121,505	87.1	42.8	71.9
Australia	36,120	81.0	27.6	28.7
Israel	66,961	78.8	34.9	34.1
Peru	55,496	77.3	20.3	31.7
France	120,215	74.3	22.8	13.9
Argentina	68,887	70.9	24.2	25.3
II. Close to U.S. Average				
England	442,499	74.6	16.4	14.3
Netherlands	103,136	67.6	20.3	8.3
Germany	849,384	67.3	14.9	6.2
Colombia	143,508	62.8	14.6	29.6
Canada	842,859	61.8	14.3	9.8
Cuba	607,814	54.9	16.1	6.3
III. Below U.S. Average				
Soviet Union	406,022	47.2	15.7	21.1
Guatemala	63,073	42.7	6.9	40.1
El Salvador	94,447	41.4	6.5	51.3
Yugoslavia	152,967	41.1	10.2	7.4
Greece	210,998	40.4	9.5	12.9
Laos	54,881	32.2	6.5	97.2
Dominican Republic	169,147	30.1	4.3	31.0
Italy	831,922	28.6	5.3	4.0
Portugal	211,614	22.3	3.3	21.7
Mexico	2,199,221	21.3	3.0	33.0

SOURCE: U.S. Bureau of the Census (1984).

[a] Persons 25 years old and over.

backgrounds, formerly unauthorized immigrants tend to depress reported educational levels for their respective nationalities. The same is true of Dominicans, many of whom came by crossing surreptitiously the Mona Passage into Puerto Rico or were visa overstayers. The remaining low-education groups are older immigrants, such as the Italians and the Portuguese, the majority of whom came in earlier migration periods.

Diversity among contemporary immigrants is not limited to their education and modes of entry, but also includes the process through which they insert themselves in the host community and labor market, that is, their modes of incorporation. This concept encompasses three different levels of reception: First there is the government stance toward different national inflows. In the United States some groups, such as refugees, are granted special resettlement assistance; others are granted legal entry and have access to the same general social programs available to the native born; still others are actively persecuted, their claims for asylum are routinely denied and, if legalized, are under an inferior legal status that limits their entitlements for extensive periods.

A second reception level is that involving civil society and public opinion. For a variety of historical reasons, a few immigrant minorities have been greeted with open arms in America; others have arrived with little fanfare, and their presence has been mostly a matter of public indifference; still others have been highly unpopular and their arrival actively resisted in their places of settlement. Haitian "boat people" and Mariel refugees arriving in South Florida during the early 1980s are prime examples of the latter situation (Portes and Stepick 1985). Refugees from the 1956 Russian invasion of Hungary and the first (1960–1962) exiles from Castro's Revolution in Cuba are examples of the first.

Barring such specific historical circumstances, white and English-speaking immigrants tend to experience the least amount of resistance from the American mainstream, while those who are phenotypically or culturally distinct endure much greater social distance and discrimination (Marger 1991: 126–129). This second dimension of public acceptance, indifference, or rejection is not necessarily dependent on the first, or governmental, reception. For instance, the large number of unauthorized Irish immigrants in Boston have generally been accorded a favorable reception, despite their illegal status. By contrast, perfectly legal Iranian and Ethiopian refugees and Jamaican immigrants have endured much greater discrimination (Tumulty 1989; Cichon et al. 1986).

The third reception level is that of the ethnic community itself. Some immigrants belong to nationalities too small to form distinct communities and, hence, find themselves dispersed among the native born. Others join communities composed primarily of immigrant workers. These communities offer some comfort against outside prejudice and the shock of acculturation commonly experienced by new arrivals. However, even if sizable, such communities provide few opportunities for upward mobility, because the assistance that they can give to newcomers seldom goes further than finding them a manual, low-paid job. Still other immigrants are lucky enough to join communities where their co-nationals have managed to create a substantial entrepreneurial presence. These communities, referred to in the literature as ethnic enclaves, are characterized by a large number of interlinked small- and medium-sized firms. Enclaves tend to offer new arrivals an option to dead-end jobs on the low-paid or secondary labor market and better opportunities for economic ascent than those available to immigrants of comparable human capital who join working-class communities (Wilson and Martin 1982; Stepick 1989; Zhou 1992).

The combination of these three levels is the mode of incorporation of a particular immigrant group into American society. If one assumes, for illustration, that positive official reception is defined by active government assistance and that societal reception is determined by the phenotypical/cultural characteristics of each immigrant nationality, it is possible to cross-classify these dimensions in a typology of modes of incorporation. This is done in Table 15.5. Ethnic community, in this table, is classified according to the size of a particular nationality and their under- or overrepresentation in small entrepreneurship, as indicated by average self-employment rates. Small groups lacking any visible concentration in the United States are defined as having no community; those that have sizable concentrations, but where business owners are underrepresented, are classified as working-class communities.

Cell entries in Table 15.5 illustrate the context of reception encountered by new immigrants of a particular nationality in 1980. The absolute number of persons from that group residing in the United States in 1980 is in parentheses, followed by median household incomes in 1979 and percentage of adults who completed 4 years or more of college. Illustrative of the significance of contexts of reception are Ethiopians and Ghanians—both small nonwhite groups of very recent arrival. Despite their very high levels of education and some governmental assistance to Ethiopians as political refugees, their economic situation in 1980 was poor with incomes much below the national average. These cases can be fruitfully contrasted with those of Argentines, Cubans, and Jamaicans.

Argentines are also a recently arrived group lacking any significant concentration anywhere in the country. Being white and of European extraction, Argentines mix easily, however, with the native white population, avoiding the discrimination meted out to African immigrants. Neither Cubans nor Jamaicans are particularly notable for their high levels of education, and most Jamaicans are black, yet both groups possess sizable and entrepreneurially oriented communities in their respective principal places of destination. Cubans, mostly in Miami, and Jamaicans in New York commonly manage to turn their human capital into business pursuits by taking advantage of the favorable context created by earlier arrivals (Portes and Bach 1985: chap. 6; Marshall 1983). This advantage is reflected in their higher incomes, both in absolute terms and in relation to average human capital. Thus, while each percent increase in college graduates was associated with a $324 increase in 1979 median incomes for Ghanaians and a still lower $267 for Ethiopians, the figure for Cubans was $1,014 and for Jamaicans, $1,390.

Table 15.5 / Modes of Incorporation of Recent Immigrant Groups in the United States[a]

I. Government Policy	Admission, But No Support		Active Resettlement Support[b]	
II. Societal Reception	Neutral[c]	Discriminatory[d]	Neutral[c]	Discriminatory[d]
III. Ethnic Community				
None	Argentines[e] (68,887) $18,892/24.2%	Ghanaians (7,564) $12,862/39.7%	Albanians (7,831) $13,572/7%	Ethiopians (7,516) $11,093/41.6%
Working-Class	Italians (831,922) $13,376/5.3%	Mexicans (2,199,221) $12,747/3.0%	Polish (418,128) $13,748/10%	Laotians (54,881) $5,634/6.5%
Entrepreneurial-Professional	Greeks (210,998) $16,103/9.5%	Jamaicans (196,811) $15,290/11%	Cubans (607,814) $16,326/16.1%	Vietnamese (231,120) $12,521/12.9%

[a] Adapted from Portes and Rumbaut (1990: 91) based on data from U.S. Bureau of the Census (1984).
[b] Awarded to legally arrived rufugees since 1980.
[c] Assumed to be accorded to white immigrants.
[d] Assumed to be experienced by nonwhite and non-Western immigrants.
[e] Cell entries are representative nationalities of each type of incorporation. Figures in parentheses are absolute numbers counted in the 1980 census; dollar figures are median household incomes in 1979 dollars; percentage figures are the proportion of persons 25 years of age or older who completed 4 or more years of college.

INCOME AND POVERTY

Table 15.6 presents individual and family incomes for the immigrant and native-born population of the United States in 1979. Data in this table suggest reasons why "immigration" and "poverty" are not closely associated concepts in the research literature. Immigrant incomes are below those of the native born, but not by a very large margin. European-born men had greater earnings than American men in 1979, and Asian families topped the average American family, a result of the greater propensity of Asian immigrants to pool incomes. Only Latin American immigrants fell significantly below on both measures, a result to which we will return later.

Diversity in modes of entry and incorporation is well reflected in the wide disparity in average incomes among immigrant nationalities. Table 15.6 presents median household incomes for (1) the 12 wealthiest foreign-born groups with a population of at least 20,000, (2) the 12 groups of at least this size with most similar incomes to the U.S. average, and (3) the 11 poorest nationalities of at least 20,000. Together the groups enumerated represent 66 percent of the total immigrant population. In 1979, Asian Indians were the wealthiest immigrant group in the United States, followed by Filipinos. Seventy percent of the highest income nationalities came from Asia and Africa. Only one Latin American (Argentines) and one European (Dutch) group are represented in this category. With the exception of some Chinese who arrived as refugees, all these groups are formed by regular immigrants. They all have high levels of human capital, and, in the case of the Chinese and the South Koreans, they have developed dynamic entrepreneurial communities in different parts of the country.

The same is true for Cubans, a group composed mostly of former refugees that tops the mid-income category. The remaining groups in this category are mostly regular immigrants from very diverse geographic backgrounds— Europe, Canada, East Asia, and South America. Also included are Jamaicans, the only black group of any size to reach household incomes comparable with the U.S. average. As noted earlier, Jamaicans are known for their entrepreneurial orientation in their principal places of destination.

Table 15.6 / Median Household Income of Selected Nationalities and Regions: 1979

Region or Country	N (000s)	Median Male Income[a]	Median Household Income
Total U.S.	226,545	$12,192	$16,841
All Foreign-Born	14,080	10,542	14,588
Europe	4,743	12,344	14,768
Africa	200	11,003	14,407
Asia	2,594	11,412	18,417
Latin America	4,372	9,019	13,748

Table 15.6 / (continued)

Region or Country	N (000s)	Median Male Income[a]	Median Household Income
I. Above $18,000			
India	206		25,644
Philippines	501		22,787
Indonesia	29		21,855
Egypt	43		21,118
Pakistan	31		20,067
Israel	67		19,063
Argentina	69		18,892
Australia	36		18,848
Netherlands	103		18,563
China	286		18,544
Taiwan	75		18,271
Hong Kong	80		18,094
Korea	290		18,085
II. Close to U.S. Average: $15,000–$17,000			
Cuba	608		16,326
France	120		16,104
Greece	211		16,103
Brazil	41		16,067
Japan	222		16,016
Thailand	55		15,998
United Kingdom	669		15,994
Canada	843		15,953
Germany	849		15,790
Colombia	143		15,583
Ecuador	86		15,402
Jamaica	197		15,290
III. Below $13,000			
Mexico	2,199		12,747
Vietnam	231		12,521
El Salvador	94		12,261
Iran	121		11,344
Dominican Republic	169		10,130
Soviet Union	406		10,021
Sweden	77		9,903
Finland	29		9,640
Cambodia	20		9,292
Nigeria	26		6,927
Laos	55		5,634

SOURCES: Bouvier and Gardner (1986: Table 8); U.S. Bureau of the Census (1984).

[a]Workers aged 15 or older.

At the bottom of the income distribution are an array of nationalities topped by the largest immigrant group, Mexicans, followed by Vietnamese and Salvadorans. Irregular modes of entry distinguish these groups, including surreptitious entrants, visa overstayers, and would-be asylees. They also include, however, a number of regular immigrants and regular refugees. The European groups included are either formed by an elderly population, survivors of earlier migration waves (Swedes, Finns), and/or include a sizable group of recent refugees (Soviets). Recent refugees are also common among other impoverished nationalities such as Iranians, Vietnamese, Laotians, and Cambodians.

The economic situation of Iranians and Nigerians is noteworthy since, as seen in Table 15.4, they figure among the most highly educated immigrants. Their low incomes may be attributed to their recency in the country, outside discrimination, and small numbers that, by 1980 at least, precluded the emergence of a protective ethnic community. Studies conducted during the 1980s reported a rapid development of small firms among Iranians in Los Angeles (Light 1991) and Dominicans in New York (Portes and Guarnizo 1991). Given the high concentration of these groups in the respective cities and apparently rapid business growth, it is possible to expect an improvement in their economic position during the decade.[3]

No similar development has been observed among Mexican and Salvadoran immigrants or among Cambodian and Laotian refugees. These four nationalities comprise today the most sizable foreign groups among whom poverty is common and, for this reason, merit additional comment. Lower than average incomes among the Latin-origin immigrant population are a consequence of the enormous weight of Mexicans, and to a much lesser extent Salvadorans, in the regionwide averages. As seen in Table 15.6, immigrants from Argentina, Cuba, and other Latin American countries have attained or surpassed U.S. average household incomes. Mexican poverty in the United States is the result of the continuous inflow across the border of a mass of unauthorized workers of modest educational and occupational backgrounds. At present, a substantial proportion of the Mexican-origin population of the United States is composed of formerly unauthorized immigrants and their descendants. The same is true of Salvadorans, although they are primarily first-generation immigrants.

The latest census data on the Spanish-origin population of the United States reflects the modest backgrounds of the Mexican-origin groups and its consequent failure to approach economic parity. These data are presented in Table 15.7. The immigration-driven character of the Mexican-origin group is reflected in its average youth and in its high level of labor force participation. College graduates among Mexican-origin adults are only one-fourth of the U.S. average, while Mexicans are heavily overrepresented among those with less than an elementary school education. As a result, Mexicans concentrate in the bottom rungs of the labor market, their mean family income lags by more than $13,000 the national average, and they are more than twice as likely to be living in poverty.

Among Spanish-origin groups, only Puerto Ricans, mostly a mainland-born

Table 15.7 / **Demographic and Labor Market Characteristics of Spanish-Origin Groups in the United States: 1990**

Variable	Total U.S. Population	Mexican Origin	Puerto Rican Origin	Central and South American Origin	Cuban Origin
Median Age	32.8	24.1	27.0	28.0	39.1
Percent 55 Years and Older	20.6	8.7	12.8	8.0	28.5
Percent College Graduates[a]	21.3	5.4	9.7	15.6	20.2
Percent less than 5 Years of Schooling[a]	2.4	15.5	9.7	8.8	5.8
Percent Male Labor Force Participation[b]	74.6	81.2	69.2	83.7	74.9
Percent Female Labor Force Participation[b]	57.2	52.9	41.4	61.0	57.8
Percent Male Unemployment[b]	5.9	8.6	8.2	6.9	6.3
Percent Female Unemployment	5.1	9.8	9.1	6.3	5.1
Percent Professional—Executive Occupation (men)	26.0	8.3	11.2	12.2	25.9
Percent Professional—Executive Occupation (women)	26.4	14.2	23.1	14.1	22.1
Percent Lower Blue-Collar or Service Occupation (men)[c]	30.1	46.8	45.1	51.1	32.2
Percent Lower Blue-Collar or Service Occupation (women)	25.5	42.7	30.8	52.4	28.7
Mean Family Income ($)	41,506	27,488	26,682	32,158	38,497
Percent Families in Poverty	10.3	25.7	30.4	16.8	12.5
Percent Female-Headed Families	16.5	19.6	38.9	25.0	18.9

SOURCE: U.S. Bureau of the Census (1991).

[a]Persons 25 years and older.
[b]Persons 16 years and older.
[c]Lower blue collar: operators, fabricators, and laborers.

minority, do worse.[4] Although the educational profile of Puerto Ricans is somewhat better, their levels of labor force participation are significantly lower, while the relative numbers of female-headed and poor families are much higher. Central and South Americans are a foreign-born category that includes Salvadorans. As seen above, this nationality has modes of entry and class backgrounds similar to Mexicans, thus depressing the average figures. Even then, Central and South Americans as a whole do much better economically than either Mexicans or Puerto Ricans, a result owed to the inclusion in this category of better educated and more affluent immigrants from Argentina, Colombia, Chile, and other countries.

Among Spanish-origin groups, only Cubans have reached parity with the U.S. population.[5] As seen in Table 15.7, Cubans are much older on the average than other Latin groups and even than the total U.S. population. This increases their average work experience. Their education is also higher than other Spanish-origin minorities, and they have been more entrepreneurially oriented. Results of this last pattern will be examined in greater detail below. The relative economic success of Cubans has been attributed to the considerable resettlement assistance that they received as refugees from the U.S. federal government (Pedraza-Bailey 1985). However, other refugee groups have received even more generous official aid without its being translated into significant economic advancement. This is the case of Southeast Asian refugees, particularly Laotians and Cambodians.

Table 15.8 presents data from a random sample of Southeast Asian refugees residing in San Diego in 1983–1984. The data show the extremely low levels of education among Hmong (from Laos), Khmer (Cambodians), and Chinese Vietnamese and the rural origins of the first two groups. These are predominantly peasant minorities displaced by the various regional wars during the 1960s and 1970s and whose marketable skills and contact with Western culture were very limited prior to departure. Hence, official assistance has focused primarily on teaching these refugees language and basic work skills and gradually introducing them to the American labor market. As shown in Table 15.8, in 1984 the process still had a long way to go: Over 75 percent of Chinese Vietnamese and Khmer families were living below the poverty level, and the figure among the Hmong was an astonishing 88 percent; labor force participation among these groups barely reached one-third of eligible adults.

There is evidence, however, that, with the passage of time, significant improvements have taken place in labor force participation as well as declines in the poverty rate among Southeast Asians (Gold 1992; Rumbaut 1990). Among

Table 15.8 / Demographic and Labor Market Characteristics of Southeast Asian Refugees in San Diego County: 1984[a]

Variable	Hmong	Khmer	Vietnamese Chinese	Vietnamese
Average Years of Education	1.7	4.9	6.6	9.8
Percent Rural Origin	89.9	55.0	4.4	5.1
Percent Jobless[b]	81.6	78.3	69.3	59.9
Percent out of Labor Force	64.2	70.8	61.4	40.1
Percent Families Below Poverty Line	88.3	81.0	76.6	61.3
Annual Family Income	9,876	8,118	9,150	12,163
N	109	120	114	157

SOURCE: Rumbaut (1989: Table 4).

[a]Random samples of adult women and men from a universe of approximately 40,000 Southeast Asian refugees living in San Diego in 1983. A follow-up was conducted in 1984 retrieving 68 percent of the original sample. The present data are for 1984.
[b]Unemployed actively seeking work plus those out of the labor force.

the Vietnamese, in particular, there have been notable improvements coinciding with the rapid growth of small firms and the regrouping of this minority in certain areas, particularly in California. In 1979, the census already detected rapid economic improvement among the Vietnamese who had been in the country 10 years or more. While family poverty among Vietnamese immigrants who arrived during 1975–1979 was a whopping 36 percent, it declined to only 9 percent among those who came during 1970–1974 and 6.8 percent among pre-1970 arrivals (Gardner et al. 1985: 34). Hence, it is possible to expect significant improvements in the economic condition of Southeast Asians when new census figures are released, although it is not likely that groups such as the Hmong and Cambodians have escaped poverty altogether.

Haitians have not been mentioned so far, because, in 1979, the Haitian-born population of the United States had average annual household incomes above the threshold of $13,000. Unauthorized Haitian migration, most of it coming by sea, accelerated during the 1980s, transforming the Haitian immigrant profile. A random sample of 500 post-1980 Haitian arrivals interviewed in southern Florida in 1983 yielded extraordinarily high rates of unemployment and poverty. Thirty-six percent of Haitian males and 81.4 percent of females were jobless. Only 3 percent of the would-be asylees had held a steady job since arrival. Median family income was a paltry $7,200 per year, and 59 percent of respondents lived below the poverty level (Stepick and Portes 1986: 339–341).

A follow-up conducted 3 years later indicated significant improvements in labor force participation, but still income levels were very low. With modest levels of education averaging only 4.6 years and very limited knowledge of English, Haitians lacked the human capital necessary to compete in the southern Florida labor market. To this must be added their tenuous legal status and widespread discrimination for reasons of color and culture. A weak and resourceless ethnic community did not compensate for these barriers, leading to one of the most precarious situations faced by any immigrant minority during the last decade. Along with Mexicans, Salvadorans, Laotians, and Cambodians, Haitians comprise today one of the poorest foreign-born groups and one of those for whom the future looks least enviable.[6]

IMMIGRANT ENTREPRENEURSHIP

Since Ivan Light (1972) noted the fact for the first time, specialists in immigration have emphasized the greater propensity for self-employment among the foreign born. Following Light's initial formulation, immigrant entrepreneurship was originally attributed to the discrimination faced by newcomers in the American labor market, forcing many of them to seek marginal niches for survival. This view of immigrant small business as a simple alternative to destitution is still predominant among many social scientists, despite recent evidence showing that self-employment can also serve as a vehicle for economic progress.

First, the association between immigration and self-employment remains as prominent today as when Light first noticed it. Not all foreign-born groups are inclined toward entrepreneurship, but among those who are, the rate of self-employment frequently exceeds twice the figure for the domestic population and three times that for native-born minorities. In 1980, the rate of self-employment per thousand population in the U.S. was 48.9; Korean, Japanese, Chinese, Cuban, Greek, Lebanese, and Asian Indian immigrants surpassed that figure by 20 percent or more (Fratoe and Meeks 1985). Second and more important is the relationship between entrepreneurship and earnings. There is evidence of a positive association at both individual and aggregate levels. Table 15.9 presents preliminary data illustrating the relationship between family incomes and self-employment among major ethnic groups. The correlation between self-employment and median income for these groups is both positive and highly significant (.53).

A similar positive relationship is found at the individual level, yet many scholars continue to insist that ethnic small enterprise is a refuge from labor market discrimination and poverty (Sanders and Nee 1987; Bates and Dunham 1991; Gordon 1992). Alternatively, it is argued that the positive association between self-employment and earnings is entirely accounted for by the higher human capital of the entrepreneurs.[7] The latter conclusion raises the question of why should the best-endowed immigrants choose small business if the latter is, as depicted in the same writings, a mere alternative to destitution. Be that as it may, the issue is significant enough to deserve additional attention since its resolution has significant theoretical and policy implications.

If the entrepreneurial route among immigrant minorities is a mere consequence of labor market discrimination, then the obvious course is to try to

Table 15.9 / Self-Employment and Family Income Among Ethnic Minorities: 1986

Ethnic Groups[a]	Total Population: 1980	Median Family Income: 1979	Mean Family Income: 1979	% Self-employed 1980
Korean	357,393	20,459	24,670	11.9
Japanese	716,331	27,354	30,527	7.9
Chinese	812,178	22,559	26,600	7.2
Cuban	806,223	18,245	21,577	5.8
Asian Indian	387,223	24,993	29,591	5.7
Other Hispanic	3,113,867	16,230	19,297	4.5
Mexican	8,678,632	14,765	16,962	3.5
Filipino	781,894	23,687	27,194	2.7
American Black	26,091,857	12,627	15,711	2.4
Vietnamese	245,025	12,840	15,271	2.3
Puerto Rican	2,004,961	10,734	13,411	2.2

SOURCE: U.S. Bureau of the Census (1983).

[a] Self-identification of national or ethnic origin.

reduce the latter so as to allow immigrants to reap full returns for their individual human capital. On the other hand, if entrepreneurship yields significant economic payoffs, then the alternative suggests itself of supplementing antidiscrimination measures with programs in support of small business development among ethnic minorities, including the most downtrodden. To examine this question, we conducted an individual level analysis of four of the most entrepreneurially oriented foreign-origin groups, based on data from the 1980 census. These groups are Cubans, Chinese, Japanese, and Koreans. The analysis is limited to males, aged 25–64 who worked at least 160 hours and earned a minimum of $500 in 1979.[8] Both foreign-born and foreign-origin individuals are included, although the former comprise between 75 and 95 percent of all groups, except the Japanese. Table 15.10 presents socioeconomic and demographic characteristics for each group, classified by employment status. Without exception, average earnings of the self-employed exceed by a significant margin those of salaried workers. The difference ranges from $10,800 per year among Cubans to $12,500 among Koreans. Differences in annual median household incomes are more attenuated but run consistently in the same direction.

A notable result is that differences in years of education between the self-employed and employees are trivial in most of these groups, contradicting the conclusion that earnings differentials are due to the higher human capital of entrepreneurs. Differences in knowledge of English tend to favor the latter, but they are not large. The principal characteristics differentiating workers and entrepreneurs are marital status and length of U.S. residence. In all groups, the self-employed are much more likely to be married and much less likely to be recent immigrants. A final important difference is hours worked: In agreement with the literature on entrepreneurship, the self-employed consistently work more hours both per week and in the course of a year (Green and Pryde 1990).

These preliminary tabulations do not suffice, however, to clarify whether the observed positive relationship between self-employment and earnings is entirely accounted for by other factors. To examine this question, we regressed average earnings on the set of independent variables associated with the human capital function plus self-employment. Also included are variables uniquely relevant to immigrants, such as knowledge of English and length of U.S. residence. Definition of variables and measures of central tendency are presented in Table 15A.1.

Results for each group are presented in three columns: (1) the gross effect of self-employment, (2) the net effect of self-employment controlling for human capital variables and marital status, and (3) the net effect of self-employment controlling for all these variables plus annual hours worked. Control for the latter variable is problematic since a higher work effort is a well-known and integral part of the entrepreneurial role. Hence, controlling for it statistically eliminates one of the defining characteristics of entrepreneurship. We include this variable, nevertheless, for the sake of comparability with earlier results.

The set of human capital predictors plus immigration-related variables does a good job in predicting annual earnings, accounting for between one-fourth

Table 15.10 / Characteristics of Self-Employed and Waged Males Among Selected Foreign-Origin Groups: 1980[a]

Variable	Cuban Self-employed	Cuban Employee	Chinese Self-employed	Chinese Employee	Japanese Self-employed	Japanese Employee	Korean Self-employed	Korean Employee
Mean Earnings, 1979 ($)	26,253	15,393	27,937	16,711	31,987	20,679	29,963	15,393
Median Household Income 1979 ($)	29,090	22,110	31,202	25,005	38,063	30,010	29,165	23,015
Mean Years of Education	12.7	11.7	14.2	14.1	14.2	14.3	16.0	14.9
Percent Speaking English Well	72.3	66.7	84.2	80.6	94.2	94.5	80.8	73.5
Percent Foreign Born	94.7	92.4	79.4	74.6	20.4	22.6	95.6	92.6
Percent Immigrated Between 1975–1980	1.9	3.5	14.4	20.1	4.1	11.8	27.3	44.7
Median Age	46.0	45.0	42.0	37.0	48.0	39.0	41.0	52.0
Percent Married	91.4	79.1	90.6	75.6	87.0	70.8	93.6	86.2
Mean Hours Worked in 1979	2,395	2,027	2,453	1,986	2,377	2,067	2,274	1,951
Mean Hours per Week Worked in 1979	48.1	41.8	49.5	41.7	47.1	41.7	47.8	42.1
N	675	7,386	596	7,667	486	6,703	297	2,127

SOURCE: U.S. Bureau of the Census, Public Use Microdata Five Percent Sample (1980). Authors' tabulations.

[a] Limited to males, aged 25 to 64 who worked at least 160 hours and earned a minimum of $500 in 1979.

Table 15.11 / **Ordinary Least Squares Regressions of Annual Earnings on Self-Employment and Human Capital Variables for Four Foreign-Origin Minorities: 1980[a]**

Predictor[b]	Cubans[c]			Chinese[c]		
	I	II	III	I	II	III
Self-Employed	10,859	7,990	6,704	11,226	8,324	6,776
	(22.3)	(17.6)	(15.0)	(20.0)	(17.5)	(14.4)
Education		707	687		803	840
		(18.0)	(18.0)		(20.0)	(21.4)
Work Experience		274	228		569	510
		(6.5)	(5.6)		(14.9)	(13.6)
Work Experience Squared		−3.6	−2.8		−7.9	−6.7
		(4.5)	(3.5)		(10.0)	(8.8)
Managerial/Professional		5,296	4,709		5,424	4,425
Occupation		(13.0)	(11.8)		(10.4)	(8.7)
Technical/Precision		955	806		2,473	1,990
Occupation		(2.6)	(2.2)		(4.5)	(3.7)
Sales/Admin. Support		−423	−719		−1,115	−1,820
Occupation		(1.2)	(2.1)		(2.3)	(3.8)
Knowledge of English		2,482	2,266		2,861	2,863
		(7.8)	(7.3)		(7.5)	(7.7)
Immigrated after 1975		−4,406	−3,424		−5,439	−4,056
		(6.4)	(5.1)		(16.7)	(12.7)
Central City Resident		−1,498	−1,183		−2,170	−2,083
		(5.9)	(4.8)		(8.4)	(8.2)
Married		2,186	1,701		1,089	790
		(6.2)	(5.0)		(3.1)	(2.3)
One Child or more Present		1,430	1,262		1,960	1,683
		(5.0)	(4.5)		(6.8)	(6.0)
Hours Worked			4.3			4.0
			(21.1)			(20.9)
R(2)	.058	.223	.264	.046	.340	.374
N		8,061			8,263	

SOURCE: U.S. Bureau of the Census, 1980 Public Use Microdata Sample.

[a]Males aged 25–64 who worked at least 160 hours and earned a minimum of $500 in 1979.
[b]See Table 15A.1 for variable definition and means.
[c]Figures are rounded unstandardized regression coefficients; t ratios in parentheses.

and two-fifths of total variance in the dependent variable among the four groups. Effects of education, occupation, and work experience are all highly reliable and in the predicted direction. Since the dependent variable is regressed without logarithmic transformation, coefficients express the annual dollar increment or decrement of a unit change in each predictor. Although the analysis contains several interesting results, for our purposes the central one is the effect of self-employment. As seen in Table 15.11, the gross effect of this variable is

Table 15.11 / (*continued*)

	Japanese[c]			Koreans[c]	
I	II	III	I	II	III
11,309	9,215	7,995	12,585	8,243	6,890
(18.0)	(16.3)	(14.3)	(13.1)	(9.5)	(8.2)
	931	947		549	551
	(14.7)	(15.2)		(5.2)	(5.4)
	1,028	967		714	538
	(20.3)	(19.4)		(5.9)	(4.6)
	− 16.8	− 15.5		− 13.2	− 9.8
	(15.9)	(14.9)		(4.9)	(3.8)
	5,907	5.438		6,842	6,263
	(11.9)	(11.2)		(7.6)	(7.2)
	2,523	2,410		1,500	1,580
	(5.1)	(5.0)		(1.7)	(1.8)
	1,402	1,070		− 1,026	− 1,152
	(2.9)	(2.2)		(1.2)	(1.4)
	3,313	3,203		2,828	2,122
	(5.1)	(5.0)		(3.8)	(3.0)
	4,262	4,222		− 5,968	− 5,369
	(8.7)	(8.8)		(9.3)	(8.7)
	− 1,097	− 1,011		− 2,302	− 1,998
	(3.8)	(3.6)		(4.1)	(3.7)
	2,948	2,411		2,030	1,618
	(7.6)	(6.3)		(2.1)	(1.8)
	1,815	1,794		2,211	1,934
	(5.2)	(5.2)		(3.1)	(2.8)
		4.4			5.8
		(17.0)			(14.3)
.043	.248	.277	.066	.281	.336
	7,189			2,424	

very strong, reproducing the finding from the earlier tabulations. This effect is not entirely accounted for by differences in other predictors.

The introduction of human capital and immigration-related variables cuts down the self-employment effect by between 19 and 33 percent. As expected, the addition of hours worked further reduces this coefficient to between 57 and 70 percent of its original value. This last result reflects again the intimate association between entrepreneurship and a higher work effort. In no instance, however, is the self-employment effect reduced to insignificance. Even after statistically equalizing the samples on 13 different predictors, entrepreneurs continue to have a significant advantage in earnings. This finding contradicts earlier dismissals of self-employment as irrelevant to the economic mobility of minorities or as a spurious consequence of human capital differences. We interpret it instead, along with results presented above, as signaling the significance of ethnic enterprise as an avenue for gaining the upper hand in the American economy, both collectively and individually.[9]

CONCLUSION: THE DECADE OF IMMIGRATION

Passage of the 1990 Immigration Act and the fading deterrent capacity of the 1986 IRCA indicate that the last 10 years of the century will probably surpass the first 10 as the "decade of immigration." Despite restrictionist voices, heard with increasing frequency during the 1980s, the overall sense of the U.S. Congress and administration is that the effects of immigration on society and the economy are benign. In signing the inclusionary 1990 immigration bill, President Bush declared that it would be "good for families, good for business, good for crime fighting, and good for America."[10] Indeed, the bill appeared to respond to recent objections to immigration raised by different constituencies by *increasing* the number of immigrants said to be missing from the pre-1990 inflow without reducing earlier categories.

Overall, the ceiling on legal immigration is raised so that it can increase from its pre-IRCA (1987) level of 600,000 to 700,000 between 1992 and 1994 and 675,000 thereafter. To satisfy criticism that the "quality" of immigrants was not as high as it could be in terms of education and professional experience, the bill sharply increases admissions under occupational preferences from 58,000 to 140,000 per year and reserves the vast majority for skilled and professional immigrants. In practice, the number of such workers that will arrive under this preference is much less, because it also includes their spouses and children. In the past, only about 40 percent of occupational preference immigrants have been the actual workers (Fix and Passel 1991).

To assuage complaints that the current inflow has become dominated by Asians and Latin Americans, the 1990 bill reserves 55,000 visas for a new "diversity" category designed to encourage immigration from other parts of the world. In practice, a large proportion of these visas will be absorbed, at least during the first years, by Irish immigrants, many of whom already reside in the country illegally. The decline of Western European immigration during the last two decades has not been due to the dearth of visas, but to the rapidly improving economies of those countries, especially relative to that of the United States. The availability of the new "diversity" visas is not likely to reverse this trend, although it may encourage new inflows from Ireland, the Eastern European nations, and the former Soviet Union.

The law recognizes for the first time the category of immigrant entrepreneurs, reserving 10,000 visas for persons who invest $1 million or more and employ in their firms at least 10 workers. This floor is lowered to $500,000 for foreign investors who establish businesses in depressed areas, for whom 3,000 visas are set aside. Given past trends in entrepreneurial immigration, it is likely that this category will be dominated by Asians. Given past practice, it is not certain that these entrepreneurs would prefer to hire the unemployed native born over their own co-nationals and other immigrants.

These changes in immigration law are not accomplished at the cost of other admission categories, which are either preserved or increased. Admission of immediate relatives of U.S. citizens remains unlimited. There is a new "cap" on family-related admissions of 520,000 per year in 1992–1994 and 480,000 thereafter. Although the latter figure represents an increase of 45,000 over previously authorized levels, it is likely to be soon pierced, because the law sets a *floor* of 226,000 for other relative admissions to prevent immediate kin of citizens from crowding them out. In addition, the prior limit of 25,000 per country per year is waived for immediate relatives of U.S. permanent residents. Given that most such visas will go to recent immigrants from Asia and Latin America, its effect will be to increase, not reduce, the preponderance of these regions in the legal inflow (Fix and Passel 1991).

More remarkable still are provisions designed to ease family reunification for beneficiaries of the IRCA legalization program. The law reserves 55,000 visas per year for 3 years for immediate relatives of those legalizing under IRCA. In addition, it bars the deportation of all spouses and children of the IRCA legalizees who were already in the country on May 5, 1988. The exact number of beneficiaries of this "family fairness" provision cannot be estimated exactly but will likely reach the hundreds of thousands.

Finally, and largely at the insistence of human rights advocates and the government of El Salvador, the 1990 act grants "safe haven" to an estimated 500,000 Salvadorans already residing illegally in the United States for a minimum of 18 months. This period can be extended subsequently. If one adds IRCA legalizees, their immediate relatives in and out of the country, Salvadorans and Irish currently unauthorized, the combined IRCA and 1990 acts will bring "above board" a number that can be estimated conservatively at 4 million. This is in addition to the newly expanded limits for legal immigration.

Despite the efforts by Congress to regularize the vast unauthorized immigrant population and to deter new illegal entries, all evidence indicates that, after an initially successful period, the deterrent features built into IRCA are failing to have the desired effect (Papademetriou et al. 1991). This is suggested by the increasing number of apprehensions of surreptitious entrants by INS and the Border Patrol after an initial decline in 1987–1988. A number of detailed field studies conducted in cities throughout the country point in the same direction (Bach and Brill 1991). Barring draconian changes in enforcement, the unauthorized flow is likely to continue and even increase during the coming years.

Hence, it is not an exaggeration to say that the 1990s are likely to be the century's decade of immigration and that several cities are slated to repeat the experiences of the 1910s, when half or more of the urban population was foreign born or of foreign parentage. This massive inflow will be diverse, but not along the national lines explicitly promoted by the "diversity" provision of the 1990 act. Despite it, Mexico, Asia, and the Caribbean will continue to predominate among sources of immigration. Diversity will rather be in modes of entry and incorporation as outlined above. Hence, it is possible to expect a growing number of prosperous communities of immigrant entrepreneurs and professionals alongside a large number of poorly educated immigrants filling menial jobs and clustering in impoverished inner-city neighborhoods. New unauthorized immigrants from Mexico and Central America, as well as sizable groups of earlier refugees and would-be asylees, will be in the latter category.

It is too soon to tell just how this massive inflow will affect the American labor market and what consequences it would have for native-born minorities. There is a notable disparity, however, between the rationale in Congress for expanded immigration and the employment opportunities for the latter groups. Increased immigration was justified in the debates preceding the 1990 Act by a supposed "mismatch" between rapidly growing labor demand in this decade and the coming century and a shortage of domestic workers. This position, advocated by an influential Hudson Institute report (Johnston and Packer 1987), stands in stark contrast with high levels of unemployment and poverty among native-born blacks, Puerto Ricans, and other minorities. It would seem as if the idle labor potential of these groups was discounted or held to be unemployable by proponents of the "mismatch" thesis.

It is not yet clear what the employment of a growing mass of low-wage immigrant workers would do to the economic situation of the native born. The preference for more motivated and more docile immigrant workers manifested by employers in a number of field studies may accelerate the displacement of domestic minorities and increase their already high unemployment levels. Alternatively, the economic dynamism promoted by the presence of the newcomers may open supervisory and other positions for English-speaking personnel that can provide a mobility path for domestic minorities. The balance between these contradictory trends is uncertain at present.

The propensity for business creation and the development of ethnic enclaves by certain foreign groups will have beneficial consequences for their members, for reasons explained earlier. However, it is not probable that these benefits will extend to domestic minorities given the well-known propensity of immigrant entrepreneurs to hire and promote their own. The emergence of vibrant ethnic entrepreneurial communities may have the effect, however, of energizing native-born minorities into attempting to follow the same path. Already a number of black community leaders and academics are advocating the reinvigoration of black business communities that effectively disappeared following integration. For these authors, the abandonment of the autonomous economic base provided by ethnic enterprise in the rush to enter the social and economic mainstream was a tragic mistake that must now be corrected.[11]

We believe that such efforts are pointed in the right direction, but note that the conditions making for the success of immigrant enclaves may be difficult to reproduce among large native-born minorities. Elsewhere, we have analyzed the unique combinations of human and social capital underlying the emergence of successful immigrant entrepreneurship (Portes 1987; Portes and Sensenbrenner 1991). It is a task for future policy and research to examine when such conditions can be reproduced among other minorities, native and foreign born, and when this is the case to devise programs for supporting such efforts. Along with policies designed to improve individual education and skill acquisition among impoverished groups, the promotion of those collective networks on which viable ethnic enterprise is always grounded can offer an important path for economic mobility in America.

Table 15A.1 / **Variables Included in Earnings Regression**[a]

Variable	Operational Definition	Cubans	Chinese	Japanese	Koreans
Dependent					
Earnings in 1979	Wage, salary, and self-employment income in 1979	$16,303	$17,521	$21,443	$18,921
Independent Variables					
Education	Years of school completed	11.820	14.136	14.248	15.035
Work experience	Age − (Education + 6)	26.595	19.378	21.060	18.250
Work experience squared		863.175	539.949	602.655	417.524
Immigrated after 1975	Coded 1 if so; 0 otherwise	0.034	0.197	0.113	0.425
English ability	Coded 1 if "good" or better; 0 otherwise	0.672	0.807	0.945	0.744
Marital status	Coded 1 if currently married; 0 otherwise	0.802	0.767	0.719	0.871
Presence of children	Coded 1 if living with children under 17; 0 otherwise	0.493	0.515	0.423	0.714
Hours worked in 1979	Mean hours worked per week multiplied by weeks worked in 1979	2,058	2,020	2,088	1,991
Self-employment	Coded 1 if self-employed or employee of own firm; 0 otherwise	0.084	0.072	0.068	0.123
Central city	Coded 1 if residing in central city area; 0 otherwise	0.420	0.592	0.460	0.491
Managerial/professional occupation	Executive, managerial, and professional occupation coded 1; 0 otherwise	0.246	0.421	0.394	0.366

Table 15A.1 / *(continued)*

Variable	Operational Definition	Cubans	Chinese	Japanese	Koreans
Technical/precision pro-duction workers	Technicians and pre-cision production workers coded 1; 0 otherwise	0.222	0.156	0.237	0.211
Sales/administrative oc-cupation	Sales, administrative support, and busi-ness service occu-pation coded 1; 0 otherwise	0.299	0.348	0.241	0.231
Laborers	(Reference category: operators, trans-portation workers, and laborers)				
N	Number of cases	8,061	8,263	7,189	2,424

SOURCE: U.S. Bureau of the Census, Population and Housing, 1980 Public Use Microdata Sample.

[a]Limited to males aged 25–64 who worked at least 160 hours and earned a minimum of $500 in 1979.

ENDNOTES

1. The apprehension figure in Table 15.1 is for 1990, but the same distributional pattern has existed since the early 1970s. In every year, Mexico consistently accounted for 90 percent or more of deportable aliens.

2. Reasons for this pattern have been examined at length elsewhere. See Portes and Rumbaut (1990: Chap. 1) and Portes (1990).

3. The acceleration of Dominican immigration during the 1980s may partially dilute this effect by adding large numbers of low-income recent arrivals. Hence, higher average incomes may be expected only among longer-term residents.

4. All Puerto Ricans are U.S. citizens by birth and, hence, they cannot be properly labeled immigrants. Figures in Table 15.5 exclude the Puerto Rican population in the island.

5. Figures in Table 15.5 do not come from the 1990 census, but from the March 1990 *Current Population Survey* and, hence, are subject to sampling fluctuations. The census published the standard errors of estimates making it possible to compute the statistical significance of differences. Difference-of-means tests show that Cuban fam-ily incomes, poverty levels, and percent of female-headed families are not signifi-cantly different from U.S. averages.

6. Haitians arriving in southern Florida in 1980–1982 were designated by the govern-ment "entrants, status pending." Although most asked for political asylum, their claims were generally denied, making them ineligible for resettlement assistance.

While many 1980–1982 entrants were eventually adjusted to permanent residence, the government actively discouraged new arrivals. A marine interdiction program was implemented by the Reagan Administration that deployed the U.S. Coast Guard to prevent new refugee boats from reaching Florida. By 1985, the flow had turned to a trickle. As foreign, Creole-speaking blacks, Haitians who managed to remain in southern Florida faced discrimination from all segments of the local community, including black Americans. They were accused of being carriers of tuberculosis and AIDS and were barred, for a time, from being blood donors and restaurant employees. Although their situation improved subsequently, Haitians remain among the weakest and most impoverished ethnic communities in the area (see Stepick 1989; Portes and Stepick 1985).

7. Borjas (1990: 164–166) reports, for example, that self-employed immigrant men earn fully 48 percent more than waged immigrants, but says that the difference is entirely accounted for by differences in human capital. The analysis presented later gives reasons to doubt this conclusion.

8. Self-employment among female workers is exceptional. The other specifications are designed to limit the analysis to working-age and employed adults.

9. Ethnographic examples among Cuban, Chinese, and Dominican immigrants illustrating the same point are presented in an earlier paper. See Portes and Zhou (1991).

10. *Interpreter Releases* 67, Dec. 3, 1990. P. 1359 quoted in Fix and Passel (1991: 10)

11. See Butler (1991), Green and Pryde (1990), and Bendick and Egan (1991).

REFERENCES

Bach, Robert L., and Howard Brill. 1991. *Impact of IRCA on the U.S. Labor Market and Economy*. Report to the U.S. Department of Labor, Institute for Research on International Labor, State University of New York, Binghamton.

Bates, Timothy, and Constance R. Dunham. 1991. "The Changing Nature of Business Ownership as a Route to Upward Mobility of Minorities." Paper presented at the conference on Urban Labor Markets and Labor Mobility sponsored by the Urban Institute, Arlie House, Virginia, March.

Bendick, Marc, and Mary Lou Egan. 1991. "Business Development in the Inner City: Enterprise with Community Links." Community Development Research Center, New School for Social Research, February.

Borjas, George J. 1990. *Friends or Strangers, the Impact of Immigrants on the U.S. Economy*. New York: Basic Books.

Bouvier, Leon F., and Robert W. Gardner. 1986. "Immigration to the U.S.: The Unfinished Story." *Population Bulletin* 41:51.

Butler, John S. 1991. *Entrepreneurship and Self-Help Among Black Americans*. Albany: State University of New York Press.

Cichon, Donald J., Elzbieta M. Gozdziak, and Jane G. Grover. 1986. "The Economic and Social Adjustment of Non-Southeast Asian Refugees." Report to the Office of Refugee

Resettlement. Washington, D.C.: Department of Health and Human Services, mimeographed.

Fiedler, Tom. 1991. "Politically, we'll hardly recognize the place at all in '92." *The Miami Herald*. Viewpoint Section, October 6, p. 5C.

Fix, Michael and Jeffrey S. Passel. 1991. "The Door Remains Open: Recent Immigration to the United States and a Preliminary Analysis of the Immigration Act of 1990." Program for Research on Immigration Policy, The Urban Institute and the Rand Corporation, Working Paper.

Fratoe, Frank A., and Ronald L. Meeks. 1985. "Business Participation Rates of the 50 Largest U.S. Ancestry Groups: Preliminary Report." (June). Washington, D.C.: Minority Business Development Agency, U.S. Department of Commerce, mimeographed.

Gardner, Robert W., Bryant Robey, and Peter C. Smith. 1985. "Asian Americans: Growth, Change, and Diversity." *Population Bulletin* 40 (October):1–43.

Gold, Steven J. 1992. *Refugee Communities*. Newbury Park, Calif: Sage Publications.

Gordon, Ian. 1992. "The Impact of Economic Change on Minorities and Migrants in Western Europe." Paper presented at the conference on Poverty, Inequality, and the Crisis of Social Policy, Joint Center for Political and Economic Studies (September).

Green, Shelly, and Paul Pryde. 1990. *Black Entrepreneurship in America*. New Brunswick, N.J.: Transactions.

Immigration and Naturalization Service. 1987. *1987 Annual Report*. Washington, D.C.: U.S. Government Printing Office.

———. 1991. *1990 Statistical Yearbook*. Washington, D.C.: U.S. Government Printing Office.

Johnston, W. B., and A. E. Packer. 1987. *Workforce 2000: Work and Workers in the 21st Century*. Indianapolis: The Hudson Institute.

Light, Ivan. 1972. *Ethnic Enterprise in America: Business and Welfare Among Chinese, Japanese, and Blacks*. Berkeley: University of California Press.

———. 1991. "The Iranian Ethnic Economy of Los Angeles." Department of Sociology, University of California-Los Angeles, unpublished manuscript.

Marger, Martin N. 1991. *Race and Ethnic Relations*, 2nd ed. Belmont, Calif.: Wadsworth.

Marks, Carole. 1991. "The Urban Underclass." *Annual Review of Sociology* 17:445–466.

Marshall, Dawn I. 1983. "Toward an Understanding of Caribbean Migration." In *U.S. Immigration and Refugee Policy*, edited by M. M. Kritz, 133–53. Lexington, Mass.: D.C. Heath.

Papademetriou, Demetrios G., Robert L. Bach, Howard Brill, Deborah A. Cobb, Roger G. Kramer, Briant L. Lovell, Martina Shea, and Shirley J. Smith. 1991. *Employer Sanctions and U.S. Labor Markets: First Report*. Washington, D.C.: Bureau of International Labor Affairs, U.S. Department of Labor.

Pedraza-Bailey, Silvia. 1985. *Political and Economic Immigrants in America: Cubans and Mexicans*. Austin: University of Texas Press.

Portes, Alejandro. 1987. "The Social Origins of the Cuban Enclave Economy of Miami." *Sociological Perspectives* 30 (October): 340–372.

———. 1990. "From South of the Border: Hispanic Minorities in the United States." In *Immigration Reconsidered*, edited by V. Yans-McLaughlin, 160–184. New York: Oxford University Press.

Portes, Alejandro, and Robert L. Bach. 1985. *Latin Journey: Cuban and Mexican Immigrants in the United States*. Berkeley: University of California Press.

Portes, Alejandro, and Luis E. Guarnizo. 1991. "Tropical Capitalists: U.S.-Bound Immigration and Small Enterprise Development in the Dominican Republic." In *Migration, Remittances, and Small Business Development*, edited by S. Diaz-Briquets and S. Weintraub, 101–131. Boulder, Colo.: Westview Press.

Portes, Alejandro, and Rubén Rumbaut. 1990. *Immigrant America: A Portrait*. Berkeley: University of California Press, p. 91.

Portes, Alejandro, and Julia Sensenbrenner. 1991. "Embeddedness and Immigration: Notes on the Social Determinants of Economic Action." Paper presented at the thematic session on Immigration, meetings of the American Sociological Association, Cincinnati.

Portes, Alejandro, and Alex Stepick. 1985. "Unwelcome Immigrants: The Labor Market Experiences of 1980 (Mariel) Cuban and Haitian Refugees in South Florida." *American Sociological Review* 50 (August):493–514.

Portes, Alejandro, and Min Zhou. 1991. "Gaining the Upper Hand: Economic Mobility Among Immigrant and Domestic Minorities." Paper presented at the conference on Poverty, Inequality, and the Crisis of Social Policy, Joint Center for Political and Economic Studies, Washington, D.C.

Rumbaut, Rubén G. 1990. "The Structure of Refuge: Southeast Asian Refugees in the United States, 1975–85." *International Review of Comparative Social Research* 1 (Winter): 95–127.

———. 1991. "The Agony of Exile: A Study of the Migration and Adaptation of Indochinese Refugee Adults and Children." Paper presented at the conference on Refugee Children, National Institute for Child Health and Human Development, Bethesda, Md.

———. 1992. "The Americans: Latin American and Caribbean Peoples in the United States." In *The Americas: New Interpretive Essays*, edited by A. Stephan. New York: Oxford University Press.

Sanders, J. M., and Victor Nee. 1987. "Limits of Ethnic Solidarity in the Enclave Economy." *American Sociological Review* 52:745–773.

Stepick, Alex. 1989. "Miami's Two Informal Sectors." In *The Informal Economy: Studies in Advanced and Less Developed Countries*, edited by A. Portes, M. Castells, and L. Benton, 111–131. Baltimore: Johns Hopkins University Press.

Stepick, Alex, and Alejandro Portes. 1986. "Flight into Despair: A Profile of Recent Haitian Refugées in South Florida." *International Migration Review* 20 (Summer):339–41.

Tumulty, Karen. 1989. "When Irish Eyes Are Hiding . . ." *Los Angeles Times*. January 29.

U.S. Bureau of the Census. 1983. *1980 Census of Population General Social and Economic Characteristics—U.S. Summary*. Washington, D.C.: U.S. Department of Commerce.

———. 1984. *Socioeconomic Characteristics of the U.S. Foreign-Born Population Detailed in Census Bureau Tabulations*. Washington, D.C.: U.S. Department of Commerce.

———. 1991. *The Hispanic Population in the United States: March 1990.* Washington, D.C.: U.S. Department of Commerce.

Wilson, Kenneth, and W. Allen Martin. 1982. "Ethnic Enclaves: A Comparison of the Cuban and Black Economies in Miami. *American Journal of Sociology* 88 (July):135–160.

Woodrow, K. A., J. S. Passel, and R. Warren. 1987. "Preliminary Estimates of Undocumented Immigration to the United States, 1980–1986: Analysis of the June 1986 Current Population Survey." *Proceedings of the Social Statistics Section of the American Statistical Association.*

Zhou, Min. 1992. *New York's Chinatown: The Socioeconomic Potential of an Urban Enclave.* Philadelphia: Temple University Press.

Chapter 16

THE IMPACT OF ECONOMIC CHANGE ON MINORITIES AND MIGRANTS IN WESTERN EUROPE

Ian Gordon

T HE EXPERIENCE OF ethnic minorities in Western Europe represents an interaction between two main sets of factors. First is the continuing perception that particular ethnic groups do not "belong" and may appropriately be treated differently from the mass of workers or citizens in the country. Second, there are changing economic circumstances and forms of organization, which condition countries' appetite for such marginal labor and the types of economic niche toward which it is channeled.

The present "minority" populations in Europe reflect major postwar waves of international migration into the leading industrial economies of the welfare states. Earlier migrant groups have almost all achieved a high degree of economic and political integration. This has not, however, been the case with postwar immigrant flows, which have increasingly been made up of groups ethnically, culturally, and socially distinct from the majority of the host population. In the years immediately after the war, the largest group of migrants was from Eastern Europe into West Germany. By the 1950s this was overtaken by a northward flow from declining rural areas in the eastern Mediterranean, accompanied by some longer-distance movement of darker-skinned migrants from former colonies. In the 1960s and early 1970s, as these flows subsided, and in some cases reversed, labor migrants were drawn from increasingly far afield, with a growing proportion of Muslim and Asian groups. Even after the first oil price crisis, rising unemployment, and bans on further migration, growth in these populations continued either through illegal migration or the entry of immigrants' families to the labor market. Several of the countries of the northern Mediterranean that were originally strong sources of emigration themselves started to receive substantial immigration particularly from Africa. Most recently the fall of socialism in Eastern Europe has revived the westward flows halted in the late 1940s, and these seem set to be the dominant group of European migrants in the 1990s.

At least until this recent shift, the trend for successive waves of migrants to be drawn from further afield, and from more "alien" populations, reflected a logic whereby the employers initiating the various flows looked beyond the boundaries of the currently integrated European market in search of cheaper sources of labor. Continuing price advantages for this labor depended on its remaining in some respects "distinct" from the host population.

One manifestation of this distinctness is the issue of citizenship. There are substantial differences in the legal basis of residence both as between the countries of immigration and between migrants from different origins. Some groups from ex-colonial territories already possessed a form of citizenship affording varying rights of residence, political participation, and social welfare; other groups of "guest workers" were admitted on a limited, strictly temporary, basis, with none of these rights; the presence of other migrants has been quite outside the law. Most migrants occupy positions between these extremes. De facto, however, it is clear that migrant populations have tended to enjoy—and were expected to enjoy—fewer of the fruits of the full employment and state welfare that, at least up to the late 1970s, governments of these nations undertook to provide for their citizen electors. The new migrant flows from Eastern Europe, of various sorts of "German" and of other nationalities, are presenting subtle new gradations of such citizenship rights, together with new challenges to the rights of earlier waves of ethnically more distinct migrants. Growing nationalist and racist sentiment in Europe also threatens the position of "aliens."

The retreat from commitment to full employment and the welfare state in many European states since the late 1970s underlines the fact that it was always contingent upon certain economic conditions. The extent to which these conditions have actually been undermined is a matter of dispute, however, as is the inevitability of the retreat. Similarly, while it is clear that there are important links between the ending of the Keynesian-welfare state era in Europe and that of the mass importation of labor, it is questionable whether both can be simply ascribed to the needs of changing forms of economic organization.

The focus of this chapter is primarily on labor market issues, and the marginality of migrant and minority groups as evidenced by their exposure to unemployment. First the European experience of immigration and incorporation of ethnic minorities is summarized. Then three different perspectives on the role of minorities and migrant labor are outlined and applied to an examination of the differing labor market experience of these groups and the changing ways in which they have been incorporated in the labor market, or established their own economic niches.

MINORITIES IN EUROPEAN LABOR MARKETS

The European experience of immigration since the war displays some elements of commonality, notably in its timing, with heavy levels of inflow of labor from southern Europe and former colonies from around 1960, rising to a peak in the early 1970s before being suddenly checked in 1974. In Britain the flow had actually been severely curtailed during the 1960s, while Dutch immigration policy only changed in 1980. The general pattern is clear, however, reflecting both a common economic experience (notably in reactions to the recessions following the oil price rises) and internal political responses to the social implications of growing ethnic minority communities. The growth of these communities was not expected, since the labor flows were believed to be temporary. In fact, not only did a large proportion of migrants start to settle, but attempts at repatriation after 1974 were relatively unsuccessful, this period seeing not only low rates of return but also a great upsurge in the migration of dependents, adding substantially to the minority populations, and, sooner or later, to the labor force. Faced with a choice between permanent settlement and permanent return, a high proportion chose the former option. Increasingly, acceptance of the reality of settlement has led toward a policy set combining strict control with efforts at improved integration.

In other respects, however, there has been a considerable diversity of experience, both as between ethnic groups and as between receiving countries. One aspect of this diversity is the concentration of specific migrant groups in different countries (e.g., Algerians in France, Turks in Germany, West Indians and South Asians in Britain, Italians in Belgium and Germany, but not in the Netherlands). The common factor underlying this diversity is that all the flows depend on the construction and maintenance of specific networks, through the activities of governments, recruitment agencies, and the migrant groups themselves.

There are problems in comparing the significance of minority workers in the European economies because of the multiplicity of different categories that are used to record them—referring variously to place of birth, nationality, residence status, and family origins. These differences in definition signal varying concerns about the position of the various minorities as well as significant national variations in their legal status. There are also significant gaps in the data, especially for illegal migrants, giving rise to particular uncertainty about the size of the immigrant population in Italy.

The most recent Organization for Economic Cooperation and Development (OECD) report presents estimates of the foreign population in seven European nations (not including the United Kingdom), which range between 3 percent of the total population (in Norway) and 15 percent (in Switzerland), and averaging 7 percent in France, Germany, Belgium, and the Netherlands (SOPEMI 1990). The Swiss figure excludes the equivalent of another 2–3 percent among seasonal and frontier workers, but half of its foreign population actually comes from the homelands of the three language communities represented among Swiss nationals. From the four main non-European origins, the Muslim countries of Turkey, Algeria, Tunisia, and Morocco, there were some 4 million residents, almost all of them in France, Germany, Belgium, and the Netherlands, where they represented some 3 percent of the population. In addition to such groups, however, the ethnic minority populations of the United Kingdom, the Netherlands, and France contain large numbers of migrants from former colonial territories (and their children) either automatically entitled to metropolitan citizenship or electing for naturalization. The overall ethnic minority population of the Netherlands has been estimated at about 600 thousand (or 4 percent), of whom over a third are Dutch nationals, including a substantial number from Southeast Asia and from the Caribbean (SOPEMI 1983). In the United Kingdom the total size of the ethnic minority population in 1985–1987 was estimated at 2.4 million or 4.5 percent of the resident population, of whom about half came from South Asian family origins and a quarter from the Caribbean, while about 1 million were born in the United Kingdom (SOPEMI 1990). In France, where the second generation does not acquire citizenship until adulthood, counts of the foreign population still capture most of the ethnic minorities. In addition to North Africans there are again a significant proportion of Asians (from Laos, Cambodia, and Vietnam). By the standards of many parts of the United States, however, levels of overseas migration and the proportion of ethnic minority population groups remain relatively low in all the European Community (EC) countries.

THREE PERSPECTIVES ON THE ROLE OF IMMIGRANT MINORITIES

Analyses of the roles of these groups in Western Europe, and of poverty among them, have been undertaken from a range of different perspectives, some of which focus on migration as the key issue, while others are more concerned with minority status. Many of the principal differences among these, in terms of explanation and prescription, can be captured by a summary of three simple approaches, leading to quite different accounts both of the incidence of poverty among minorities, and the brake on immigration imposed in the mid-1970s.

Market Economics

Strong positive cases for labor immigration have been made both by neoclassical economists such as Julian Simon (1989) and from a more Keynesian perspective by Charles Kindleberger (1967). The latter was particularly influential in postwar Europe, supporting the view that only with an elastic labor supply (unavailable from indigenous sources) could faster industrial growth be achieved without the risk of inflation cutting off future investment. West German economic success, with extensive use first of migrants from the East and then of Turkish *gastarbeiter*, represented the paradigm of the Kindleberger thesis, while the British "stop-go" industrial growth experience could be seen as the price of a much more restrictive approach to immigration.

A characteristic of this market economic perspective is advocacy of the free use of migrant labor in whatever activities it would be most productive, rather than its assignment to specific economic roles, or any form of discrimination. And it would be seen as being in the collective interest that the state should ensure equal opportunities in both employment and education.

From this perspective, how migrants prosper depends essentially on what they bring with them, in terms of financial, human, and cultural capital, including their skills, entrepreneurial ability, industry, and familiarity with the language. If a particular group is poorly endowed in these respects, they would be overrepresented in poorly paid employment. And, by domestic standards at least, they are particularly liable to be poor if they bring larger families and/or spouses who are traditionally kept out of waged employment. In a competitive labor market, however, there is no expectation that migrants be particularly vulnerable to unemployment, unless minimum wage provisions restrict their employment opportunities. But, if employment is allocated on the basis of job rather than price competition (Thurow 1983), unskilled migrants *are* liable to get "bumped down" into unemployment in times of general demand deficiency.

Temporary "guest workers" seem to be a particularly attractive form of immigration, if they allow the receiving economy to avoid the costs of reproducing its labor supply, or of supporting the inactive, and to minimize its social responsibilities. A demand for skilled and efficient labor may be harder to satisfy in this way, however, and it is not clear that such migrants should be repatriated in time of recession. When unemployment is simply a reflection of demand deficiency and is expected to last for some period of time, repatriation might yield advantages for the native population. (Although this would also remove a source of consumer demand.) If, however, unemployment is essentially a means of bringing inflation under control, the withdrawal of an effective component of the labor supply (i.e., active members of the reserve army) would be self-defeating and might well require higher unemployment among the indigenous labor force.

From this perspective, the effective ending of legal immigration to the European industrial economies after 1974 appears to have been simply a mistake (like the earlier, and more obviously political, halt to British immigration from the Commonwealth).

Ethnic Discrimination

Another quite different starting point is the recognition that increasingly during the postwar period, immigrant labor has been drawn from origins that are not only much poorer than the receiving economies but ethnically and culturally quite distinct from the majority of the home populations. These migrants are not just additional "pairs of hands" but different ones—distinctively cheap (whatever their level of human capital), subject to prejudices about their abilities or suitability, and perceived as "outsiders" by incumbent groups with established interests to protect. These characteristics are obviously linked and a reflection of some important attributes of real (rather than idealized) labor markets. Central to the latter are a limited number of strategies that are used by employers to mitigate the inherent managerial problems of first identifying the potential productivity of quite heterogenous units of labor and then ensuring that this potential is actually delivered. Among these strategies three important components, used in varying combinations, are a reliance on stereotypes, the use of particular recruitment networks, and the creation of internal labor markets.

The unequal treatment, and uneven distribution, of ethnic minorities in the labor market is a visible indicator of how these components may combine to produce varying degrees of submarket closure and systematic patterns of disadvantage over and above any real differences in human capital at the individual level. The processes both draw on and reinforce racist ideologies and, combined with the latter, alter the chances that investment in training or education will be seen as worthwhile by the individuals concerned or those who allocate the relevant opportunities.

The sense of difference, that immigrants (or their children) are outsiders, is also crucial in the political sphere, affecting the perceived entitlement to rights fought, worked, or paid for by the host community, and the degree of solidarity or rivalry recognized by others in economically similar situations. Guest worker, or similar, status clearly reinforces such an insider/outsider distinction in the economic as well as the political sphere, making it more difficult to treat migrants simply as additional "pairs of hands" and fully to exploit their potential. If migrants are then "crowded" into particular (lower) segments of the labor market, there is likely to be conflict with those indigenous workers remaining in these segments, or others "bumped down" there during recession, whose pay and security are both liable to suffer while the benefits of cheap labor are felt by the majority.

Poverty among migrant groups is then the expected outcome of processes of exclusion and marginalization, from which the protected majority of workers benefit, through a stabilization of their employment opportunities.

From this perspective, the halt to legal immigration in the mid-1970s was essentially political (rather than economic) in its basis, a reaction both to fears about the growth of an "alien" population who could not be full citizens of the host society, and to the rising tide of racism among the indigenous population. This view is lent support by the introduction of British immigration control as far back as 1962 and the ending of large-scale Commonwealth immigration 6 years before the first oil price crisis; the initiation of the French ban also dates from 2 years before the crisis.

Labor Market Restructuring

A third approach accords a much more active role in shaping the history of European labor migration to the behavior of employers and the ways in which their labor market strategies have been modified by changing economic circumstances within the postwar period.

The initiation of long-distance movements of workers from cheap-labor economies was in large part the outcome of recruitment activities of major employers responding to specific labor problems and of governments acting on their behalf. Subsequently, chain migration, with information transmitted along ethnic networks, may have made the process more or less self-sustaining, but in the face of political opposition to further "invasions," continued pressure from employers could be critical to the maintenance of an open door.

The original needs of employers related to sets of jobs that were being abandoned by an increasingly educated indigenous labor force, in the context of more or less full employment. The problem with these jobs might be that they were dirty, dangerous, stressful, and/or poorly paid, but it was also crucial that employers could neither solve this labor problem at that time by transferring the activities concerned to cheap labor areas (because the goods or services were untransportable), nor by mechanization, rationalization, or paying higher wages. Circumstances change, however. The transfer of labor intensive production to cheap-labor countries has become increasingly feasible, both politically and economically. The abandonment of full-employment policies has created a homegrown reserve army of labor. And the consequent shift in the balance of industrial power has allowed employers to intensify labor and achieve productivity gains without replacing their workforce. Perhaps more fundamentally, the shift to less stable product markets since the early 1970s and to a slacker labor market has reduced employers' interest in cultivating internal labor markets in favor of a growing pursuit of "flexibility." Recruitment of a replacement labor force can be a costly strategy, and the investment is only likely to be worthwhile if the immigrant workers remain both distinct and attached to their original employers. Employers are only likely to take the initiative in recruiting overseas in sectors that could offer fairly stable employment opportunities, as opposed to highly competitive secondary sector activities. With flexible employment strategies in place, labor importation becomes a less relevant strategy for industrial employers.

De-industrialization of employment and the loss of manual jobs in restructured transport and distribution activities involves a growing polarization of employment opportunities within the service sector, especially in the most advanced regions. On the one hand stable employment opportunities are increasingly concentrated in sectors such as business services and professional occupations, which tend to require formal educational qualifications, and for which traditional labor migrants would be ineligible. On the other hand, service jobs free of the demand for certification come to be found in the burgeoning private consumer services (and related trades, such as the fashion garment industry), characteristically in small establishments within highly competitive industries manned by the secondary labor market. Within this sector there *can* be a considerable demand for immigrant labor (as Sassen-Koob [1984] has shown), but the channels of recruitment are quite different from those supplying most of the primary industrial demand of the earlier period.

From this perspective, then, another explanation can be developed of the halt to labor importation in the mid-1970s, in terms of the changing requirements of primary sector employers who were its major protagonists (Cohen 1987). But the restructuring argument also suggests that there could have been *growing* opportunities over this period for less organized migration into secondary sector jobs, which continue to have an appetite for cheap labor.

There is also a distinctive explanation of poverty among minority groups, relating to the manner in which particular groups get incorporated into the labor market. For the original migrants the key fact is that they were mostly recruited to fill specific job slots rejected by domestic workers. But the danger of poverty is particularly acute when a minority comes to be heavily dependent on unstable secondary employment, because this can provide its own basis for their economic marginalization, over and above that arising from ethnic discrimination and lack of human capital.

The Changing Role of Minorities in European Labor Markets

Ethnic minorities have occupied a number of distinctive roles in those European economies with substantial immigration during the postwar period. These include sometimes important roles as middlemen entrepreneurs and in businesses servicing ethnic enclaves, as well as that of replacement labor, taking over jobs abandoned by a traditional labor force (Ward 1985). The last category has clearly been the most important for the principal immigrant groups. However, it needs some further disaggregation to distinguish at least three main types of employer seeking replacement labor: (1) public sector organizations; (2) other primary employers with a degree of market power, notably within the manufacturing sector; and (3) secondary employers in more competitive sectors, notably in construction and private consumer services, but also in the clothing trades.

Within each of these sectors the demand has been essentially for manual or service workers, rather than for white-collar labor, which is why producer services, with their predominantly white-collar labor force, do not figure in this typology of migrant employers. In the two primary sectors seeking replacement labor, the loss of domestic workers often reflected poor employment conditions or shift requirements as much as low pay. Some of the jobs (e.g., in iron-working) could nevertheless attract "skilled" status, while most of them were fairly stable jobs. Conditions of access varied, and public sector jobs would not be available to foreigners in some countries (e.g., in France). In the secondary sector access was clearly easier, but typically pay, security, and advancement would all be worse.

The original distribution of minorities across these sub-labor markets varied both by country and by the immigrant group concerned. On the one hand, in West Germany manufacturing industry was clearly the major employer of foreign labor, with above average proportions not only in some of the more noxious process industries and in the declining textile sector but also in engineering and electrical manufacturers, where there was considerable growth during the period of large-scale immigration. Construction was also an important employer of foreign workers, but there were relatively few in any of the service sectors. Although most of the migrants occupied relatively low-level manual jobs, the sectoral pattern of employment reveals a distinct skew toward what should be primary labor markets. In France, on the other hand, the bias in employment of foreign workers has been more toward construction and services. When immigration was at its peak, some 30 percent of new migrants were going into building or public works; this sector together with (private) health services had by far the highest proportion of foreign wage earners in their labor force, at over 30 percent (SOPEMI 1975). That was roughly double the proportion of foreign workers in those sectors in Germany, despite the generally lower proportion of foreign workers in France. Overall a substantially larger share of French immigration appears to have been directed toward secondary labor markets (Lebon 1988). This tendency has been carried much further in the recent waves of immigration to Italy from Africa and Asia, involving between a half and 1 million illegal migrants, mostly confined to insecure jobs in the black economy, notably in agriculture, hotels and catering, street trading, building, and the steel industry (SOPEMI 1988). In Greece and Spain, too, recent immigration appears to have been largely directed to the secondary labor market.

A third situation is represented by the United Kingdom, where there is as much variation within the black/Asian population as a whole as there is between this group and the white majority. Afro-Caribbeans have been overrepresented in the metal trades and public services (mostly "primary" sectors in labor market terms), those from Pakistani or Bangladeshi origins were relatively concentrated in the more competitive parts of manufacturing and in private consumer services (mostly secondary), while those from India were heavily represented across a range of manufacturing activities as well as in private consumer services. None of these minorities, however, had an above average share of construction employment, which has been a traditional sector for Irish migrants (Cross 1989).

Over the past 20 years the situation in Europe has changed in several respects. First, the overall balance of employment has shifted, with many of the primary jobs in heavy industry being casualties of recession and industrial restructuring. Much of the new employment has developed in producer services or high-technology industries to which immigrants have not been recruited. Second, the minority communities have themselves changed, with settlement and the entry into the labor market of a new generation with potentially different education and aspirations. And there has been a tendency for more of the recent migrants to be drawn from non-European origins.

Evidence on changes in the labor market position of the earlier cohorts of immigrants is patchy. In the French case it is argued that employment trends among those immigrating up to the early 1970s have increasingly paralleled those among French natives, with a similar impact from economic crisis and restructuring, although migrants' chances of unemployment were exacerbated both by racism and illiteracy (Palidda 1988).

In the United Kingdom one study of occupational mobility among middle-aged men found greater change between 1971 and 1981 among South Asians and Caribbeans than the indigenous population, but with a slightly greater chance of downward than of upward movement for the minorities (Stuart 1989). A second (London-focused) study, following changes of employment over this same period, shows substantial evidence of convergence in the distribution of whites and of Afro-Caribbeans, with a virtual end to the latter's overrepresentation in manufacturing and a shift into the public sector. There was less convergence in the case of Indians and none for Pakistanis and Bangladeshis, the group with the most distinctive distribution at the outset. All three minorities showed (relative and absolute) shifts into public sector employment, but Indians maintained and Pakistanis increased their overrepresentation in manufacturing, while the latter group failed to make any progress into higher white-collar jobs (Cross and Waldinger 1992).

For the 1980s, data for France, Belgium, West Germany, and the Netherlands show a major shift in the balance of foreign worker employment, from mining, manufacturing, and construction (accounting for 65 percent of their jobs in 1980) toward services (which had 41 percent of the total by 1986). In West Germany, despite the sharpest fall in foreign-worker industrial employment, a clear majority of their jobs were still in manufacturing, and only a third in services, whereas in the other three countries half of the jobs were now in this sector (EUROSTAT 1988).

The impact of these shifts in labor market role has been felt more strongly among the second generation and recent waves of migrants, who have perforce been seeking jobs during this period of recession and restructuring. Those born and/or raised in the receiving country might have been expected to have educational qualifications and command of the language that would secure better employment opportunities than their migrant parents. However, the educational experience of the second generation has often been unsatisfactory. Against a background of environmental disadvantages, institutional racism, and doubts about the likely rewards for qualifications, educational attainments have been uneven. In the United Kingdom, for example, the message of a series of studies has been that South Asian children (with the exception of poorer Bangladeshi communities) have been producing results at least comparable with those of white children, but that West Indians have been doing significantly worse. Access to vocational training, through apprenticeships or the better government schemes has also frequently been denied to young workers from minority communities (Jenkins 1988).

In the labor market one effect of recession and of high unemployment has been to increase the value of access to *informal* information networks. This would seem to favor members of reasonably close-knit communities, provided that sufficient of their members were in employment, or running their own businesses (as in the British Asian communities). Indeed, ethnic networks have been used by employers from both minority and majority groups to create extended internal labor markets (Manwaring 1984), although an effect is likely to be the preservation of the status quo in terms of the sectoral distribution of minority workers. On the other hand, where labor market entrants from minority communities consciously reject the type of "shit job" taken by their parents' generation and take their chances in the open, they are particularly likely to end up either in unstable jobs or in the black economy. Wilpert's study (1988) of young Turks in Germany, for example, concludes that they are substantially more likely than the original migrants to end up in these segments of the labor market. And those who cannot get work permits have no choice but to enter the black economy. Indeed, settlement has removed from the younger generation the option exercised by some of their predecessors to return home when faced with unemployment in the receiving country. For this reason also, unemployment has been especially high among young members of all the minority groups.

Unemployment

Unemployment data provide the best available evidence on the relative vulnerability of migrants and minorities to economic distress, but even this is subject to biases reflecting the varying legal situations and entitlements of foreigners in particular countries. Thus, in Switzerland unemployed migrants have been liable to lose their residence permits; in Austria recorded unemployment among foreigners is depressed because of their ineligibility for unemployment support; and in Germany during the 1970s, unemployment among those guest workers with reasonable prospects at home was successfully contained by return migration, even though foreign workers were clearly absorbing a high proportion of the job losses. (In France, too, it is clear that the great bulk of net job losses between 1973 and 1985 were absorbed by foreigners.) In general, however, it is evident that, since the first oil price crisis (although possibly not before then), foreign workers have been much more likely to experience unemployment than their domestic counterparts.

Unemployment in Europe has been highly age specific, with a disproportionate incidence both among the very young, who need to establish themselves in the labor market when there are few openings, and among older workers, who find it particularly hard to regain employment after the loss of a job. The age distribution of minorities still involves relatively few of the latter group, but growing numbers of young (second-generation) workers, who have faced particular problems of unemployment in the 1980s. Overall, however, the age composition of the minority labor force cannot account for much of its higher exposure to unemployment. Ultimately this has to be explained in terms of some combination of, on the one hand, deficiencies in human capital and, on the other, labor market discrimination. But these factors are mediated by the specific labor market positions allocated to different minority groups. In particular, outcomes are contingent on whether the groups are concentrated in declining sectors (or occupations) or in relatively unstable types of secondary labor market employment. In fact, many of the industrial jobs to which first-generation migrants were recruited—in textiles or iron foundering, for instance—have been in chronic decline over the past decade. It is also true that most minorities have found secure jobs rather harder to achieve than their indigenous counterparts. A number of British studies have shown that when other factors (such as age, qualification, and so on) are controlled for, black and South Asian workers still exhibit significantly higher unemployment rates. This continues to be true even when the skill level of the last occupation, the growth performance of the last industry, and its stability characteristics are controlled for (Buck and Gordon 1987). In fact these conditioning factors also tended to boost the chances of unemployment among the minority groups, as did their relative lack of educational qualification and concentration in public-sector housing tenures. After control for these factors (together with age and marital status), the risk of unemployment (in 1981) for blacks and South Asians was still more than double that of the white population.

This proportionate relationship (holding across three sets of areas with varying overall levels of unemployment) implies that the gap between minority and majority unemployment rates is substantially greater in times and places where the general labor market is slack. Similar conclusions are suggested by time series evidence; for example, in Belgium foreign workers have accounted for a fairly consistent 15 percent of unemployment ever since the mid-1970s (compared with a 6 percent share of the labor force). In other places there seems to have been little or no excess of unemployment among migrant populations prior to the recessions of the 1970s. And in the United Kingdom the recovery of the mid-1980s appears first to have had an impact among blacks and South Asians, with a particularly sharp reduction in unemployment among West Indian males. Like other disadvantaged groups, ethnic minorities and migrants have clearly suffered particularly from the passing of full employment in Europe. This follows not merely from concentration in vulnerable sectors and occupations, but also from their weak competitive position coupled with increased scope for employers to discriminate in a slack labor market.

There have been considerable differences in the experience of different minorities. In particular, non-European migrants have tended to face higher unemployment. In the Netherlands, for example, it has been those from Surinam, Molucca, and the Antilles (apparently irrespective of nationality) who have fared worst, with unemployment rates of around 21 percent in 1980, as compared with 14 percent for other foreigners and 7 percent for natives (SOPEMI 1981). However, the high unemployment among Turks and Moroccans at least has been attributed to low levels of schooling, with 90 percent of the unemployed having only primary-level education (SOPEMI 1985). In France also ethnic differences are large, with unemployment among North Africans around twice the average for foreigners.

In the United Kingdom only those minorities from black or South Asian ethnic origins have experienced unemployment rates significantly above those for native whites, but these higher rates apply to the British born as well as immigrants. Within these categories there have again been substantial differences, with those from West Indian, Pakistani, or Bangladeshi origins having the highest risks of unemployment, while Indian unemployment rates are now close to those of whites. Evidence from the 1986 Greater London Living Standards Survey, which allowed respondents to choose their own categorization of ethnic origins, found a further distinction, with those West Indians who identify themselves as "black British" having unemployment rates no higher than whites of comparable age and education.

In Germany the pattern of variation by national origin has been rather different. Over a number of years Italians as well as Turks have displayed the highest unemployment rates (typically at least double the national average), followed by Greeks and Yugoslavs, with Spaniards and Portuguese having rates close to the national average. The high rate among Italians may have reflected their freedom, as EC citizens, from the need to acquire work permits (normally only available to residents of other minorities when EC job-seekers are unavailable). But in Belgium, too, there has been a strikingly high rate of unemployment among Italians. In 1981, for example, 27 percent of Italian workers were totally unemployed, as compared with 14–19 percent among other Mediterranean groups and about 10 percent for Belgians and other EC migrants.

There is clear evidence then that non-Europeans, and to a lesser extent those from Mediterranean origins, have suffered disproportionately from high European unemployment levels during the past decade. There is also a general tendency for the largest migrant groups in each country (Turks and Italians in Germany, Italians in Belgium, Algerians in France, Turks and Moroccans in the Netherlands) to experience the highest rates of unemployment. This may reflect the more supportive environment that larger communities can provide for their temporarily unemployed members, but it is also probably connected with particular selection mechanisms in the recruitment of migrants for specific labor market roles. Except in the United Kingdom (during the mid-1980s), there is disturbingly little evidence of a closing of these gaps in unemployment rates. Indeed there has been an increasing divergence between 1986 and 1989 in Belgium, Germany, and the Netherlands, in each of which overall unemployment was declining (SOPEMI 1990). This tendency may well reflect the shift of the minority labor force toward unstable secondary jobs and the particular problems being encountered by the second generation.

Minorities as Marginal Citizens

The legal and social status of migrants and minorities, in terms of their general acceptance as full and equal citizens, is important for several reasons. It may directly affect entitlement to state or social support (or the probability of taking up such support) and, thus, the level of real incomes. Uncertainties about rights to continued residence or employment weaken the bargaining power of those involved and, thus, increase chances of exploitation, poor wages, working conditions, and so on—and also diminish the incentives to make investments in specific human or cultural capital. And formal status may be a significant indicator of social attitudes to the groups concerned, particularly of the extent to which they are perceived as "outsiders," which can be important in hiring and other potentially discriminatory situations.

Within Europe the legal status of migrant groups has varied considerably, as have the implications that a particular status confers, and its transmission to subsequent generations. In France, the Netherlands, and the United Kingdom, migrants from ex-colonies have benefited (to a degree that was never intended) from rights to residence, naturalization, and/or political participation. In Germany, Austria, and Switzerland, on the other hand, where colonial connections have been weaker or absent, most labor migrants have been guest workers, originally with strictly temporary rights to residence and employment, no right to political participation, and extremely limited rights to naturalization.

There have been changes in these rights over time, bringing about some convergence. The security of residence of Commonwealth citizens in the United Kingdom has been weakened over the years, while French governments have made increasing efforts to promote repatriation. In Germany, on the other hand, through the 1980s there has been a transition to a situation in which over 90 percent of migrant workers (including those from outside the EC) enjoy a consolidated status, with permission to remain in the labor market even if there are German or other EC workers available, or if they have experienced spells of unemployment. Their families still need, however, to obtain a first work permit when they enter the labor market. In Switzerland, too, there has been some stabilization of the migrant labor force, with a considerable reduction in the proportion of seasonal and frontier workers. Widespread evidence of dissatisfaction among the younger generation, including urban riots in France and elsewhere, has also prompted some action to promote integration and better living conditions.

As far as the marginality of minorities is concerned, however, social attitudes and prejudices may be as important as legal status. In all of the receiving countries, there is evidence of racist or xenophobic attitudes that affect the security of migrants and their offspring, restrict the legitimacy of expressions of their interest, and color administrative and allocative decisions. At the most basic level the effects can be seen in the very real fear of attack among the South Asian community in the United Kingdom. In France it was actually the experience of racist attacks that led initially to the first suspension of migrant flows by the *Algerian* government in 1973.

A recent Eurobarometer opinion survey indicated that in four of the five main immigrant countries in the EC, between 40 and 50 percent of the population think there are too many foreigners living in their country (the exception being the Netherlands, where the proportion was 30 percent; see Table 16.1) (Eurobarometer 1989). Rather fewer people found their presence actively "disturbing," and (across the EC as a whole) the commonest complaint, against all the evidence, was that the presence of foreigners increased unemployment for nationals. In three of the countries (Germany, France, and the United Kingdom), opinions were evenly divided as to whether the presence of non-EC residents was a good or bad thing for the country's future. In Belgium a clear majority thought it a bad thing, but in the Netherlands a decisive majority saw it as a good thing. Across the EC as a whole the view that non-EC residents were bad for the country was shared by a third of those among the majority, who claimed to disapprove of racist movements, as well as by a half (only) of

**Table 16.1 / Attitudes to Immigrants and Minorities
in European Community (EC) Countries**

Country	Percentage of Non-Europeans in Population	Percentage Believing Too Many Residents of Another Race	Attitudes to Racist/Antiracist Movements	Attitudes to Rights of Immigrants in the EC
Germany	5.3	37	73	+13
United Kingdom	4.5	44	75	−4
Netherlands	4.0	27	87	—
France	3.9	43	74	−3
Belgium	3.8	43	69	−8
Italy	1.8	33	86	+28
Denmark	1.8	34	76	−20
Luxembourg	1.0	12	82	+22
Ireland	0.6	3	75	+31
Greece	0.6	15	92	+30
Portugal	0.5	16	80	+34
Spain	0.3	10	87	+50

SOURCES: A: Eurobarometer (1990) *Public Opinion in the European Community*, No. 34 Brussels: Commission of the EC. B: Eurobarometer (1989) *Survey: Racism, Xenophobia and Intolerance*, Brussels: Commission of the EC.

NOTES: *Column 1:* data relate to the percentage of non-EEC foreigners in the population (source B) except for the United Kingdom and Netherlands where they are estimates of the ethnic minority population; the Italian estimate has been revised on the basis of the 1990 SOPEMI report. *Column 2:* 1988 survey data, from source B. *Column 3:* scaled figure incorporating data, from source B, on approval/disapproval of racist and antiracist movements; range = 0–100, high values support antiracist activity. *Column 4:* data represent percentages favoring extension of rights, *minus* percentages favoring restriction, 1990 survey data from source A.

those approving of the latter. Only one in ten of the population actually approved of racist movements, but in France, Germany, Belgium, and the United Kingdom, a further 20–30 percent opposed antiracist activity, implying a view that immigrants should keep out of politics. Again, attitudes in the Netherlands appear substantially more liberal than in the other main countries of immigration. Interestingly, Dutch respondents were the most likely to claim involvement with other nationalities, races, and cultures at *work*—although not so conspicuously among friends or in the residential neighborhood—suggesting that this greater liberality may extend to employment practices also. Belgium was at the other extreme in this respect among the main immigrant countries— three-quarters of respondents claiming there was nobody from another culture at their work—as it was in terms of the proportions claiming to be "disturbed" by the presence of people from another race. The Netherlands was also the only one among the five receiving nations in which significantly more respondents wanted the rights of foreigners to be improved rather than restricted: The reverse was clearly the case in Germany, Belgium, and the United Kingdom.

Within each of these nations, a large proportion of the population saw fascists as threatening to their way of life (60 percent or so, as compared with around 35 percent in the other EC countries) (Eurobarometer 1988). The significance of this concern, however, may well be not so much in a sense of watchfulness over the growth of extremist politics (hardly a realistic threat in the United Kingdom, for example) as a nervousness over the divisiveness of "racial" issues—a fear that serves further to disempower minorities.

ETHNIC ENTREPRENEURSHIP

One possible response to exclusion from full economic or social citizenship is the adoption of an entrepreneurial role in order to capitalize on those of a community's resources of labor, capital, and information that have been undervalued by indigenous business. Recent American studies have highlighted success stories of such ethnic entrepreneurship among new waves of immigrants including Cubans, Koreans, and Chinese arriving in the United States in the 1960s, 1970s, and 1980s (Portes 1991). Among immigrants to Europe over this period, evidence of a similar burgeoning of entrepreneurship based on close intra-community ties can be found—notably among South Asians settling in Britain—although for various reasons it is a smaller-scale phenomenon among most immigrant minorities in Europe (Waldinger et al. 1990).

In Europe the scale of business activity among migrant groups has been constrained by more institutional barriers than in the United States. A key example involves the terms of entry imposed on immigrant workers in countries such as Germany and the Netherlands. In West Germany, as a consequence, only 2 percent of foreign nationals were self-employed in 1980. There is evidence, however, of a considerable increase since then, particularly among Turks, many of whom have now worked in Germany long enough to acquire residence permits free from these restrictions and have benefited from a liberalization of conditions for business formation. In the Netherlands also about 2 percent of the ethnic working population were active as entrepreneurs in the mid-1980s, with a higher proportion (5–6 percent) among Turks and a very low proportion of Moroccans and Moluccans. In France and Britain limitations on self-employment among immigrants have been much weaker or nonexistent. In France 6 percent of foreign nationals are estimated to be self-employed, with strong entrepreneurial activity being reported among European, African, and Asian immigrant groups, although the level of self-employment among French nationals is three times as great (Waldinger et al. 1990). In Britain the rate of self-employment among ethnic minorities is substantially higher (16 percent in 1987–1989 according to the Labour Force Survey), and above the average for the white population (12 percent). There are big differences among the minorities, however, with a very much higher proportion among South Asians (21 percent)—whether from India, Pakistan, Bangladesh, or East Africa—than for Afro-Caribbeans (7 percent). In fact, South Asian migrants to Britain represent the one substantial example of entrepreneurial "success" among European minorities to set alongside the well-documented cases of the Japanese, Chinese, Cubans, and Koreans in the United States.[1]

It must be noted that the extent of entrepreneurship among immigrant groups in the United States is extremely variable. Portes and Zhou demonstrate clearly that among the four main entrepreneurial minorities, a relatively high rate of business participation is accompanied by self-employed earnings that are about a third higher than for their employed counterparts (in terms of qualification levels, occupation, etc.). These higher earnings presumably reward their entrepreneurial capacities, risk taking, and financial investments in the business, and cannot be assumed to be available to other workers who might set up in business.[2] In general the self-employed within each group emerge as possessing educational and other characteristics that ought to provide better than average rewards in the labor market. They are generally not the most disadvantaged members of their communities, but they may well be those who suffer most from discriminatory processes in the open labor market through unrecognized qualifications, etc. Comparisons *between* minority groups also show a positive correlation among average levels of educational attainment, mean income of the self-employed, and the extent of participation in self-employment. At the bottom end of the scale in 1980, self-employment among Afro-Americans, Puerto Ricans, Mexicans, Vietnamese, Dominicans, Jamaicans, and Caribbean groups other than Cubans was in the range of 1–2 percent, while the average earnings of those in self-employment were in the range of $11–15,000.

The levels of entrepreneurship within particular population groups are not fixed, however, a point that is clearly illustrated by British experience since 1979. Over this period there has been a remarkable revival of self-employment, with growth in all sectors except agriculture and an overall increase in numbers of two-thirds by 1990. Ethnic entrepreneurs have fully shared in this expansion. Between 1981 and 1987–1989 the Labour Force Survey shows an increase from 19.5 percent to 25.5 percent in the proportion of South Asian males in self-employment, a growth of 6 percentage points compared with 4 for whites and Afro-Caribbeans. This was a particularly remarkable increase given that two-thirds of South Asian businesses were in distribution and catering (Waldinger et al. 1990: 87), the sectors that have shown the slowest overall growth in self-employment. However, the real breakthrough in South Asian business ownership seems to have occurred in advance of this general revival, at some point between 1971 and 1981. Over this period the self-employment rates for men born in India or Pakistan moved from a level about 3 percentage points *below* the national average (Waldinger et al. 1990: 82) to 7 percentage points *above* the average (according to the Labour Force Survey). This rise occurred over a period of rapidly rising unemployment in the country as a whole when marked ethnic disparities in unemployment were emerging. The likelihood is that it was in large part a defensive response at this time. Most of the growth took the form of entry into (what was then) a declining sector of self-employment, retailing, and catering, notably in inner-city areas in niches vacated by white-owned businesses, in which Asian entrepreneurs were able to survive only on the basis of long hours of work, minimal rewards. This strategy was, however, pursued by few Afro-Caribbeans for various reasons, including their stronger expectations of social and economic integration, and the greater importance of public sector employment as a role model for West Indians (as for Afro-Americans in the United States) ever since their arrival in the United Kingdom.

A South Asian business community has now developed in Britain, including substantial businesses in a wider range of sectors and offering much of the infrastructure of economic and social support associated with the concept of "ethnic entrepreneurship." Both the economic and political climate were supportive of such small business development through the 1980s, in tune with the growing demand for flexibility in meeting specialized needs. However, most of the businesses are very small, crowded into insecure and poorly rewarded sectors of the economy, and seem to offer no better prospects of occupational advancement for the majority than the marginal jobs to which immigrants had previously been assigned as employees. There are many individual stories of entrepreneurial success, but there is little evidence of economic success for the South Asian community (or communities) as a whole (Robinson 1990). People of Indian origins continue to do relatively well, in terms for example of unemployment rates, but those from Pakistan or Bangladesh still experience very high unemployment despite rates of self-employment comparable to the Indians. Since the depths of the last recession, their relative position has improved, but by no more than that of Afro-Caribbeans, who display much lower rates of entrepreneurship. Presumably the growth of South Asian businesses has had some impact on levels of poverty in the community. Data do not exist to show this, however, and the simple facts demonstrate only the weak economic position of many in that community. For example, in a recent London survey of living standards, 49 percent of South Asians reported themselves as "finding difficulty managing on their income," compared with 29 percent for the population as a whole (Greater London Living Standards Survey 1986).

European governments, like their U.S. counterparts, have been particularly keen to encourage ethnic entrepreneurship as a strategy for addressing minority unemployment that did not require either an extension of state activity or obvious sacrifices from other groups, and which was supportive of current free-market ideologies. This approach has also been encouraged by the evidence of entrepreneurial success among some recent immigrant groups and the lack of any single-factor explanation as to why their success could not be matched by other minorities. The success of individual entrepreneurs is no guarantee of a lifting of living standards among the poorer members of a particular community, however. That would depend on the ability of their businesses to generate substantial numbers of additional jobs of a kind to which minorities are denied access in the mainstream labor market and to provide alternative avenues of career advancement, rather than a segregated version of the secondary labor market. Caution is appropriate until such gains can be demonstrated, because an emphasis on the value of self-reliance among such groups, and on ethnicity as a resource, can too easily divert attention from the need actively to promote integration and equal opportunities in the labor market.

At an operational level also, recent evaluation of minority business development policies, in Europe as well as the United States, severely questions their effectiveness (Waldinger et al. 1990). Such policies are seen as of very limited relevance to the problems of the unemployed in minority communities, because of the overall ceiling on self-employment opportunities and because the unemployed are not well integrated into the relevant social networks. Policy implementation suffers both from the inability of government reliably to select good commercial prospects, and because formal bureaucratic systems conflict with the informal social structures on which ethnic enterprise depends. Moreover, in so far as the entrepreneurial success of recent immigrants reflects the specific circumstances of their migration, and their lower economic and social expectations, the example cannot be directly translated to the situation of other minority groups, or even to second and third generations of these groups (Waldinger et al. 1990). There is a useful role for governments to play, particularly in continental Europe, in reducing the barriers to small business development, which especially affects immigrant minorities. To have any substantial impact on minority poverty, however, they also have to enforce much broader equal opportunities policies in relation to employment and education.

CONCLUSION

A theme in recent OECD reports on international migration has been that of increasing convergence in national experience of, and policies toward, migrant labor, especially within western Europe. It has been argued that this convergence also extends to a comparison between Europe and the United States (Miller 1988). The basis of this claim is the transition since the early 1970s from a situation in which advanced European economies encouraged labor immigration, with the provision that this should be on an essentially temporary basis, not requiring integration of ethnic minorities, to one where it is widely accepted that the migrant communities are here to stay and need integration, although future migration should be highly restricted. Miller compares this shift with the earlier shift in U.S. policy from the "Bracero" era (1942–1964), when temporary migration of Mexican workers was legally promoted, to the resumption of permanent immigration, which presumes integration. The difference, of course, is that in Europe since the mid-1970s legal immigration has essentially been limited to family reunifications, with no mass movement of primary workers comparable with that in the United States. Nor, in the old European receiving countries, has there been an equivalent replacement of legal temporary migration by unauthorized flows. The foreign labor force in France, West Germany, Belgium, and the Netherlands together has scarcely changed since the mid-1970s, while the United States has absorbed 8–10 million new immigrants.

In neither region, however, can it be said that recent policies have been intended to encourage substantial immigration of normal workers, and the growing numbers of refugees are widely regarded as a problem. There have been signs of a modest revival in migrant flows during the late 1980s and pressure from some groups of German employers for a relaxation of controls. Whatever the economic case may be, the current political climate of prejudice makes any return to open migration from outside the EC appears to be quite out of the question. But in any event, structural changes in the economy, and the pursuit of labor market flexibility, point to a rather different form of labor migration from that experienced in the 1960s. The essential precondition for that, however, is a substantial reduction of the level of unemployment across Europe, not simply through macroeconomic developments, but through labor market initiatives directed at the reintegration of disadvantaged groups. Young workers from many, but not all, of the migrant communities are prominent among these and becoming more politically self-conscious than other marginalized groups.

The experience of minorities in Europe has varied among countries, groups, periods, and generations. The common factor has been an economically and politically weak position with a particular exposure to the risks associated with economic recession. Neither recent immigrants nor the second generation are immune to the problems of marginality, although their forms change. Limited or inappropriate stocks of human capital explain only part of the employment disadvantage experienced by individuals from ethnic minorities, and there is evidence of discrimination discouraging investment in human capital. However, some of the more successful groups, such as Indians in the United Kingdom, do seem to be characterized by a higher average level of educational attainment, and at this level it may have a significant effect on ethnic stereotyping. No policy initiatives appear to have been strong enough to make any real difference to the employment position of European minorities, and it is not possible to point to models of policy development here deserving consideration by U.S. policymakers.

The European experience does show that it does not require the particular history of Afro-Americans to account for severe economic disadvantage among ethnic minorities. New immigrant groups can as readily be assigned to economically marginal roles and an incomplete citizenship if they are perceived both as outsiders and as inferior. The consequences depend substantially, however, on the state of the overall labor market, becoming particularly severe in the context of chronic unemployment. Structural shifts in the economy change the form of the problem, but de-industrialization is not its cause, nor is a "flexible" service-orientated economy its answer. The latter has changed the character of international migration and opened up new niches for ethnic enterprise, but its proliferation of marginal, unstable jobs is unlikely to reduce poverty within minority communities. That aim still requires determined action to overcome discrimination and improve access to mainstream employment.

ENDNOTES

1. Indeed the rate of self-employment among British South Asians is now well above the 1980 census estimates for any of these ethnic groups across the United States as a whole and comparable with estimates quoted for Cuban refugee concentrations in the Miami area. Even the "low" proportion cited for Afro-Caribbeans, against the background of generally higher levels of self-employment in Europe, is actually higher than published 1980 census estimates for Cubans in the United States—about five times the corresponding figure for Afro-Americans and three times the U.S. average for Jamaicans (who are the main Afro-Caribbean group in the United Kingdom).

2. Failure rates are high for all new businesses, but average earning figures for the self-employed inevitably exclude the losses of those who are no longer self-employed.

REFERENCES

Buck, Nick, and Ian Gordon. 1987. "The Beneficiaries of Employment Growth; the Experience of Disadvantaged Groups in Expanding Labor Markets." In *Critical Issues in Urban Economic Development Vol. II*, edited by Victor Hausner. Oxford: Clarendon Press.

Cohen, Robin. 1987. *The New Helots: Migrants in the International Division of Labor*. Aldershot: Avebury.

Cross, Malcolm. 1989. "Blacks, Asians and Labor Market Change." Paper presented to the ESRC seminar on Social Change: Theories, Concepts and Issues, University of Surrey.

Cross, Malcolm, and Roger Waldinger. 1992. "Migrants, Minorities and the Ethnic Division of Labor." In *Divided Cities*, edited by Susan Fainstein, Ian Gordon, and Michael Harloe. Oxford: Blackwell.

Eurobarometer. 1988. *Public Opinion in the European Community*, No. 30. Brussels: Commission of the European Community.

―――. 1989. *Survey: Racism, Xenophobia and Intolerance*. Brussels: Commission of the European Community.

EUROSTAT. 1988. *Employment and Unemployment 1988*. Luxembourg: Statistical Office of the European Community.

Greater London Living Standards Survey. Unpublished tabulations from 1986 survey data supplied by Prof. P. Townsend, Bristol University.

Jenkins, Richard. 1988. "Discrimination and Equal Opportunity in Employment; Ethnicity and 'Race' in the United Kingdom." In *Employment in Britain*, edited by Duncan Galie, 310–343. Oxford: Blackwell.

Kindleberger, Charles P. 1967. *Europe's Postwar Growth: The Role of Labor Supply*. Oxford: Oxford University Press.

Lebon, A. 1988. "La main d'oeuvre étrangère en France à la fin de 1985: composition et rôle économique"("Foreign Labor in France at the End of 1985: Composition and Economic Role"). Paper presented to the International Conference on Economic Change and Immigrant Workers in the Industrial Countries, Vaucresson, France.

Manwaring, T. 1984. "The Extended Internal Labor Market." *Cambridge Journal of Economics* 8:161–187.

Miller, M. 1988. "Valeur et limites de la notion de la convergence dans les études de la migration internationale" ("Value and Limits to the Convergence Thesis in International Migration"). Paper presented to the International Conference on Economic Change and Immigrant Workers in the Industrial Countries, Vaucresson, France.

Palidda, S. 1988. "Mutations et immigration: ethnicité, ethnic business? Ou simple rentabilisation des ressources specifiques au plan économique et politique, entre formel et informel" ("Change and Immigration: Ethnicity, Ethnic Business or Ordinary Exploitation of Specific Resources for a Political and Economic Plan, Between Formal and Informal"). Paper for the International Conference on Economic Change and Immigrant Workers in the Industrial Countries, Vaucresson, France.

Portes, Alejandro. 1991. "Gaining the Upper Hand: Old and New Perspectives in the Study of Foreign Born Minorities." Paper prepared for the conference on Poverty, Inequality and the Crisis of Social Policy, Joint Center for Political and Economic Studies, Washington, D.C., September.

Robinson, Vaughan. 1990. "Boom and Gloom: The Success and Failure of South Asians in Britain." In *South Asians Overseas: Migration and Ethnicity*, edited by Colin Clarke, Ceri Peach, and S. Vertovec, 269–296. Cambridge: Cambridge University Press.

Sassen-Koob, Saskia. 1984. "The New Labor Demand in Global Cities." In *Cities in Transformation*, edited by Michael P. Smith, 139–171. Newbury Park, Calif.: Sage.

Simon, Julian L. 1989. *The Economic Consequences of Immigration*. Oxford: Blackwell.

SOPEMI. Annual. *Continuous Reporting System on Migration*. Directorate for Social Affairs, Manpower and Education, Paris: Organization for Economic Co-operation and Development.

Stuart, Angus. 1989. "The Social and Geographical Mobility of South Asians and Caribbeans in Middle Age and Late Working Life." Working Paper 81, Social Statistics Research Unit, City University, London.

Thurow, Lester. 1983. *Dangerous Currents*. New York: Random House.

Waldinger, Roger, Howard Aldrich, Robin Ward, and Associates. 1990. *Ethnic Entrepreneurs: Immigrant Business in Industrial Societies*. Newbury Park, Calif.: Sage.

Ward, Robin. 1985. "Minority Settlement and the Local Economy." In *New Approaches to Economic Life*, edited by Bryan Roberts, Ruth Finnegan, and Duncan Gallie, 198–212. Manchester: Manchester University Press.

Wilpert, C. 1988. "D'une generation à l'autre: position professionelle et reproduction sociale des descendants de travailleurs immigrés en republique féderale d'Allemagne" ("From One Generation to the Next: Professional Position and Social Reproduction Among the Children of Migrant Workers in West Germany"). Paper presented to the International Conference on Economic Change and Immigrant Workers in the Industrial Countries, Vaucresson, France.

Chapter 17

THE COMPARATIVE STRUCTURE
AND EXPERIENCE OF URBAN EXCLUSION:
"RACE," CLASS, AND SPACE
IN CHICAGO AND PARIS

Loïc J. D. Wacquant

URBAN INEQUALITIES—among classes, racial or ethnic groups, households, cities, and neighborhoods—in advanced nation-states such as the United States, France, Great Britain, or the Netherlands have increased noticeably over the past two decades. Persistent joblessness, material deprivation, and ethnoracial tensions are on the upswing throughout much of Western Europe and North America as segments of the urban population of these countries appear to have become increasingly marginalized and segregated economically, socially, and spatially. Thus, while American inner cities have experienced rapidly accelerating dislocations and degradation since the 1960s, many traditional working-class towns and boroughs in Europe have also undergone sharp decline.[1] American social scientists and public policy analysts have grown alarmed about the rise and consolidation of a predominantly black "underclass" believed to be trapped in the urban core and increasingly cut off from the rest of society (e.g., Glasgow 1980; Wilson 1987, 1989). On the other side of the Atlantic, mounting concern has been expressed over the spread of "new poverty," the constitution of "immigrant ghettos," and the threat that these pose for citizenship, national solidarity, and the public order (e.g., Paugam 1991; *Le Monde* 1990; Benyon 1984; Room 1987).

Is this to say that America and Western Europe are converging with respect to the formation of urban enclaves of entrenched poverty where housing blight, joblessness, educational failure, and ethnic/racial discrimination cumulate into constellations equally impervious to policy intervention? This chapter begins to explore this issue by means of an analytically guided comparison of the distinctive position, composition, and experiences of two persistently poor urban "communities"—or spatial enclaves of extreme poverty—in France and the United States: the black ghetto of Chicago and a declining working-class estate of the outskirts of Paris. Two central questions anchor this investigation: How does the *social structure* of concentrated socioeconomic exclusion vary across these sites? What commonalities exist in the *daily experiences and perceptions* of their residents? A third, subsidiary, question raised by this chapter may be phrased curtly as follows: Is the alleged process of "ghettoization" of European working-class boroughs comparable to that of the black inner city in America—and, if not, what can their differences teach us about the causal dynamics of the plight of the American ghetto today?[2]

SETTING AND DATA

These queries are addressed by drawing parallel sociographies of the black ghetto neighborhood of Woodlawn in Chicago and of the public housing concentrations (*cité* or *grands ensembles*) of La Courneuve in the outer ring of Paris. The two countries selected, the United States and France, are particularly interesting in that they diverge notably in the degree to which (1) they regulate the lower segments of the labor market and have elaborated policies to absorb and redistribute the social costs of the restructuring of their economy, and (2) they provide their citizens and residents with minimum standards of living and segregate social provision from "welfare."[3]

On the one hand, the French state has developed perhaps the most extensive array of industrial reconversion, unemployment, and training policies of the European Economic Community and has traditionally been strongly interventionist in the labor market. Notwithstanding the recent trend toward labor "flexibility," France has a rigid system of industrial relations regulated by a dense network of legislative restrictions and centralized collective bargaining (Piore and Sabel 1984; Grahl and Teague 1989). This country has also evolved a wide set of welfare, family, and social policies that strongly counteract market pressures, including universal health care coverage and family allowances, and a national guaranteed minimum income plan. This is in notable contrast with the American "semi-welfare state" (Katz 1987: x), which severely limits social citizenship and is essentially designed not to deflect but to prop up market sanctions. The United States typifies a laissez-faire attitude with regard to both welfare and labor market regulation. On the side of the labor market, the United States is characteristically noninterventionist, granting considerable political and administrative leeway to firms for the setting of wages, work conditions, and entry into or exit from the workforce. It does very little to macro-manage labor supply and demand and even less to micro-manage them, spending a pittance on job placement, training, and creation[4] and failing to develop the administrative capacity to implement any systematic active labor market policy (Janoski 1990). Due to its historic bifurcation from social provision (a legacy of the late and partial institutionalization of the American welfare state in the New Deal era), welfare consists essentially of inadequately funded and highly stigmatizing, means-tested programs that target politically vulnerable, dependent populations (Susser and Kresnicke 1987).

The two cities of Chicago and Paris were chosen because both are "world cities" that dominate leading regional nodes of the emerging global economy (Feagin and Smith 1987). Both have suffered heavy manufacturing job losses due to de-industrialization and witnessed a sweeping transformation of the spatial and social organization of production and consumption forms (Boyer 1986) at a time when "minority" or immigrant populations were consolidating their presence in them. Both have been subjected to intense media and scholarly scrutiny. Chicago is widely portrayed as emblematic of the plight of the contemporary black ghetto and as one of the major breeding grounds of America's alleged "permanent underclass" (*Chicago Tribune* 1986). The Parisian Red Belt, in turn, epitomizes the degradation of the *banlieue* where the social problems that have increasingly beset working-class *cités* in the last decade have taken a particularly acute turn (Hérodote 1986). Together, then, Paris and Chicago offer a "strategic research site," as Robert K. Merton would say, for inquiring into the comparative economic and political logics of urban "ghettoization."

This chapter is based, for the American case, on firsthand research on Chicago's ghetto conducted over the period 1986–1991 (as part of an ethnographic investigation of the social world of black boxers on the city's South Side Black Belt) and on data gathered by the Urban Poverty and Family Structure Project at the University of Chicago.[5] On the French side, it relies on existing monographs and census data on La Courneuve and neighboring *banlieues* of Greater Paris and on documentation gathered during several field visits to La Courneuve (in September and November 1990 and in May and June 1991), supplemented by intensive consultation with urban researchers and public officials in charge of France's "Neighborhood Social Development" program. In addition to primary knowledge of these sites, I draw selectively on existing case studies, ethnographies, and reports on structurally comparable poor neighborhoods in each of these two countries.

Three caveats should be entered from the outset. First, the diverse data used to contrast Woodlawn with La Courneuve were not produced for the same purposes and by the same information-generating apparatus. They are, to varying degrees, only imperfectly correlated with the reality they seek to capture (a reality that is also changing rapidly) and with one another. A full comparative analysis of these two sites would require systematic, specially designed, long-term field work; in the absence thereof, the present analysis should be regarded as tentative and exploratory. Second, this comparison is, by choice, skewed: It contrasts an exaggerated French situation with an average black American ghetto area. La Courneuve is a classical working-class "Red Belt" city archetypal of the cumulative decline of large public housing projects in the French urban periphery. It is something of an empirically realized ideal-typical case in that it accentuates numerous traits of France's *cités*: The size and density of its settlement, its physical compactness and relative social homogeneity, the volume of its immigrant population, and its degree of economic hardship are all unusually high by national standards.[6] By contrast, although Chicago has one of the country's largest and most degraded ghettos, the neighborhood of Woodlawn is, by

Chicago standards, a moderately poor ghetto area: It ranked only 13th on the scale of poverty among Chicago's 26 Community Areas with at least 20 percent of their population living under the federal poverty line in 1980 (out of a total of 76 such areas) and 10th from the bottom on the hierarchy of median household income. It is by no means the most destitute section of Chicago's Black Belt (see Wacquant and Wilson 1989b). This design, contrasting an extreme French case with a median section of the American ghetto, will allow us to argue *a fortiori:* Whatever differences are found between La Courneuve and Woodlawn have every likelihood of being even more pronounced between an average poor urban area in France and the generally more degraded inner-city neighborhoods of the United States.[7]

Third, the problems of terminology that any comparative research encounters are exacerbated here by the fact that the phenomena under examination are, for a good part, *discursively* constituted. Words such as the "poor," the "excluded," the "marginal," "slum," *cité,* "ghetto," or the "underclass" are not and cannot be neutral, descriptive terms (Verdès-Leroux 1978, Ward 1989, Gans 1991). They are crucial ingredients of the reality they claim to capture, as well as symbolic weapons and stakes in the classification struggles through which various agents—including, crucially, academics and policymakers—seek, consciously or not, to act upon reality by acting upon its representation. Whether we like it or not, sociological discourse about poverty partakes of this struggle and is inescapably enmeshed in and penetrated by the "ordinary theories of poverty" (Ogien 1983) that ordinary people and political actors draw on to define its nature, causes, and possible remedies. Terminological difficulties, therefore, are coextensive with and revealing of political assumptions that should not be pushed under the rug but brought out in the open.[8] Cross-national comparison compounds this difficulty because the terms proper to each country are also excerpted from different semantic spaces and traditions. The fact that, very roughly put, Europeans have emphasized a language of class, labor, and citizenship when considering urban hardship, while American discourse has been framed by "supply-side" views of poverty anchored in the vocabularies of family, race, and individual (moral and behavioral) deficiency, makes the question of terminology even more touchy. It would be not only naive but dangerous to make such differences disappear with the sleight of hand of translation (e.g., by straightforwardly equating "inner city" with *banlieue* and "ghetto" with *banlieue*). Ideally, then, brackets should be inserted every time a term is used that is subject to discrepant, sometimes even opposed, definitions and usages and refers back to different symbolic spaces, each with its own social history and structure.[9] Although this will not be done for the sake of readability, the reader should constantly bear this in mind.

As we shall see, the lived experiences of the inhabitants of poor neighborhoods on both sides of the Atlantic exhibit striking similarities, owing to their structural position at the bottom of their respective social orders. Yet, because the ghetto and the *cité* are the products of discrepant urban and class/racial legacies, and because in addition they are inserted into different state structures and welfare regimes, they are also *institutionally* quite different from one another, and they are likely to remain so despite bearing the same press of deindustrialization and economic disarticulation. These institutional differences also account for the sizable gaps in rates of poverty, degree of material hardship, and intensity of exclusion between the periphery of Paris and Chicago's inner city. Indeed, comparison with the degraded enclaves of the French *banlieue* highlights the specificity of ghetto poverty in the United States: its racial character, its extreme concentration and depth, perpetuated by the breakdown of public institutions in the urban core, all of which find their main roots in state policies of benign neglect or outright abandonment (Wacquant 1992b).

WOODLAWN: A BLACK URBAN BANTUSTAN ON CHICAGO'S SOUTH SIDE

Racial Changeover and Selective Depopulation: Woodlawn Joins the Ghetto

The neighborhood of Woodlawn is a section of Chicago's South Side ghetto located about eight miles from the downtown Loop. It is bounded, to the north, by the predominantly white, affluent enclave of Hyde Park, home of the University of Chicago; to the west and south by the poor all-black communities of Englewood, Greater Grand Crossing, and South Shore; and to the east by the green expanses of Jackson Park along Lake Michigan. Viewed on a city map, Woodlawn would seem like a parkfront community with excellent access routes downtown via Lakeshore Drive and the Illinois Central train tracks, with ample cultural and social amenities within close reach and vast tracts of underdeveloped land for economic and residential expansion. All of this might lead one to expect that it is a prosperous and growing neighborhood. Nothing could be further from the truth.

In the decades since the end of World War II, Woodlawn has gone from a stable and economically viable white community to a dilapidated pocket of segregated poverty and despair.[10] Between 1960 and 1980 (the last year for which credible statistics are available), its population fell from 81,000 to a mere 36,000 as the percentage of black residents shot from 38 to 96 percent. In less than three decades, the neighborhood was in effect emptied of its white population as black migrants from the South moved into the area en masse following the redrawing of the color line on the city's South Side (Hirsch 1983).[11] The presence of Hispanics (of Mexican and Puerto Rican origin), who make up nearly 15 percent of Chicago's 1980 population, is negligible, as is that of other ethnic or national categories such as Asians and Middle Easterners. Today's Woodlawn is a *homogeneously black ghetto* neighborhood that is studiously shunned by whites. Indeed, a white person is such an unusual sight on the streets of the neighborhood that police will routinely stop her to ask if she got lost—or to check if she is entering the area to purchase drugs.

The mass exodus of whites in 1950–1965 was soon followed by the outmigration of much of the small Afro-American elite of the middle and working classes. From 1970 to 1980, while some 17,000 black residents moved out, the number of craftsmen, foremen, and operatives dropped from 5,417 to 1,584 (a 70 percent cut), that for white-collar employees (sales and clerical together) decreased by one half from 4,287 to 2,161, and the ranks of managers, professionals, and technicians thinned from 2,152 to 1,798. The resulting workforce is much less industrial and more service-dependent than that of the city as a whole: Only 18 percent of the area's employed workers are in manufacturing, and 52 percent are classified in white-collar occupations, compared with 27 percent and 54 percent, respectively, for the entire city. In 1970, there was 1 blue-collar worker for every 7 residents; by 1980, this figure had dropped to 1 for every 14 Woodlawnites.

Migration, housing deterioration, and rising unemployment have conspired to leave mired in this neighborhood a population not only exclusively black but also younger, poorer, and with a more imbalanced sex ratio than in previous decades. In 1980, 37 percent of Woodlawn's inhabitants were below 20 years of age compared to 21 percent three decades before, and 55 percent were females.[12] Single-parent families were twice as common as two-parent households by then. Indeed, 6 of every 10 households were reported as headed by solo females in 1980, nearly double the proportion of a decade before.

The Ubiquity of Joblessness, Welfare Receipt, and Poverty

The official unemployment rate doubled in the 1970s to reach 19 percent, twice the city average of 9.8 percent. But this rate takes no account of all those who, discouraged or exasperated by discrimination and racial steering into the secondary labor market, dropped out of the labor force altogether to join the informal economy. It thus hides a more dramatic statistic: that half of the adult males and two women in three do not hold a job, putting Woodlawn's 1980 employment ratio (employed persons over total population) at a paltry 28 percent. The purge of employment slots is reflected in the sudden decline of government-sponsored jobs for teens, young adults, and even seniors; by some estimates, over 15,500 full- and part-time positions were lost to Woodlawn in the last quarter century (Belizario 1984). Of those still active in the labor force, 31 percent held clerical and sales positions, and 24 percent were employed as private household or service workers in 1980. Nearly all of them worked outside the neighborhood.[13]

As a result, 1 family in 3 lived under the official 1980 federal poverty line ($9,885 for a family of three in 1989), a rate equal to that for all blacks in Chicago but twice the municipal figure of 16.8 percent. The median family income in Woodlawn barely topped $10,500 per annum, half the city average and only 60 percent of the national figure for Afro-Americans. Only 8 percent of households incurred an annual income of $30,000 or more, a third of the city rate, and nearly half of them did not incur any earnings whatsoever. Fully 44 percent of the neighborhood's 1980 population had to rely on public assistance to survive, translating into a total of 16,000 individuals on the welfare rolls (compared with 2,323 in adjacent Hyde Park for a ratio of 7 percent). Some 10,400 of them received Aid to the Aged, Blind and Disabled; 9,100 were on Aid to Families with Dependent Children and 2,300 on General Assistance; an additional 1,200 received food stamps independently of a welfare grant.

The prevalence of public aid receipt helps explain the high incidence of extreme poverty, because the value of the standard Illinois AFDC and food stamps package is grossly insufficient to lift its recipients even close to the poverty line—the maximum public aid grant for a family of three barely corresponds to the average cost of a one-room apartment in Chicago. Receiving welfare in Illinois, as elsewhere in America, is tantamount to *enforced destitution* (Susser and Kresnicke 1987). To branch out and travel outside to get jobs is not easy: Only 39 percent of Woodlawn's households possess a car, and 17 percent have no telephone. Public transportation is at once costly, impractical, and unsafe. The "Jeffery" express bus line that joins the far South Side and Hyde Park to the downtown Loop avoids going into Woodlawn.

Because of the rampant poverty that grips most of the city's South Side and the paucity of job openings, drug peddling, prostitution, and purse snatching are common on the streets of Woodlawn. Teenage "crack prostitutes" can be spotted near the IC train tracks, where the Apostolic Church of God, a wealthy middle-class religious organization, is bracing to build a multi-million-dollar chapel in a gentrifying borderline section of the neighborhood. Groups of jobless men, young and old, are busy "killing time" at streetcorners or near the entrance of liquor stores at all hours of the day and night.[14] Homelessness has also increased noticeably over the past decade, touching both lone individuals and families with small children. A shelter for homeless mothers and children is in operation, but it accommodates barely a third of the calls received for emergency shelter alone.[15] Several privately run soup kitchens operate throughout the year, but they are inadequately funded and cannot satisfy demand. Perhaps a third of the area's families suffer from chronic malnutrition. Many of the single unemployed men who can be seen drifting through the streets of the neighborhood "squat" abandoned buildings, although the latter are often unfit for human habitation. In the wintertime, when temperatures drop below freezing level for weeks on end, many of them "check into" the prison system to get free shelter and food. Crime, diseases, substandard nutrition and living conditions, as well as the absence of proper health care, contribute significantly to shorten life expectancy in Chicago's ghetto: In the 1970s, Woodlawn recorded some 6,000 deaths for an initial population of 53,200, for a staggering cumulative mortality rate of 11 percent.

The Destruction of Housing and Waning of the Economic Fabric

Like so many inner-city neighborhoods across America, Woodlawn suffers from severe "housing famine" (Wallace 1989). Many families are forced to double or triple up in cramped apartments because of the lack of affordable housing

/ **549**

outside of the ill-reputed public housing projects run by the Chicago Housing Authority, from which everybody desperately tries to stay away. This is due, first, to the massive destruction of the area's housing stock in the last quarter century and, second, to the subsequent dearth of public and private construction. During the 1960s and 1970s, thousands of arsons wiped out countless residential and business buildings throughout the area—an average of nearly a 100 fire calls a month was the norm during these decades. These arsons were part of a variety of insurance scams engineered by absentee "slumlords" and by banks who sought to "milk" their declining real estate holdings for all the tax money they were worth. Thus, it was not rare for the same building to experience two or three fires, sometimes in the same week or month.[16]

Over 4,500 units were officially demolished in the 1970s alone and a mere 554 were added (1 percent of the city's new construction). As a result, there were about 15,800 dwelling units left in the neighborhood as of 1980, half the number recorded in the 1960 census. Woodlawn was home to 300 public housing units—10 times the number located in adjacent Hyde Park but only 8 percent of the neighborhood housing stock. The quality of the latter mirrors the dilapidated state of the neighborhood: Over two-thirds of the units predate World War II; subdivided apartments with shared toilets as well as peeling-paint and cockroach- and rat-infested buildings can be found on most blocks. A mere 5 percent of the units in Woodlawn are occupied by their owner, while another 10 percent are officially vacant. The median value of owner-occupied housing stood at $26,617 in 1980, compared with $47,200 for the city and $98,000 in neighboring Hyde Park.

According to Belizario (1984), the early 1980s again saw the gutting of hundreds of buildings along the central corridor of 63rd Street. Today the once busy stores and prosperous retail outlets—the neighborhood boasted over 800 commercial and industrial establishments in 1950—are either empty, burned out, or boarded up. The Woodlawn Business Association estimates that only about 100 of them are left today, if one generously counts the smattering of tiny catering places, barber shops, and thrift stores with no more than one or two employees. The commercial strip has been reduced to a long tunnel of charred stores, vacant lots littered with broken glass and garbage, and dilapidated buildings left to rot in the shadow of the elevated train line. At the corner of 63rd Street and Cottage Grove Avenue, the handful of remaining establishments that struggle to survive are huddled behind wrought-iron bars. The Asian and Middle Eastern ("Arab") shopkeepers who have taken over much of the area's retail trade employ hulky security personnel who stand guard in front of their establishments during opening hours. The only enterprises that seem to be thriving are liquor stores and currency exchanges, "banks of the poor" where one can cash checks, pay bills, and buy money orders for a fee.[17]

Throughout the past three decades, numerous plans for the redevelopment and renewal of Woodlawn have been proposed by The Woodlawn Organization and other community groups, but all in vain. The area continues on its downward slide. The recent resurfacing of 63rd Street, which cut off all road traffic for nearly 2 years at the reported cost of some $20 million, has not triggered a single new business opening. The tenor of advertising billboards on the walls of crumbling buildings is a good indicator of the downright oppressive and depressed atmosphere of the neighborhood. One group of brightly covered posters, by far the more numerous, blares the merits of hard liquor ("Vampin' with the brothers," "Misbehavin'—Canadian Mist," "Be Cool: Smirnoff Vodka"), beer, or cigarettes. Another group, in somber colors and graphic pictures, highlights their destructive effects and warns against the plague of drugs, street violence, and school failure: "Addiction is Slavery: Say No to Drugs," "No School, No Future," "Stop Black-on-Black Crime."

LA COURNEUVE: A STIGMATIZED WORKING-CLASS CITÉ OF THE PARISIAN PERIPHERY

An Aging "Red Belt" Suburb in Decline

The city of La Courneuve is a traditional working-class town located in the northeastern suburbs of Paris,[18] midway between the capital and the international airport of Roissy-Charles de Gaulle, in the heavily industrial *département* of Seine-Saint-Denis.[19] This densely urbanized municipality, emblematic of the Parisian "Red Belt" (Stovall 1990), harbors a mix of small, independent brick homes, two massive public housing estates knows as *les Quatre mille*, a smattering of small shops, as well as large factories, warehouses, and rows of newer apartment buildings in the renovated downtown. Its housing stock is old and heavily subsidized: Two-thirds of the units were built before 1962, and nearly half are administered by the HLM (Low-Income Housing) authority; only a fifth are owner-occupied.

Long a stronghold of the French Communist Party (the latter has controlled city hall since World War II, and its house representative until the early 1970s was none other than Waldeck Rochet, the general secretary of the Party), La Courneuve has seen its population decline since the mid-1970s after two periods of sustained growth in the interwar years and the 1960s.[20] Its residents numbered an estimated 32,500 in 1988, down from 33,700 in 1982 and 43,300 in 1968—a loss of one-fifth over a 20-year period. According to 1982 census figures, one-fifth of the city's inhabitants are of foreign nationality, with a notable presence of immigrants from North Africa. The country of origin of foreigners breaks down as follows: 52 percent from Algeria and an additional 8 percent from other Maghrib countries (Morocco and Tunisia in particular), 15 percent from Portugal, 12 percent from Spain and Italy, with the remainder coming from black Africa and Asia. The proportion of foreigners in La Courneuve is close to the average for the Seine-Saint-Denis (17 percent), but, as in other peripheral working-class towns of the Greater Paris, it has increased steadily in recent years so that there has occurred an absolute and relative concentration of the immigrant population in the city since 1975.[21]

Although it has tended to age over the years, the population of La Courneuve remains, on the whole, somewhat younger than that of the region, a third of the residents being under age 20 (as against 27 percent for the latter). The typical household is also larger than the regional average: Half comprise more than two members, and 1 in 10 counts at least 6 persons, compared with 42 percent and 3 percent, respectively, for the Ile-de-France. Because foreign households are larger than those of native French residents, only 16 percent of the city's households are headed by a person of foreign nationality. (La Courneuve ranks ninth among cities of the *département* on that scale.) The model family is composed of both parents and 1 or 2 children, though Préteceille (1988: 143) calls attention to what is, by French standards, a "particularly high rate" of female-headed families: 6.2 percent.

A Working Class Decimated by De-industrialization

With an employment ratio (number employed over total population) of 47.7 percent, a figure similar to that of the *département* of Seine-Saint-Denis as a whole, La Courneuve is one of the most heavily working-class communities of the Parisian Red Belt: 38 percent of its labor force is comprised of manual workers, compared with 33 percent for the Seine-Saint-Denis and 25 percent for Greater Paris. White-collar employees make up another 36 percent of the employed population. Thus, three-fourths of the city's inhabitants belong to the working and lower middle classes. Not surprisingly, 80 percent of all families are estimated to have incomes below the regional average (which, it should be noted, is the highest in the country).

La Courneuve has suffered very heavily from de-industrialization as the shift to postfordist services and manufacturing "split" the local industrial space and dispersed sites of production and residence throughout Greater Paris.[22] Most of the large companies still in operation (mainly in chemical processing, industrial equipment, and aeronautical construction) were first implanted there during the interwar years, when the city was at the cutting edge of industrial technology. Industrial growth peaked in the 1960s and industry declined rapidly afterward:[23] In 1968, the town boasted 170 industrial firms providing over 17,700 jobs or one factory job for every 2.35 residents; by 1984, these figures had fallen to 126 firms employing a modest 7,000 workers, for a ratio of one job for every 4.7 Courneuvois. In the last decade, 70 percent of job losses have come in industry, while 59 percent of newly created positions have been in commerce and transportation.

The growing discrepancy between a workforce trained in traditional, smoke-stack industrial occupations and the labor demand of new, predominantly service- and "high-risk"-oriented firms explains in part why the latter tend to locate elsewhere as they experience increasing difficulties finding skilled workers in the immediate area. Plant closings have left a gaping vacant hole at the heart of the city and laid over 50 acres of industrial land to waste, half of which are presently occupied by abandoned factories. This industrial wasteland has attracted real estate speculators, much to the concern of municipal authorities.

Soaring Unemployment and the Expansion of Public Assistance

As a result of factory layoffs and closings, joblessness has soared, particularly among working-class youth. The number of unemployed more than doubled between 1979 and 1984 alone, escalating to 3,355 for 16,300 employed by 1986—a 16 percent official unemployment rate, twice the national average. Half of the registered jobless population is under 30 years of age; one-third have no academic credentials and another third only a primary school degree.[24] Some 2,300 young residents of La Courneuve (80 percent of them from the public housing estate of the *Quatre mille*) are registered at the local Youth Employment Council. Although 9 of every 10 hold either the baccalaureate or a 3-year vocational degree (*Certificat d'Aptitude Professionnelle*), only a fraction (15 percent) are able to find employment and then hold mostly precarious part-time jobs.

Not surprisingly, given the combination of extensive family and social programs provided by the French welfare state (see Lefaucheur this volume) and municipal patronage disbursed by the local PCF "machine," social services enjoy a large clientele.[25] For the year 1990, nearly half of the city's households were entitled to state family allowances by virtue of having children, and 28 percent also received housing assistance. A total of 554 persons (out of some 720 applicants, including 369 residents of the *Quatre mille*) were recipients of the recently instituted national guaranteed minimum income (RMI) in 1989; 525 requests for free medical coverage by the *département* were also granted (out of 734 applications). In addition, a total of 1,443 families were awarded assistance under the program "Social Aid to Childhood," half of them single-parent households; 1,128 families (out of 1,470 who applied) were given "First-need assistance," for an average yearly grant of $350 while another 645 households received a "Monthly Grant" of $700 on average.[26] Half of these families had been found to have insufficient financial resources to provide adequate standards of living for their children, including 6 percent with no income whatsoever to report.

The Infamous Project of the *Quatre mille*

The low-income housing estate or *cité des Quatre mille* consists of two massive high-rise projects, the "*Quatre mille* South" and the "*Quatre mille* North," sprawled over several acres. It is composed of 32 concrete "rods" (as they are called locally) of 16 stories and 4 towers of 26 stories comprising a total of 3,667 housing units—of which 1,000 were recently renovated under the ongoing Neighborhood Social Development program.[27] The *cité* was built from 1957 to 1964, and, for over two decades, it remained the property of the city of Paris, which used it as a "dumpster" for its so-called "problem population" (*mal logés*) and for ridding itself of poor residents displaced by the urban renewal of the eastern boroughs of the capital. Residents of La Courneuve are keenly aware of this and readily point out that "Chirac [the Mayor of Paris since 1978] sent us all the families he wanted to get rid of" (Avery 1987: 28; also Guglielmo and

Moulin 1986). After a bitter and hard-fought political battle, the Communist municipality finally wrestled control of the project in 1984. Since then, management of the *Quatre mille* has remained a bone of contention and a major stake in the guerrilla tactics of the PCF against the central government.

The estate initially posted a housing stock of just over 4,000 units (whence its name) designed to accommodate a population of about 17,500 comprised mainly of repatriates from the former French Algeria, displaced residents of the suburban "slum camps" of the 1950s, and migrant workers. Much like the public housing projects of Chicago, the *cité* was beautiful when it was inaugurated. Its creation was greeted with enthusiasm and accompanied by a vibrant celebration of *grands ensembles* (high-rise projects) invoking the popular, frugal, but warm conviviality of the largely imaginary working-class suburbs of yesteryear (Bachmann and Basier 1989: 38). A city official reminisces (author's interview): "When I arrived in La Courneuve from [the rural province of] Limousin in 1964, I thought I was in the United States, it was so big and beautiful! I truly marveled at the sight of the towers."

Ten years later, the positive image of the "blue city" had been overlaid by an imagery of fear and anonymity as the *cité* became the haven of the most disadvantaged residents of La Courneuve. As of 1984, 790 or 22 percent of 3,603 housing units were occupied by households of foreign origin, and one in five were behind in payment of their rent. Fully 46 percent of the residents were under age 20, and the average household size of 3.9 persons was substantially larger than the city average of 2.9. Together, the loss of jobs, depopulation, and bad reputation of the project account for the nearly 500 units that are presently vacant. With a 30 percent unemployment rate, the highest of all "sensitive neighborhoods" in the country according to city documents, half of the households from the *Quatre mille* experience the plague of long-term joblessness.

One of the assets of La Courneuve is its location: It takes but a few minutes on the train to reach Paris to the south or Roissy and Charles de Gaulle Airport to the north. Yet the *Quatre mille* itself is wedged in between the downtown area and the surrounding industrial wastelands, alongside the RER (regional rapid transit) train line. The project is not directly connected to the flow of commercial and cultural activities in the city. It tends to lead its own life and has developed a distinct atmosphere, one that "is peaceful but depressed, friendly but isolated, without pretentions but conscious of a definite repute" (Avery 1987: 76). The first impression upon entering the estate is one of oppression and an overwhelming sense of vacuousness despite the lively street scene—children playing on the lawns and running about with their mothers, the amicable tone of the nearby group of men overheard arguing about car repairs and sports events, residents walking to and from local stores with their pets in tow. Perhaps the single largest cause of the heavy feeling of gloom that pervades the *Quatre mille* is the dilapidated state of the housing stock. Because of structural deficiencies (due to their hasty building with cheap materials) and lack of proper maintenance, most buildings are unpleasant by sight and use. Cracks in the walls of apartments create a feeling of insecurity, elevators smell of urine, while staggering quantities of identical doors and windows can be traumatizing. The unusually high levels of noise, dirt, and graffiti, owing to the large proportion of youngsters among residents, also contribute to the bleak, somber atmosphere of the project:

> Facing four thousand identical doors, combined with the fact that a number of entrances are not lit and stink, certainly discourage visits. People are suspicious of one another, perhaps by necessity. People often complain of isolation. However, there is also a very relaxed side in everyday behavior, which can be observed for instance in the attitude of those women who go to the bakery in their nightgown and slippers, or who continually shout intimate confidences to their dogs. (Avery 1987: 77–78)

EXPERIENTIAL SIMILARITIES AND STRUCTURAL DIFFERENCES BETWEEN GHETTO AND *CITÉ*

This comparative sketch of La Courneuve's *Quatre mille* and Chicago's Woodlawn reveals several experiential commonalities and parallel demographic trends but also significant structural differences between the French working-class *cité* and the black American ghetto. I discuss each of these in turn before turning to a brief diagnosis of the distinctive makeup and trajectory of these two urban forms.

Stigmatization and the Cumulation of Social Ills

There are, first, remarkable similarities in the subjective experiences of the people of Woodlawn and La Courneuve. On both sides of the Atlantic, an atmosphere of drabness, monotony, and despair prevails; life in these poor urban enclaves is felt to be slowed down, dull, and insecure. Both sites are sharply demarcated from their respective urban setting and closely identified with failure, downward mobility, and prolonged marginality by residents and outsiders alike. People in La Courneuve's *grands ensembles* and in Woodlawn are keenly aware of having been relegated to a degraded territory that inferiorizes them and where they face a closed future with little chance of getting ahead unless they manage to move out. Thus, the inhabitants of the *Quatre mille*, taking over the representation of the press, refer to the *cité* as "the city of fear," "the garbage can of Paris," a "chicken coop" (*cage à poules*), or a "reservation" (Avery 1987: 13). Youths from La Courneuve and other Red Belt projects will greet visitors by saying; "The *cité*? All you're gonna find here is shit, everything's rotten here" (cited in Pialoux 1979: 19–20).

Residing in Chicago's ghetto is likewise a public mark of social inferiority, because today's urban core contains only those dispossessed segments of the black community that cannot escape its blighted conditions. Indeed, given a choice, three in four residents of Chicago's historic Black Belt would like to move out of their neighborhood, and 82 percent rate the latter as a "bad or very bad" place to live, with half listing gangs as a "big problem" to contend with. Fully two-thirds expect their area to continue to deteriorate or to remain as dilapidated at best (Wacquant 1992b). This sense of relegation is conveyed in the following remark by a 28-year-old man struggling to raise his two children on a part-time janitorial job at a Woodlawn fast food store:

> In the typa environment that I live in, right now, it's jus' that you gotta go through a lot—I live aroun' *drug dealers*, I live aroun' peoples tha's *using drugs*, I live aroun' people that *stick people up*, taking thin's from peoples. You know, everybody's tryin' to get out—'s *like the ghetto: Everybody's tryin' to get out*.[28]

A sense of social indignity and isolation is thus shared by Woodlawnites and Courneuvois, as a result of the *powerful territorial stigma* attached to residence on Chicago's South Side and in a declining Red Belt project. Residents of both locales believe that this stigma adversely affects their economic and social opportunities, reducing their chances for employment, housing, and even friendship or interpersonal contacts (Wacquant 1994). Responses to this stigmatization run the gamut from mutual avoidance and self-deprecation to invidious distinctions and withdrawal, but each involves recognition of the social stain attached to membership in such a community, and all concur to undermine the conditions for collective action and solidarity.

Second, a number of morphological trends and "deviations" from their larger surroundings are common to Woodlawn and La Courneuve, due to the *self-feeding cumulation of social dislocations* in these isolated enclaves. Both areas have suffered large-scale housing deterioration and severe depopulation: We noted that La Courneuve lost 20 percent of its residents in 1968–88, while Woodlawn saw its population decrease by 55 percent over 1960–1980 and, according to preliminary returns from the 1990 census, by an additional 30 percent in the 1980s. Both neighborhoods contain large and increasing concentrations of foreigners on the one side, of "minorities" on the other: The proportion of immigrants—or of families publicly perceived or assimilated as such even though they in fact hold French citizenship, as is the case with the *beurs* (French-born youths of North African descent)—in La Courneuve is one of the highest of the Parisian inner ring and rising, while Woodlawn's population has been virtually all black for over two decades. Both neighborhoods also have a skewed age structure, due to an overrepresentation of teenagers, and a distorted household distribution, with a stronger presence of "solo parents" or female-headed households than elsewhere.

Woodlawn and La Courneuve are also similar in that both neighborhoods suffer from unusually high unemployment rates—twice the citywide figure for the former and double the national average in the latter. Not surprisingly, the occupational composition of both neighborhoods is substantially lower than that of their respective city, with a predominance of factory workers in declining industries on the French side and of deskilled service jobs on the American side. This is the result of industrial restructuring, both locales having lost thousands of jobs in the secondary sector of the economy. To sum up, the *evolution* of the HLM towns of the Parisian Red Belt and of the South Side of Chicago over the last two decades or so would seem to bear *prima facie* evidence of an objective and subjective convergence between them.

Structural Differences Between *Cité* and Ghetto: Class Fragmentation Versus Racial Exclusion

Behind these apparently converging trends, however, significant *structural contrasts* remain between La Courneuve and Woodlawn that point to the different institutional logics and closure mechanisms that command urban decline and recomposition on each side of the Atlantic. To anticipate: in the French *cité*, the driving force is one of *working-class fragmentation* in the context of a twofold movement of socioeconomic and spatial dispersion of the group that has brought about the end of traditional "worker territories" (Tripier and Tripier 1991: 299–302; Magri and Topaloff 1989). On the American side, the core process is one of *hyperghettoization* characterized by the spatial conjugation of color and class exclusion and produced by the twofold withdrawal of market and state from the urban core (Wacquant 1992b).

Size, location, and levels of hardship.   First, it should be noted that La Courneuve is a relatively small site in the midst of a varied, if declining, industrial and urban landscape. One can cross its "ghetto" in 10 minutes on foot and escape it for more congenial surroundings. By contrast, Woodlawn is but one piece of a considerably larger and expanding urban kilt—the South Side of Chicago covers several tens of square miles—which is totally segregated racially and uniformly depressed economically, save for the anomaly of Hyde Park.[29]

These differences in size and ecological location point to the different scales of hardship that apply in each site. Comparable official unemployment statistics hide huge gaps in labor force participation and economic exclusion: In La Courneuve, nearly half of all residents still hold jobs in spite of the upsurge in unemployment, whereas only one in five Woodlawnites is employed in the wage economy. Families depending on public assistance (as opposed to universally available social redistribution programs), although large by French standards, remain a minority in La Courneuve; even in the *Quatre mille* itself, most families are headed by a wage earner. This is not so in Woodlawn, where nearly half of all households depend on welfare for survival and where most residents have to "hustle" in the underground economy to make ends meet.

Similarly, homelessness, while visibly on the rise, is not a major issue in La Courneuve, even though the municipality has the reputation of being "a refugee land" for transients and tramps. Certainly, it does not affect large numbers of families with children as it does in Woodlawn and in most American inner cities. Neither are hunger and malnutrition sufficiently widespread in this Red Belt town for warranting municipal intervention. The city has no public or private soup kitchen, such as the famous *restaurants du coeur* sponsored by the late comic Coluche; all children get free meals in the public schools, and social workers periodically distribute packages to households in need. In Woodlawn, malnutrition and hunger are common among school-age children, and public and private pantries cannot meet local demand for food assistance. Thus, similar "deviations" and trends in the incidence of selected social dislocations can obscure massive differences between the French *cité* and the American ghetto. One statistic is indicative of how wide this gap can be: The proportion of "female-headed households" in Woodlawn is exactly *10 times* that of La Courneuve.[30]

Ethnic heterogeneity and social divisions. Although the projects of La Courneuve house significant and growing numbers of foreigners,[31] to the point where they are publicly misperceived as "Arab ghettos" (Bachmann and Basier 1989), their population is in fact highly *heterogeneous both ethnically and socially.* Some 20 nationalities are represented in the *Quatre mille,* and no one group dominates or sets the tone for the neighborhood because "native white" French families make up a large majority (about three-fourths) of the residents. Indeed, this very diversity, and the dispersion of modes of life and social trajectories it implies, is a major source of the internal conflicts of which the *banlieue* has been the scene in recent years. It brings into physical co-presence groups that are not used to sharing the same territory and scarce public facilities and for whom living in HLM projects has different, even opposite, meanings.

By comparison, Woodlawn is not only increasingly homogenous in terms of class but, most distinctively, *entirely segregated racially.* Whites and blacks do not mingle or interact on the South Side of Chicago. Most Woodlawnites never encounter any member of another racial group in the course of their daily round. This is because the ghetto is not simply a low-income neighborhood but a particular institutional configuration or *clustering of exclusionary mechanisms*—in the housing, labor, marriage, and cultural markets—*based on skin color.* People in the *Quatre mille,* including immigrant families (for whom access to public housing generally represents a promotion rather than a downward slide), end up there because they lack the economic means for moving into better neighborhoods. In particular, the overrepresentation of North African families in these projects stems essentially from their low class distribution. People on the South Side of Chicago, on the other hand, are trapped not simply because they are poor but first and foremost because they are (categorized as) *black.*

This is reflected in the different principles of division that structure the representations and actions of residents of Woodlawn and La Courneuve. The kind of "us/them" relation of dichotomous opposition between whites (and middle-class blacks whom ghetto residents symbolically assimilate to whites)[32] and poor blacks that shapes the perception and practices of people on the South Side of Chicago has no equivalent in degraded French housing projects. Although there has occurred an incipient "racialization" of space over the past decade (Calogirou 1989; Body-Gendrot 1993), due to the concentration of immigrant families of North African descent in some HLM estates, the central organizing cleavage of the *cité* does not oppose foreigners and natives but "youth" and adults. Youths are perceived by older residents as the main source of insecurity, vandalism, and delinquency. They, in turn, complain of being locked in a "dump" where grown-ups disrespect them and show no concern over the paucity of employment and entertainment opportunities they suffer. In a major study of the survival strategies of young men in several declining *cités*, Dubet (1987: 327) found that "in spite of a markedly racist climate, the social relations of youth are not organized on a [national and ethnic basis]. The unit of activity is the pluri-ethnic neighborhood and groups of youth reflect this diversity."[33] This is because

"French youth and immigrant youth do not live separately in the *cité*, each on their side of the ones against the others. They explain that they have gone through the same schools, the same games, the same *galère* ["drifting"]. They share, to various degrees of course, the same rage and the same exclusion." (Dubet 1987: 130–131)

On Chicago's South Side, color awareness is ubiquitous, whites totally absent from the daily universe, and racial apartheid encompasses all realms of life and consciousness. There is the black world of the ghetto and the *terra incognita* of the white world, "as distant from [the former] as Mars and Earth, a white world with different codes of speech, dress, and conduct. Boys from the projects [are] made to feel like trespassers there, alien and, because they are black, presumptively dangerous" (Monroe and Goldman 1988: 100).

State penetration, organizational decline, and the erosion of public space. Another major contrast is that between the strong presence of the state and the relatively dense organizational ecology of La Courneuve—the *Quatre mille* is the home of a plethora of grass-roots and public organizations[34]—and the concurrent state retrenchment and institutional debilitation that plague ghetto neighborhoods such as Woodlawn. Being a racial reservation, the latter has been largely abandoned by public authorities, and this has led to the continual degradation of facilities and services such as transportation, schools, health care, and commercial outlets (Wacquant 1992b). More specifically, while La Courneuve appears to suffer from an *overpenetration* of state agencies and public organizations that tend to isolate their users by drawing them away from other (especially private) organizations, Woodlawn suffers from the *withdrawal* and breakdown of public institutions.

The divergent relations of these enclaves of poverty to their respective states also accounts for the sharp differences observed in the areas of housing and crime. In La Courneuve, the city and government have been conducting a massive urban rehabilitation program designed to improve living conditions and to strengthen the commercial and organizational fabric of the *cité* since 1984. In Woodlawn, there has been virtually no construction or renovation since the 1960s, and nearly half of the housing stock has disappeared in the last three decades. The French *cité* and the American ghetto are both viewed as "dangerous places" in which violent crime and delinquency are commonplace and create a climate of fear and insecurity. Yet, they differ sharply in the frequency, degree of social embeddedness, and nature of criminal activities prevalent in them, as well as in the impact that these have on the organization and flow of daily life (Wacquant 1994). Put briefly, in La Courneuve, there is a widespread feeling of insecurity rooted in the ecology of the neighborhood and fueled by petty youth delinquency, but public safety is not a major issue.[35] In point of fact, rates for most crime categories are lower there than they are in Paris— murders, for instance, are a rarity. In Woodlawn, actual physical danger pervades everyday life. Houses are barricaded behind bars, and residents organize their daily round to avoid having to go out or to use public transportation. The incidence of homicides and street violence (shootings, muggings, rape, and battery) in Chicago's ghetto has reached levels comparable with that of a civil war and caused the virtual disappearance of public space.

Woodlawn and La Courneuve may both be poor and bleak neighborhoods undergoing decline and dislocation, but they still differ profoundly in the mechanisms that sort, articulate, and accumulate various forms of exclusion in them. In Chicago, *state abandonment acts as a major determinant and racial segregation as a crucial prism that concentrates hardship* in poor black areas, compounding a color line and a class line. Racial enclaves such as Chicago's South Side, Boston's Roxbury, or New York's Harlem are unknown in France—and in all of Europe for that matter. In the Greater Paris, as in the rest of France, "there are no neighborhoods entirely occupied by a single ethnic group" (Dubet 1989: 31). Moreover, locales containing high percentages of immigrants do not overlap with the most disadvantaged areas because foreign families are widely distributed in space and mixed with the French-born population (Leray 1990). Ethnic concentration is essentially an offshoot of the concentration of immigrant households at the bottom of the class structure, not the result of a racial division of physical and social space.

Alhough they increasingly manifest themselves in the guise of racial enmity or xenophobia directed primarily against immigrants from the Maghrib, the rising tensions observed in France's working-class *banlieues* in recent years are not primarily ethnic. They are caused by the demise of historic "worker territories," which has deprived the working class of its conventional means of collective reproduction and expression (Verret 1992). Immigrants enter into this picture to the extent that their integration into French society has traditionally operated via their incorporation into the working class and its organizations (most notably the Communist Party and the CGT union), the crisis of the latter rendering the former more protracted and contentious.

Yet the most remarkable difference between La Courneuve and Chicago's South Side is arguably the following: Whereas the ghetto subproletariat continues to experience continued downward mobility and an absolute worsening of its condition, in France the overall situation of immigrants is, at least in relative terms, improving and "becoming more similar to that of French workers" (Dubet 1989: 109–110). So that, in the American inner city, alienation and confrontation are fueled by the growing social *distance* between ghetto blacks and the rest of society. In the French *cité*, tensions arise out of growing social *proximity* between immigrant and native residents.

The Sociopolitical Articulation of "Race," Class, and Space

The difference between Chicago's South Side and the degraded working-class projects of the Parisian periphery, then, is not simply one of scale, intensity, and depth of deprivation, but more importantly hinges on the different institutional machineries and closure mechanisms that manage and allocate the costs of the ongoing economic restructuring within each of these societies. The American inner city is not simply much poorer and much meaner than the French *banlieue*: It is a different urban form altogether, specific to the United States, in which race functions as the primary template of social and spatial division. Thus, while it may be proper to speak of "pockets of immigrant poverty" or "ethnic concentrations" in France (and in other European countries such as the Netherlands or even England), it is misleading—or to say the least very premature—to announce the formation of ghettos there in the sense that this term takes by reference to the situation of blacks in the American city. And if it is true that "welfare states are key institutions in the structuring of class and social order" and that their "organizational features help determine the articulation of social solidarity, divisions of class, and status differentiation" (Esping-Andersen 1990: 56), then we have good reasons to expect that the fate of poor urban enclaves will continue to differ significantly in France and the United States.

Indeed, the recent policy responses offered in this regard by the American federal and local governments and by the French state (and the regions and municipalities that enjoy increased autonomy under the new "decentralized" administrative regime) could hardly be more contrasted. In France, rising social tensions and citizen discontent within and around the *cités* have ushered in a phase of unprecedented state activism. Central government reaction to decline and unrest in the *banlieue*—and to the concurrent rise of LePen's extremist National Front on the electoral stage—has been two-pronged. On the specifically urban front, in late 1990, the Rocard administration announced the creation of a Ministry of Urban Affairs entrusted, among other duties, with expanding and implementing the state's Neighborhood Social Development scheme, a comprehensive package of housing, educational, crime prevention, job training and search assistance programs, youth activities, and beefed-up public services designed to ameliorate the ecology and social life of 400 officially designated "sensitive neighborhoods" across the country.[36] The second, nonurban, component of state intervention has centered on the creation, by a unanimous vote of Parliament in 1988, of a national guaranteed minimum income plan and stepped-up expenditures on employment and training schemes aimed in particular at youth and the long-term unemployed. Concurrently, at the city and regional level, local experiments with programs of "social solidarity" have multi-plied in the past decade, with the aim of mending the holes left in the social safety net of the state (Paugam 1991).

In the United States, by contrast, the policy reaction to the worsening plight of urban blacks has been one of continued abandonment and punitive,contain-ment in the crumbling racial enclaves of the inner city. The first component of this policy of urban laissez faire includes decreased funding for large cities, "welfare reform," a euphemism for welfare reduction (especially at the state level where public aid budgets are being cut back with a ferocity that exceeds that of the Reagan federal rollbacks of the early 1980s), and a reorientation of big-city priorities away from the provision of social services to its poorest resi-dents in favor of direct support for private capital accumulation. On the repres-sive side, several variants of "workfare" have been designed to force poor mi-norities into the substandard and casual employment slots offered by the secondary segments of the new service economy, while the War on Drugs has given added momentum to a *de facto* penal policy that has already led to a tripling of the incarcerated population in two decades.

The contrast between France and the United States is perhaps best captured in the terminology employed by state officials to frame their policies or lack thereof. In Paris, even the Right has adopted the language of national *solidarity* and bemoans the growth of inequalities in the city under Mitterrand. In Wash-ington, D.C., while then-President Bush spun his lyrical evocations of "a thou-sand points of light," liberals and conservatives vied to monopolize claims to individual *compassion* (the modern word for what used to be called charity). So we might conjecture that, their experiential parallels notwithstanding, the trajectories of the black American ghetto and of France's degraded working-class *cités* will continue to differ to the extent that they embody different historical urban, class, and racial legacies and so long as the state structures that "process" them diverge in their ideology, institutional capacity, and political commitment to reduce inequalities and to foster social justice in the city.

Research and writing for this paper would not have been possible without the cooperation of numerous individuals and institutions that provided data, suggestions, lodging, and other material and intellectual assistance. First thanks go to Katherine McFate of the Joint Center for Political and Economic Studies, who not only commissioned this study and patiently waited for successive re-formulations of its first results, but helped give it focus and purpose.

In France, I received invaluable help from Claire Guignard (Haut commissa-riat à l'intégration), Nicole Smadja (Préfecture de région Ile-de-France), Sonia Serkoff (librarian with the Commissariat au Plan), Nicole Tabard (socioecono-mist with INSEE), M. Galibourg (Direction départementale de l'équipement for the Seine-Saint-Denis in Bobigny), and from G. Duchatelet (Caisse nationale des allocations familiales). Mme Delahaye (Municipality of La Courneuve) was kind enough to give me access to numerous unpublished municipal reports and to take me on tours of the 4000 housing project, while the staff of the documentation center of the city of La Courneuve offered crucial library support; without them, this study simply would not exist. Monique Pinçon-Charlot and Michel Pinçon of the Centre de sociologie urbaine (CSU-CNRS) supplied useful additional data and a sounding board for my interpretations of them. I also benefited from discussions with Michel Pialoux, Michel Wieviorka, Didier Lapeyronnie, Yvette Delsaut, and Abdelmalek Sayad. And I thank Nonoessa Bushronde, Roscoe Muniste, and Tonton and Tata Odile for housing and affection while in Paris.

Much of the data on Chicago's ghetto was gathered while I was a member of the Urban Poverty Project at the University of Chicago under the direction of William Julius Wilson, whose intellectual companionship and support have been most rewarding through the years. The comments and reactions of Godfried Engbersen, Roger Lawson, Alex Portes, Guy Standing, Jaap Timmer, Peter Townsend, and other participants in the conference meetings stimulated me to rethink and recast many of my arguments—I hope for the better. Last, to my informants from the South Side of Chicago, who shall remain anonymous, goes my heartfelt gratitude for the incisive tutorials on race and class in American society they have given me: They are without match on university campuses.

ENDNOTES

1. On the American urban core, see McGeary and Lynn (1988), Wacquant and Wilson (1989a), and Harris and Wilkins (1988). See Pinçon (1987), Durand (1984), Dubet (1987) on France; Harrison (1985) and Mack and Lansley (1985) on Great Britain; and Engbersen, van der Veen, and Schuyt (1987) and Oude (1987) on the Netherlands.

2. A fuller analysis of this question is offered in the companion piece to this essay (Wacquant 1994).

3. See Esping-Andersen (1990) for a broad contrast of the corporatist and liberal welfare state regimes of France and the United States, respectively, and O'Higgins and McFate (1991) for a comparison of their labor market policies and levels of expenditures.

4. Of all advanced industrialized nations, only Japan and Switzerland spend proportionately less than the United States; France spends roughly three times as much as a percentage of her gross national product.

5. The Urban Poverty and Family Structure Project is a multidisciplinary research project directed by William Julius Wilson at the University of Chicago. Its main empirical components are a multistage, random probability sample of 2,490 residents of Chicago's poor neighborhoods (defined as census tracts with at least 20 percent poor persons in them in 1980) conducted in 1986–1987; a set of intensive, semistructured interviews on perceptions of opportunity and inequality with a subsample of 164 respondents; a series of repeated genealogical interviews with select informants in key black, white, and Hispanic neighborhoods; an interview survey of a stratified sample of 185 employers in the Greater Chicago area. The financial support of the Ford Foundation, the Carnegie Corporation, the U.S. Department of Health and Human Services, the Institute for Research on Poverty, the Joyce Foundation, the Lloyd A. Fry Foundation, the Rockefeller Foundation, the Spencer Foundation, the

William T. Grant Foundation, the Woods Charitable Fund, and the Chicago Community Trust for this research is gratefully acknowledged.

6. As can be seen from Tabard and Aldeghi's (1988) statistical profile of poor French urban areas (the 400 "sensitive neighborhoods" covered by the state's Neighborhood Social Development plan).

7. Need I emphasize that the purpose of the chapter is not to try to establish the "superiority" of either country with respect to their treatment or forbearance of urban poverty but, rather, to uncover the common socio-logic and specifics of each through their methodical empirical confrontation? Because poverty is a sociopolitically constructed reality, each situation can be normatively evaluated only within its own national historical and institutional context: Levels of hardship tolerable here are deemed unacceptable there; degrees of inequality or redistribution found desirable or normal on one side of the Atlantic may be found excessive or undesirable on the other side; forms of public intervention or market sanctions are readily accepted and administratively feasible in one case, not in the other, etc.

8. As was made plain at the international conference on "Poverty, Immigration and Urban Marginality in Advanced Societies" (organized by the Maison des sciences de l'homme and the Russell Sage Foundation), held at the Maison Suger in Paris in May 1991, where American and European scholars were forced to explicate, to one another and to themselves, moral preconceptions and conceptual commitments that normally remain safely undiscussed (see conference proceedings and summary).

9. See Wacquant (1992a) for an attempt to analyze the pitfalls involved in the importation of an "Americanized" notion of "ghetto" in the recent French debate about the ongoing crisis of the *banlieues*.

10. This sketch of Woodlawn draws on Chicago Fact Book Consortium (1984), Brune and Camacho (1983), Belizario (1984), and field observations and interviews conducted by the author. For a more detailed description of a similar process of urban involution and destruction in other Chicago ghetto neighborhoods, see Duncan (1987) on North Kenwood (the area just north of the University of Chicago) and Wacquant and Wilson (1989b) on the West Side community of North Lawndale.

11. If not for the fierce resistance of the University of Chicago (the single largest landlord on Chicago's South Side) and its enormous political clout, which allowed it to shape urban renewal legislation so as to funnel public funds to the protection of its private interests, there is good reason to believe that the whole South Side would be an all-black territory today. In the 1960s and early 1970s, much of the area comprised between 60th and 61st Street, Drexel and Blackstone was bought by the university and the traffic grid reorganized so as to create a buffer zone between Hyde Park and the Midway, a blockwide avenue bordered by open lawns, which marks the southern boundary of Hyde Park, was restricted to a few arteries and buildings demolished to make room for the university facilities or to create vacant lots that served as a "no-man's land"—all in an effort to isolate and "protect" Hyde Park (see "Hyde Park: A Neighborhood on the Hill" in Hirsh 1983).

12. Such sex imbalance is common to poor black neighborhoods, not only in Chicago, but throughout America, due in good measure to the high rates of incarceration and violent deaths among young black males (see Gibbs 1989). Note that the proportion

of older residents is also increasing in Woodlawn: Persons ages 65 and over were 9 percent in 1970 and 15 percent in 1980.

13. A modest 200 Woodlawnites are reported as self-employed and only 900 walk to work, many of them to the University of Chicago, where they mostly fill menial jobs in the plant, hospitals, and laboratories.

14. They are the so-called street-corner men described in so many ethnographies of the ghetto (Anderson 1978, Hannerz 1969, Liebow 1967).

15. A broad-brush statistical portrait of homelessness in Chicago can be found in Rossi (1990), although it misses a very sizable chunk of the phenomenon by virtue of its overly narrow operational definition and limiting survey technology.

16. Arsons were so common that the "going rate" was public knowledge on the street: $500 for an empty building, more for one with residents. Occasionally, buildings were also set on fire as part of extortion schemes designed to coax their owners into paying "protection" money to local gangs on pain of seeing their property go up in flames. Added to accidental and "insurance" fires were the arsons deliberately committed by demolition companies to economize on trucking and dumping costs. On the linkages between inner-city arsons, the policies of banks and insurance companies, organized crime, shady landlords, and corrupt public officials, see Brady (1983).

17. "Currency exchanges" are the only formal financial institution left in the area since the last bank of the community closed its facility in the early 1970s to relocate in the downtown Loop.

18. Unless otherwise specified, the figures for this profile of La Courneuve and of the housing project of the *Quatre mille* are drawn from a variety of census reports, city and regional documents and brochures, including Direction départementale de l'équipement (1988, 1989), Ville de La Courneuve (1988, 1989, 1990), and from Avery (1987), Préteceille (1988), and Bachmann and Basier (1989).

19. In terms of Tabard's socio-occupational typology of townships, La Courneuve falls in the category of "*communes* with skilled workers undergoing rapid depopulation." Of the 40 *communes* of Seine-Saint-Denis, 31 are working-class counties, 13 of which fall into this category (Bessy 1990: 63). Four of the six contiguous municipalities of Aubervilliers, Saint-Denis, Stains, Le Bourget, Bondy, and Noisy Le Sec are of the same type.

20. After three decades of stagnation, La Courneuve's population increased rapidly (by over 60 percent) in the 1960s due to the construction of HLM high rises. Close to 6,400 people, or 16.8 percent of the 1975 population, moved out during the 1975–1982 period.

21. Foreigners composed 16 percent of the city's population in 1975 and 11 percent in 1968 (Préteceille 1988: 114, 164). This trend can be observed in other "Red Belt" towns with large HLM concentrations. It reflects in part the improved access of foreign immigrants to public housing (Dubet 1989).

22. This process is described in Browaeys and Chatelain (1974–1975) and Fourny (1986).

23. The year 1980 was the first in the history of the city in which industry provided less than half of total employment (Avery 1987: 162).

24. This figure includes individuals who have not held a job with regularity and, therefore, cannot sign up for unemployment.

25. The figures that follow are excerpted from Centre communal d'action sociale, *Bilan d'activités 1989*, Ville de La Courneuve, mimeo, 37 pp., 1989.

26. *Secours de premier besoin* is an emergency public assistance grant given under the program of "Social Aid to Childhood" to families who experience severe financial difficulties on suggestion of a social worker.

27. Buildings take the form of long blocks of concrete, either 4 or 16 stories high and nearly 200 yards in length, which bear the names of famous artists and scientists (Verlaine, Villon, Balzac, Braque, Curie, Debussy, etc.)

28. For moving testimonies of the indignity of relegation in the black ghetto, see Monroe and Goldman (1988) and Duncan (1987).

29. The concurrent spatial expansion of racial segregation and of poverty in Chicago is charted on maps found in Brune and Camacho (1983) and Wacquant and Wilson (1989b: 86–87).

30. Another statistic revealing of this gap is that for infant mortality. Whereas La Courneuve's rate is similar to that for the Greater Paris region and has been cut in half over the past two decades (falling from around 17 deaths per 1,000 live births in 1968 to 8 per 1,000 in 1982), the infant mortality rate of many ghetto areas in Chicago has been rising in recent years and now exceeds 30 per 1,000, three times the rate for whites in Illinois.

31. As is the case with all public housing in France. Nationally, the presence of foreigners in HLMs has increased steadily over the past three decades, from 5.9 percent in 1968 to 15 percent in 1975 and 23.6 percent in 1982 (Dubet 1989).

32. One of my Woodlawn informants put it thus: "Louie, to make it in Chicago, you gotta talk white, act white, and think white—that's the only way."

33. The absence, or muted character, of racial consciousness in the French working-class *cité* has been noted by numerous other researchers, including Avery (1987) on La Courneuve, Calogirou (1989), Pétonnet (1978), and Moreau de Bellaing (1988).

34. See Avery (1987: 52–54) for a partial roster and Wacquant (1994) for further discussion.

35. Any outsider (such as this author) can freely come and go in and out of the *Quatre mille*, walk into buildings, and talk to residents and groups of youths outside. I did not experience any nervousness or tension, and certainly no sense of danger, during my field visits to La Courneuve. This is not the case in most areas of the South Side of Chicago, where a white person is readily identified as a potential prey and, even if versed in the code of street behavior, takes real risks as to his (and even more so her) safety.

36. Various versions of this urban program have been in operation since 1982. The scale, funding, and number of sites has expanded steadily over the years (from 23 experimental locations to the 400 current locations covering the entire national territory). See Lenoir et al. (1989) for a historical synopsis and a preliminary evaluation of the effects of this policy, which has slowed down and even reversed decline in a number of neighborhoods.

REFERENCES

Anderson, Elijah. 1978. *A Place on the Corner*. Chicago: The University of Chicago Press.

Avery, Desmond. 1987. *Civilisations de La Courneuve: Images brisés d'une cité*. Paris: L'Harmattan.

Bachmann, Christian, and Luc Basier. 1989. *Mise en images d'une banlieue ordinaire*. Paris: Syros.

Belizario, Nelson. 1984. *Profile of Woodlawn*. Report prepared for the Donor's Forum, mimeo, 47 pp. + 7.

Benyon, John (ed.). 1984. *Scarman and After: Essays Reflecting on Lord Scarman's Report, the Riots and their Aftermath*. Oxford: Pergamon Press.

Bessy, Pascale. 1990. *Typologie socioprofessionalle de l'Ile-de-France: 22 types de communes*. Paris: INSEE.

Body-Gendrot, Sophie. 1993. "Migration and the Racialisation of the Postmodern City in France." In *Racism, the City and the State*, edited by Malcolm Cross and Michael Keith (pp. 77–92). London: Routledge.

Boyer, Robert (ed.). 1986. *Capitalisme fin de siècle*. Paris: Presses Universitaires de France.

Brady, James. 1983. "Arson, Urban Economy, and Organized Crime: The Case of Boston." *Social Problems* 31–1 (October).

Browaeys, Y., and P. Chatelain. 1974–1975. "Marché du travail et espace ouvrier en région parisienne." *Espaces et société* 13–14 (Oct-Janv).

Brune, Tom, and Eduardo Camacho. 1983. *A Special Report: Race and Poverty in Chicago*. Chicago: The Chicago Reporter and the Center for Community Research and Assistance.

Calogirou, Claire. 1989. *Sauver son honneur*. Paris: L'Harmattan.

Chicago Fact Book: Consortium. 1984. *Local Community Fact Book: Chicago Metropolitan Area*. Chicago: Chicago Review Press.

Chicago Tribune (staff of the). 1986. *The American Millstone: An Examination of the Nation's Permanent Underclass*. Chicago: Contemporary Books.

Direction départementale de l'Equipement. 1989. "Contrat de Plan Etat-Région: Réunion du 8 Septembre. Premiers éléments d'informations récentes sur quartier des '4000'." Mimeo.

Dubet, François. 1987. La galère. *Jeunes en survie*. Paris: Le Seuil.

———. 1989. *Immigrations: qu'en savons-nous? Un bilan des connaissances*. Paris: La documentation française.

Duncan, Arne. 1987. *The Values, Aspirations, and Opportunities of the Urban Underclass*. Cambridge, Mass.: Department of Sociology, Harvard University, unpublished B.A. honors thesis.

Durand, Claude. 1984. *Chômage et violence*. Paris: Editions Galilée.

Engbersen, Godfried, Romke van der Veen, and Kees Schuyt. 1987. *Moderne Armoede: Overleven op het sociaal minimum*. Leiden: H.E. Stenfert Kroese B.V.

Esping-Andersen, Gösta. 1990. *The Three Worlds of Welfare Capitalism*. Princeton, N.J.: Princeton University Press.

Feagin, Joe, and Michael B. Smith (eds.) 1987. *The Capitalist City*. London: Blackwell.

Fourest, Alain. 1985. "Quel développement pour quel quartier?" *Annales de la recherche urbaine* 26: 5–9.

Fourny, Marie-Christine. 1986. "Politiques locales et désindustrialisation en proche banlieue parisienne." *Hérodote* 43: 123–139.

Gans, Herbert H. 1991. "The Dangers of the Urban Underclass: Its Harmfulness as a Planning Concept." In *People, Plans and Policies: Essays on Poverty, Racism and Other National Urban Problems* (pp. 328–343). New York: Columbia University Press.

Gibbs, Jewelle Taylor. 1989. "The New Morbidity: Homicide, Suicide, Accidents and Life-Threatening Behaviors." In *Young, Black and Male in America: An Endangered Species*, edited by Jewelle Taylor Gibbs (pp. 258–293). New York: Auburn House Publishing Company.

Glasgow, Douglas. 1980. *The Black Underclass*. New York: Random, p. 370.

Grahl, John, and Paul Teague. 1989. "Labour Market Flexibility in West Germany, Britain and France." *West European Politics* 12 (April).

Guglielmo, Raymond, and Brigitte Moulin. 1986. "Les grands ensembles et la politique." *Hérodote* 43: 39–74.

Hannerz, Ulf. 1969. *Soulside: Inquiries into Ghetto Culture and Community*. New York: Columbia University Press.

Harris, Fred, and Roger W. Wilkins (eds.). 1988. *Quiet Riots: Race and Poverty in the United States*. New York: Pantheon.

Harrison, Paul. 1985. *Inside the Inner City*. Harmondsworth: Penguin Books.

Hérodote 1986. "Aprés les banlieues rouges?" *Hérodote: Revue de géographie et de géopolitique* 43 (thematic issue, October–December).

Hirsch, Arnold. 1983. *Making the Second Ghetto: Race and Housing in Chicago, 1940–1960*. Cambridge: Cambridge University Press.

Janoski, Tomas. 1990. *The Politics of Unemployment: Active Labor Market Policies in Germany and the United States*. Berkeley: University of California Press.

Katz, Michael B. 1987. *In the Shadow of the Poorhouse*. New York: Basic.

Lefaucheur, Nadine. "French Policies Towards Lone Parents: Social Categories and Social Policies." Chapter 7 in this volume.

Le Monde. 1991. *La ville et ses banlieues. Le Monde: Dossiers et documents*. 1985 (February).

Lenoir, Noëlle, Claire Guignard-Hamon, and Nicole Smadja. 1989. *Bilan/Perspectives des contrats de plan développement social des quartiers*. Paris: La documentation française.

Leray, Rudy. 1990. "Les quartiers sensibles de la région parisienne." *Insee Première* 61 (April).

Liebow, Elliot. 1967. *Tally's Corner: A Study of Negro Streetcorner Men*. Boston: Little, Brown, and Company.

Mack, J., and S. Lansley. 1985. *Poor Britain*. London: Allen and Unwin.

Magri, Susanna, and Christian Topalov (eds.). 1989. *Villes ouvrières, 1900–1950*. Paris: L'Harmattan.

McGeary, Michael G.H., and Lawrence E. Lynn, Jr. (eds.). 1988. *Urban Change and Poverty*. Washington, D.C.: National Academy Press.

Monroe, Sylvester, and Peter Goldman. 1988. *Brothers: Black and Poor. A True Story of Courage and Survival*. New York: Morrow.

Moreau de Bellaing, Louis. 1988. *La misère blanche. Le mode de vie des exclus*. Paris: L'Harmattan.

Ogien, Ruwen. 1983. *Théories ordinaires de la pauvreté*. Paris: Presses Universitaires de France.

O'Higgins, Michael, and Katherine McFate. 1991. "Integrating Labor Market and Social Policy Programs." Conference paper for "Poverty, Inequality and the Crisis of Social Policy" in Washington, D.C., September.

Oude, Engberink. 1987. *Minima zonder marge, de balans drie jaar*. Rotterdam: Municipality of Rotterdam.

Paugam, Serge. 1991. "Les statuts de la pauvreté assistée." *Revue française de sociologie* 32–1: 75–102.

Pétonnet, Colette. 1978. *On est tous dans le brouillard. Ethnologie des banlieues*. Paris: Galilée.

Pialoux, Michel. 1979. "Jeunesse sans avenir et travail intérimaire." *Actes de la recherche en sciences sociale* 26–27: 19–47.

Pinçon, Michel. 1987. *Désarrois ouvriers*. Paris: L'Harmattan.

Piore, Michael J., and Charles F. Sabel. 1984. *The Second Industrial Divide: Possibilities for Prosperity*. New York: Basic Books.

Préteceille, Edmond. 1988. *Mutations urbaines et politiques locales*, vol. 1. Paris: Centre de sociologie urbaine.

Room, Graham. 1987. *"New Poverty" in the European Community. A Summary of Twelve National Reports Prepared for the European Community*. Bath: Center for the Analysis of Social Policy, University of Bath.

Rossi, Peter H. 1990. *Down and Out in America*. Chicago: The University of Chicago Press.

Stovall, Tyler. 1990. *The Rise of the Paris Red Belt*. Paris: University of California Press.

Susser, Ida, and John Kresnicke. 1987. "The Welfare Trap: A Public Policy for Deprivation." In *Cities of the United States: Studies in Urban Anthropology*, edited by Keith Mullings (pp. 51–68). New York: Columbia University Press.

Tabard, Nicole, and Isa Aldeghi. 1988. *Transformation socioprofessionnele des communes de l'Ile-de-France entre 1975 et 1982*. Paris: CREDOC.

Tripier, Maryse, and Pierre Tripier. 1991. "Monde ouvriers, aujourd'hui et hier." *Sociologie du travail* 2: 293–303.

Verdès-Leroux, Jeannine. 1978. "Les 'exlus.'" *Actes de la recherche en sciences sociales* 19: 61–65.

Verret, Michel. 1992. "Où va la classe ouvrière française?" In *Ouvriers, ouvrières. Un continent morcelé et silencieux*, edited by Guy-Patrick Azemar (pp. 21–33). Paris: Editions Autrement.

Ville de La Courneuve. 1988. "Ilot sensible de La Courneuve: bilan 1982–1986." City of La Courneuve, unpublished report.

———. 1989. "Bilan d'activités. Service communal d'action sociale." Mimeographed.

———. 1990. "Contrat de Plan Etat-Région. Dossier de candidature." City of La Courneuve, unpublished report.

Wacquant, Loïc. 1992a. "Pour en finir avec le mythe des 'cités-ghettos.'" *Les annales de la recherche urbaine* 52 (September): 20–30.

———. 1992b. "Redrawing the Color Line: The State of the Ghetto in the 1980s." In *Social Problems*, edited by Craig Calhoun and George Ritzer. New York: McGraw-Hill.

———. 1994. "Dangerous Places: Violence and Isolation in Chicago's Ghetto and the Parisian 'Balieue.'" Forthcoming in *Urban Poverty and Family Life in the Inner City*, edited by William Julius Wilson. Oxford: Oxford University Press.

Wacquant, Loïc J.D., and William Julius Wilson. 1989a. "The Cost of Racial and Class Exclusion in the Inner City." *Annals of the American Academy of Political and Social Science* 501 (January): 8–25.

———. 1989b. "Poverty, Joblessness and the Social Transformation of the Inner City." In *Welfare Policy for the 1990s*, edited by David Ellwood and Phoebe Cottingham (pp. 70–102). Cambridge, Mass.: Harvard University Press.

Wallace, Roderick. 1989. "Homelessness, Contagious Destruction of Housing, and Municipal Service Cuts in New York City." *Environment and Planning* 21: 1585–1603.

Ward, David. 1989. *Poverty, Ethnicity, and the American City, 1840–1925*. Cambridge: Cambridge University Press.

Wilson, William Julius. 1987. *The Truly Disadvantaged: The Inner City, the Underclass and Public Policy*. Chicago: The University of Chicago Press.

Wilson, William Julius (ed.). 1989. "The Urban Underclass: Social Science Perspectives." *Annals of the American Academy of Political and Social Science* 501 (January).

Chapter 18

IMMIGRATION, MARGINALITY, AND FRENCH SOCIAL POLICY

Sophie Body-Gendrot

T O WHAT EXTENT is the French response to immigration, social policy, and hard-core urban problems different from other industrial countries? Unique historical and institutional factors mold the French perception of the nation, of the way foreigners are and should be integrated in society, and of what immigration policy should be. However, as is the case elsewhere in Europe, France is now at a turning point, and change seems imminent.

THE HISTORICAL CONTEXT

A Fictitious Entity

For a long time, the French perceived their country as ethnically homogeneous. In contrast to the experience of America, a nation that ritually celebrates its immigrants, in most works "in search of France," the contribution of foreigners to the building of the nation is forgotten. Instead, the centrality, continuity, and unitary identity of France is emphasized. Until recently, research on a variety of topics (the workplace, working-class history, the family, housing, and education) scarcely took account of the presence of a foreign-born population. Few French people have been aware of the extent to which immigrants and their children have left their marks on the cities in which they have settled and in turn helped shape the nation.

One explanation for this is that even though immigration began as early as the thirteenth century, the first substantial influx did not occur until the mid-nineteenth century—as the institutional and territorial formation of the nation-state was completed. Immigration remained, therefore, an external phenomenon for the French, despite its massive volume. In the nineteenth and early twentieth centuries, demographic concerns (French birthrates fell earlier than in other European countries) and economic and military interests (marked losses due to wars) inspired a policy of expanding immigration to compensate for labor shortages in agriculture and, later, in industry.

Yet immigration was not perceived as a fundamental element of the constitution of France for nineteenth century policymakers. The more central issue of majorities and minorities at that time involved the incorporation of culturally distinct regions, counties, and villages into one culturally united matrix. This integration was accomplished by the Third Republic (1975–1940) via powerful institutions—the school system, the army, the Catholic church, the welfare system, and political parties—which are today in crisis. Foreigners were not identified as such in these cultural spaces, which were themselves fragmented into tiny social enclosures (Weber 1976).

The migration of the peasantry to cities incorporated both French and foreigners, who then became part of a massive working-class proletariat that lived on the margins of the nation. At that time, the social cleavage was based on class; externality was not linked to nationality, partly because cultural differences were kept within the private sphere and were not politically recognized. Yet, according to the census, in 1931 France was the leading country of immigration in the world, with foreigners—mainly from neighboring countries and Eastern Europe—comprising 6.6 percent of the population (Noiriel 1988: 21).

Another characteristic of France was the state's denial of ethnicity. Although certain researchers see an "ethnicization" of foreign populations and emerging communities of "ethnic groups," the situation of immigrants in France has traditionally differed from that of other countries. In the United States, for instance, "ethnics" are American citizens who share the civic culture of the nation. As such, they lobby to defend their interests, and the political system frequently responds to their pressure. By contrast, the French constitution gives no legitimate recognition to intermediary bodies, such as ethnic groups or minorities, that might fragment the political community. The French Revolution proclaimed that the nation was "One and Indivisible," and, therefore, attempts to exert ethnic pressures have been discouraged. Ethnicity exists, of course, but it has been confined to the private sphere.

The notion of "republican integration" used by the French can be summarized by the words of the Duke of Clemont-Tonnere during the Revolution: "All should be given to Jews as individuals and all should be refused to Jews as a nation" (then meaning a social group). This is the basis of secularization (*laicité*) in France. At the end of the nineteenth century, the same assertion was made in the National Assembly regarding the Italians settled in France. The constitution of "communities" is considered as a "threat," and the individual integration of second generations is emphasized. (Recently, the State Council, the highest judicial jurisdiction, denied the recognition of the "Corsican people" within France.)

According to a French specialist on Islam, the French state has one particular idiosyncrasy: The public domain does not tolerate the emergence of cultural entities that might assume a partnership role with the state. Only individual functional skills are given credit, not ethnic identities. For the state, newly emerging minorities do not constitute a priori ethnicities or communities (Etienne 1987: 308). France shelters "aliens," "guestworkers," or "immigrés" but recognizes only French citizens after these individuals become naturalized citizens. Unlike the British or American experience, once citizenship is obtained, nothing legally and statistically distinguishes the former alien from the old-stock French. The state, in short, does not actively participate in racial or ethnic formation.

This preeminence of the French nation over communities is defended as a way to prevent the formation of "benignly neglected" ethnic ghettos. Yet those who cannot or do not want to submit themselves to the naturalization process become discrete and insular minorities in France with no effective political voice. No ethnic vote, no political machine, exists to foster their interests.

Realities Versus Principles

Of course, there have been exceptions to these rules. Groups have mobilized, relying upon their ethnicity, and have forced the state to take their specific demands into account. Specific programs, combining police and welfare functions in a policy of social and spatial segregation, were set up for the first "colonial workers" who came to work in France from Algeria before World War II in the 1920s. More recently, the case of the Harkis shows how the state has at times recognized ethnicity and implemented specific measures directed at immigrant groups.

Harkis are Algerians who sided with France during and after the colonial war of independence (1954–1962). Their number has been estimated at around 250,000. When decolonization occurred in 1962, large numbers of Harkis, considered traitors by other Algerians and abandoned by France, were tortured and massacred by the Algerian Liberation Front. Thousands nevertheless managed to escape to the south of France (despite prohibitions on their immigration from French authorities eager to prevent a mass exodus) and were settled in hastily established army camps.

Military authorities sought to ease the cultural transition, but little visibility was given to these operations because army personnel feared retaliation from nationalist Algerians living in France. In the next two decades, between a third and a half of the Harkis were able to leave the camps and assimilate into French society. But today around 100,000 Harkis remain marginalized, illiterate, and among the poorest people in France. More than two-thirds of these people are unemployed, and, among the young, 80 percent are school dropouts (Faivre 1990; *Le Monde* July 8, 1991). Between 4,000 and 5,000 thousand are still in the camps, an extreme example of social marginalization and exclusion.

During the summer of 1991, Harkis violently protested their official "oblivion," and the government hastily passed a number of special measures to speed their integration. That year was marked by a number of wider confrontations between immigrant youths and the police in an array of cities and by growing public and media pressures for more distinct immigrant-targeted measures. Faced with waning support for the tradition of republican principles of integration, the government created a Higher Council on Integration and appointed a

French secretary for integration—a former citizen of Togo, M. Kofi Yamgnane—within the Ministry of Social Affairs (renamed Social Affairs and Integration). As was the case in the United States in the 1880s, an increasingly politicized "immigration crisis" began to provoke significant institutional as well as ideological change (Body-Gendrot and Schain 1991).

NEO-RACISM IN FRANCE

In setting the context for this discussion, another distinctive feature of the French situation needs to be stressed. Racism in France is not based on theories of biological superiority, on the "cult of blood," or on a mystical Volksgeist, but on cultural distinctions (Balibar and Wallerstein 1988). This helps explain why, in a recent poll, 18 percent of French respondents expressed apprehensions about living near an African immigrant worker, but the number climbed to 31 percent in the case of an Arab immigrant worker. As Kristeva (1988) put it, there is hardly any country in the world where you feel more like a foreigner than in France, however well treated you are.

Cultural distinctions (based on class) are part of the social fabric of France. The idea, therefore, that French traditions and culture would have to "step down" in order to accept Islam as a component of French culture is unbearable for the more conservative elements of society, still eager to preserve "the universal cultural mission" of France. Such ideologies create hierarchies based on the degree to which various groups resist cultural assimilation. Hence, Moslems who require prayer rooms and mosques, hallal meats, and koranic scarves for girls find themselves looked down on to a much greater degree than francophone Africans (who were brought up in French missionary schools). The paradox is that the more immigrés become legally part of the French nation, the more racist stereotypes stigmatize their distinctiveness.

The French Social Policy of Integration

An important date in the development of French policy on immigration is 1974 (since then there has been a policy, even if its priorities have not been respected). That year there was consensus among all political parties about the need to close the doors of immigration. The timing was favorable: The previous year, Algeria had stopped the emigration of its workers in order to protest racist crimes occurring in France, and other major European countries had already adopted a restrictive policy. The defense for more restricted immigration policy was twofold. First, the living condition of immigrants settled in France needed to be improved (before new workers came in); and second, fiscal constraints required that immigration stop and illegal workers be expelled.

In reality, immigration was not completely stopped. To improve the living conditions of immigrants, family reunification was encouraged, and this led to a steady influx of family members from North Africa. Political refugees, students, and persons with specific skills required by the economy were also admitted. On the whole, an average of 30,000 foreigners still settle in France each year. Paradoxically, despite the policy changes of the 1970s, immigration issues have become more visible in the 1980s and 1990s, as the presence of numerous immigrant families in low-income neighborhoods on the periphery of cities has become more noticeable (Table 18.1). Rising birthrates in these areas (French family size averages 1.9 children per family, while foreign families have between three and four children per family), the problems of lone parents unable to adjust to the new cultural environment, and the visibility of polygamous African families (mostly from Senegal and not exceeding more than 15,000 persons), have made housing an important issue in political debates on immigration.

The Housing Issue in the 1980s and 1990s

In the mid-1970s, the government decided to set aside one-tenth of the tax on firms' assessments reserved for general housing construction for immigrant housing. The motive was concern for immigrants' welfare, as stated in the 1974 policy mentioned earlier. It was argued that the integration of foreign families would be accelerated by decent housing. Their situation urgently needed to be improved, and several targets were established.

In the 1970s, around 150,000 single foreign workers lived in hostels in poor conditions. More units were required, and physical improvements were needed in the existing units. Officials running the units were often viewed as hostile to the workers (if not openly racist), and the existing rules literally allowed little space for personal or collective expression. Workers who were not in hostels were frequently housed in private, single-room occupancy hotels run by unscrupulous landlords. To counteract this latter situation, the central government launched a campaign against slum landlord exploitation by levying heavy penalties on those who exploited immigrants. A slum clearance policy, accompanied by urban renewal of low-income neighborhoods, was also devised (similar to

Table 18.1 / Foreigners in France: 1931, 1968, 1975, and 1982[a] (in thousands)

	1931	1968	1975	1982	1990
All Foreigners	2,720	2,620	3,440	3,680	3,597
Percentage of Population	6.6	5.3	6.5	6.8	6.3
European Nationals	2,460	1,880	2,000	1,750	1,475
Percentage of Foreign Population	90	72	61	47	41
African Nationals	110	650	1,190	1,570	1,619
Percentage of Foreign Population	4	25	34	43	45
Other Nationalities	150	90	160	360	503
Percentage of Foreign Population	6	3	5	10	14

SOURCE: INSEE, Recensements de la population.

[a] Rounded numbers.

the Housing Law of 1949 in the United States). Finally, in line with the traditional French assimilation strategies, foreign families were dispersed in public social housing to avoid a concentration of foreigners that would result in ghettoization (Weil 1990).

These well-intentioned measures encountered numerous economic and structural obstacles. Soon after the decisions to improve the semipublic hostels, rent strikes erupted in protest of living conditions in the hostels, the lack of prayer rooms, the prevailing racism of the management, etc. Such strikes, the first signs that isolated migrant workers could become organized, had paradoxical effects. To reduce social tensions, priority was shifted to the improvement of existing units at the expense of much needed new construction for additional accommodations. Second, the control of slum landlords was not effectively executed at the local level. Few landlords have been prosecuted, and, when they have been, judges have been lenient in sentencing them. As is often the case, local bureaucrats have not been eager to carry out a policy that they did not help construct. Third, urban renewal came to mean, in effect, immigré removal. Immigrants were dispersed to overcrowded adjacent neighborhoods, which meant further environmental and social deterioration in these areas. While $100 million was provided for housing dispersal each year between 1975 and 1980, cutbacks in social housing at the same time led to public housing authorities filling the dwellings that the French (and upwardly mobile immigrant families) had deserted with poor immigrant families.

At the same time, the effects of the recessions and fiscal crises of the 1970s and 1980s were most deeply felt at the local level. Mayors, eager to reduce their welfare expenditures, began to refuse the settlement of new foreign families (and even of black French families from the Caribbean). Or they sent them to "reservation areas," their poorest "dump" estates where maintenance had been nonexistent for years due to unpaid rents (Body-Gendrot and Schaine 1991). As new decentralization laws were passed in 1982 and 1983, the powers of mayors were further enlarged, and they now control a major portion of public housing. They can refuse to allocate housing to a family if it is deemed too large for the size of the apartment or if the family income is too low. They also have more police functions concerning the settlement of foreigners, because they sign the various permits required to allow family members to stay temporarily with relatives. With such controls, mayors are in a position to identify illegal residents. Many even refuse marriage authorizations, if papers are deemed not in order.

Thus, these developments have had the effect of fragmenting French and foreign working classes—not so much in the workplace, but in poor neighborhoods. With de-industrialization and urban pauperization hitting the French, large cities have become the loci of transnational change, anticipating the major transformation of the nation-states and what some are already calling "the end of national societies" (Lapeyronnie 1993). Such change heightens tensions in social relations. In areas most adversely affected—that is, socially homogeneous areas with differentiated ethnic populations—people attempt to create symbolic distance within the space they live in.

In France, the resulting tensions and new hierarchies of social relations are also the product of privatization policies pursued in the aftermath of the oil crisis (Bourdieu et al. 1989). In housing, these policies were characterized by a marked shift away from general subsidies for the construction of social housing toward more targeted government support for the private sector. Particular stress was placed on encouraging the building of detached or semidetached family homes in areas where the most problematic and stigmatized high-rise projects were found.

Very soon, new tensions arose between the mobile segments of the French working class (which had access to these homes and wanted to change the image of their neighborhoods) and the multi-racial, poorer new families increasingly trapped in older, social housing. The proximity of the hopeful and the hopeless in tight spaces gives rise to violence—and each year reports of angry small homeowners shooting at noisy French or foreign youths make the newspaper headlines.

Table 18.2 gives an indication of the marked differences between the housing situation of French and immigrant households. While 56 percent of French households are homeowners, more than two-thirds of immigrant households are tenants, and around half of these are in social housing. Among North African immigrants, one in every two households is in social housing, compared with one in six among French households. Whereas the average dwelling space for each member of a French family is 33.5 square meters, an immigrant lives in 20 square meters and in the Parisian region in 16 square meters. In this region, 13.8 percent of single foreign workers live in overcrowded hostels or on work sites (Guillon 1995). Overcrowding and poor amenities are also marked features of the privately rented housing. Almost two-thirds of immigrants in private housing live in buildings more than 40 years old, and one-quarter have no personal sanitary facilities (compared with 11 percent of the French who live in privately rented housing).

Table 18.2 / Housing Situation, by Nationality

Nationality	Owners and Owners-to-be	Social Housing Tenants	Rental Market Tenants	SRO Tenants	Farmers, Shareholders	No Rent	Total
French	56.3	16.1	19.1	0.9	0.5	7.1	100
Total Immigrants	22.4	33.2	30.4	4.9	0.3	8.8	100
Portuguese	28.7	25.0	33.5	1.0	—	11.8	100
North African	9.9	49.3	27.3	7.2	—	6.3	100
Total Population	54.3	17.1	19.7	1.2	0.5	7.2	100

SOURCE: Taffin. *Economie et Statistiques*, p. 64.

Besides a heavy reliance on social housing, immigrants have come to be disproportionately dependent on other state interventions in the housing area. With per capita incomes of roughly one-half those of French households, immigrant households are typically heavily dependent on state housing allowances to cover part of their rent. Immigrant tenants in social housing receive, on average, a benefit amounting to 53 percent of their rent. Likewise, the very few immigrant families who become homeowners are often recipients of housing allowances and other linked state support (Taffin 1991: 65).

Efforts to avoid ghettoization have led to other forms of government intervention over the past decade under the auspices of the National Commission for the Social Development of Neighborhoods. Created in 1984 as a public-private partnership to upgrade the bleakest neighborhoods, the commission's aim has been to induce French families to return to such neighborhoods or not to leave them. But its actions have also embraced wide-ranging measures targeted, in effect, at the immigrant population. These included programs to combat school failure and delinquency as well as antiracist training. The commission has given rise to an Inter-Ministerial Delegation on Cities to coordinate the actions of a variety of ministries aimed at upgrading "sensitive" (working-class/immigrant) neighborhoods.

Despite such policies, including new forms of partnership in 1993, the profile of the targeted areas remains grim. In June 1991, a report on Parisian suburbs highlighted the multiple and cumulative nature of the disadvantages facing the poorest neighborhoods—old, poorly maintained buildings, abandoned industrial sites, and increasingly inadequate transportation, which left them isolated from the metropolis (Lelévrier and Noyé 1991). The ravages of unemployment and the crisis in public service delivery are now being compounded by a growing indebtedness among families, due in part to the recent efforts to spread homeownership. If the suburbs of the inner circles around Paris continue to attract upwardly mobile groups, growing poverty and exclusion seems an inescapable fate for those in the outer circles. A similar report for the Ministry of Urban Affairs reached the same conclusion in a survey of 400 targeted areas: Apart from schools, the lack of public services (police, justice, hospitals, employment agencies) was described as "flagrant" (*Libération* 10.9.91: 31).

Immigrants in the Labor Force

According to the Ministry of Labor, in 1990 there were 1.7 million immigrant workers in the French labor force, that is, 1 in every 14 actively employed persons in France is an immigrant. The major sources of immigrant labor are southern Europe (Portuguese, 27 percent; Spanish and Italians, 13 percent) and North Africa (Algerians, 16 percent; Moroccans, 11 percent). Two-thirds of all immigrant workers are male, more than half are aged under 55, and 68 percent had no high school education compared with 34 percent of French workers.

As Table 18.3 shows, immigrants have suffered disproportionately from unemployment during the 1980s, although there are marked variations by country

Table 18.3 / Unemployment Rates in France, by Nationality: 1980–1990

Year	Algerians	Moroccans	Spanish	Portuguese	All Foreigners	French
1980	15.2	9.1	7.0	5.6	9.3	5.9
1981	20.3	12.6	6.3	5.8	11.2	6.8
1982	25.1	17.7	10.4	7.5	14.9	7.4
1983	22.9	18.8	9.6	8.7	14.9	7.6
1984	24.5	24.7	10.2	8.8	16.7	9.0
1985	26.6	23.6	12.1	11.0	18.5	9.7
1986	24.3	22.9	11.7	11.9	18.7	9.7
1987	28.8	23.9	13.2	10.8	18.9	10.2
1988	27.3	26.6	14.5	10.6	18.6	9.6
1989	26.6	23.2	13.1	9.3	17.7	9.1
1990	28.1	23.3	9.6	8.3	16.8	8.7

SOURCE: Enquête Emploi, O. Marchand, *Economie et Statistiques* (April 1991).

of origin. The hardest hit have been North African workers, especially Algerians, whose overall levels of unemployment are almost three times those of French workers in 1992 (44 percent of them versus 32 percent of the French have been unemployed for more than a year). Portuguese workers, by contrast, were able to rely on their own local networks and were by 1990 better protected from unemployment than the French. Nonetheless, given their general lack of skills and mediocre chances of apprenticeship and training, teenagers of foreign origin are particularly vulnerable to unemployment (28 percent were unemployed in 1990). High unemployment rates are found too, among immigrant women: In 1990 one in four women was unemployed compared with one in seven male immigrants.

Table 18.4 shows that a distinct shift occurred during the 1980s in the kind of employment in which foreigners are found. Between 1983 and 1990 120,000

Table 18.4 / Job Changes in Service Industries: 1983–1989

	Change in Total Jobs	Change in Jobs Held by Immigrants	Immigrant Share of All Jobs in 1989
Services to Firms	+19	+7	7
Services to Individuals	+15	+32	5
Hotels and Restaurants	+6	+18	10
Transportation	−2	+19	5
Insurance	−3	−43	2
Retail Trade	−3	+15	5
Auto Repair	−12	−3	8
Wholesale Trade	−13	−19	4

SOURCE: Ministry of Labor, Labor Force Survey (1989).

industrial jobs disappeared in France; there are now fewer foreigners in manufacturing (36 percent) than in services (37.5 percent) (Maurin 1991). The profile of employed foreigners has moved closer to that of the French, although concentrations of foreigners in certain sectors, notably hotels and restaurants, are still visible.

This shift to tertiary jobs has been accompanied by a rapid growth in immigrant-owned businesses, trends that reflect the mutations of the postindustrial economy that favor the integration of immigrants into the economy via business creation. The steady decline in the number of unskilled jobs in the automobile and building industries, the penetration of foreigners into the service sector, and increasing unemployment, especially among women, are all factors that have increased the share of self-employed or non-wage work and of underground activities. The increasing emphasis on subcontracting and changes in patterns of consumption that have required "flexible" producers who can adjust quickly to diversified urban demands have also increased job opportunities among foreigners.

In 1982, there were 62,000 immigrant-owned businesses in France. By 1989, the number had climbed to 90,000, and businesses established by foreigners in 1989 accounted for 61 percent of all new owner-run firms in France (*Le Monde* Feb. 10, 1991). Included under this heading are the activities of new Asian entrepreneurs, who have made significant inroads in the computing and electronics fields, and of Italians, who have a quasi-monopoly in sections of the construction trade and organize import-export transactions. The Portuguese, who have traditionally been more interested in creating their own businesses than any other foreign group, have taken advantage of the huge public works projects started by President Mitterand to become contractors. As I have shown in previous research, the growing number of North Africans, including immigrant women, pursuing entrepreneurial strategies is also noticeable (Body-Gendrot 1992). In 1989, about 39,000 North Africans owned their own businesses.

Other immigrants—Africans, Turks, Lebanese, Poles, Pakistanis—are also engaging in entrepreneurship, but so far they have pursued individual strategies of mobility. Poles and Lebanese, for instance, have the same profile as French entrepreneurs and do not cater exclusively to their own communities. Africans, by contrast, mainly serve their community but still on a small scale and often in the underground economy (Pallida 1991). Although the government encourages these trends with grants and training schemes, the French have not yet come to recognize the significance to the economy of this burgeoning entrepreneurship.

Exclusion, the New Priority

The youth riots that occurred in 1981 in the suburbs of Lyon revealed the shortcomings of education and training policies for young people. What was to be done about those who were school dropouts? Several types of action were elaborated by the central government. Sixty-one local "missions" were created to deal with job training, health, and housing among those young people in trouble. In 1982, an "antiriot" campaign was launched in 11 regions. Some 10,000 teenagers were involved in employment schemes with Club Med (the teenagers were employed as temporary actors, clerks, and staff) and the Ministry of Defense and others.

In 1983, after a new racial crime in the suburbs of Lyon, a commission of investigation further documented the deficiencies of traditional institutions in helping foreigners become more integrated into French society: Problem children were concentrated in certain schools that had dismal performance records, the police were either invisible or brutal, judges were absent, and social workers were burnt out (Weil 1991: 263). A comprehensive delinquency prevention program was established in 21 areas, which relied on the cooperation of various local actors. Some of the results, particularly those relating to judiciary and police reform, were positive. Rates of incarceration were reduced, and police began to assume a more cooperative role in a number of neighborhoods. Yet deeper problems have persisted.

When the French Secretary of National Education set a new target for French students—that 80 percent should graduate with a baccalaureate degree—this was hailed as a major advance. However, the problem in France today concerns the 10–20 percent of students who will not get any diploma and who will feel *more* marginalized as more of their peers receive higher levels of training for the newly emerging labor market. The chances that dropouts will be integrated into the labor market will be further reduced. It is not surprising that youths of French stock and of foreign origin reveal deep feelings of frustration, despair, and hatred in interviews (Bourdieu 1991). The only way that they can resist "public oblivion" and exert pressure is to resort to violence, a violence conveyed on television screens each evening to a French audience that does not live near them and feels increasingly estranged from them (Body-Gendrot 1993).

French sociologist Alain Touraine says correctly that the major problem in France today comes neither from labor relations nor capitalist exploitation. "Today," he remarks, "the problem is not exploitation, it is exclusion. French society based on classes carried with it conflicts and inequality, the laissez faire society that France is becoming now carries ghettos within it. . . ." (Touraine 1991). The French labor movement mediated conflicts that went beyond production relations. It embraced the problems of immigrants' integration and marginalization. Today, the labor movement has collapsed, and the dual "socioeconomic" concept has fallen apart. Economies have become transnational. As a consequence, "social" logic takes on a new dimension: It gives a meaning to new identities based on the collective experience of exclusion. In France, this is not synonymous with racial discrimination, except in a broad sense when people mix together "Arab" versus French. In most of the 400 neighborhoods targeted as especially "sensitive," however, French working-class families live together with immigrant families and are frequently in the majority. The young people who express their frustration in burning, looting, and fighting with the police represent a mix of races and cultures.

Are all the funds, all the public policies that have been developed in France to assist decaying neighborhoods and drifting populations simply show windows? Probably not. They have the merit of slowing down the physical and social deterioration of these neighborhoods. They have benefited important proportions of French and foreign low-income residents who have begun to form embryonic middle-class enclaves. As for the young causing the unrest, their violence can be interpreted as nihilist and/or as a desire to become more integrated in French society. When they marched in the streets in the fall of 1990 to protest the lack of safety in schools, they were, in fact, asking the state to provide the order that would allow them to finish high school and prepare for the future. Violence targeted at property and stores might be seen as expressions of the same feelings. Sometimes, those who were marching and those who were breaking into buildings were brothers and sisters in the same family.

French policy is now at a turning point. National solidarity promoted by those at the top of the social order, which was the motor of progress in France for most of the postwar period, is in decline. In its place, the fragmentation of interest groups seems to prevail, and these changes are influencing state policies. "Compassion fatigue" among the general population is expressed in the success of the xenophobic National Front. If these tendencies persist, the feelings of marginality among the disenfranchised can only increase, and there can be no end to violence in the near future.

REFERENCES

Body-Gendrot, S. 1982. "Urban Social Movements in France and the U.S." In *Urban Policy Under Capitalism*, edited by Fainstein and Fainstein. Beverly Hills, Calif.: Sage.

———. 1993. *Ville et violence*. Paris: Presses Univeritairis de France.

———. 1993. "Pioneering Moslem Women in France." In *The Rise of Global Cities and Community Mobilizations*, edited by R. Fisher and J. Kling. Beverly Hills, Calif.: Sage.

Body-Gendrot, S., and M. Schain. 1991. "National Policies, Local Policies: A Comparative Analysis of the Development of Immigration Policies in France and in the United States." In *Immigration and Ethnicity in France and the U.S.*, edited by D. Horowitz. New York: New York University Press.

Bourdieu, P. 1991. "L'ordre des choses." *Actes de la recherche en sciences sociales*, December: 7–19.

Bourdieu, P., and Christin R. 1990. "La construction du marché. Le champ administratif et la production de la 'politique du logement.'" *Les Actes de la recherche en sciences sociales*, March: 81–82.

Etienne, B. 1987. *L'islamisma radical*. Paris: Hachette.

Faivre, M. 1990. "Une histoire douloureuse et controversée." *Hommes et Migrations* 1135: 13–20.

Guillon, M. 1995. *Etrangers et immigrés en Ile de France*. Paris: L'Harmattan.

Kristeva, J. 1988. *Etrangers à nous-mêmes*. Paris: Fayard.

Lapeyronnie, D. 1993. *L'individu et les minorités*. Paris, PU7.

Lebon, A. 1991. "Recensement de 1990: premiers résultats par nationalité." *Migrations-Société*, 3:16–17, July-October 7–14.

Lelévrier, C., and C. Noyé. 1991. "Quartiers en difficulté." *Regard sur 1'Ile de France*, INED, June 12.

Marchand, O. 1991. "Autant d'actifs éstrangers en 1990 qu'en 1980." *Economie et Statistiques* 242:31–38.

Marie, C. V. 1992. "Les étrangers dans l'espace économique français. Une nouvelle donne." *Revue européene des migrations internationales* (special comparative issue on French ethnic business) 8:1.

Maurin, E. 1991. "Les étrangers: une main d'oeuvre à part?" *Economie et Statistiques* 242:39–51.

Noiriel, G. 1988. *Le creuset français*. Paris: Le Seuil.

Pallida, S. 1992. "Des immigrés créateurs d'entreprises. Un apport à l'économie français." *Revue européene demigrations internationales* 8:1.

Sayad, A. 1991. "Immigration in France: An 'Exotic' Form of Poverty." In draft paper presented at Washington, D.C.: Joint Center for Political and Economic Studies.

Taffin, C. 1991. "Le logement des étrangers en France." *Economie et Statistiques* 242:63–68.

Touraine, A. 1991. "Face à l'exclusion." *Esprit*, February.

Tribalat, M. 1991. "Combien sont les Français d'origine étrangère?" INSEE, *Economie et Statistiques* 242:17–30.

Weber, E. (1976). *La fin des terroirs*. Paris: Le Seuil (transl. *Peasants into Frenchmen*).

Weil, P. 1991. *La France et ses étrangers (1930–1990)*. Paris: Calmann-Levy.

Chapter 19

POVERTY, IMMIGRATION, AND MINORITY GROUPS: POLICIES TOWARD MINORITIES IN GREAT BRITAIN

Colin Brown

BACKGROUND

Citizenship and History

THE ETHNIC MIX of minorities in the British population and the history of their development differ greatly from the makeup and evolution of minorities in the United States. Probably the most obvious difference is in the timing. Minority groups identifiable by skin color are relatively new to Great Britain, but other differences are equally important. To understand the present social position of the minorities, it is vital to comprehend why their families came to Britain and the conditions under which that migration occurred.

Great Britain owes much of its identity to migrants and invaders whose cultural and genealogical roots extend throughout continental Europe and the Middle East. But the principal ethnic minority groups today, the populations of Asian and Afro-Caribbean origins,[1] have been in the country for less than 50 years. Of course, there were small numbers of nonwhite residents before: Britain, with its eventful past as a center for maritime trade, slave dealing, and colonial expansion, has become home to people from many parts of the world over the centuries, and the untold history of blacks and Asians has only recently begun to emerge (Fryer 1984; Vadgama 1984; Visram 1986). But settlement of these groups in substantial numbers happened only after World War II. The preconditions for that migration stem from an earlier phase in Britain's history, the time of the British Empire. All of the populations living in the colonies were subjects of the British monarch, a concept that embraced the entire citizenship and nationality policy of the "mother country": There was no distinction between subjects, so an Indian living in Britain had the same rights as a native Londoner, and, crucially, there were no restrictions on immigration. When the

empire began to break up, and the newly independent countries began to develop their own nationality laws, Britain established a two-tier citizenship
throughout the Commonwealth (a political federation of Britain, its colonies,
and ex-colonies, still headed by the monarch) to preserve that universal status:
all inhabitants remained subjects of the crown despite their new nationalities,
and they therefore continued to have right of entry into Britain. This was the
1948 British Nationality Act. At the same time, the Act maintained freedom of
immigration within the Commonwealth and laid the legal basis for its later
control.

In the late 1940s and the 1950s, immigration began from the Caribbean and,
later, from the Indian subcontinent. The reason was the availability of jobs. The
postwar expansion of the British economy resulted in a serious labor shortage,
prompting employers to take on migrant workers, although immigrants were
seen as a last resort after the failed search for indigenous white workers. One
employer of the time explained this approach to recruitment: "The big influx of
labor began in 1954. At this time you couldn't get an armless, legless man never
mind an able-bodied one" (Rose et al. 1969). Another employer stated, "We
haven't got to the point where we have to take them on. I suppose if things
got bad enough we would "(Daniel 1968).

Most of the jobs available to newcomers were at the bottom of the pile. The
economic improvement allowed white workers to move up, leaving to immigrants the less pleasant jobs. Where new jobs were generated, immigrants were
again recruited to fill the lower-paid vacancies, especially in the public services.
But the legal status of immigrants was secure: As British subjects they had the
right to stay and settle. In some other European countries, labor shortages were
solved by importing labor in a different way, by giving migrant workers only a
temporary right to stay and few citizenship rights. When the economy slowed
down and jobs became more scarce, those countries were able to reduce their
migrant labor pool simply by withdrawing their right to stay, but in Britain
this could not happen. Later, in response to growing white hostility to black
settlement, laws were passed in Britain to reduce immigration, but the immigrants who did come mostly stayed.

The economic nature of this relationship between Britain and immigrants
from its former colonies is revealed in the geographical distribution of the minority ethnic communities, which are still concentrated mainly in the areas of original settlement. Very old black communities exist in the western ports of Liverpool and Bristol, a reminder of those cities' involvement in the slave trade,
but most of the more recent minority settlement has been in the major conurbations where workers were required.

Commonwealth migrants were mostly from the Indian subcontinent (India,
Pakistan, and Bangladesh) and the Caribbean (Jamaica, Trinidad and Tobago,
Barbados, other smaller islands, and Guyana, on the South American mainland), but there were smaller groups from Africa, the Mediterranean countries,
and Hong Kong. Other groups of migrant workers in Britain who are from
non-Commonwealth countries do not have the same rights as those from the

Commonwealth and must rely on work permits for their residence; although their numbers are much smaller, they comprise an important but hidden and poorly treated part of the labor force in London, working mainly in the domestic, hotel, and catering sectors.

Demography

The best information on the size and characteristics of the minority ethnic populations in Great Britain comes from the annual Labor Force Survey. England, Wales, and Scotland together form Great Britain, the geographical base for most of the data in this chapter. (Great Britain with Northern Ireland is termed the United Kingdom.) The total population of Great Britain is nearly 55 million. Minority ethnic groups comprise about 2½ million people, 4.7 percent of the total. This includes about half a million Afro-Caribbeans and 1⅓ million Asians. Overall, the minority population is growing: from under a million in the 1960s to 1½ million in the mid-1970s, and passing 2 million at the beginning of the 1980s (Table 19.1).

The minority population is relatively young, and over 40 percent of it is

Table 19.1 / Size and Composition of Ethnic Minority Population of Great Britain

(a) Ethnic Minority Population to Nearest 100,000

Year	Number	Percentage of Great Britain Population
1951	200,000	0.4
1961	500,000	1.0
1971	1,200,000	2.3
1981	2,100,000	3.9
1986/88	2,600,000	4.7

(b) Most Recent Estimates of Individual Groups

	Population Size 1986/88
Indian	787,000
Pakistani	482,000
Bangladeshi	108,000
Afro-Caribbean	495,000
African	112,000
Chinese	125,000
Arab	73,000
Other	163,000
Mixed	287,000

SOURCES: For section (a), Census and Labour Force Surveys. For section (b), Labour Force Survey.

British-born. Although the varied timing of the initial migration of the various ethnic groups means that their age patterns are complex, they all differ considerably from the white population in the proportions of elderly people and children among them (Tables 19.2 and 19.3). One in five whites is over age 60, compared with only 1 in 20 among the minorities, and only 18 percent of whites are aged under 15, compared with 32 percent among the minorities. Two other notable features in the age distributions are the evidence of the earlier migration of Afro-Caribbeans (the relatively large population aged over 44) and the very large proportion of children (over 40 percent) among the Pakistanis and Bangladeshis.

Traditionally, men predominate in migrant worker populations. This was at first the case for the Commonwealth immigrants in Britain (although less so for Afro-Caribbeans than for Asians), but now there is overall parity. Only among the Bangladeshis (the most recent immigrant community) and the African and Arab groups is there still a noticeable imbalance.

Family size and structure also differ among the minorities. Overall, minority household sizes are larger and more likely to comprise horizontally or vertically extended families, especially among Asians (Table 19.3). As more Asian people become elderly, the vertically extended household is likely to become even more common. (Abandonment of elderly people to live on their own is traditionally frowned upon among Asians.) Among Afro-Caribbeans there is a substantial proportion of lone-parent families, mostly headed by women. Lone parenthood is relatively common in the Caribbean (although often followed by marriage later in life) but was less typical among blacks in Britain in earlier days when, in the absence of community and family networks to provide support and childcare, the nuclear family was a refuge. Later, with more established communities, lone parenthood again began to increase. Nearly one in five Afro-Caribbean households is a lone-parent family with dependent children—nearly a third of all Afro-Caribbean families with children.

Table 19.2 / Age Distribution of White and Minority Groups

	Percent					
	White	Minority	Afro-Caribbean	Indian	Pakistani	Bangladeshi
Under Age 5	6	12	10	11	15	20
5–14	12	20	14	18	26	27
15–24	15	20	24	19	19	16
25–34	14	18	16	20	16	15
35–44	14	12	9	14	10	8
45–59	17	13	20	14	11	13
60+	21	5	7	5	2	2

SOURCE: Labour Force Survey, 1986–1988.

Table 19.3 / Household Size and Type, by Ethnic Group

	White	Afro-Caribbean	Indian	Pakistani	Bangladeshi
Average Household Size (1985/87)	2.5	2.7	3.9	4.6	5.2
Percentage of Households with Children (1982)	31	57	67	83	82
Percentage of Lone-Parent Households (1982)	3	18	4	3	7
Percentage of Pensioner-Only Households (1982)	29	2	3	a	a
Percentage of Extended Households (1982)	4	8	18	21	18

SOURCES: Labour Force Surveys and Policy Studies Institute Surveys.

[a] Denotes less than 0.5 percent.

Geography

Members of the minority population live mainly in urban areas around London and other major cities, with the metropolitan counties[2] accounting for 70 percent of minorities but only 23 percent of the general population. London and the West Midlands (around Birmingham) are the areas most heavily populated by minorities. Within cities the residential patterns of minorities are highly clustered: the closer the geographical focus, the greater the degree of segregation observed, both between minorities and whites and between different minority groups. However, considerable numbers of black and Asian people live away from the main centers of settlement: Those in the thin tail of the geographical distribution are relatively isolated from their communities, and there are observable differences in their employment and housing conditions.

The 1982 Policy Studies Institute (PSI) survey suggested that that year the residential pattern of the minority communities in Britain was very similar in many ways to that of earlier years, with surprisingly little net interurban movement away from the original patterns of settlement, and very slow net intraurban movement. Further evidence of a generally stable geographical distribution of ethnic minority population comes from research linking census returns from 1971 and 1981, despite a relatively high individual rate of movement of Asian households (Robinson 1991). Natural growth and continued immigration have generally led to the consolidation of geographical communities and to local population densities of minority groups. Even so, ethnic residential concentrations are rarely very high, and although streets and groups of streets may have a majority of Afro-Caribbean or Asian households, for example, in most cases the minorities are correctly described as minorities at both local and national levels.

In the general population the trends in internal migration have been an overall drift to the south, a substantial move away from the cities, and, paradoxically, gentrification of city centers (Robinson 1991). This last factor has augmented the social complexity of British cities: The inner areas of London, for example, which account for over one-fifth of Britain's ethnic minorities, are extremely mixed in terms of both class and race. Although some of the larger public housing developments can easily be recognized as the territory of the poor, they are rarely far from streets of owner-occupied houses with high market values. There is little evidence of a drift away from cities by ethnic minorities, although some residential spread into suburban areas, particularly among Asians, is expected to be visible when the results of the 1991 census are analyzed in detail.

At the individual level, there is evidence of relatively high rates of mobility by Asian families, but not by Afro-Caribbean families. One reason for this difference is the lack of an easy mechanism in public housing for movement between different areas; Asians, who are predominantly owner-occupiers, can buy and sell on the private housing market, whereas many Afro-Caribbeans are council tenants and find it hard to move.

Jobs and Unemployment

Manual labor predominated in the employment profile of the early immigrants. In the mid-1960s, 9 out of 10 immigrant workers were in blue-collar jobs, irrespective of whether they had been manual or nonmanual workers before migration (Daniel 1968). They were drawn into some sectors of the economy more than others, especially into manufacturing, transport and communications, and the health service. Individual industries tended to recruit migrants from particular groups, so ethnic concentrations intensified. For example, Asian men were more likely than Afro-Caribbean men to have jobs in industrial manufacturing, while the reverse was true in public transport. These patterns have left a deep stamp on the labor market position of ethnic minorities, and, although the picture today is more complicated, it is easy to see how job opportunities for blacks and Asians have continued to be limited by these entrenched inequalities and by racial discrimination.

Employment patterns of black and Asian people in Britain shifted during the 1980s but have not converged with those of whites, and the extent and direction of the changes have been limited both by the inequalities of the original migrant recruitment and by persistent racism. These complex changes are discussed next under four headings: unemployment, self-employment, job levels, and racial discrimination.

Unemployment

The major feature of ethnic minority experience in the labor market in the past decade has been mass unemployment: The overall jobless rate of minorities continued to climb during the early 1980s, passing the 20 percent mark in 1983 and not falling below it again until 1987 (Table 19.4). The rise in unemployment among minority workers is always greater than among the rest of the workforce, and during the period the overall rate for minorities almost doubled the white rate. Separate comparisons of unemployment rates among people with particu-

Table 19.4 / Unemployment Rate, by Ethnic Group

Year	Whites	Ethnic Minorities
1981	9.5	16.7
1983	11.2	20.9
1984	11.4	21.4
1985	10.9	20.7
1986	10.8	20.0
1987	10.5	17.1
1988	8.5	13.5
1989	6.9	12.0

	White	Afro-Caribbean	Indian	Pakistani/ Bangladeshi
Men, 1989	6.9	15.1	9.9	21.4
Women, 1989	6.8	13.6	8.6	[a]

SOURCE: Labour Force Survey.

[a]Denotes data not available.

lar levels of qualifications have shown that the ethnic differences cannot be explained by educational differences—in fact, the unemployment gap between whites and minorities is greater among people with higher qualifications. In some respects the areas inhabited by black and Asian people appear to affect their employability, in that many live in locations high in local unemployment. But a comparison of the regional distribution of whites and minorities leaves the conclusion that, overall, the geographical differences are as likely to favor the minorities as to disadvantage them. Even at a local level, the high-unemployment districts are often within the same "travel-to-work areas" as districts with much lower unemployment—suggesting that ethnic minorities live among other disadvantaged people, rather than a simple causal relationship between their residential location and their high unemployment.

Behind the overall unemployment rate for minorities have been some important differences between ethnic groups and among age groups. The unemployment rate among Afro-Caribbeans and among Pakistanis and Bangladeshis has been much higher than among Indians; and for young people the rate has been much higher than for older people. Among Afro-Caribbeans aged 16–24, unemployment exceeded 30 percent for a time, and it exceeded 40 percent among Pakistanis and Bangladeshis in that age group.

After 1986, unemployment began to fall as the job supply improved, and the gap between whites and minorities began to close. This was partly the result of a general economic improvement in Britain, and also partly because of the country's changing population structure: The "demographic downturn" means that the number of 16–19-year-olds available for employment will fall by nearly 600,000 between 1987 and 1995. The kinds of jobs that young, inexperienced people would usually fill are the same as those to which ethnic minorities have been recruited, and the shortage of workers in this part of the market benefits the ethnic minorities—in numbers of jobs, but not necessarily in the quality of jobs.

Self-Employment

Self-employment has increased considerably among Asians since the mid-1970s. Now about a quarter of economically active Indian men in Britain are self-employed, almost double the proportion for white men. The figure for Pakistanis and Bangladeshis (17 percent) is less startling but is still higher than average. By contrast, among Afro-Caribbeans the proportion of self-employed is lower than average.

British Asian business development is noteworthy because much of its success is the result of two factors: first, the strong network of social, religious, economic, and family ties within the Asian communities; and second, the ability of the self-employed to circumvent the impediments that face minority workers in mainstream employment. Racial discrimination is largely avoided, not confronted. And in many areas the Asian business community has reached the critical mass required to generate its own employment market, insulating ordinary employees from racial discrimination. In this way a "marginal" economic existence has been transformed into an asset rather than a disadvantage; the excluded have beaten an exclusive path to progress.

Job Levels

The large number of unemployed minorities, as well as the relatively large group of self-employed Asians, make it very difficult to see trends in the gap between the job levels of white and minority workers. The high unemployment rate interferes with the comparisons over time because it has affected some types of jobs more than others: Were it not for the job losses, many unemployed persons would appear in the tables in lower-level occupations, so their "removal" has artificially inflated the percentage of individuals in better jobs. The self-employed also cause problems, because in the available statistics they are included with employees and are classed in the top occupational categories; therefore, the move into self-employment raises the proportion of Asians in "top jobs" by definition and might be misinterpreted as evidence of better treatment of Asians in society at large and at the hands of white employers. Thus, perversely, two processes involving minorities moving outside the mainstream of employment (voluntarily or involuntarily) can give the impression that minorities are becoming more closely integrated into the mainstream. Among those who are employed, there has been a drift upward in the average job levels of blacks and Asians over the 1980s. The general shift away from manufacturing and toward services is particularly apparent in the changing industrial profile of minority workers. The improvement in job levels among employees is largely due to changes in the job patterns of young people. Overall, however, the gap between white and minority job levels is still large: Among black and Asian workers, there is still a disproportionately large number of semiskilled and unskilled manual workers.

Racial Discrimination

There was no evidence during the 1980s that discrimination decreased in Great Britain. Results of repeat bogus application trials by the Policy Studies Institute (PSI) in 1984 and 1985 in London, Birmingham, and Manchester indicated that the minimum level of employer discrimination was no lower than in 1973 and 1974 (Brown and Gay 1985; McIntosh and Smith 1974). In this study at least one-third of private employers were found to discriminate against Asian applicants, Afro-Caribbean applicants, or both. A less systematic but more dramatic illustration of racial discrimination was provided in a series of British Broadcasting Corporation (BBC) Television programs in 1988, relating the experiences of two men, one black and one white, searching for work and accommodation in Bristol. Using hidden cameras and microphones, the program revealed discrimination on a wide scale. In 1990 a set of application tests conducted by *Today* newspaper also demonstrated that discrimination was still common. In addition to these reports of direct, deliberate discrimination, research in the late 1980s and in 1990 detailed the disadvantages still suffered by ethnic minorities in employment because of both direct and indirect discrimination. Such discrimination is of particular concern because it acts to block entry into and progress within higher-paying professional occupations. Equally worrying is evidence that young blacks and Asians have been excluded from the parts of government training programs that are most likely to lead to permanent employment, and also have been diverted by the Careers Service away from employers that choose to exclude minorities (Cross and Smith 1987; Wrench 1990). At all levels of employment, therefore, there is evidence of continuing widespread discrimination.

The 1982 PSI survey showed that the overall impact of the employment differences between whites and minorities resulted in a male earnings differential of 10–15 percent; among women the results were more complicated, suggesting a much smaller differential. Local surveys and the small sample of minority group members in the annual General Household Survey have been used by economists to carry out multivariate analyses of earnings differentials (Blackaby 1986; Chiswick 1980; Dex 1986; McCormick 1986; McNabb and Psacharopoulos 1981; Stewart 1983). Their findings have generally shown that differentials increase with educational attainment. There is also evidence that among younger people, the differentials are falling, although it should be noted that these analyses take no account of the large ethnic differences in the numbers now jobless; these differences tend artificially to inflate the quality of minority jobs.

/   593

Household Income from Earnings

Scant research has been conducted on household incomes of minority ethnic groups in Britain, and there has been no attempt to estimate and compare levels of poverty in the different communities. Again, the most detailed information comes from the 1982 PSI survey (despite the fact that its analysis of household income was very limited), which confirmed that the poorer jobs and higher unemployment rates of ethnic minorities resulted in comparatively large proportions of families on low earned incomes and relying on state benefits.

To compare the white and minority populations irrespective of age is unhelpful, because the huge ethnic difference in the proportion of retired people distorts the comparison of households lacking a wage earner. However, if the comparison excludes households in which all members are above retirement age, it can be seen that there are more households without a wage earner among minorities than among whites, principally because of minorities' greater rates of unemployment (Table 19.5). In 1982, 14 percent of non-elderly white households lacked a wage earner, whereas the figures for Afro-Caribbean and Asian households were 21 percent and 18 percent, respectively. Because minority households tend to be larger than white households, the impact of joblessness is exacerbated. In the study, the overall number of dependents per earner within the minority groups was much higher than among whites: 50 percent higher for Afro-Caribbeans and over 100 percent higher for Asians. If these findings are combined with the ethnic differentials in earnings, one sees how much less is available to each person in minority households. Table 19.5 illustrates, for households with at least one wage earner, the impact of the different wage levels and household sizes. For clarity it gives separate figures for different types of families. For three out of the four family types, the income available to each person is between 14 and 40 percent lower in the minority groups than

Table 19.5 / Support from Earned Income, by Ethnic Group in Great Britain: 1982

	White	Afro-Caribbean	Asian
Percentage of Households without any Earners	14	21	18
Number of Dependents per Earner	1.2	1.8	2.7
Median Weekly Earnings Divided by average household size (£ per person)[a]			
Lone parents	20	24	21
Extended households	46	37	27
Others with children	37	32	27
Adults without children	59	51	50

SOURCE: Policy Studies Institute Survey, 1982.

NOTE: Table excludes pensioner-only households.

[a] Households with at least one earner.

in the white group. The one exception is the lone-parent family, because a larger proportion of ethnic minority lone mothers work full-time rather than part-time and, therefore, bring home a larger wage. Overall, about half of all lone parents, irrespective of ethnic group, have some type of job.

Education and Training

Overall, the educational qualifications of the minority populations are lower than those of whites, but the patterns are complex: There are differences between generations (especially between the immigrant and British-born cohorts) and gender. In general, a substantial minority of Asian people speak English poorly, although this is strongly related to age and to whether their early schooling was in Britain or abroad. Nearly all Asians born in Britain speak English fluently, usually as one of several languages.

Table 19.6 gives an indication of the differences in qualification among people of working age. Pakistanis and Bangladeshis stand out, along with Afro-Caribbean men, as relatively poorly qualified. Note that among the Indian population there is a wide spread of qualification levels: Although the proportion of people without qualifications is larger than among whites, the proportion with substantial qualifications is also high. From the start of the migration, the Indian group has spanned a wider range of social backgrounds than the other minority groups.

Table 19.6 / Education Qualifications, by Ethnic Group

	White	Afro-Caribbean	Indian	Pakistani/ Bangladeshi
Percentage with No Qualifications				
Men				
Aged 16–24	25	32	17	46
Aged 24–44	28	38	35	63
Aged 45–64	46	68	53	72
Women				
Aged 16–24	23	21	24	63
Aged 25–44	39	36	49	78
Aged 45–59	63	74	74	91
Percentage with Higher Qualifications (above A level)				
Men				
Aged 16–64	14	5	19	8
Women				
Aged 16–59	12	12	12	4

SOURCE: Labour Force Survey, 1985–1987.

Educational research has focused on the continuing ethnic differences in examination results, with particular attention paid to the underachievement of Afro-Caribbean pupils. However, recent research suggests that a convergence of results has begun. Even the earlier differences are now seen to be less dramatic than they appeared at first, because minority pupils with poor qualifications often stayed on after the minimum school-leaving age or took part-time education courses to enhance their skills. Recent research has also shown that differences between schools outweigh ethnic differences within schools by a substantial factor, suggesting that the poor overall performance of blacks is largely the result of school differences.

The education system in Britain is undergoing major changes including a restructuring of the examination system and of the national core curriculum. Schools are being given the right to opt out of local government control and to become self-governing. There is a danger that this move may lead to greater social polarization within education, favoring parents who are better able to work the system. Already the drive toward "parental choice" has led some white parents to challenge local education authorities by trying to move their children to all-white schools, arguing their case on cultural and racial grounds. So far, they have succeeded, with encouragement from the press and, to a degree, from the government.

Britain has a set of ever-changing skills training programs, spawned by the recent years of high unemployment and the mismatch between the supply and demand of skills sought by employers. The programs, organized by the government's Training Agency, have been of great importance to those leaving school at the end of the normal compulsory period. The most prominent has been the Youth Training Scheme (YTS), established in 1983 to provide 1–2 years' on-the-job training for 16- and 17-year-olds; by 1990 over 2 million young people had completed the YTS. The program is now revised to increase the emphasis on providing formal training. (The YTS was previously criticized as being a vehicle that allowed employers to exploit cheap sources of labor.) There is evidence that ethnic minority school leavers have been discriminated against in the administration of the YTS (Cross and Smith 1987). Local management of Training Agency programs is being transferred to new Training and Enterprise Councils (TECs), business-led bodies whose role also includes building links between education and industry and business training programs; there will be 82 TECs nationwide.

Housing

Two forms of housing dominate in Britain: Most homes are owner-occupied or rented from the local governing body, and there is a strong relationship between tenure group and income. Private tenancy is now a marginal tenure, accounting for less than 10 percent of dwellings and occupied by people at the top and the bottom of the income ladder and by those needing temporary

Table 19.7 / Distribution of Housing Arrangements, by Ethnic Group in Great Britain: 1983–1985

	Percent				
	White	Afro-Caribbean	Indian	Pakistani	Bangladeshi
Owner-Occupied	59	39	77	74	35
Council-Rented	28	47	11	16	45
Other	12	13	11	9	19
Total	100	100	100	100	100

SOURCE: Labour Force Survey.

accommodation. Within this pattern, the ethnic minority groups have diverse housing characteristics of their own (see Table 19.7).

In the past, tenure patterns among minorities have been linked to income to a lesser extent than among the general population, with many poor Asian households buying cheap (in those days), run-down properties in the inner areas. Now the relationship between income and tenure is becoming more conventional; for example, over four-fifths of black lone parents live in public housing. As mentioned previously, one special problem associated with council housing is its restriction on labor mobility. Once housed, a tenant faces considerable difficulties if he or she needs to move across the boundaries of local authorities, because the authorities are administratively separate. Even to move to another part of London is a complex and lengthy process.

The quality of housing within the tenure sectors has been found to be consistently lower among minorities—in terms of age, type of dwelling, amenities, and number of persons per room. The gap is closing, however; over the years, British housing standards have shown such large overall improvements that in absolute terms there has been a substantial increase in the quality of minority housing.

Research has shown that blacks and Asians still face considerable discrimination in all sectors of housing. But the housing world has seen other changes in the last few years that also have implications for the minorities. Government policy is changing the role of the council sector: Dwellings are being sold to tenants at a discount, and the stock is not being replaced, thus severely restricting the ability of local authorities to maintain a supply of good properties to let. During the 1980s over a million council homes were sold, and between 1971 and 1986 the council sector shrank from 31 percent of all dwellings in Britain to 26 percent. For new households who are not in a special needs category, such as the homeless, there is little hope of obtaining a council tenancy, and even the homeless are often put into temporary accommodation in poor hotels. In the owner-occupied sector, housing prices rocketed during the 1980s, making it very difficult for people to become first-time buyers even with a high income: Between 1979 and 1989 average housing prices almost trebled nationally, and in London, where prices were already higher, the increase was even greater. Families already on the ladder of home ownership have been relatively safe from the problems caused by this increase (unless they want to move to London), but young people are finding accommodations increasingly hard to find. Homelessness is increasing, with the problem especially severe in London. At present, the impact of this development on blacks and Asians is hard to assess because of a lack of official statistics. The fact that both main housing sectors are now so difficult to enter, and are becoming harder to move within, must be affecting so young a population. From the information available, we know that in London the rate of homelessness among minorities is four times higher than among whites (Mullins 1990).

POLICY RESPONSES TO RACIAL DISCRIMINATION

From the mid-1960s to the mid-1970s, legal moves were made to control racial discrimination in Great Britain. Three Race Relations Acts progressively outlawed discrimination and established the mechanisms and institutions of enforcement. The first Act, passed in 1965, did not cover employment or housing, both of which were addressed in the second Act, in 1968. The third Act, passed in 1976, changed the basis of enforcement. Until then, the procedure for handling discrimination complaints was a system of conciliating aggrieved parties handled by a central agency, the Race Relations Board. The new Act enabled individuals to take cases of alleged discrimination to industrial tribunals or county courts to seek damages and replaced the Race Relations Board (and another body, the Community Relations Commission, which had worked in other ways to foster good race relations) with the Commission for Racial Equality (CRE). The CRE assisted individual complainants with litigation and was also given powers to act as an enforcement agency by mounting formal anti-discrimination investigations and issuing nondiscrimination notices to those found in breach of the act. The 1976 Act also outlawed policies and practices that were discriminatory in outcome, regardless of their formulation and original intent; therefore, the grounds for action included both direct and indirect discrimination.

All three acts were products of Labor administrations, responding in part to liberal and left-wing pressure to balance the immigration injustices on non-white populations with moves to reduce the by then obvious systems of discrimination and segregation. Politicians felt that the base on which the Race Relations Acts rested was the end of immigration; they believed public support for (or, more accurately, public acquiescence to) legal measures to promote racial justice could only be maintained by assuring white people that "colored" immigration would be firmly controlled. The formula had such appeal that it gained broad support in Parliament and in the country, but at its heart was the familiar notion that immigrants were undesirable if they were not white. The government's challenge to racism within Britain's borders, therefore, was built on an official endorsement of racism at those borders. The significance of this contradiction has been more than formal: For most of the white population, the primary (and most popular) element of the policy has been the ending of nonwhite immigration, a strategy that conforms with the opinion that black and Asian people cause problems by their mere presence in the country. The principal strength that antidiscrimination legislation can draw from the twin-plank policy is pragmatic (equality in exchange for an end to immigration) rather than moral, because moral opposition to racism has so clearly been abandoned in the immigration plank of the policy.

The impact of the Race Relations Acts on discrimination, although at first encouraging, has in the long term been disappointing. Openly discriminatory advertisements disappeared after the 1965 and 1968 acts, and a public mood that discrimination was no longer acceptable did reduce its extent (possibly helped by an unrealistic alarm about the powers of the Race Relations Board); the second PEP study (Smith 1977) revealed evidence of a general reduction. But it was not the beginning of a steady erosion: Later research has indicated that direct discrimination has become set at a lower but still substantial level. The Commission for Racial Equality has for several years been calling for changes in the law to make it easier to enforce both by individuals and the Commission itself.

The 1976 Race Relations Act contains provisions for positive action, but these are limited when compared with those operating in the United States. Specially designated training bodies may offer training to minorities who are underrepresented in a particular type of work; employers may also provide encouragement and training to such minorities; employers may recruit people from a specific ethnic group if they are providing welfare services to that group; and arrangements can be made to help minorities with special needs gain access to services. These positive action provisions have been used most widely by local authorities.

GEOGRAPHICALLY BASED POLICY RESPONSES TO DEPRIVATION AND RACIAL INEQUALITY

A number of public policy initiatives over the past 25 years have aimed resources at deprivation in the inner cities. In many respects this would appear to be the only area in which needs of minority groups have been incorporated into mainstream policy considerations. In fact, however, the process has worked the other way around: Much of the thinking behind these initiatives has race as its starting point and has used geography as a politically acceptable proxy for race because of fears about objections to "reverse discrimination." Unfortunately, in practice the geographical focus tends to take over in substance as well as in appearance.

The Urban Programme was established in 1968, largely in response to political disquiet about race relations, although its administration was area based rather than targeted toward ethnic groups. It provided funds to help local authorities with educational and social projects in inner-city areas; the program had some initial impetus to address racial disadvantage, but this fizzled out, and in the first decade of the program's existence only 5 percent of its funds were devoted to projects explicitly aimed at reducing racial inequality. A reorganization of the program in the late 1970s targeted selected authorities for special attention. Again, racial disadvantage was intended to be on the agenda, but in practice few projects benefited minorities directly. Only in the wake of urban unrest in 1980 and 1981 was there a serious redirection of funds toward areas and projects helpful to minorities, and during the first half of the 1980s the share of the expanding Urban Programme resources going to minority projects rose from 3 percent to 15 percent; moreover, the large increase in the scale of the general program to over £300 million in public funding per year had an indirect beneficial impact on minorities, as intended. More recent developments, however, in which policy has been to shift the balance away from social projects to economic development projects, have been accompanied by a reduction in the ethnic contribution to 11 percent in 1988 and 1989.

The other important area-based policy comes from Section 11 of the 1966 Local Government Act. This section of the act originally provided for a subsidy for extra staff in local authorities where the numbers of resident Commonwealth immigrants necessitated special provisions. The policy therefore had an explicit ethnic focus. Local authorities had to apply to the Home Office, arguing their case for extra posts. By the end of the 1980s, Section 11 was under attack from many quarters, for several reasons. Some authorities failed to apply for funds that they should have claimed from the central government; others made successful claims but failed to direct the funds toward the needs of minority groups; others used the funds for race relations work that technically fell outside the terms of Section 11; and the "immigrant" threshold for determining eligibility for funding was agreed to be out of date, because by then so many ethnic minorities were British-born. Consequently, in 1988 the Home Office conducted a review of Section 11 and established new arrangements (effective in October 1991) for funding projects in local authorities with substantial minority populations (Home Office 1988, 1990).

It is not yet clear what the changes will mean in the lives of ethnic minorities to whom the funding is ultimately directed. The government states that the purpose of Section 11 is "to meet certain needs particular to ethnic minorities that prevent full participation in the mainstream of national life. Barriers to opportunity arise in a number of areas, particularly through differences of language in educational attainment, and through economic, social and cultural differences" (Home Office 1990). The policy is therefore aimed at problems caused by ethnic difference rather than discrimination. Most of the money will continue to be spent on education, but the aims will be to improve skills, confidence, and motivation, with particular attention to English language and mathematics skills. Grants will no longer be used for projects that foster cultural, artistic, or linguistic traditions, and there will be no funding of mother-tongue teaching except as part of programs pursuing the main policy objectives. Projects will make more use of the voluntary sector and ethnic self-help groups, particularly in the area of social services. Other projects will be encouraged in the areas of employment training and business development, and, in a radical departure, the government will accept Section 11 applications directly from local Training and Enterprise Councils, rather than through local authorities—a move that will divert some of the funding away from local political control, to be administered by business-led bodies instead.

Section 11 is the most substantial ethnically targeted public program, funding some 12,000 posts, with total funding in at about £100 million per year. The 1988 Home Office review estimated that the new arrangements might reduce costs by a quarter over the ensuing 5 years and suggested that this money could be used either for other Section 11 projects or simply to make the whole scheme cheaper.

BRITISH ETHNIC MINORITIES IN THE 1990s

Clearly the 1990s will be a period of major change for British ethnic minorities. Each of the following issues needs to be taken into account when one considers what the future will bring these populations and what chances there are for lessening racial inequality.

The Aging of the Minority Population

Until recently a very small percentage of the minority population was over retirement age. Now the picture is changing rapidly. Although the minorities' average age will remain younger than the national average for years to come, the cohort of first-generation immigrants is now reaching retirement, and a considerable number of elderly dependent relatives have come to live with their minority families in Britain. Pensioners are the poorest section of the population nationally, and it is possible that this income disadvantage will be compounded with racial disadvantage and discrimination to make this a doubly deprived group.

Changes in Education

As outlined earlier, both the educational characteristics of the minority populations and the structure of the British education system are experiencing considerable change. Young blacks and Asians are coming to the labor market better equipped than ever before to compete for jobs, although it is still true that the return on personal educational investment is lower for them than for whites. The consequences of the current educational reforms for minorities can only be speculated on, both because so many aspects of the system are being modified simultaneously and government directives on the practical implementation of those reforms are being announced so frequently that it is difficult to predict the impact of the whole package. As indicated earlier, moves to give greater parental choice over schools might in some ways help minority pupils, but one consequence may be a drift toward racially segregated schooling.

Further Integration with Europe

The implementation of the Single European Act in 1993 and the creation of the new European Union, following the Maastricht Treaty, involve three important developments for Britain's minorities. First, labor mobility within the European labor market is likely to increase, the consequences of which are unclear. (Will it mean greater opportunities on mainland Europe or increasing competition in Britain from new migrant workers?) Second, the drive toward homogeneity of European legislation and immigration policy has important political implications. "Equal opportunity" in the European political arena usually means women's rights, race is seldom mentioned, and hardly any countries have operative laws to combat racial discrimination. This chapter has expressed a fairly critical view of British policy, but it should be noted that British legislation takes a clear stand against racial discrimination, and there must be some anxiety as to whether closer European ties will spread these laws or dilute their operation. Third, free movement within Europe means that borders of Europe will become hardened to immigration. There are already indications that the political base for unity between the disparate European peoples may be a new hostility toward the southern border with Islam.

Political Representation of Minority Groups

In the 1980s Asians and blacks were for the first time in Great Britain elected in numbers to serve on local councils. Four were elected to the national parliament in 1987 and eight in 1991. These were political breakthroughs. In the 1990s the trend can be expected to continue, although the extent to which policies and practices have changed as a result of the work of these politicians is not clear. Certainly they have been able to raise the profile of race issues at both the local and national levels.

Continued Development of Ethnic Business

The development of the Asian business community was extraordinary during the late 1970s and 1980s. Its level of activity is now self-sustaining and able to offer employment to others in the community. There are some signs of business development within the Afro-Caribbean community, but these are starting from a low base, with a lower-than-average self-employment rate. There can be little doubt that Asian business will be an important element in the development of future prospects for Asian workers; whether the same will be true for Afro-Caribbeans remains to be seen.

Changes in Demand for Labor

Ethnic minorities in Britain are particularly vulnerable to the vicissitudes of the economy. Increases and decreases in labor demand produce wild swings in black and Asian unemployment rates, and during periods of high unemployment minority workers are especially vulnerable to racial discrimination, simply because employers have more applicants to choose from. The fall in both white and minority unemployment rates in the late 1980s seemed to herald an improvement in the job market, but the employment prospects of minorities worsened again in the recession of the early 1990s. Underneath the economic changes is a medium-term demographic change: There is a shortage of younger workers, and minorities are bound to benefit to some extent from this. In the longer term, there is no reason yet to believe that the cyclical opening and closing of the labor market will fundamentally affect the disadvantaged position of ethnic minorities.

Racism and Discrimination

Although much research is devoted to the mechanisms by which racial disadvantage operates in Great Britain, a bedrock of individual and collective antipathy to nonwhites must be acknowledged. In Britain there is no evidence that individual racial discrimination has decreased since the 1970s; in fact, what evidence we have suggests that it remains at the same level. Racial attacks on black and Asian people continue at an alarming level, and there is also evidence of a rise in organized violent anti-Semitism, orchestrated partly on a European basis. Many local and national political developments suggest that racial hostility toward blacks and Asians is growing, or becoming bolder, rather than declining. Without a major initiative from the political center, it is difficult to see how matters can improve.

ENDNOTES

1. American and European colleagues will, I hope, forgive the British for their inconsistent, inaccurate, and changing use of terminology in race relations. Nonwhite people with family origins in the Indian subcontinent (India, Pakistan, Bangladesh, and Sri Lanka) are referred to as Asian. (But people with origins elsewhere in Asia are not usually referred to as Asians.) People with African racial origins whose families come more recently from the Caribbean are referred to as Afro-Caribbeans. People of African origin from Africa are referred to as Africans or black Africans. All people with African racial origins are referred to as black (whether from Africa or the Caribbean). In Britain's not-too-distant past, Afro-Caribbeans, Africans, and Asians were all described, by some, as blacks; this usage is now becoming unfashionable, although there is still political debate about it among some researchers and activists.

2. The metropolitan counties were large, administrative areas including the conurbations of London, Birmingham, Manchester, Liverpool, Newcastle, and the urban centers

of Yorkshire. They were abolished as political units by the government during the 1980s, but they persist in the work of researchers because of their usefulness in analyzing urban geography.

REFERENCES

Blackaby, H. 1986. "An Analysis of Male Racial Earnings Differential in the UK, Using the General Household Survey." *Applied Economics* 18.

British Broadcasting Corporation. 1988. "Black and White" (television documentary).

Brown, C. 1984. *Black and White Britain: The Third PSI Survey.* London: Heinemann/ Gower.

Brown, C., and P. Gay. 1985. *Racial Discrimination: 17 Years After the Act.* London: Policy Studies Institute.

Chiswick, B. R. 1980. "The Earnings of White and Coloured Male Immigrants in Britain." *Economica* 47.

Cross, M., and D. Smith, eds. 1987. *Black Youth Futures: Ethnic Minorities and the Youth Training Scheme.* London: National Youth Bureau.

Daniel, W. W. 1968. *Racial Discrimination in England.* Harmondsworth: Penguin Books.

Dex, S. 1986. "Earnings Differentials of Second Generation Indian and White School Leavers in Britain." *Manchester School of Economic and Social Studies*, no. 2.

Fryer, P. 1984. *Staying Power: The History of Black People in Britain.* London: Pluto Press.

Haskey, J. 1990. "The Ethnic Minority Population of Great Britain: Estimates by Ethnic Group and Country of Birth." *Population Trends*, HMSO, no. 60.

Home Office. 1988. *A Scrutiny of Grants Under Section 11 of the Local Government Act, 1966.* London: HMSO.

———. 1990. *Section 11 of the Local Government Act, 1966: Grant Administration: Proposals.* London: HMSO.

Labour Force Survey (published annually). London, HMSO. Additional data also published periodically in *Population Trends* (see Haskey above) and in *Employment Gazette*, monthly, HMSO.

McCormick, B. 1986. "Evidence About the Comparative Earnings of Asian and West Indian Workers in Great Britain." *Scottish Journal of Political Economy* 23:(2).

McIntosh, N., and D. J. Smith. 1974. *The Extent of Racial Discrimination.* London, Political and Economic Planning.

McNabb, R., and Psacharopoulos, G. 1981. "Racial Earnings Differentials in the UK." *Oxford Economic Papers: New Series* (33) 3.

Mullins, D. 1990. "Reports: Housing and Urban Policy." *New Community* 17 (1).

Robinson, V. 1991. "Goodbye Yellow Brick Road: The Spatial Mobility and Immobility of Britain's Ethnic Population." *New Community* 17 (3).

Rose, E. J. B. et al. 1969. *Colour and Citizenship: A Report on British Race Relations.* London: Oxford University Press.

Smith, D. J. 1977. *Racial Disadvantage in Britain: The PEP Report.* Harmondsworth: Penguin.

Stewart, M. B. 1983. "Racial Discrimination and Occupational Attainment in Britain." *The Economic Journal* 93.

Vadgama, K. 1984. *India in Britain: The Indian Contribution to the British Way of Life.* London: Robert Royce.

Visram, R. 1986. *Ayahs, Lascars and Princes: Indians in Britain 1700–1947.* London: Pluto Press.

Wrench, J. 1990. "New Vocationalism, Old Racism and the Careers Service." *New Community* 16 (3).

ETHNIC MINORITIES IN THE NETHERLANDS

Justus Veenman

AN OVERVIEW OF POSTWAR EMIGRATION/IMMIGRATION POLICY

T HE NETHERLANDS has one of the highest population densities in the world. Covering only 16,000 square miles, it is inhabited by approximately 15 million people, on average 950 inhabitants per square mile. Given this fact, it is hardly surprising that a succession of Dutch governments has encouraged emigration. An active emigration policy was pursued in the first decades after World War II, and between 1945 and 1960, more than half a million Dutch people left the country for residence abroad—particularly in Canada, Australia, and the United States.

However, despite governmental attempts to encourage emigration, the Netherlands also received a significant number of immigrants from (former) Dutch colonies, especially Indonesia, during the same period. More than 300,000 immigrants trickled in from 1945 to 1960, and most were integrated into Dutch society without great trouble. The Moluccans were the only exception to this rule.

In 1951, a group of about 12,500 Moluccans arrived in Holland. Among them were 3,500 soldiers who had been in the Dutch army in the Dutch colony of Indonesia and fought against the nationalist army. The Moluccan soldiers and their families had refused to recognize the right of the new Republic of Indonesia to occupy the area they referred to as the free Republic of the South Moluccans, and, in order to avoid civil strife during the struggle over independence, the Dutch government ordered the soldiers to come to Holland with their families. Intended to be a temporary measure, the Moluccans were given collective accommodations, often in former concentration camps and monasteries.

Although some people still claim the situation is "temporary," more than 35,000 Moluccans currently reside in Holland. About 40 percent are housed in areas that are almost exclusively Moluccan ("Moluccan quarters") in more than 50 small towns scattered around the country. The first generation of Moluccans did not speak Dutch; they are visibly distinct (South Pacific islanders) from the native Dutch and are somewhat different culturally (more collectivist-oriented, stronger family ties, etc.). Although the government provided them with vocational training, they tended to take lower-paid jobs because of language and educational deficiencies. The integration of the Moluccans into Dutch society was, and is, problematic. The overall difficulty lies in the fact that many first generation Moluccans remain strongly oriented toward their home islands.

Other immigrants came from the Caribbean territories in the Kingdom of Holland—particularly Surinam and the Dutch Antilles. Migration from Surinam began in the 1880s but was largely limited to members of the upper class, who were attracted to Holland by its educational opportunities. It was not until after 1954, when the Surinamese and Antilleans were granted rights of residence equal to those of the indigenous Dutch, and Holland's economy was flourishing, that immigration from the Caribbean colonies to the Netherlands expanded rapidly. Most of the Surinamese and Antilleans share a common language, culture, and religion with the native Dutch. However, Surinam especially had large populations of African slaves and Asian contract-workers, so these immigrants are racially distinct. As with the earlier immigrants, the more recent waves of immigrants from the territories came to Holland primarily to obtain higher education, and those who stayed after graduation were typically able to find better-paid jobs.

Overall, from the end of the second World War through the 1960s, Holland sent a larger number of emigrants than the number of immigrants it received. Since then, the ratio has shifted, because of an increased rate of immigration among three distinct groups: the Caribbeans, the Mediterraneans, and political refugees. In 1974 and 1975, the approaching independence of Surinam caused a politically inspired boom in migration of Surinamese to Holland, because many Surinamese believed the option of permanent residence in Holland would be removed after independence. (In fact, the Dutch government has for some years continued to give Surinamese easy access to the country, on humanitarian grounds.) With the surge in Surinamese immigration that lasted until 1980, the overall number of Caribbean immigrants living in Holland rose rapidly between 1960 and 1976—from 12,700 to 128,000. By 1988, a total of over 260,000 Caribbean immigrants resided in the Netherlands; roughly 200,000 of these were Surinamese. The immigrants who arrived after 1975 have had a harder time finding work, partly because of the economic recession in Holland and partly because of the new immigrants' educational and language deficiencies.

The Mediterraneans comprise a second and larger part of the growing immigrant population in Holland. This group includes guest workers from southern European countries such as Spain, Portugal, Italy, Greece, and Yugoslavia, as well as countries like Turkey and Morocco. These latter two countries have contributed the largest number of immigrant workers: The number of immigrants from Turkey and Morocco tripled in just 8 years, increasing from 64,000 in 1968 to 190,000 in 1976. Most were recruited by Dutch employers in a period of economic growth to fill temporary labor shortages that resulted from a booming economy as well as from a structural shortage of low-skilled (low-wage) workers among the native Dutch. The character of this immigration has had far-reaching social consequences.

Unlike some other Western European governments, the Dutch government does not set limits on the duration of a guest worker's residence permit, and during the 1970s, an increasing number of immigrant workers decided to take up permanent residence in Holland. This created a tension between the stated objective of governmental policy (that Holland should be a country of emigrants) and practical reality. The tension became more pronounced as "chain migration" occurred (the wives and children of guest workers followed them into the country after a few years), and the Dutch government accepted "family reunification" as a social fact. By 1988, there were more than 370,000 Mediterraneans in Holland; about 180,000 of these were Turks, and about 140,000 were Moroccans. Turks and Moroccans found their integration in Dutch society more difficult than the 50,000 southern European immigrant workers, who also entered the country when labor demand was expanding. The Turks and Moroccans differ in language, culture, and religion from the native Dutch. The religious distinction is especially notable: Most of the immigrants are Islamic, and a significant number are fundamentalist Muslims.

The third and smallest group of recent immigrants to the Netherlands are political refugees. Since World War II, about 30,000 political refugees from around the world have been admitted to the country. Although an increasing number have requested asylum in recent years, more are denied admittance today than in the past.

Nonetheless, net immigration in Holland is still increasing. According to recent figures of the Netherlands Central Bureau of Statistics, there were 51,000 immigrants to the Netherlands in the first half of 1990 (up from 42,000 persons in the first half of 1989), and emigration declined by 1,000—from 28,000 to about 27,000—during this period. In other words, in the first half of 1990, there were almost two immigrants in Holland for each emigrant out of Holland.

Table 20.1 shows the relative size of the principal minority groups in the Netherlands today. Altogether, ethnic minorities comprise less than 5 percent of the Dutch population, a smaller proportion than the minority populations of Germany, France, Belgium, the United Kingdom, or Switzerland. Despite this, the country has frequently been described as a "multiethnic society," especially by scholars concerned with the social position of ethnic minorities. These scholars tend to conduct their research in the larger cities, where most of the Dutch universities are located and where ethnic minorities are overrepresented (e.g., about 20 percent of Amsterdam's total population belongs to an ethnic minority). In fact, it is more accurate to say Holland is a country with some multiethnic cities, rather than a multiethnic society.

However, this distinction may be somewhat moot, in that the Dutch government has adopted the social scientist's definition of the situation and behaves as though Holland were indeed a multiethnic society. A main objective of current government policy is "the realization of a society in which the members of ethnic minorities, individually as well as collectively, have sound and equal opportunities, and a social position that is equivalent to that of the indigenous Dutch" (*Minderhedennota* 1983: 5). This broad objective has been delineated in three goals:

1. to further the emancipation and participation of ethnic minorities in Dutch society, not only by strengthening their self-respect and self-assurance but also by influencing Dutch society in such a way that there are permanent chances for the ethnic minorities to develop themselves;

2. to diminish the social and economic disadvantages of ethnic minorities; and

3. to prevent or, if necessary, to fight discrimination and to improve the legal status of ethnic minorities (*Minderhedennota* 1983: 5).

Although these are fine words, finding concrete ways to implement them is difficult. This chapter evaluates whether actual policy practices of the Dutch government have helped to further these objectives. Special attention is given to whether the second aim—reducing the social and economic disadvantages that ethnic minorities face, especially in the labor market, has been achieved. This emphasis corresponds to the Dutch government's stated priorities. However, before we evaluate the impact of government practice, a brief review of the demographic characteristics and geographic distribution of ethnic minorities in Holland today will follow.

CHARACTERISTICS OF ETHNIC MINORITIES IN HOLLAND

Researchers face serious problems in attempting to describe accurately the demographic and geographic characteristics of ethnic minorities in Holland. The general public in Holland is suspicious of official attempts to collect data on peoples' backgrounds, for fear that this information will be abused by authorities—a legacy of experiences during World War II. As a result, the Netherlands

Table 20.1 / Ethnic Minorities in the Netherlands: January 1, 1989

Country of Origin	Number
Surinam	209,000
Turkey	177,000
Morocco	140,000
Antilles	66,000
Moluccan Islands	35,000
Spain	17,000
Italy	16,000
Yugoslavia	12,000
Portugal	8,000
Greece	4,000
Other (e.g., Vietnam 6,000)	30,000

SOURCES: Ankersmit et al. (1990) and Wetenschappelijke Raad Voor het Regeringsbeleid (Scientific Council for Government Policies (1990); data are from the Central Bureau of Statistics.

Central Bureau of Statistics is very reluctant to use the birthplace of a person's parents as a criterion of identification in nationwide surveys. Because nationality and place of birth are the main indicators of minority identity, official statistics cannot be used to ascertain the characteristics of ethnic minorities in Holland.[1] The problem of identification is compounded in the case of minorities with Dutch nationality (i.e., Antilleans, Moluccans, and Surinamese). For these groups, data must be collected through special surveys. This is also the case for political refugees, who, because of their special status, cannot be identified by nationality alone. Such problems do not apply to Mediterraneans. However, because Mediterraneans represent such a small percentage of the general population, data from national surveys often do not provide samples of a size large enough to allow researchers to generalize about the Mediterranean population with statistical reliability. Because of the costs involved, it is not always possible to increase the minority subgroups in national surveys to obtain a representative picture of their condition.

As a result of this problem, the Dutch government regularly subsidizes special surveys on one or more of the nation's ethnic minorities. However, the data from these surveys typically have a shortcoming. The Central Bureau of Statistics takes a representative sample of the general population, but the special minority survey samples are primarily drawn from the bigger cities, where most ethnic minorities live. Samples are drawn this way for purely financial reasons. This means the data collected cannot be considered representative of the national population as a whole; rather, they give information about the position of minorities relative to the position of the indigenous population in large cities.

Demographic Characteristics

Table 20.2 illustrates the growth in population among the four largest ethnic minorities in the Netherlands. As will be evident, the 1970s witnessed a substan-

Table 20.2 / Growth in Population Size of Four Largest Ethnic Minority Groups in the Netherlands (in thousands)

Minority Group	1971	1981	1989
Turks	30	139	177
Moroccans	21	83	140
Surinamese	38	165	209
Antilleans	18	40	66
TOTAL	107	427	592
Percentage of Total Population	0.8	3.0	4.0

SOURCES: Van der Erf (1989); the Netherlands Central Bureau of Statistics.

tial increase in the numbers of Turks, Surinamese, and Moroccans, mainly as a result of immigration. Only the Moluccans did not fit this pattern.

After the 1951 initial immigration of 12,500 Moluccans, only a few hundred more came to Holland. However, the fertility rate of the first generation of Moluccans was high, and return immigration to Indonesia was low, so that today there are more than 35,000 Moluccans in the Netherlands. The second generation of Dutch-born Moluccans has adopted the Dutch fertility rate, so that the current "net replacement rate" for Moluccans is only 0.5—below the 0.7 replacement rate of the Dutch (Veenman 1989: 41).

Other ethnic groups have also adopted the lower Dutch fertility rates. Some interpret this as a sign of *"assimilation"* to Dutch values and morals, whereas other observers suggest that it is just the result of improved access to contraceptives (Schrool 1989: 55–69).[2] Recent studies indicate that both factors are relevant. Whatever the reason, fertility rates affect the age structure of different minority groups.

Table 20.3 contains information on the present-day age structures of ethnic minorities in Holland. As the table shows, the age structure of the Moluccans comes closest to that of the general Dutch population, although there are somewhat more young people and fewer old people among the Moluccans. The other minority groups have a significantly younger population than the Dutch— but this is common among immigrant groups.

Data on household size and family structure are shown in Tables 20.4 and 20.5, respectively. For Antilleans, household size approximates most closely the pattern of the total population, although there are more single persons among them, probably due to the fact that many Antilleans in Holland are students. The Surinamese immigrants have somewhat larger families than the Dutch population, but they are much more likely to live in families headed by a lone

Table 20.3 / Age Structure of Ethnic Minorities and of the Total Population in the Netherlands

Age	Minority Group (%)					Overall Population (%)
	Turks	Moroccans	Surinamese	Antilleans	Moluccans	
0–15	34	41	27	24	27	18
15–30	35	27	34	36	22	25
30–50	25	25	29	32	29	29
50–60	6	7	7	6	11	15
65+	0	0	3	2	11	13
TOTAL	100	100	100	100	100	100

SOURCES: Ankersmit et al. (1989; data as of January 1, 1988). Labor Force Survey of Moluccans (1990, forthcoming). Data on Turks, Moroccans, Surinamese, Antilleans, and the total population are from the Netherlands Central Bureau of Statistics. The Labor Force Survey of Moluccans was conducted in 32 cities with concentrations of Moluccans and included 6,000 persons. Nevertheless, the data are not, strictly speaking, "representative" of the entire Moluccan population in Holland.

Table 20.4 / **Household Size of Ethnic Minorities and**
                of the Total Population in the Netherlands: 1986

Household Size	Minority Group (%)					Overall Population (%)
	Turks	Moroccans	Surinamese	Antilleans	Moluccans	
1	11	20	25	36	13	28
2	12	7	21	22	23	30
3	16	12	20	17	21	15
4	23	11	16	17	23	19
5	17	13	12	6	12	6
6	22	39	6	3	7	2
TOTAL	100	100	100	100	100	100

SOURCES: Van Praag (1989; data as of 1986) and Labor Force Survey of Moluccans (1990, forthcoming). The data on Turks, Moroccans, Surinamese, Antilleans, and the total population are from the Netherlands Central Bureau of Statistics—not from the "registers of population" but from a nationwide survey on housing, with raised portions of the earlier-mentioned ethnic minorities (respectively, N = 584, 315, 634, and 109; for the total population, N = 46,730). For data on Moluccans, see source note to Table 20.3.

parent. Almost a third of the Surinamese and about a fifth of Antilleans live in lone-parent households (Table 20.5). (This means that more than half of Surinamese families with children and 40 percent of Antillean families with children are headed by a lone parent.) The same pattern occurs in Surinam and the Dutch Antilles and may be related to the historical prohibition against slave marriages in the colonies.

By contrast, Turks and Moroccans have the largest households and few single-parent families. Over half of all Moroccan families and almost 40 percent of Turkish families have three or more children (Table 20.4). Not more than 3 percent and 6 percent of these households, respectively, are headed by a single parent (Table 20.5). About half of Turkish and Moroccan one-person households contain married men, who came to Holland as guest workers and left their families in their home country. Because there has been a strong tendency for "family reunification" lately, it is likely that the percentage of one-person households among these Mediterranean groups will diminish as more males bring their families to live in Holland.

The southern European Mediterranean population has an age distribution roughly similar to that of the Dutch population. About 17 percent are under 25 years old. However, there are many fewer elderly among them (less than 2 percent, compared with 13 percent in the Dutch population); over 41 percent are in the 30–50 age category, compared with only 29 percent of the total population in Holland (Ankersmit et al. 1989; data from the Netherlands Central Bureau of Statistics). The family size of southern European Mediterraneans approximates that of the Moluccans (i.e., families are larger than Dutch families but smaller than Turkish families). Only 1 in 10 families contains 5 persons or more. There are many more childless married couples among southern European Med-

/ **613**

Table 20.5 / Family Structure of Ethnic Minorities and the Total Population: 1986

	Minority Group (%)					Overall Population (%)
	Turks	Moroccans	Surinamese	Antilleans	Moluccans	
One Person	11	20	25	36	13	28
Married Couples without Children	10	4	8	6	17	22
Married Couples with Children	68	70	29	28	55	39
Single Parent	6	3	32	21	13	7
Other Relatives in Household	5	1	1	1	1	0
Nonfamily Household	1	3	5	5	1	5
TOTAL	100	100	100	100	100	100

SOURCES: Van Praag (1989; data as of 1986) and Labor Force Survey of Moluccans (1990, forthcoming). The data on Turks, Moroccans, Surinamese, Antilleans, and the total population are from the Netherlands Central Bureau of Statistics—not from the "registers of population" but from a nationwide survey on housing, with raised portions of the earlier-mentioned ethnic minorities (respectively, N = 584, 315, 634, and 109; for the total population, N = 46,730). For data on Moluccans, see source note to Table 20.3.

iterraneans than among Turks or Moroccans (17 percent vs. 10 percent and 4 percent, respectively), and the proportion of lone-parent households is only about 8 percent, which is comparable with the percentage of lone-parent households in the general population (Van Praag 1989: 25–35). Southern Mediterranean immigrants appear to be more similar to the native Dutch in family size and structure than to other immigrant groups. (Data problems in identifying "political refugees" preclude detailed demographic breakdowns on them.)

Geographic Distribution of Minorities

The residential distribution of ethnic minorities across regions is quite uneven in Holland. There are 17 cities in the country with more than 100,000 inhabitants. Mediterraneans are very concentrated in the larger cities. Among Mediterraneans, Moroccans are the most concentrated; roughly half live in the four largest cities (Amsterdam, Rotterdam, The Hague, and Utrecht). Among southern Europeans, 42 percent live in the four largest cities, as do 37 percent of Turks. Although strictly comparable data on Surinamese and Antilleans are not available,[2] some estimates indicate that at least 60 percent of the Surinamese live in these four cities (a quarter live in Amsterdam), whereas only about a third of Antilleans live in these cities (Van Praag 1989: 25–35; data from the Netherlands Central Bureau of Statistics at the beginning of 1988).

Exact data on the residential distribution of Moluccans are not available because Moluccans cannot be identified in the "registers of population." However, because Moluccans were originally accommodated in special "Moluccan quarters" in small cities spread over the country, they tend to be underrepresented in cities with over 100,000 inhabitants. For this reason, their situation has been very different from that of other ethnic minorities in Holland. However, nowadays, there is a tendency for young Moluccans to leave their place of birth and move to the larger Dutch cities, so their residential distribution is beginning to look more like that of other minority groups.

Within cities, ethnic residential segregation in the strict sense of the word does not exist, that is, there are no districts that include *only* immigrants. Although there are concentrations of minorities within the larger cities, especially within the older quarters of inner cities, the quality of the buildings is good, and the environment does not in any way resemble the ghettos of inner cities in the United States.[3]

The past two decades have seen a growing concentration of Turks and Moroccans in the largest cities, but they are not becoming more overcrowded in the same districts where they have been historically clustered. Rather, minorities are spreading out, so that they now comprise a majority of the population in a larger number of urban districts than previously. This is partly the result of public policies that distribute available housing according to need and family size rather than income. If a large family has a low income, it can rent a large dwelling (if it is available), even if the family does not have the money to pay the market rent; the Dutch government will subsidize rent to a certain level (about f. 250 monthly) with an "individual rent subsidy." To get this subsidy, only two criteria must be met: (a) The gap between taxable family income and the rent must not be above a certain amount, and (b) the size of the family must correspond to the size of the dwelling that is available. However, a process of deregulation of housing has been going on recently, and this has resulted in looser enforcement of the strict rules about dwelling size. Moreover, there is political pressure to reduce the amount of the rent subsidy as well as to reduce public assistance levels. Both these developments are reducing the housing available to the poor and may result in more overcrowded conditions in the future.

The Surinamese and Antilleans have a different housing pattern than Turks and Moroccans. They are increasingly likely to rent moderate income flats outside the inner cities, and so are residentially clustered outside of city centers (Van Praag 1989: 25–35; analysis is based on data from the National Housing Survey, 1985–1986).

Always the exception, the Moluccans were deliberately segregated by residence when they came to Holland. As described earlier, they were placed in special "Moluccan quarters" within smaller towns. Although about 60 percent of all Moluccans lived in these quarters in the 1960s, today the percentage has diminished to about 40 percent, due to the government's decision not to enlarge these enclaves and the tendency of young Moluccans to leave their place of birth. Of course, the two factors are related: Because there are not enough accommodations available within "Moluccan quarters," young Moluccans who want to live independently are almost always forced to leave these neighborhoods. But many young people are also voluntarily looking for accommodations within Dutch society (Veenman 1990a: 283).

THE SOCIAL POSITION OF ETHNIC MINORITIES

Educational Achievement

The most recent data on the educational level of different ethnic groups, shown in Table 20.6, demonstrate the differences between the educational qualifications of the native Dutch and ethnic minorities. Turks and Moroccans are the most educationally disadvantaged. Fully 90 percent of Moroccans have only a primary education or less, and more than half have had no formal education; 62 percent of Turks have only a primary education, and 15 percent have no education. Thirty-four percent of the Surinamese, 30 percent of Moluccans, and 31 percent of Antilleans have only a primary education, compared with 20 percent of the indigenous Dutch. Thus, although the Caribbean groups have higher educational qualifications than the Turks and Moroccans, they still lag behind the indigenous Dutch. Almost a third of the Dutch have at least a senior secondary education degree, but only 14 percent of Surinamese and 7 percent of Moluccans do. The education levels of Antilleans most closely approximate

Table 20.6 / Educational Attainment of Ethnic Minorities and the Total Population

Educational Level	Percent					
	Turks	Moroccans	Surinamese	Antilleans	Moluccans	Indigenous Dutch
No Education	15	54	5	4		0
Primary Education	62	36	34	27	30	20
Junior Secondary Vocational education	7	3	15	21	40	19
Junior Secondary General education	8	4	22	15	12	12
Senior Secondary Vocational education	3	1	9	8	11	13
Senior Secondary General education and grammar schools	4	2	8	16	4	17
Higher Vocational Colleges	1	1	5	7	3	11
University education	0	0	1	2	0	8
TOTAL	100	100	100	100	100	100

SOURCES: Veenman (1990b) and Labor Force Survey of Moluccans (1990, forthcoming). The data for all groups except Moluccans are for 1990; the data for Moluccans are for 1988.

Dutch education levels, although only 2 percent of Antilleans attend a university, compared with 8 percent of the native Dutch.

The educational qualifications of young people are higher than those of their elders. This is true for all groups—including natives. However, the young indigenous Dutch are improving their educational attainment much more rapidly than young people of other ethnic groups, so that the *difference* in educational levels between the indigenous Dutch and ethnic minorities has grown. Antilleans are the only exception to this pattern—they are gradually closing the educational gap between themselves and the indigenous Dutch (Braat and Veenman 1990: 87–107).

Several factors are of special significance in explaining differences in educational attainment. The first has to do with the moment an individual arrives in Holland. Young people who do not participate in the Dutch educational system from the first year on appear to have a difficult time "catching up" in school. Many of them also have great difficulty acquiring the Dutch language; this obstructs learning. But even those immigrants who speak Dutch well and are familiar with the school system still tend to lag behind the indigenous Dutch (Roelandt and Martens 1990: 19–41). Many minority youths are from the lowest socioeconomic strata, and this is strongly correlated with lower achievement levels. However, even minority children with good language skills who enroll in the Dutch educational system early perform less well in school than indigenous Dutch children of the same age, gender, and social class (Roelandt and

Martens 1990: 19–41). So it would appear that, while social class is the most important factor in determining school achievement, cultural aspects and racial discrimination probably also contribute to lower performance among minority children.

Public and "special" religious schools in Holland have the same funding levels and curriculum. There is some concern about the level of minority concentration in some urban schools in the center of the largest cities, and recent policy reforms are directed at improving the quality of these schools—by spending more money on them and by providing them with better equipment and facilities.

Labor Market Activity

Given these educational differences, one would expect certain minority groups to be especially disadvantaged in the labor market. Table 20.7 shows that unemployment rates among minorities are three times as high as among the indigenous Dutch. Unemployment rates do not differ greatly *between* minority groups, however, and diverge somewhat from the pattern that one would expect according to educational levels.

If unemployment were strictly related to educational level, one would expect Antilleans to have the lowest unemployment rates, followed by Surinamese, Moluccans, Turks, and Moroccans. However, Moluccans have the lowest unemployment rates, followed by Surinamese, Antilleans, Turks, and Moroccans.

When one examines long-term unemployment, education appears to be more important (Table 20.8). In 1990, fully three-quarters of unemployed Moluccans had been unemployed for over 2 years, compared with 60 percent of Moroccans and half the Turks and Surinamese. Only a third of the unemployed Antilleans had been unemployed for over 2 years—about the same proportion as in the general population.

Table 20.7 / **Level and Amount of Unemployment Among Ethnic Minorities and of Total Population**

Minority Group	Unemployment Rate	Numbers Unemployed
Turks	37	950
Moroccans	40	664
Surinamese	33	716
Antilleans	34	444
Moluccans	26	2,414
Indigenous Dutch	11	883

SOURCES: Veenman (1990b) and Labor Force Survey for Moluccans (1990, forthcoming; see source note to Table 20.3).

Table 20.8 / **Duration of Unemployment Among Ethnic Minorities**

	Percent Unemployed for		
Minority Group	0–12 Months	12–24 Months	>24 Months
Turks	22	20	58
Moroccans	16	24	60
Surinamese	25	20	55
Antilleans	42	22	36
Moluccans	14	10	76
TOTAL POPULATION	54	13	33

SOURCES: Veenman (1990b) and Labor Force Survey for Moluccans (1990, forthcoming; see source note to Table 20.3).

Multivariate analysis attempting to explain unemployment rates of ethnic minorities indicates that education level, occupational identification, gender, age, and regional labor market conditions explain only one-third of the difference between unemployment rates of the indigenous Dutch and respective minority groups (Niesing and Veenman 1990b: 41–69). Although one cannot conclude that all remaining differences in unemployment are due to discrimination,[4] these results and those of many other studies of discrimination in the Dutch labor market make it clear that discrimination is an important causal factor in high minority unemployment rates.[5]

There is no such division between work and living as there is in the larger cities of the United States. Employment opportunities are greatest in and around the largest cities where the highest concentration of ethnic minorities is found. Moreover, public transportation is good and not too expensive. Thus, residential segregation does not appear to be an important factor in high minority unemployment rates. On average not more than 3 percent of minorities are self-employed, so ethnic enterprises and/or business development do not appear to be an alternative to discrimination in the general labor market.

Income Levels and Sources of Support

Holland's complex tax and subsidy system makes disposable income the best way to compare the income of individuals and groups. The 1988 national survey of Turks, Moroccans, Surinamese, Antilleans, and indigenous Dutch (which samples the population of 10 cities with a large proportion of minorities) contained questions on income. (The following income figures refer to *net* monthly income.) The indigenous Dutch enjoy the highest income level. Their average disposable income is f. 1,740 a month. The average minority household has a monthly income of about 80 percent of the Dutch average: Turks (81.9 percent), Surinamese (81.4 percent), Moroccans (81.2 percent), and Antilleans (77.6 percent). However, the various groups differ widely with respect to family structure and *source* of income as Table 20.9 shows.

Labor income is the most important source of income for 65 percent of the indigenous Dutch, 47 percent of the Turks and Surinamese, and 41 percent of the Antilleans and Moroccans. However, this may reflect the fact that minority groups have lower average earnings than the indigenous Dutch rather than differences in work effort. About 20 percent of all households in Holland earned over f. 2,700 in net monthly income in 1988, but only 8 percent of Antillean, 6 percent of Surinamese, and 1 percent of Turk and Moroccan households did so (Table 20.10). Differences in earnings between ethnic group households increase even more when one restricts the comparison to working males, because Surinamese and Antillean females work more hours and so have more earnings than indigenous Dutch females (Table 20.11).

To explore the factors related to earnings differences, the earnings of heads of households working at least 30 hours a week were regressed on educational level, occupation, whether or not the job was a supervisory position, work experience, age, and length of time in Holland. These factors explain 98 percent of the difference in earnings between indigenous Dutch and Turks, 87 percent of the difference between Surinamese and Dutch, 81 percent of the difference between Antilleans and Dutch, and 78 percent of the difference between Moroccans and Dutch. These findings suggest that there is little racial discrimination with regard to wages in Holland. Rather, differences in basic human capital and in occupation explain most wage differences. Strong government regulation of Dutch wage inequality apparently has been helpful in preventing wage discrimination based on ethnicity, even if the government has not been successful in preventing discrimination in hiring (Veenman 1990b: 122–124).

Although there are some differences in the level of support that various groups receive from the government when they are not working, minority groups do not appear to be in a disadvantaged position with respect to government assistance. Family size and family structure are important factors in determining income support levels, and, because minorities are more likely to have larger families and/or be part of a lone-parent household than indigenous Dutch households, they are likely to qualify for relatively generous income support. This is demonstrated by the fact that most minority households have about the same disposable income (78–81 percent of the Dutch average) despite markedly less reliance on earnings income.

Housing

Although minority districts in Holland are *not* like urban ghettos in the United States, minority groups are overrepresented in the older quarters of larger cities in Holland where smaller, cheaper dwellings of a somewhat lesser quality are found. Turks and Moroccans, who have large families and limited means, tend to be concentrated in these areas, apparently because they have greater difficulty utilizing the allotment of publicly subsidized dwellings than

Table 20.9 / Average Net Monthly Income of Ethnic Minorities and Indigenous Dutch from Various Income Sources: 1988 (in guilders)

Income Source	Turks (f.)	Moroccans (f.)	Surinamese (f.)	Antilleans (f.)	Indigenous Dutch (f.)
Occupational Earnings	1,629	1,718	1,773	1,853	2,037
Unemployment Benefit	1,300	1,232	1,181	1,073	1,186
Social Welfare	1,215	1,214	1,195	1,166	1,173
Disability Pension Benefit	1,471	1,440	1,358	—	1,576

SOURCE: Veenman (1990).

Dash (—) denotes not enough observations.

Table 20.10 / Net Monthly Earnings of Ethnic Minorities and of the Total Population (percentage of each group in various earnings categories): 1988

Minority Group	f. 1,100	f. 1,100–1,900	f. 1,900–2,700	f. 2,700	Percent (n)
Turks	13	61	25	1	100 (565)
Moroccans	6	71	23	1	100 (364)
Surinamese	14	49	31	6	100 (409)
Antilleans	9	48	35	8	100 (261)
TOTAL POPULATION	15	32	33	20	100 (614)

SOURCE: Veenman (1990b).

Table 20.11 / Net Monthly Earnings of Male Household Heads, by Ethnic Group and Earnings Category: 1988

Minority Group	f. 1,100	f. 1,100–1,900	f. 1,900–2,700	f. 2,700	Percent (n)
Turks	0	60	40	0	100 (300)
Moroccans	1	70	28	1	100 (203)
Surinamese	2	47	44	7	100 (136)
Antilleans	1	42	51	6	100 (83)
TOTAL POPULATION	2	22	47	29	100 (223)

SOURCE: Veenman (1990b). Because of reluctance on the part of Moluccans to give information on income, this question was not asked in the Labor Force Survey of Moluccans, and data are not available here.

do the Surinamese and Antilleans. These latter groups have better knowledge of Dutch institutions (and so, are more likely to utilize the government rent subsidies that are available) and they have smaller families—which makes it more likely that housing of an appropriate size will become available (Roelandt and Veenman 1989). As a result, the Surinamese and Antilleans have gradually managed to improve their position in the housing market. Because they improved their position at a time when the housing stock was increasing, this improvement has not been at the expense of other groups.

Summary

Ethnic minority groups in Holland are disadvantaged in various areas of social life. First, their educational attainment levels lag behind those of native Dutch (although the degree varies greatly by ethnic groups). The lower educational levels of minorities are related to migrational characteristics such as age at arrival and familiarity with the Dutch language, but social class is also correlated with school achievement. This means that immigrant children's educational deficits are tied to their parents' problems. As mentioned earlier, all young people are improving their educational levels, but the native Dutch are increasing their level of education more than young minorities, so differences between native Dutch and minorities (with the exception of the Antilleans) are growing. Given the current state of the Dutch labor market and labor demand, the growing differences in educational attainment between natives and immigrants are likely to result in large differences in employment rates in early adulthood.

Research suggests that the higher rate of unemployment experienced by ethnic minorities cannot be explained by differences in educational level, occupational experience, gender, age, or residence. Employer discrimination, either deliberate or unconscious, appears also to restrict minority access to jobs.

By contrast, discrimination against minorities is less evident with respect to wages and housing. In Holland, both wage levels and access to housing are highly regulated. Wage levels are regulated by collective bargaining agreements among employers, workers, and the government that result in collective labor contracts that are applied to all employees in the same segment of the labor market (e.g., dockworkers or bank employees). The housing market for low-income families in the larger cities is regulated by local governments. Because low-income housing units (those that rent at less than f. 750 per month) are allocated by local governments in most of the larger cities, private prejudice (among property owners) is not allowed to play a role in determining the distribution of housing.

Nonetheless, growing educational gaps and unemployment rates have left minorities in the same position of *relative* disadvantage that they were in a decade or two ago. A study of the "professional prestige" of successive age categories in each ethnic group conducted in 1990 found almost no improvement across age groups. Minorities have not been able to rise up the occupational ladder in Holland. The housing sector seems to be the only sector in which the gap between minorities and the native Dutch is closing (especially the case for Surinamese and Antilleans).

DUTCH POLICIES THAT TARGET ETHNIC MINORITIES

Antidiscrimination Policies

Successive Dutch governments failed to enact specific policies aimed at ethnic minorities until about 1975, because they refused to accept the reality that Holland had become a country with more immigrants than emigrants and that most immigrants were permanently settling in Holland. The arrival of large numbers of Surinamese in the mid-1970s brought a change in attitude, and specific legislation to assist these immigrants was introduced. Although these first acts were supposed to be of a temporary nature, it became clear as time passed that more systematic policies would be required to further integrate minority groups into Dutch society. This was the starting point of a policy of "integration while preserving the identity" of ethnic groups.

This initial policy toward immigrants was based on the idea that ethnic minority groups should have the opportunity to participate fully in Dutch society but would not be asked to diverge too much from their own culture; preserving their cultural identity would allow them to return to their country of origin if they desired. With this in mind, instruction in the home-country language and culture was introduced in the Dutch educational system. During the period 1975–1983, the government also encouraged the establishment of specific minority organizations on the assumption that these organizations would simultaneously assist the integration of minorities in Dutch society and help maintain the groups' culture. In the educational system, more teachers were hired to teach minority students; in the labor market, special vocational training for minorities was introduced; and in the housing market, attempts were made to remove the barriers to using housing programs and to allocate more public housing to large families. Gradually, policies focusing on the integration of ethnic minorities into Dutch society began to receive greater emphasis.

This shift of focus culminated with the publication of the *Minderhedennota* in 1983, the most important government document on ethnic minorities.[6] It proposed three ways to advance integration: (1) further the emancipation and participation of ethnic minorities in Dutch society, (2) prevent discrimination, and (3) diminish social and economic differences. Discrimination was legally prohibited, and laws were enacted to give minorities more equality and protection in such areas as suffrage and civil service employment. However, the most emphasis was placed on the third goal of diminishing social and economic inequality, and the government became more concerned with ensuring equal access to the benefits of the welfare state.

The Dutch government began to monitor systematically the effectiveness of various government policies designed to diminish minority disadvantage—

especially those associated with the labor market and the educational system. A separate directorate within the Ministry of the Interior was established to coordinate the policies of the Departments of Labor, Education, and Housing as they affect minorities. However, the policy of creating a separate directorate was criticized, mainly by the personnel of established departments, who argued that all public programs were meant to include ethnic minorities.

Eventually, the strategy of special targeted policies was abandoned in favor of emphasizing universal, general policies (with special programs for minorities that were intended to "supplement" general measures). The new objective was to *assimilate* minorities into Dutch society rather than encourage cultural plurality.

At the same time that these reforms were implemented, the government embarked on a policy of decentralization, partially the result of an ideology of the "state stepping back" and partially the result of an urgent desire to reduce government spending in the midst of the recession of the early 1980s. As local governments at the municipal level became increasingly involved in the design and implementation of housing, welfare, and training policies, it was determined that they should have more influence over the content of policies toward minorities. This change also reduced the influence of the directorate responsible for minority programs. Although specific policies for ethnic minorities still exist in Holland, they have become less pronounced, because of the new emphasis on integrating minorities in more universal programs and the shift toward decentralization. Both these changes are connected to the reduction in government spending on social programs and the charge that ethnic minorities have become too dependent on government assistance or, as critics charge, have "been hugged to death."

Defenders of special programs point out that the social position of ethnic minorities in Holland is still very tenuous, particularly with regard to their labor market position. Since the recession ended in 1984, the unemployment rate of the indigenous Dutch has declined, but unemployment among ethnic minorities has continued to rise. Available evidence suggests that this development is not a function of the characteristics of the minority labor force but the result of labor market selection processes. Thus, it is argued, the social position of ethnic minorities will not improve without government intervention.

The Limitations of Government Intervention

This discussion leads to the question: What are the limitations of government intervention in improving the social and economic position of ethnic minorities? The question is especially relevant with respect to the labor market, because government intervention in this arena confronts the ideology of a free enterprise system. Because there has been little political support in recent years for the government increasing the demand for labor, government programs have emphasized improving the labor supply (i.e., improving the human capital of workers). Most measures to improve the employment of minorities have focused on improving the qualifications of ethnic minorities in order to make them "more attractive" to employers. Unfortunately, while many unemployed minorities have invested their time in government training programs, most have not succeeded in finding a job. As a result, many became discouraged, stopped actively searching for work, and became part of the long-term unemployed. The status of being one of the long-term unemployed then, creates another strike against minorities. When vacancies do open up, employers do not want to take individuals who have been unemployed for long periods. Nowadays, Dutch employers are looking for new employees in eastern European countries like Poland and the former German Democratic Republic, instead of from among ethnic minorities in Holland.

The only solution to this problem would be government intervention on the demand side of the labor market, that is, public policies that actively promote the hiring of minorities. But here we confront the limitations of government influence. Employers in Holland have made it clear that they oppose measures like affirmative action, contract compliance, and Employment Equity Acts (like the one implemented in Canada). The Dutch labor system is a tripartite corporatist system (comprised of labor unions, employers' organizations, and the government), and policy makers have not yet been willing to run the blockade raised by private employers. Direct government job creation has been confined to the public sector, and there are strict rules against interfering in the private sector. The number of new jobs created has not kept pace with the number of job-seekers, and those private jobs that have been created have the characteristics of the "secondary labor market." Ethnic minorities are the victims of the government's unwillingness to influence the labor market. Because employment directly affects income and housing opportunities and indirectly affects children's educational achievement, this limitation thwarts the attempts of ethnic minorities to become more socially integrated and leaves them increasingly economically marginalized.

Because Holland has almost no experience of a third generation of ethnic minorities, it may be too early to predict a gloomy end. Holland has a well-developed social security system, which keeps the vast majority of the population close to a socially determined average living standard, and this may justify some optimism. On the other hand, it also presents a danger—ethnic minorities could become dependent on government support for prolonged periods, and this could result in a different sort of social marginalization.

Concluding Observations

Although containing only a small percentage (less than 5 percent) of ethnic minorities, the Netherlands nevertheless has been characterized as being a multiethnic society by scholars and politicians alike. Since the end of the 1970s, this characterization has been institutionalized by successive Dutch governments that have designed, organized, financed, and implemented special policies to help ethnic minorities. However, the characterization also reflects at least some degree of tolerance toward new ethnic minorities by the native Dutch. The *Minderhedennota* document (1983) certainly set forth noble intentions regarding the fair treatment of ethnic minorities in Holland.

Nonetheless, a number of negative trends in the social position of ethnic minorities can be observed in recent years. The economic recession of the 1980s was marked by mass unemployment and a growing hostility toward immigrants. The recession also created fiscal pressures for the government that put pressure on the Dutch to reduce welfare state expenditures. The concept of social solidarity that provides the justification for the welfare state tends to be questioned during periods of economic hardship, particularly when the individuals most in need of assistance are new, ethnic minorities. Feelings of solidarity are stronger when the assisted group is very similar to the population that is taxed for transfer programs. Consequently, in recent years there has been an attempt to emphasize general policies that affect the entire citizenry and a perceptible reluctance to establish new policies aimed only at ethnic minorities. However, universal programs are not able to reduce the growing gap between the educational and employment levels of minorities relative to the indigenous population. Fiscal constraints limit the public money available for social policies for minorities, and the free enterprise ideology draws a line between government interference and the labor market. However, it is important to remember that when the government has been able and willing to use its influence on behalf of ethnic minorities—as has been the case with housing policy—a reduction in inequality has been the result.

ENDNOTES

1. The Netherlands Central Bureau of Statistics is even more reluctant to use a so-called subjective identification criterion, namely, the question of whether the person concerned considers himself a member of a minority group. This method has been used in the United States by the Bureau of the Census and in Great Britain's Census and Labour Force Survey. At present, the Netherlands Central Bureau of Statistics is working on what has been called the "register counting." This means that the "registers of population" of every Dutch city are being checked to count the number of inhabitants born outside Holland. Unfortunately, the results of this counting are not yet available.

2. The data will be available after the "register counting" of the Netherlands Central Bureau of Statistics is completed.

3. Some Dutch social scientists do use the term *ghetto* to refer to some urban sectors in Dutch cities, out of what seems to be an urgent desire to employ concepts and terms that have proven useful in the American context. Unfortunately, this desire is not always coupled with a critical eye, for the Dutch "ghetto" and the American ghetto are by no means equivalent.

4. Referring to this point, Mincer (1979: 279) once called the applied analysis "a measure of our ignorance."

5. Among these studies are: employment tests by Bovenkerk (1977: 58–76), postal surveys among employers by Veenman (1985), and research among applicants by Veenman (1985).

6. The basic recommendations in the government documents were first formulated by the Scientific Council for Governmental Policies in 1979. There was then a large and time-consuming political debate, which involved a number of minority organizations. As a result of this debate, the *Minderhedennota* was written and published in 1983. The most important impetus to the writing of this government document on ethnic minorities was the growing awareness that most migrants did not return to their home country, but stayed in Holland: The need for a more formal policy finally became clear.

   Later, in 1989–1990, there was a new moment of awareness: Migrants not only stayed here, but kept coming. Holland really had become an immigration country. This meant "new" problems had to be solved. From that moment on, the debate had focused more and more on *obligations*. ("If migrants want to come and stay here, they have to assimilate.") The moment in which the government consciously decides *not* to assist minorities who are unwilling to assimilate has not yet arrived, but the perspective is not very different: Assistance is especially targeted on those who are willing to assimilate.

REFERENCES

Ankersmit, T., Th. Roelandt, and J. Veenman. 1989. *Minderheden in Nederland, Statistisch Vademecum 1989 (Minorities in the Netherlands: Statistical Handbook, 1989)*. The Hague: Staatsuitgeveri en drukkerij.

———. 1990. *Minderheden in Nederland, Statistisch Vademecum 1990 (Minorities in the Netherlands: Statistical Handbook, 1990)*. The Hague: Staatsuitgeveri en drukkerij.

Bovenkerk, F. 1977. "Rasdiscriminate op de Amsterdamse arbeidsmarkt" ("Racial Discrimination in the Amsterdam Labor Market"). In *Arbeidsmarkt en ongelijkheid (Labor Market and Inequality)*, edited by J. J. Hoof and A. Martens, 58–76. Meppel: Boom.

Braat, H., and J. Veenman. 1990. "Sociale ongelijkheid en sociale mobiliteit" ("Social Inequality and Social Mobility"). In *Ver van huis, Achterstand en achterstelling bij allochtonen (Far from Home, Arrears of, and Discrimination toward Ethnic Minorities)*, edited by J. Veenman, 87–107. Groningen: Wolters-Noordhoff.

Maillat, D. 1987. "Long-term Aspects of International Migration Flows: The Experience of European Receiving Countries." In *The Future of Migration*. Paris: Organization for Economic Cooperation and Development.

Mincer, J. 1979. "Comment." In *Women in the Labor Market*, edited by C. B. Lloyd, E. S. Andrews, and C. L. Gilroy, 278–285. New York: Columbia University Press.

Minderhedennota (Governmental Document on Ethnic Minorities). 1982. The Hague: Staatsuitgeveri en drukkerij.

Neising, W., and J. Veenman. 1990a. "Achterstand en achterstelling in het inkomen" ("Arrears and Discrimination in Incomes"). In *Ver van huis, Achterstand en achterstelling bij allochtonen* (*Far from Home, Arrears of, and Discrimination toward Ethnic Minorities*), edited by J. Veenman, 69–87. Groningen: Wolters-Noordhoff.

————. 1990b. "Achterstand en achterstelling in het inkomen" ("Arrears and Discrimination in the Labor Market"). In *Ver van huis, Achterstand en achterstelling bij allochtonen* (*Far from Home, Arrears of, and Discrimination toward Ethnic Minorities*), edited by J. Veenman, 41–69. Groningen: Wolters-Noordhoff.

Roelandt, Th., and E. Martens. 1990. "Ongelijke kansen in het onderwijs: social herkomst, migratie, en ethniciteit" ("Unequal Chances in Education: Social Origin, Migration, and Ethnicity"). In *Ver van huis, Achterstand en achterstelling bij allochtonen* (*Far from Home, Arrears of, and Discrimination toward Ethnic Minorities*), edited by J. Veenman, 19–41. Groningen: Wolters-Noordhoff.

Roelandt, Th., and J. Veenman. 1989. *Minderheden in Nederland Positie op de woningmarkt* (*Minorities in the Netherlands Position in the Housing Market*). Rotterdam: Erasmus Universiteit Rotterdam.

Schrool, Jeannette J. 1989. "Het kindertal van Turkse en Marokkaanse vrouweden in Nederland: 'assimilate'?" ("The Number of Children of Turkish and Moroccan Women in the Netherlands: Assimilation?"). In *Demografisch onderzoek naar minderheden* (*Demographic Research among Ethnic Minorities*), edited by C. S. Van Praag, 55–69. Alphen aan den Rijn: Samsom.

Van der Erf, R. F. 1989. "Beleidsrelevante migrantngroepen demografisch bezien" ("A Demographic Look at Migrant Populations, Relevant for Minority Policies"). In Van Praag, C. S. (ed.), *Demografisch onderzoek naar minderheden* (*Demographic Research among Ethnic Minorities*), edited by C. S. Van Praag, 11–24. Alphen aan den Rijn: Samsom.

Van Praag, C. S. 1989. "Huishoudens en huishoudensvorming bij etnische minderheden in Nederland" ("Households and the Formation of Households within Ethnic Minorities in the Netherlands"). In *Demografisch onderzoek naar minderheden* (*Demographic Research among Ethnic Minorities*), edited by C. S. Van Praag, 25–35. Alphen aan den Rijn: Samsom.

Veenman, J. 1985. *De arbeidsmarktproblemmatiek van Molukkers* (*Labor Market Problems of Moluccans*). Rotterdam: Erasmus Universiteit Rotterdam.

————. 1989. "Molukkers in Nederland: een demografische speurtocht" ("Moluccans in the Netherlands: A Search for Demographic Data"). In *Demografisch onderzoek naar minderheden* (*Demographic Research among Ethnic Minorities*), edited by C. S. Van Praag, 36–47. Alphen aan den Rijn: Samsom.

————. 1990a. *De arbeidsmarktpositie van allochtonen in Nederland, in het bijzonder van Molukkers* (*The Labour Market Position of Migrants in the Netherlands, with Special Reference to the Moluccans*). Groningen: Wolters-Noordhoff.

————. 1990b. *Ver van huis, Achterstand en achterstelling bij allochtonen* (*Far from Home, Arrears of, and Discrimination toward Ethnic Minorities*), edited by J. Veenman. Groningen: Wolters-Noordhoff.

————. 1991. *Ear large weg, Molakkers op de arbeidsmarkt* (*A Long Way to Go, Moluccans in the Labor Market*) (Rotterdam, ISEO).

Wetenschappelijke Raad voor het Regeringsbeleid (Scientific Council for Government Policies). 1990. *Allochtonenbeleid* (*Minority Policy*). Gravenhage: Staatsuitgeveri en drukkerij.

Part V

THE FUTURE OF SOCIAL POLICY

Chapter 21

TRAMPOLINES, SAFETY NETS, OR FREE FALL? LABOR MARKET POLICIES AND SOCIAL ASSISTANCE IN THE 1980s

Katherine McFate

A S ECONOMIC RESTRUCTURING left larger numbers of citizens outside the mainstream labor force, and policymakers faced the prospect of a growing number of marginalized "prime age" workers, a new policy orthodoxy began to take shape. The main outlines of the doctrine are as follows. Traditional social-assistance programs are too passive; they allow citizens to withdraw from the workforce for long periods. But in a dynamic, rapidly changing economy, a prolonged period of joblessness can lead to skill deterioration and reduce an individual's real and perceived "employability." A better way to help people adjust to economic restructuring would be to reshape income support safety nets to create social trampolines that help able-bodied individuals bounce back into the labor market. Labor market policies need to focus less on income support and more on active integration programs.

The "active society" approach mandates that priority be given to "training, placement and rehabilitation programmes for the unemployed, the inactive and those on welfare in order to break dependency cycles, reduce inequality in access to jobs, and generally integrate people into the mainstream of productive activity" (OECD 1990:7). It argues for the better coordination of various income support programs and labor market policies so that individuals are encouraged to return to (or enter) the workforce as rapidly as possible. Reversing twentieth century trends toward reduced working hours and the expansion of leisure (at the family as well as the individual level), this strategy advocates the "full mobilization of the labor supply." It conveniently overlooks the dramatic decline in *demand* for low-skilled labor that occurred over the last decade and a half in most Western democracies.

The canons of labor market policy in the 1980s spoke to improving the labor supply. There was an emphasis on increasing the work effort of the poor, not on increasing the demand for low-skilled labor. Policy reforms focused on the "work disincentives" buried in income support programs rather than on growing wage inequality. Government officials worried more about the quality of workforce preparation than about the quality of work.

This chapter gives an overview of the policy reforms of the 1980s (some of which are discussed in more detail in Parts II and III of this volume). Income support for the jobless has become more conditional in most countries; in some nations, benefit receipt has been restricted. In countries without the institutional networks and commitment to active labor market policies at the beginning of the decade, little progress was made in integrating the agencies responsible for administering public placement, training, and income support programs. Instead, the fragmented, temporary, and sometimes contradictory nature of the reforms that were enacted in the 1980s tended to mirror the turbulence and insecurity of the labor market rather than mitigate its impact.

THE GENDER QUESTION: WHO IS EXPECTED TO WORK?

Although the rhetoric of the active society supports increased female participation in the paid labor force, "full mobilization of the labor supply," like "full employment," is a culturally determined term. As Table 21.1 shows, the composition of the paid workforce varies significantly by age and gender across nations,[1] and large cross-national differences in the work behavior of women are still evident. In the United States, Canada, the United Kingdom, and France, at any given time, about a third of women in their "prime years" are not active in the paid labor force—presumably because they are primarily involved with family-related responsibilities. About half the women in Germany and the Netherlands and 60 percent of prime age women in Italy are not in the paid labor

Table 21.1 / Average Percentage of Population not in the Paid Labor Force in the 1980s, by Gender and Age[a]

Country	Males Aged			Females Aged		
	15–24	25–54	55–64	15–24	25–54	55–64
United States[c]	36.6	12.1	34.7	44.9	35.3	59.6
Canada	40.7	12.8	34.1	44.1	38.1	68.2
United Kingdom[c]	36.0	14.9	37.7	40.3	36.4	65.1
Italy[b]	64.3	11.3	62.8	74.5	60.1	89.6
France	59.4	9.1	49.6	70.5	38.0	69.1
Netherlands	46.4	12.1	55.0	50.6	51.4	84.9
Germany	42.8	12.2	43.7	51.6	48.1	77.4
Sweden[c]	36.5	6.6	25.6	36.8	13.6	41.2

SOURCE: OECD *Employment Outlook 1992.* Table 2.7.

[a]The nonemployment rate is defined as the sum of persons not in employment (unemployed + inactive) as a percentage of the working age population. It is calculated over the period 1980 to 1989.
[b]Italy: age groups are 14–24, 25–59, and 60–64.
[c]Sweden, United Kingdom, United States: age groups are 16–24, 25–55, 55–64.

force. Only Sweden approaches the active society goal of full female labor force participation: at any time, eight of every ten Swedish women are in the paid labor force in their prime child-rearing years.[2]

However, the *strength* of female attachment to the paid labor force varies as widely as overall participation rates. Three-quarters of the women who work in the United States, Canada, and France work full-time. Although only 44 percent of women are in the labor force in Italy, almost 90 percent of these work full-time. While 80 percent of Swedish women are in the labor force, less than 60 percent work full-time. In both Germany and the Netherlands, a little over half of all prime age women are in the labor force, but almost 70 percent of the German women work full-time compared to less than 40 percent of Dutch women (Table 21.2).

Thus, the work expectations for women still vary widely. Although government policies can affect the labor force attachment of mothers, cultural norms have been fairly resistant to change. Nonetheless, there seems to be a grudging movement toward the view that at least mothers of school-aged children should have some involvement in the paid workforce. Proponents point out that it becomes increasingly difficult to reenter the paid workforce after years of inactivity,[3] so they argue it is better to encourage some part-time work throughout the child-rearing years if a mother is expected to enter full-time employment after her children are grown.

But the growing social consensus supporting working mothers obscures divergent trends in labor market demand. The (so far) fairly robust demand for high-skilled labor makes it desirable for educated mothers to remain in the labor force from a societal point of view (even if it may not be deemed desirable by

Table 21.2 / Women and Work at the End of the 1980s

Country	Female Labor Force Participation Rate 1989[a]	Percentage of all Female Workers who Worked Full-Time in 1990[b]	Percentage of Female Part-Timers who Worked 20 Hours or Less per Week in 1988[c]
United States	68.1	74.8	N.A.
Canada	67.3	75.6	N.A.
United Kingdom	64.8	56.2	67.4
Italy	44.3	89.1	58.5
France	56.1	76.2	55.4
Germany	55.8	69.4	61.1
Netherlands	52.0	38.3	72.6
Sweden	80.6	59.5	N.A.

SOURCES:
[a] *Employment Outlook 1992.* Table H, p. 276.
[b] *Employment Outlook 1991.* Table 2.9, p. 46.
[c] *Employment Outlook 1991.* Table 2.10, p. 48.
N.A. = Not Available.

the family or the individual mother). Governments want to encourage highly educated female workers to remain in the labor force during their child-rearing years: their productive capacity is high and their contributions to the private economy and tax coffers will be critically important as Western societies age.

Yet, if the wages of low-skilled women are equal to or less than the costs of childcare, there is little economic reason for them to work, and we are likely to find that highly educated mothers have higher labor force participation rates than do low-skilled mothers. Indeed, this differential is already evident among lone mothers in most countries and creates a sociopolitical dynamic very detrimental to interests of poor women. When the government provides special income assistance to nonworking mothers (over and above family allowances or advance child support), it can be accused of subsidizing nonwork. In means-tested systems, this sets the stage for attacks on social-assistance benefit levels and for calls for work requirements for poor mothers in the name of vertical equity.

Clearly, the way women balance child-rearing responsibilities and participation in the paid labor force will remain an important issue for labor market policy in the 1990s. Will governments encourage more women to work in those nations where work expectations have been limited? If they do, what effect will the influx of women into an already overcrowded low-wage labor market have on wage policies and employment security?[4] Will we see a movement toward the adoption of some version of the Swedish model, in which almost all women are attached to the paid labor force, but a substantial proportion work only part-time? Can the Swedish model work if the state is *not* the primary employer of part-time female workers? Or will full mobilization of the labor supply be so strictly interpreted that all adults will be expected to work full-time, regardless of their family responsibilities or earnings potential? If this happens, will the necessary investments in public childcare services be forthcoming?

Weighing the costs and benefits of these various approaches to female labor force participation will depend on social judgments of the importance of work, child-rearing, reproductive rights, and basic fairness. But the work behavior of educated women will play an important role in these evaluations. As long as a significant proportion of educated mothers choose not to enter the paid workforce, the work behavior of poor mothers will not be questioned. But as the proportion of middle-class mothers who work reaches majority status, then work demands on poor mothers are likely to increase even if the demand for their labor does not.

The degree to which women are included in efforts to fully mobilize the labor force frames the policies described below. Although there is a tendency to view programs aimed at the long-term unemployed as programs targeted at low-skilled male workers, this need not be the case. In fact, the three general strategies described below (reducing income support, an increased emphasis on job search and training, and work creation schemes) have included women—mothers—as well as men.

INCOME ASSISTANCE: A DISINCENTIVE TO WORK?

During the 1980s, critics of the generous income support programs provided in Europe argued that these programs contributed to Europe's higher unemployment rates and to long-term unemployment in two ways. First, these programs increased the social costs of labor, thereby making employers reluctant to create more jobs. New research (Abraham and Houseman 1993; Blank 1993; Blank and Freeman 1993; Burtless 1987) has found the connection between poor job growth and the generosity of social protection programs in Europe to be tenuous.[5] Nonetheless, the orthodoxy among European policymakers in the 1980s was so powerful that many countries reformed their labor market institutions to allow employers greater flexibility in their treatment of workers. France, Germany, and the United Kingdom weakened their laws against arbitrary dismissal; the Netherlands, the United Kingdom, and France decentralized the collective bargaining process and/or wage agreements. But there is little evidence that the increased flexibility afforded to employers by these changes significantly increased private job creation efforts.

The second criticism of Europe's generous social-assistance programs is that they slow workers' adjustment to economic change. They encourage/allow workers to withdraw from the labor market for a while instead of immediately looking for new employment. And research from a number of countries has shown that the longer an individual remains unemployed, the harder it becomes for that person to find employment (de Neubourg 1991). Whether this is a function of skill deterioration or the stigma employers attach to long-term joblessness is not clear.

If the generosity of income support programs creates the disincentives to work that critics claim, we would expect the countries with the most generous programs to have the highest rates of long-term unemployment. Table 21.3 shows the broad array of income support available to individuals rejected by the labor market. Sweden's unemployment insurance system provides the most generous wage replacement rate—the unemployed receive 90 percent of their previous wages—but unemployment benefits last only a year. The Netherlands and France have the longest-lasting unemployment benefit schemes, and wage replacement rates are high. Canada and Germany provide benefits close to the replacement rate provided in France (about 60 percent), but individuals can receive unemployment benefits for only one year. The United States and Italy provide benefits for a maximum of 6 months. Italy and the United Kingdom provide the lowest benefit levels (only about 15 percent of an average production worker's earnings). All the Western states examined here except for the United States and Italy provide a second tier of income support for individuals who exhaust their unemployment insurance benefits.

If the availability of support encourages labor force withdrawal, then the Netherlands and France should have the highest rates of long-term unemployment. In fact, Italy—the country with the most meager, short-term assistance—

Table 21.3 / Unemployment Insurance and Assistance Benefits for a Prime-Age Employed Worker[a]

Country	Benefit Type	Qualifying Conditions and Maximum Duration of Benefits[b]			Initial Relation to Earnings[c]	Initial Gross Replacement Rate of Average Production Worker's 1988 Earnings[d]		
		Reference Period	Employment Record	Maximum Benefit Duration	Formula	Single	With Spouse	
							At Work	Dependent
United States	Unemployment insurance	1 year	20 weeks[e]	26 weeks	Proportional	50	50	50
Canada	Unemployment insurance[f]	1 year	27 weeks	50 weeks	Proportional	60	60	60
	Social welfare			Indefinite	Fixed	23	0	37
United Kingdom	Unemployment insurance	1 year	11 weeks[g]	52 weeks	Fixed	16	16	26
	Guaranteed minimum income			Indefinite	Fixed	16	0	26
Italy	Unemployment insurance	1 year	2 years	6 months	Proportional	15	15	15
France	Unemployment insurance	24 months	12 months[h]	30 months	Linear	59	59	59
	Unemployment assistance	10 years	5 years	Indefinite	Fixed	26	19[i]	26
	Guaranteed minimum income			Indefinite	Fixed	23[j]		
Germany	Unemployment insurance	4 years	3 years	12 months	Proportional	58	58	58
	Unemployment assistance			Indefinite	Proportional	52	0[k]	52
Netherlands	Unemployment insurance	5 years	3 years	36 months	Proportional	70	70	70
	Guaranteed minimum income			Indefinite	Fixed	40	0	58
Sweden	Unemployment insurance	12 months	5 months	60 weeks	Proportional	90	90	90
	Social welfare			Indefinite	Fixed	27	0	44

SOURCE: *Employment Outlook 1991.* Tables 7.2, 201.

[a] The table refers to the system on 1 January 1989 and to a worker 40 years and 1 day old (except in a few countries, the same rates apply at other ages between 25 and 50 or 55). For Canada and the United States, actual provisions vary by region (an approximately representative case is shown). The married person cases refer to a couple without children. Provisions for couples with children may be different.

[b] To qualify for the maximum duration of insurance benefits, the worker must have had the employment record listed during the reference period listed, counting the reference period up to the time of entering unemployment.

[c] See Table 7.A.1., p. 228, *Employment Outlook 1991* for details of how benefits in some countries fall during a prolonged spell of unemployment.

[d] This replacement rate refers to benefits before tax (and also before other benefits such as housing benefit, and without any reductions due to income testing of assistance benefits, other than with respect to spouse's earnings), as a percentage of previous earnings also before tax, when the person and spouse in work have 1988 Average Production Worker (APW) level of earnings. The gross replacement rate can be less than the percentage rate of benefit when there is a ceiling to insurable earnings that is below the APW level.

[e] States in the United States have their own eligibility rules. Many use earnings level as a qualifying condition for UI receipt.

[f] In Canada, due to a 1990 change in the law, an employment record of 27 weeks will now give 50 weeks of benefit only in regions with an unemployment rate above 14 percent.

[g] To qualify for insurance benefits in the United Kingdom, earnings in the last tax year must have been at least 50 times the lower limit (£41 per week as of January 1, 1989). At the Average Production Worker level of earnings, this required about 11 weeks of work but in lower-paid jobs more work would have been required.

[h] If a person with 6 months' employment in the last 12 months has 10 years' employment in the last 15 years, he/she can receive 30 months' maximum benefits.

[i] This benefit (ASS-the "solidarity benefit") is means-tested and is paid up to a maximum amount each month of ff4650 for a single person and ff9300 for a couple (January 1989). This limit leads to only a partial withdrawal of the benefit when the working spouse is at the 1988 Average Production Worker level of earnings.

[j] The Revenu Minimum d'Insertion (RMI) was passed in 1988, primarily to provide coverage for single individuals without a work history. However, initial evaluations showed a good number of older single mothers used the benefit.

[k] Some unemployment assistance payments may be available to a person whose spouse is in full-time work. Any excess of the working spouse's own earnings over his/her hypothetical needs (DM150 per week, DM650 per month) is deducted from the assistance payment to the nonworking spouse. This mechanism extinguishes benefit unless the working spouse has low earnings or the nonworking spouse had high earnings when in work.

wins this dubious distinction. About 70 percent of the unemployed in Italy had been unemployed for more than a year in 1989 (OECD 1992). About half of the unemployed in both the Netherlands and Germany are long-term unemployed, even though unemployment benefits in the Netherlands last three times as long as unemployment assistance in Germany. The United Kingdom and France have similar rates of long-term unemployment (41–44 percent), but France's unemployment insurance benefits last three times as long as those in the United Kingdom and are four times as generous. The "benefits-encourage-withdrawal" argument doesn't hold up on the basis of cross-national evidence.

Still, on an individual basis, the argument remains persuasive: If the government provides income support close to what one would earn in wages, there is little incentive to leave assistance for work, particularly among the least skilled, who may find little intrinsic enjoyment in the kind of jobs to which they are relegated. In the 1980s, policymakers spent a good deal of time worrying about what the appropriate income gap between workers and nonworkers should be. The countries used here to illustrate the debate on this issue, the Netherlands and the United States, are at opposite poles in terms of the overall generosity of their income support programs. Yet both reformed their policies to increase the gap.

Basic minimum assistance levels in European countries are often pegged to wages, in order to keep the income of an unemployed person within socially acceptable norms. The social democratic view holds that individuals who find themselves without occupation are already penalized; to force severe income deprivation on them as well serves no purpose. Poverty demoralizes the unemployed and reduces their capacity to search for work. Minimum income support is part of a general strategy of keeping inequality within reasonable boundaries through solidaristic wage policies and the like.[6]

In the Netherlands, unemployment rose rapidly in the early 1980s—about one in ten workers were unemployed, over half for over a year. About a third of households headed by a young person had no earners, and a large proportion of these households were entirely dependent on assistance (Chapter 1 in this volume; de Neubourg 1991). Jobless individuals in the Netherlands who did not qualify for or had exhausted their unemployment benefits could receive monthly income assistance equal to about 40 percent of the average worker's wages (Table 21.3).

In the mid-1980s, some researchers identified a "culture of dependency" among indigenous young Dutch people in Amsterdam and Rotterdam (Engerson et al. 1987). These young people doubled up in households, illegally pooling resources so that they had a combined household income of more than a single working person. Committed to a so-called alternative lifestyle (typically in the arts), they were willing to trade a minimal income for freedom from paid work. While these individuals represented only a small minority of those receiving assistance, they showed that the system was supporting people who *chose* not to work.

Growth in the proportion of long-term unemployed ethnic immigrants in the largest Dutch cities also fueled charges that Dutch income support was too generous. A steady flow of about 50,000 North African migrants a year continued to arrive in Holland in the 1980s, in spite of double digit unemployment. Although studies showed that most migrants came for purposes of family reunification and hoped to work, the influx provoked popular outcries that these immigrants were settling in the Netherlands because of the country's generous and accessible public assistance programs.

So, as joblessness and dependency rose, policymakers decided to "de-link" social assistance from wage levels (de Neubourg 1990). For some period of time, inflation will be allowed to erode the real value of social assistance in the Netherlands. Wages, however, continue to be inflation-adjusted, so over time the wages–assistance gap has increased. Presumably, the minimum assistance allowance will be allowed to fall to about the 25 percent (of the average production worker's salary) that appears to be the unacknowledged norm in most countries (OECD 1991: 228).

The United States, the classic example of a "residual welfare state" (Titmuss 1974), has no guaranteed minimum income assistance for childless adults, nor is the income support that is available to the poor wage-linked or inflation-adjusted. In fact, the only income support available to childless adults who have exhausted or been ruled ineligible for unemployment benefits[7] is General Assistance (GA). GA is not a federal program: it is available statewide in only 8 of the 50 states; another 16 states have county-based GA programs. In most locales, GA provides very meager income support—often less than 40 percent of the *minimum* wage.[8] Public assistance for childless adults in the United States is so low that few people argue it is a disincentive to work.

The same cannot be said for Aid to Families with Dependent Children (AFDC), the major income support program for poor families, which is calculated according to family size. The real value of AFDC benefits was allowed to erode in most states for most of the decade, declining on average by about 40 percent. However, the federal minimum wage was also untouched between 1981 and 1989. As a result, by 1988, the combined maximum AFDC and Food Stamp benefits for a family of three provided a higher monthly income than full-time minimum wage employment in 34 states.

This spawned a debate about how to remove work disincentives from AFDC and to "make work pay." Critics of the income assistance program called for reduction in support levels, and state legislatures in California and Wisconsin did reduce benefits. But at the national level, Congress focused on the positive incentives for work, increasing the Earned Income Tax Credit, an income supplement for low-wage workers. The Family Support Act, passed in 1988, mandated that states provide more employment and training options for AFDC adults and encourage them to look for work. However, without a healthcare guarantee and continuously subsidized childcare, a low-skilled lone mother of several children would find no economic advantage in working—assuming she could find full-time work. Enrollment in the AFDC program continued to climb in the 1990s as job growth stagnated.

The United States and the Netherlands present two very different kinds of social protection systems, yet they illustrate the same problem—the difficulty in setting a minimum income level that allows citizens in an affluent society to maintain an acceptable living standard without undermining the motive to work. As a growing proportion of Western citizens age into dependent status, the fiscal burden of supporting large numbers of unemployed able-bodied workers is likely to create more pressure to reduce or restrict income support. In most European countries, it has proved socially unacceptable to openly cut benefits, but we may see more nations resort to inflation-erosion to depress social-assistance benefits in the 1990s. The question is, how far will this be allowed to go? How much will the "social costs of labor" be reduced before European policymakers believe they are competitive with other countries? How much inequality between workers and the jobless can be allowed to exist without fundamentally undermining the concept of national solidarity or social citizenship (Marshall 1950)?

PUBLIC EMPLOYMENT SERVICES: THE KEY TO ACTIVE LABOR MARKET POLICIES

A national public employment service (PES) has two major functions. First, it helps to reduce frictional unemployment by matching potential employers with employees as rapidly as possible. Second, it helps workers adjust to structural changes in the economy by encouraging/assisting those who try to move from declining sectors of the economy to dynamic industries. In the process of performing these tasks, the PES may also promote more equity in employment insofar as it moves disadvantaged workers closer to the front of the employment queue. Although many Western nations have established or strengthened antidiscrimination legislation in recent years (see Part III), most public employment services in the 1980s were more concerned with employment matching and structural adjustment than with equity issues.

The effectiveness of any placement service depends on its ability to identify and fill labor market vacancies. Employers must notify the PES of vacancies and use public agencies to recruit a broad range of workers for PES to have an effective role. Today, only Sweden, Italy, and France legally require employers to report openings to the public employment service. Sweden gradually extended compulsory notification of vacancies and mandated that firms notify the employment exchanges about planned layoffs in the 1980s (Standing 1988: Chapter 5). Both Sweden[9] and Italy also ban the use of profit-making placement agencies (Table 21.4). In effect, these countries are trying to create a public employment service monopoly on placement services. But even in Sweden, it is estimated that only about two-thirds of all job openings come through the public employment office.[10] In most other countries, the figure is between a tenth and a third (OECD 1990:27). Improving the labor market coverage of public employment services would presumably improve the government's abil-

Table 21.4 / Public Employment Services in the 1980s

Country	Percentage of GDP Spent on PES and Administration, 1988[1]	Unemployed Persons per Staff in Public Employment Office, 1988[2]	Employers Required to Notify Public Employment Offices of Vacancies?[3]	Profit-Making Placement Agencies Legal?[4]
United States	.06	N.A.	No[a]	Yes
Canada	.20	213	No	Yes
United Kingdom	.15	53	No	Yes
Italy	.08	N.A.	Yes	Banned
France	.12	271	Yes[b]	For temp work only
Germany	.24	86	No	For temp work only
Netherlands	.08	152	No[c]	Yes
Sweden	.21	14	Yes[d]	Banned

SOURCES:
[1] *Employment Outlook 1992.* Table 2.B.1.
[2] *Employment Outlook 1991.* Table 7.7., p. 213.
[3] *Employment Outlook 1991.* Table 7.11.
[4] *Employment Outlook 1991.* Table 7.11.

[a] U.S. firms with government contracts of $10,000 or more are required to report vacancies to the public employment service.
[b] All vacancies for external candidates must be reported to the public employment service.
[c] In the Netherlands, there is no requirement in general law to notify vacancies to the public employment service, but some collective agreements specify that employers notify vacancies to the public employment agency. Private sector placement agencies need permits; but the effective degree of restrictions appears low.
[d] The public employment service must be notified of all vacancies in Sweden except those for management staff, for occasional employment (less than 10 days), and those to be filled by existing employees.
N.A. = Not Available.

ity to place the unemployed quickly. Yet few nations have attempted to control information on the employer side of the recruitment process.

The public resources available to assist the unemployed vary a great deal by country. Germany, Sweden, and Canada spend about three times more on public employment services than do the United States, Italy, and the Netherlands (Table 21.4). Yet these differences do not fully capture the real distribution of resources within a particular country. In Canada, France, and the Netherlands, less than 30 percent of the staff of the public employment services are engaged in "active" labor market policies—i.e., in providing employment-related services to clients (OECD 1990:31). The vast majority only process unemployment benefit claims. As column 2 in Table 21.4 shows, most public employment services simply do not have the staff to provide real job placement or counseling to the unemployed.

Instead of investing in more staff or improving coverage of vacancies, most public employment services tightened up restrictions on the receipt of unemployment insurance and/or established special procedures or programs for the long-term unemployed (Table 21.5). The United Kingdom may have developed the most elaborate procedure.

Table 21.5 / Constraints on Unemployment Insurance/Assistance Receipt

Country	Minimum Waiting Period?[1]	Waiting Period if Voluntarily Quit?[2]	Sign-on or Reporting Procedure?[3]	Scheduling of Intensified Interviews?[4]
United States	1 week	Disqualifies[a]	Every 1–2 weeks	
Canada	2 weeks	6 weeks		
United Kingdom	3 days	1–26 weeks[b]		Every 6 months
France	None	Disqualifies[c]	Monthly, by post	4th and 13th months of unemployment
Germany	None	12 weeks	No regular procedure	At least after 1 year
Netherlands	None	None	Maximum 3 months, by post[d]	After 3 years
Sweden	None	4–10 weeks	No regular procedure[e]	Unemployed over 6 months get priority

SOURCES:
[1] *Employment Outlook 1991.* Table 7.5.
[2] *Employment Outlook 1991.* Table 7.6.
[3] *Employment Outlook 1991.* Table 7.8.
[4] *Employment Outlook 1991.* Table 7.9.

NOTE: Italy was not included in the study from which this information was taken.

[a] Ten states have no waiting period. Complete benefit disqualification applies to voluntary quits in all but five states.
[b] There was a maximum disqualification of 6 weeks until 1986 in the U.K. Between 1986 and 1988, the disqualification was 13 weeks.
[c] A worker may argue before a bilateral commission that there were legitimate reasons for quitting. If this case is not brought to or accepted by the commission, no benefits are paid.
[d] The local labor office may require more frequent reporting or reporting in person.
[e] In Sweden, the employment officer and unemployed job-seeker set the next appointment date at each visit.

Under the Restart initiative, established in 1987, an unemployed person is given a mandatory interview appointment schedule with a "new client advisor" with whom to develop a "back to work" plan on application for unemployment benefits. After 3 months, if the individual is still unemployed, he or she must participate in a job search and/or job review workshop that typically lasts 2 days. If, after 6 months, the individual has still not found employment, he or she may join a Jobclub[11] or receive employment training (which covers a broad range of training and typically lasts about 6 months). If the individual is still unemployed after 2 years, he or she can be required to participate in a mandatory week-long Restart course. Restart courses are designed for those deemed "non-job-ready," who need help with motivation or other assistance.

The British government deemed Restart a success because (a) about 10 percent of the unemployed stopped claiming benefits when they were asked to come in for an interview (the government assumed these claimants had other income and were fraudulently claiming benefits); and (b) there was a large fall in unemployment in the United Kingdom in 1986–89 that some analysts attribute to the program because ". . . long-term unemployment fell much more than short-term unemployment; and there was rapid growth in low-earning and unskilled employment, which might be expected from a strategy which succeeds in getting the unskilled unemployed into work" (OECD 1992:147). One of the unspoken goals of these kinds of reforms appears to be to encourage low-skilled workers to adjust their expectations downward and accept whatever wages the labor market offers. Although these tactics may reduce unemployment and speed some structural readjustment, it hardly seems the kind of adjustment most citizens would find comforting.

Staff and fiscal resources devoted to public employment services are important, but appropriate institutional networks are perhaps the most critical element of a nation's ability to operate active labor market policies. There has to be some coordination between the agency that registers the unemployed, public placement services, and training or retraining programs. Sweden is undoubtedly the leader in active labor market policies: It consistently spends more on active measures than on unemployment benefits. As a result, registered unemployment was kept at 3 percent or less through the 1980s while 5 percent of the labor force were in active labor market programs during the height of the recession (Meidner 1991).

Sweden is able to achieve this because it has an integrated yet flexible administrative structure for its labor market policies. All programs are operated through a centralized tripartite authority—the National Labour Market Board (NLMB)—comprised of private employers, the government, and unions. Of the 10,000 staff employed by the labor market administration, only 500 are at the central agency in Stockholm. The rest work in over 300 local employment service offices and institutes for vocational rehabilitation in twenty-four county labor boards across the country which are responsible for formulating policy. The local LMBs follow guidelines set by the central authority, but they choose measures and programs that seem most applicable to local conditions. This allows local boards to shift investments quickly from one measure to another, depending on market conditions. Although place-specific monitoring is built into the system, Swedish policies emphasize training for the national labor market, and mobility grants are used to encourage workers to move to jobs.[12]

In the past, Sweden relied on a full array of active measures. However, the advent of a more conservative government at the end of the decade has resulted in an ideological shift, and training programs are now being emphasized at the expense of job creation schemes.

The public employment service of a country is the command center of active labor market policies. A national or regional system for identifying job shortages, emerging skill demands, and labor surpluses must be in place if a government is to effectively place citizens in activities that have the potential to improve their employment prospects. Unfortunately, few of the nations without developed capacities in these areas invested in upgrading their public employment services in the 1980s.

"If We Train Them, Jobs Will Come."

In the 1980s, the mantra of the active society was "training, more training." If the problem was that there were not enough jobs for low-skilled workers, then the solution was to train them into being skilled workers. Raising the skill levels of the jobless would not only increase their employability, it would also improve the productivity of the workforce and increase national competitiveness.

By the end of the decade, at least 1 percent of the workforce in every country examined here was participating in a training program for the unemployed. It has been estimated that enrollment in training programs reduced the unemployment rate in Germany, Canada, France, and the Netherlands by between .5 and 1 percent (OECD 1990:37). In Sweden, about 2 percent of the labor force enrolls in training annually (Meidner 1991).[13] At the end of the decade, most of the countries examined here spent between .28 and .55 percent of their GDP on training programs, with the exception of the United States, which spent only .12 percent and Italy and Sweden, which spent .72 and .90, respectively (Table 21.6). Four countries—Germany, Sweden, Italy, and France—significantly increased total spending on public training; public spending on training in the United States actually dropped.[14] Italy almost doubled its overall spending, quadrupling the money devoted to youth training programs. (See Pugliese, Chapter 13 in this volume, on these programs.) France increased its training expenditures on every target group somewhat. Germany doubled its spending overall, tripling expenditures on unemployed adults, as a result of the new obligations it acquired with Reunification. Sweden significantly increased its

Table 21.6 / Public Expenditures on Training (as a percentage of GDP)

Country	Unemployed Adults 1985–1986	Unemployed Adults 1991–1992	Employed Adults 1985–1986	Employed Adults 1991–1992	At-Risk Youth 1985–1986	At-Risk Youth 1991–1992	General Youth 1985–1986	General Youth 1991–1992	Total Public Spending on Training Programs 1985–1986	Total Public Spending on Training Programs 1991–1992
United States	.12	.09	—	—	.03	.03	—	—	.15	.12
Canada	.32	.34	.01	.02	.03	.02	—	—	.36	.38
United Kingdom	.07	.15	.02	.02	.02	—	.24	.18	.35	.35
Italy[a]	.06	.03	—	—	.22	.26	.10	.43	.38	.72
France[b]	.22	.28	.03	.05	.05	.08	.12	.14	.42	.55
Germany	.15	.44	.05	.03	.04	.04	.01	.01	.25	.52
Netherlands[b]	.19	.22	—	—	—	.01	.04	.05	.24	.28
Sweden	.48	.77	.02	.02	.21	.11	—	—	.71	.90

SOURCE: OECD *Employment Outlook 1992*. Table 2.B.1.

[a] 1988 is most recent year.
[b] 1990 is most recent year.

spending on unemployed adults, but reduced training expenditures on at-risk youths. The United Kingdom redistributed training funds from youth programs to training for unemployed adults during the second half of the decade.

The investment in training programs is based on an unproven leap of faith and a shaky assumption. First, and most importantly, the training solution is grounded on the assumption that employers will change the way they organize production when the skill level of workers improves, and that a supply of highly skilled labor will create a demand for itself. There is little empirical evidence to support this view (see Osterman, this volume).

Second, the success of training as a strategy for improving the match between demand and supply trusts the ability of public employment services to accurately predict the emerging demand for different kinds of skilled labor, and its capacity to key this information into the national training system so that low-skilled workers can be prepared for these emerging jobs. Although most national labor offices have become more proficient at predicting labor demand (at least short-term), national public training systems have not been notably successful at producing workers to fill predicted shortages.

In the early- and mid-1980s, youth unemployment was a serious problem in most European countries (see Part III in this volume). Since youth joblessness was heavily concentrated among the least educated (OECD 1989), governments everywhere have encouraged young people to stay in school longer and upgrade their educational credentials, with varying degrees of success. France was a notable leader in this regard, increasing the proportion of 18 year olds who remained in school by 44 percent and the percentage of 19 year olds who stayed in school by over 65 percent in just 6 years (Faure 1991).[15] The proportion of young people leaving school with no qualifications was also cut in half in the 1980s. In Sweden and the United Kingdom, the government disqualified young people under age 18 from receiving unemployment benefits to encourage 16 and 17 year olds to continue school or training.

Most national training systems also focused more attention on the school-to-work transition in the 1980s, attempting to involve private employers more closely in training young people in order to ensure the relevance of the work skills learned. The German "dual system" became the implicit or explicit model for most European apprenticeships or internships.[16] In modern apprenticeship systems, training takes place partly in schools and partly in enterprises. Reforms have focused on measures to improve the quality of training, with stricter curriculum enforcement and more classroom instruction, but the extent and nature of actual training activities differs widely—both between and within programs.

Unfortunately, governments cannot replicate the most unique aspect of the German system: private employers' commitment to providing apprenticeship slots and real training to young people. And even the German system has undergone significant reforms during the last decade (see Casey, Chapter 12 in this volume). The school-based parts of most German certification programs now take up 1 or 2 days per week and the practical training for which employers are responsible has been upgraded (with some public support), and more enterprise training takes place in special training workshops and other institutions than in the past too.

The deep division between general education and vocational tracks found in European upper-secondary schools reflects and reinforces the rigidity of the labor markets into which trainees are sent (Leibfried and Allmendinger 1991; Osterman, Chapter 11 in this volume). But as these labor markets become more flexible and occupational structures change more rapidly, vocational training is proving a less reliable path to occupational security. As more and more young people in France and Great Britain transitioned from school to unemployment in the 1970s and 1980s, both countries experimented extensively with special youth training and work experience programs.

In France, youth employment-training contracts and internships were established in 1975 and reformed annually. In 1981, a generalized plan for young adults was devised which included the earlier programs and established work initiation internships (SIVP), special school-based internships for the least qualified school leavers (DIJEN), and socially useful work programs (TUC) for young people. Over two million French young people entered one of these programs between 1986 and 1988; by 1987, about 9 percent of all 16–24 year olds in France were in some kind of transition program (Faure 1991).

In the United Kingdom, the Work Experience Programme, a scheme that gave youths temporary jobs, was replaced by the Youth Opportunities Program (YOP) for 16–18-year-olds and the Special Temporary Employment Programs (STEP) for those aged 18 and over in 1978. In 1983, YOP was replaced with the Youth Training Scheme (YTS), which offered school-leavers 12 months of work experience combined with 13 weeks or more of off-the-job training. By 1984, there were about 300,000 youths in YTS and over 33,000 in YOP (Standing 1989). The employment services also became involved with two school-based vocational training programs—the Technical and Vocational Education Initiative (TVEI) and the Non-Advanced Further Education (NAFW) scheme.

The criticisms of the youth initiatives in both countries were surprisingly similar (Faure 1991; Standing 1989). The programs were set up quickly on a large scale, leading to a great deal of administrative confusion about rules and eligibility. Both trainees and participating employers had difficulty keeping up with frequent rule changes. But the most serious criticism was that the training provided to young people was of uneven quality and sometimes lacking altogether. As in Italy (see Pugliese, Chapter 13 in this volume), there were charges that some employers were taking advantage of the government subsidies to acquire extra labor, but providing little useful training. (In 1989, SIVP rules were changed to prevent the "moral abuse" of these internships by employers (Faure 1991).)

In fact, most "training" programs for unemployed young people are designed to only provide work experience. This is true for Canada, the Netherlands, Sweden, France, the United Kingdom, and Italy (OECD 1990:43). The

Table 21.7 / Measures for Unemployed or Disadvantaged Youth: 1988

Country	Participants Starting per Year as Percentage of the Labor Force	Public Outlays		
		Total as Percentage of GDP	US $ per Starting Participant[a]	Outlay per Participant as Percentage of Average Income[b]
United States	0.6	0.03	1,800	9
Canada	0.6	0.02	1,200	6
United Kingdom	0.02	0.01	7,300	46
France	1.4	0.06	1,800	11
Germany	0.4	0.04	4,200	21
Netherlands	0.2	0.03	4,500	28
Sweden	0.6	0.09	5,800	29

SOURCE: OECD 1990: Table 8.

NOTE: Italy was not included in the study from which this information was taken.

[a] The conversion to United States dollars has been made using average 1988 exchange rates.

[b] Average income: annual GDP per capita.

differences in cost per participant shown in Table 21.7 are primarily the result of differences in the stipends given to young people and/or the subsidies provided to employers.

Although school completion rates have improved in most Western states in the past 20–30 years, a significant proportion of young people still leave school without basic educational qualification each year. Thus, we are continuing to create an influx of low-skilled "at-risk" young people even as we puzzle over what to do with their parents and older siblings. For the truth is that no nation has sorted out how to improve basic competency and teach vocational skills to large numbers of minimally qualified adults in a way that moves them out of the "least skilled" category and up in the hiring queue.

Most national training programs were established in the 1960s and 1970s to deal with skill shortages and mismatches. To be effective, vocational training must *anticipate* market developments and train for them. Unfortunately, most national training systems do not have strong records of being future-oriented in the skills taught, and many do not have well-established links to employers in the private market (Castro and Andrade 1990). Thus, there is an inevitable lag between the technology and techniques used on the job and those taught in large publicly funded institutions. Developing vocational courses is time-consuming and can be capital-intensive, when equipment is involved. There is a natural tendency for public training to outlive its relevance. As a result, most vocational training provided in public institutions is not state-of-the-art. But most long-term unemployed or those low-skilled individuals at risk of becoming long-term unemployed have not had the opportunity to test the vocational training system thoroughly. As Table 21.8 shows, training courses tend to be short-term and relatively inexpensive.

Table 21.8 / Training for Unemployed Adults and Those At-Risk: 1988

Country	Participants Starting per Year as Percentage of the Labor Force	Average Duration in Months	Public Outlays		
			Total as Percentage of GDP	US $ per Starting Participant[a]	Outlay per Participant as Percentage of Average Income[b]
United States	1.0	3.5	0.05	1,800	9
(including Perkins Act)	[6.4]	—	.11	650	3
Canada	1.1	6	0.22	7,000	37
United Kingdom	1.4	—	0.22	5,000	31
France	2.3	2.5	0.28	4,600	27
Germany	1.5	8	0.25	7,200	37
Netherlands	2.3	4	0.20	3,500	22
Sweden	1.7	5	0.54	12,000	60

SOURCE: OECD 1990: Table 5.

NOTE: Italy was not included in the study from which this information was taken.

[a] The conversion to United States dollars has been made using average 1988 exchange rates.
[b] Average income = annual GDP per capita.

Most countries introduced special reorientation programs for the long-term unemployed in the 1980s. An OECD report observed:

> These schemes aim principally at improving motivation, life skills and job search techniques, and at providing general information about the operation of the labor market. They may involve a limited amount of skill instruction or actual work experience, but not usually to the extent that the participants can subsequently exercise a particular skill or occupation. . . . Examples of this kind of measure are to be found in the U.K. in the Wider Opportunities Programme, the CBB programme in the Netherlands, the AFG programme in Germany, . . . and the recently introduced special modular training courses for the unskilled longterm unemployed in France. . . . In Sweden,[17] the AMI-A centers mount special courses for hard to place unemployed, lasting in some cases up to 24 weeks (the average is about 11 weeks) . . . while this program involves skill instruction, the main emphasis is on improving behavior and attitudes (OECD 1988: 34).

Large-scale public training programs have not been able to significantly improve the skill levels of large numbers of the unemployed, especially those with the lowest educational attainment levels. Training, while politically attractive because it promises a win-win strategy for all, has proved an elusive elixir.

WORK CREATION STRATEGIES

Using public funds to stimulate the demand for labor was not a particularly popular policy in any Western democracy in the 1980s, even though job creation schemes and public sector employment are considered part of "active" labor market policies. As Table 21.9 shows, most national governments cut spending for job creation in the second half of the decade. Today, only Germany and Sweden spend significant sums on work creation, and only Germany increased spending, primarily due to its unique problems in finding employment for workers in the former East Germany. Although not a major part of the economic orthodoxy of the 1980s, these programs merit review.

Public Subsidies to Private Employers

In the late 1970s and early 1980s, a number of European governments embraced wage subsidy schemes or "marginal stock" subsidy plans that allowed private employers to receive a weekly or monthly subsidy for each additional worker taken on above a specific base point. The subsidies could be a fixed sum per hour per worker (an arrangement that automatically favors the least skilled) or could be for a percentage of the normal wage for the occupation. They were usually for a limited period and/or gradually declined over time. Like the other programs examined thus far, they had the goal of expanding the total number of employment slots and of placing disadvantaged groups in employment. Target groups varied significantly, but a majority of programs favored the long-term unemployed.[18] Other schemes target relatively broad and varied groups. Employer subsidy schemes in Germany target older workers; in France, part-time workers are targeted. The Targeted Jobs Tax Credit in the United States defines nine categories of disadvantaged adults and youngsters.

Table 21.9 / Public Expenditures on Work Creation Programs (as a percentage of GDP)

| | Types of Work Programs | | | | | | Total Spending on Work Creation Programs | |
| | Private Employer Subsidies | | Self-Employment Schemes | | Direct Public Sector Job Creation | | | |
Country	1985–1986	1991–1992	1985–1986	1991–1992	1985–1986	1991–1992	1985–1986	1991–1992
United States	.01	—	—	—	.01	.01	.02	.01
Canada	—	—	—	—	.02	.02	.02	.02
United Kingdom	—	—	.03	.03	.19	.01	.22	.04
Italy[a]	—	—	—	—	—	—	.00	.00
France[b]	.02	.03	.04	.02	—	.01	.06	.06
Germany	.05	.04	—	—	.12	.20	.17	.24
Netherlands[b]	.02	.02	—	—	.04	.03	.06	.05
Sweden	.10	.03	.01	.01	.32	.11	.43	.15

SOURCE: OECD *Employment Outlook 1992.* Table 2.B.1.

[a] 1988 is most recent year.
[b] 1990 is most recent year.

France, the United Kingdom, and the Netherlands each established subsidy schemes in the late 1970s. The first French scheme provided an incentive premium for employers who hired older workers. This was followed by employment and training contracts (CEF), which emphasized employment and training for young workers (Caspar 1988). The subsidies continued into the 1980s. The Netherlands also introduced a number of marginal stock schemes in the 1970s, which targeted various disadvantaged groups but consolidated them into a single program to assist hard-to-place unemployed in 1981 (OECD 1988b). Germany has two employment subsidy programs: a small program for older workers and the Integration Assistance Subsidy for "hard to place" unemployed persons. The latter program had a throughput of approximately 53,000 in 1986, 40 percent of whom were long-term unemployed. The general program is short-term, providing subsidies of 50 percent of the wage costs of the previously unemployed for 6 months. (The new recruits are supposed to be hired as permanent employees.) The program for older workers provides more generous subsidies of up to 70 percent of wage costs for 2 years.

The sums in Table 21.10 represent average accumulated subsidy payments per participant in the subsidy schemes in operation today. The subsidies are paid over varying periods, typically for 4, 6, or 12 months. Germany and the Netherlands pay the most subsidies per starting participant, but as is now a familiar pattern, Sweden makes the heftiest long-term commitment.

Marginal stock plans, in effect, give employers the task of administering work programs for the unemployed; their reward is the wage subsidies they receive in return. Initially, there was a great deal of concern about how much of a subsidy would be required to make the administrative costs to employers worthwhile. As it turns out, only certain kinds of employers find these schemes attractive.

To be able to effectively supervise and utilize new workers, a firm has to be doing well enough to afford extra supervisors and/or equipment. In other

Table 21.10 / Subsidies to Regular Jobs in the Private Sector: 1988

Country	Persons Starting per Year as a Percentage of the Labor Force	Public Outlays		
		Total as Percentage of GDP	US $ per Starting Participant[a]	US $ per Participant Place and Year[a]
United States	0.5	0.01	500	—
France[b]	0.2	0.01	1,900	—
Germany	0.2	0.02	5,900	8,700
Netherlands	0.3	0.04	5,300	4,000
Sweden[c]	0.4	0.04	4,600	13,700

SOURCE: OECD 1990: Table 9.

[a]The conversion to United States dollars has been made with average 1988 exchange rates.
[b]Some measures are excluded.
[c]Subsidies to construction during the winter are excluded.

words, it needs to be on the verge of expansion. And only employers in industries or firms that rely on relatively unskilled labor find wage subsidies a counterbalance to the cost of training new workers (especially if the subsidies only last for a period of months). In other words, the policy is likely to create substantial windfall effects for employers of low-wage workers, employers who would have recruited new workers for these jobs even without a subsidy. One report suggested that the windfall effects may be as high as 80 percent: they are typically between 20 and 50 percent (OECD 1990).[19] The take-up on these schemes increased significantly in periods when employment was expanding, fueling complaints about windfall profits.

Critics also expressed concern that wage subsidies could have a negative impact on skilled workers in affected industries. Fixed wage subsidies give an advantage to the employers of low-wage labor. A firm employing more highly skilled labor would be at a distinct market disadvantage if competing against a firm employing low-skilled, low-wage labor because the latter would have a greater proportion of its production costs subsidized. Thus, employer wage subsidies could result in an industry-wide "displacement" of high wage workers by low-wage workers even if no enterprise-level displacement took place.

As experience with marginal stock plans grew, so did skepticism about their ability to generate new job growth. An OECD report characterized employment subsidy schemes as follows:

> There has been a lack of clarity in relation to objectives, particularly where governments simultaneously tried to achieve the twin aims of promoting equity and employment growth. As a result, in a number of countries these measures in particular have been subjected to almost continuous alteration and restructuring, frequently in an ad hoc manner without reference to an overall guiding strategy (OECD 1988:58).

The report concluded that employment subsidy schemes may yet have a role to play in encouraging more *equitable* recruitment—i.e., in moving some groups up in the hiring queue—but that they are not much use in generating new employment overall. With this caveat in mind, France recently increased funding for youth subsidy schemes. Despite their initial enthusiasm for marginal stock programs, most governments reduced investment in these schemes in the 1980s.

Encouraging Self-Employment

If private employers do not want to hire certain groups of workers, why not have these workers "hire themselves"? Why not help them establish their own small businesses or microenterprises? This became a popular approach to job generation in the 1980s. At least seventeen countries established programs to encourage the unemployed to take up self-employment in the 1980s. Programs now exist in Denmark, Finland, France, Germany, Ireland, the Netherlands, and the United Kingdom.

Programs are generally targeted at and open only to unemployed persons who have already received benefits for a certain length of time. Under these schemes, the unemployed are typically allowed to take some or all of their benefits in a lump sum (as start-up capital) rather than receive monthly support, although they may be paid an allowance for a fixed period during the initial stages of business establishment. For example, in the Netherlands, participants receive a substantial initial lump sum (25,000 guilders) and draw a weekly allowance. (For more specifics of the programs, see Table 21A.1.)

The largest self-employment schemes are in France and the United Kingdom. Between 1979 and 1987, over 330,000 French citizens had participated in a self-employment program for the unemployed. Over half a million Britons participated in the Enterprise Allowance Scheme (EAS) in the United Kingdom between 1983, when it was introduced, and 1990.

Self-employment in the United Kingdom almost doubled in the 1980s, growing faster than in any other OECD country (OECD 1992: 172–173). This is partially the result of the EAS, and partially the result of the fact that the costs of entering self-employment in the United Kingdom are relatively low. The benefits from salaried employment are not much greater than one would get from self-employment in the United Kingdom. Job security and employers' social security contributions are relatively low,[20] and self-employed individuals are eligible for a wide range of social security benefits, including National Health Service.

Evaluation studies of self-employment schemes in France and the United Kingdom show that between 50 and 60 percent of the participants in these programs remained in business for over 3 years. However, the British evaluations judged that only about one-quarter of the surviving enterprises would not have been started if EAS support was not available. A sustained net effect in terms of job creation would seem to be in the order of 12–15 percent of total participants, or 60,000 jobs in 7 years (OECD 1992: 46). This is not inconsequential, but expanded numbers appear unlikely.

Self-employment schemes deliberately take up the most interested, capable, and enterprising among the out-of-work. Sometimes these individuals are required to have their own capital to enter the program. Participants in the schemes tend to resemble the existing self-employed population more than the unemployed, and this is especially true of the participants whose businesses survive. They are likely to be older, male, married, skilled, to have had previous work experience, and to have been out of work for less than 6 months. Moreover, a large percentage have a relative who is self-employed (OECD 1992b: 175). Less select groups of unemployed persons are likely to have higher failure rates.

Although self-employment schemes are very popular with governments, we would be remiss if we did not raise questions about the quality of this employment. While many workers might think they would relish the idea of being "their own boss," self-employed individuals typically earn less than salaried employees and work longer hours. With over half of all small businesses failing, these individuals work in conditions of maximum risk. While certainly better than being jobless, programs that promote self-employment add to the overall insecurity of the workforce.

Public Work Creation

Before the 1980s, most European countries spent a good portion of their active labor market moneys on special public employment programs. The jobs created were usually temporary and not meant to compete with regular employment. Although some large public investment projects still exist, recent job creation initiatives have concentrated on service jobs or the maintenance of local infrastructure. By the 1990s, only Germany and Sweden spent significant sums on direct job creation (Table 21.11), and with the advent of a more conservative government in Sweden, there has been a dramatic shift away from relief work to training.

Most public work programs are organized and administered by local bodies but financed by central governments.[21] Protections and compensation vary broadly across national (and even regional) boundaries. In continental Europe, participation in work programs has been targeted at the long-term unemployed, variously defined, with special provisions for young people. In the United Kingdom, Community Programs (temporary work programs) were set up for anyone over age 25 who had been unemployed for 12 of the last 15 months. If the person was under 25 years old, he or she needed to be unemployed only for 6–9 months. In France, the TUC program created a year-long subsidized employment slot for unemployed young persons. Programs in the Netherlands target individuals unemployed for at least a year. In the "plough-back project" in the Netherlands, participants are paid a full wage (local governments can recoup the cost of the unemployment benefits that would have been received by the participants from the central government).

Sweden has a long tradition of using temporary relief work as a tool of

Table 21.11 / Direct Job Creation (public or nonprofit): 1988

| | Participants as Percentage of the Labor Force | Public Outlays | | |
| | | Total as Percentage of GDP | US $ per Starting Participant[a] | US $ per Participant Place and Year[a] |
Country	Persons Starting per Year			
United States	0.1	0.01	3,700	5,100
Canada	0.2	0.02	3,800	—
France	0.2	0.01	2,200	4,700
Germany	0.5	0.16	13,800	14,800
Netherlands	0.1	0.03	9,100	9,600
Sweden	0.8	0.17	7,800	18,600

SOURCE: OECD 1990: Table 11.

[a] The conversion to United States dollars has been made using average 1988 exchange rates.

countercyclical fiscal policy. Public infrastructure and other projects deemed socially useful are first identified, designed, and inventoried. Relief projects are chosen by the National Labor Market Board and generally last 6 months. To qualify for public relief employment, a worker must be unemployed for at least 6 months or, if less than 25 years old, 4 months. Priority is given to those suffering the longest unemployment spells. Wages are equal to the comparable level for the relevant skill category and are subsidized at 50 percent. Since 1980, only public and nonprofit organizations can be sponsors. In 1986, there were four times as many Swedes in direct job creation programs as in training, but the number in work programs steadily declined after the conservative government came in. Enrollment fell from a peak of 58,800 in 1983 to 19,200 in 1986 to 8,000 in 1990 (Meidner 1991).

Germany's main job creation program, ABM, was created in 1969. Target groups are specified by the labor office in each state or *Lander*. Approved sponsors receive central government funding to cover a portion of project costs. Most of the time, between 50 and 75 percent of a worker's wages (the standard market rate) are subsidized, but in regions with high unemployment, up to 90 percent of wages can be subsidized and projects can also get loans for equipment and supplies. Although projects are generally funded for 1 year, they may be extended to 2, and if a sponsor commits itself to offering permanent employment to ABM employees, the project may be extended to 3 years. Sponsors are usually local governments, but a growing share are not-for-profit organizations.

Between 1970 and 1991, average ABM enrollments grew from less than 2,000 to more than 80,000, due to Reunification. However, at its peak, ABM enrollment never represented more than .3 of the labor force or about 5 percent of the unemployed in 1989 (Worden and Vroman 1992).

The United States and Canada also established Community Work Experience Programs (CWEP) for public assistance recipients in the 1980s. In the United States, AFDC or Food Stamp recipients can be asked to perform socially useful community service work in a nonprofit or public agency for a certain number of hours per week (their grant divided by the minimum wage) as a condition of income assistance. After 9 months, they must receive the average wage for that occupation, but most slots do not last this long. Less than 13,000 individuals (out of a caseload of almost 460,000 eligible individuals) were enrolled in work experience programs in 1991 (U.S. Committee on Ways and Means 1993).

We see, then, that there are two general models of public work creation today. In the older, Social Democratic model, relief work is used in countercyclical fashion. Market-comparable wages are paid to relief workers. Working conditions and worker protections are assured by the unionized local government employees who supervise the work. In the newer version, individuals are assigned to a nonprofit organization responsible for providing them with work experience. The individuals in these assignments tend to be paid minimum wages (or substantially less if they are young people on training stipends). Their rights and responsibilities tend to be less defined. With both kinds of work programs, the government may be involved in creating temporary, insecure employment outside the mainstream of society.

Moreover, since these public work programs are the domain of the "least employable," the individuals who end up in them are not only the least skilled and least experienced; they are also likely to be members of groups that suffer employment discrimination in the private market. This raises concerns that they have the potential to reinforce instead of restrain market inequalities. Insofar as income for subsistence is contingent on participating in work schemes, these policies create an essentially involuntary kind of work activity that may segregate, stigmatize, and more permanently marginalize vulnerable groups.

In a democratic, free society, we should perhaps judge these programs according to (a) whether the activity adds to the social product/has real value; and (b) whether the activity makes the individual more likely to be able to move into the mainstream economy and enhances the individual's prospects for future earnings. Local governments in Sweden and Germany would attest to the value the work programs described above provide. The value of some of the other work programs for the long-term unemployed is less clear-cut.

The research evidence regarding the second goal is mixed. An OECD evaluation panel found that participation in temporary public sector jobs does improve future job chances, but the effect was not large (OECD 1988: 48). By contrast, controlled-experimental design evaluations of work experience programs in the United States found that some participants had *lower* employment rates as a result of participating in CWEP programs because the time spent in work programs took time away from the search for work in the private sector (Gueron and Pauly 1991).

WORK, ENTITLEMENTS,
AND THE POSTINDUSTRIAL WELFARE STATE

Twenty-five years ago, the president of the United States, a Republican, proposed a guaranteed income for all American families; today a Democratic president has proposed changing the one federal income support program for the non-elderly into a work-based system. Although the United States has long been known as the most miserly of welfare states, this policy shift is not unreflective of the change in the debates about work and entitlements that has occurred over the past 20 years (Heclo, Chapter 22 in this volume). The emphasis on work is not simply a function of politicians reading the demographic trends and realizing that new taxpayers are needed to support an aging population. Governments are increasingly concerned about the social and political repercussions of long-term idleness.

Twenty years ago, an active goal of many policymakers was to increase the leisure of the populace. Today, most worry that without the "discipline of work," individuals will lapse into a state of alienated detachment or turn to antisocial behavior (crime, substance abuse, etc.). In Europe, young people have been the special target of policy initiatives, the fear being that they will become habituated to a life of idleness or irregular, erratic employment. This led to a number of different schemes for integrating them into the work world, whether through subsidized training with the private sector or "socially useful" activities directed by nonprofits or local authorities. In the United States, poor urban minorities have been the particular target of concern. The long-term unemployed, many of whom have long work histories, have garnered somewhat less attention, but the policy response has been the same: increase the supervision of their activities. The belief that individuals outside the labor market can and will find constructive ways to occupy their time has vanished.

It may not be accidental that "work as an integrative force" has emerged as a theme in public policy debates as our societies become more racially and ethnically diverse. For some observers work symbolizes an individual's willingness and/or ability to assimilate to the mainstream culture. The irony is that this litmus test has been created at a time when more and more native-born white citizens are unable to pass.

Political and social concerns about idleness and dependency have led national governments to create a variety of special training and employment activities for those low-skilled citizens that the market rejects. In large measure, however, the effect of these work and training programs is to replicate and further blur the differences between "regular" or "secure" employment and other activities. Developments in both the private economy and in public policies raise a host of difficult questions about the future of work, about our vision of what work should be. What constitutes a *real* job today? A job with health and retirement benefits? A job that pays a "family" wage? If so, then ever-growing numbers of part-time, self-employed individuals and service sector employees aren't in "real" work. What distinguishes public sector employment from public works schemes? The level of wages paid? The length of the job? The work performed? The conditions of work? Does the use of nonprofits as employers decrease participants' security and protections?

The forms of work in Western societies are changing, and we do not yet have a language to clearly delineate these mutations, let alone a clear understanding of the role that government can or should play in the transformation. (For one view, see Esping-Anderson 1991.) This is the real challenge for the 1990s.

Where have the groping policy reforms of the 1980s left the countries examined here? Has the active society approach been implemented more broadly? Do we have a few more trampolines than safety nets at the end of the decade than we had at the beginning?

Realizing the vision of the active society requires a heavy investment of public moneys and an integrated infrastructure of labor market institutions. Without both, active labor market policies cannot be effective. At the beginning of the decade, only a few of the countries examined here had the institutional networks in place to implement active labor market policies (Sweden, Germany, and the United Kingdom to a lesser degree). No massive new investments, program initiatives, or organizational transformations were started by those nations without such an infrastructure.

Although the new conservative government in Sweden has shifted resources from public relief to training and has allowed unemployment rates to reach unheard-of proportions, the generosity of Sweden's unemployment benefits and training grants is likely to keep inequality in check, at least in the short-term. If long-term unemployment is allowed to grow, the political climate may change.

Germany was content to define full employment rather narrowly in the 1980s (males between their late twenties and early fifties) and was financially able to support a rather large dependent population. Unification and recent changes in the international climate have changed this and we may see greater efforts to mobilize the educated labor supply and trim back social benefits in the future.

The government in the United Kingdom briskly stepped up the integration activities of the Manpower Services Commission in the 1980s (despite its ideological disdain for government intervention) while simultaneously encouraging inequality to increase with other policies. This appears to have resulted in a great deal of program activity directed at the unemployed without improving their chances for economic advance to realms outside the secondary labor market.

France has focused its policy activity on the young, actually mending an apparent rift in its social protection net in the 1980s with the passage of the RMI (Guaranteed Minimum Income). Although a large number of programs were designed to help new labor market entrants become more integrated into the workforce, there is little evidence that they had much effect in the face of sagging demand.

Governments in the Netherlands and Canada have shared the rhetoric of the active society, but they have failed to invest the financial or organizational resources to make the changes a reality.

In the United States and Italy, where the jobless have always been left to rely more on family and private charity (Titmuss 1974; Therborn 1986), there was an apparent willingness to watch the unskilled free fall from the market even if family and community supports were not available to cushion the fall.

Trampolines require strong, flexible safety nets. To bounce back into the mainstream, one cannot be allowed to fall too close to the ground or languish there too long. The commitment to labor force integration must be accompanied by a commitment to income equality, or at least the creation of income floors that save the jobless from severe financial decline. Economic degradation does not spawn initiative. Work requirements do not promote a work ethic or feelings of inclusiveness.

Looking forward to the next century, it is hard to be optimistic about policy trends that emphasize work in the context of a weakening commitment to equality/social solidarity. As Standing notes, the "right to employment" can quickly become an "obligation to work." How would this obligation square with the principles of a democratic polity or a free market economy? How would a work-based system like Sweden's operate in a country without strong unions or labor protections?

The specific policies that emerge to cope with new work forms over the next decade are likely to be as tentative and diverse as those of the 1980s. Their content will be shaped by decisions that are ultimately moral and political in character. Social policies are determined by our vision of the kind of society we want to live in, and by the social groups that have the power to realize their vision.

ENDNOTES

1. Two-thirds of men in Italy and over half the men in the Netherlands over 55 years of age are not active in the paid labor force. High rates of inactivity among older men are also evident in France and Germany, demonstrating the use of early retirement schemes in these countries in the 1980s as a way to facilitate restructuring. The age of retirement can be redefined as 55 years old, so that "full mobilization" only applied to those younger than this new cut-off.

   In the 1980s, several countries (the United Kingdom, the Netherlands, France) lifted the lower boundary of the labor force, disqualifying 16 and 17 year olds from unemployment coverage per se. (Young people can still receive a training stipend, but not unemployment benefits.)

2. Table 21.1 shows that Sweden is the only country with a long-standing norm of female workers—almost six out of ten women 55 to 65 years of age were in the paid workforce compared to 15 to 40 percent of older women in other countries.

3. This argument is more persuasive when applied to skilled workers than to low-skilled women relegated to work in the secondary labor market. In the latter case, re-entry problems are more likely to be the result of declining demand for unskilled labor than the result of "deteriorating" skills.

4. Between 1975 and 1988, female labor force participation in the Netherlands grew by 61 percent, but the number of unemployed women rose from 42,000 to 267,000 during this period. After the recovery of 1984–85, unemployment didn't decline for several years because of the high unemployment rates of women (Price Waterhouse 1990).

5. "There is little empirical evidence that labor market flexibility is substantially affected by the presence of social protection programs, nor is there evidence that the speed of labor market adjustment can be enhanced by limiting these programs" (Blank 1993:3).

6. In keeping with this ideal, France actually established a new income support program in 1988—the guaranteed minimum income ("Revenue Minimum d'Insertion" or RMI). Established for jobless people who had not worked long enough to establish a right to Unemployment Insurance or Solidarity assistance, the program grew out of concern about a "lost generation" of young people who unsuccessfully tried to enter the labor market in the late 1970s and early 1980s at the height of France's worst mass unemployment. RMI explicitly states that its goal is to prevent the social marginalization of these individuals by providing them with a minimum source of

income. However, RMI is not unconditional—individuals are required to sign an "insertion contract" with local authorities that outlines the steps they will take to prepare to enter the workforce.

RMI is means-tested in that it takes into account other social assistance that an individual or household receives (like family and housing allowances); RMI "fills in" up to a certain minimum. The base amount of RMI is low so as to "avoid competing excessively with the disposable income of individuals earning SMIC" (CERC 1989). The program guidelines, however, clearly establish incentives to combine RMI with part-time work. A recipient can earn up to FF2000 before income support is reduced due to earnings. (He/she receives 100 percent of the first FF500; 60 percent of the next FF500; 40 percent of the next and 20 percent of the next FF500.)

About 700,000 households representing 1.5 million people were assisted by RMI in its first 2 years of operation. Almost 80 percent were single, 68 percent were single and childless. Half were under 35 years of age and one in ten were homeless when they entered the program. After 2 years, a third of those who had entered the program had left, most because they earned enough to surpass the base income level of RMI. About 82,000 RMI participants returned to work in 1990, but 52,000 were on publicly subsidized work contracts. An evaluation noted that not all these jobs resulted in a permanent job or "durable insertion," but that "all have [helped participants] reestablished links to the working world" (CERC 1989).

7. Only 40 percent of unemployed Americans actually receive unemployment benefits.

8. By way of illustration, GA levels in the District of Columbia declined in real value by 40 percent between 1980 and 1988. In 1988, GA provided about $165 per month to a single adult, less than 33 percent of what an individual working full-time at minimum wage would earn in a month, and less than 9 percent of average monthly earnings in the metropolitan area.

9. Sweden prohibited private employment services in 1936 and enacted a law that employers must report all vacancies in 1978.

10. About 90 percent of all registered vacancies are filled through the employment service in an average of 3 to 4 weeks. It takes an average of 5 months for job-seekers to find places (Meidner 1991: 348).

11. Jobclubs are group job search programs designed for those deemed "job ready." Individuals in Jobclubs usually participate for four half day sessions a week. The first 2 weeks involve structured training about how to look for and apply for jobs. The unemployed person graduates to a "resource area" with telephones, resume materials, etc., and the job search becomes an exercise in group encouragement and reinforcement. (In fact, the government had to put a time limit of 4 or 5 months on the Jobclubs to limit their use as social clubs.)

There are about 1,000 Jobclubs in Great Britain today, each of which serves about 150 people a year. Keeping with the conservative government's commitment to privatization, only 200 are administered directly by the Employment Service; subcontractors are used to provide services at the other 800 at a cost of about $45,000 per club per year. The placement-into-jobs rate from the Jobclubs was about 50 percent for those who completed the course, but nonattendance was high.

Job search clubs are also part of official employment programs in France, Canada, and the Netherlands. These kind of job clubs were used by a number of state welfare offices in the United States over the 1980s as a key component of welfare-to-work programs. Evaluations suggest that the success of these programs ultimately depends on the demand for labor in the local labor market (Gueron and Pauly 1991).

12. It should be noted that mobility grants tend to be used more by employed individuals changing jobs than by the unemployed. And they do not appear to be more popular in recessionary periods (Standing 1986).

13. Typically, about 200,000 individuals in a labor force of 4 million are in training, public relief work, subsidized employment, sheltered employment, or some other labor market program.

14. There is no evidence that private investments in training—especially for low-income workers—increased either (Lynch 1993).

15. In 1988–89, 71 percent of 18-year-olds in France and 52 percent of 19-year-olds were still in school (Faure et al. 1991).

16. As Casey (this volume) points out, even the much-admired dual-system in Germany had to step back and revamp its system in the face of heavy unemployment in the early 1980s.

17. In Sweden, unemployed or at-risk persons are eligible for training free of charge through the employment service office in one of two ways. The employment service provides stipends/benefit payments to an unemployed adult attending courses within the regular school system—about 290,000 students receive this kind of training a year (Meidner 1991: 351). Alternately, an unemployed person can attend one of the public vocational rehabilitation centers (AMU centers) that were built around the country in the 1960s and 1970s. About 100,000 students are enrolled in about 100 training centers around the country at any given time. Training is tailored to individual needs and can vary in length from a few days to a year or more, but the average length of AMU training is about 5 months. AMU training is the alternative most used by the long-term unemployed.

18. From time to time Canada, Sweden, the U.K., and the U.S. have used nontargeted schemes but have since abandoned them.

19. (R. Lindley 1980). "Employment Policy in Transition," *Economic Change and Employment Policy*, in R. Lindley, ed. London: Macmillan, 1980.

20. Total social security contributions paid by the self-employed in the United Kingdom are less than in other countries—24 in the U.K. compared to an average of 31 percent in other countries.

21. This tends to create an inherent conflict in objectives: local communities tend to be more concerned with the successful completion of the community projects being financed than with the employment experience of participants.

Table 21A.1 / Summary of Selected Self-Employment Schemes for the Unemployed: 1990–1991

Characteristics	Canada	France 1	France 2	Netherlands	United Kingdom
1. Title of Program/Measure	Self-Employment Incentive Option (SEI).	Start-Up Allowance (Starttiraha).	Departmental Fund for Youth Initiatives (FDU).	Self-Employment Scheme for the Unemployed (Bz).	Enterprise Allowance Scheme (EAS) for Great Britain.
2. Eligibility Criteria	Reside or have been employed in a selected community. Be eligible for or in receipt of social assistance or unemployment insurance benefits. Present plan and have necessary personal funding.	Be unemployed and in receipt of or eligible for unemployment benefit. Sufficient training or experience to be judged capable of self-employment. Viable plan for beginning enterprise.	Be either a registered job-seeker under 25, or be unemployed for at least 1 year. Present a valid proposal.	Be aged 18–65 and unemployed or threatened with unemployment. Be a (potential) beneficiary of a social allowance and lacking other means of subsistence. Present a valid business plan.	Be unemployed and in receipt of a benefit. Be over 18 and under 65. Have been out of work for at least 6 weeks. New business, with day-to-day control.
3. Financial Aid Offered	Can$ 200 per week for a maximum of 52 weeks, in lieu of social assistance or unemployment insurance. Applicant must invest 25 percent.	Minimum of FF 10,750 (US$ 1,800) if only 1 year's employment in the last 2 years. Maximum FF 43,000 (US$ 7,200).	Between FF 10,000 and FF 100,000 (US$ 1,500–15,000), depending on the circumstances of the proposer and interest in the plan.	Income supplement at social assistance rate, 6–18 months, maximum. Gld 2,300 p.m. (US$ 1,150). Loan of up to Gld 40,000 over 10 years at commercial rates.[a]	£20–£90 per week (US$ 35–158) for 26–60 weeks.[a]
4. Other Aid and Assistance	Last resort business financing and advice.	Exemption for extra 6 months from social security contributions. Access to professional advice through "cheque book" system.	Advice through "cheque book" system.	Supplementary tax relief, offsetting investments against tax liability and tax losses against later profits. Access to training and advice.	Information, advice, and counselling services by TECs.
5. Expenditure and Coverage Data	Budget 1989/90 Can$ 17 million. Participants 1987/88 451 persons	Expenditure: 1989: FF 1.750 million. Total participants: 1989: 55,000 (est.)	Expenditure: 1988: FF 150 million (US$ 25 million). Total participants: 1988: 6,000	About 1,360 applications accepted per year.	Expenditure: 1989/90: £270 million (US$ 270 million). Participants: Sept. 1989 nearly 80,000

[a] Information for 1992.

REFERENCES

Abraham, K. G., and S. N. Houseman. 1993. "Does Employment Protection Inhibit Labor Market Flexibility? Lessons from Germany, France, and Belgium." Paper prepared for the NBER/Ford Project. "Social Protection vs. Economic Flexibility: Is There a Tradeoff?"

Blank, R. 1993. "Public Sector Growth and Labor Market Flexibility: The U.S. vs. the U.K." Paper prepared for the NBER/Ford Project. "Social Protection vs. Economic Flexibility: Is There a Tradeoff?"

———. 1993. "Social Protection vs. Economic Flexibility: Is There a Trade-off?" Paper prepared for the Working Under Difficult Rules Conference. Washington, D.C.: NBER.

Burtless, F. 1987. "Jobless Pay and High European Unemployment." In *Barriers to European Growth: A Transatlantic View*, edited by R. Lawrence and C. Schultze. Washington, D.C.: The Brookings Institution.

Casey, B. 1994. "Apprentice Training in Germany: The Experiences of the 1980s." Chapter 12 in this volume.

Caspar, M.-L. 1988. "Employment-cum-training Contracts in France: The 1977–85 Record." *International Labour Review* 127:4.

Castro, M., and A. Cabral de Andrade. 1990. "Supply and Demand Mismatches in Training: Can Anything Be Done?" *International Labour Review* 129:3.

Engbersen, G., R. van der Veen, and K. Schuyt. 1987. *Moderne Armoede: Overleven op het sociaal minimum*. Leiden: H.E. Stenfert Kroese B.V.

Esping-Anderson, Gosta. 1990. *The Three Worlds of Welfare Capitalism*. Princeton, N.J.: Princeton University Press.

Euvard, F., J. Lion, and S. Paugam. 1991. *The RMI Beneficiaries' Chances of Economic and Social Insertion*. Paris: CERC.

Faure, J-L. 1991. "The School to Work Transition in France: Programs to Promote the Occupational Integration of Young People in a Period of High Unemployment." Paper presented at Joint Center for Political and Economic Studies conference on Poverty and Social Marginality, January, Paris.

Faure, J-L., D. Brunson, J-M. Charbonnel, and G. Charlot, with J-J. Silvestre. 1991. *Les rémunérations des jeunes a l'entree dans la vie active*. Paris: CERC.

Gueron, J., and E. Pauly. 1991. *From Welfare to Work*. New York: Russell Sage Foundation.

Heclo, H. 1994. "The Social Question." Chapter 22 in this volume.

Kamerman, S., and A. Kahn. 1991. *Mothers Alone*. Princeton, N.J.: Princeton University Press.

Lawson, R. 1986. "Income Support During Unemployment: Comparison in Western Europe, 1945–1986." In *Yearbook of Social Security in Europe*. Deventur: EISS.

Leibfried, S., and J. Allmendinger. 1991. Comments on "Young Workers in Germany," presented at Joint Center for Political and Economic Studies conference on Poverty and Social Marginality, January, Paris.

Lindley, R. 1980. "Employment Policy in Transition." *Economic Change and Employment Policy*. London: MacMillan.

Lynch, L. 1993. "Payoffs to Alternative Training Strategies at Work." Paper prepared for the Working Under Different Rules Conference. Washington, D.C.: NBER.

Marshall, T. H. 1950. *Citizenship and Social Class.* Cambridge: Cambridge University Press.

McQuaig, Linda. 1992. *Canada's Social Programs Under Attack.* Toronto: Atkinson Charitable Foundation.

Meidner, R. 1991. "The Role and Potential of Active Labour Market Policy: The Swedish Experience." Chapter 17, in *In Search of Flexibility: The New Soviet Labour Market,* edited by Guy Standing. Geneva: ILO.

de Neubourg, Chris. 1990. *Unemployment and Labor Market Flexibility: The Netherlands.* Geneva: ILO.

Organisation for Economic Co-operation and Development (OECD). 1988a. *Employment Outlook.* Paris: OECD.

———. 1988b, *Measures to Assist the Long-Term Unemployed: Recent Experiences in Some OECD Countries.* Paris: OECD.

———. 1989b, *Employment Outlook,* Paris: OECD.

———. 1990a, *Labor Market Policies for the 1990s,* Paris: OECD.

———. 1990b, *Lone-Parent Families: The Economic Challenge,* Paris: OECD.

———. 1991b, *Employment Outlook,* Paris: OECD.

———. 1992b, *Employment Outlook,* Paris: OECD.

Osterman, P. 1994, "Is There a Problem with the Youth Labor Market, and If So, How Should We Fix It?" Chapter 11 in this volume.

Pugliese, E. 1994. "Special Measures to Improve Youth Employment in Italy." Chapter 13 in this volume.

Smith, S., and M. Lipsky. *Nonprofits for Hire: The Welfare State in the Age of Contracting.* Cambridge: Harvard University Press.

Standing, G. 1986. *Unemployment and Labor Market Flexibility: The United Kingdom.* Geneva: ILO.

———. 1988. *Unemployment and Labor Market Flexibility: Sweden.* Geneva: ILO.

———. 1989. "European Unemployment, Insecurity and Flexibility: A Social Dividend Solution." ILO Working Paper No.23, Geneva: ILO.

———. 1991. "Toward Economic Democracy and Labour Flexibility? An Era of Experimentation." *In Search of Flexibility: The New Soviet Labour Market,* edited by Guy Standing. Geneva: ILO.

Therborn, G. 1986. *Why Some Peoples are More Unemployed Than Others: The Strange Paradox of Growth and Unemployment.* London: Verso.

Titmuss, R. M. 1974. *Social Policy: An Introduction.* London: Allen & Unwin.

U.S. House of Representatives, Committee on Ways and Means. *Overview of Entitlement Programs, 1993 Green Book.* Washington, D.C.: U.S. Government Printing Office.

Worden, K., and W. Vroman. 1992. "Job Creation in Germany, Belgium and Sweden." Unpublished paper. Washington, D.C.: The Urban Institute.

Chapter 22

THE SOCIAL QUESTION

Hugh Heclo

S OME TIME in the early 1990s the United States tipped over the edge, demographically speaking, into the twenty-first century. We reached the point
where a majority of Americans will spend more of their lives in the next
century than in the twentieth century.

There are other ways of marking how that new century is already with us.
The next century's first high school and college graduating classes are now in
grade school. So, too, is much of the early twenty-first century's prison population. The new century's first teenage dropouts, unwed mothers, and youth
offenders have now left the toddler stage. Those who will retire in the early
part of the twenty-first century have already gone a long way to shape their
future by gaining or losing a foothold in today's job market.

This chapter tries to use the past to help think about the emerging future of
social welfare policy. Some of the conditions described in this volume are hardly
new; others seem a more recent development. In either case, any action on our
social problems will have to take account of the legacy created by the long
historical struggle to shape the interests, institutions, and ideas of a modern
industrial society. To declare our situation "postindustrial" scarcely means starting from a clean slate.

If there has been a direction to our century's struggle, it seems to have been
mainly a question of expanding presumptions of inclusiveness, of assuming
that more people matter and that they matter as equals in aspirations for social
welfare. Clearly this movement should not be romanticized or exaggerated.
Data presented in the preceding chapters show an immense gap between the
rhetoric of social citizenship and the reality of daily life. In what follows I will
take this gap and its supporting data as given. It is the public conversation
about social citizenship itself that I wish to explore. We have, on both sides of
the Atlantic, become more self-consciously inclusive societies. However, the
nature of that inclusiveness—the terms on which it has been achieved—may
have diminished rather than expanded our moral sensitivity to the needs of
fellow citizens. That dismal thought, and what might be done about it, is the
theme of this chapter.

THE OLD SOCIAL QUESTION AND THE NEW

At the beginning of this century, socialists took it as an article of faith that history had a direction. So, too, did their opponents in the capitalist classes and liberal reform movements. Those on the political Left could foresee the struggle of the working class leading to the eventual triumph of scientific socialism. Defenders of capitalism looked forward to the worldwide spread of free markets and individual enterprise, invigorated by an unabashed imperialism. Liberal reformers and those who would later be labeled as social democrats counted on public education and a gradual amelioration of conditions to shape a more just society. The moral seems to be that when people find a direction to history, it almost always happens to be one that supports their own side.

Before there were modern social policies, there existed what was widely referred to as "the social question" or "worker problem" in Europe and North America. An exasperated Bismarck once remarked, "Germany's unity has developed so much new energy and created new interests and points of view. But oh! the social question! It makes all governments shudder" (Engelberg 1990). From roughly the last third of the nineteenth century onward, politicians, social agitators, civic leaders, pioneers in the young social sciences, and many others were preoccupied with the problem of what to do about a rapidly emerging industrial workforce and its accompanying economic and social changes. And this in turn provoked broad debate among intellectuals about the nature of modern society, the role of government, and the place of the individual in such a society. The force of that ideological clash still reverberates around the world, although with a diminished intensity and an ascendancy of economic and political liberalism that some have mislabeled as "the end of history."

Of course what was being talked and fought about was not simply one particular social formation called the industrial working class but a host of interconnected social, economic, and political issues that took various forms and occasioned different responses depending on the country in question. There is no need here to try to summarize a complex story that historians have told with increasing skill in recent years (see, e.g., Skocpol 1991; Castles 1989; Flora et al. 1986). But because the United States has too often been considered an exception to that story, let me repeat the definition of the social question offered by the American Progressive Herbert Croly in 1909:

> By the social problem is usually meant the problem of poverty; but great inequalities of wealth are merely the most dangerous and distressing expression of fundamental differences among the members of a society, [differences] of interest and intellectual and moral standards. In its deepest aspect, consequently, the social problem is the problem of preventing such divisions from dissolving the society into which they enter—of keeping such a highly differentiated society fundamentally sound and whole. In this country the solution of the social problem demands the substitution of a conscious social ideal for the earlier instinctive homogeneity of the American nation. (Croly 1909: 139)

This, I think, goes to the heart of the social question that prompted so much argument and policy development over the last 100 or so years—to protect and reconcile both individual diversity and social union. Twenty years before Croly wrote, William Graham Sumner, that most self-assured of Social Darwinians, observed that "what seems to be desired now is a combination of liberty for all with an obligation of each to all." And while he harrumphed that reformers should mind their own business and stop trying to fix society, Sumner went on to do exactly the opposite by preaching his own version of "social duty" as a way of dealing with the situation. Sumner asked a very modern question: "Can we get from the state security for individuals to pursue happiness in and under it, and yet not have the state itself become a new burden and hindrance only a little better than the evil it wards off?" (Sumner [1883] 1987: 113). Crusty conservatives, like everyone else, were caught up in the inescapable social question of their time.

The fact of a growing industrial workforce provided more than just another occasion for philosophical reflection on the ancient problem of reconciling individual and collective welfare. At the dawn of this century, perhaps more than ever before, *conscious* choices about how to organize society were being required. And these choices were being posed as the old faiths in traditional authority were losing their grip on the masses. The domestic turmoil of the years leading up to World War I, the uncertainties of the interwar years—all this is a rich and complex story in every country. Rather than trying to summarize the particulars, let me skip ahead to characterize the general outcome. Looking back from the 1990s, it seems fair to say that by the onset of the Cold War in the last half of the 1940s, the overall shape of a settlement to the old social question had become clear in both Western Europe and North America. This settlement found expression in new social legislation, in expanding administrative activities, and in a gradual moderation in the political argument about government's social welfare responsibilities. Later developments in the postwar period would entrench and enlarge upon the pattern, which had only haltingly emerged through painful trial and error in more austere times. Three features in this settlement of the social question are worth recalling.

First, at the center of social welfare stands the male breadwinner and the family dependent on his earnings. The prevailing view that developed was that if this basic unit of society could be made more economically secure, most of the threatened community disorganization would be defused. The way in which many industrializing nations structured their pension, unemployment compensation, health insurance, and other laws generally made clear that the male worker was regarded as the linchpin of family well-being and social welfare more broadly.

Second, financial security against income loss and not economic equality as such became the main focus of efforts to settle the social question. Claims for greater economic equality and share-the-wealth schemes were continually stalemated at the level of practical politics. By contrast, the risks associated with lost wages were a reality of everyday life on which both manual workers and the growing ranks of middle-class, white-collar employees could eventually find common ground. In this situation the economic status of women and minorities was generally an afterthought tacked onto the income safeguards for male workers in the economic mainstream.

A third feature was an eventual recognition of the nation-state as the appropriate arena for the organization of social welfare institutions. In every modern welfare state there developed an important break with the older poor law tradition and its locally run mixture of charity and coercion. Outcomes of the political battles varied somewhat in different nations, but by the mid-twentieth century it was always *national* legislation that was in question. By then it had become taken for granted that people would look to the national level and not particular localities—much less any international class-based regime—for solutions to social problems. Postwar social insurance laws are a leading example.

Earlier chapters suggest how each of these three elements in the settlement of the old social question is now open to challenge. Changes in family structure and women's role in the labor market are perhaps the most obvious change.[1] (The following statistics apply to the United States, but general trends are similar throughout democratic welfare states.) Between 1960 and 1988, births to unmarried mothers in the United States rose from 5 percent to over 25 percent of all live births. One-parent families that stood at 6 percent of all families with children in 1960 were at 26 percent by 1986. Thirty years ago less than one-third of all marriages involved at least one previously married partner. Today about one-half of all marriages have at least one previously married spouse. Such statistics reflect the fact that unwed motherhood, divorce, separation, and reconstruction of family and household units have become much more acceptable than they were 30 years ago, as well as the fact that married women have chosen to have fewer babies and more paid employment outside the home. Between 1960 and 1988 the proportion of married mothers with jobs rose from 26 percent to 62 percent (Jencks and Peterson 1991: 58). These changes have gone far to undermine the traditional premise that treated the economic status of women and children as the simple by-product of a husband's income support. As others have noted, every married woman is a potential single mother, and every child is a potential member of a one-parent family. At present rates, of all children born in 1980, 60 percent will spend part of their childhood living with only one parent. This can be one of the surest routes into poverty and social marginalization.

The second element to come under challenge is the focus on security against income loss. While this obviously remains an important objective of major government programs, the concept of income insurance is rooted in industrial-era assumptions about family "breadwinners" with decent employment earnings that might be interrupted. Today a combination of international and domestic economic changes is casting doubt on this traditional conception of a "normal" working life. The problem of income loss as such is often less central than the prior problem of gaining access to viable employment careers in the first place. This applies not only to women and the growing ranks of minorities in the labor market, but also to white males in what are no longer stable manufacturing sectors and especially to young people trying to gain a foothold in the labor market. For example, between the years 1967 and 1987 (both relatively good years for the economy), the proportion of American men with steady jobs[2] declined across all adult age groups and at virtually all education levels. For men with only high school diplomas, the decline was from 85 to 74 percent, while for high school dropouts the proportion with steady jobs fell from 77 to 59 percent (Jencks and Peterson 1991: 53). The decline was less dramatic for college graduates, but even there, especially for those over 35, there was a reduction in those with steady work from roughly 91 to 87 percent. The official poverty rate, although only a crude approximation of the social marginalization that can occur, reflects the severe difficulty of many young adults trying to gain a foothold in the contemporary labor market. Households with heads aged 30–55 had a poverty rate of about 15 percent in 1979 and 16 percent in 1986. By contrast, households headed by persons aged 20–29 had a rate of 17 percent in 1979 and, after 4 years of economic recovery, a poverty rate of 25 percent in 1986. In 1979, 15 percent of young couples with children were poor, but by 1986 the proportion stood at 28 percent. One-half of the overall increase in poverty between 1979 and 1987 occurred among two-parent families (Bane and Ellwood 1989: 1047–1048).

In short, structural economic changes are challenging the older idea of secure career lines—especially in routine production jobs and especially for those without good college degrees—where there is a living wage to support a family and the main problem is to ensure against interruptions to that income.

The third element of the old settlement now in question concerns national policy structures and boundaries. As a focus for social welfare institutions, the nation-state seemed appropriate when national economies were more self-contained and national societies—at least in terms of their dominant cultural powers—were more or less homogeneous.[3] Today that national focus is under immense pressure as national welfare states are being pulled in two opposite directions.

On the one hand, global economic interdependencies and major cross-national migrations of people and capital are straining the ability of national welfare state institutions to control their own destiny. Sweden's current situation is only one of many indications that "welfare stateism" in one country is becoming increasingly problematic. Some of the challenges posed by these transnational forces are obvious. (The Western welfare states are a magnet for increasingly mobile people from poorer, overpopulated regions; a lowering of social standards to protect wages, health, safety, and the environment can occur because of competition among global corporations and states seeking to attract business investment.) Other pressures are more indirect but still real (problems of financing national social programs and coordinating domestic policies amid interest rates that are driven by international financial markets).

At the same time, subnational forces are pulling in the opposite direction. Demands to decentralize services and increase local policy control have grown increasingly powerful in the past two decades. At first many of the demands seemed to arise from technocratic desires to economize and rationalize public management. But we can now see that the forces at work go deeper. Citizen-activist groups have become a permanent part of the political landscape in their attempt to break centralized professional monopolies and empower local interests. Perhaps most important of all has been the reassertion of ethnic identities and cultural rights of nations within nations. Increasingly in our time, policy history is being made less by what nations do and more by virtue of what is done to nations by diverse groups championing resegregation.

In one sense the "social question" has always remained the same conundrum—a problem of reconciling our individual and social welfare, of creating a Oneness from the Many and using this more perfect Union to enhance the individuality of the Many. And yet it also seems true to say that in an earlier era, this challenge was mainly expressed in a clash of rather distinct and raw economic interests. What is "new" about the new social question is that the perennial conundrum of individual and social welfare is being revisited amid growing cultural confusion. Economic interests still contend with each other, of course, but they do so in a context where there is much greater uncertainty about who we are and what understandings we share with each other. The new social question has cultural overtones in the sense that the meanings of things relevant to people's life together—of family, work, community, national identity—have become contested ground more than shared premises. We dispute the traditional ideal of family and "breadwinners," many seeing these as yokes from which to be liberated; so, too, with the once simple faiths in a good job defined as a living wage or the nation as the unquestioned source of social identity. Contemporary social institutions organize our lives into more and more extended webs of mutual dependence; we counter with greater parochial insistence on personal, group, and lifestyle interests. We become both more ensnarled and more unattached (Sandel 1984; Taylor 1989).

I have spoken of three elements in coping with the social question of the past century. There was a fourth element in the settlement that had to do less with interests and institutions and more with the realm of social ideas as such. This was the idea of what came to be labeled social citizenship, and it formed an important part of the pattern for trying to reconcile welfare at the individual and collective levels. Can this hopeful and expansive concept help in meeting the social challenge of our own time?

THE CAREER OF A CONCEPT

Writing shortly after the end of World War II, the British sociologist T. H. Marshall ([1949] 1965) described what became an influential schematization for describing three stages in the development of citizenship rights. By his account, the past 200 years had witnessed a successive expansion of such rights. First came civil/legal rights, as the early capitalist system evolved institutions to protect property ownership, equality before the law, and basic civil liberties. In the nineteenth century, political rights were gradually added so as to extend political participation to the middle and, later, working classes. By the time he was writing in the late 1940s, Marshall perceived that there was underway a consolidation of welfare claims, yielding a form of social citizenship comparable with the equal legal and political citizenship of earlier times. The new rights of social citizenship were aimed not merely at attacking poverty at the bottom of society but at restructuring the overall provision of welfare in a more equal and just manner so as to express the solidarity of a national community. For Marshall, the outstanding illustration of such mutual caring for shared needs was Britain's National Health Service.

Marshall's conception of social citizenship matters, although not because policymakers or the mass public read essays by sociologists. It matters because his schema for social citizenship gave expression to a more or less widely held—if vague—view of how social welfare policy should be thought about. Perhaps the outstanding embodiment of this aspiration (40 years before globalization became a faddish term) was the Universal Declaration of Human Rights, which was adopted by the then still U.S.-dominated General Assembly of the United Nations in 1948. The lofty phrases brook few qualifiers: "Every one, as a member of society . . . is entitled to the realization . . . of the economic, social, and cultural rights indispensable for his dignity and free development of his personality" (Article 22). Every member of society is entitled to "just and favorable conditions of work," to "just and favorable employment" (Article 23). Everyone should have the right "freely to participate in the cultural life of the community and to share in the scientific advances and its benefits" (Article 27).

Empty rhetoric? Over 40 years later we may smile, some wryly and some ruefully, at these hopeful assertions of rights. Still, I think that a fair reading of postwar social policy shows that these words express an idea of social inclusion that has been an important—no, a *defining*—aspiration in North America and Western Europe. Seen against the long backdrop of earlier centuries, the presumption for inclusion—the idea that everyone should matter in the ongoing struggle for social welfare—is a remarkable, unique development. If we go back no farther than the beginning of this century, it is abundantly clear that the debate on the social question across both sides of the Atlantic contained vocal defenders of the time-honored idea that certain people did *not* matter. They did not matter in very deliberate, concrete ways. Those in what were referred to as "the lower orders" should know their place and not expect that the good things in life were meant for them or their children.

Despite America's preferred self-image as a classless society, we should recall that this same theme of certain people not mattering, and certainly not counting for as much as those in "good society," was prominent here (quite apart from the pervasive racism of the time). Thus, in nineteenth century America, popular manuals for self-improvement made a clear distinction between the standards appropriate for clerks or others engaged in "headwork" and those with a "common mind" destined for manual labor. For example, in a typical nineteenth century American volume of advice for manual workers, we learn that taste for the fine arts is beyond their reach:

> Labor requires strained, forced and violent motions. This race of men walk not for pleasure, but to perform journeys of necessity. They take advantage therefore of bending the body forward, and assisting their motion by a sling with their arms. Their low station, their wants and their drudgeries, give them a sordidness and ungenerosity of disposition, together with a coarseness and nakedness of expression; whence their motions and address are equally rude and ungraceful.

Another popular manual counsels artisans and other manual workers to cultivate domestic pleasures, avoid unions, ignore theories of equal rights, and read for pleasure and self-improvement rather than to rise in the world (Blumin 1989: 131–132).

In contrast, by the mid-twentieth century there was a widespread assumption that all citizens should be integrated into the mainstream institutions of social life. The obvious gaps between that aspiration and actual performance were regularly documented in the years after Marshall wrote, but that does not deny the power of his observation. Such gaps were not a source of complacency, nor were they publicly endorsed in any of the developed countries. Several generations earlier the deprivation and marginalization of large numbers of people had been routinely accepted and defended. This change in the working assumptions about who should be considered in and out of the community was a social fact, no less real than statistics on poverty. By midcentury it had become generally unacceptable to argue that certain people in one's nation are in some sense so irretrievably "different," so essentially inferior, that they should not count and can be forgotten by public policy. So, too, today, as this volume shows, many persons are being left behind and treated, in practice, as if they were disposable. But it is widely regarded as beyond the bounds of acceptable public debate to contend that this exclusion is the way things *should* be. The titles of our contemporary exposés speak of people who are "forgotten," "hidden," or "silent." So what? many of our ancestors would have asked; some people and their problems should be forgotten and hidden from good society. Today even leading conservative critics of the welfare state routinely stake out claims for social inclusion that 100 years ago would have been regarded as naive romanticism, if not rank socialism. Thus, in the 1980s, America's most "conservative" of modern presidents blithely endorsed (in a backhanded way to be sure) a social safety net strung by the federal government and spoke of catastrophic health insurance as "the last full measure of security for all" (Reagan 1982: 261; Klein and O'Higgins 1988). Public pandering by an elected politician? Perhaps, but the revealing point is the public expectations to which pandering is deemed required. Or on a more intellectual level, consider Friedrich A. Hayek writing to counter "the mirage of social justice":

There is no reason why in a free society government should not assure to all protection against severe deprivation in the form of an assured minimum income, or a floor below which nobody need to descend. To enter into such an insurance against extreme misfortune may well be in the interest of all; or it may be felt to be a clear moral duty of all to assist, within the organized community, those who cannot help themselves. (Hayek 1976: 87)

Some will scoff that this whole business of social citizenship and its presumption for inclusion is merely a rhetorical smokescreen—worse, that in writing about such ideas as if they were real, one becomes an apologist for what are in fact racist and class-ridden societies. This, it seems to me, is a cramped and short-sighted view, one that sees only the failings of the here and now and misses the long-term power of social aspirations. It is akin to arguing that the aspirations guiding the antislavery movement for over 100 years did not really matter until, in 1888, the 3,000-year-old institution of slavery was finally outlawed everywhere in the Western world. Both the "is" of existing conditions and the "should" of things hoped for count among the facts of a people's existence. Thus, decades of hard-nosed, social science research have shown that American slavery was a profitable, efficient, and economically viable institution. In the end, its downfall had to do less with economics and more with ideas, ideas so alive that even from a distance of over 100 years, the ostensibly objective cliometricians (social scientists calculating the rates of return on people-ownership) are left feeling, as one put it, "the dirtiness of the business rubbing off on them" (Johnson 1989).[4] Such is the power of certain social aspirations, themselves a harbinger of social citizenship.

What exactly is this idea of an inclusive citizenship of social rights? In fact it is nothing very "exact" as far as a philosophical doctrine goes. But then neither were the concepts of civil and political rights as these acquired historical force in earlier centuries. Because we might operate without a formal philosophical framework does not mean there is no framework at all. Social citizenship was, as Marshall clearly recognized, a general idea that evolved in conjunction with the problems of an industrializing workforce amid a rough-hewn democratic order. Each of the Western democracies had its own painful version of the story to tell, but social citizenship was a concept that emerged from a caldron of Euro-American history involving domestic turmoil, economic depression, and total war. For many people, these were shared experiences not only in the sense that almost everyone went through them but also in the sense that one could—in various circumstances—feel a part of something of great importance being done in common. The sentiment of social citizenship can be stylized as a middle ground between self-interested exchange and selfless altruism. A brief word on each position is in order.[5]

Economic markets are, of course, the preeminent instance of self-interested exchange. The mutual dependence that exists (through the division of labor, contracts, buying and selling, and so on) is mechanical and impersonal. Market efficiency depends precisely on the hard bargains that can be driven only among strangers, not people one feels attached to as neighbors, family, or friends. In the marketplace I affect and am affected by others, but if the relationship with those others ends, I feel nothing. The reciprocity that exists is prudential; I do as I would be done by because it is in my self-interest to behave in that way. The playing out of this logic leads to problems of free ridership, the prisoner's dilemma in game theory, and all the other classic puzzles of collective action in a presumed world of egoists without a central authority.

At the other extreme, an appeal to altruism involves self-sacrifice for the sake of others, a giving without thought of consequential returns. Here we move well beyond the realm of reciprocity or even mutual dependence, because there is a loss of self in some higher purpose that goes beyond such considerations of return and mutuality. Altruism gives without receiving, shares without calculating, loves without requiring love.

The practical-minded reformers whose action cumulated into a response to the old social question were only too familiar with the power of economic markets to disrupt and distort human relations. But they were also under no illusion about the prospects for altruism in the workaday world. What many reformers seemed to have in mind, and what the experience of economic depression and world war pushed the thinking of other people toward, was a social sentiment that went beyond self-interested mutual exchange but that was less morally demanding than self-sacrificial altruism. Economic markets were a design for inclusiveness without social attachments; communal utopias (guild socialism, Communism, and so on) were a design for inclusiveness without individual liberty. Events had shown there was another way of thinking. Inclusiveness could mean individuals doing things for the sake of what they realize they have in common. This was a kind of mutual dependence and reciprocity based on feelings of solidarity. But no "new socialist man" would be required. Alongside rights by which individuals could pursue and protect their particular interests, there were also rights through which people could express their joint interest in a life together. Social citizenship in a national community envisioned a people who, being neither saints nor economic egoists, cared about each other's fate. This view fit nicely, of course, with widespread sentiments favoring the nation as a source of social identity. The idea of rights as a means to social union was certainly not a new idea. Today we tend to forget how, at the founding of American government as well as at other times, advocacy of political rights was grounded in such unity-enhancing claims.[6] Rights of self-government could turn mere inhabitants and subjects into citizens sharing a fate, could make the nation more of a nation. What the twentieth century view of social citizenship added was a commitment to national welfare programs to deal with the shared insecurities of an industrial age.

It would be farfetched to think that social policies were created and expanded simply as a result of fraternal sentiments. That clearly is not what happened in either Western Europe or North America. The purpose of the discussion to this point is to suggest that there was a certain coherence to the welfare state legacy carried into the Cold War period, that along with the institutions and interests there were some orienting ideas in this legacy, and that the vague notion of an inclusive social citizenship was a central idea that seemed to make sense relevant to the social question—to make sense as a background aspiration if not as an immediate description of fact.

One might ask why it made sense. Why should a society aspire to this inclusiveness? Certainly many reasons can be and were given in the first half of this century. The historical experiences of worldwide depression and wars were certainly important. Some have emphasized the role of the trade union movement and its political representatives in pushing solidarity onto the national agenda. There have also been many reasons given of a prudential nature as to why risk-averse individuals should join together to pool risks, making binding commitments and evolving institutions of cooperation.

These and many other factors are no doubt relevant. However, if one tries to be faithful to the history and looks at the actual people who fought for the idea of inclusiveness and the welfare state apparatus we take for granted, then I think there is no escaping the seminal importance of moral and religious convictions. This goes beyond the obvious fact that religious groups, church leaders, and their offspring were often major players in the agitation to deal with the social question. The closer one looks at the lives of the men and women involved in every country, the clearer it becomes that those pushing for changes that academics would later label as social citizenship were people with deeply ethical commitments, usually of a religious nature (Lacey 1989; Kloppenberg 1986). The project they set for themselves, each in his or her own way, was to bring social practice into closer alignment with religious/ethical principles of sympathy, brotherhood, and a just humanity. Their opponents—more powerful than we can now really recall—argued that relations of sympathy and sentiment were exclusively private, interpersonal affairs; "society" was at its best when it simply cleared the way for self-interested exchanges and other capitalist acts between consenting adults. The founding fathers and mothers of social citizenship championed an opposite view. Society was seen as a fundamentally moral enterprise. Moral/religious standards applied not only to individuals but also to the way a society comports itself. A situation where people are affected by each other but feel nothing for one another may be an economy, but it is not what reformers thought a society should be.

The early social reformers and their descendants in the pre–Cold War era spoke with many voices, but there was a common overtone. Their answer to the social question—how to hold society together amid vast destabilizing changes—embodied a moral vision of mutual concern across all groups and classes in a truly national society. For such reformers, many of them pioneers in the young social sciences, scientific knowledge and religious belief pointed in this common direction. Their high-mindedness can grate on our modern ears. What did they really mean in talking about "social righteousness" or "a society under moral obligation" or a "borderland in which theology, ethics and economics meet"?[7] Perhaps their apparent obscurity says as much about us as about them. Of course, reactions to the social question grew out of political calculations, economic interests, and so on. Nonetheless, I think we miss something very important if we overlook or dismiss the fundamentally ethical/religious impulses that underlay social reformers' presumption for inclusion. They acted on the belief that the social club must include everyone, because, at the end of the day, that was the morally right thing for a society to try to be.

Notwithstanding its aura of legitimacy, there have proven to be considerable difficulties in applying the idea of an inclusive social citizenship. Here there is space only briefly to identify three general issues. One set of problems was inherent in trying to attach the essentially political concept of citizenship to issues of social welfare. Throughout its history, the term *citizen* has been as much about exclusion as inclusion, a boundary-drawing word setting apart some people from others. To be an inhabitant or even a functionally essential member of the community did not make one a citizen. Unlike subjects, citizens were those sharing in the power of governing the community. As Aristotle put it, the virtue of a citizen lies in knowing "how to govern like a freeman and how to obey like a freeman. . . ." The citizen's liberty is not freedom from government but freedom through self-government.

Applying this fundamentally political concept to the sphere of social welfare raises a difficult question: If everyone is a social citizen, what is it they do that makes them such? What is a citizen-like sharing of power as applied to social relations? If it means no more than partaking in collective consumption or passively sharing risks against income loss, then clearly we risk draining much of the core meaning from the term citizenship. The problem is compounded by the fact that under modern conditions, the provision of social welfare is often in the hands of large-scale bureaucracies and self-contained professions. In terms of mutual concerns and duties, the actual experience of social citizenship in everyday life seems to boil down to little more than an obligation to pay taxes and otherwise support government welfare measures (Plant 1988). And yet the very idea of a "social" *citizen* implies someone personally engaged in much deeper social ties expressing what we have and owe in common. The general absence of such relationships—in fact a contrary surge toward self-absorbed privatism—has not escaped the attention of contemporary advocates of social citizenship. However, so far their proposals for some new form of time tax or "national service" requirement have gone nowhere.

There is an additional problem for social citizenship in that greater inclusiveness increases the probability of fewer shared standards. Given the fact of human diversity, efforts to expand membership in the social club are likely to reduce the range of things that everyone in the club can be expected to have in common. This dilemma of inclusiveness is certainly an old theme in political philosophy, one that was prominently before the Founding Fathers as they debated the terms of union under the American Constitution. As every U.S. schoolchild used to know, Madison reversed over 1,000 years of conventional thinking on the subject by arguing that a large republic would be more stable and desirable than a small republic with its more homogeneous, shared interests. According to his argument, what I have called the dilemma of inclusiveness was actually an advantage. Encompassing a large variety of interests, parties, and sects would not only make it more difficult for any majority to combine in oppressing minority rights. It would also mean, more positively, that ". . . a coalition of a majority of the whole society could seldom take place on any other principles than those of justice and the general good" (*The Federalist*, no. 51). Political citizenship in such a system might seem to require a minimal sense of fellow feeling among the participants, and it is easy to see how such an arrangement became an invitation to contemporary notions of procedural liberalism. But America's early political leaders understood that a stronger glue was necessary. They worked hard to promote a reverence for the national political symbols of free constitutional government that might bind such a people together.

If we transfer to the plane of social citizenship, the aspirations clearly become more substantive than procedural, more about rights to have something than to do something. Rather than offering Madisonian advantages, the play of more unshared interests directly challenges the central thrust of an inclusiveness based on people's realization of what they should have in common. On this plane it is no easy matter to find the social equivalent of the political symbols— the Nation, the Constitution, the Republic, etc.—for gluing together a diverse people's citizenship attachments. Political patriotism is one thing, but what might social patriotism be? Typically we are left with the rather lame phrases of politicians (a Folkhem, New Deal, Fair Deal, Great Society, Social Market Economy, and so on) or else with a more scary vision of ethnic/racial/sectarian unity that actually threatens the moral reach of social citizenship. Hence, there is no contradiction in what many people seem to feel about the trajectory of postwar Western societies. These societies have become more encompassing in terms of a concern for all inhabitants and more problematic as communities of shared standards and valuations, more inclusive and more splintered.

Far from being a hypothetical puzzle for academics, the dilemma of inclusion has been played out in increasingly vivid terms during the years since World War II. Because social citizenship was seen to go hand in hand with the open politics of a mass democracy, there arose the inescapable question as to how far such an idea could be grounded in the understandings of ordinary people going about their everyday social, political, and economic business. Socially, and in the abstract, the terms of inclusion were clear enough—a comprehensive pooling of risks, a fellow feeling of solidarity among a people concerned with their welfare in common as a nation. In postwar practice, the social standards that could be realistically shared on any extensive basis were those that dealt with enhancing individual security and equalizing opportunities for personal and group advancement. Such social valuations were not a strong basis for even a fixed supply of fraternal attachments across the nation. And yet the logic of inclusion meant that successively *more* empathy would be required to bring in outlying groups that would be even less like "us." Toward the end of the queue for membership in the social club stood those with differences based on race, on physical or mental disability, and on nontraditional views of gender relationships, among others.

On the political front, the problems went beyond social diversity as such to the realities of bargaining and compromise in the open democratic processes of the postwar Western world. Social programs that might be inspired (rationalized, some will say) by ideas of solidarity could be most easily adopted through interest group politics. I do not think this means that the moral vision of social citizenship was a hypocritical facade. But it does mean that high-minded aspirations, translated as they had to be into democratic politics, produced outcomes that represented less a thickening of social ligatures and more a moveable feast of ad hoc, interest group deals. Typically, in postwar practice, political reality required that solidaristic policies (e.g., comprehensive social insurance) offer major benefits to coalitions of middle-class interests above and beyond whatever they might do to help the poor (Baldwin 1990). Postwar economic growth both facilitated these political bargains and also gave a decidedly individualistic, consumerist cast to social welfare provisions. In their early evolution during the first half of this century, reforms to deal with the old social question did not assume rapid economic growth. In fact, they were rather restrained in their expectations about improvements in employment and wages. But the welfare state programs born in austerity matured and expanded in mass consumption societies. The unexpectedly strong economic growth of the postwar years made social programs relatively easy to pay for and also made the Depression and wartime era appeal to solidarity seem slightly antiquated. In the early 1960s, T. H. Marshall could lament how the drive for self-enrichment in an affluent society was supplanting the welfare state consensus of the 1940s. By 1972 Marshall, noting a pervasive "short-sighted egotism," was arguing that "the ethos of the normal processes of political and industrial democracy is out of harmony with the spirit required for taking policy decisions at operational level in the field of welfare" (Marshall 1972:20). So much for any natural succession of stages from civil, to political, to social citizenship.

My general point is that, while by midcentury the idea of social inclusion had gained in public acceptability, the postwar world has provided a weak institutional context for giving substantive meaning to such inclusiveness. Institutional attachments that have generally receded in importance are those requiring a person actually to do something in conjunction with others: Political parties, unions, neighborhood schools, and military conscription are examples. As opposed to institutions of personal obligation, "soft" institutions requiring little more than passive involvement—the mass media, spectator sports, and welfare state programs themselves—have become the common landmarks of social life. Horrible as the Depression and world wars were, it is important to note that it has now been two generations since people in Western societies have been asked to sustain, and personally experienced, shared sacrifices for the common good. Those "national" experiences that have occurred have tended to divide rather than unite the countries affected (e.g., involvements in Korea, Indochina,

Algeria, etc.) Or else they have been short-lived "civic surges" that melt away with surprising speed (e.g., U.S. feats in space, the Persian Gulf War). This means that few people under age 50 can fully appreciate the notion of a society-wide solidarity as part of their personal experience.

The legacy of social citizenship has also been weakened by its very accomplishments. One obvious fact is that reforms typically produced government involvement that over time could show itself bureaucratic and self-interested, rather than the benign expression of solidarity reformers might have hoped for. But the problem also goes deeper. Because reformers succeeded in creating a huge structure of social welfare programs, and because one's obligation generally amounts to an impersonal tax duty to help pay for these programs, we can find it easier to disassociate ourselves from whoever may be in need. This has been a favorite theme of welfare state critics over many years, and we would do well in present circumstances to take the concern seriously. Most of us will try to look after our own, but if there are other people with problems, it has become easy to assume there are programs available that can absolve our indifference. The fact of unmet needs can be interpreted as a sign that bureaucrats and their programs are not working properly. This may of course be at least partly true, leaving us with the reality of both people in need and public indifference. Attitudes toward the homeless are an example. Exposed to the wretchedness it is someone else's job to remedy, we pass by. In this way, we make moral insensitivity a requirement of daily living.

Finally, we should recognize that the idea of social citizenship grew out of an intellectual community that has fundamentally changed. Early in this century one could assemble on both sides of the Atlantic an intellectual quorum around certain fundamental beliefs. These included the idea that there are discoverable truths in the social and natural sciences; that these truths do together produce human progress; that scholarship, religious belief, and political activism are mutually reenforcing; that enlightenment values are real, nonsubjective, and timeless. Here is not the place to discuss how that intellectual consensus fell apart. The important fact is that it did, leaving us with the current tumult of "postmodernist" attacks on hegemony, canonical truth, and commonalities (Rorty 1989; West 1989; Novick 1988). Social citizenship is an idea that presumes a common narrative in society. However, intellectual trends since the end of World War II have been more or less in the opposite direction. Belief in progress or objectivity has come to be regarded as hopelessly naive among serious thinkers, or as it is sometimes called, the chattering class (a term that itself denotes how intellectuals are now seen as more fit for ridicule than for leadership in the public conversation about social problems). It has been in intellectual fashion to argue that "shared vision" is a code word for oppression and that membership in racial, ethnic, and gender groups constitutes the most fundamental truth of each individual's experience. While the social problems described in this book fester, intellectual circles have become more interested in debating whether "texts" have any definable meaning or whether Alice Walker should have a place on Western Civ. course reading lists.

The result has been a gradual and important shift in how we frame and think about the social question. As secularization gathered force throughout this century, the separation of knowledge and belief did not, as many of its advocates had hoped (Westbrook 1991), lead to a transfer of religious energies into political and social action. It led to a hermeneutics of suspicion against anyone who dares to speak out about social purpose as founders of the social citizenship idea once so self-confidently did. The very thought of high-minded community leaders guiding the debate on social reform sounds quaint and more than a little embarrassing to modern ears. Social policy has become grounded in policy analysis and particular interests. It is a game played by politicians, group spokesmen, and technocrats, not moral leaders. Perhaps for this reason we are long on unread papers about policy problems and short on reasons and convictions why we should do anything about them.

THE EMERGING DEBATE

In words not much different from those quoted above from 100 years earlier, one of America's leading liberal intellectuals looks forward to a society where all people are ". . . secure in their individuality and cooperative in their citizenship" (Walzer 1989). The social citizenship ideal is not dead, but it certainly seems to have fallen on hard times. Critiques from the Left and Right during the 1970s foresaw a crisis of democratic welfare states. These works have taken their rightful place on the remainder lists, a curiosity considering the missing critiques of state socialism that actually was collapsing in crisis. Conservative efforts to transform the mixed-economy welfare state have had their day in the sun during the 1980s, scored some modest changes, and receded before the inescapable complexity of reality. A stalemate born of mutual exhaustion between critics and defenders of modern social policy seems to have settled in, reenforced by the paralyzing power of structural budget deficits. In each country the impasse in the democratic–mixed-economy welfare state has it own form on its own particular plateau, but the overall result is the same. We began this century expecting the triumph of an "ism" and end it living with a hyphenation.

It is certainly possible that the political debate will remain stalemated, yielding a *de facto* choice to do little or nothing about the social marginalization described in this book. While not a pleasant thought, a case might be made that modern societies can continue to function, and most people do quite well, while a significant number of people are treated as if they were disposable. Few would publicly endorse such a position, but inertia may effectively produce the same result. Down this road lies a society of separatism, where the more privileged parts have in effect seceded from the other parts. As the daily news suggests, there are in fact powerful forces pushing in this direction, and they can be found among both the privileged and those eager to exploit the misery and resentments of people at the social margins. Racism, a general contempt for poor people, and—most powerful of all—indifference are sweet comforts in that they make it easier for us to go through life without caring about each other.

In my view this dismal result is not particularly likely for two reasons. First, as the eruption of the underclass debate itself suggests, the Western welfare states are open systems that invite and accept scrutiny of themselves. The drift toward separatism will not proceed without vigorous debate and social self-examination. Admittedly, this can produce the touching academic illusion that if we know the facts, we will do something about them. Nevertheless, there is an inherent bias against complacency in a society where people are being constantly reminded of how they are shaping the community they and their children will have to live in. Openness to self-scrutiny is at least a partial counterweight to indifference.

The second reason stalemate may not be permanent is that the presumption for inclusion cannot be easily cast aside. It is a defining feature of our Western identity. Hypocrisy may abound in these matters, but there is historical momentum behind the idea that all human beings should be treated equally with respect, that each person has an innate right to pursue happiness in freedom. It is an idea, developed in opposition to hierarchical conceptions of society, that has evolved through a long series of painful struggles in Western history, and we will not be able blithely to step outside that cultural framework. On the contrary, there is an expansiveness to the idea of equal individuals living in freedom that can fit all people and that clearly, as this century shows, represents an immense challenge to more rigid, fixed patterns of social organization (Naipaul 1991). If we are not for this positive idea of inclusion, for it in a fundamental, self-defining way, then who are we? To deny this idea is to deny precisely the better part of our cultural identity, which has constantly challenged racist, sexist, imperialist, exclusivist tendencies—those tendencies that multiculturalists wish to define as the sum total of the white Eurocentric legacy.

Thus, however vague and buffeted by postwar trends it might be, the aspiration for inclusiveness remains a fundamental premise of Western societies. This being so, some observers predict that the current political stalemate will be succeeded by a turn in the policy cycle that will produce a new period of reform and government activism, or what in the U.S. context is sometimes referred to as a Progressive revival. If this is true, we may expect the emerging debate to recycle rhetorical categories that are quite similar to those used by conservatives in attacking social programs during the 1970s and 1980s. Progressive critics will point out the deleterious, unforeseen consequences of market forces, the dangers of government inaction rather than action.[8] There may even be efforts to rehabilitate the idea of progress.

A number of different proposals have been put forward in recent years, all aimed at dealing with modern versions of the age-old problem: to harmonize the production of wealth with the distribution of welfare. Most can be distinguished in terms of how far they seek to guide or transcend the workings of the labor market and whether they are directed toward some groups or everybody. Here there is room for only a cursory review.

One set of approaches focuses on the compensation of labor. Proposals for a "share economy" point mainly toward the widespread adoption of profit sharing (or comparable devices), so that the average cost of labor (cost per worker) actually falls when more workers are hired (Weitzman 1985). Under such a system, which finds some precedent in Japan, employers have an incentive not to lay off workers but to use them more imaginatively; because labor is cheaper at the margin under a share system than under a wage system, labor is likely to be in short supply, employers are under pressure to improve working conditions and labor markets, and full employment is more compatible with low inflation. Of course, all this only very indirectly confronts the problems of those in the nonprofit or low-profit sectors as well as those outside the work-force altogether. A more extensive, societywide system of wage earner funds has been proposed and implemented on a modest scale in northern Europe. In this view, the compensation of labor should include an extraction from profits to be collectively owned and managed by representatives of workers and other social interests. The rationales offered for such an approach have ranged from encouraging wage restraint and increasing net investments to setting in motion a new form of economic democracy that would transcend the traditional welfare state (Esping-Andersen 1985; Heclo and Madsen 1987).

Another set of approaches deals less with labor compensation and more with integrating or reintegrating those who are outside the labor market. Publicly funded income support is seen to be inadequate not only because of the obvious budget constraints but, more importantly, because paid work is considered the central means of de-marginalizing people and bringing them within the social mainstream (McFate, this volume). In the Western European setting, this has normally translated into advocacy of active labor market policies available to the entire working-age population. In the United States, the approach has been more narrowly conceived. The 1988 Family Support Act, with its emphasis on work requirements, demonstrated the U.S. tendency to confine the newfound concern for moral obligation, values of work, and so on to those who are on public assistance. Still, the problem of positive integration (as opposed to inclusion achieved by removing barriers) hovers over a Europe increasingly sensitive to racial and underclass issues. This is one aspect of the cultural dimension of the new social question mentioned earlier.

Another tack takes off from the perceived failings of the labor market to argue for what is in effect a broader, cultural renegotiation of the whole meaning of work. In this view, modern labor markets in their increasingly flexible, postindustrial form are unable to generate income security for most people. Broad, publicly provided guarantees of support are claimed to be necessary. Of course, modern welfare states already have institutionalized a variety of income guarantees. The problem, reformers say, is that such guarantees are invariably conditional on employment-related circumstances or on falling into some bureaucratically defined category of need. Under contemporary employment conditions, this traditional conditionality is said to divide the labor force into a core of

well-paid, relatively secure workers with good employer benefits and high public income guarantees against a periphery of low-paid, occupationally insecure
workers and would-be workers with poor or nonexistent employer benefits and
chintzy, stigmatizing social welfare programs. The latter, short end of the stick
is usually held by women, minorities, migrants, and others who have been
left behind. What some reformers propose is a basic income/general minimum
income/citizenship income guarantee/guaranteed annual income (choose your
term) approach. Whereas the first two proposals I have mentioned urge changing the compensation structure and/or individual access and competence relative to the social mainstream of the labor market, this approach essentially
suggests moving the mainstream. There are, however, some important variations.

In its least radical form, the guaranteed citizen income is a refurnished version of the older conservative proposal for a negative income tax, a device for
eliminating a host of social welfare bureaucracies while more efficiently providing to all workers the equivalent of a minimum wage (another marker of how
the doctrine of inclusiveness had seeped into even pro-market conservative
thought in the 1940s) (Moynihan 1973).[9] In its more recent guise, the object of
conservatively oriented negative income tax ideas seems to be to make the
periphery of the labor market more inhabitable while pushing for greater wage,
employment, and management flexibility in the core (Myles 1985). The problem
in all this is that such wage subsidies for low-paid and intermittent workers are
also subsidies for low-wage employers and would-be low-wage employers.

It is the more far-reaching "citizenship income" proposals that actually challenge the mainstream view of labor markets. Thus, one plan calls for greatly
reducing the linkage between income security and employment by creating a
single citizenship income paid to all individuals (tax credits for income earners
and cash payments for nonearners) regardless of social or economic status. This
would be part of a "social dividend strategy" providing new ways of organizing
a community-wide sharing of surplus profits (Standing 1989). Another plan
proposes a comprehensive general income insurance to finance all periods of
voluntary or age-determined nonwork in the labor market (Rehn 1977). Individuals would have drawing rights across the life cycle for utilizing these personal
accounts (within certain limits). This, it is contended, would allow people to
break up the conventional compartmentalization of life histories into study,
work, and retirement, because these are now imposed by labor market institutions and welfare state bureaucracies. Envisioned is a "security by wings" (as
opposed to "security under shells") that would counteract the polarization of
the labor force between those who enjoy income security as long as they stay
put and those whose formal freedom consists of marginal employment and
insecurity. Still others argue that strategies of monetary income guarantees are
at best incomplete and at worst counterproductive to deal with exclusion and
social marginalization (Liebfried 1990). In this view, true integration requires
that any income security strategy be fully coupled with the systematic creation

of opportunities to participate in other central areas of social life—education, cultural institutions, labor markets, and so on. And so we come back again to our old friend, the concept of social citizenship.

In coming full circle on the subject, perhaps we can see at least one thing more clearly. Responding to the data in this book is not simply a matter of figuring out what to do. It is a matter of establishing convincing reasons—reasons with political and moral traction in the larger society—as to why to do anything at all.

In my view, those expecting an imminent turn in the policy cycle toward progressive reform are being far too optimistic. For one thing, there is now a deeply embedded cynicism about the ability of government programs to produce desired social changes. This is the result, not only of conservative rhetoric, but of hard experience as well-meaning efforts have collided with the unforgiving complexity of social reality. Early social reformers acknowledged critics' arguments that government can be dangerous and bumbling. But, they could argue, government will never do anything well unless it is given important things to do in addressing the social question.[10] Today we are far from an era of do-nothing government, and reformers cannot make the same argument. Having seen reform transmogrify into postwar bureaucracy, many people accept the idea both that government has useful things to do and that it is bumbling and dangerous as it tries to do them.

In the second place, reform has become far more difficult to manage politically than it was earlier in this century. Earlier periods of progressive change had about them a strong element of paternalism. Elite leaders were confident in, and others were more or less diffident about questioning established social institutions and processes, much less the right of leaders to lead. Much of that has changed, especially since the radical onslaught of the 1960s. More open, fluid forms of public participation and less acceptance of any established authority are facts of political life that will be with us for the foreseeable future.[11] Policy struggles that were once like large set piece battles between forces of change and reaction are now more like continuous guerilla warfare, where the lines are fluid, and every group advocate carries a marshal's baton in his or her knapsack. Followership isn't what it used to be.

A third reason for doubting the cyclical prospects for reform is the reduction in external threats. Closing ranks as a nation has always been an appeal that makes sense when facing some foreign foe. Early in this century, arguments about "national efficiency" were frequently used to justify social reform measures that could be claimed to improve the manpower stock against competing countries. In the 1940s, social citizenship in democratic welfare states was counterposed to the rebarbarizing movements of totalitarian regimes. And we tend to forget how often (at least in the United States) social reform initiatives in the late 1950s and early 1960s were grounded in Cold War claims of standing up to the Russians (Sundquist 1968). Today there is no easily identifiable foreign threat pressuring us to act on our interests as one people.

Of course one can immediately object that there are threats aplenty. The example usually cited is the challenge posed by international economic competition. The trouble is that while a Japanese or Korean face can be put on the problem, global competition is even more abstract and difficult to mobilize around politically than is our perennially unmet challenge of foreign energy dependence. At least with energy dependence, virtually all Americans share a perceptible stake in the outcome. No one likes gas lines or high energy costs, but that shared stake has not been sufficient to lead to any significant action. International economic competitiveness is another slow-motion crisis, but in this case it is not clear there is a shared stake—not unless we are already willing to think of ourselves as a single society. Thus, in July 1991 the U.S. government's Commission on Achieving Necessary Skills reported that "more than half our young people today leave school without the knowledge or foundation required to find and hold a good job."[12] But the other side of the coin is that almost half of American youth probably are prepared and can expect to be part of an internationally competitive labor market. This same bifurcation characterizes the existing adult workforce. It seems to be an important reason for the growing economic inequality among Americans in the 1970s and 1980s, even among those with jobs (Reich 1991). Far from pulling us together, the foreign economic challenge has an immense potential for pulling us even further apart.

It might be argued that it is the internal rather than external threat that may drive us to serious reform. The bloodless academic language of "social marginalization" can translate into urban killing fields and a palpable decline in personal security for everyone. And history does provide instances where a logic of self-defense has prompted social reforms. A prime example is initiation of the world's first national social insurance in Bismarckian Germany a little over 100 years ago. But reform through fear is a doubtful basis for building social cohesion. Recent experience suggests that fears generated by today's clashes among groups of have-nots are more likely to redouble efforts by the privileged to buy self-protection, private security firms being one of the few consistent growth industries in the last 30 years. Likewise, the same logic is at least as likely to produce punitive reactions as preventive investments in human beings. Other things being equal, the easiest, and therefore most likely, answer to the social question is always to insist on ways of protecting "us" from "them."

In short, there are major obstacles to any presumed turn in the policy cycle toward progressive social reforms, even after taking account of dreary budget prospects. Where does this leave us? If inclusiveness is central to our self-understanding as a society, if stalemate in the debate between ideological stick figures of conservatism and liberalism is unlikely to endure, and if we cannot count on seemingly automatic cycles of reform, then what is the emerging social policy debate all about? Contrary to the view of those who think social life only becomes more complex and imponderable, I think we have become very good at answering many different kinds of questions. Compared with what was known 100 years ago during the debate on the old social question, our state of knowledge is striking. We can answer questions about what is happening in the economy or what are the living conditions of poor people with astonishing detail. We know how to bring a healthy baby into the world, how to keep it well, how early childhood development affects preparedness for school, and answers to any number of other questions that were only dimly perceived at the beginning of this century. It is the "why should" questions that have become so difficult for us. Whatever we know about the facts of social marginalization, why should we do anything about them? Why should we care for each other? Why should I not just live as I like? The "why should" questions are the ones that touch the moral will of a community.

There was a time when we felt surer in answering the "why should" questions, a time when reformers remembered the name of prejudice and self-absorption and called it sin. Here is the way the Lutheran teacher John Vannorsdall expressed such convictions:

> It's the sense that there was a design, an intention for . . . this humankind. A oneness with other human beings, even a bond with those now dead and with those who are yet to be born. A connection which goes beyond race and beyond nation state and beyond the folkways which bind together a town or a culture. A sense that what I am, these other humans are also. What they need and desire for their living is what I need. That we need one another . . . there is a sense that justice is something more than a term I made up to guarantee my survival, that it is a giving and receiving activity which is appropriate to what I am as human being. (Vannorsdall 1991: 5)

I am not suggesting there was a golden age of social reform when everyone agreed on social citizenship as universal brotherhood. Neither am I arguing that society must achieve a cast iron moral consensus before we can do anything about the growing problem of social marginalization. What I mean to say is that the emerging debate on social reform, no less than those debates of earlier periods, is at its heart a struggle to define our moral identity. And because of how Western society and thought has changed in this century, we find that an extremely awkward and difficult task to undertake.

Our nearest precedent and legacy for doing this work comes from the 1960s, and it is scant help. The 1960s generation represented not only the last major reform era but also the most secular of the "great awakenings" that have punctuated our history. To be sure, the civil rights movement was energized by precisely the older tradition of religious commitment I have referred to earlier. But this was not characteristic of the larger liberal reform community with which civil rights leaders were in uneasy alliance. If there was a moral vision in 1960s liberalism, it was somehow too small, for we were too soon left tired and bruised. Society came to seem simply a collection of irritable group sensitivities.

The presumption for inclusion has become commonplace, but we lack any working sense of what the terms for that inclusion should be. The tendency, therefore, is toward a negative inclusiveness, a milky pluralism that amounts to a meaningless head count of whoever happens to be on the scene. Society is seen as a cultural open bar, an inclusiveness of "anything goes" rather than a bringing together around shared commitments. But if that is the case, and if anything beyond it is "imposing values," then why *should* we care about each other, care in any real, action-forcing way? If the "why should" question cannot be seriously addressed in public judgment and even lacks meaning for postmodernist ears, then the opponents of the early social reformers have won the final word. Society *is* without moral meaning. Indifference is the privileged perspective.

The idea of social marginalization makes no sense unless we believe there is a social centeredness from which we evaluate conditions of life at the margins. And to evaluate is to stand for something—not necessarily the same thing as imposing values. The emerging debate is much like the feeling in too many of our cities. It is a feeling that there is no middle territory between glitz and grit, between a cultural pablum of negative inclusiveness and the lockstep inclusiveness of moral fascism.

It need not be this way unless we, being a fundamentally free people, want it to be. And if we do not want it to be, there is more than enough history to strengthen faith in the middle territory. We cannot go back to the days of the old social question, but after all that modern society has been through, there is recoverable material to help us deal with the new social question. New world orders have been proclaimed, faded, and been forgotten. What lasts? Not much, it seems, but some things: not The Truth, but usable truths for imperfect human purposes. Truths such as the realization that there can be no collective security without collective justice—that tolerance is a positive commitment, not simply indifference or the absence of prejudice—that the most honest skepticism is one that questions its own self-doubt—that, after all the horrors of the twentieth century, experience does vindicate human empathy (Berlin 1990).

The emerging debate is not simply about a policy problem. Policy talk, the language of policy options, among policy people, moves us only a very little way. The emerging debate is about a moral problem, one that many people will have to be engaged in more deeply. For the essential issue is not even what is the right thing to do. The real social question is, What is the right thing we should want to be?

I am grateful to Tony Rees, Roger Lawson, and Stephan Liebfried for helpful comments on an earlier draft of this paper.

ENDNOTES

1. Unless otherwise noted, the following statistics are taken from earlier chapters in this volume.

2. This term refers to year-round, full-time employment and excludes inmates of institutions and members of the armed forces.

3. This is not to deny the obvious demographic fact that the nation at the time was far from homogeneous. By 1920, one-third of the U.S. population was foreign born or had at least one foreign-born parent. The point is that the nation's dominant cultural powers were self-confident and cohesive enough successfully to insist that there was a common culture to which individuals from whatever group would assimilate as part of one people; thus, Woodrow Wilson during World War I: "You cannot become thorough Americans if you think of yourself in groups. America does not consist of groups."

4. Robert Fogel, as quoted in Michael P. Johnson, "Upward from Slavery," *The New York Review of Books* (Dec. 21, 1989): 53.

5. Some general reviews of these and related concepts are Amitai Etzioni, *The Moral Dimension* (New York: Free Press, 1988); Jon Elster, *Nuts and Bolts for the Social Sciences* (Cambridge: Cambridge University Press, 1989); Morton Hunt, *The Compassionate Beast* (New York: Morrow, 1989). A more comprehensive, four-fold framework is discussed at great and stimulating length in Alan Fiske's, *The Structures of Social Life* (New York: Free Press, 1991). For a discussion of important variations in the citizenship notion, based on different historical trends among developed nations, see Bryan S. Turner, "Outline of a Theory of Citizenship," *Sociology* 24:2, May 1990: 189–217. A thoughtful reflection on the meaning of citizenship in the U.S. is Judith N. Shklar's *American Citizenship* (Cambridge: Harvard University Press, 1991).

6. As James Wilson put it at the U.S. Constitutional Convention, "the right of suffrage, properly understood, properly valued, and properly exercised, in a free and well constituted government, is an abundant source of the most rational, the most improving, and the most endearing connection among the citizens." Quoted in Robin W. Lovin, "Equality and Covenant Theology," *Journal of Law and Religion* 2:2, 1984: 260.

7. The phrases are taken from a text "for youths of high school attainment" by Richard T. Ely, a founder of the American Economic Association and Christian reformer. Ely is emblematic of any number of other leaders through whom one can trace two or three generations of cumulative social reforms on both sides of the Atlantic. Richard T. Ely, *The Social Law of Service* (New York: Eastin and Mains, 1896). B. G. Rader, *The Academic Mind and Reform: The Influence of Richard T. Ely in American Life* (Lexington: Heath, 1966).

8. A fuller discussion of such similarities is in Albert O. Hirschman's *The Rhetoric for Reaction* (Cambridge: Harvard University Press, 1991): chap. 6.

9. Daniel Moynihan. *The Politics of a Guaranteed Income* (New York: Random House, 1973). For an earlier rationale of the negative income tax see George Stigler, "The Economics of Minimum Wage Legislation," *American Economic Review* (June 1946): 364–365.

10. Thus, the American economic reformer Henry Carter Adams argued in 1887 that the American state was like a sick man in the days of treatment by "the leech and the lance." By bleeding government of effective power, he said, the laissez-faire philosophy had reduced it to "feebleness and disintegration." Quoted in John A. Garraty, *The New Commonwealth* (New York: Harper & Row, 1968): 328.

11. This is a common theme across policy areas in virtually all the OECD countries. See, for example, Arnold Heidenheimer, Hugh Heclo, and Carolyn Adams, *Comparative Public Policy* (New York: Harper & Row, 1968): 328.

12. Quoted in David Broder, "An American Paradox," *The Washington Post* (July 14, 1991).

REFERENCES

Baldwin, Peter. 1990. *The Politics of Social Solidarity: Class Bases of the European Welfare State 1875–1975.* Cambridge: Cambridge University Press.

Bane, Mary Jo, and David Ellwood. 1989. "One Fifth of the Nation's Children, Why Are They Poor?" *Science* September: 1047–1048.

Berlin, Isaiah. 1990. *The Crooked Timber of Humanity.* New York: Knopf.

Blumin, Stuart M. 1989. *The Emergence of the Middle Class.* Cambridge: Cambridge University Press.

Broder, David. 1991. "An American Paradox." *The Washington Post* July 14.

Castles, Francis G., ed. 1989. *The Comparative History of Public Policy.* Oxford: Oxford University Press.

Croly, Herbert. 1909. *The Promise of American Life.* New York: Macmillan.

Elster, Jon. 1989. *Nuts and Bolts for the Social Sciences.* Cambridge: Cambridge University Press.

Ely, Richard T. 1896. *The Social Law of Service.* New York: Eastin and Mains.

Engelberg, Ernst. 1990. *Bismarck.* Berlin: Siedler Verlag.

Esping-Andersen, Gosta. 1987. *Politics Against Markets.* Princeton: Princeton University Press.

Etzioni, Amitai. 1988. *The Moral Dimension.* New York: Free Press.

Fiske, Alan. 1991. *The Structures of Social Life.* New York: Free Press.

Flora, Peter, et al., eds. 1986. *State, Economy and Society in Western Europe, 1815–1975.* London: Macmillan.

Garraty, John A. 1968. *The New Commonwealth.* New York: Harper & Row.

Hayek, Friedrich A. 1976. *The Mirage of Social Justice.* Chicago: University of Chicago Press.

Heclo, Hugh, and Henrik Madsen. 1987. *Policy and Politics in Sweden.* Philadelphia: Temple University Press, chap. 6.

Heidenheimer, Arnold, Hugh Heclo, and Carolyn Adams. 1968. *Comparative Public Policy.* New York: Harper & Row.

Hirschman, Albert O. 1991. *The Rhetoric for Reaction.* Cambridge: Harvard University Press, chap. 6.

Hunt, Morton. 1989. *The Compassionate Beast.* New York: Morrow.

Jencks, Christopher, and Paul E. Peterson, eds. 1991. *The Urban Underclass.* Washington, D.C.: Brookings Institution.

Johnson, Michael P. 1989. "Upward from Slavery." *The New York Review of Books* December 21: 53.

Klein, Rudolph and Michael O'Higgins. 1988. "Defusing the Crisis of the Welfare State." In *Social Security: Beyond the Rhetoric of Crisis,* edited by Theodore R. Marmor and Jerry L. Mashaw. Princeton: Princeton University Press.

Kloppenberg, James T. 1986. *Social Democracy and Progressivism in European and American Thought, 1870–1920.* New York: Oxford University Press.

Lacey, Michael J., ed. 1989. *Religion and Twentieth-Century American Intellectual Life.* Cambridge: Cambridge University Press.

Liebfried, Stephan. 1990. "Poverty, Marginalization and Social Exclusion in the Europe of the 90s." Paper presented to EC Seminar on European Welfare Regimes in Transition, April 23–25, 1990, Alghero.

Lovin, Robin W. 1984. "Equality and Covenant Theology." *Journal of Law and Religion* 2:260.

McFate, Katherine. "Trampolines, Safety Nets, or Free Fall?" Chapter 21 in this volume.

Marshall, T. H. 1949. "Citizenship and Social Class," Alfred Marshall Lectures given at Cambridge University in 1949; reprinted in Marshall, *Class, Citizenship, and Social Development.* New York: Doubleday, 1965: chap. 4.

———. 1972. "Value Problems of Welfare-Capitalism." *Journal of Social Policy* 1:1.

Moynihan, Daniel. 1973. *The Politics of a Guaranteed Income.* New York: Random House.

Myles, John. 1985. "Decline or Impasse: The Current State of the Welfare State." *Studies in Political Economy* 26:92.

Naipaul, V. S. 1991. "Our Universal Civilization." *New York Review of Books* January.

Novick, Peter. 1988. *That Noble Dream.* Cambridge: Cambridge University Press.

Plant, Raymond. 1988. "Needs, Agency, and Welfare Rights." In *Responsibility, Rights and Welfare,* edited by J. Donald Moore. Boulder, Colo.: Westview Press.

Rader, B. G. 1966. *The Academic Mind and Reform: The Influence of Richard T. Ely in American Life.* Lexington, Mass.: D. C. Heath.

Reagan, Ronald. 1982. "State of the Union, 1982." *Vital Speeches of the Day.* 48 (n. 9).

Rehn, Gosta. 1977. "Toward a Society of Free Choice." *Comparative Public Policies,* edited by Jerzy Wiatr and Richard Rose. Wroclaw: Ossolineum.

Reich, Robert B. 1991. *The Work of Nations.* New York: Knopf, chap. 17.

Rorty, Richard. 1989. *Contingency, Irony, and Solidarity.* Cambridge: Cambridge University Press.

Sandel, Michael J. 1984. "The Procedural Republic and the Unencumbered Self." *Political Theory* 12: 1.

Shklar, Judith N. 1991. *American Citizenship.* Cambridge: Harvard University Press.

Skocpol, Theda. 1991. *Protecting Soldiers and Mothers: The Politics of Social Provision in the United States 1870–1920.* Cambridge: Harvard University Press.

Standing, Guy. 1989. "Labor Market Analysis and Employment Planning," *World Employment Programme Research Working Paper no. 23.* Geneva: International Labor Organization.

Stigler, George. 1946. "The Economics of Minimum Wage Legislation." *American Economic Review* June: 364–365.

Sumner, William Graham. 1987. "State Interference." *North American Review* 145: 113. *What the Social Classes Owe Each Other.* New York: Harper & Brothers [1883], chap. 8.

Sundquist, James L. 1968. *Policies and Policy: The Eisenhower, Kennedy and Johnson Years.* Washington, D.C.: Brookings Institution.

Taylor, Charles. 1989. *Sources of the Self: The Making of the Modern Identity.* Cambridge, Mass.: Harvard University Press.

Turner, Bryan S. 1990. "Outline of a Theory of Citizenship." *Sociology S* 24: 189–217.

Vannorsdall, John. 1991. *The Best of John Vannorsdall.* Chicago: Evangelical Lutheran Church, Office of the Bishop.

Walzer, Michael. 1989. "Socialism Then and Now." *The New Republic.* November 6: 78.

Weitzman, Martin. 1985. *The Share Economy.* Cambridge, Mass.: Harvard University Press.

West, Cornel. 1989. *The American Evasion of Philosophy.* Madison: University of Wisconsin Press.

Westbrook, Robert B. 1991. *John Dewey and American Democracy.* Ithaca, N.Y.: Cornell University Press.

Chapter 23

POVERTY, SOCIAL RIGHTS,
AND THE QUALITY OF CITIZENSHIP

Roger Lawson and William Julius Wilson

"NEW POVERTY" IN EUROPE AND NORTH AMERICA

T HE CHAPTERS in this volume leave little doubt that the period since the
late 1970s marks a watershed in poverty, inequality, and social policy on
both sides of the Atlantic. With the erosion of the protective systems of
social and economic cooperation erected in the earlier postwar era, a growing
section of the workforce is now more likely to be exposed to the vagaries of the
labor market. Economic insecurity has been accompanied by family breakdown
and inferior and uncertain forms of public assistance. For an increasingly vulnerable minority population, the prospects are a life more or less detached from
the broader economic and social experiences of mainstream society.

On both continents, a variety of economic, social, and political forces have
been producing powerful new configurations of inequality. Described as "the
new poverty," these recent forms of inequality reflect changes in the size and
composition of economically marginal groups, the crystallization of racial cleavages among them, a downward turn in their life chances, and an increase in
their social and political isolation.

In contrast to the period between the 1940s and 1970s, poverty rates have not
only been rising in most Western societies, they have grown disproportionately
among the younger sections of society and the prime-age workforce. The most
significant rises have occurred, as the data from the Luxembourg Income Study
(LIS) reveal, among the more vulnerable younger families and their children,
particularly among the increasing numbers of lone-parent families.

The period since the late 1970s has also seen a hardening of racial cleavages,
especially among the more disadvantaged segments of the population. In the
United States, deindustrialization, the growing plethora of low-wage and part-
time jobs, rising unemployment, and the rolling back of greatly needed social
and urban programs have affected all economically marginal groups. But the
urban black poor have been particularly devastated, mainly because their plight
has been compounded by their spatial concentration in deteriorating inner-city

/   **693**

ghettos (Wilson 1987, 1991). In Western Europe, links between race or minority status and social exclusion and deprivation have also become increasingly evident over the past decade, and they have been compounded by the upsurge of xenophobia and racism since the late 1980s.

What most characterizes the "new poverty" is that it affects the life chances of the poor more acutely than in the recent past. It has involved qualitative changes in the status, social relations, and expectations of the poor and does not just represent new forms of material inequality and deprivation. Terms like *feminization* and *racialization* of poverty and various explanations of poverty, which now center around labor market processes and work relationships, are used to convey or demonstrate these changes. In Europe, especially, efforts to treat poverty in the 1960s focused mainly on providing adequate services and benefits. Today, the new poor are exposed to more grudging, bureaucratic forms of welfare that many would regard as denying them the dignity and status essential to their social citizenship (Vincent 1991).

In the tougher environment on both sides of the Atlantic, the "moral worth" of the poor (i.e., their willingness to work, sexual arrangements, and honesty) is subjected to more detailed scrutiny in means-tested programs. Recent research in the United Kingdom (Dean and Taylor-Gooby 1993) has shown how changes in the official orientation to welfare tend to strengthen claimants' inclinations to view the state as adversary and to reduce the likelihood of their cooperation with the authorities. Rather than the creation of a "dependency culture," in the sense propounded by conservative theorists, the research pointed to an emerging " 'captivity culture': claimants may be trapped unwillingly into dependency, and policies intended to promote 'independence' may serve in practice to sustain state dependency as a 'manageable' phenomenon." It should come as no surprise that the reactions of many poor people to such trends have been a willingness to "fiddle" the system to some degree and, among some, to turn to an alternative social economy based on illicit or semilegal activities and earnings.

Furthermore, the social and political isolation of the poor has become more marked in the 1980s and 1990s. In the United States, poverty has become more urban, more concentrated, and more firmly implanted in inner-city neighborhoods in large metropolises, particularly in older industrial cities with immense and highly segregated numbers of black and Hispanic residents. Even the most pessimistic observers of urban life in America during the ghetto riots of the 1960s hardly anticipated the massive breakdown of social institutions in these neighborhoods and the severity of the problems of joblessness, family disruption, teenage pregnancy, failing schools, and crime and drugs that now involve many of those who live in the inner city. These social dislocations derive in part from macro-structural changes in the broader society, most notably from the declining labor market opportunities for the poor (Wilson 1987).

An important aspect of the urban poor's predicament is the way the dwindling presence of nonpoor families has deprived ghetto neighborhoods of key resources, including structural resources, such as a social buffer to minimize the effects of growing joblessness, and cultural resources, such as conventional role models for neighborhood children. The absence of these resources increases social isolation (as reflected, e.g., in the rapidly decreasing access to job information network systems), which further reinforces already weak labor force attachment. Moreover, a social context that also includes poor schools, a lack of legitimate employment opportunities, and a depletion of other social resources increases the probability of illegal or deviant activities. This weakens attachment to the legitimate labor market even further (Wilson 1987, 1991).

Europe and the United States provide a sharp contrast on the issue of urban inequality. No European city has experienced the level of concentrated poverty and racial and ethnic segregation typical of American metropolises. Nor does any European city include areas that are as physically isolated, deteriorated, and violence prone as the inner-city ghettos of urban America. As Loïc Wacquant's comparison of La Corneuve in Paris and Woodlawn in Chicago in this volume suggests, there is, as yet, no real European equivalent of the plight of the American ghetto. Nevertheless, the omens are not always as favorable as they appear in La Corneuve. In France and in other parts of Europe, many inner-city communities and outer-city public housing estates have been cut off from mainstream labor market institutions and informal job networks, creating the vicious cycle of "weak labor force attachment," growing social exclusion, and rising tensions. As in the United States, evidence is now accumulating that once this process gets under way, it has serious consequences for the socialization of the next generation (Ashton and Maguire 1991).

Although these European communities are more mixed than in the United States, their population is invariably drawn disproportionately from various ethnic minorities. Trends in a number of European countries suggest the beginnings of a social polarization in the cities that has been characteristic of American metropolises, featuring a growing gap in the concentration of social problems between some areas and others.

Moreover, European research has been documenting how poverty, as it becomes more concentrated, multiplies forms of deprivation, and leads to a qualitative and not just material deterioration of conditions. A study of *Poverty and Labour in London*, conducted in the 1980s, notes the growing inequalities between boroughs in social and health conditions, particularly in the "geography of death." It also found

> a lot more evidence of hostile and fearful relationships within local communities than did a corresponding team 17 years ago. The volume of concern about safety on the streets, burglaries and muggings has gained a major grip and affects ordinary people deeply in an increasing number of communities. . . . This makes poverty worse because it isolates people and stultifies community support and the readiness of others to offer . . . services to mitigate or compensate for the privations which old people and unemployed people experience. (Townsend et al. 1987: 52)

Given these developments, it should not be surprising that in several quarters and with increasing frequency, European observers have been warning that if present trends continue, in a few years cities in Europe will feature ghettos that resemble those in the United States. However, when such comparisons are made, differences in the social and political organization of American and European cities are rarely taken into account.[1] In American cities, groups can be more easily separated by income, race, and ethnicity because of differences in land use policy, housing policy, the organization of social policy, and federal urban policy. Municipalities in the United States have much greater autonomy than do those in Europe. They have much greater control over population movements and urban developments. Through zoning and other measures ostensibly designed to ensure a community's health, they have the power "to determine what kinds of people can live and what kinds of business activities can be conducted within their borders" (Weir 1993: 18).

A major factor in the movement to create separate political jurisdictions has been the organization of social policy that reflects the greater autonomy of localities in the United States. This is particularly true with respect to education. Given the middle class's long-established norm of enrolling its children in public schools, a strong impetus for groups to separate themselves by income, and/or by race, has been the traditional use of local property taxes to finance education.

Also, federal government policies have contributed to the growth of local fragmentation. On the one hand, the building of numerous federally financed freeways and the creation of federal government programs to subsidize private homeownership in order to meet the postwar housing demands contributed substantially to the growth of suburban communities, including many new political jurisdictions. On the other hand, the federal government "bowed to local opposition to subsidize housing that might promote integration" (Weir 1993: 19). Indeed, opposition from organized community groups to the building of public housing in their neighborhoods and de facto federal policy to tolerate extensive segregation against blacks in urban housing markets have led to massive, segregated housing projects that have become ghettos for the minorities and disadvantaged (Sampson and Wilson 1994). Accordingly, because local acceptance dictated federal housing policies, public housing was overwhelmingly concentrated in the overcrowded and deteriorating inner-city ghettos—the poorest and least socially organized sections of the city and the metropolitan area. In America, public housing represents a federally funded, physically permanent institution for the isolation of families by race and class and, therefore, has contributed to the isolation of many minority residents in inner-city ghettos in recent years.

Finally, since 1980, a fundamental shift in the federal government's support for basic urban programs has contributed to the worsening conditions of the urban ghettos in the United States. Spending on direct aid to cities, including general revenue sharing, urban mass transit, public service jobs and job training, compensatory education, social service block grants, local public works, economic development assistance, and urban development action grants, was sharply cut during the Reagan and Bush administrations. The federal contribution to city budgets declined from 18 percent in 1980 to 6.4 percent in 1990. In addition, the latest economic recession, which began in the Northeast in 1989, sharply reduced urban revenues that the cities themselves generated, thereby creating budget deficits that resulted in further cutbacks in basic services and programs, and increases in local taxes.

Unlike during the Ford and Carter presidencies, in which countercyclical programs, such as emergency public service jobs, emergency public works and countercyclical cash payments were used to fight recessions, there was no anti-recession legislation in 1990 and 1991 to combat economic dislocations in urban areas. As Demetrios Caraley (1992) has pointed out, if the antirecession package voted by Congress in 1976 and 1977 had been introduced during the early 1990s, it would have amounted to $17 billion dollars in 1990 dollars.

Caraley (1992) also noted that the combination of the New Federalism, which resulted in sharp cuts in federal aid to local and state governments, and the recession created for many cities, especially the older cities of the East and Midwest, the worst fiscal and service crisis since the Depression. Cities have become increasingly underserviced, and many are on the brink of bankruptcy. Therefore, they have not been in a position to combat effectively three unhealthy social conditions that have emerged or become prominent since 1980: (1) the outbreaks of crack-cocaine addiction and the murders and other violent crimes that have accompanied them, (2) the AIDS epidemic and its escalating public health costs, and (3) the sharp rise in the homeless population not only for individuals but for whole families as well.

Although these unhealthy social conditions are present in many neighborhoods throughout the city, the high jobless and socially unstable inner-city ghetto areas are natural breeding grounds for violent crime, drug addiction, AIDS, and homelessness. Life in inner-city ghetto neighborhoods, already imperiled by unprecedented levels of joblessness and social disorganization, has become even more difficult in the face of these new epidemics. Fiscally strapped cities have had to watch in helpless frustration as these problems—the new urban poverty, the decline of social organization of inner-city neighborhoods, the rise of unhealthy social conditions, the reduction of social services—escalated during the 1980s and made the larger city itself seem like a less attractive place in which to live. Accordingly, many urban residents with the economic means have followed the worn-out path from the central city to the suburbs and other areas, thereby shrinking the tax base and further reducing city revenue.

As Margaret Weir (1993) has pointed out, in 1960 the nation's population was evenly divided among cities, suburbs, and rural areas. By 1990, both urban and rural populations had declined, leaving suburbs with nearly half of the nation's population. The urban population dipped to 31 percent by 1990. And as cities lost population, they became poorer and more minority in their racial and ethnic composition, so much so that in the eyes of many in the dominant white population, the minorities symbolize the ugly urban scene left behind.

Today, the divide between the suburbs and the city is, in many respects, a racial divide. For example, whereas 68 percent of all the residents in the city of Chicago were minority in 1990, 83 percent of all suburban residents in the Chicago metropolitan area were white. Across the nation, whereas 74 percent of the dominant white population lived in suburban and rural areas, a majority of blacks and Hispanics resided in urban areas in 1990.

These demographic changes are associated with the declining influence of American cities. The shift of the population to suburban areas made it possible to win national elections without a substantial urban vote. Suburbs cast 36 percent of the vote for president in 1968, 48 percent in 1988, and a majority in the 1992 election. The sharp drop in federal support for basic urban programs since 1980 is associated with the declining political influence of cities and the rising influence of electoral coalitions in the suburbs.

These aspects of the American political system (land use policy, housing policy, the organization of social policy, and federal urban policy) contribute to greater racial differences and "make the problems of racially-identified concentrated poverty more extreme and intractable." (Weir 1993: 2). Consider, by comparison, Britain and France, two countries that also have a significant number of citizens who are members of racial minorities and who tend to be concentrated in deteriorated areas.

In Britain, the strong central government has exerted a good deal of control over population movements and urban development. Local authorities have little autonomy in the highly centralized British political system. Until recently the only local source of revenue to which they had access was the property tax levied on businesses and property owners. Thus, unlike in the United States, the quality of local public schools is far less determined by the resources of local governments and, therefore, the association between schooling and residence is not as strong. Because of lack of autonomy and of discretion in financing, competition between local jurisdictions is far less apparent than in the United States.

Furthermore, unlike in the United States, where the federal government subsidized suburban home ownership to satisfy postwar housing demands, the rebuilding of housing stock in Britain occurred mainly through the construction of public housing. "By the end of the 1970s, a third of British households lived in 'council housing.' The very size of the British sector made some level of income mixing inevitable" (Weir 1993: 21). Moreover, council housing in Britain was less concentrated in certain locations. The government's aim to decentralize the urban population resulted in the construction of council housing outside the central city. By the late 1980s, although 43 percent of council housing was located in poorer inner London, 29 percent was located in central London and 23 percent in outer London.

Although the postwar population sorting in Britain did affect racial mixing, the sharp racial concentration so characteristic of cities in the United States did not occur because public housing was not deliberately segregated. With the absence of preexisting ghettos, many public housing units were built in working-class neighborhoods that were not defined racially. Moreover, opportunities for the working class to move to suburban owner-occupied housing were restricted because of limited financing and less favorable tax treatment of mortgages (Weir 1993).

A somewhat different pattern prevails in France. French cities tend to be more desirable as places to reside, with the more disadvantaged segments of the population concentrated in the suburbs. Overseen by the central planning agency, the public housing program, traditionally populated mainly by the lower middle classes and working classes, has recently opened up to immigrant minorities, and their representation in public housing has gradually increased since 1970. Fourteen percent of the French population now resides in public housing, and the proportion of immigrants in public housing has reached 30 percent in some estates (Weir 1993).

Although poor ethnic and racial minorities are often concentrated in suburban high-rise public housing, which leads to problems of physical isolation, French land use and housing policies controlled population movements more and permitted more mixing of people by income, ethnicity, and race than in either Britain or the United States (Weir 1993).

However, recent population movements and government action in Britain and France that have increased concentrated poverty and racial/ethnic segregation suggest a growing convergence between these countries and the United States. Just as the promotion of home ownership by the United States government in the 1950s increased sharply the suburbanization of the middle class, so, too, has the central government's promotion of home ownership more than a decade later in both France and Britain contributed to the suburbanization of the middle classes there. Moreover, as the barriers to their entry have been removed, the minority poor have become more concentrated in public housing in both countries (Weir 1993).

These two developments have separated populations along racial and ethnic lines in a manner that resembles historic racial sorting in the United States. And the problems associated with the construction of high-rise public housing have contributed to the growing segregation of the British and French minority populations. "Difficult to maintain, many of the housing blocks quickly became dilapidated, undesirable places to live, propelling those who were able to find housing elsewhere" (Weir 1993: 24–25).

Nonetheless, for the reasons discussed earlier, it is unlikely that Britain and France will eventually experience the degree of income and racial segregation that characterizes metropolitan areas in the United States. The central government's control over the formation of new political jurisdictions in Britain and France reduces the opportunities and incentives for the spatial separation by race and income. Structural arrangements, such as local control over education and taxation, and political arrangements that enable localities to incorporate and to resist federal government efforts to site public housing are far fewer in the two European countries. Accordingly, the "tipping" phenomena so characteristic of the ghettoization process in American cities is far less likely to develop in France and Britain. When the "tipping" mechanism is triggered, it is much more likely to be restricted to, say, a particular public housing project and can be more easily reversed by government interventions. As Weir (1993: 26) has observed, "In neither country have residents had the same incentives or opportunities to act on their racial antipathies as in the United States."

Finally, in neither Britain nor France has suburbanization been associated with the abandonment of cities as residential areas. In France especially, governments have "continued to treat cities as a national resource to be protected and nurtured" (Weir 1993: 25). These arguments are presented not to suggest that the new poverty in Europe does not represent some fundamental and major change in the system of inequality but rather to indicate that different structural and political arrangements in European countries reduce the likelihood that American-style ghettos will emerge in the near future.

POLICY LESSONS FROM THE UNITED STATES

So far we have drawn attention to the emergence of the new poverty on both continents, the various economic, social, and political forces associated with it, and the special problems and challenges it presents. However, the chapters in this volume also raise important questions about variations between countries in the extent to which problems of poverty and inequality are addressed. Foremost among these are questions about the dismal record of the United States. Although poverty and inequality have increased in Europe and in Canada, the most severe consequences of the social and economic dislocations of the past two decades have occurred in the United States. This was already readily apparent in the late 1970s but became more pronounced during the 1980s, when the Reagan administration pursued policies aimed at improving the living standards of the broad middle class and relied on economic growth to trickle down and take care of the problems of the poor.

The comparisons based on the LIS data illustrate the effects of these policies. By the second half of the 1980s, the American poverty rate among the nonelderly population rose to more than double that of most European countries and to almost three times the level in West Germany. Even when the elderly are included, the United States had the highest national poverty rate of all 13 countries represented in the LIS data base (Rainwater 1991). Even more significant were the changing depth or severity of poverty in the United States and the sharply divergent patterns of poverty concentration between racial minorities and whites.

In recent years, the United States Census Bureau established what might be called "the poorest of the poor" category, that is, those individuals whose annual income falls at least 50 percent below the officially designated poverty line. In 1975, 30 percent of all the poor had incomes below 50 percent of the poverty level; in 1988, 40 percent did so. Among blacks, the increase was much sharper, from 32 percent in 1975 to nearly half (48%) in 1988 (U.S. Bureau of the Census 1988).

As the comparisons with Europe suggest, these trends can be seen as the outcome of a distinctive response to poverty that has long prevailed in the United States. As Rainwater (1991) has noted, "America's various wars on poverty, unlike those of some continental European countries, have been particularly preoccupied with the situation of the very worst off in society, with the situation of the lower class rather than that of the working class more broadly." This difference has been reflected in the way antipoverty and social policy agendas have been structured. In most European welfare states, the prevailing view for much of the postwar period has been similar to that described by a French official. "A policy for the poor," he suggested, "is a poor policy . . . the general principle underlying steps to help the most disadvantaged is to ensure that they get the maximum benefit from programs which apply to the population as a whole. Rather than specific measures, the idea is to pay specific attention to groups in difficulty within the context of general measures" (Lion 1984).

By contrast, most American "welfare" and antipoverty programs, including the Great Society's War on Poverty programs in the 1960s, have emphasized targeting and means testing rather than universalistic social policy. As such, they have been relatively autonomous arrangements for the "poor" that have developed largely in isolation from broader national concerns with employment or indeed from macroeconomic interventions more generally. Politically and institutionally they have been sharply differentiated from mainstream social policies, especially social security, health, and housing, for the "stable" working class and middle class. Moreover, the American response to poverty has been typically characterized by a predilection for "programs" rather than "policy" and especially for decentralized and fragmented programs and experiments.

A number of excellent historical studies have shown that the American approach to poverty is part of the peculiar policy legacy of the New Deal (see, e.g., Weir, Orloff, and Skocpol 1988; Katz 1986, 1989; Patterson 1981). These studies demonstrate how the development of nationwide social security programs under the New Deal marked an important extension of social citizenship to the "deserving" working class (i.e., workers with good job prospects and the ability to pay regular contributions). These programs were not only backed by a strong federal bureaucracy, they also had a broad base of public support, including support from the middle classes who gained from the improvements in social security entitlements.

However, the New Deal did much less to address the problems facing people with low skills and status, including many blacks migrating out of the rural South, who were prone to bouts of joblessness, low and fluctuating incomes, and poor health. Policy initiatives that would have rebounded to their benefit, such as attempts to establish a firm national commitment to full employment or to a nationwide health care program, were notably unsuccessful in the 1930s and 1940s. As Paul Osterman's chapter notes, the United States also lacked the combination of laws, union power, and customs used in Europe after 1945 to raise the bottom of the labor market. Instead, under the New Deal system, efforts to combat the real threat of poverty among the weakest sections of society were confined to a number of disjointed, second-tier programs grouped under the rubric of "welfare." With much weaker administrative capacities than social security, the fate of these programs was largely dependent on the altruism of the nonpoor.

The historical analysis shows how the development of second-tier "welfare" programs from the New Deal not only restricted the scope of antipoverty initiatives but also reinforced traditional concerns with the "undeserving poor" and, more importantly, images of the poor and of many black Americans as a class apart in American society. In many important respects, the Great Society programs of the 1960s helped sustain these images.

Although the War on Poverty appeared to herald a new and less divisive era in social policy, its impact on social rights contrasted sharply with the extension of political and civil rights to blacks in the 1960s. The poor gained some notable improvements in welfare benefits, but from policies that did little in practice to integrate the recipients into the economic and social life of mainstream society. On the contrary, issues like unemployment and the growth of female-headed households among the newly urbanized black poor were still treated as distinctive welfare issues to be addressed through "special interest" programs. As one study puts it, "despite a greater willingness to expend resources on the poor . . . the labor economists and sociologists who became architects of the poverty programs in the 1960s saw efforts to change the behavior of the poor as the most promising route to ending poverty—for poverty was, by definition, not a national economic problem" (Weir, Orloff, and Skocpol 1988: 206). Even the more radical measures of the War on Poverty, such as the efforts in the Community Action Programs to secure poor and minority group control of social policy institutions, effectively maintained the separation of poverty policy from broader issues of social solidarity and wider economic and workplace concerns (Klass 1983).

The events of the past two decades have exposed the real weaknesses of the targeted welfare programs. As Skocpol (1988: 309) has argued, "When the political going gets rough for public social policies, as it has in the United States since the 1970s, policies that lack clear political and cultural legitimation as expressions of social compassion and collective solidarity are difficult to either defend or extend against individualist, market-oriented, and anti-statist attacks." Put another way, the most significant welfare state backlash in this period has occurred, not where social spending is highest, but in countries like the United States, where there has been a more marked "us/them" divide in social policy between programs for the broad middle mass in society and programs for the poor. As Korpi (1980) explains, this dualism "in effect splits the working class and tends to generate coalitions between the better off workers and the middle class thus creating a larger constituency for welfare-backlash.

In fact, the 'welfare backlash' becomes rational political activity for the majority of citizens."

But the welfare backlash is also activity that has been fueled by the way America's antipoverty efforts have in the long run fostered group misunderstanding and isolation and distrust of the poor. A weakening of community support for the poor—or what Alan Ryan (1992) has called "the retreat from caring"—is another of the broader themes associated with the new configurations of poverty. Ryan used the phrase in a commentary on the new "tough love" policies advocated by both Democrats and Republicans in the 1992 U.S. presidential campaign and particularly on the way even Democrats appeared to despair of the poor. The 1992 Democratic party platform took a line that 10 years earlier would have been denounced as "blaming the victim." Why this exasperated mood seemed so widespread was, to Ryan, a puzzle, given the low costs of the social programs that evoked so much hostility. However, he attributed it partly to despair at the apparent intractability of black poverty and, more specifically, to the decline of basic formal and informal institutions in ghetto neighborhoods. This placed severe constraints on welfare services in locating their clients but, more importantly, made it "harder to recruit community organizers who provide grassroots support to go with government assistance."

The problem of who now speaks for the poor is raised in Guy Standing's discussion in this volume of the dramatic erosion of trade union rights and influence on both sides of the Atlantic. As he argues, unions have sometimes been castigated for representing mainly relatively secure male employees. But, in reality, union membership has often in the past made a substantial difference for the most vulnerable groups in the labor market. His figures for the United States in the late 1980s are worth repeating: "whereas white men gained a wage premium of about 50 cents an hour from union membership, black men gained about $1.61, Hispanic men about $2.18, white women about $0.83, black women $1.23 and Hispanic women $1.53."

The retreat from caring in the United States reflects a more widespread sense of pessimism about the intractability of poverty and the failure of welfare programs than has been evident in Europe. The European comparisons indicate that much of the problem in the United States stems from the limited range of tools available for combating poverty. Without the support of more universal social services or labor market interventions, welfare programs have attempted to do too much, not too little. However, the prevalent mood in America by the 1970s and 1980s offered a very different interpretation. To many middle Americans, the nation's poorest citizens had come to be virtually synonymous with a "welfare class" posing a growing threat to the public peace and to dominant American norms. To be more specific, as a study of social standing in America in the 1970s showed, lower America was seen to be separated into two status subdivisions. At the bottom of the ladder was the welfare class, people who were described in terms of their behavioral and cultural deficiencies by the great majority of those interviewed in the study, and who were seen as being caught up in a "welfare way of life" that undermined initiative and encouraged apathy, alienation, and normlessless. Above them were people who were "lower class but not the lowest": Significantly, they were "accorded their superior standing 'because they are never on welfare' or 'only occasionally' (and 'if on, they're trying to get off')" (Coleman and Rainwater 1979).

The heavy emphasis on the individual traits of the welfare poor and on the duties or social obligations of welfare recipients is not unique to the general public. This "common wisdom" has been uncritically incorporated into the work of many poverty researchers. Throughout the 1960s and 1970s, the expanding network of poverty researchers in the United States paid considerable attention to the question of individuals' work attitudes and the association between income maintenance programs and the work ethic of the poor. They consistently ignored the effects of basic economic transformations and cyclical processes on the work experiences and prospects of the poor.

However, despite this narrow focus, these very American researchers have consistently uncovered empirical findings that undermine, rather than support, assumptions about the negative effects of welfare receipt on individual initiative and motivation. Yet these assumptions persist among policymakers, and "the paradox of continuing high poverty during a period of general prosperity has contributed to the recently emerging consensus that welfare must be reformed" (Melville and Doble 1988). Although it is reasonable to argue that policymakers are not aware of a good deal of the empirical research on the effects of welfare, the General Accounting Office (GAO), an investigative arm of Congress, released a study in early 1987 that reported that there was no conclusive evidence for the prevailing beliefs that welfare discourages individuals from working, breaks up two-parent families, or affects the child-bearing rates of unmarried women, even young unmarried women.

The GAO report reached these conclusions after reviewing the results of more than 100 empirical studies on the effects of welfare completed since 1975; analyzing the case files of more than 1,200 families receiving public assistance in four states, and interviewing officials from federal, state, and local government agencies. Nonetheless, despite the report's findings, the growth of social dislocations among the inner-city poor and the continued high rates of poverty have led an increasing number of policymakers to conclude that something should be done about the current welfare system to halt what they perceive to be the breakdown of the norms of citizenship. Indeed, a liberal-conservative consensus on welfare reform has recently emerged that features two themes: (1) The receipt of welfare should be predicated on reciprocal responsibilities whereby society is obligated to provide assistance to welfare applicants who, in turn, are obligated to behave in socially approved ways; and (2) able-bodied adult welfare recipients should be required to prepare themselves for work, to search for employment, and to accept jobs when they are offered. These points of agreement were reflected in the discussions of the welfare reform legislation passed in the United States Congress in 1988.

These two themes are based on the implicit assumption that a sort of mysterious "welfare ethos" exists that encourages public assistance recipients to avoid their obligations as citizens to be educated, to work, to support their families, and to obey the law. In other words, and in keeping with the dominant American belief system, *it is the moral fabric of individuals, not the social and economic structure of society, that is taken to be the root of the problem* (Wacquant and Wilson 1989).

The poverty tradition in the United States, including the lack of comprehensive programs to promote the social rights of American citizens, is especially problematic for poor inner-city blacks who are also handicapped by problems that originated from the denial of civil, political, and social rights to the previous generations. And their degree of current economic deprivation and social isolation is in part due to the limited nature of institutionalized social rights in the United States (Schmitter-Heisler 1991). Indeed, the effects of joblessness on all the poor in the United States are far more severe than those experienced by disadvantaged groups in other advanced industrial Western societies. While economic restructuring and its adverse effects on lower-income groups has been common to all these societies in recent years, the most severe consequences of social and economic dislocations have been in the United States because of the underdeveloped welfare state and the weak institutional structure of social citizenship rights. Although all economically marginal groups have been affected, the inner-city black poor have been particularly devastated because their plight has been compounded by their spatial concentration in deteriorating ghetto neighborhoods, neighborhoods that reinforce weak labor force attachment.

In short, the socioeconomic position of the inner-city black poor in American society is extremely precarious. The cumulative effects of historic racial exclusion have made them vulnerable to the economic restructuring of the advanced industrial economy. Moreover, the problems of joblessness, deepening poverty, and other woes that have accompanied these economic changes cannot be relieved by the meager welfare programs targeted to the poor. Furthermore, these problems tend to be viewed by members of the larger society as a reflection of personal deficiencies, not structural inequities.

Accordingly, if any group has a stake in the enhancement of social rights in the United States, it is the inner-city black poor. Unfortunately, given the strength of the American belief system on poverty and welfare, any program that would improve the life chances of this group would have to be based on concerns beyond those that focus on life and experiences in inner-city ghettos. The poor and the working classes struggle to make ends meet, and even the middle class has experienced a decline in its living standard. Indeed, Americans across racial and class boundaries continue to worry about unemployment and job security, declining real wages, escalating medical and housing costs, childcare programs, the sharp decline in the quality of public education, and crime and drug trafficking in their neighborhoods.

These concerns are reflected in public opinion surveys. For the last several years national opinion polls consistently reveal strong public backing for government labor market strategies, including training efforts, to enhance employment. A 1988 Harris poll indicated that almost three-quarters of the respondents would support a tax increase to pay for childcare. A 1989 Harris poll reports that almost 9 out of 10 Americans would like to see fundamental change in the United States' health care system. And recent surveys conducted by the National Opinion Research Center at the University of Chicago reveal that a substantial majority of Americans want more money spent on improving the nation's educational system and on halting rising crime and drug addiction.

These poll results suggest the possibility of new alignments in support of the enhancement of social rights. If a serious attempt is made to forge such an alignment, perhaps it ought to begin with a new public rhetoric that does two things: focuses on problems that afflict not only the poor, but the working and middle classes as well; and emphasizes integrative programs that promote the social and economic improvement of all groups in society, not just the truly disadvantaged segments of the population.

EUROPEAN RESPONSES TO POVERTY

While the experience of the United States suggests the need for a fundamental shift in policy away from the emphasis on targeted, fragmented, and "isolationist" antipoverty programs, the various economic crises facing European welfare states over the past two decades provide a sobering reminder of the difficulties now involved in sustaining more universal and integrative social citizenship rights. Europe's postwar commitment to universal programs and social inclusion was premised, as Guy Standing's chapter emphasizes, on assumptions of steady growth and full employment and, although this occurred in varying degrees in different countries, on improvements in a range of closely interrelated employment and labor market securities. It was also closely—and, many would now argue, too inflexibly—identified with notions of collective solidarity associated with organized "wage labor" and class-based labor movements, and revolving primarily around the risks facing the male "breadwinner." Fundamental to the postwar version of social inclusion were conceptions of citizenship that assumed a fair degree of cultural homogeneity, or at least played down the significance of historic cleavages between Catholics and Protestants or between various ethnic groups.

In the 1990s, by contrast, issues of race, ethnicity, and cultural diversity loom large in all discussions of citizenship in western Europe. The future of the European welfare states depends crucially on the ability of European countries to widen their definitions of citizenship to embrace their new minority and immigrant communities, and prevent the emergence of a racialized underclass, marginalized by the welfare state as well as the economy. However, this itself depends on the capacity and willingness of governments to revitalize "social citizenship" by combating broader marginalizing tendencies in the welfare state that have accompanied the return of mass unemployment and the growing fragmentation of European labor markets.

Since the late 1970s, increasing numbers of indigenous workers as well as immigrants in western Europe have found themselves in the "secondary labor market," with a high risk of unemployment, low skills, poor working conditions, and weak trade union protection. Many are on temporary or part-time contracts, or in the gray areas of employment where employers can evade social or labor rights. At the same time, the growth of long-term unemployment—in 1993 it constituted about half of all Western European unemployment, compared with 10–20 percent in the rest of the industrialized world—has created a substantial group more or less detached from the labor force. It includes many young people unable to enter the employed labor force, as well as those "pushed into long-term unemployment or economic activity through discouragement, illness, alcoholism, disability, drugs or crime, much of which could be linked to experience of unemployment in one way or another" (Standing 1986: 20).

An important, interdisciplinary study of poverty and marginalization in West Germany (Leibfried and Tennstedt 1985) reveals the effects of growing economic dislocations on social rights. The study shows how during the 1970s and 1980s, those that formed the "productive core" of German society and who could continue to rely on regular, stable employment consolidated their hold on the established social insurance system, the traditional nucleus of the German welfare state. Despite cuts in social insurance provisions, most of the beneficiaries of the system still enjoyed comparatively high standards of social security, health, and welfare and on the whole succeeded in preserving their relative position in the income hierarchy. By contrast, a growing German lumpenproletariat—those in more precarious employment or increasingly detached from the labor force—was effectively excluded from many of these provisions and forced to depend for its livelihood on an "alternative welfare state in reserve," mainly localized public welfare and assistance, or on family support, or on illegal forms of "self-help."

The study showed, for example, how prior to the onset of the recession in the 1970s the idea of applying for local means-tested public assistance was anathema to most German workers, and less than 1 percent of those receiving such assistance were registered as unemployed. By the mid-1980s the proportion had grown to more than 25 percent, with surveys suggesting that more than half of all the unemployed eligible for these benefits were still not applying, mainly because of feelings of shame and the stigma attached to public assistance (see, e.g., Balsen et al. 1984).

This bifurcation of the welfare state remains evident in newly unified Germany in the 1990s. Indeed, it has acquired new dimensions, as growing numbers of East Germans have been forced to depend on public assistance and—a more disturbing trend, if it persists—as Germany's large foreign population appears to have become more ghettoized and more dependent on means-tested

welfare in the aftermath of unification. Until the end of the 1970s, foreign workers and their families were much less likely than native Germans to rank among
the "official poor" receiving public assistance. Since then, but particularly in
the 1990s, the situation has changed markedly. During 1991, almost 15 percent
of all foreigners at some stage drew upon public assistance, compared with
less than 5 percent of the German population (Statistisches Bundesamt 1993).
Foreigners are also disproportionately affected by the cuts in social benefits in
the much heralded "Solidarity Pact" of 1993 aimed at diverting resources to the
former GDR. This involves major savings in benefits paid to asylum seekers
and refugees and, more generally, in means-tested poverty programs, in which
foreign workers and their families tend to be overrepresented (Schneider 1993).

Similar developments have been evident throughout western Europe, though
the form they have taken and their effects have varied from country to country.
In the United Kingdom, for example, the Thatcher governments of the 1980s
consciously accentuated the "splitting apart" of the welfare state by encouraging
the growth of tax-supported private and company-based welfare among the
middle classes and more affluent workers. At the same time, major cost-cutting
reforms in social security and housing led not only to an increased association
of residual care for the poorer sections of society with social security and housing, but also to a toughening of entitlement requirements and reducing of minimum standards for the poor. By the second half of the 1980s, around 8 million
people or one in seven of the total British population were living in households
dependent on a national means-tested and last-resort income support program.
This compared with 4 million people in 1973 and 1.2 million in 1950 (Lawson
1987). A shift toward more targeted welfare has been a feature of recent French
and Dutch policies, although with less pronounced effects than in Britain. In
the Dutch case, a period of "self-discipline" in the 1980s involved austerity
measures significantly reducing the proportion of national income allocated to
social security, more emphasis on individually earned social insurance, and a
strategy focusing benefits more on the *echta minima* (the truly needy).

While trends like these point to a growing convergence between western
Europe and the United States, it is important not to overstate the case. Despite
clear tendencies in social policy in the 1980s that appear to promote group
separation rather than social integration, a commitment to universal social services remains firmly institutionalized in most European welfare states. As a
number of chapters in this volume have shown, much of the difference between
Europe and America in the incidence of family and child poverty, particularly
among lone-parent families, can be attributed to family policy packages that
still receive wide popular support in Europe. In addition to income transfers to
all or almost all families with children, family policy packages include a range
of measures providing mothers at work, as Sheila Kamerman emphasizes in
this volume, with a "social infrastructure . . . far ahead of the United States."
Europe's commitment to publicly provided health care is another area where
efforts to contain costs and trim programs have had to contend with a deeply

entrenched popular preference for universal services, as well as strong support for universalism from health professionals. Although not a direct focus of our inquiries in this volume, differences in health care provision would seem to have a major bearing on the quality of life among the poor.

For the United States, important lessons can be learned from recent European efforts to coordinate economic and social policies, and to adjust social policies and public expectations of welfare to the new economic situation. The new policies emerging in Sweden following the much publicized defeat of the Social Democrats in 1991 are one example that will be interesting to follow. The liberal-conservative coalition that took office has introduced a wide-ranging reform package aimed at stimulating industrial restructuring and more competitiveness and "enterprise" in Swedish society through tax and public expenditure cuts and curbs on the state monopoly in social policy.

However, the Swedish reform package involves a commitment not to dismantling the welfare state but rather to revitalizing it by giving priority to those components seen to be more consistent with the obligations and rights of "active citizenship." Foremost among these components are the labor market programs pioneered in Sweden in the 1950s, programs that subsequently played a key role in one of the most effective strategies in facilitating social participation and eliminating poverty found in Europe. The programs, which have deliberately sought to avoid passive reliance on welfare among the working-age population by using alternative labor market measures, include retraining measures and publicly supported job creation in areas of high unemployment, subsidized travel for job search, paid costs for movement to a new residence, and an active labor market exchange system.

Germany is another country with a tradition of active labor market measures and close links between industries and educational institutions in its "dual" apprenticeship system. Germany sought to foster a "community of skills" and a successful partnership between economic and social policies. This partnership suffered, however, between the mid-1970s and mid-1980s, when cuts and retrenchment in public expenditures were the overriding concern of governments. Between 1982 and 1984, in the early years of Chancellor Kohl's coalition, almost half the cuts in the federal budget were in labor market and unemployment measures, creating what was dubbed "a new labor market policy without the unemployed."

As Bernard Casey's chapter shows, it also became clear in these years that Germany's much admired dual system was failing to integrate many young people into permanent, core employment. Inspired by the problems of restructuring and reskilling the former East German economy, a more determined effort has been made to revamp the provisions of the dual system since 1989. But, as Casey indicates, the situation was already improving prior to unification, partly as a result of a well-directed trade union campaign, but mainly because of successful pressure on government from two national institutes, the Federal Labour Institute and the Federal Training Institute, comprised of employers, union representatives, and government. As in Sweden, powerful, semi-independent bodies overseeing labor market and training programs and setting goals for employers have played a key role in Germany.

Paul Osterman's chapter shows how other European countries have witnessed an explosion of interest in altering the relationship between schools and the workplace, inspired partly by the German system. In countries like France, the United Kingdom, and the Netherlands, there has been a noticeable reaction against more passive, compensatory social rights for the working-age population, with their connotations of welfare dependence, and a movement to reorient social protection toward forward-looking interventions aimed at improving skills and job opportunities. This reaction includes more acknowledgment than has been given in the past to the potential of workfare and to the obligations, responsibilities, and rights of "social citizenship." But it also reflects a new interest in developing mixed packages of work and welfare in line with what the Organization for Economic Cooperation and Development (OECD) has described as the central role of public social policy in the 1990s: "to design interventions so as to maximize both the numbers of people who have opportunities for active social roles, and the duration of their lives over which they can experience such activity" (OECD 1988: 18).

While these are promising trends, their prospects of revitalizing social rights are by no means secure. So far, as McFate emphasizes, many of the new employment and training innovations have been ill-planned and poorly coordinated, partly because they have been developed in a period that has emphasized decentralized program delivery. It has become abundantly evident in the deepening recession of the early 1990s that efforts to combat the problems of economic dislocation through employment and training strategies can only be effective as part of broader national programs of economic recovery and adjustment to structural change. With European unemployment rates climbing again in 1993 to around 10 percent of the workforce, many of the new training initiatives now look more like remedial actions serving to delay the onset of unemployment.

While the recession of the 1990s has set back the prospects for more "active" social rights, it has also created situations ripe for the demagogic mobilization of racism and anti-immigrant feelings. As economic conditions in Europe have worsened, generating a widespread urban housing crisis and insecurities in the labor market, many in the majority white population have come to view the growth of minorities and immigrants as a source of the problem. The new inflow of refugees and asylum seekers from eastern and southeastern Europe has further exacerbated this feeling. Although extremist violence in Germany and France has attracted the greatest attention, heightened racial and ethnic antagonisms have been evident in most countries. In the United Kingdom, for example, 7,780 racially motivated attacks were officially reported in 1991; the total had climbed by around 1,000 a year over the previous 3 years (*Economist* 1992).

The recession has also underlined the particular vulnerability of immigrant and minority communities to economic stagnation, industrial restructuring, and the decline of traditional manufacturing. Immigrant unemployment rates are commonly more than double those of the indigenous workforce, reaching levels ranging from 25 to 50 percent in cities that have experienced unprecedented high levels of unemployment overall. At a time of growing strains on the welfare state, the minority population, thus, has become more dependent on public assistance for survival. Studies of poverty and welfare benefits show that the onus is often put on minorities and immigrants to prove their entitlement in ways that are not required of the majority, while among more recent immigrants rights are even less often secured (see, e.g., Smith 1989: 176; Townsend 1987: 56). As the German example discussed earlier indicates, immigrants are often ready and easy targets for government cutbacks, particularly when they lack citizenship and effective political voice. Moreover, many of those most acutely affected by the recession have been the second and third generation of minority youths who "often suffer from educational deficiencies, are unable to find meaningful employment and are culturally and institutionally removed from the societies of their parents. Their isolation, dislocation, and alienation have been increasing" (Schmitter-Heisler 1991).

However, as Loïc Wacquant stresses in his comparisons of urban deprivation in Paris and Chicago, we ought not to exaggerate the salience of race in European countries. The new social tensions in Europe may be manifested in xenophobia and racial enmity, but they stem primarily from the deteriorating economic and social conditions and declining organizational resources in poorer working-class neighborhoods that afflict the native populations and immigrants alike and that create situations that enhance racial antagonisms. Accordingly, if Europe is to avoid the levels of poisonous racial flareups and antagonisms that have plagued America, it will be important to generate public recognition and appreciation of the impact of these changes on the lives of the poor, including the minority poor, and on intergroup relations.

CONCLUSION

In this chapter we have argued that a new poverty has emerged on both sides of the Atlantic represented by changes in the size and composition of disadvantaged groups, the hardening of racial cleavages among them, an increase in their social and political isolation, and a worsening of their life chances. Although aspects of the new poverty are more severe in America than in Europe, recent trends in a number of European countries suggest a growing convergence of income and racial segregation between the two continents. However, as we have attempted to show, different structural and political arrangements in European countries reduce the likelihood of the emergence of American-style ghettos in the near future.

Moreover, there are still notable differences between the United States and Europe in the extent to which problems of poverty and inequality are addressed. In contrast to many European nations, the United States has not created comprehensive programs to promote the social rights of American citizens. Antipoverty programs have been largely targeted and fragmented. Instead of helping to integrate the poor into the broader economic and social life of mainstream society, they tend to stigmatize and separate them (see Schmitter-Heisler 1991).

However, recent economic crises in Europe have made it difficult to sustain programs that embody universal and integrative social citizenship rights. With the growth of mass unemployment and the growing fragmentation of European labor markets, pressures to cut back on welfare state benefits have mounted. Moreover, the increase of racial and ethnic diversity has led some to reexamine the postwar commitment to universal programs and social inclusion, a commitment originally based on conceptions of citizenship that assumed a fair degree of cultural homogeneity. Recent challenges to this commitment often reflect racial bias. As economic conditions have worsened, many in the majority white population view the growth of minorities as part of the problem. Stagnant economies and slack labor markets have placed strains on the welfare state at the very time when the immigrant population, facing mounting problems of joblessness, has become more dependent on public assistance for survival.

Nonetheless, although the conditions for the expressions of racial antagonisms have increased, as pointed out earlier, because of differences in political organization, Europeans do not have the same opportunities as Americans to act on their racial antipathies. Moreover, official and scholarly explanations of the new poverty in Europe tend to focus much more on the changes and inequities in the broader society than on individual deficiencies and behavior and, therefore, lend much greater support to the ideology of social citizenship rights. Furthermore, welfare programs that benefit wide segments of the population, including the poor and minorities, such as childcare, child allowances, housing subsidies, education, and medical care, have been firmly institutionalized in many Western European democracies. Efforts to cut back on these programs in the face of growing joblessness have met firm resistance.

However, changes in Europe are occurring very rapidly. The extent to which the multiracial and multiethnic countries there will approach the United States in the levels of racial and income segregation, belief systems on poverty and welfare, and commitment to social rights is a question that cross-cultural researchers will pursue with considerable interest.

ENDNOTE

1. In the following discussion in this section, we are indebted to the stimulating work of Margaret Weir (1993) and Demetrios Caralay (1992). Parts of this discussion are also based on Wilson (1995).

REFERENCES

Ashton, D., and Maguire, M. 1991. "Patterns and Experiences of Unemployment." In *Poor Work: Disadvantage and the Division of Labour*, edited by P. Brown and R. Scase, 40–55. Milton Keynes & Philadelphia: Open University Press.

Balsen, W., et. al. 1984. *Die neue Armut*, Cologne: Bund Verlag.

Caraley, D. 1992. "Washington Abandons the Cities." *Political Science Quarterly* 107: 1–27.

Coleman, R., and Rainwater, L. 1979. *Social Standing in America*. London: Routledge & Kegan Paul.

Dean, H., and Taylor-Gooby, P. 1993. *Dependency Culture: The Explosion of a Myth*. New York and London: Harvester Wheatsheaf.

Economist. 1992. "All Quiet on the Racial Front?" 325 (7788), December 5th–11th, London.

Freeman, R. 1983. "Public Policy and Employment Discrimination in the United States." In *Ethnic Pluralism and Public Policy*, edited by N. Glazer and K. Young, 124–144. Lexington, Mass.: D.C. Heath.

Katz, M. 1986. *In the Shadow of the Poorhouse: A Social History of Welfare in the United States*. New York: Basic Books.

———. 1989. *The Undeserving Poor: From the War on Poverty to the War on Welfare*. New York: Pantheon.

Klass, G. 1983. "Explaining America and the Welfare State: An Alternative Theory." *British Journal of Political Science* 15: 427–450.

Korpi, W. 1980. "Social Policy and Distributional Conflict in the Capitalist Democracies." *West European Politics* 3(1).

Lawson, R. 1987. "Social Security and the Division of Welfare." In *Inside British Society: Continuity, Challenge and Change*, edited by G. Causer, 77–97. New York: St. Martin's Press.

Leibfried, S., and Tennstedt, F., eds. 1985. *Politik der Armut und die Spaltung des Sozialstaats*. Frankfurt am Main: Suhrkamp.

Lion, A. 1984. "An Anti-poverty Policy or a Social Development Policy? A French Point of View." In *Anti-Poverty Policy in the European Community*, edited by J. Brown, 100–112. London: Policy Studies Institute.

Marklund, S. 1986. "The Swedish Model—Work and Welfare." *ASW Impact* December.

Melville, K., and J. Doble. 1988. *The Public's Perspective on Social Welfare Reform*. The Public Agenda Foundation, January.

OECD. 1988. *The Future of Social Protection: The General Debate*. Paris: Organisation for Economic Co-operation and Development.

Patterson, J. 1981. *America's Struggle Against Poverty*. Cambridge, Mass.: Harvard University Press.

Rainwater, L. 1991. *Poverty in American Eyes*. Luxembourg Income Study, CEPS/INSTEAD. Mimeo.

Ryan, A. 1992. "The Retreat from Caring." *The Times*, London, August 12.

Sampson, R., and W. J. Wilson. 1994. "Toward a Theory of Race, Crime, and Urban Inequality." In J. Hagan and R. Peterson, *Crime and Inequality*. Stanford: Stanford University Press.

Schmitter-Heisler, B. 1991. "A Comparative Perspective on the Underclass." *Theory and Society* 20: 455–483.

Schneider, U. 1993. *Solidarpakt gegen die Schwachen: Der Rückzug des Staates aus der Sozialpolitik.* München: Knaur.

Skocpol, T. 1988. "The Limits of the New Deal System and the Roots of Contemporary Welfare Dilemmas." In *The Politics of Social Policy in the United States,* edited by M. Weir, S. Orloff, and T. Skocpol, 293–312. Princeton, N.J.: Princeton University Press.

Smith, S. 1989. *The Politics of "Race" and Residence.* London: Polity Press.

Standing, G. 1986. *Unemployment and Labour Market Flexibility: The United Kingdom.* Geneva: International Labour Office.

Statistisches Bundeamt. 1993. *Sozialhilfe.* Wiesbaden: Statistisches Bundeamt.

Townsend, P., et al. 1987. *Poverty and Labour in London.* London: Low Pay Unit.

U.S. Bureau of the Census. 1988. "Money Income and Poverty Status in the U.S." In *Current Population Reports,* Series P-60. Washington, D.C.: Government Printing Office.

Vincent, D. 1991. *Poor Citizens.* London and New York: Longman.

Wacquant, L., and W. J. Wilson. 1989. "Poverty, Joblessness and the Social Transformation of the Inner City." In *Reforming Welfare Policy,* edited by D. Ellwood and P. Cottingham, 70–102. Cambridge, Mass.: Harvard University Press.

Weir, M. 1993. "Race and Urban Poverty: Comparing Europe and America." Center for American Political Studies, Harvard University, Occasional Paper 93-9, March.

Weir, M., Orloff, A., and Skocpol, T. 1988. "The Future of Social Policy in the United States: Political Constraints and Possibilities." In *The Politics of Social Policy in the United States,* edited by M. Weir, S. Orloff & T. Skocpol, 421–446. Princeton, N.J.: Princeton University Press.

Wilson, W. J. 1987. *The Truly Disadvantaged: The Inner City, The Underclass, and Public Policy.* Chicago: University of Chicago Press.

———. 1991. "Studying Inner-City Social Dislocations: The Challenge of Public Agenda Research." *American Sociological Review* 56: 1–14.

———. 1995. *Jobless Ghettoes: The Disappearance of Work and its Effect on Urban Life.* New York: Knopf.

NAME INDEX

SUBJECT INDEX

Entries in **boldface** refer to figures and tables.